Welcome to the universal world of play.

HANNELORE VANDENBUSSCHE

HUMAN PLAYGROUND

Why We **Play**

WRITTEN BY ROSE CASELLA

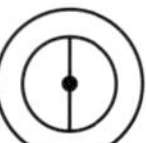

"Sport can create hope
where once there was only despair.
It is more powerful than governments
in breaking down racial barriers.
It laughs in the face of all types of discrimination.
Sports is the game of lovers."

~ Nelson Mandela ~

Preface by
Hannelore Vandenbussche

FOUNDER & PHOTOGRAPHER OF *HUMAN PLAYGROUND*

Despite my curiosity to learn about the world, school was not something I was passionate about as a child. Had it not been for my parent's encouragement, I would not have gotten my degree. It wasn't long until I discovered the world of photography and knew I wanted to be a photographer. Seeing the world through a camera lens ignited a passion in me that was fanned by my first travels.

Soon after, I was given the opportunity of a lifetime – an utterly unexpected dream project. I had the chance to work with Jimmy Nelson on his renowned *Before They Pass Away* photo book, wherein he documented unique tribes from all corners of the world. We travelled to sixteen countries and met with thirty-six different indigenous peoples, from the desolate ice fields of Siberia to the pristine tropical rainforests of Papua New Guinea. We were lucky enough to move around this beautiful blue orb and take in its beauty. But what stayed with me most were the people themselves.

Being able to tell stories is one of the main reasons I chose this profession. Stories are everywhere, everyone has something unique to express, and I discovered that I wanted to help bring some of these stories into the world. I didn't want to tell commercial stories but rather my own story – my version of how I see the world in its purity, honesty and rawness.

The one reoccurring theme I noticed during my work on *Before They Pass Away* is that no matter how isolated tribes are or their social or financial status is, they all love playing games and sports. Many of these sports were not the kind I was familiar with, like football, but instead, the games were steeped in tradition, rituals, and the pursuit of perfection or the coming of age.

In Ethiopia, I was intrigued by the donga stick fighting. Tribesmen told me stories of how men engaged in this brutal fighting tradition, sometimes resulting in death, to win the hearts of women. And in Vanuatu, an island in the South Pacific, young men land-dive from a height of 20-meters with only long vines tied around their ankles to prove their strength, bravery and manhood, which has resulted in a fair share of accidents and even deaths. A dangerous tradition based on the belief that the gods will be pleased with their efforts and reward them with a good harvest. Another fascinating story that I witnessed was in Mongolia, where children participate in a nomadic rite of passage, a 20-kilometre race. As an experienced rider, I was shocked to see six-year-old boys and girls riding horses without saddles or protective gear, with only the reins to hold onto and being led by slightly older children, nine years of age.

Learning about the wide range of reasons people play sports, whether to secure the best marriage, get more prestige, or for rituals, celebrations and honouring the gods, was so interesting that I knew I wanted to pursue this. Most of all, I wanted to understand the 'why' behind it all. The more I investigated this topic, the more I realized that there was very little documentation on why we humans play. I felt this was a story I could dedicate myself to, a project that I could make my own.

I threw myself into months of online research and began finding one compelling story after another. For example, in La Paz, Bolivia, a group of female wrestlers are using their sport to fight for gender equality within their macho-dominated system. Or the traditional camel racing of the United Arab Emirates, which evolved by inventing robot jockeys to replace child jockeys.

But there was one specific story that I couldn't shake. A Dutch psychiatrist asked me to join her on a trip to Sierra Leone to meet and document a young man who had fought as a child in the civil war and had managed to heal his trauma through yoga. In a country with little to no health care, he took on the task of helping those with similar traumatic backgrounds by teaching yoga at the only psychiatric hospital in the city. This brave young man's story showed me how sport is much more than just a physical action; it can help heal trauma. It was then that I realized that all people play, regardless of age, race, gender, culture or religion. It's not just about winning or losing; it's about how it connects us and makes us human.

The scope of this project turned out to be much larger than I could have ever imagined. I didn't want it to be focused solely on indigenous sports stories, but instead, I wanted to show the kaleidoscope of sports worldwide, from the more familiar western games to the most remote and unknown games, people and places. While photographing the world's best runners in the world – Mexico's Tarahumara people, I felt that a book wasn't enough to adequately portray the core of the story in all its glory. The *Human Playground* stories needed also to be seen as a documentary series to reveal all the rich layers of human expression.

It took me a year to find the perfect producer Isidoor Roebers, founder of Scenery, the leading production company in the Netherlands and the Benelux. He immediately believed in me and my creative vision for *Human Playground*. We were on the same wavelength. Together with the talented director and show-runner of the series, Tomas Kaan, we filmed the pilot, which we proudly and humbly delivered to Netflix – the ideal partner to bring our story to the next level.

However, one thing was missing, a narrator to tell the story with the ability to elevate the project to new heights. When we heard Idris Elba's deep, resonant voice, we knew he was the man for the job. We sent him a teaser, and fortunately, he was very impressed with the project, which goes hand in hand with his athletic background. Everything began moving forward, and our documentary series was about to be broadcasted on one of the world's largest streamers. My dream blossomed into something bigger and better than I could have ever envisioned.

As a photographer, what interests me most is people and their stories, which means I need to get close to my subjects to forge a bond of trust. Therefore I spend extended periods living with people, not just to capture their image but also to capture their essence. I work instinctually and combine reportage with on-set studio portraits. I prefer smaller lenses, allowing me to feel closer to the subject. I want to feel what they feel – the danger, the adrenaline, the joy.

One of the more challenging stories I photographed was big wave surfing in Nazaré because of the unpredictability of weather, light, wind and waves. There is zero control, and you can't ask someone to repeat an action; everything happens within a millisecond and one fast shutter speed. When I first saw the waves crashing against the Portuguese coastline, they were 'only' 10–15 meters. Imposing but not frightening. But the second time I was there, I saw the giant 30-meter waves and watched surfers run into them, wondering if they had a death wish. One wrong move and they would break in two like a match stick. Crazy! I had to see and feel it for myself to understand why they would risk their lives for it. So I got on the back of a jet ski with my camera and started photographing the surfers, the jet ski drivers and all the community of people who are part of getting everyone back safely. When I returned to land, I understood what possessed them to do something so dangerous. Because for a moment, I felt like I was one of them.

Another story where I threw myself into the thick of it was in Tajikistan for buzkashi – the sport where men on horseback frantically chase a goat carcass. This game included hundreds of men on horses running at high speeds over a giant field. I was trying to figure out the best place to get the shot I needed and thought the best place to photograph all the action would be on horseback, smack in the middle of the action. They provided me with a reasonably spirited horse, and after announcing my name and profession over the loudspeaker, I tested my horse out and started galloping across the field. The hundreds of spectators began shouting and cheering my name, "Hanna, Hanna" it was overwhelming and surreal. And to be amongst the multitude of horses and men gave me a completely different perspective than if I had taken the shot with a long lens from a safe distance.

With both the *Human Playground* book and Netflix series, I want everyone to feel and understand what goes on in the minds of these brave and talented athletes and what motivates them to play on some of the most dangerous playgrounds. What at first may seem like madness can later be understood and even admired.

Sport can be an inspiring and unifying factor that bridges the gap between people, culture, religion and economic differences breaking down prejudices and barriers. My deepest wish is for *Human Playground* to shine a light on humanity, highlighting this planet's incredible beauty and diversity.

Idris Elba

NARRATOR OF THE *HUMAN PLAYGROUND* SERIES

It was another day at the office. I was on set in Docklands, East London, shooting a show about car stunts. To be honest, I was a little scared. For some reason, that day, I was going to drive a car at 80 miles per hour, up a ramp, through the air, before crashing it head-on into four rows of parked vehicles. Why? Because something deep inside of me has always loved testing my limits. Seeing what I am capable of. From taking part in a professional kickboxing fight to breaking a historic land speed record, it's no secret that I love to play, and I'm fortunate enough to become involved in projects that allow me to explore this obsession.

Most recently, I have helped start a boxing gym for eight young adults who have challenging backgrounds because play can help you focus, it can teach you discipline. It can change your life.

Shortly before take-off, there was a knock at the door. It was the creators of *Human Playground*. They wanted to introduce me to their project and ask if I wanted to be involved. I was blown away by the scale of the story they wanted to tell. A book and TV series that scours the globe examining the many amazing games humans have invented. Hannelore showed me photos taken on her travels of a wide range of playgrounds and players. I was struck by the differences, but more so the similarities. You see, like music, play is something that unites us. No matter where we are, who we are, humans live to test our boundaries. We take each other on. We face our fears. We win, and we lose.

This book has been put together by a hugely talented team. I hope, like me, you are fascinated by the photos and find the deeper meaning hidden in these pages. Above all, when you put this book down, I hope it inspires you to pick up that racket, put on those boxing gloves or football boots, and take part in one of our most ancient rituals. These are more than just games. This is our human playground.

Tomas Kaan

DIRECTOR OF THE *HUMAN PLAYGROUND* NETFLIX SERIES

My 4-year-old son Mozes and I like to play. One minute we're playing that he is a knight much stronger than me. The next moment I'm the dragon, having captured him and tickling him until he bursts out laughing.

He can also play on his own for long periods, living in his own little world pretending that a stick is his sword. Looking at him play like this often makes me think about the similarity between his games and what I myself do in everyday life.

I have always experienced my work as a continuation of child's play. As a director, I go out into the world to meet people and record their stories. But on a more fundamental level my work is an activity where I can playfully become who I want to be, working with people who are – or will often soon become – my friends. And it is also where I physically, mentally and emotionally am challenged to get the best out of myself. To tell stories and show the world what I think is worth the effort of experiencing. With film, I can express who I am.

When I met Hannelore, she gave me a peek through her lens. And she showed me how she sees the world and what she values. The concept of her project is one of stunning simplicity. A few lines in the sand, a giant wave or a snowy mountain peak are all opportunities for us to play, and we have done that for as long as we can remember. On these playgrounds, we show the world who we are, where we have come from and maybe even where we are going.

I knew immediately that this project was a playground I wanted to contribute to. The book before you is where it all began. It is the work of one of the most playful and fantastic team players I've ever known. I am proud that Hannelore included me as one of the players on her team to translate *Human Playground* cinematically. But where I need 25 images per second, Hannelore's photography only needs 1 to tell us a story. In this book, she holds up a mirror to us and shows us ourselves in all our emotional complexity and cultural, colourful diversity.

index

The Human B
photo book cr
explores the m
which human
express who t

ayground
eatively
any ways in
 use sport to
hey are.

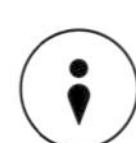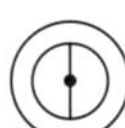

This visual collection of stories illustrates the fascinating ways humans experience play in the forms of ancient rituals and rites of passage; or while doing business, feeling pain, chasing perfection or honouring the sacred. It gives a glimpse into the most phenomenal playgrounds on the planet, the people who engage in the games and the extremes they're willing to go to. This book is not just about sports; it's about what makes us human. And just as in the *Human Playground* Netflix series, the stories in the book fall under six universal themes that shed light on why humans have such a fierce, intense drive to conquer, perfect and win.

Why do we play?

Why do humans have the urge to run, jump, surf, wrestle, dive or chase a moving ball, individually or in a team?

Human Playground focuses on specific, universal themes within a collection of the most intriguing, extreme and primal ways humans use play to express themselves. Historically, sport has been a form of entertainment, celebration and honour, but it has also been used to resolve conflicts within communities. Sport is an important connective element that binds people together regardless of social background, race, gender or belief. This book gives insight into why we need to play and into the many ways in which we do it.

ANCIENT RITUALS • Humans have been playing together for millennia. Play rooted in ancient rituals tells a story that transcends generations and individual desires; it maintains the diversity and richness of ancient knowledge and of the history that makes us what we are today. Often, these sports are not based on competition and conquering but are about participating, having fun and passing cultural practices on to a younger generation. The question is, should traditions and rituals remain static, or should they evolve with the world's changing ethics?

RITES OF PASSAGE • Human play is often about a rite of passage, a time-honoured practice that celebrates the transition from girl to woman or boy to man and demonstrates strength, bravery, skill and endurance. It documents a piece of our life journey and helps us bond with a community, family or team. It is a universal coming-of-age experience expressed in multiple ways according to various cultures and beliefs.

BIG BUSINESS • Becoming an athlete requires complete dedication and commitment. Yet many athletes cannot stay in the game without sponsors, and sponsorship forces them to work as representatives for various brands. Playing for money is not uncommon, and it's no surprise that people are willing to pay large sums of money for champion horses, camels and falcons. But should money be involved, and does it change the game and those who play it?

BREAKING THE PAIN BARRIER • Many sports require athletes to push beyond their limits to compete, overriding the usual response to pain and suffering. Crossing the pain threshold requires rigorous physical and mental training, a fine line between pleasure and pain. What motivates someone to put their life on the line to pursue victory? Perhaps it's the adrenaline rush of cheating death and rising from it with a renewed zest for life, or maybe it's simply the challenge of going further than others would dare.

IN PURSUIT OF PERFECTION • Adversity motivates many athletes to persevere, train harder and never stop chasing excellence. They toil toward perfection, continually training to be the best they can be; striving for the perfect move, the perfect body and the perfect strategy. But the pursuit of perfection can become a slippery slope of constant pressure, anxiety and obsessive thoughts. At what point does the desire for perfection help or hurt?

SACRED PLAYGROUNDS • The connection between play and the sacred goes back to the fifth century B.C. in ancient Greece, where the Olympic games were held to praise and appease the gods. Sport can be a way to celebrate, honour the sacred and preserve ancestral wisdom or Indigenous beliefs. Both spirituality and sport require sacrifice, faith, worship and even superstition. Many athletes have risen to godlike status, inspiring intense emotions in adoring followers. And the medals and trophies have become as blessed as the holy grail. The need to play may evolve and change with time, regardless of tradition, business, perfec-

tion or pain, but one sure thing is that play will be around for as long as humans walk this earth.

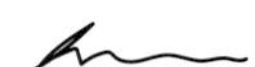

Buzkashi

CENTRAL ASIA

Horse and rider are seen as one, demonstrating
athletic ability, agility, and resilience.

Hundreds of horses' hooves thunder across the wide-open steppes of Central Asia's barren landscape, kicking up clouds of dust as men shout battle cries above the commotion in the fierce game of *buzkashi* ('goat-pulling' in Persian), also known as *kok-boru* ('blue wolf' in Kyrgyz). This ancient equestrian sport was first played by nomadic tribes in Afghanistan, Kyrgyzstan, Kazakhstan, Tajikistan and Mongolia, and few Westerners are familiar with it. It is a game played on horseback featuring two or more opposing teams competing for a headless goat carcass with which they can score points.

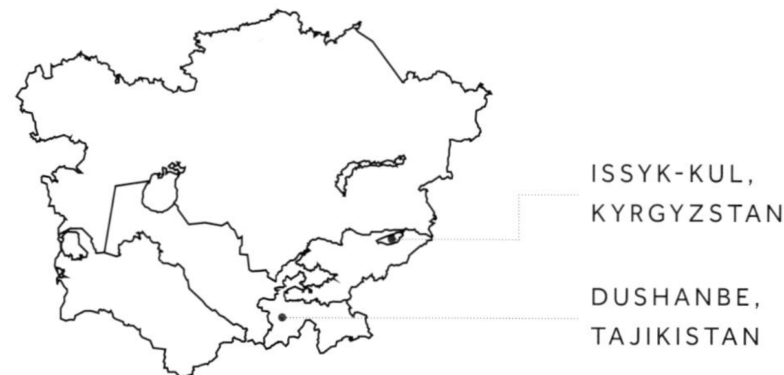

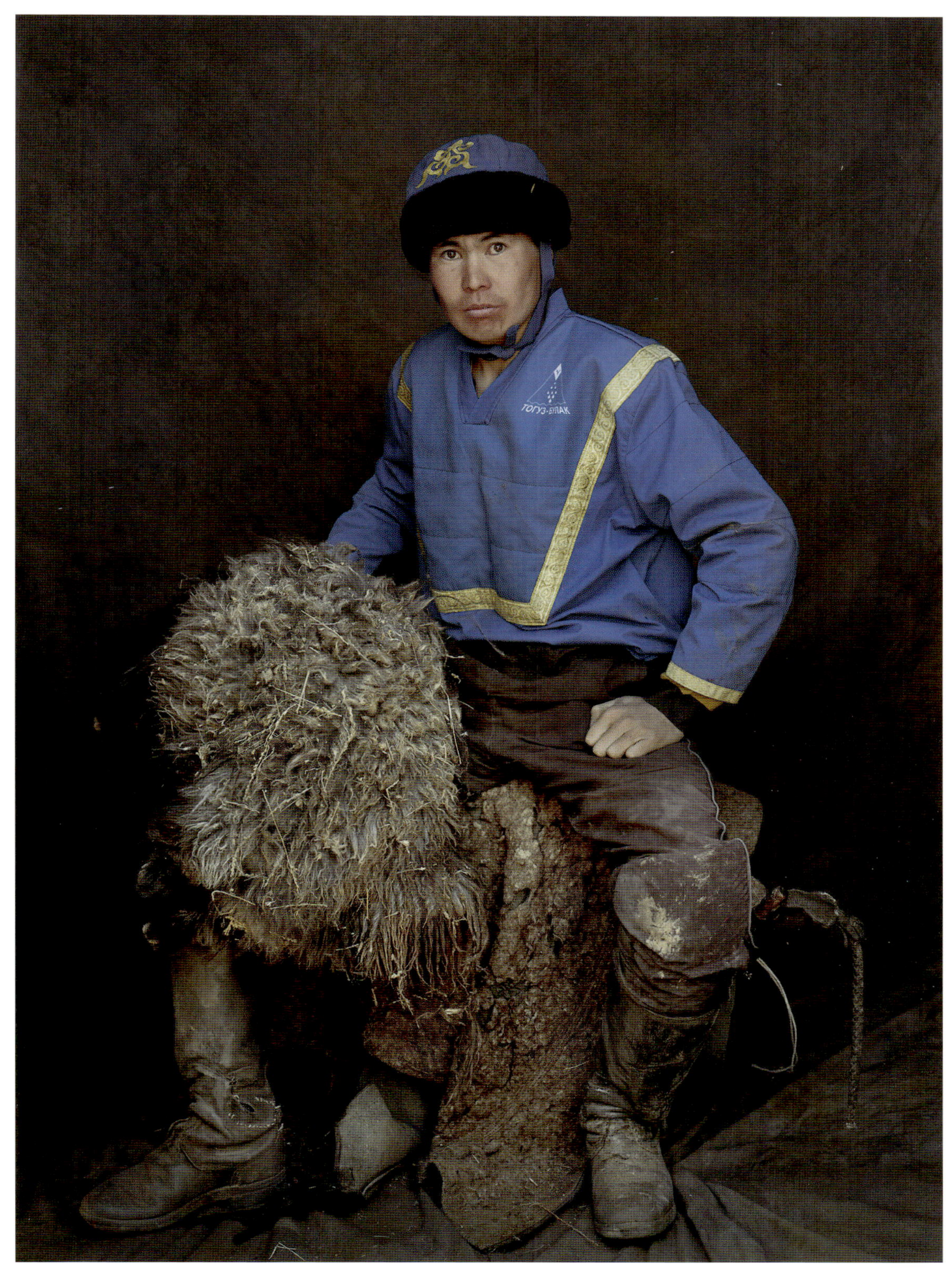

"Horses are the wings of a man."

~ old Kyrgyz saying ~

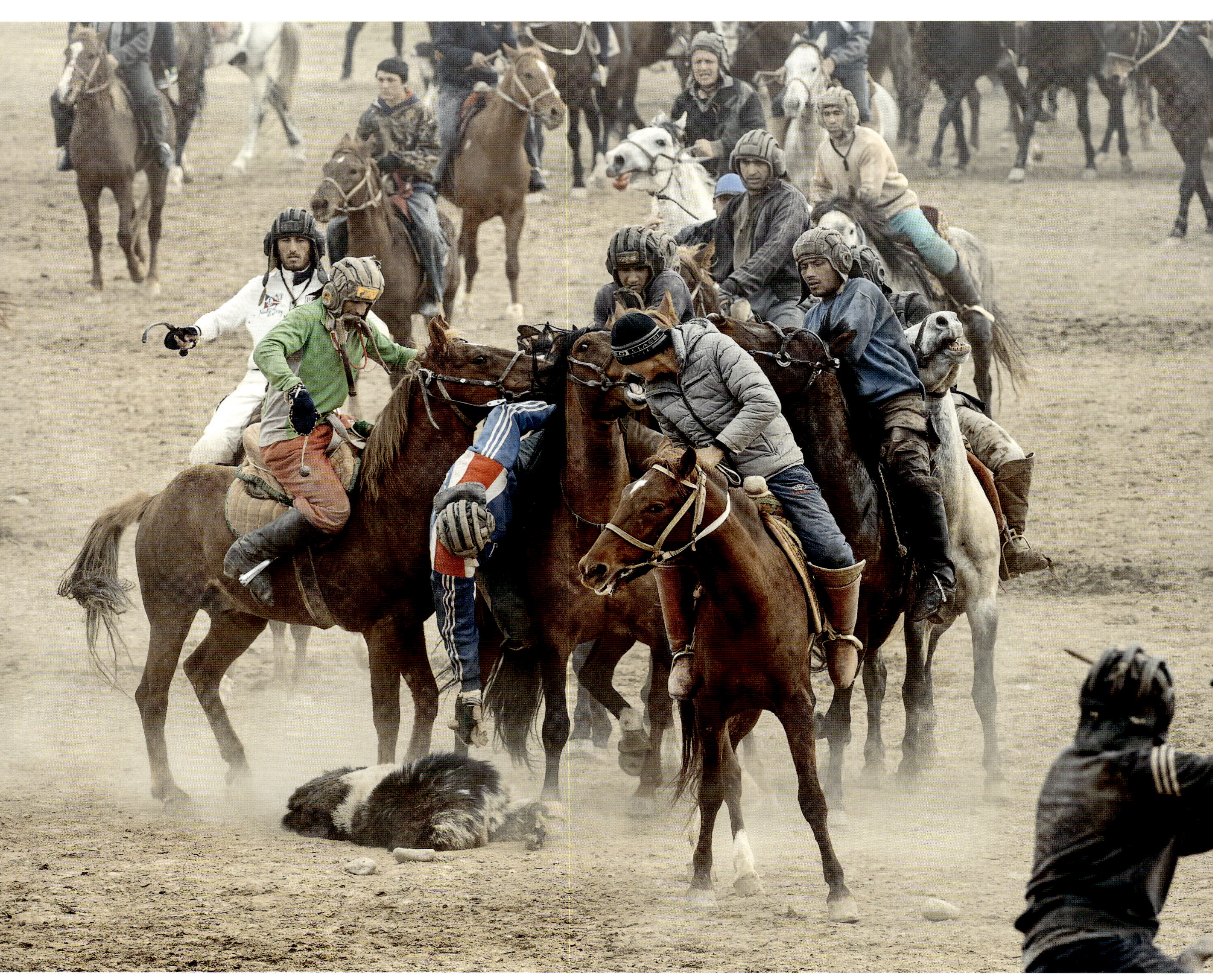

Known as the most dangerous game in Central Asia, *buzkashi* was introduced by the nomadic Turkic populations somewhere between the tenth and fifteenth centuries. There are several legends of how this ferocious game began. One suggests it was invented at a time when Afghan tribes on horseback would steal goats from other battling tribes. A Kyrgyz legend speaks of how wolves were killing their livestock, so as revenge, young men would search for the pesky predator, and when caught, they would make a game of tossing it to one another as a display of strength and bravery. The game was banned during the first Taliban and Soviet rule but has since seen a resurgence in the entire region.

The Kazakhs were the first to tame horses some 5,000 years ago, and horses have always played a vital role in nomadic traditions. Nomads are practically born on horses; it's hard to find a person, male or female, who cannot ride. It is not surprising, then, that they compete on horseback; rider and horse are seen as one, demonstrating athletic ability, agility and resilience.

Buzkashi or *kok-boru* competitions often take place on cultural occasions such as weddings, births or religious festivals. Entire villages participate, and people travel for days on horseback to attend. Many of the games are held on the *Nowruz* holidays, which is Persian for 'new day', marking the spring equinox on March 21. Before the match, a spiritual ritual is held involving prayer, blessings and the promise of fairness. The goat carcass must then be prepared by removing its head and limbs, gutting it and soaking it in water for twenty-four hours. The soaking helps keep it in one piece.

Rules of the game vary from country to country. Most games throughout Central Asia aren't supervised by a referee, yet there are some rules all must abide by. Players must keep the carcass in their hand or under their leg and can snatch it from an opponent and throw it to other players, but they must remain on their horses at all times; and players are not allowed to strike their opponents or their horses. Almost anything else goes, and many players and horses have left the game bloodied and bruised. Despite the players' superhuman athleticism their safety is not ensured. The pressure of teams of horses smashing up against one another is enough to crush bones.

The playground where this madhouse of a sport takes place can be an officially marked out area 800–1000 meters long and 20–30 meters wide, but the game is also played on large unbounded plots. Two teams of five courageous men on horseback try to heave up a twenty-kilo carcass (called an *ulak tartysh* in Kyrgyz) and race with it to one end of the field. As soon as the headless sack is yanked out of the mayhem, the race is on to the other end of the field, where the battered *ulak* is victoriously slammed into the *tai kazan* (goal). It's sheer anarchy, a wild flurry of human and animal limbs thrashing about, grasping at the lifeless goat. The winners of more traditional games receive the goat itself as a prize, to be prepared for a shared celebratory meal. The official competitions gift the champions with awards, money or domestic appliances.

To become a *buzkashi* player (a *chapandaz*) requires years of rigorous training for both man and horse. Both must be in top shape to play this physically demanding and violent sport, yet most agree that a player is only as good as his horse. Horses are carefully selected for their strength and agility, mainly stallions because of their ability to fight off rivals while riders battle for control.

While outsiders may question *buzkashi's* impact on the horses, these nomadic peoples say animals are sacred to them and that they would never do anything to hurt them. They insist that they treat them with great respect, kindness and love.

And even though ancient games seem to be disappearing around the globe, *buzkashi* is here to stay. Some say it is more popular than football. When asked why they carry on the legacy of this intense game, twenty-six-year-old player Myrzamambetov Adilet explains, "It's in our blood, it is the spirit of our ancestors, and it's the most exciting sport in the world."

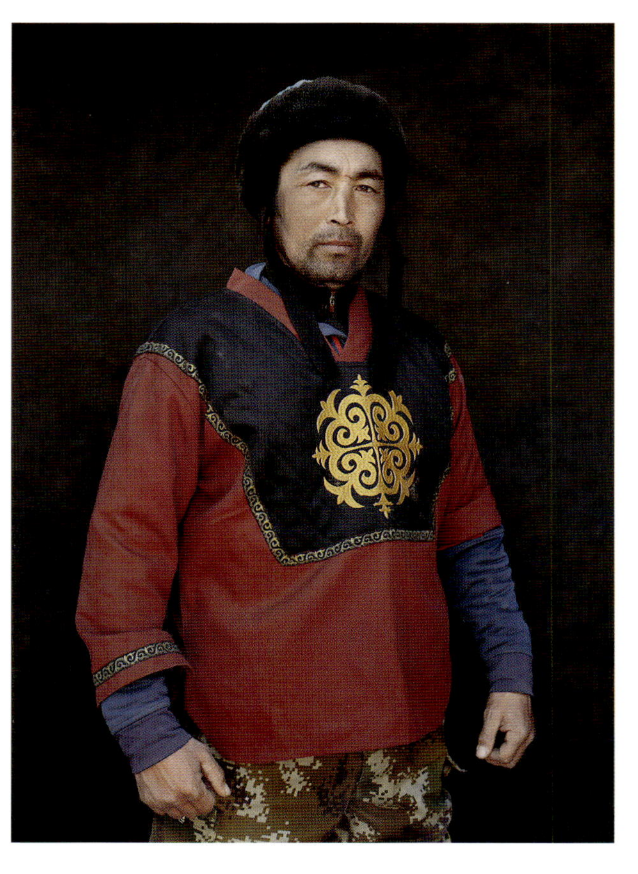
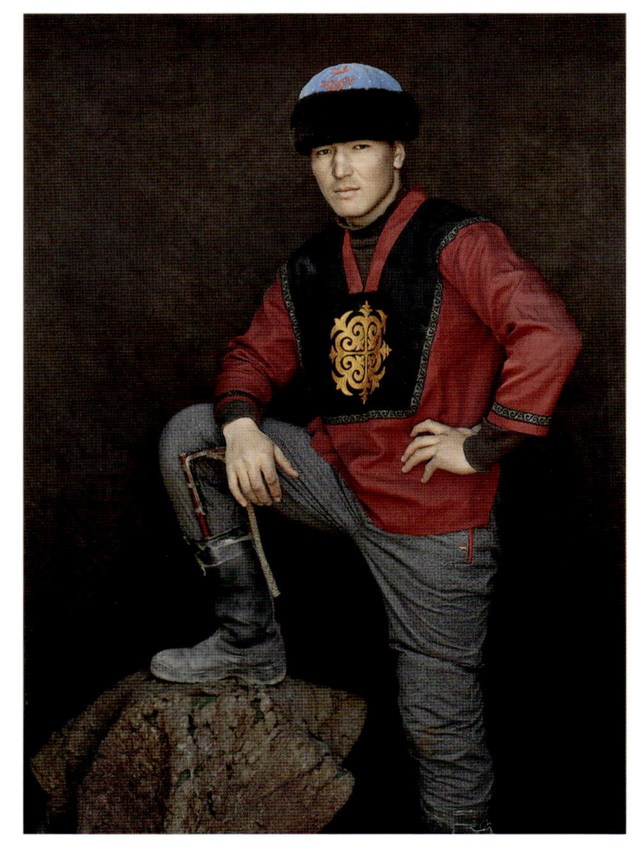
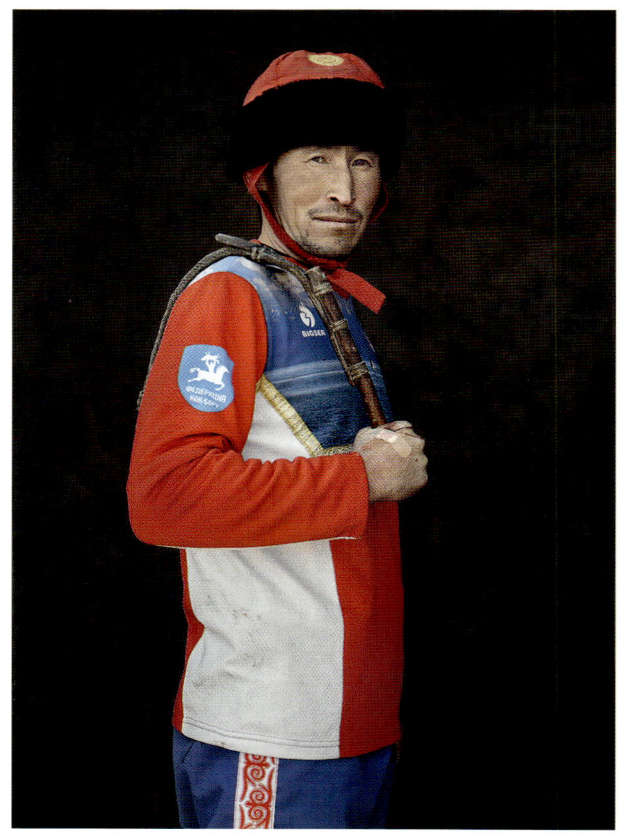
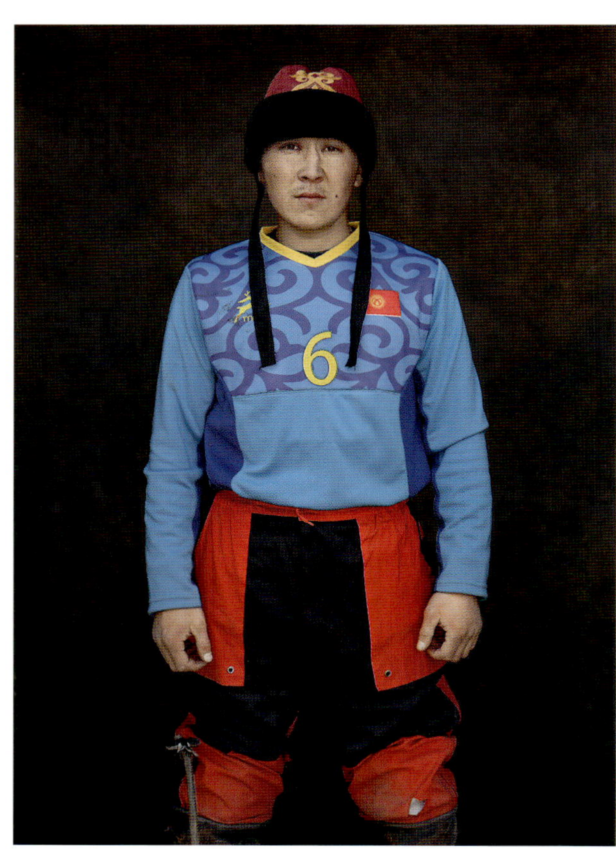

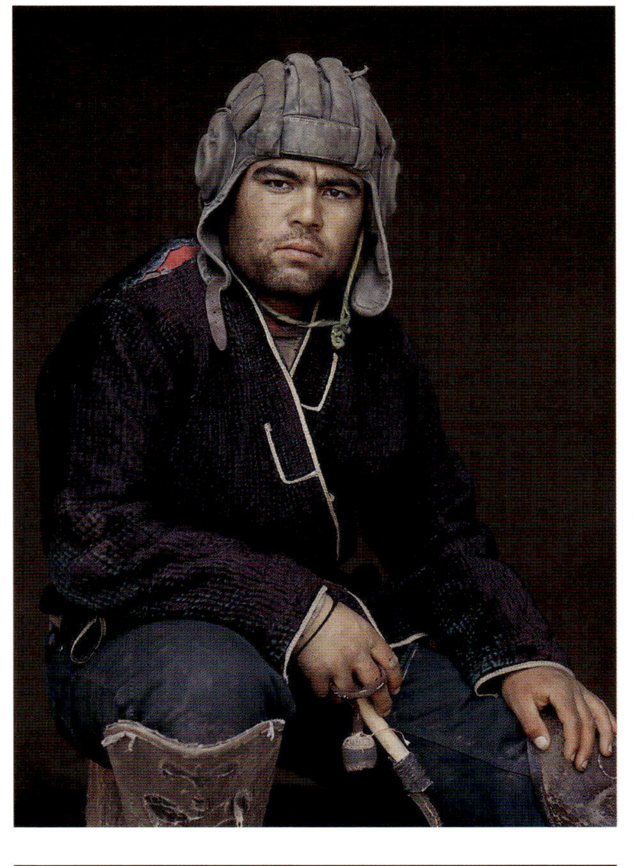
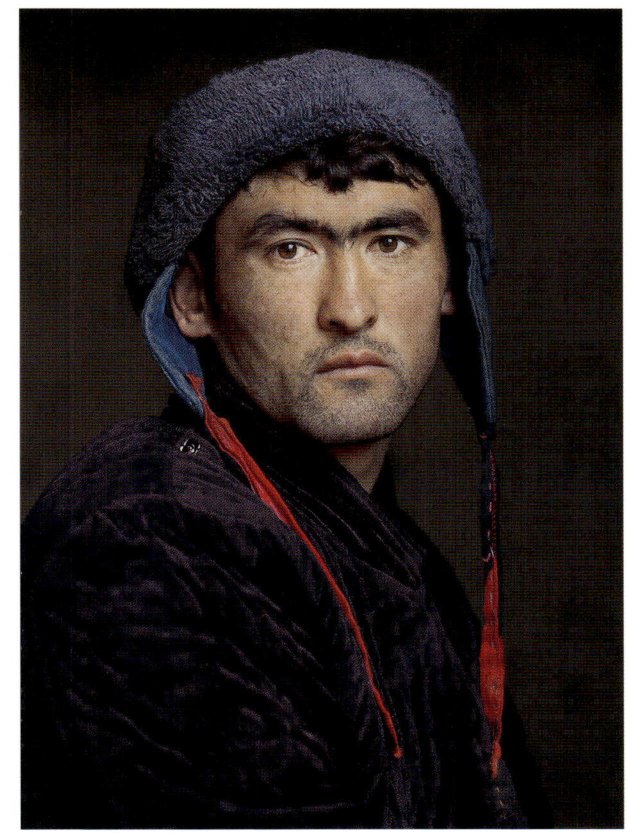
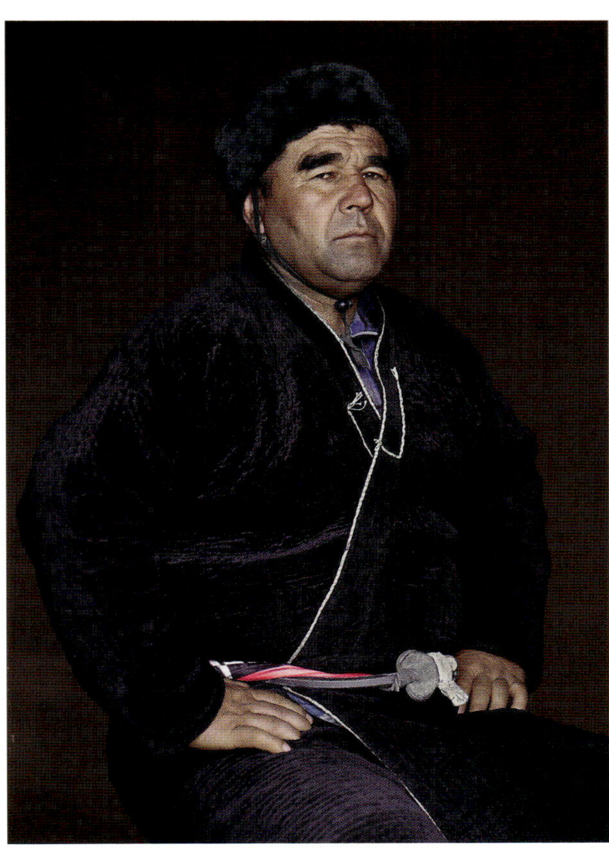
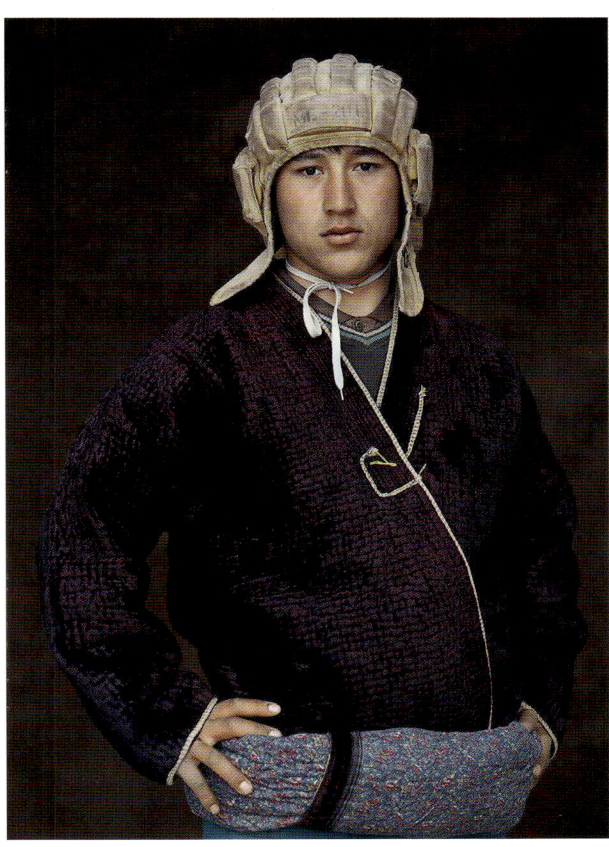

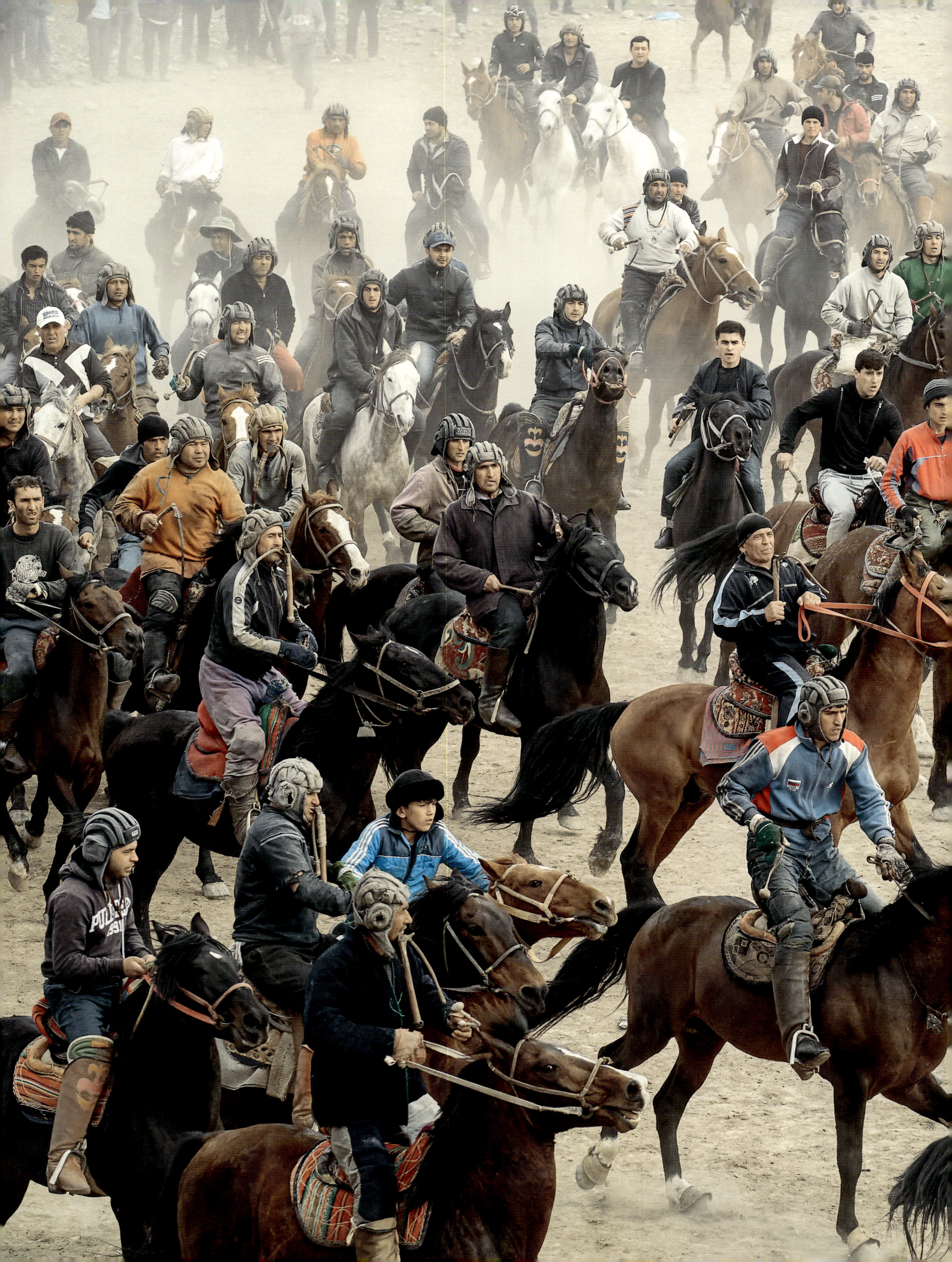

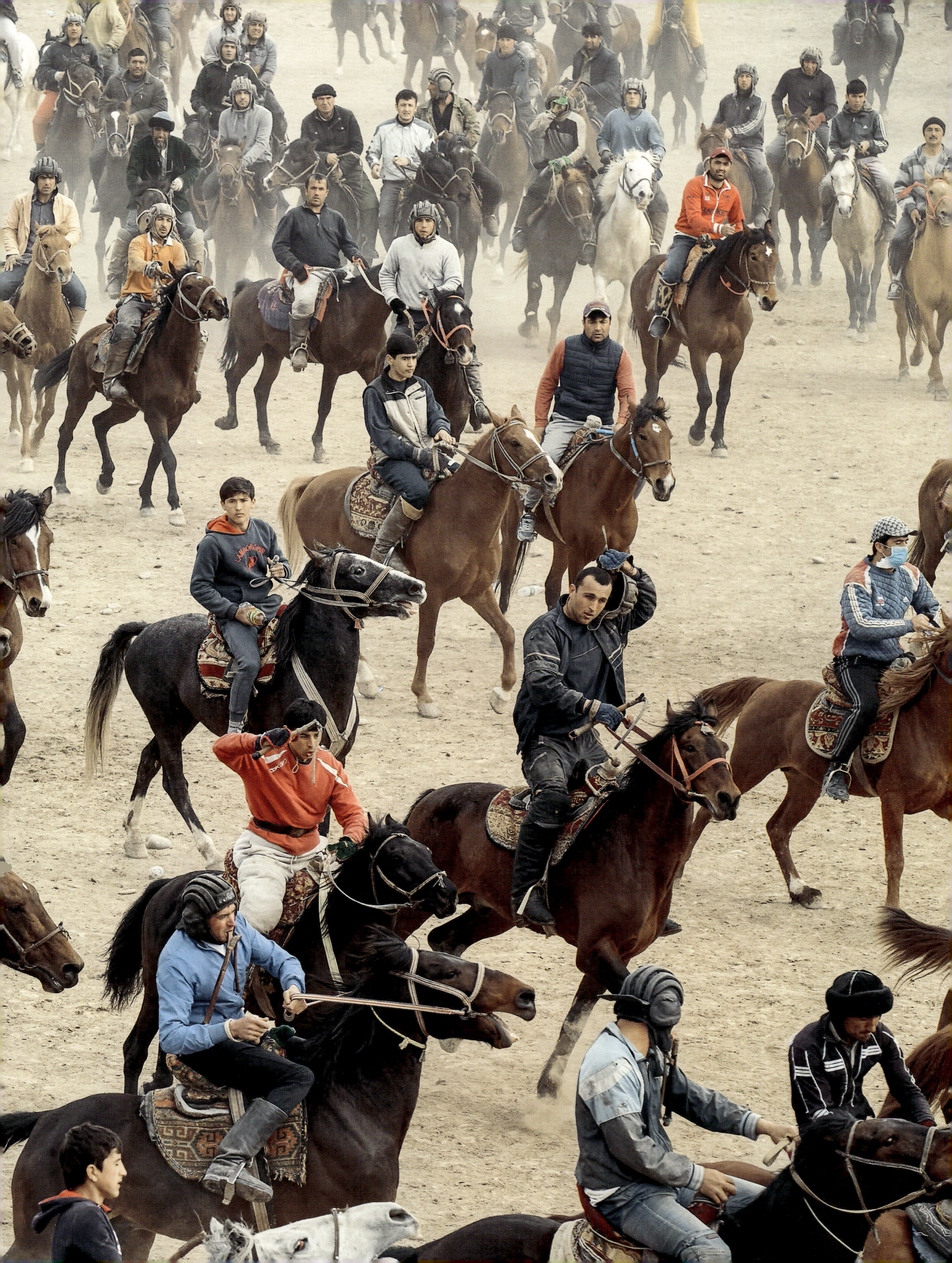

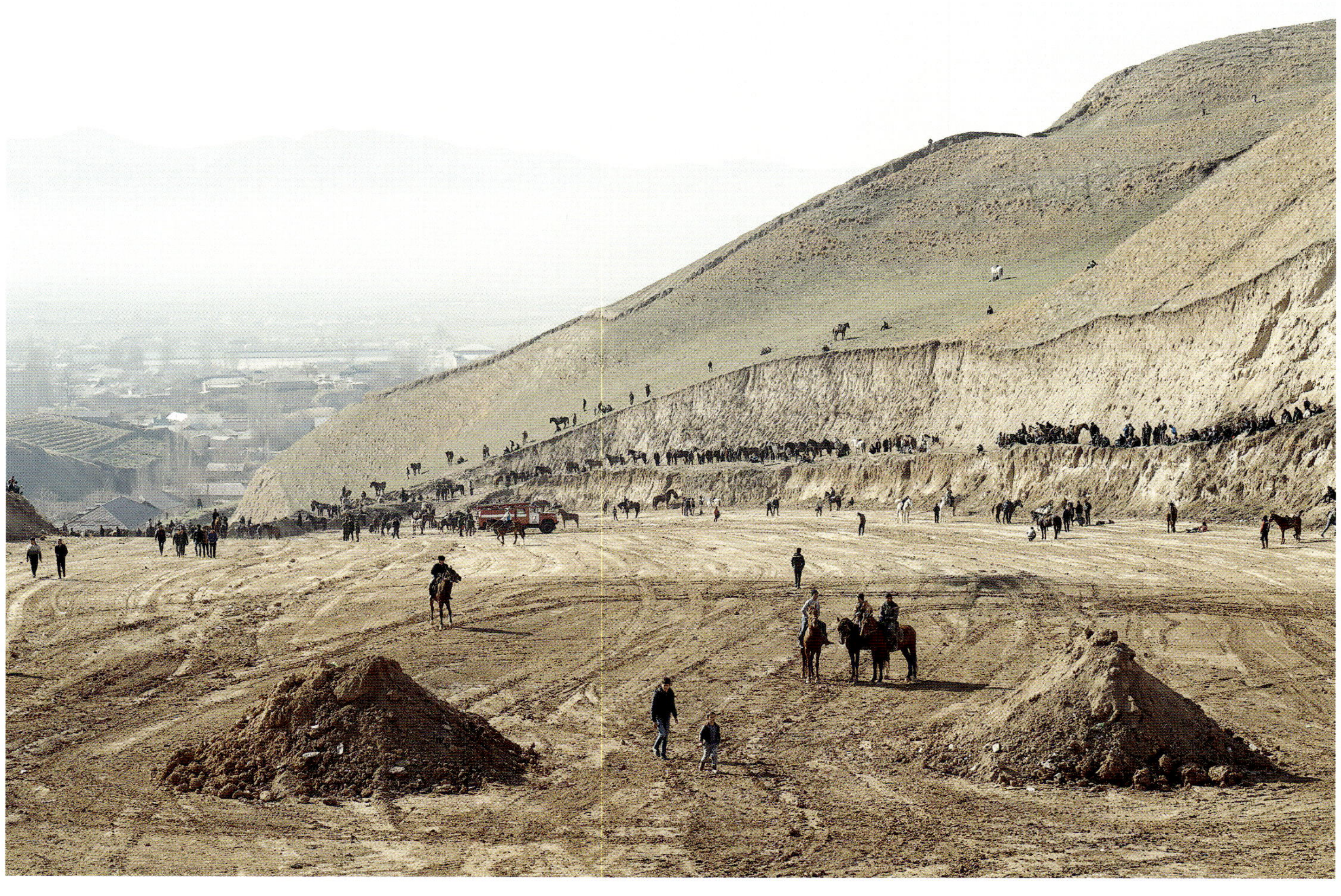

Throughout Central Asia, buzkashi games often
take place on wide-open fields without boundaries
and others on officially marked fields.

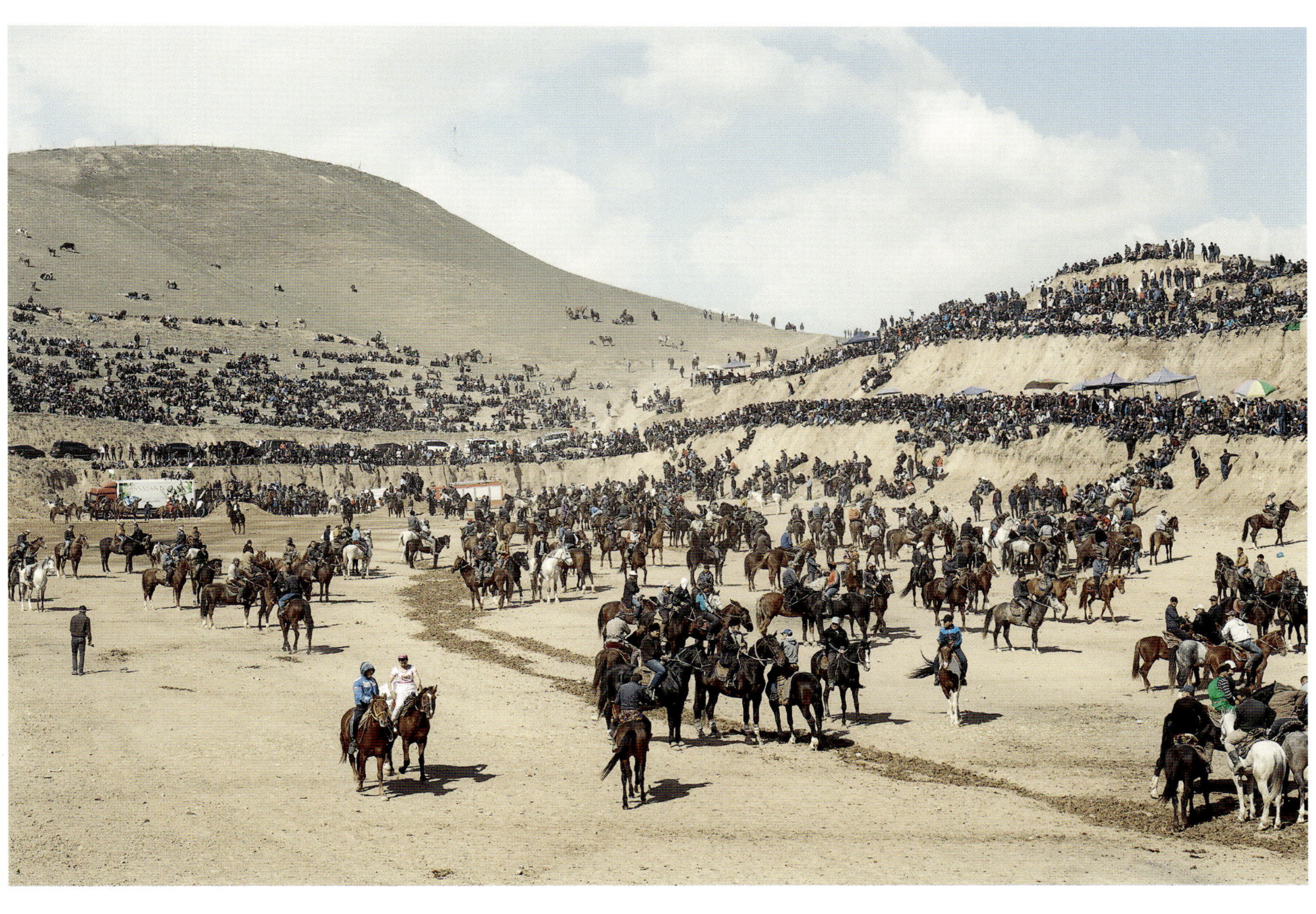

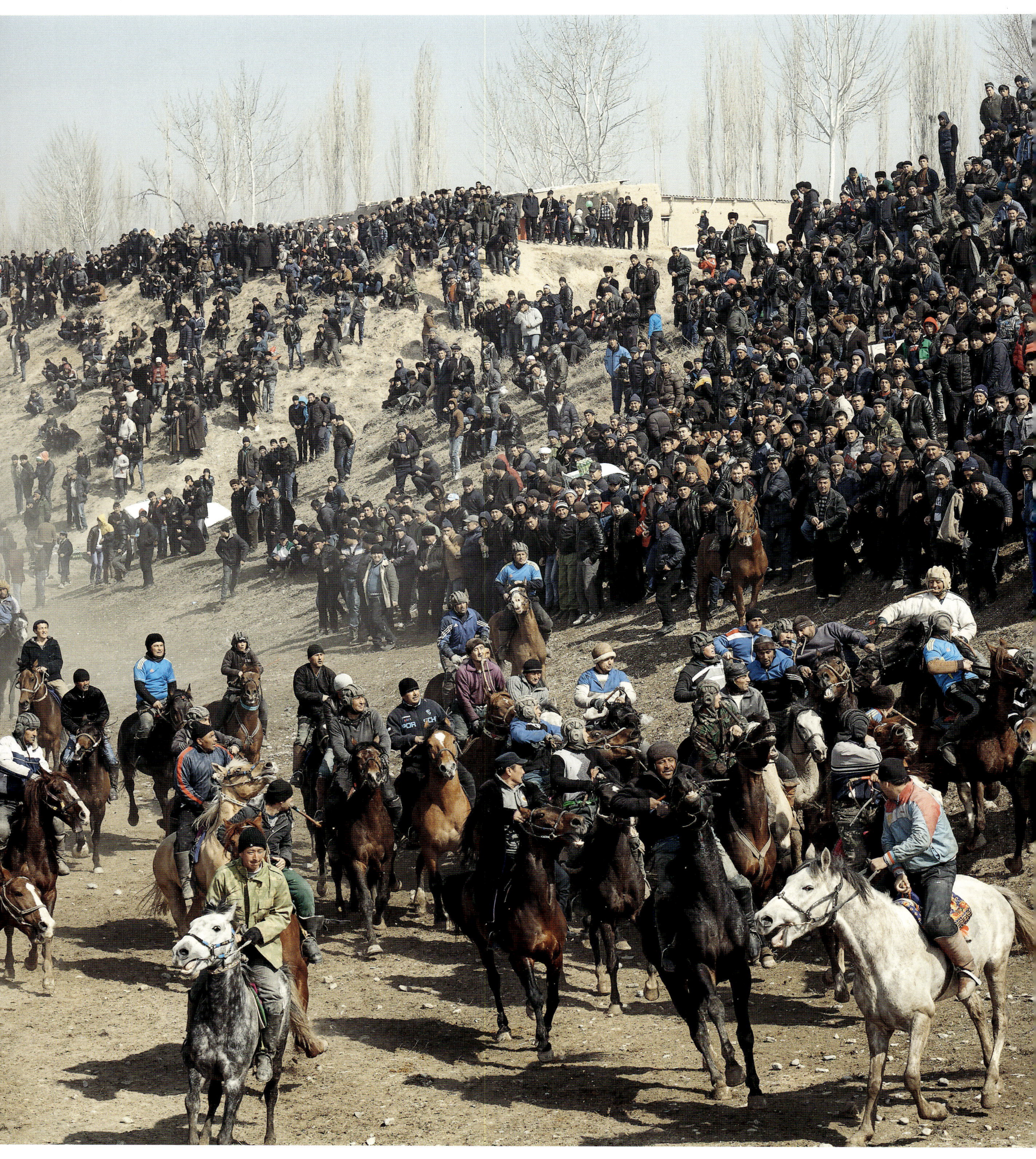

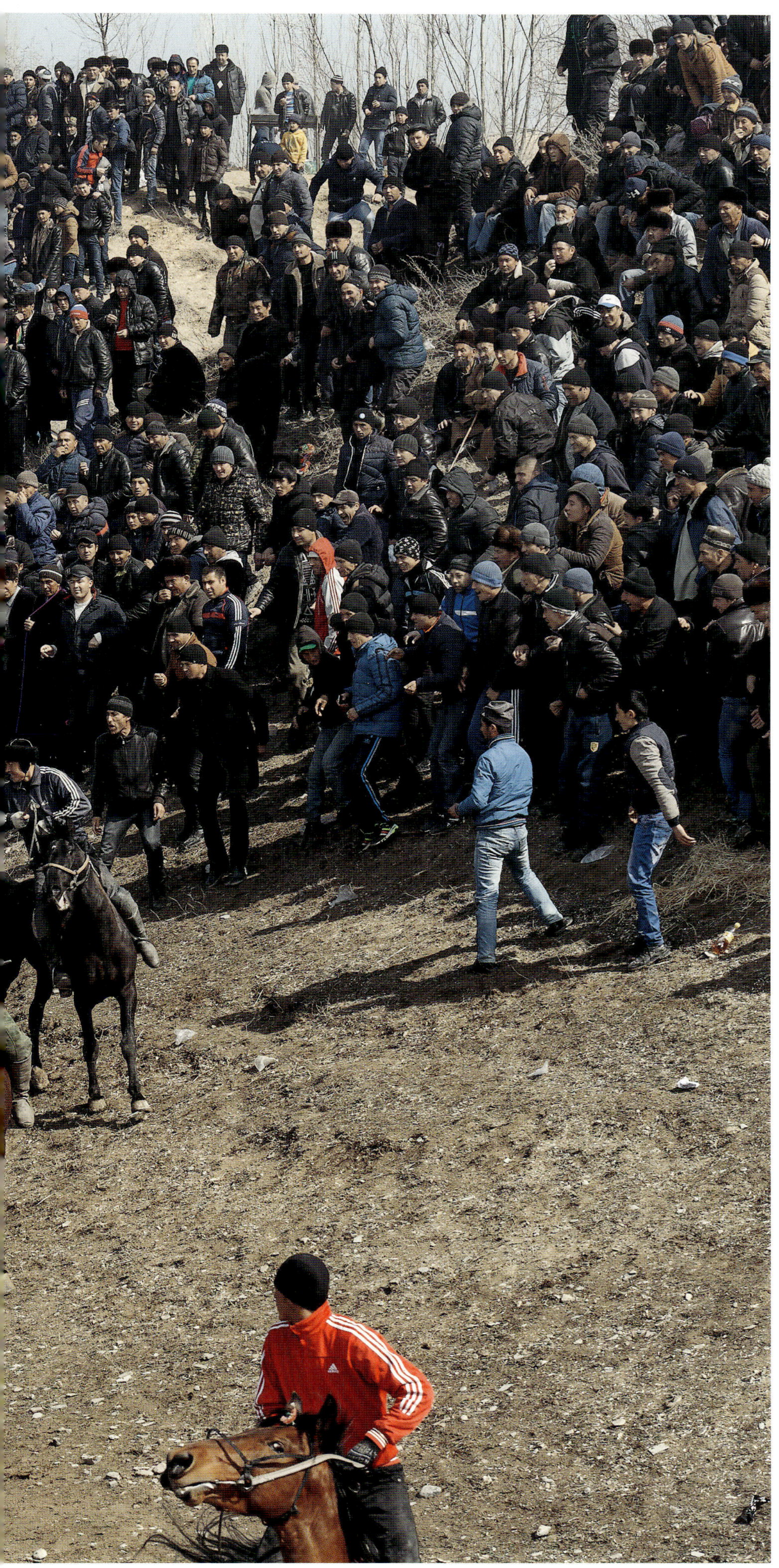

Hundreds of men on horseback try to pull the carcass away from their opponents, oblivious to the spectators or any potential dangers.

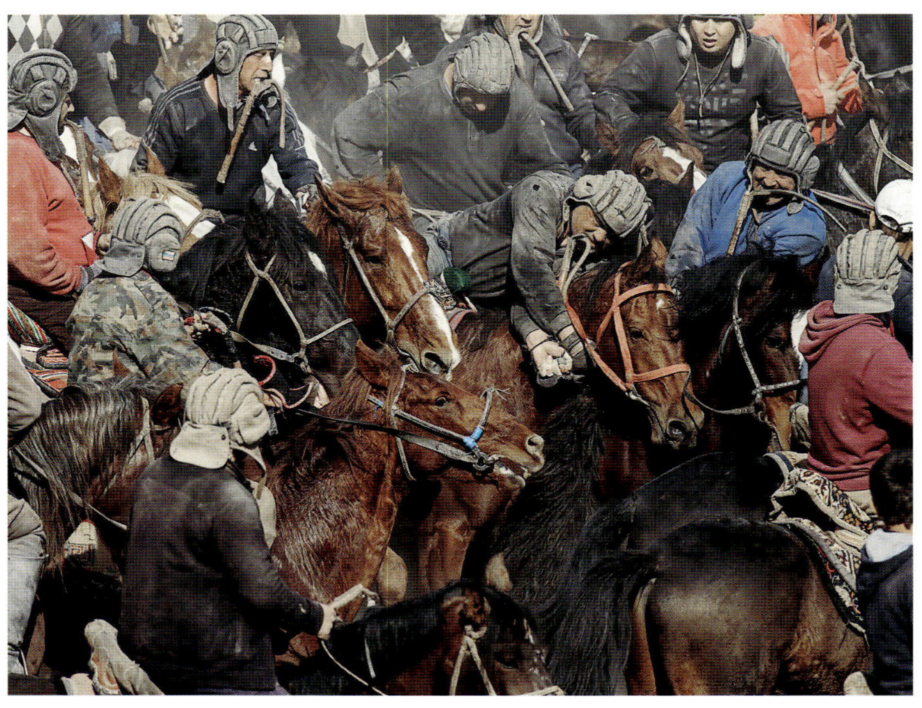

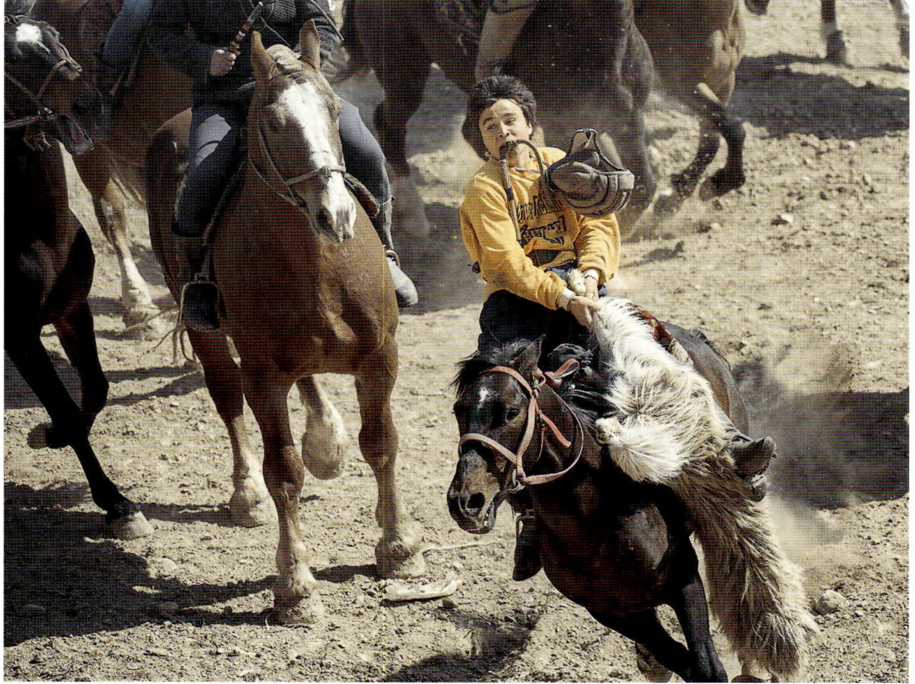

Buzkashi was once a battle exercise disguised as a sport;
today, it is still one of the most dangerous sports in the world,
having caused broken limbs and even death.

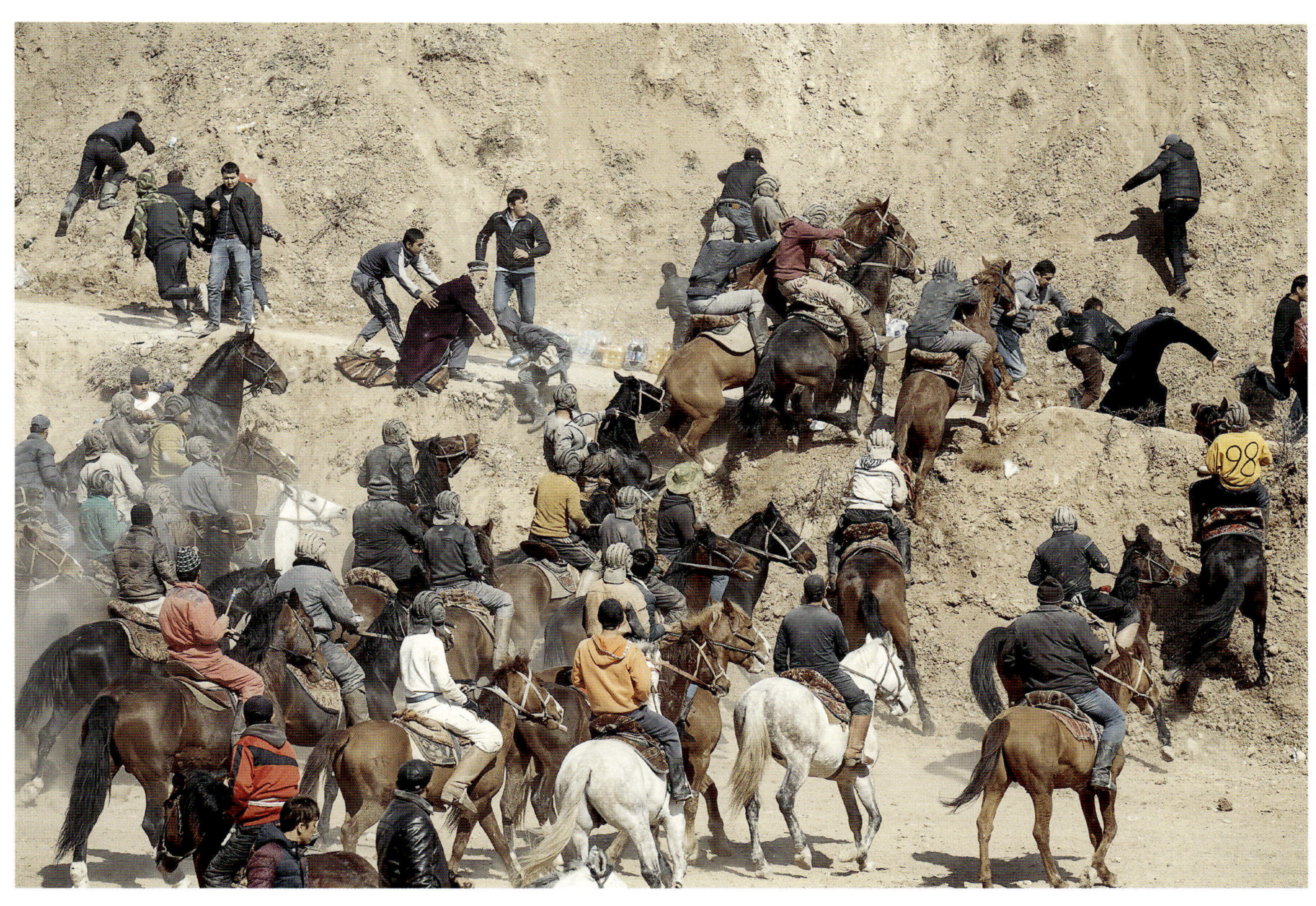

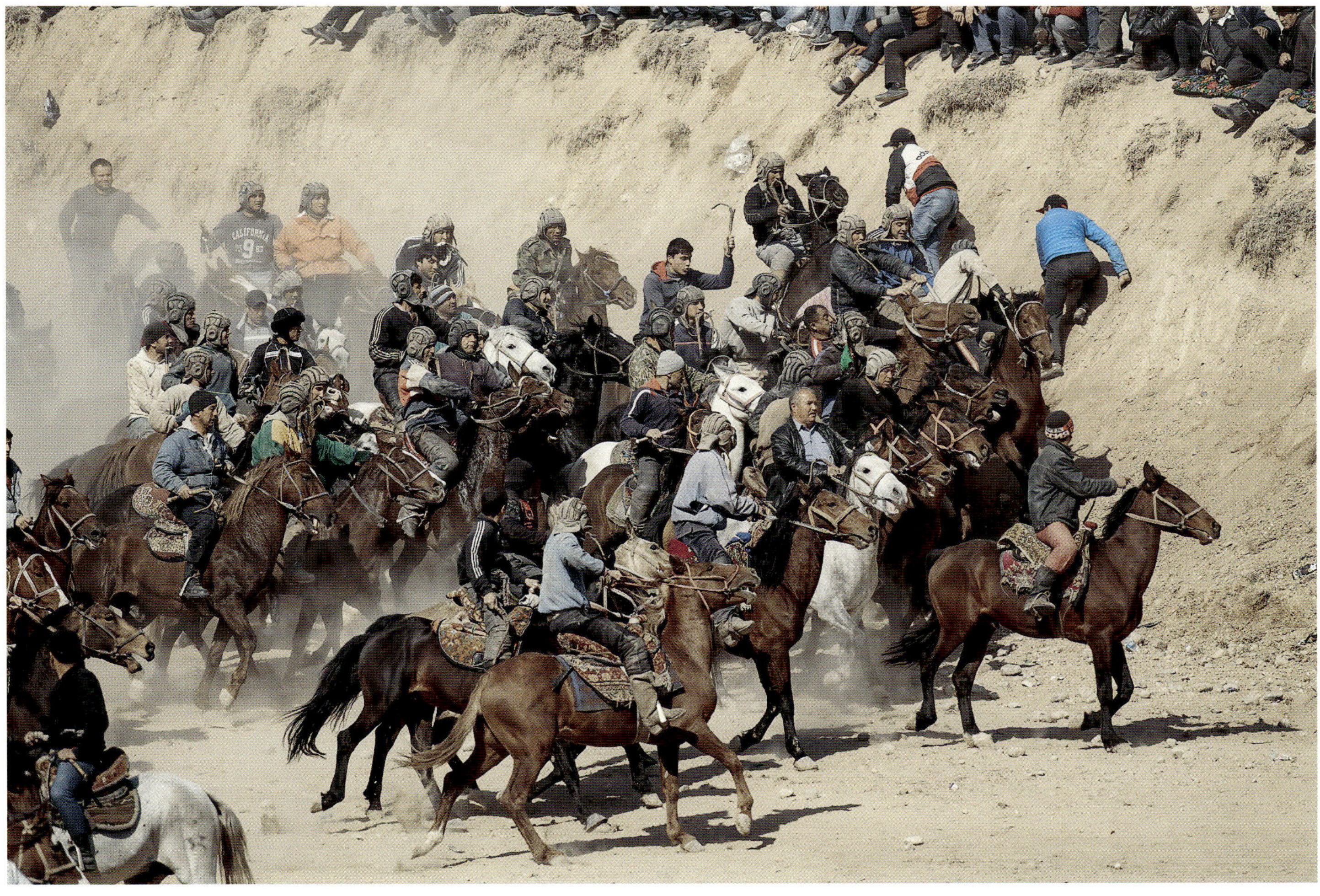

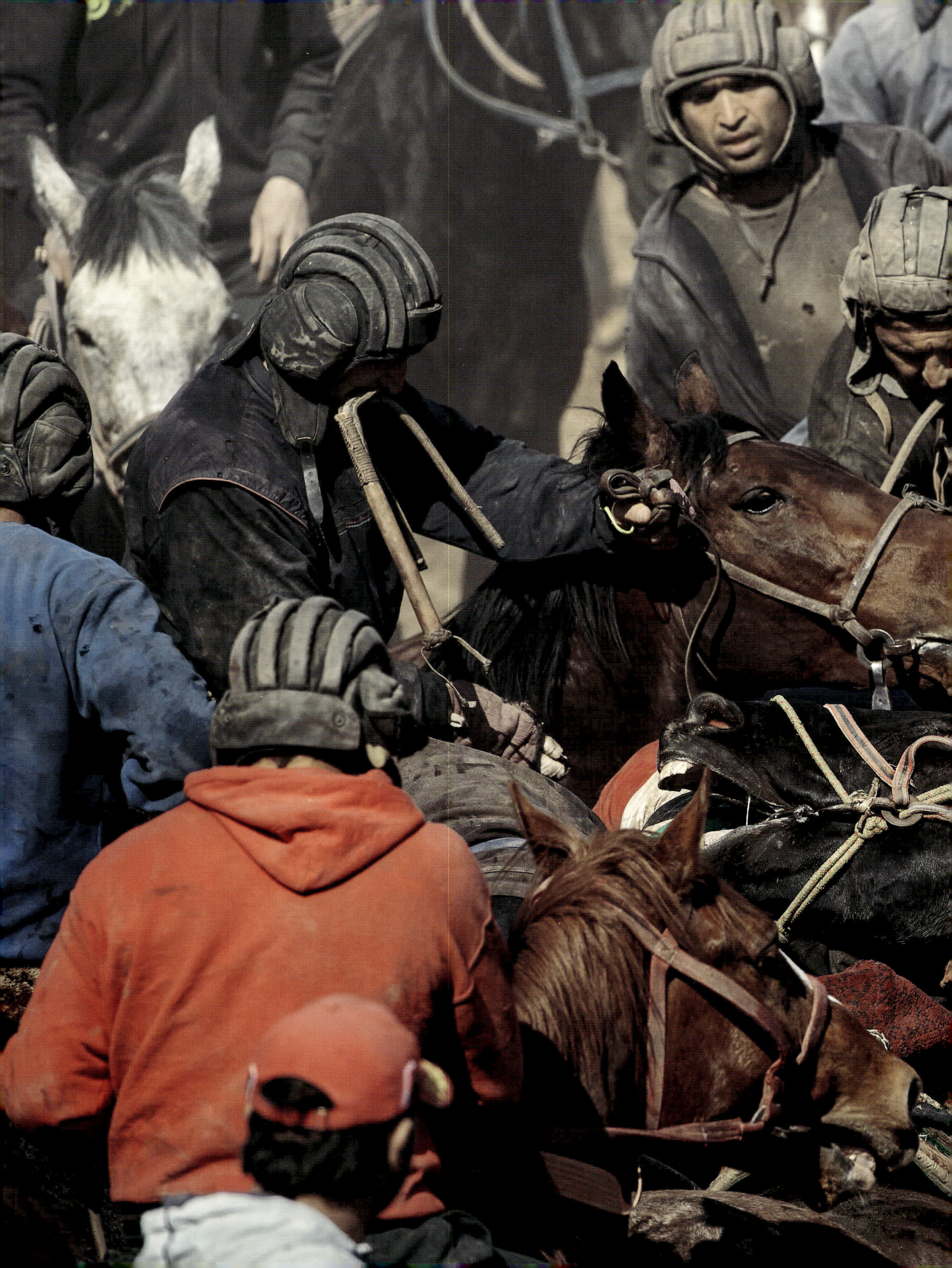

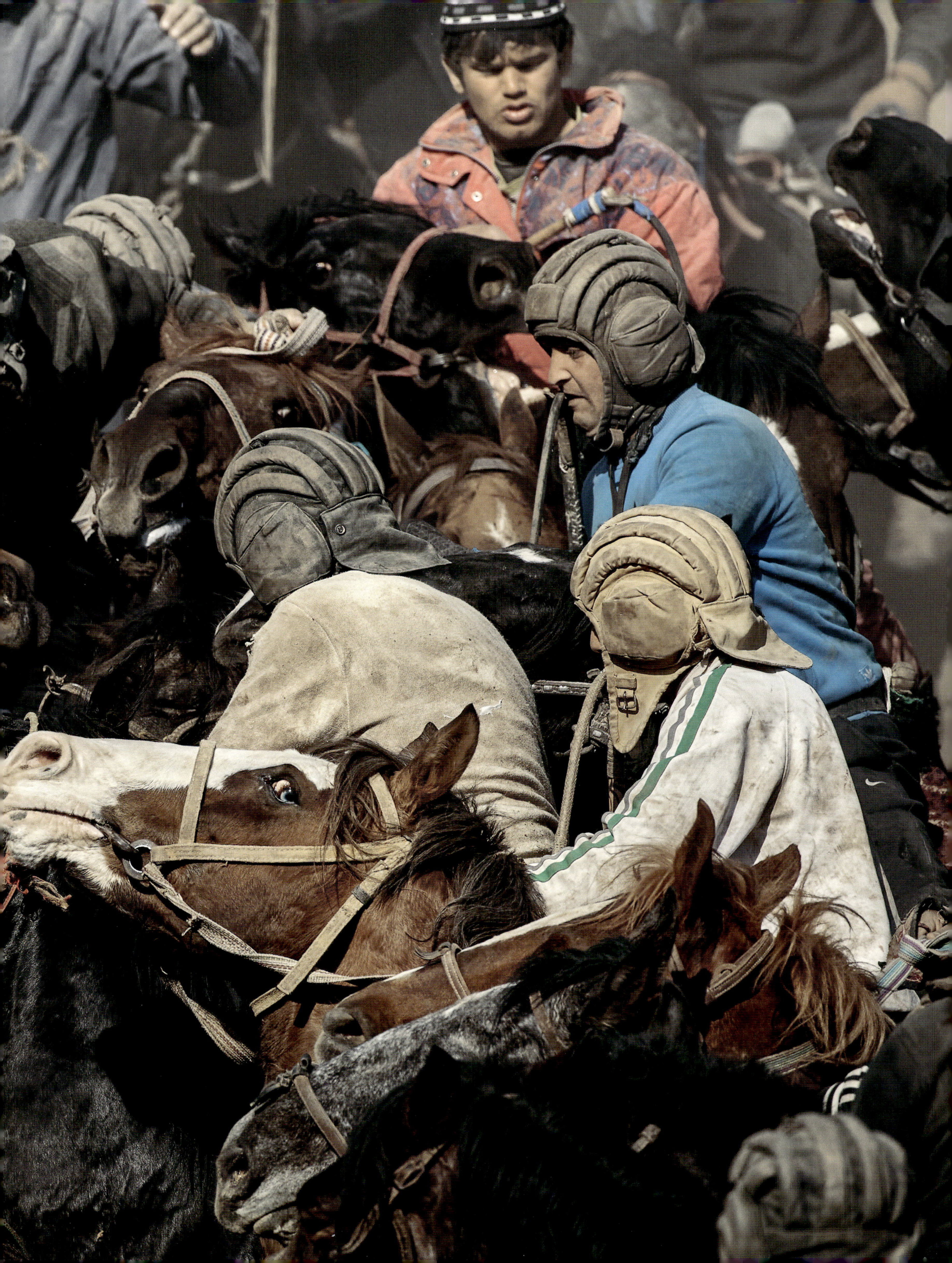

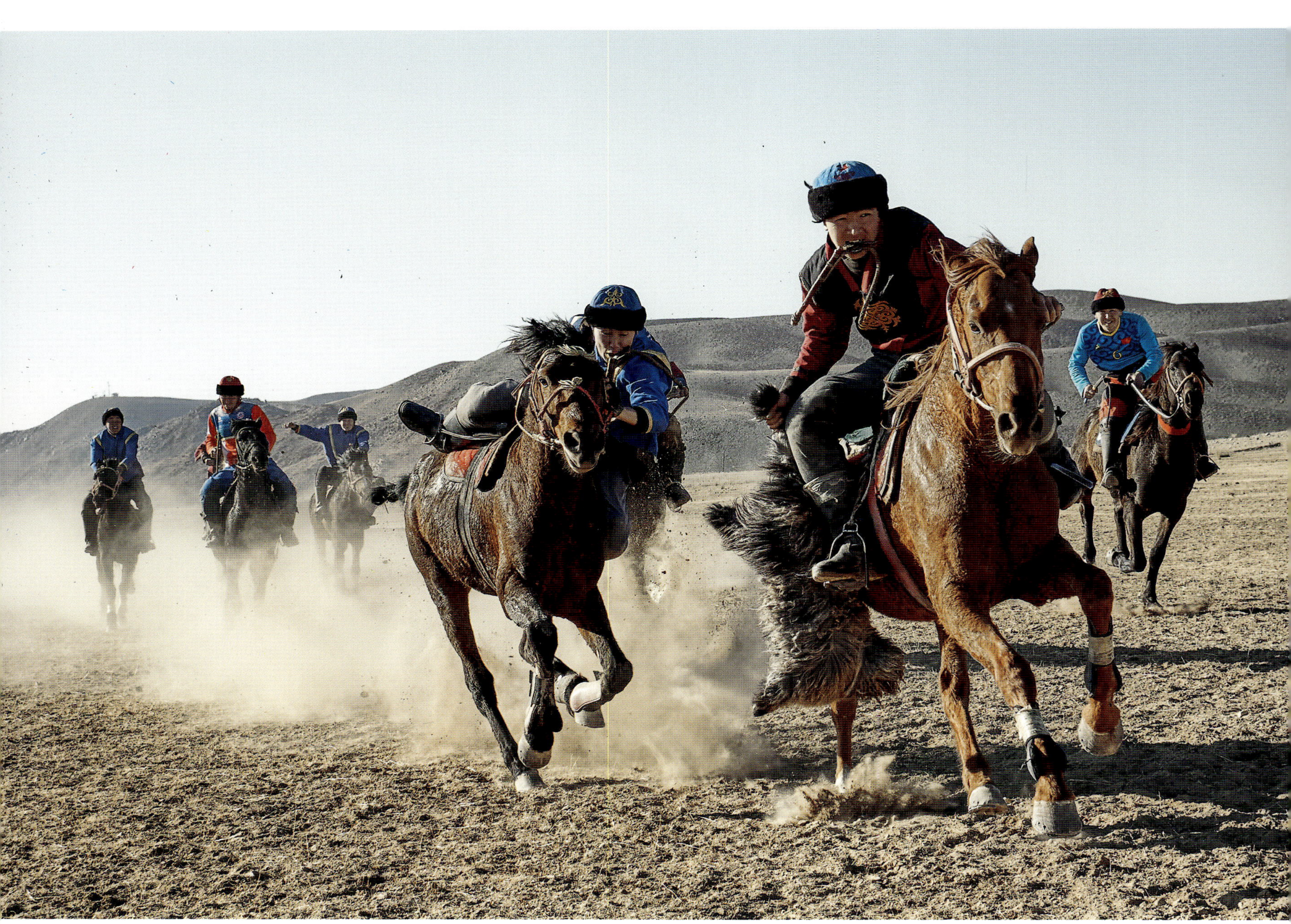

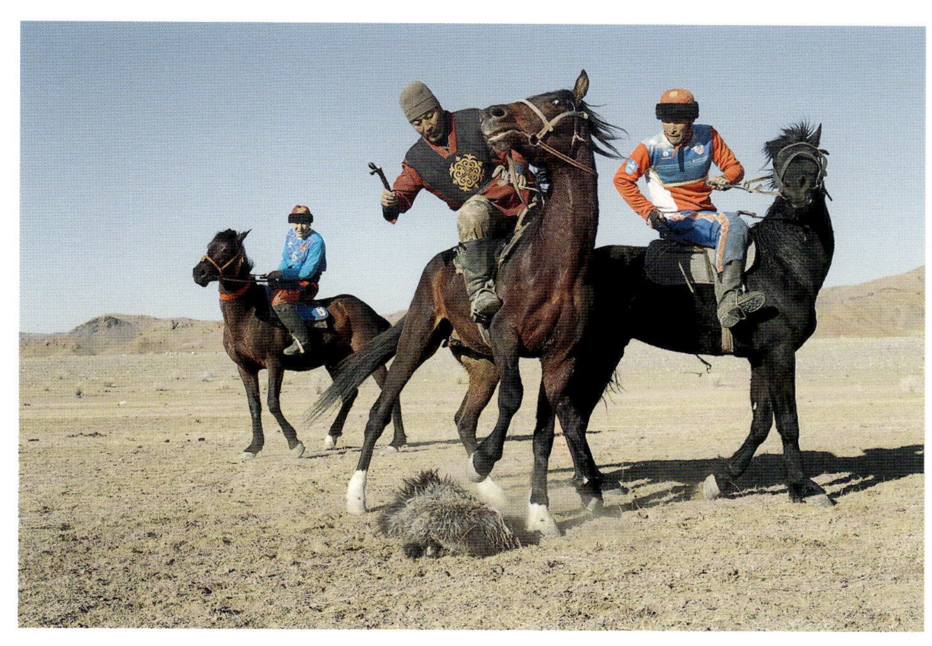

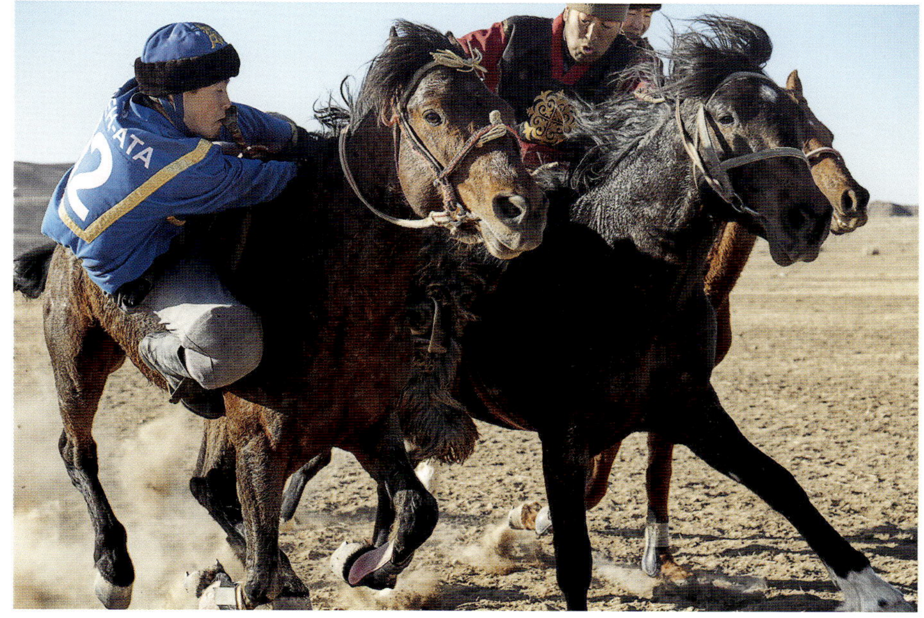

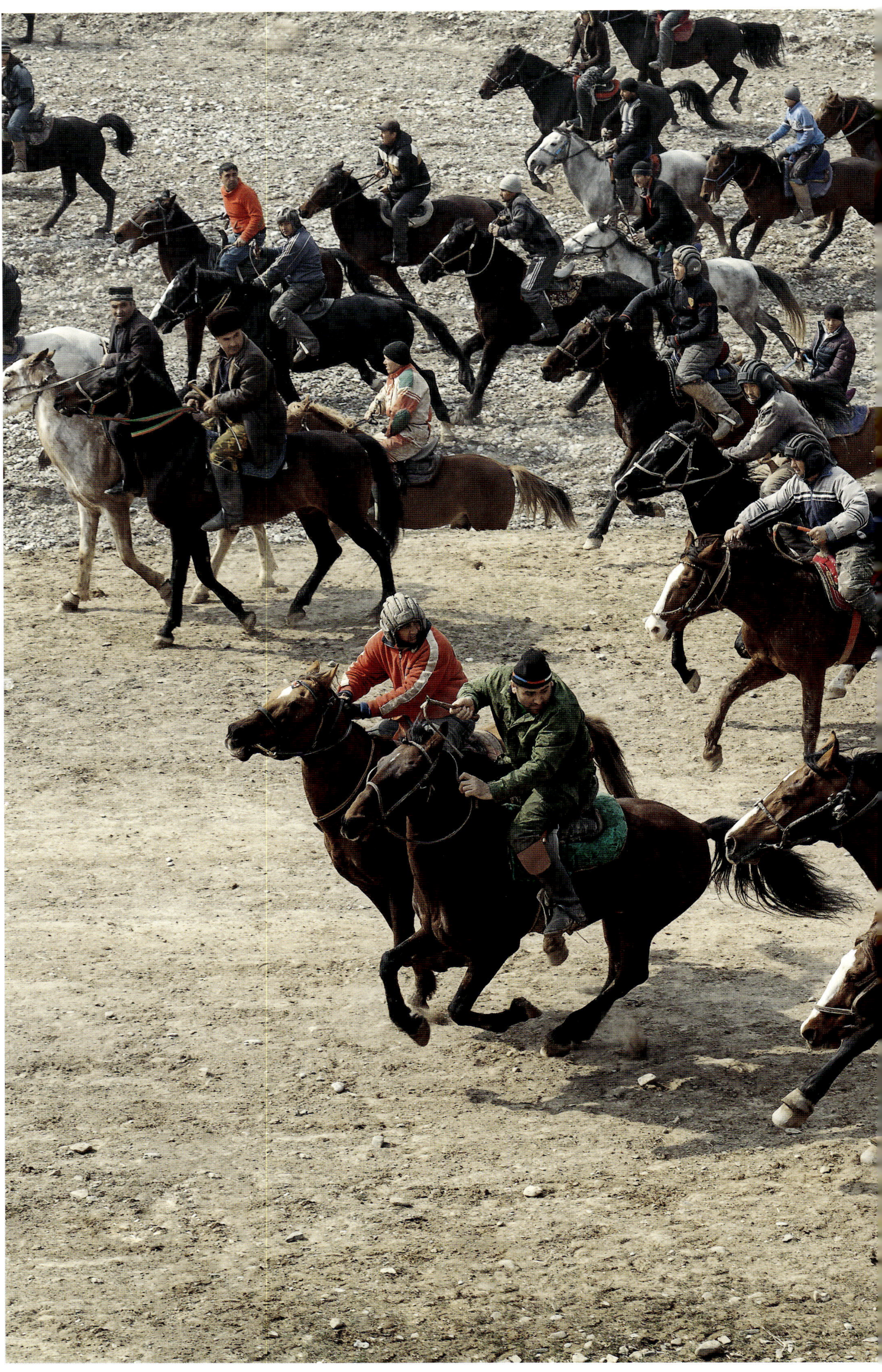

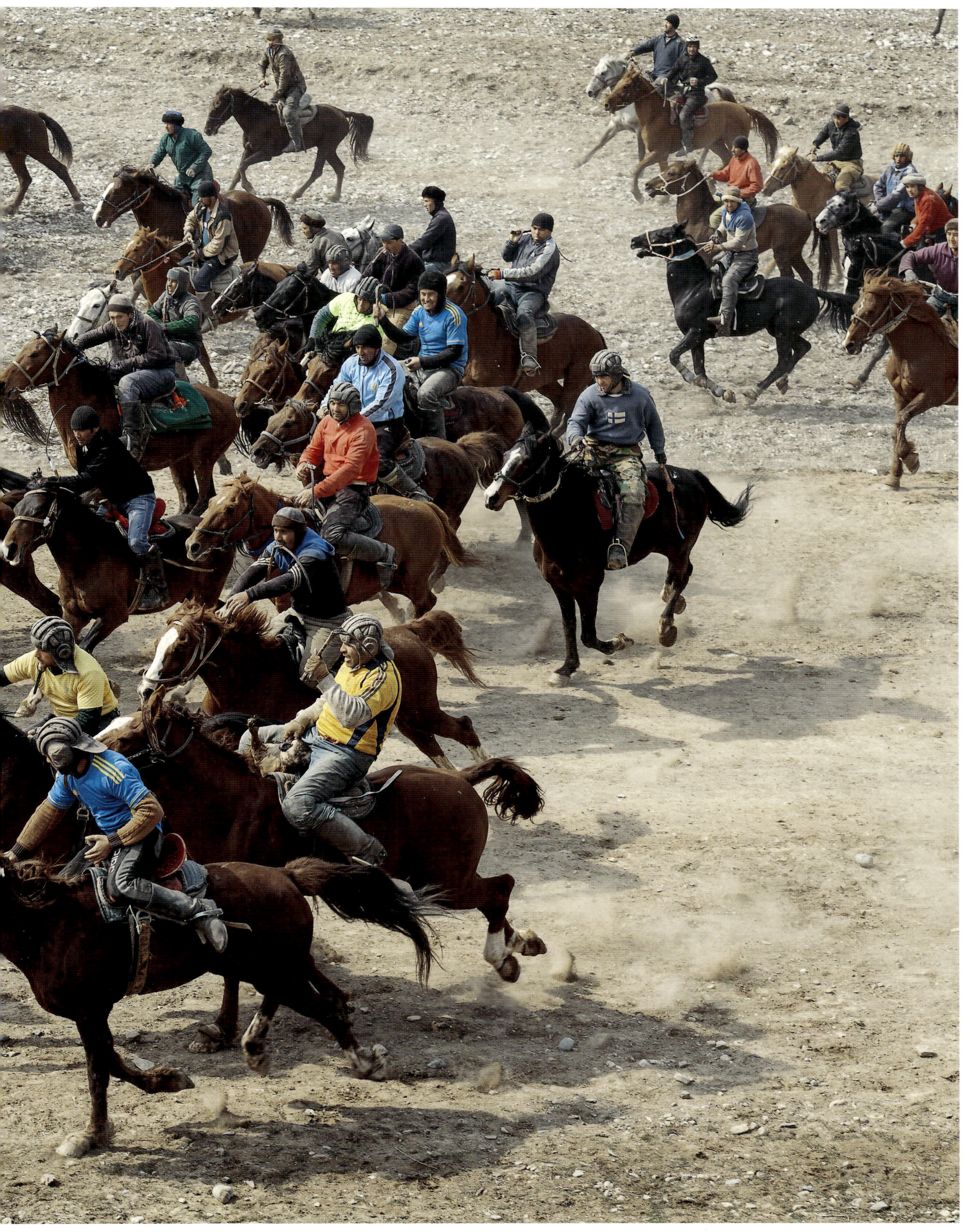

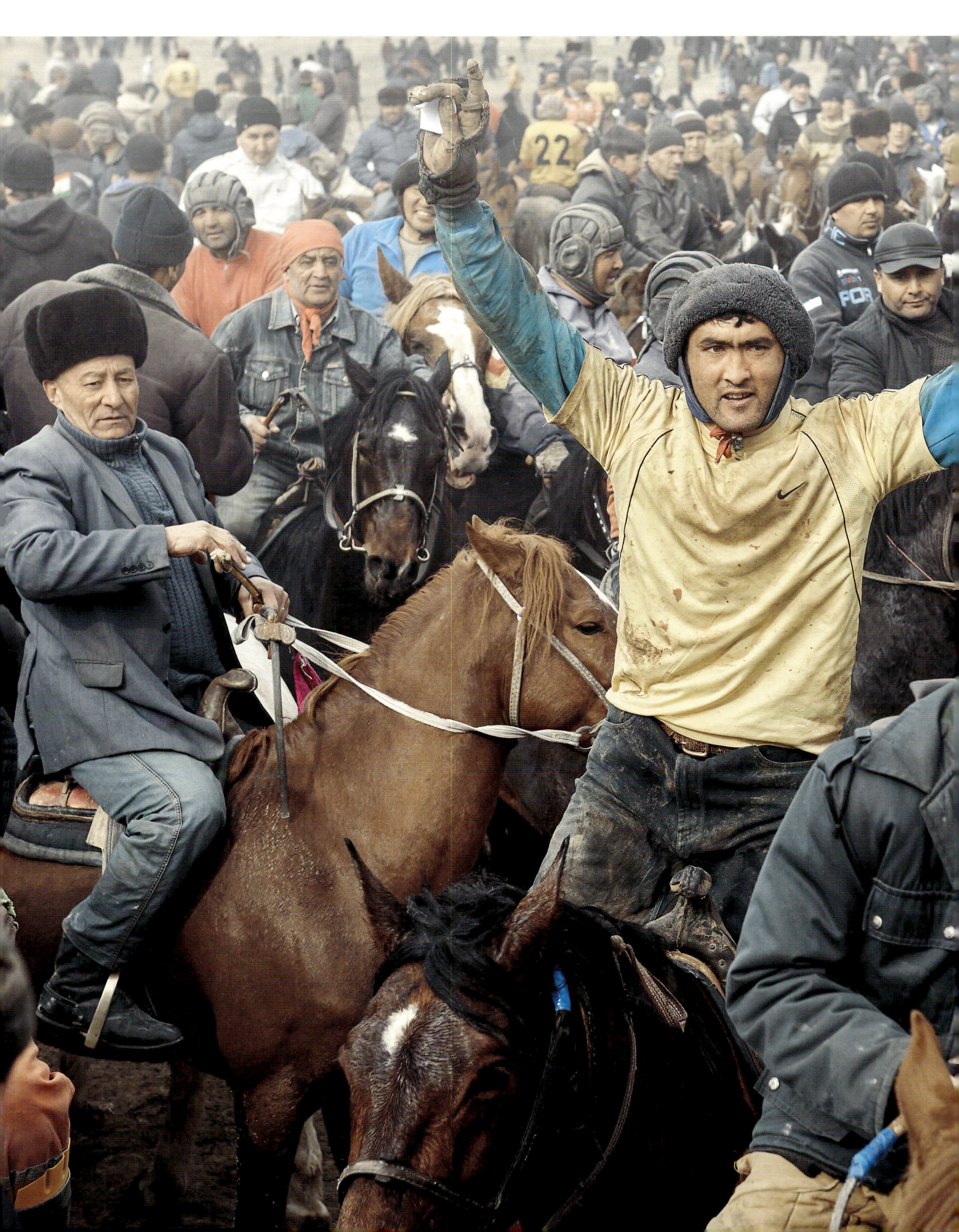

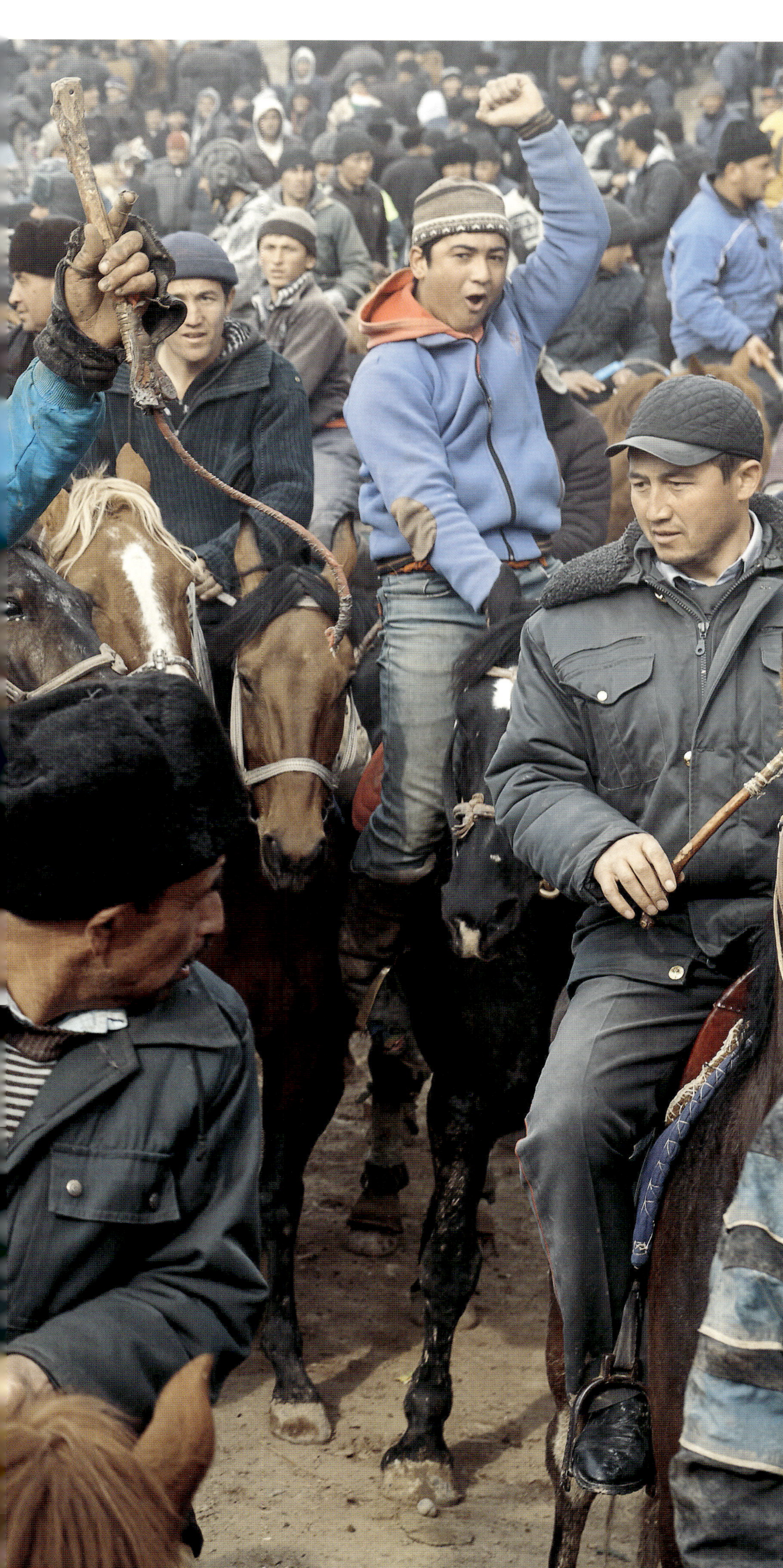

The winners' prize is often a carpet or sometimes a goat to take home.

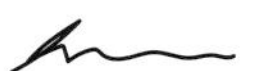

Kite Fighting

BRAZIL

*The need to play prevails as boys cling to their
vanishing innocence, dreaming of a better life.*

Glimmering like a gemstone between lush green mountains, a brilliant blue ocean and miles of golden beaches lies the *Cidade Maravilhosa* – The Wonderful City of Rio de Janeiro. Travellers, poets, musicians and artists agree it is the most beautiful place in the world. This vibrant, visual feast of a city is the playground where children from the congested *favelas* (shanty towns) stretch their arms out towards the sky, like the omnipresent Cristo Redentor, to participate in their beacon of hope – playful and perilous kite fighting.

The urge to spread our wings and soar above the ground is a fascination that goes as far back as 400 B.C. China, where kites were said to have been invented. History is full of individuals, like Leonardo da Vinci and the Wright brothers, whose sense of curiosity propelled them to reach for the skies with aerodynamic inventions. Yet the kite remains an everlasting form of aviation and nowhere is kite-flying more alive than in the pulsating city of Rio.

VIDIGAL,
RIO DE JANEIRO

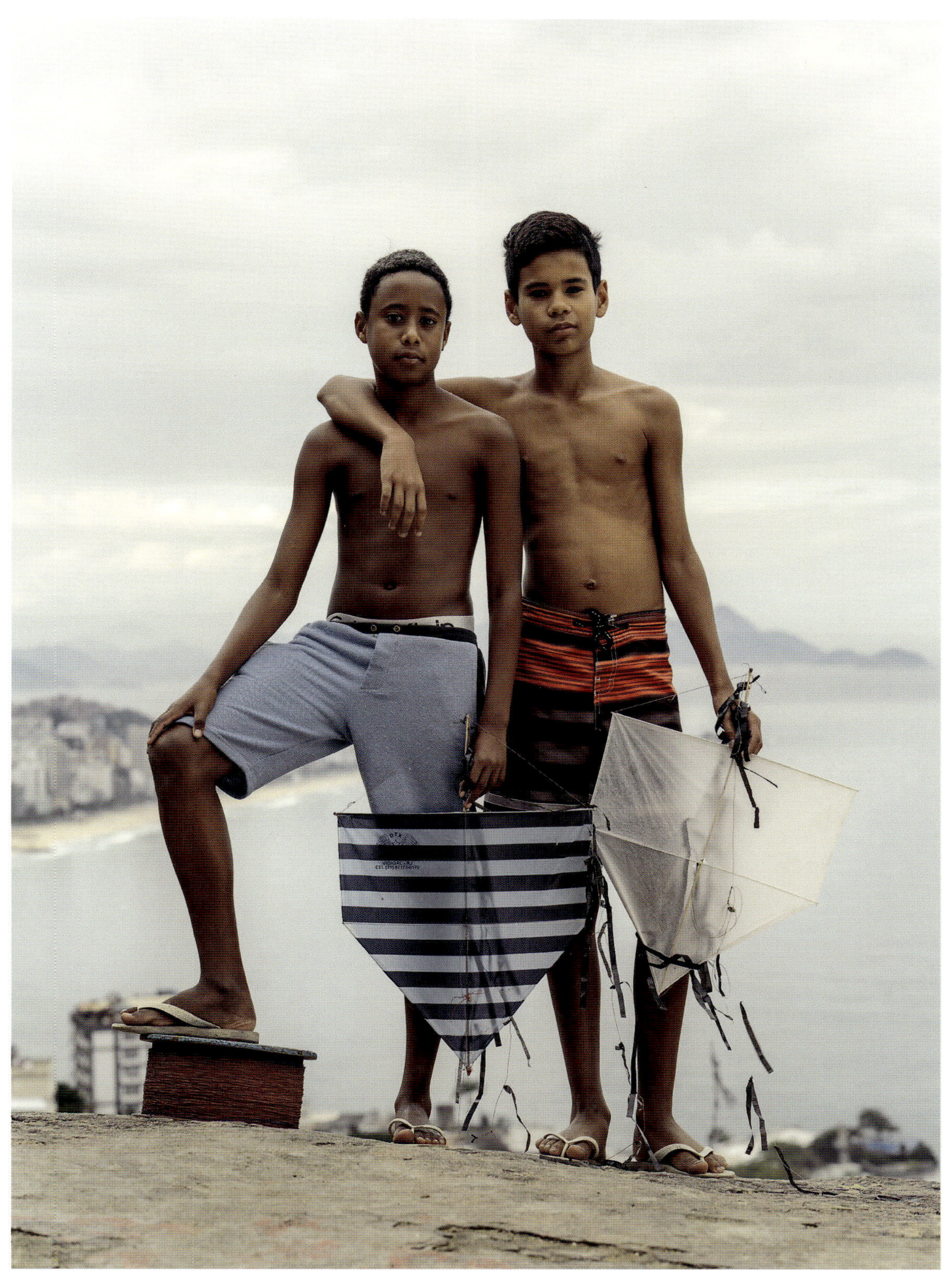

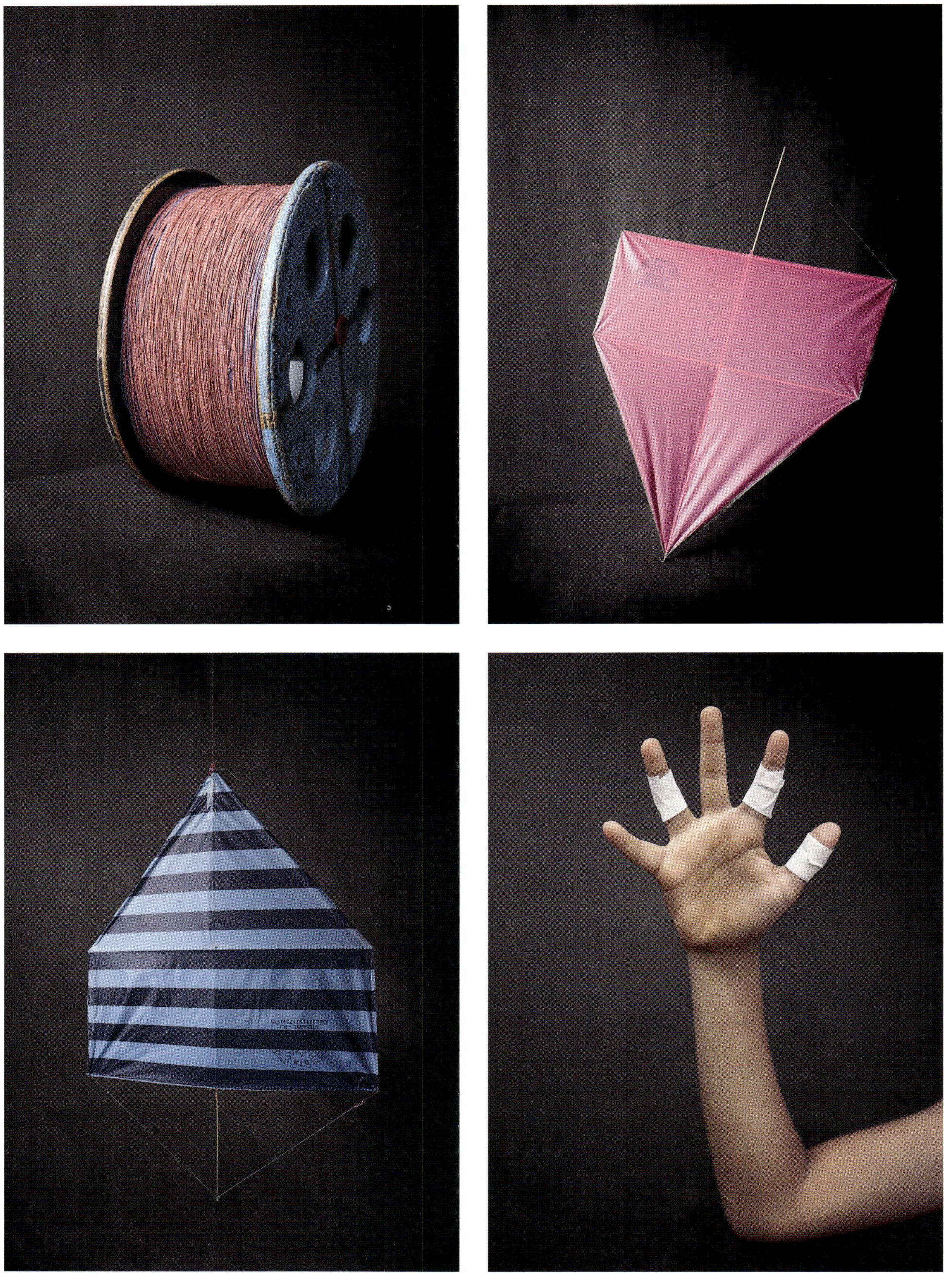

"Don't be afraid of a little opposition. Remember that the 'kite' of success generally rises against the wind of adversity, not with it."

~ Napoleon Hill ~

Only blocks away from the beach, stacked into the sprawling hillsides overlooking the city, are over a thousand *favelas* where 1.5 million of Brazil's most impoverished people live. And to make matters worse, the *favelas* are controlled by drug lords and militias, raining violence on an already downtrodden people struggling with poor health care, education and sanitation and pushing them deeper into the crevices of the land. Despite these dire conditions, residents will tell you that there is an incredible sense of community in the *favelas*; everyone knows and helps one another. And it is here in this oppressive and contradictory playground children find a way to play, escaping their harsh environment through kite fighting, Brazil's most popular sport next to soccer.

Kites (or *pipas*) are constructed from recycled materials such as plastic grocery bags that the boys find amongst the rubble. The kites are designed, decorated and shaped into triangles or diamonds. But the game turns dangerous when their kite strings are coated with *cerol* — a mixture of wax and crushed glass.

On any given day, dozens of boys leap from one rooftop to another, brimming with excitement as they help each other's kites lift off into the breeze. With seemingly infinite kite line, the boys skilfully and strategically loose them into the sky, the kites soaring ever higher, before ambushing opponents in neighbouring communities whom they've never even met. Kite fighting allows the boys to learn aerodynamics and hand-eye coordination and to feel a sense of pride and freedom, which to them is invaluable, as many get little to no formal education.

The aim of this game passed down through generations is to cut your rivals' kite strings before they cut yours. These razor-sharp lines are nearly invisible and have slit many a boy's hand. But more grievously, they've injured and even killed unsuspecting bystanders on bicycles and motorcycles. Although Brazil has banned kite fighting, not even the law can stop this hazardous sport from continuing.

In the midst of this battlefield, presided over by Icarus, the need to play prevails as boys cling to their vanishing innocence, dreaming of a better life. They hurl their kites up into the heavens, their wishes lagging behind on a wing and a prayer and longing to shine as brightly as the enchanting city they were born in.

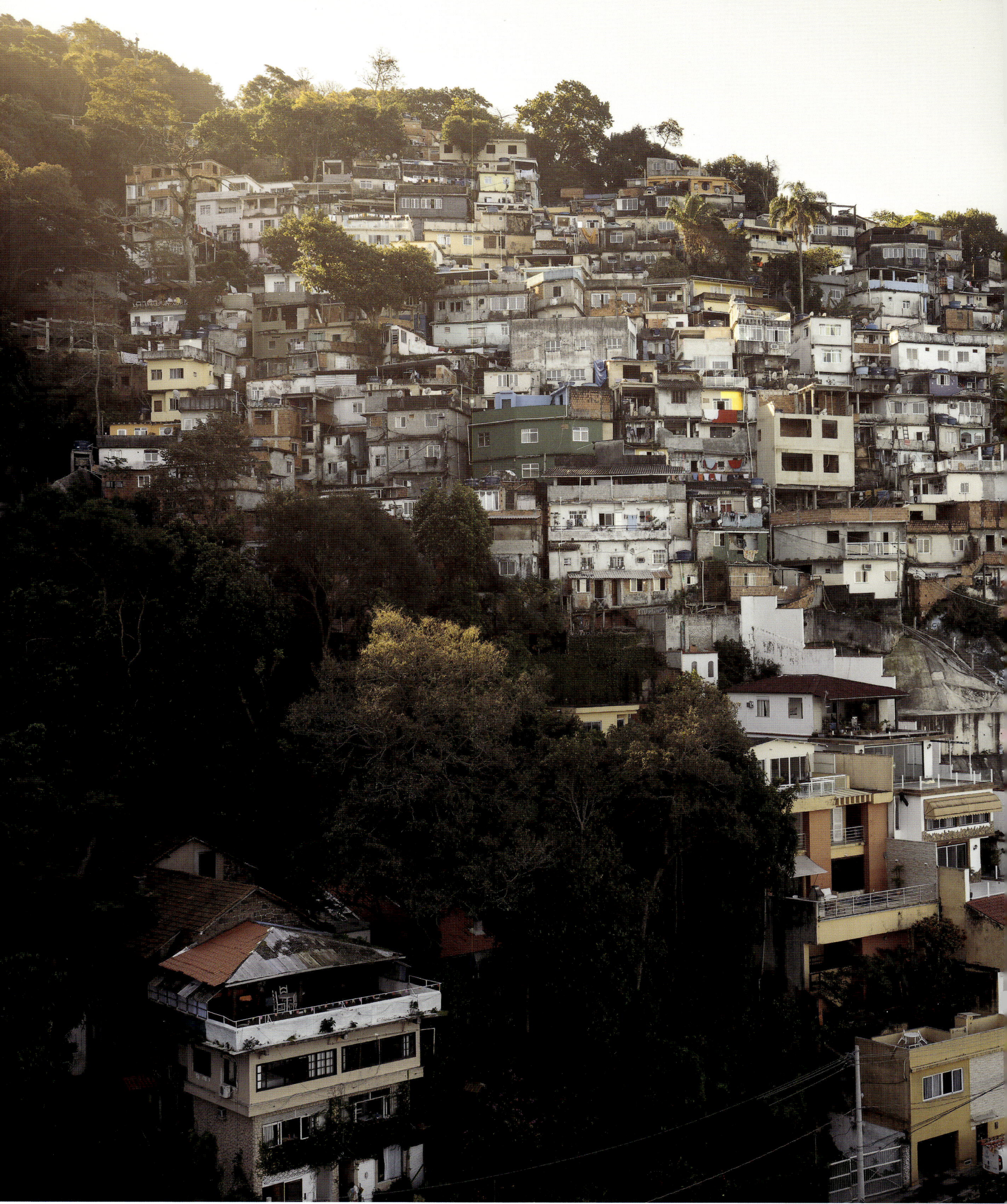

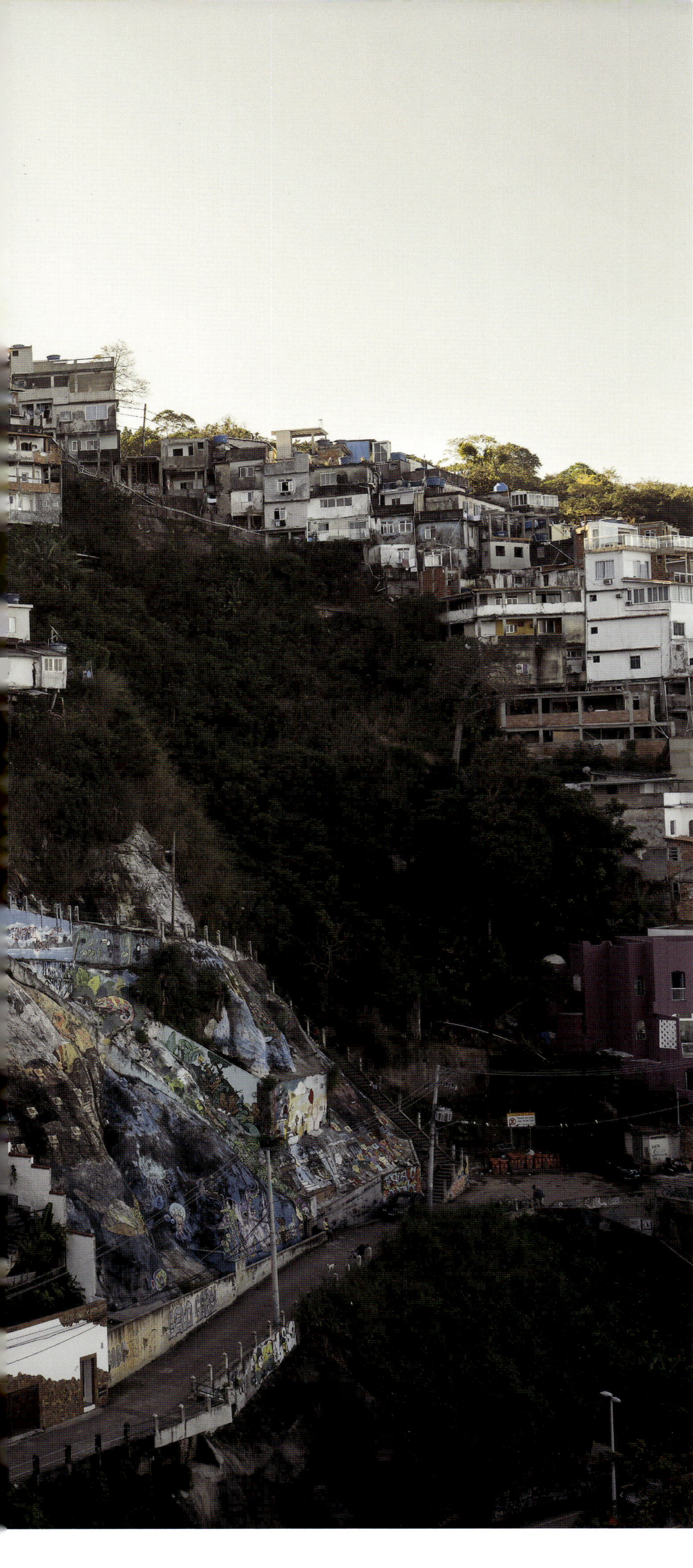

Favela Vidigal, once known as the
most dangerous favela in Rio, is now
an up-and-coming- area overlooking
the famed Ipanema Beach.

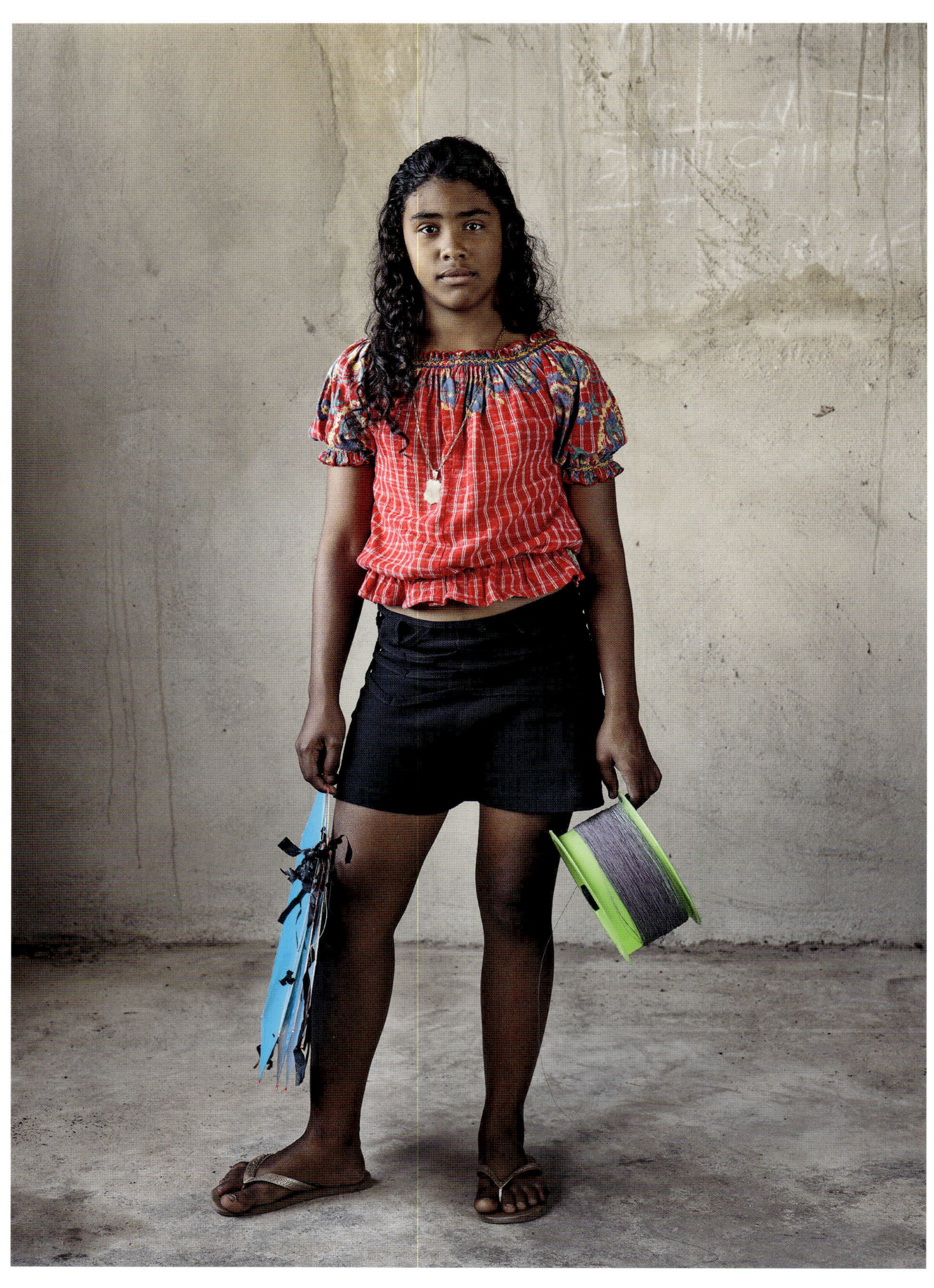

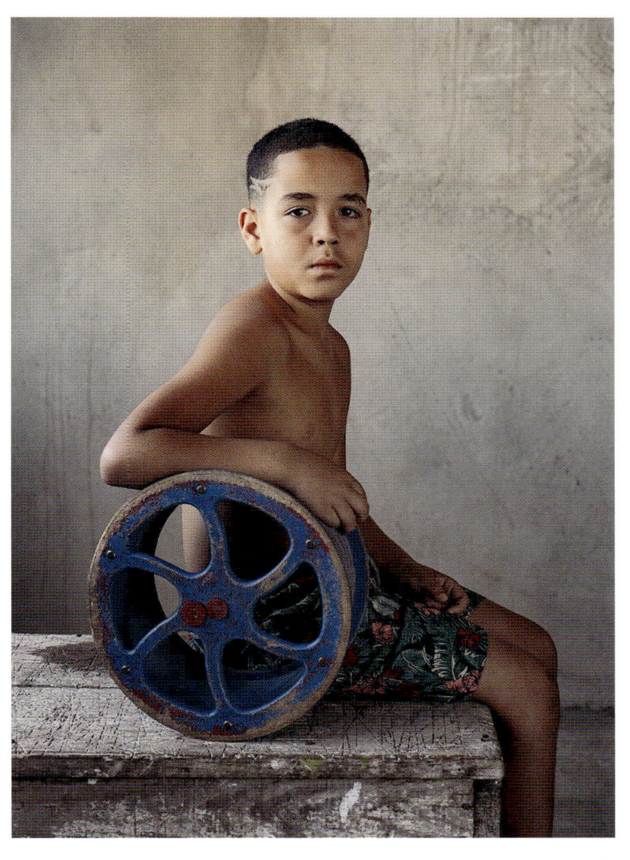
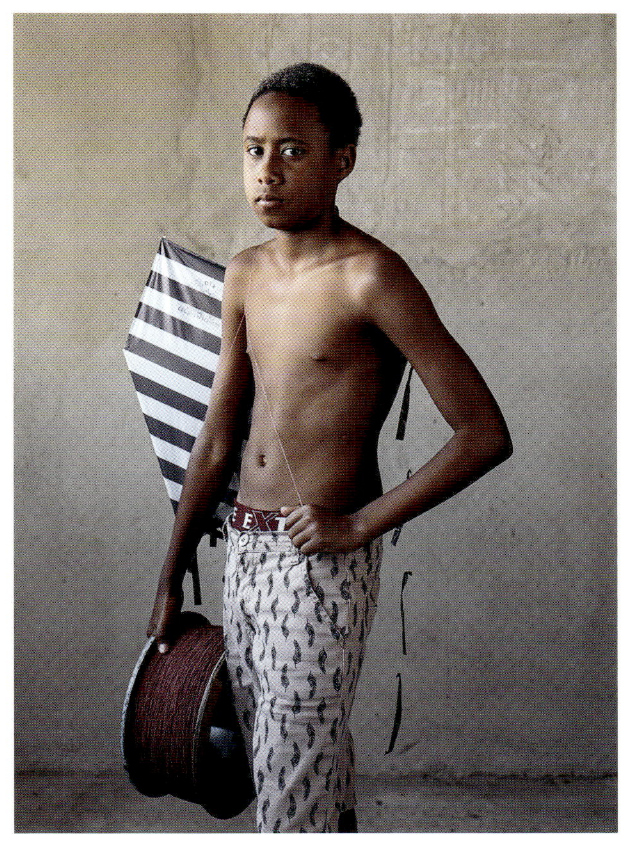
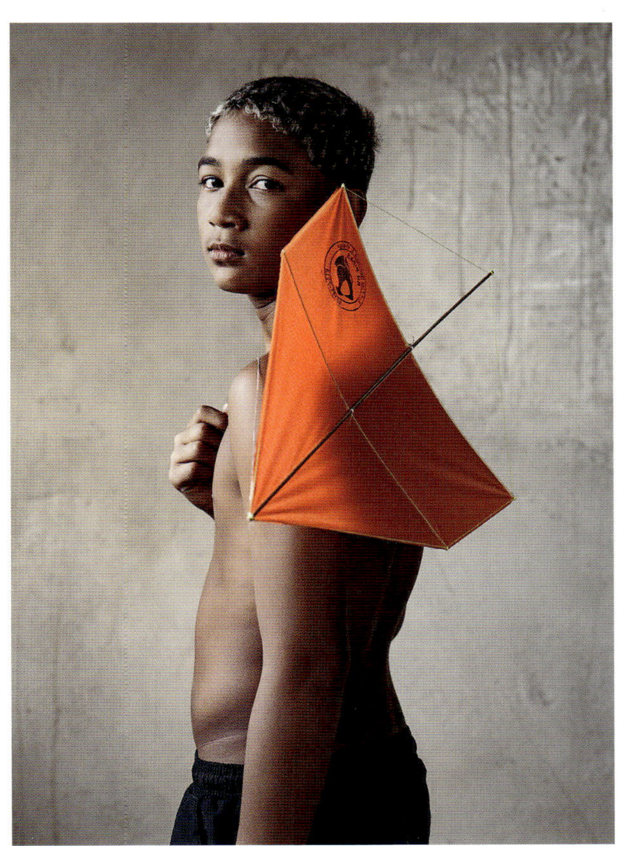
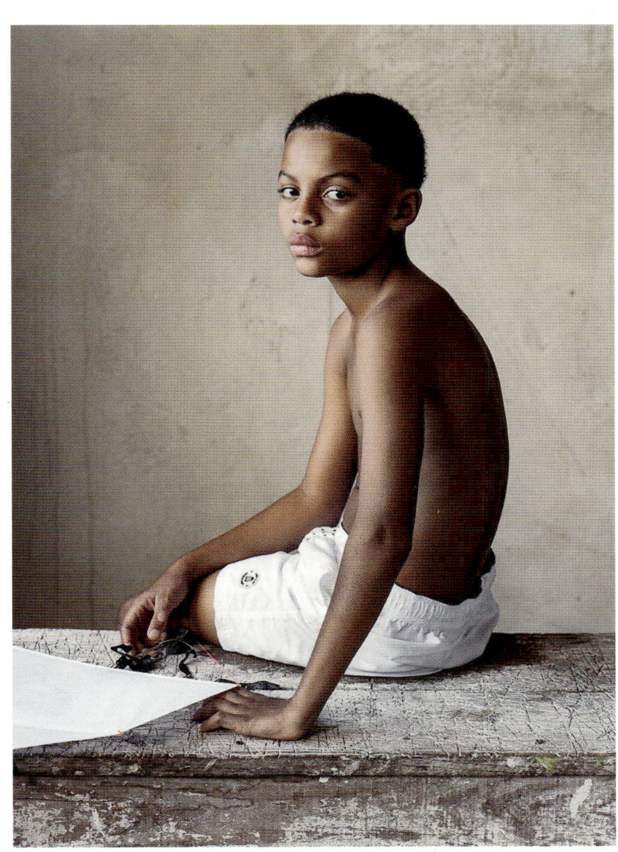

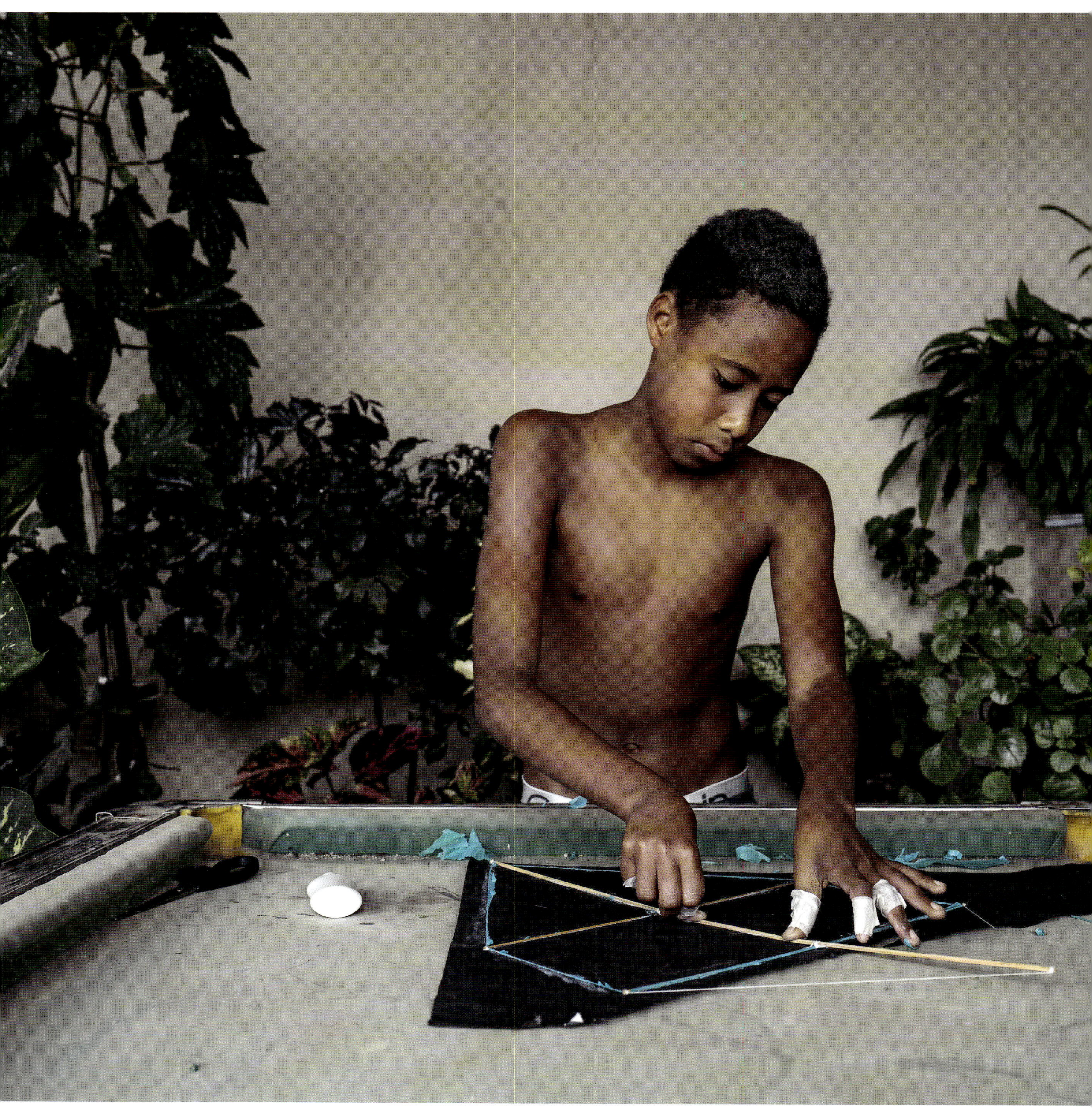

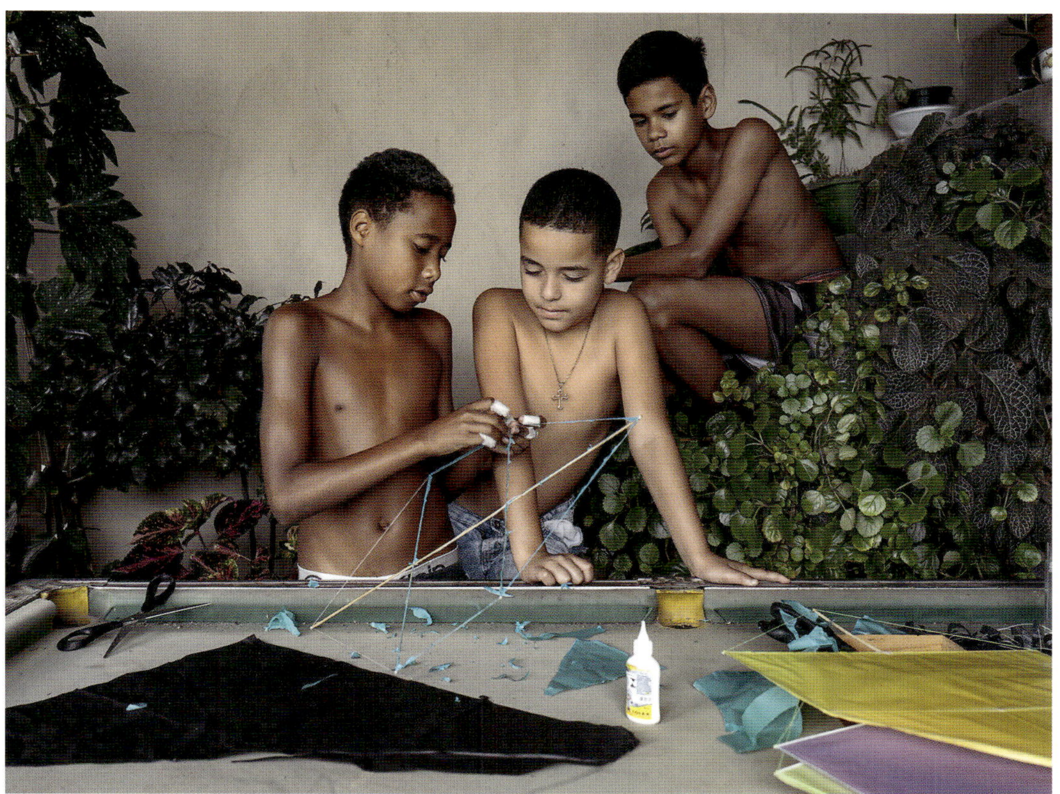

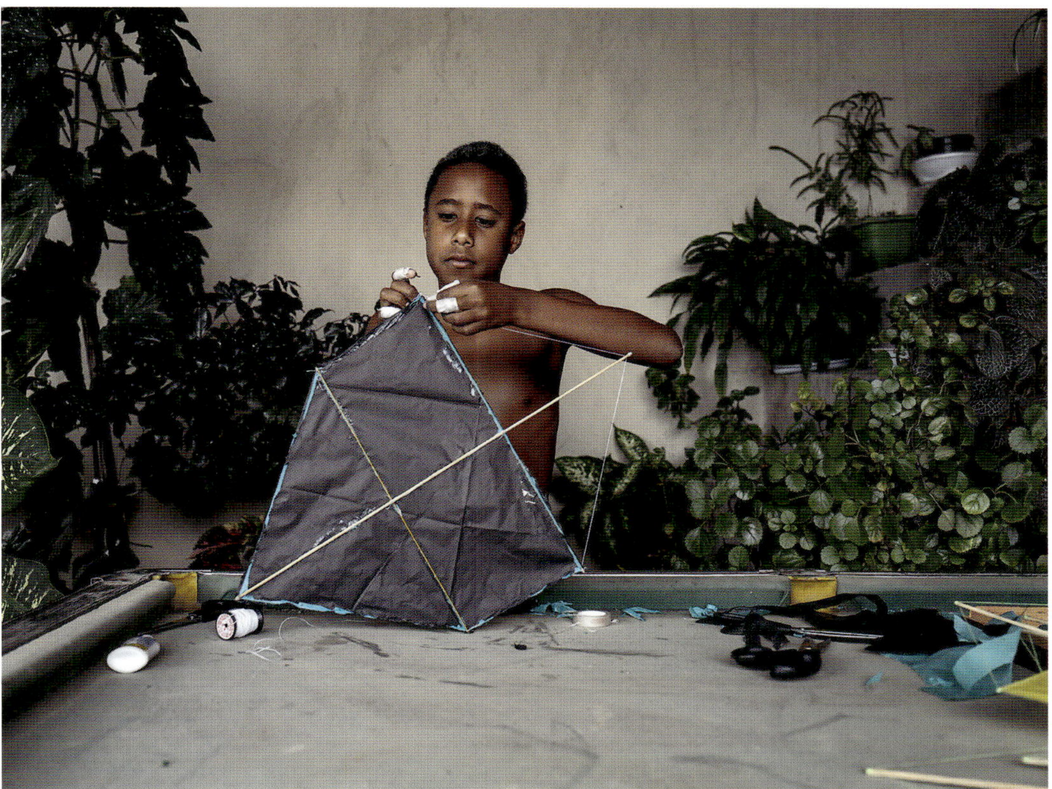

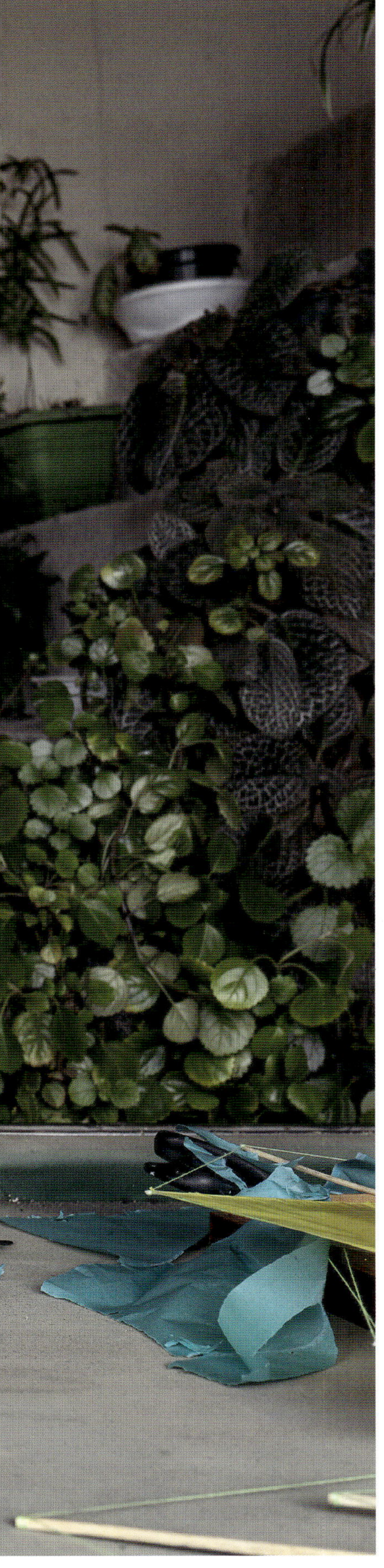

Kites (pipas) are made from whatever recycled materials the boys find
in the rubbish, decorating and shaping them into triangles or diamonds
and coating the strings with 'cerol' - a paste of wax and crushed glass.

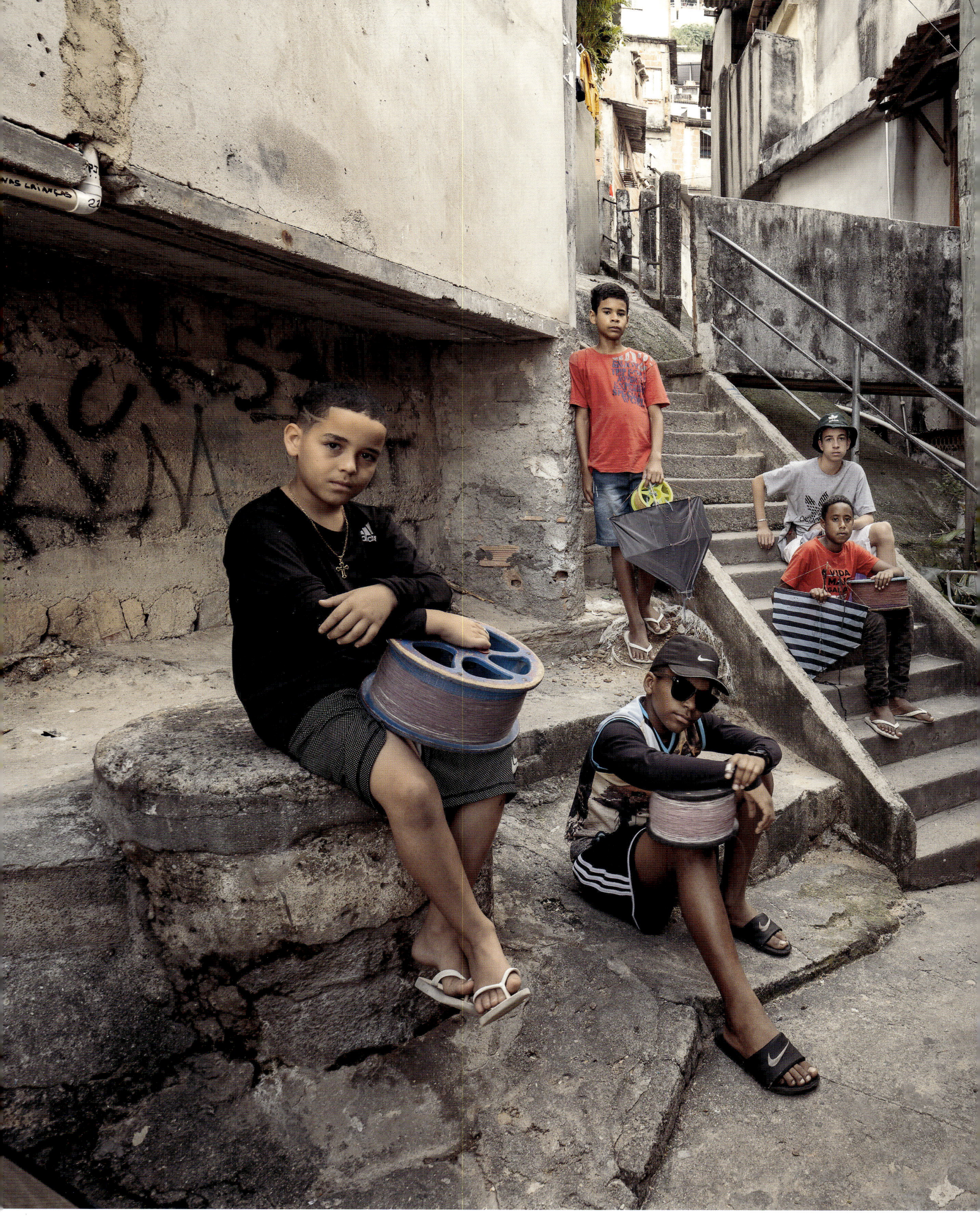

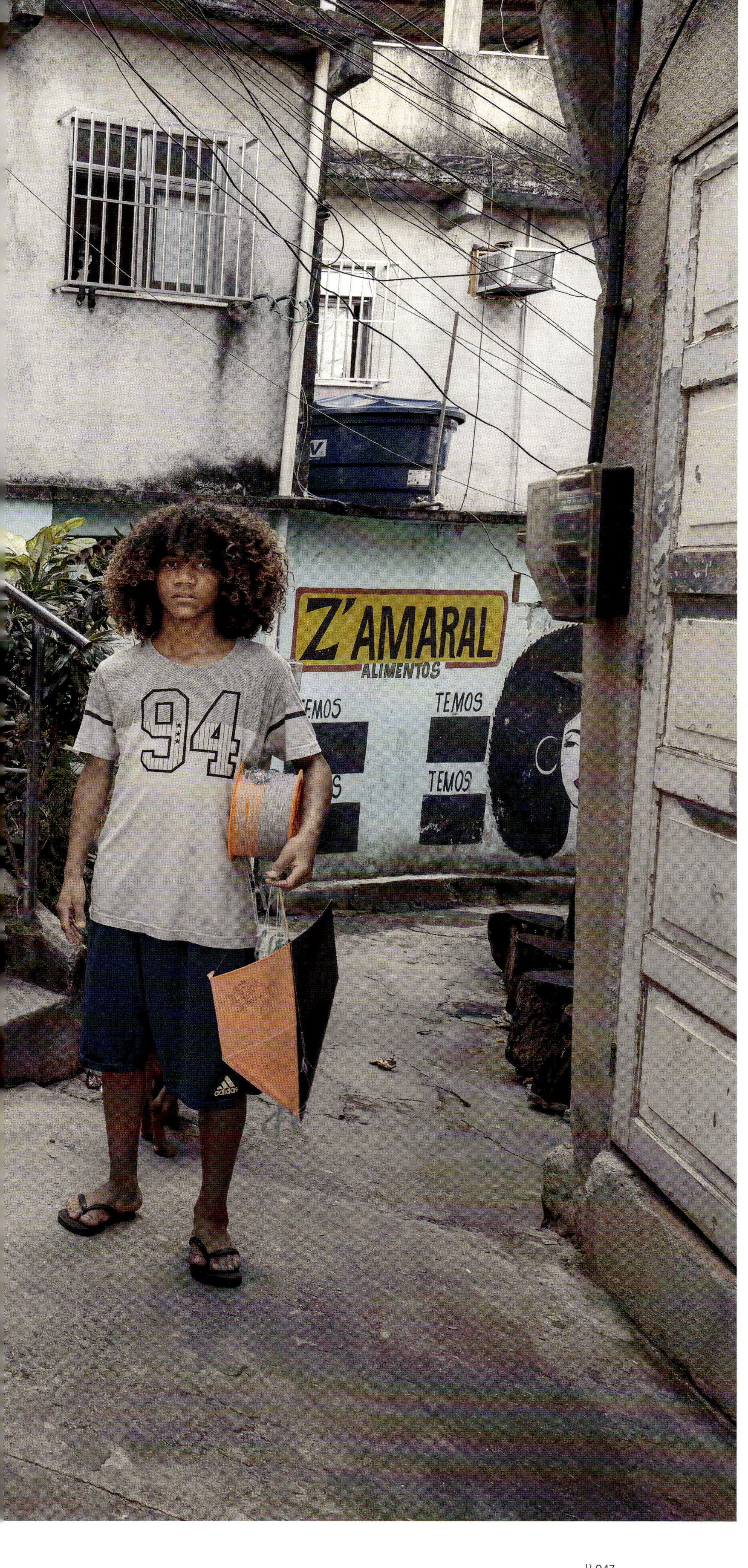

Z'AMARAL
ALIMENTOS
TEMOS
TEMOS
TEMOS
TEMOS
94

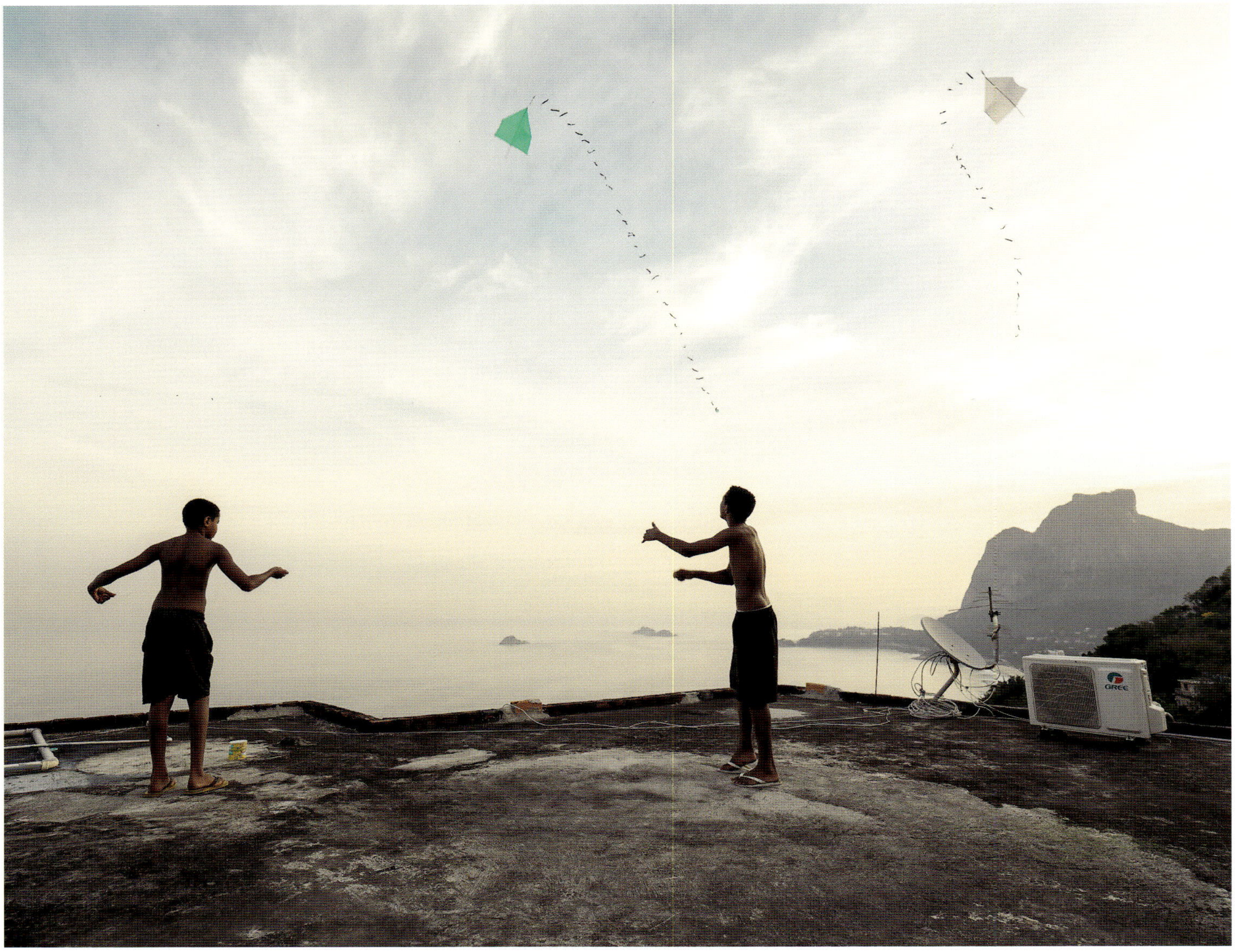

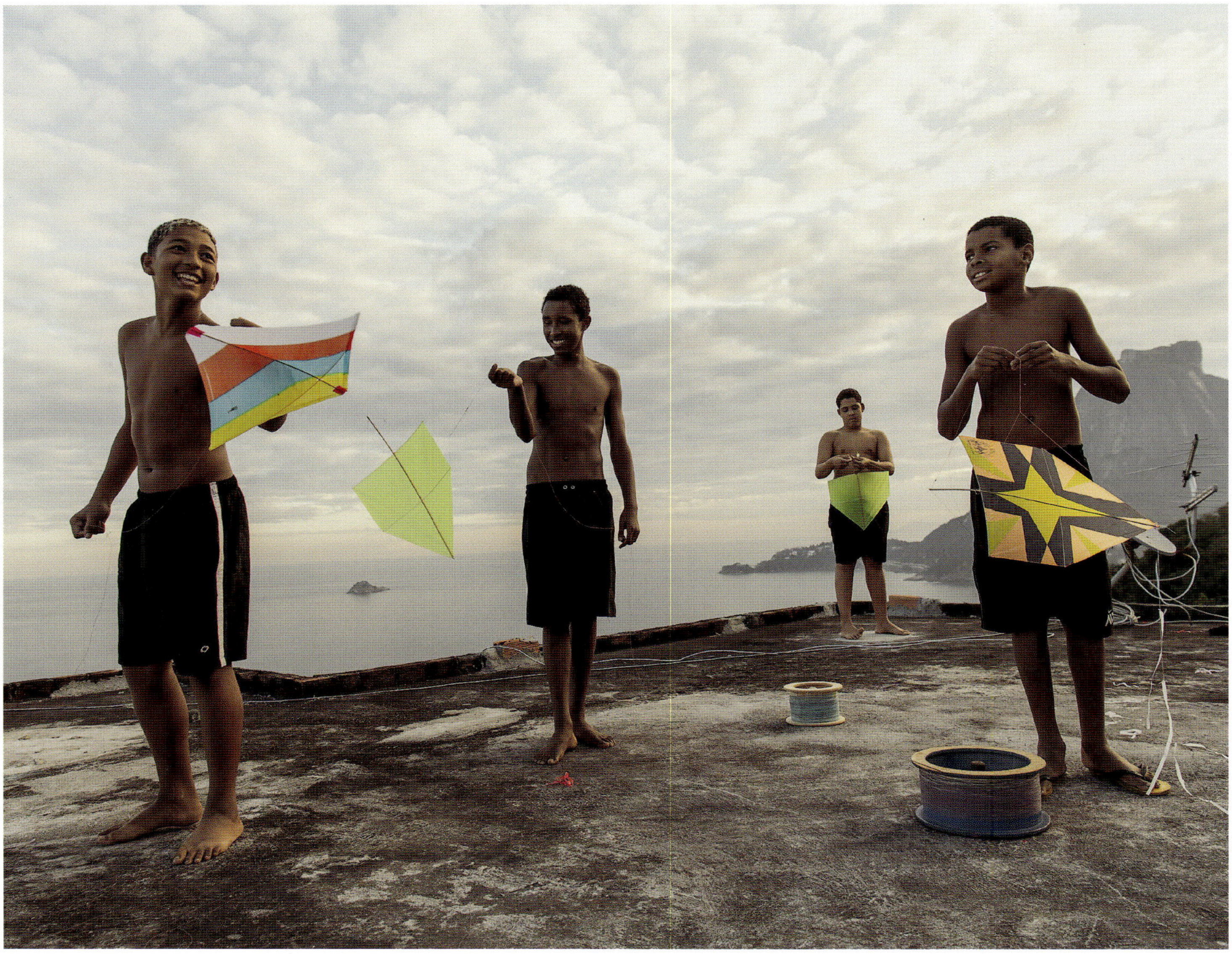

"You sometimes feel like it's a kids' game, but it's actually a game you can play at any age. You need to be super smart to keep your kite in the air and avoid people breaking your line."

~ Ian Cosenza, Brazilian surfer ~

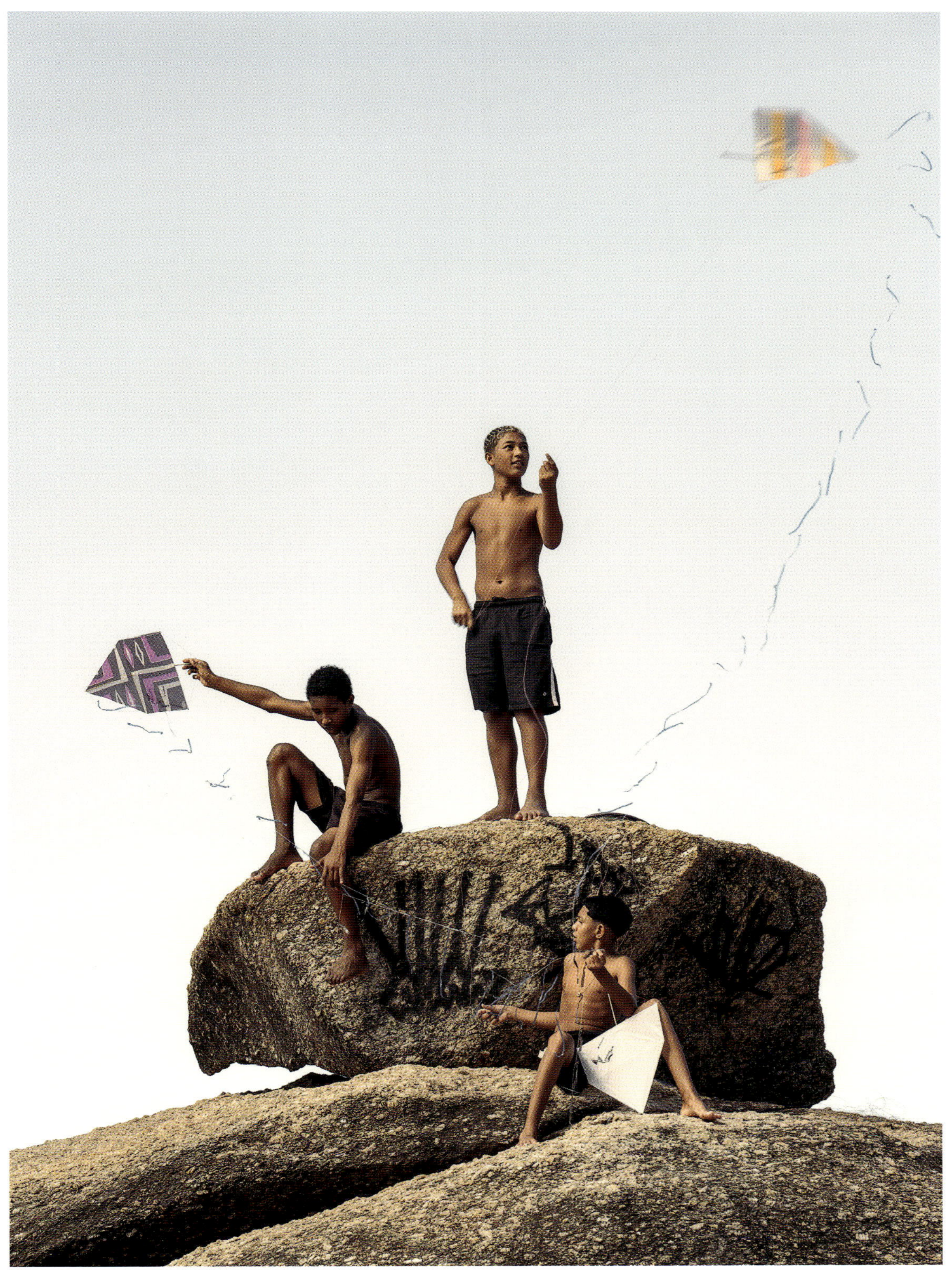

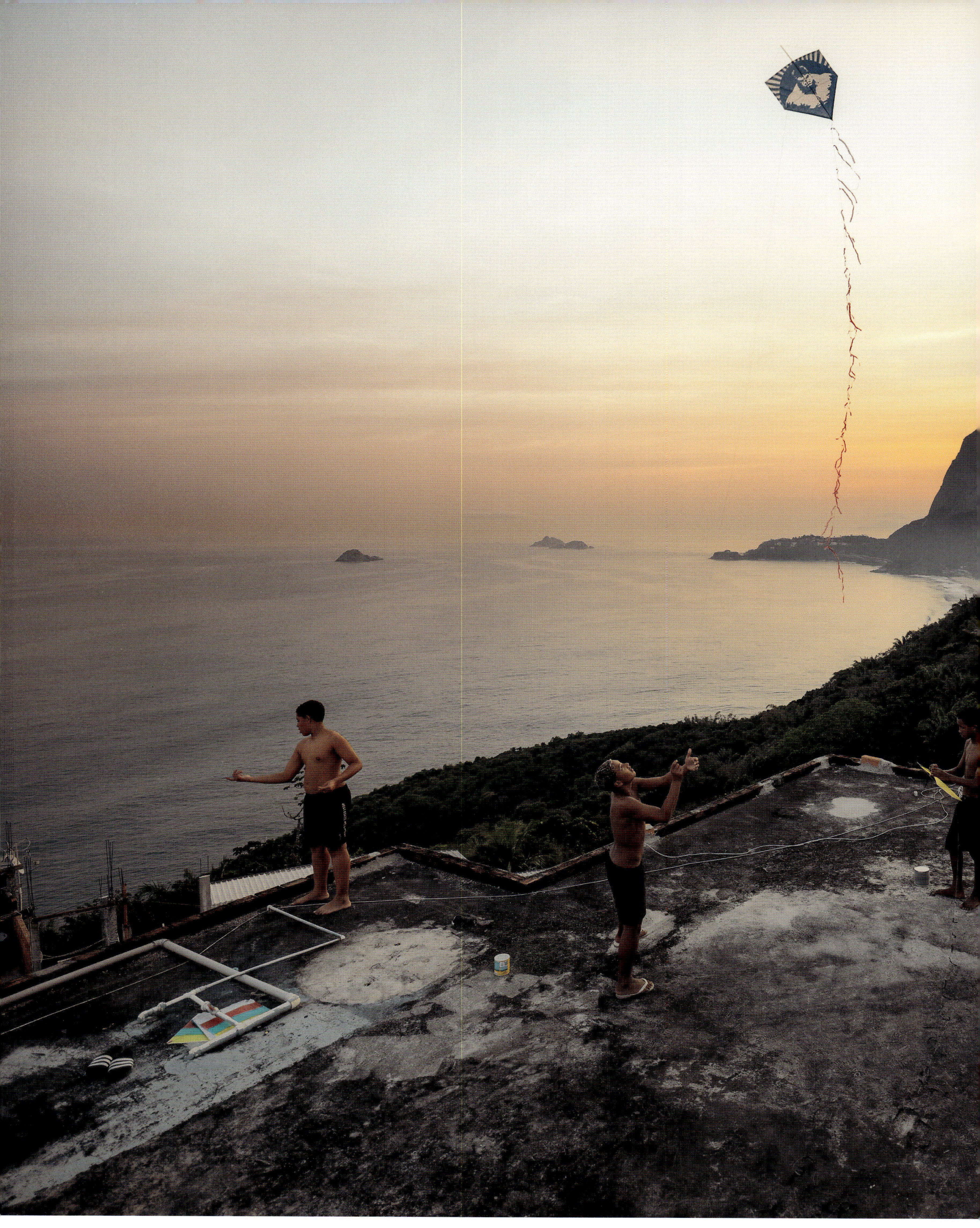

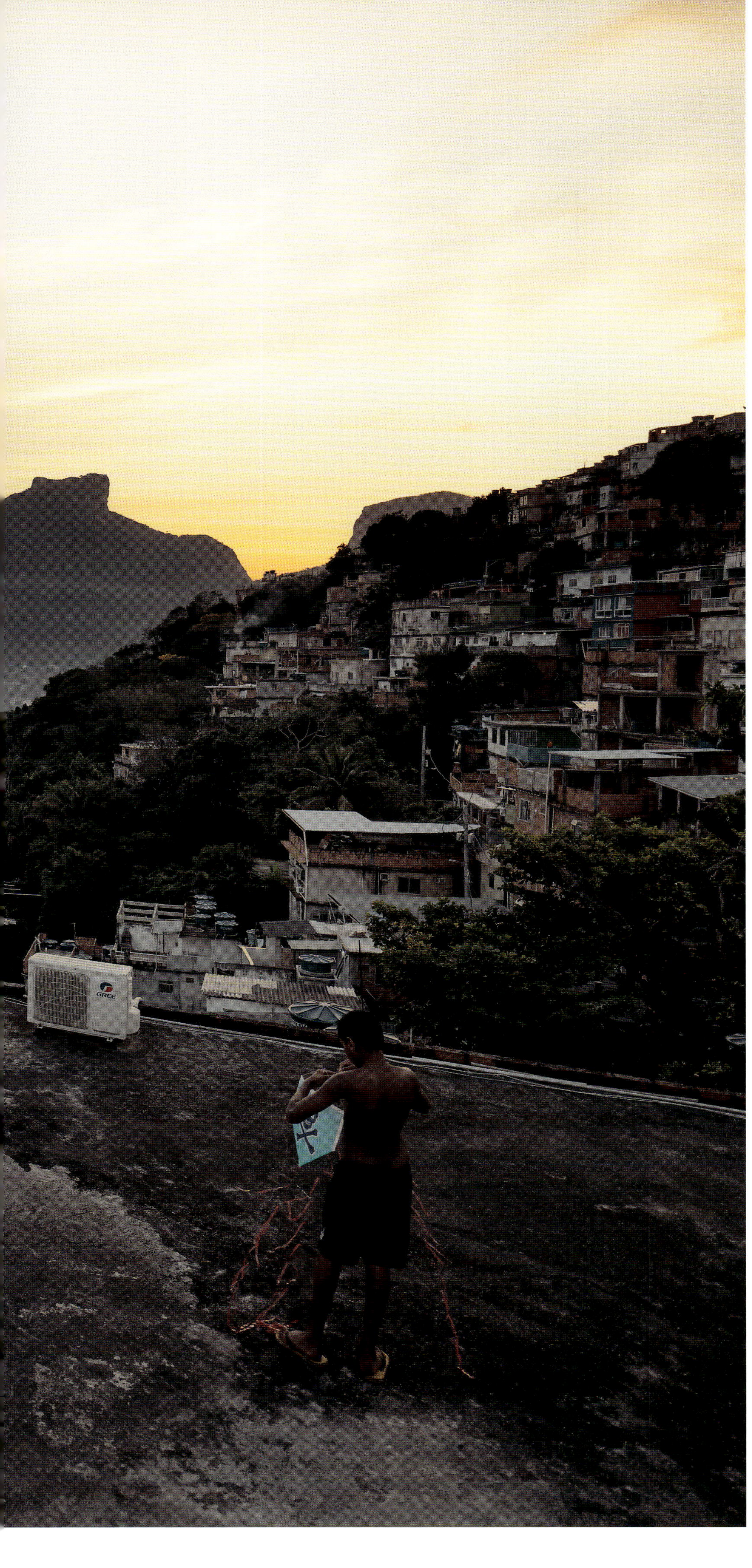

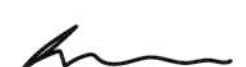

Reindeer Racing

FINLAND

*It is more than a game of speed and control, it is a
cultural heritage, a symbiotic relationship between
humans and reindeer, rooted in ethnic identity.*

Deep in the frigid, inhospitable lands above the Arctic circle live the Sami, Europe's only indigenous people who span four countries – Finland, Norway, Sweden and Russia. Reindeer
herding has been central to the Sami for over 2,000 years. And reindeer racing, more than a
peculiar, highly competitive sport, is a way of life. Galloping at an astonishing thirty to forty
kilometres per hour, these semi-wild animals charge on spindly legs around icy, snow-packed
tracks towing racers on skis as crowds gather in this frozen playground to watch Rudolph run.

The Sami people inhabited this frozen wasteland long before the Scandinavians, Rus-
sians or even the Vikings. They have always felt a close affinity to and respect for their
environment, traditionally living in harmony with animals and with nature's cycles. Sami
communities depended on reindeer for food, warmth, transportation and basic survival, and Sami are thought to have been the first in the world to herd and tame wild animals.

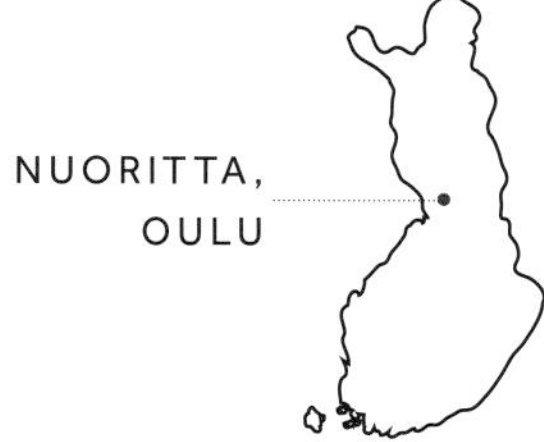

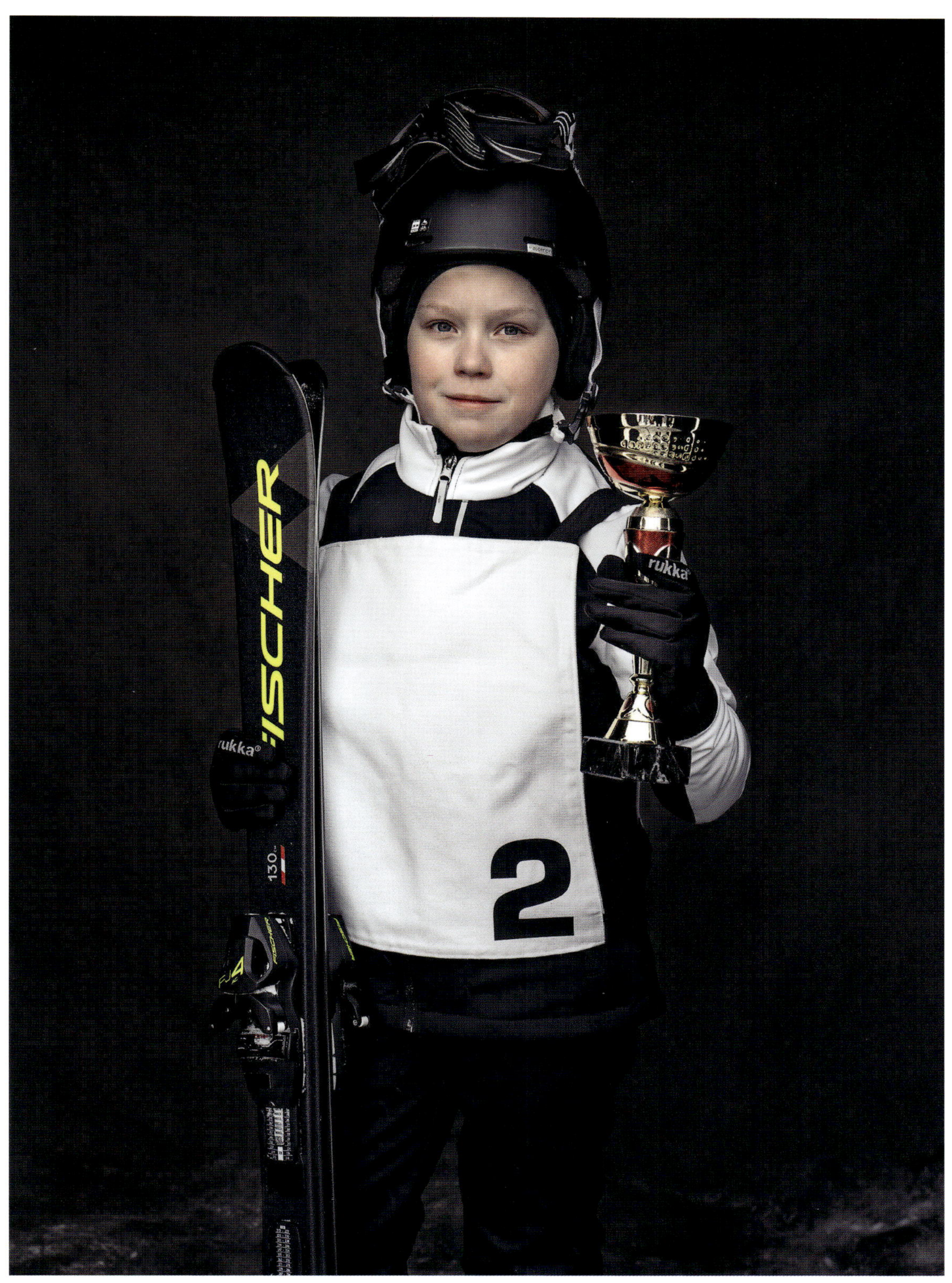

FISCHER
rukka
130
2
rukka

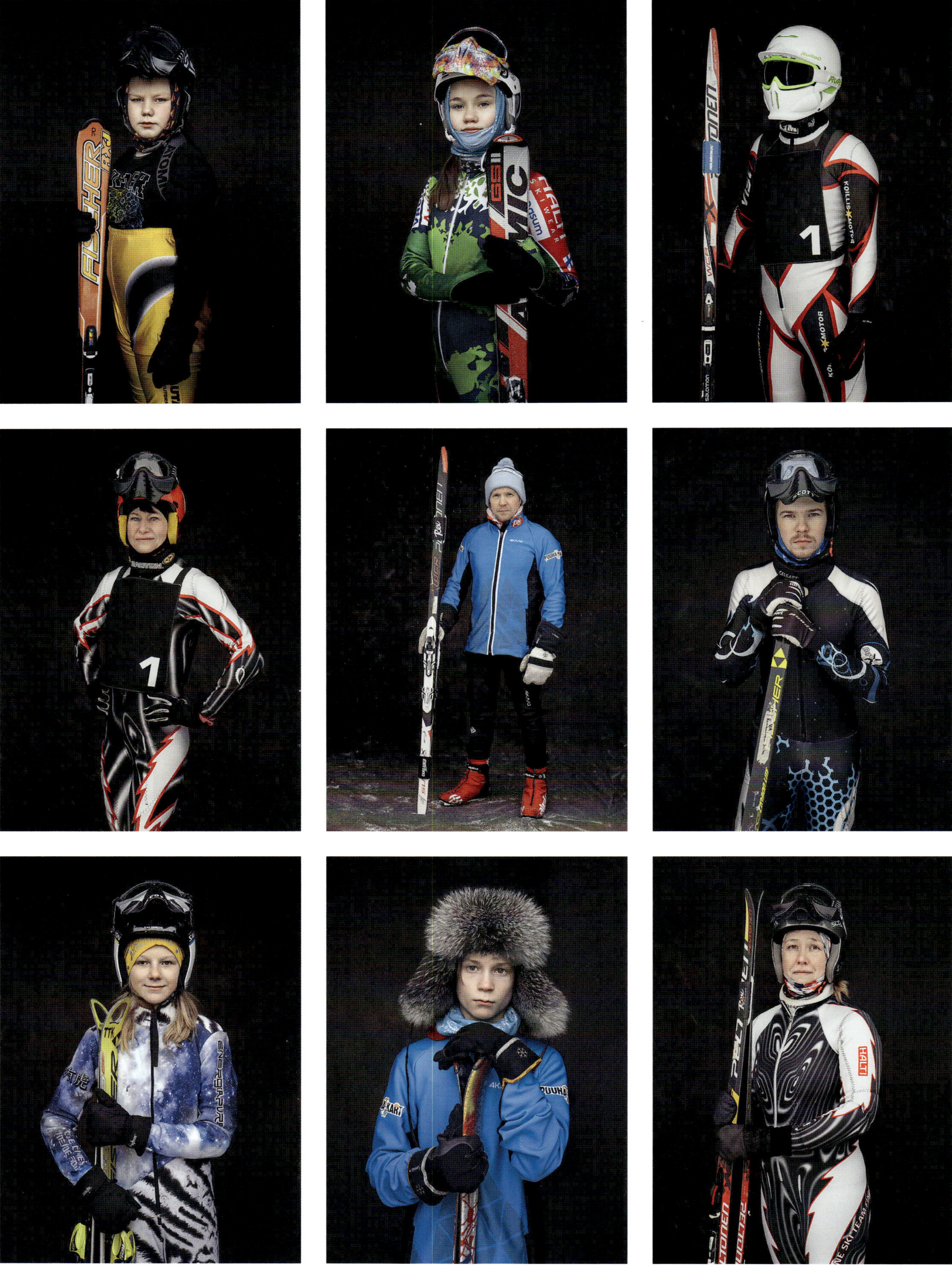

*"Reindeer racing is not just about speed;
it is about being a hundred percent in the
present moment. For one minute and twenty
seconds, you can't think of anything else."*

~ Sanna-Mari Kynkäänniemi (Racer & biologist – University of Oulu, Finland) ~

The first reindeer race took place in Finland in 1932, and the sport has persisted until today. Herding and reindeer racing go hand in hand, with herders trying to pick the fastest bull; only male reindeer race. Each herder has its own particular selection method. The fastest reindeer may have a prominent nose (better lung capacity), a muscular build or a wild temperament. Any bull could have what it takes to be the next King Reindeer, winner of the finals in Inari, Finland.

In Finland, competitions begin in mid-February and end in April. Racers put in hours of cross-country skiing to build up thigh and leg strength as well as balance. Before the racing season, they train with their reindeer at least three times a week and are adamant that they treat their beloved animals with the utmost love and respect in keeping with Sami tradition. The competitions are usually held on frozen lakes or in vast open spaces buried under a white blanket of snow. The landscape is quiet; there is nothing but pine and spruce trees for miles and miles, barely a hint of human life, interrupted only by the Falun red houses and barns that dot the horizon. In this pristine setting, you hear the muffled sound of hooves crunching over the frozen ground. The air is so cold that each exhalation from the reindeer's nostrils is visible.

Tradition meshes with the modern world on this playground as the crowds trickle in, well prepared for the subzero climate, sporting ski suits with traditionally embroidered Sami belts and real fur hats. People are so passionate about this sport that they come from all over the region, driving hours on icy roads, enduring the bitter cold for a mere glimpse of their favourite racer or reindeer, and simultaneously meeting with the reindeer community. It is an authentic local, family event with children of all ages running free amongst the snowbanks, the younger ones pulled in fur-lined sleds and vendors selling local crafts, warm coffee and snacks.

As the announcer rattles off a Finnish monologue, the racers in fluorescent racing gear prepare their freshly waxed skis and step onto scales, proving they weigh no less than sixty kilos. In the spirit of true equality, men and women compete against one another. The junior competition is held during this same event, ensuring the next generation continues the Sami tradition.

The racers take their places at the starting gate while herders wrestle the bulls into an adjacent pen. As the gates open, the reindeer rush out and speed along the icy, kilometre-long track, a flurry of fur, hooves and wagging tongues; one could almost imagine them flying up above the snow pulling Santa's sleigh. Each racer releases the rope as they cross the finish line, and the frenzied reindeer run free to the end gate, looking breathless yet fulfilled.

Reindeer racing is not for the faint-hearted. More than a game of speed and control, it is also cultural heritage: a symbiotic relationship between humans and reindeer rooted in an ethnic identity. With the modern world fast encroaching on what's left of Sami territory, the future of this ancient sport is tethered to a new generation. Hopefully, they are committed to carrying on their ancestral traditions with pride.

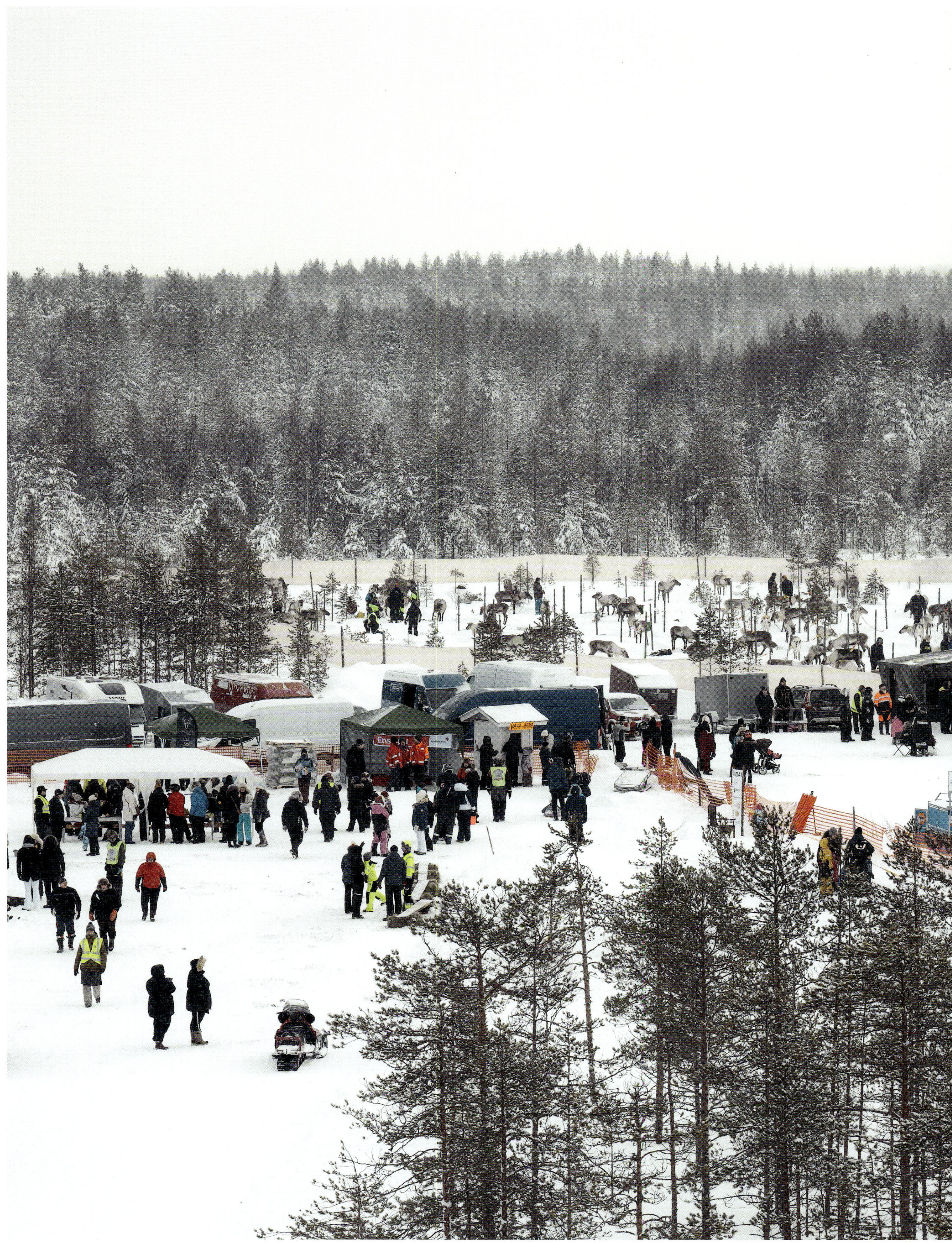

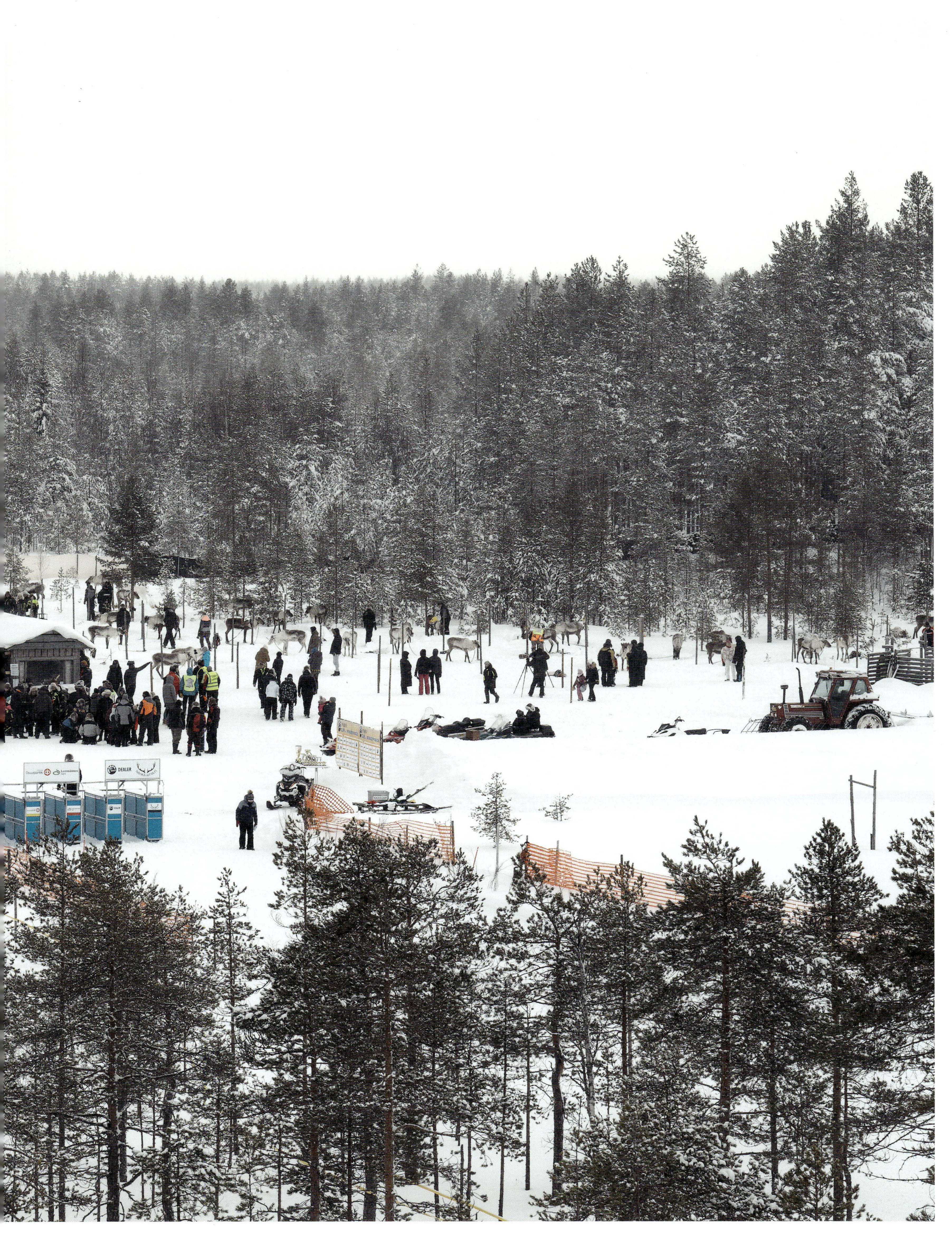

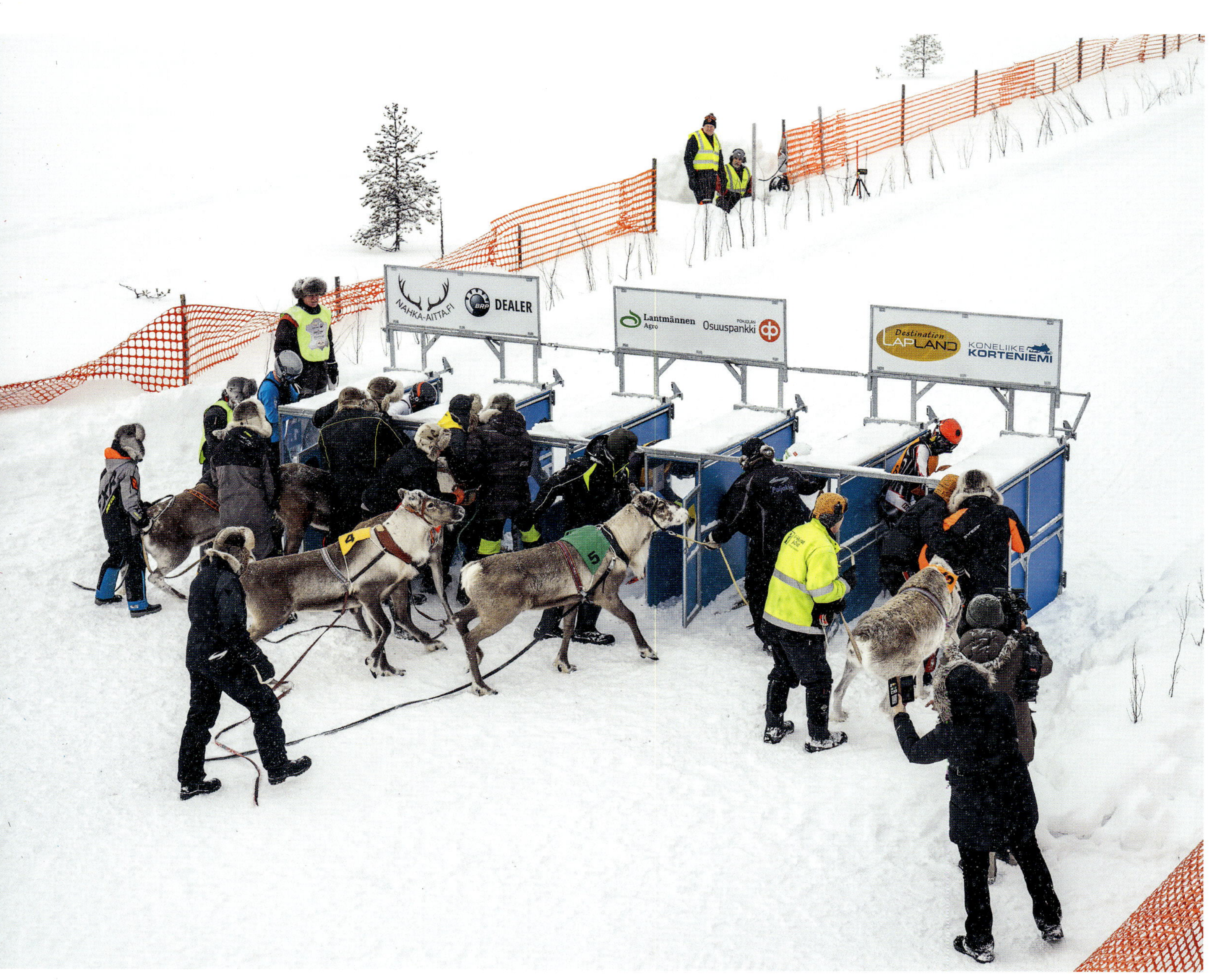

Reindeer are naturally skittish with a mind of their own, only running when they want to; therefore, they need to be well cared for if they're going to race.

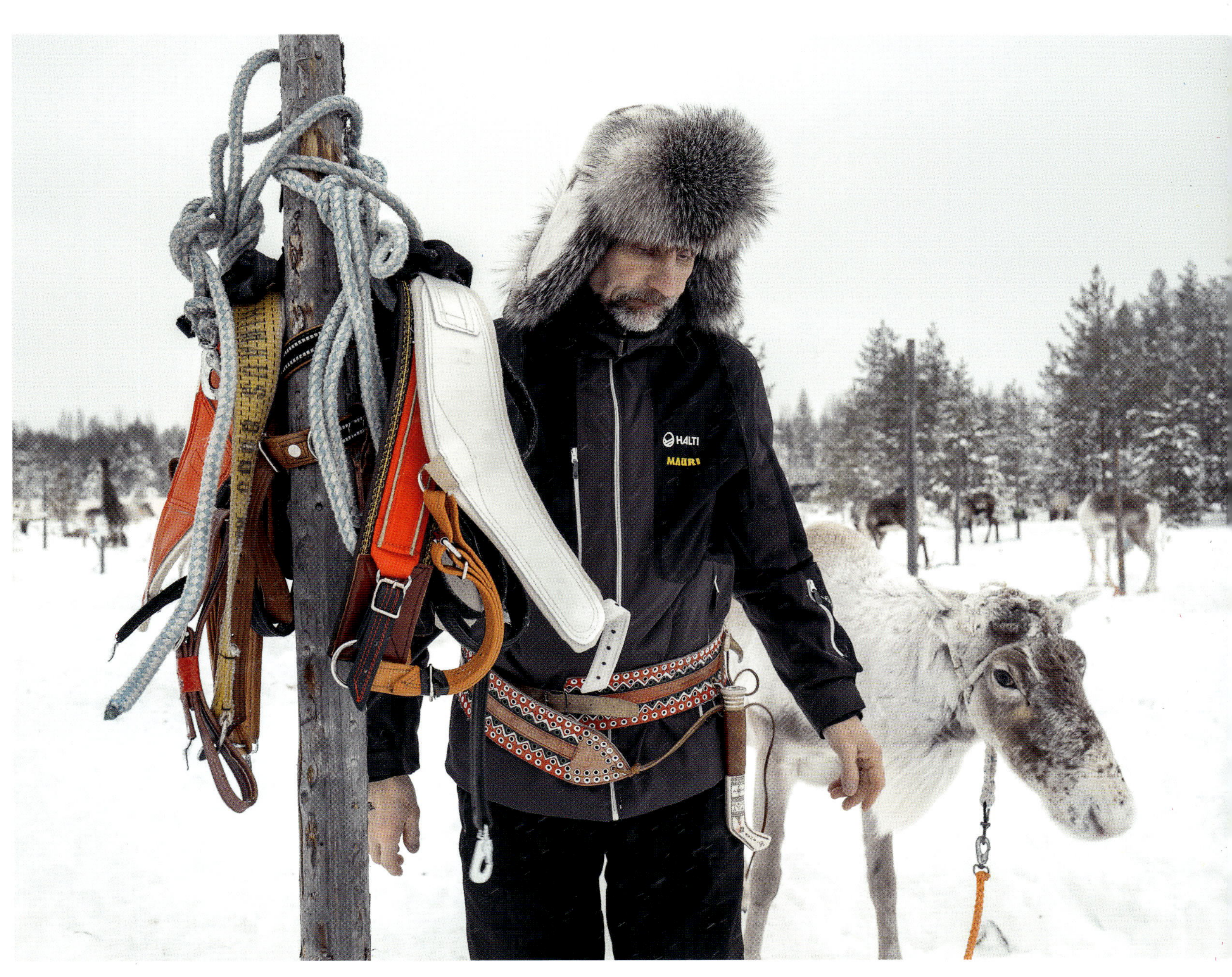

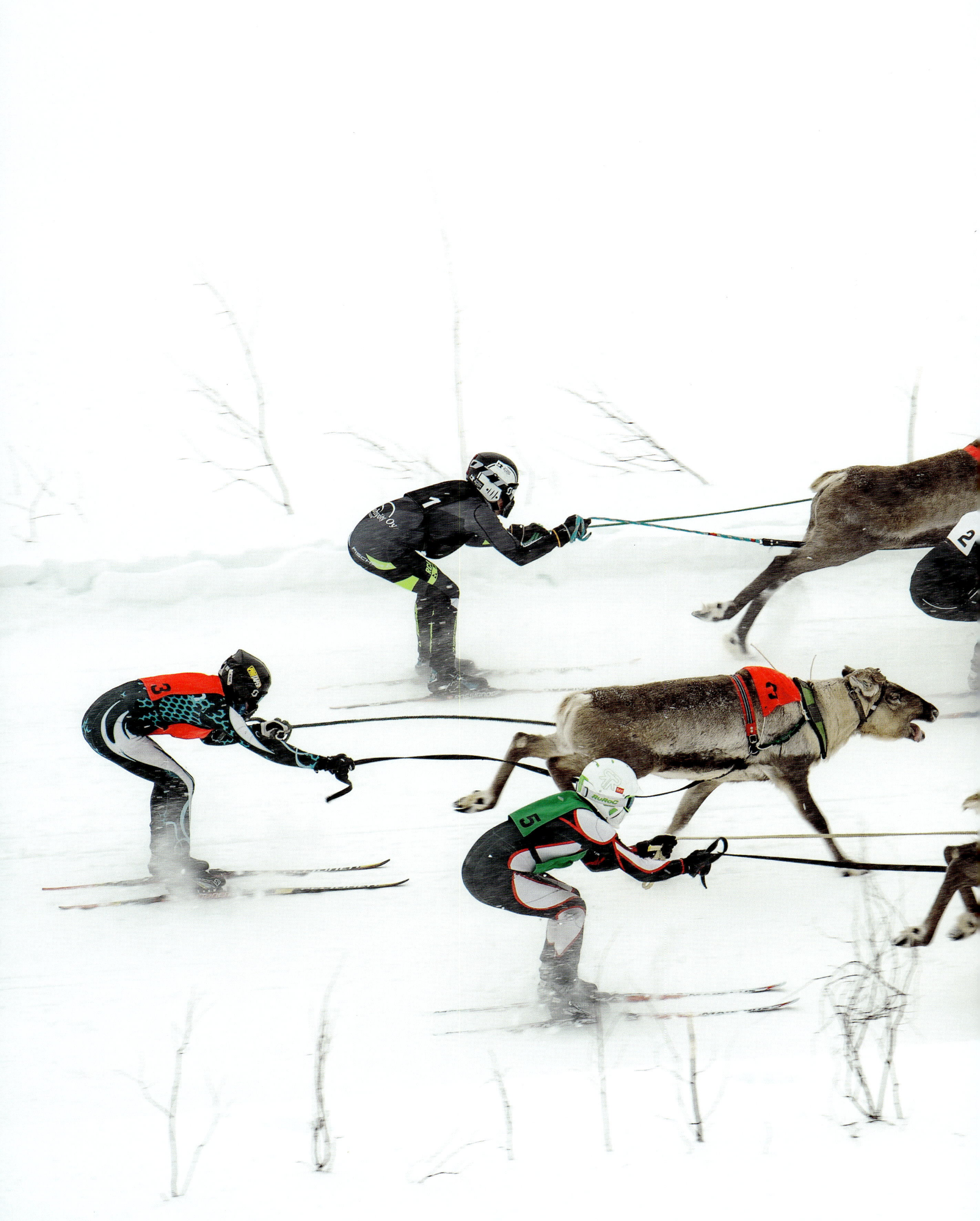

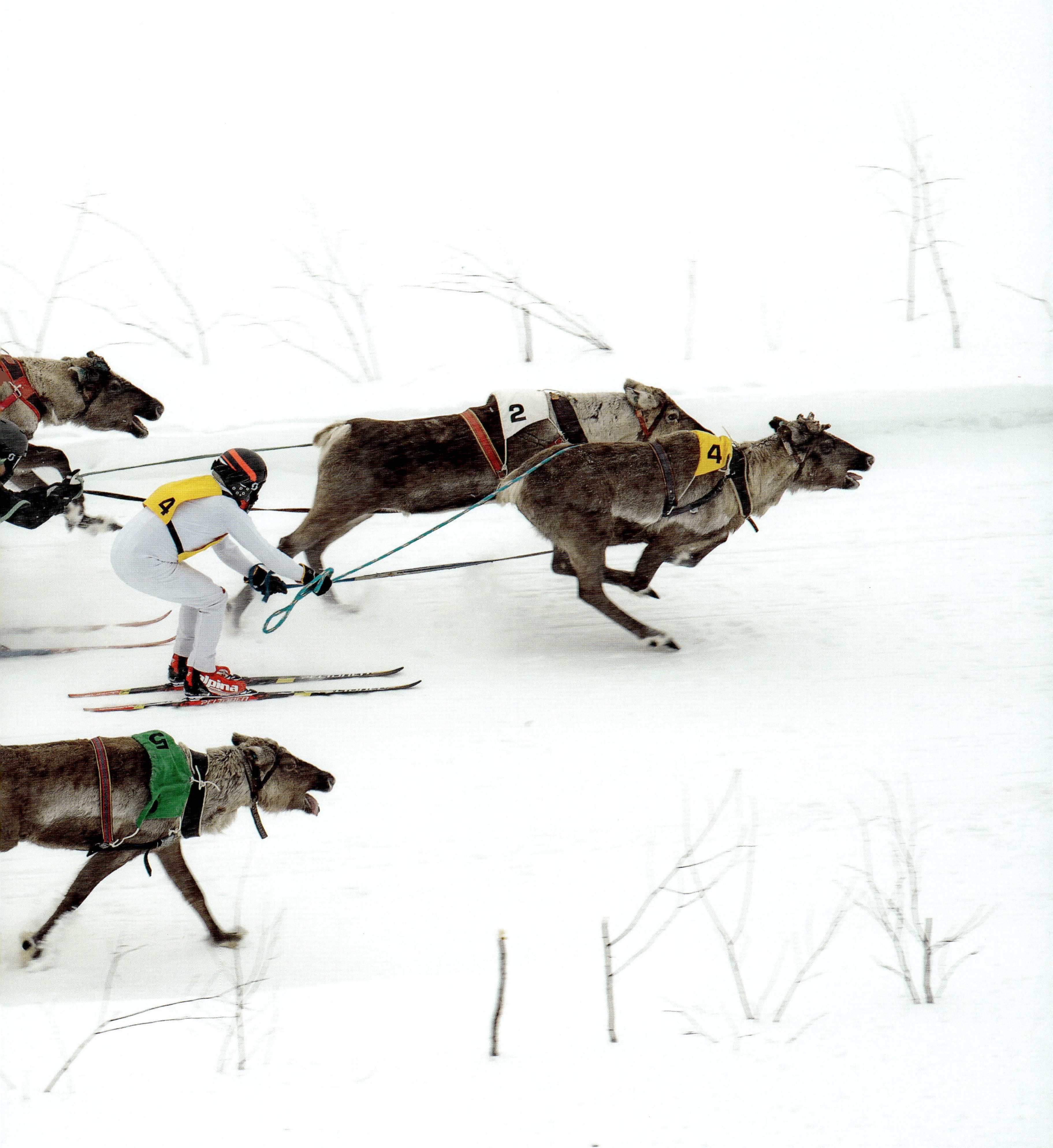

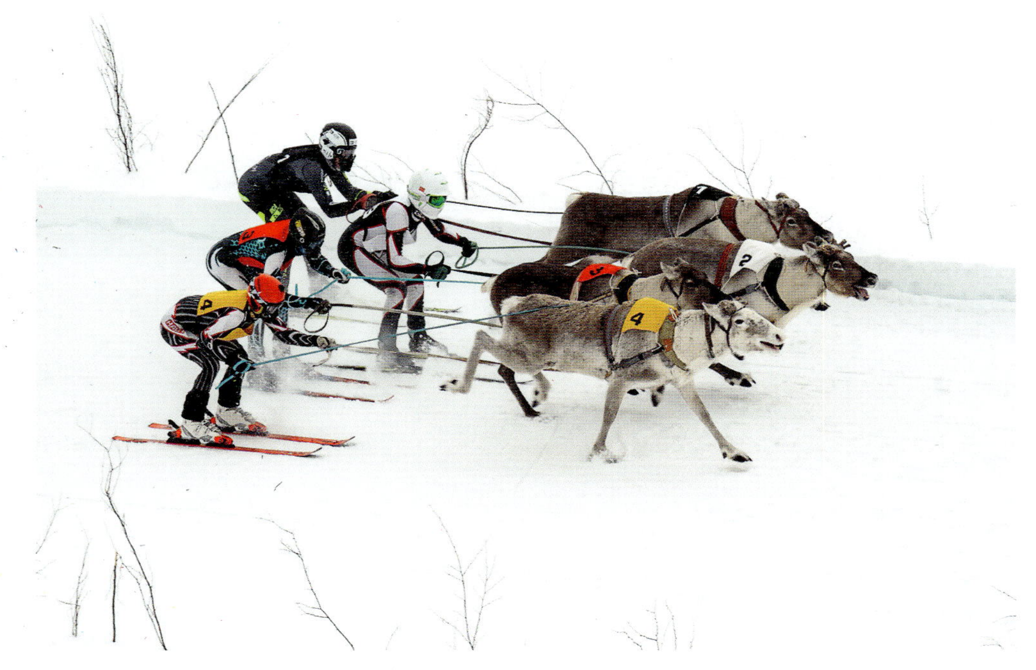

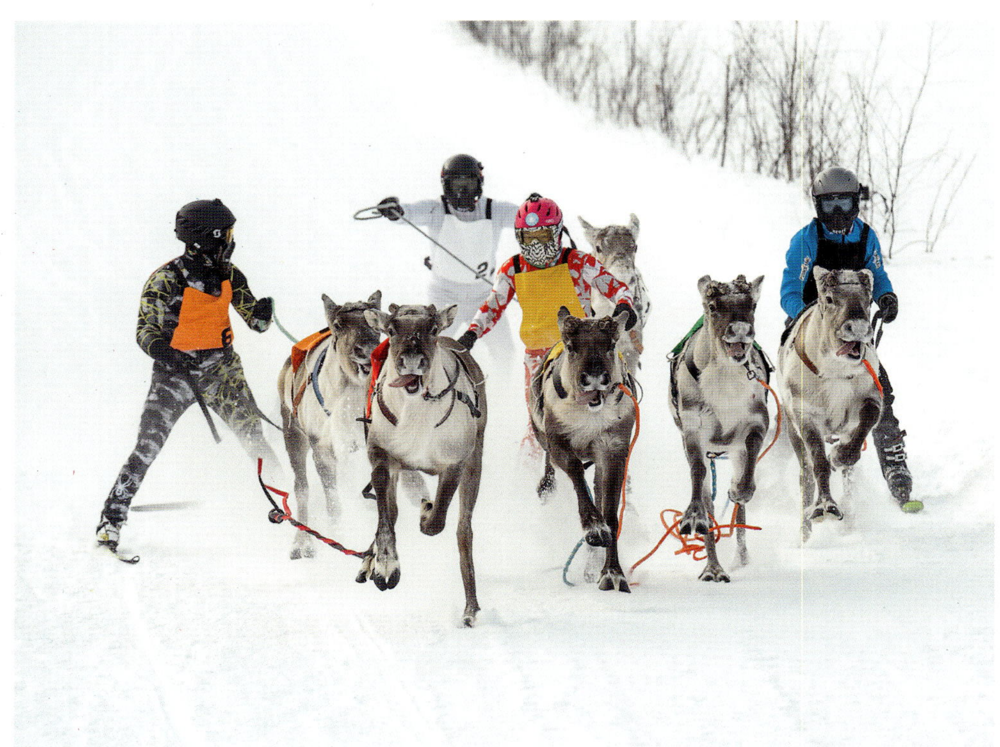

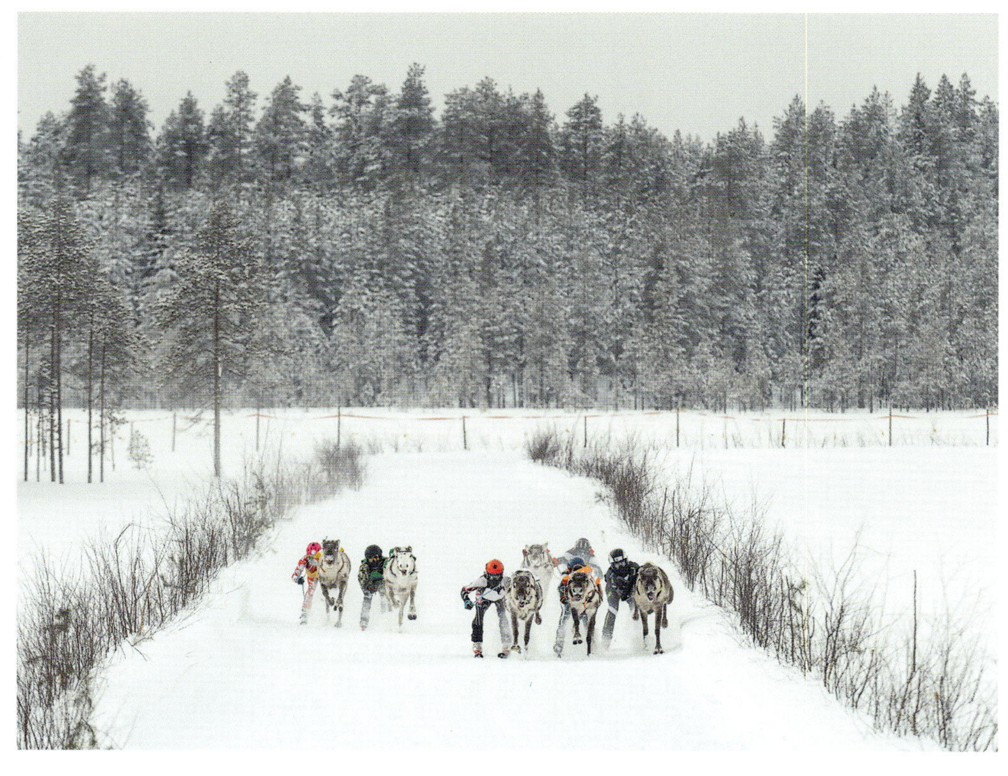

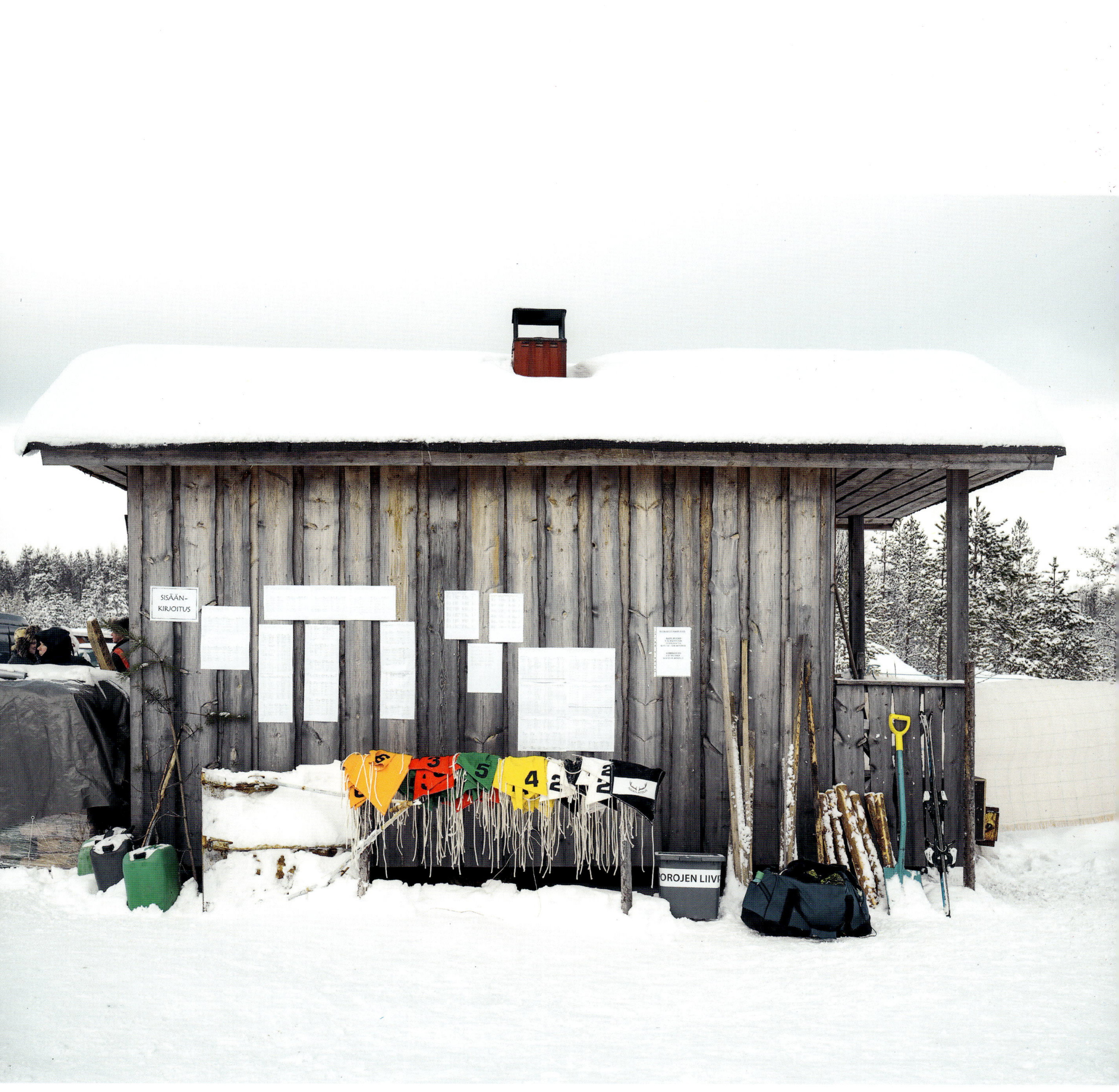

In the spirit of true equality, both men and
women, and boys and girls, compete against
one another, not separated by gender.

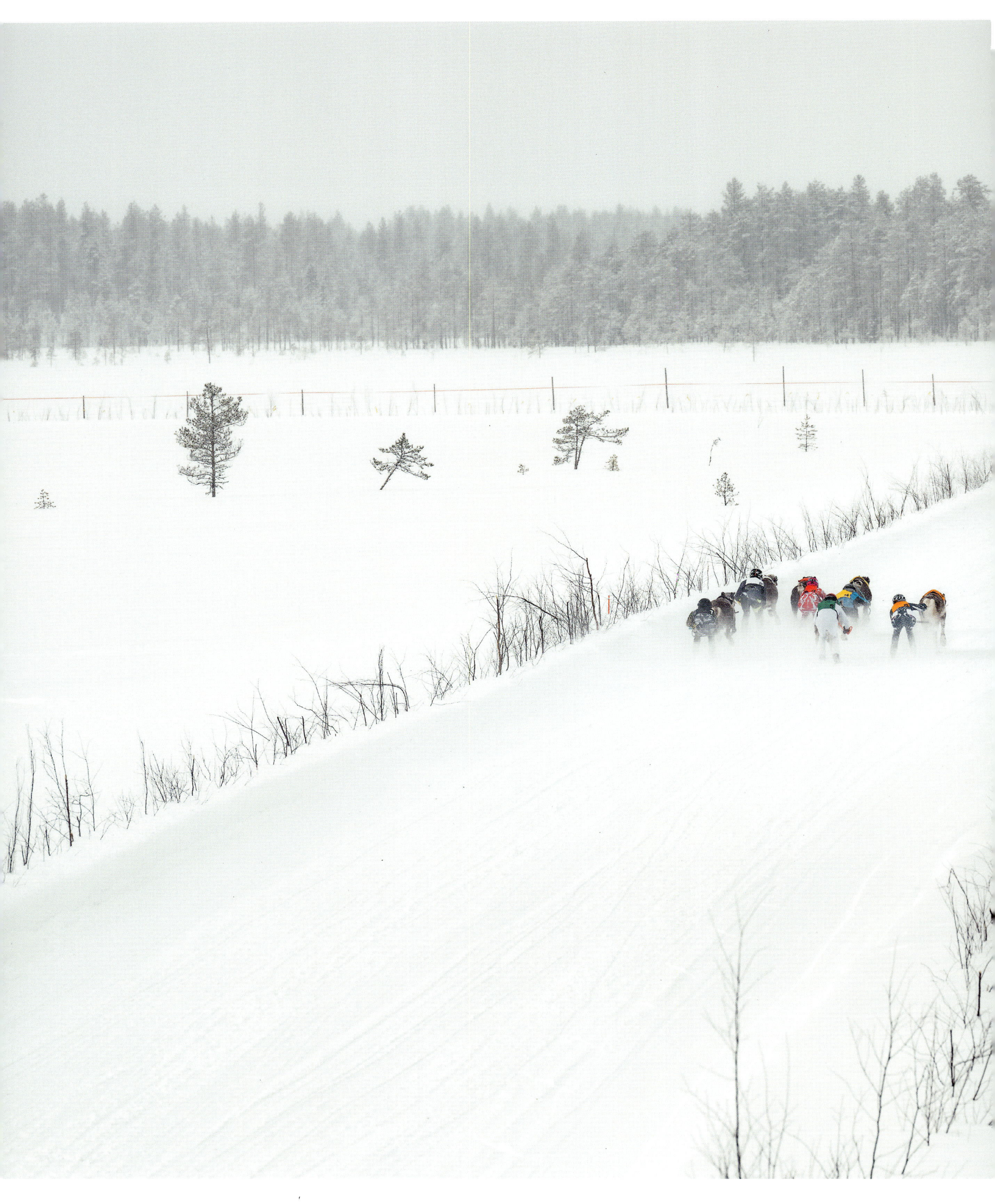

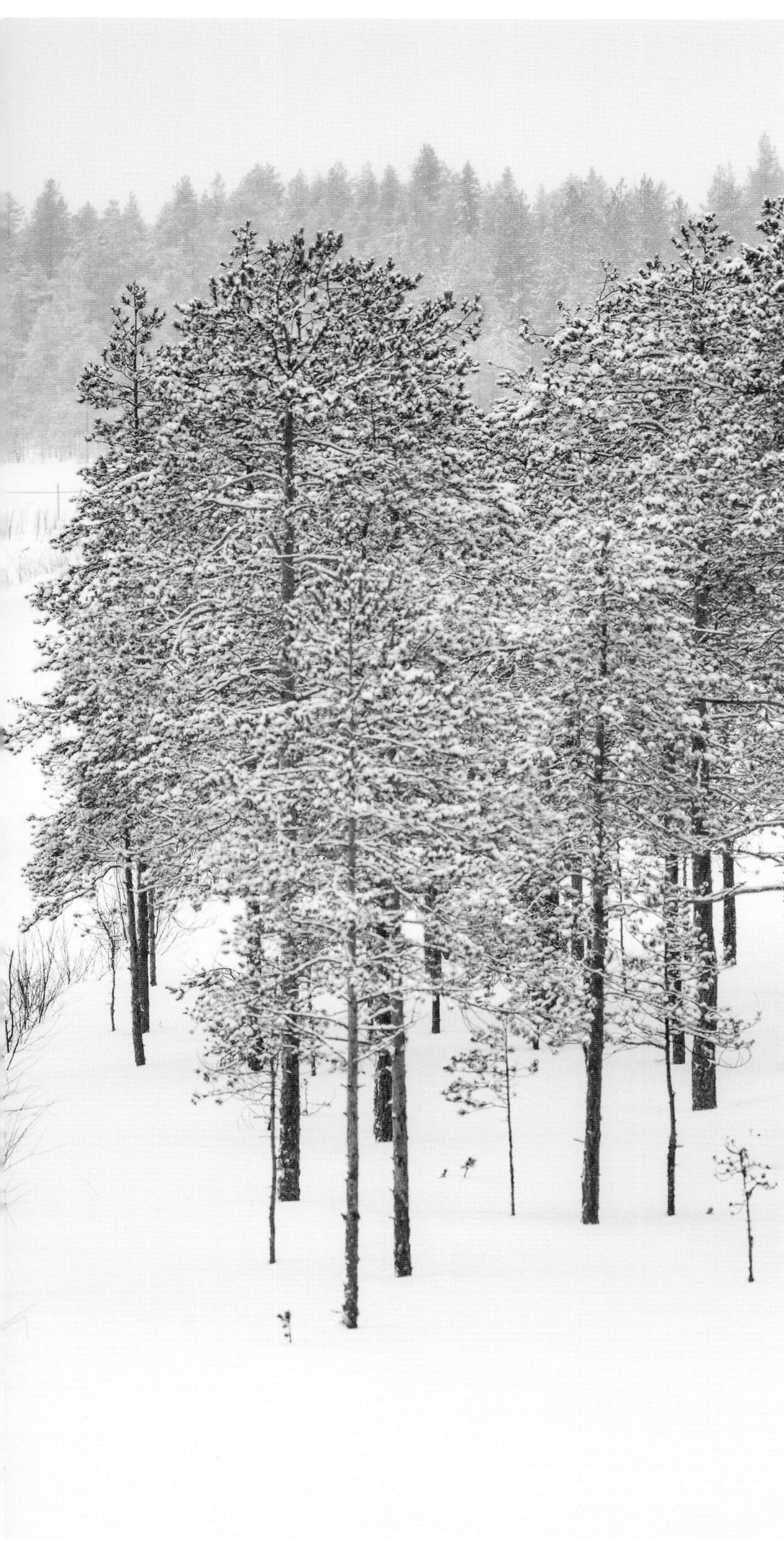

The reindeer population of
Finnish Lapland is about 200,000,
which is 20,000 more than
the human population.

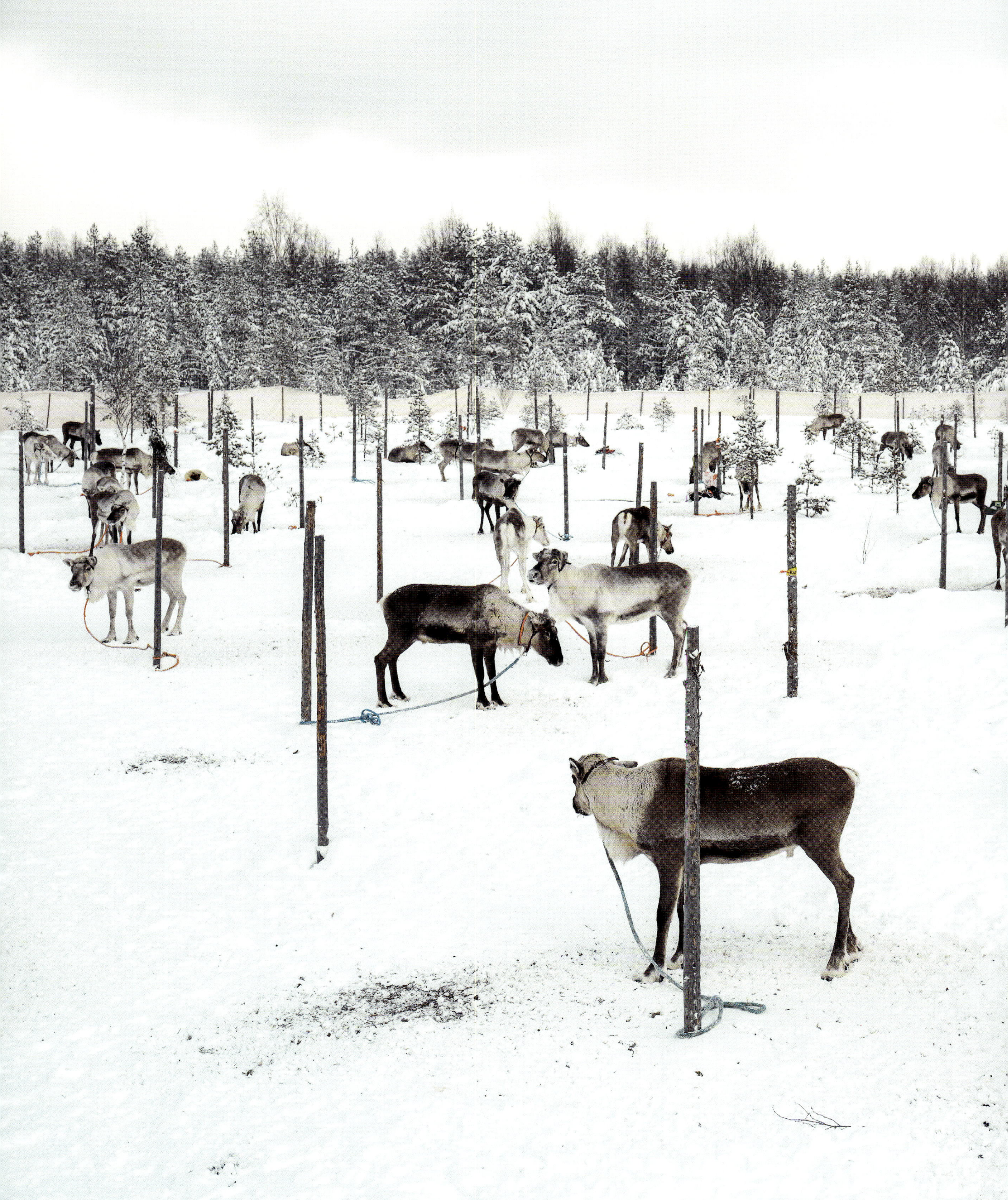

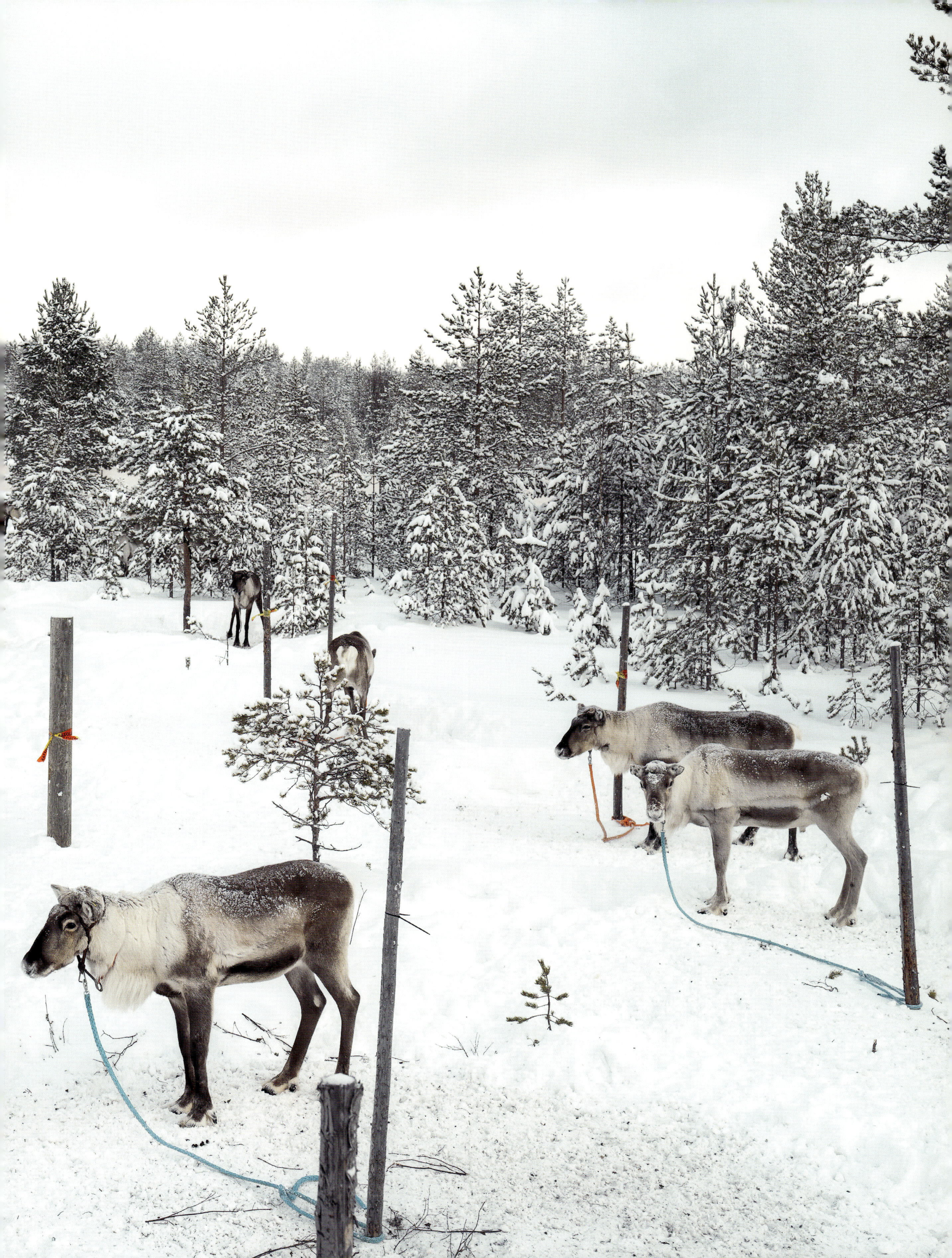

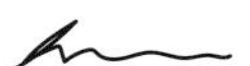

Donga Stick Fighting

ETHIOPIA

*They fight to improve their status, show strength
and bravery, settle personal conflicts, and, above all,
conquer the hearts of women.*

Off the beaten path, concealed in the lush, untamed nature of Ethiopia's Omo Valley, live the Surma, some of the fiercest but also most colourful and genuine humans on the earth. This unique indigenous people's playground is an isolated landscape in a country Europeans never colonised, where human remains date back nearly 2.5 million years.

The Suri, or Surma, tribe are a relatively unknown agropastoral people who have lived on the border of southwestern Ethiopia and Sudan for generations. They have cultural ties to the Nilotic people of Sudan and are related to Ethiopia's Mursi and other tribal groups in the area. Historically, the tribes in these outlying areas have been locked in inter-tribal rivalries resulting in years of bloodshed.

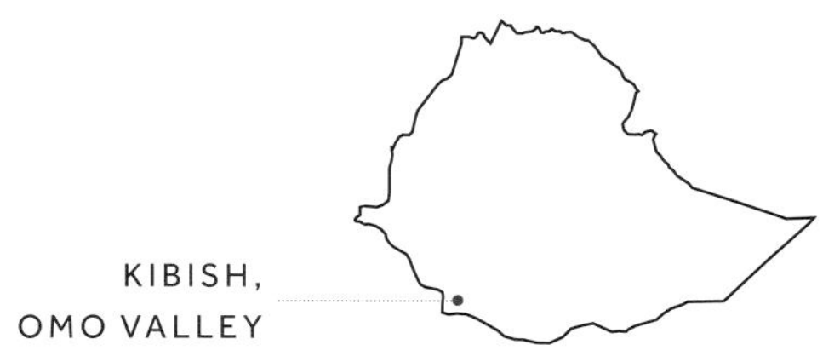

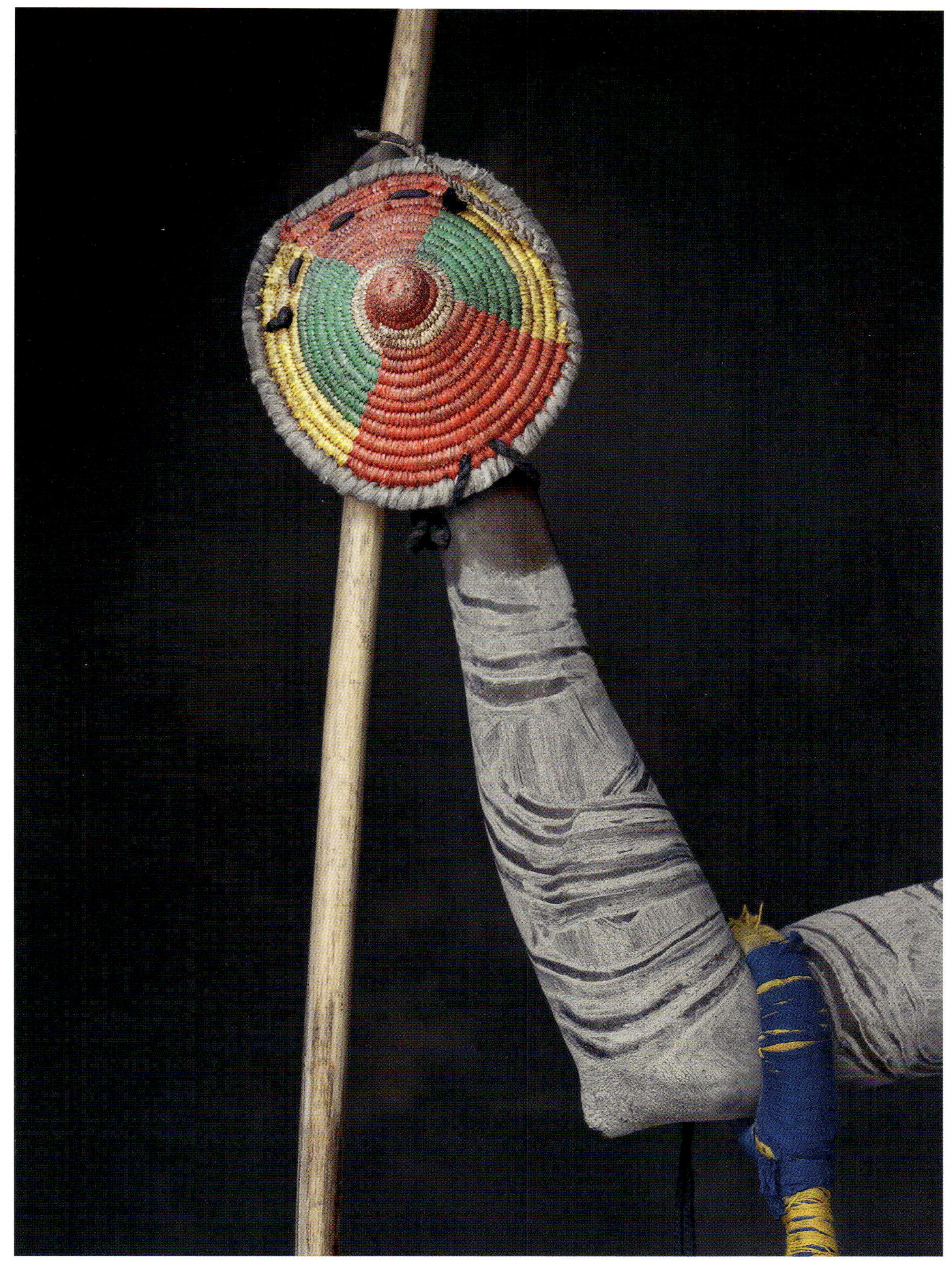

Fighters barely wear any clothes except for hand, head and
leg protection, made from thickly-woven cotton.

Driving miles and miles into this area without a single soul in sight is like going back in time, as far from civilisation as possible. Until way off in the distance, specks of movement appear. As we get closer, people peer out from the bushes, surprised by the aliens before them, yet offering the warmest and most welcoming greeting. It's hard to imagine these seemingly timid people participating in the continent's fiercest sport.

Only the most powerful male fighters participate in donga stick fighting, a ferocious battle that teeters between sport, martial art and ritual. At first glance, this self-sufficient and culturally rich tribe seems shy and light-hearted – until the stick fighting begins. Then they suddenly turn into the wildest, most brutal fighters, the gladiators of Africa with spears and AK-47s.

From the moment they're born, Surma men are groomed to fight. They fight to improve their status, show strength and bravery, settle personal conflicts, and above all, conquer the hearts of women. The champion has the fortune of marrying the most beautiful girl in the village, the one with the largest lip plate and thus the most expensive dowry. He must gift the bride's family some sixty cows and Kalashnikovs if he wants to marry her.

From a Western perspective, painful rituals such as the women's lip plates seem cruel and unjustifiable. And yet the Surma women freely choose it and see it as a sign of beauty. Some younger Surma women have decided to discontinue the practice replacing it with earplugs and body scarring instead. As with many such traditions, the younger generations choose whether it continues, changes or stops altogether.

The day before the battle, young men prepare by drinking a unique concoction made from the bark of a tree to purify their bodies. They wash and decorate themselves in a secret location and hand-paint patterns made from a mixture of chalk, clay, wood ashes, and water to intimidate their opponents and show off their attractiveness to the opposite sex. To demonstrate their bravery, some men fight naked, with no physical protection; but today, the more cautious wear head, arm and leg gear. The whole village participates in this ritualistic celebration, including women and children, who also adorn themselves with paint in honour of the festivities.

The merciless fights usually occur between two villages around the harvest, attracting large audiences. Each side puts up thirty or more fighters. You can feel the increasing tension as they move toward the battlefield. As the fighters enter a trance-like state assisted by drugs and alcohol, there is singing, chanting and firing of AK-47s. The famous stick-fighting is in full swing, and the combat reaches a crescendo: the excited crowd suddenly becomes a menacing mob. As the sun settles into the dust and bullets continue to fly, the more reserved seek safer ground.

The winners of each duel fight to the last man standing. Despite the rowdiness of the sport, there are referees present to ensure the rules are obeyed, yet severe injuries and even deaths happen. Accepting defeat is not only expected but seen as gracious. At the end of the fight, the champion is lifted into the air on a platform and victoriously delivered to his future bride as the whole village celebrates, carrying on this age-old tradition.

Here amongst the most authentic tribe in Africa, with its unique rituals and customs, fast-food tourism is barely trickling in; even so, modernity is pushing up against ancient tradition. Dams, extreme drought and national parks threaten to forever alter the lives of people who have inhabited the valley for millennia – their future rests on the precipice of progress.

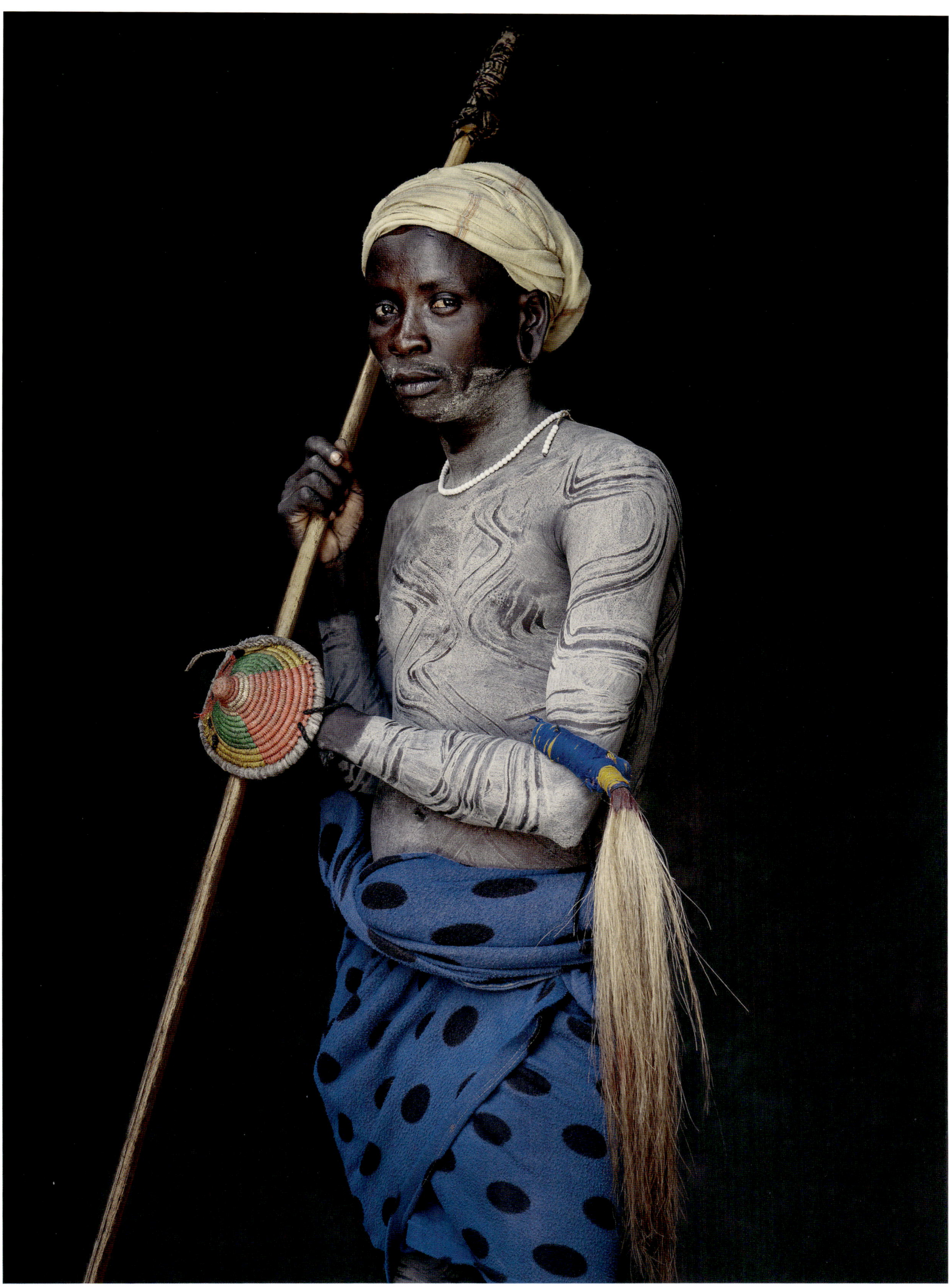

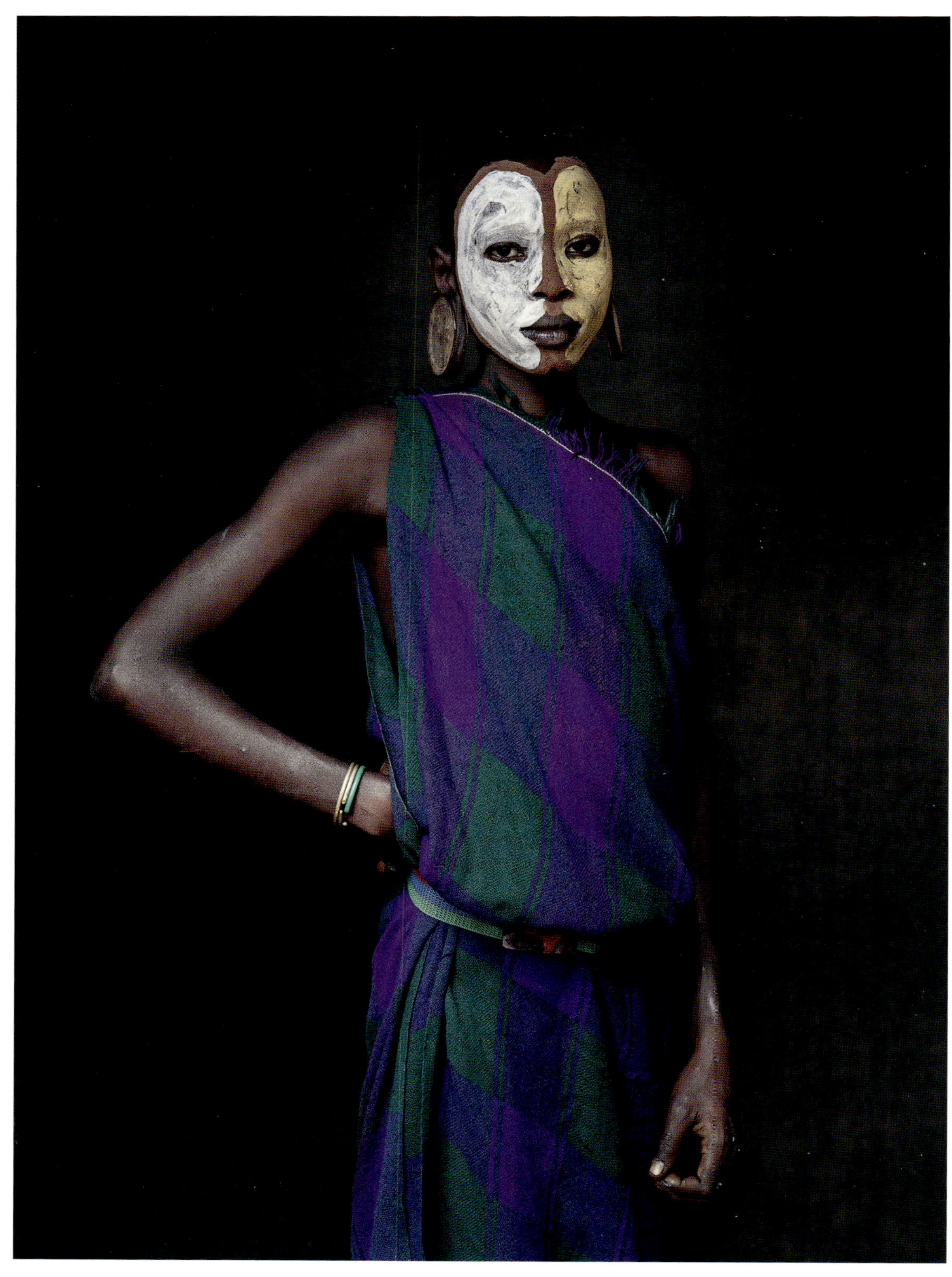

Surma woman adorns herself with face paint
and large earplugs to enhance her beauty.

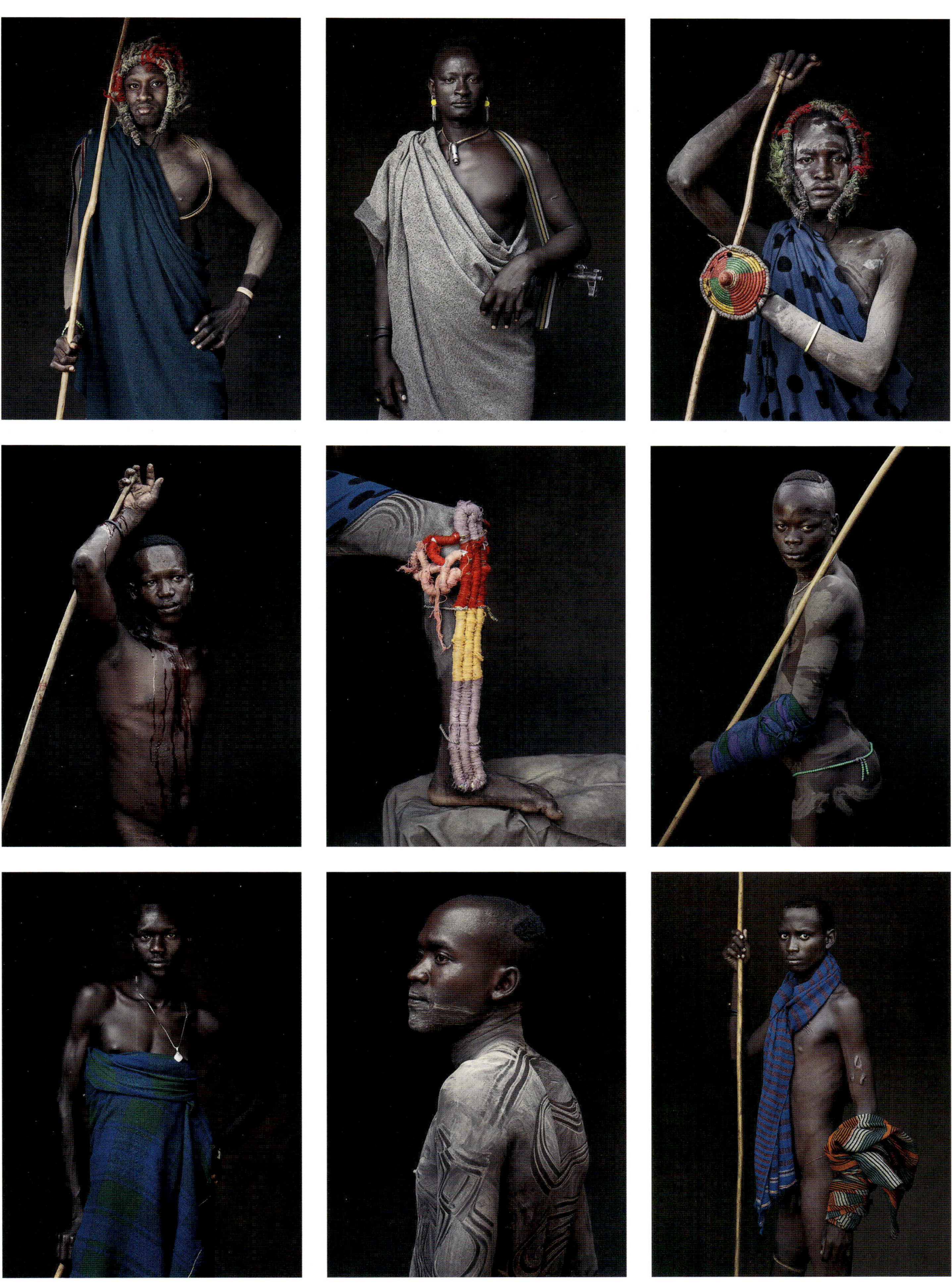

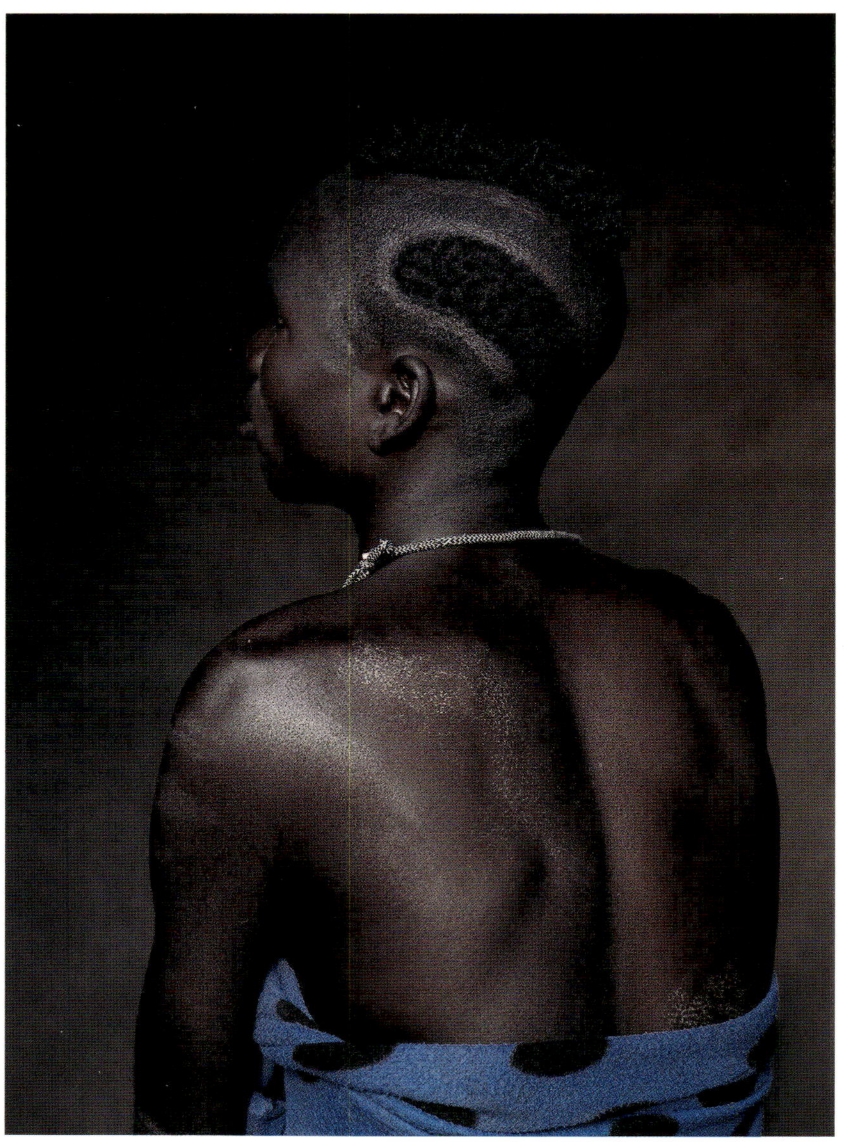

The Surma tribe still engage in the tradition of scarification
and unique hairstyling, which are seen as signs of beauty.

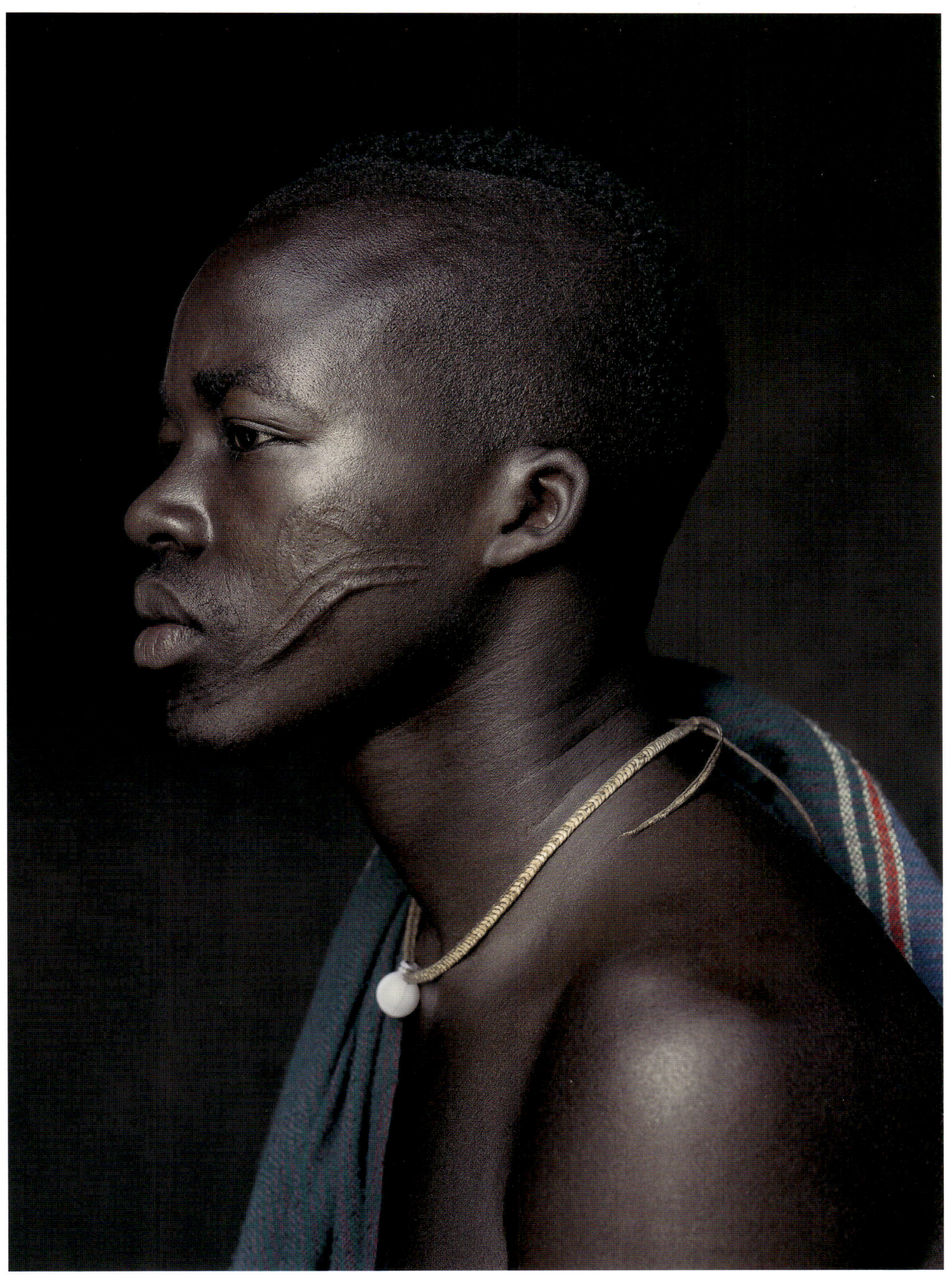

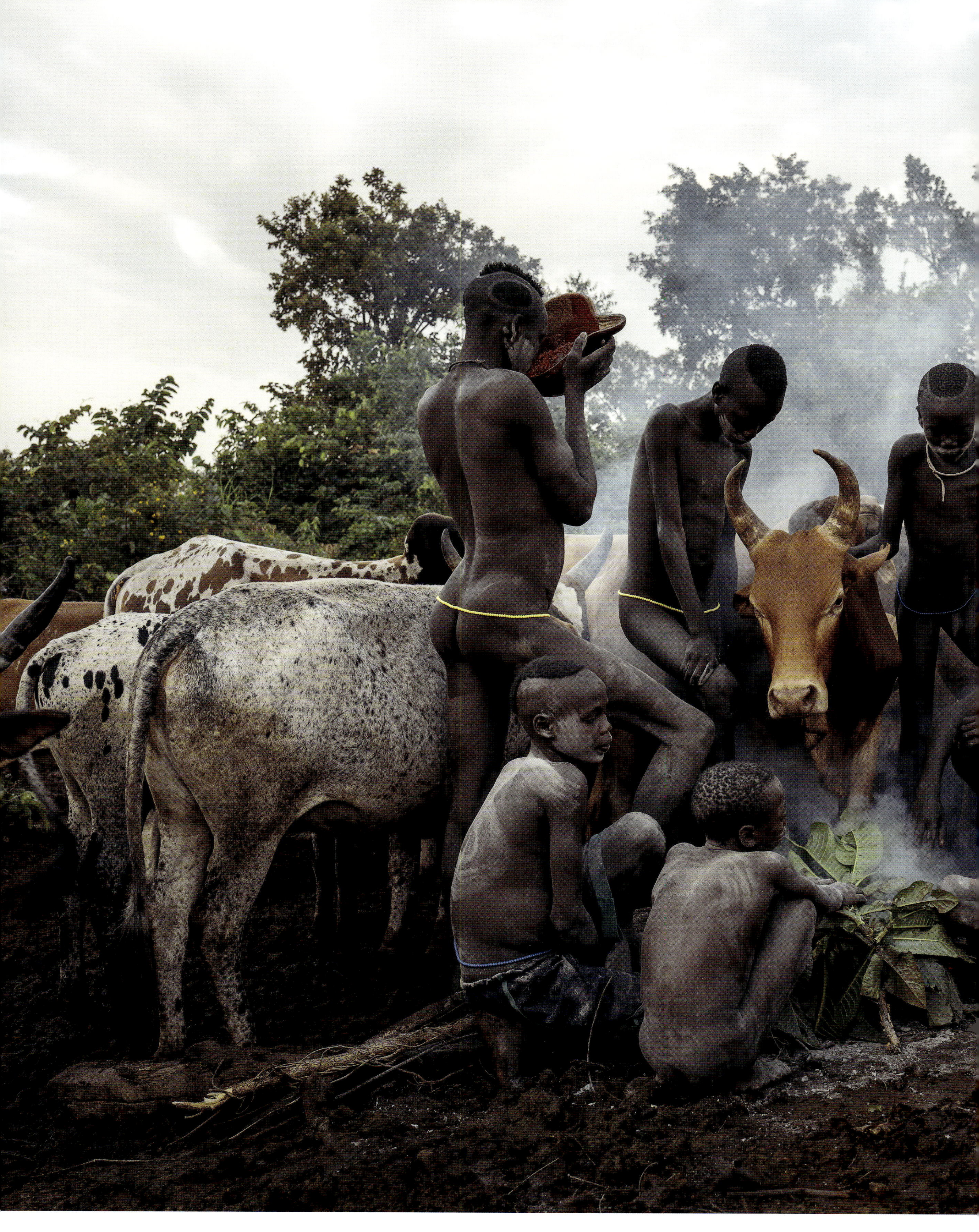

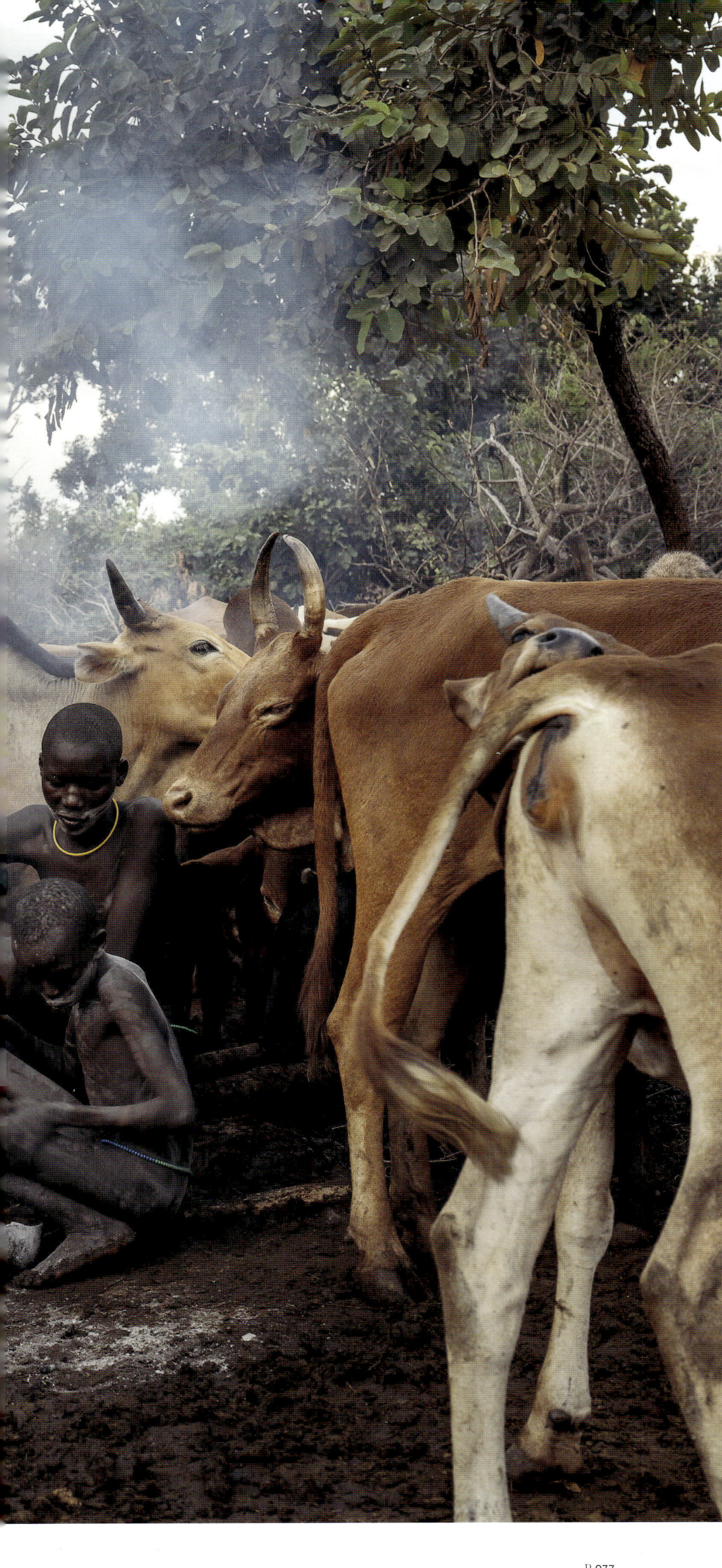

Surma men prepare for the big battle by drinking cows' blood, believed to be full of vitamins giving the men the added advantage of physical strength.

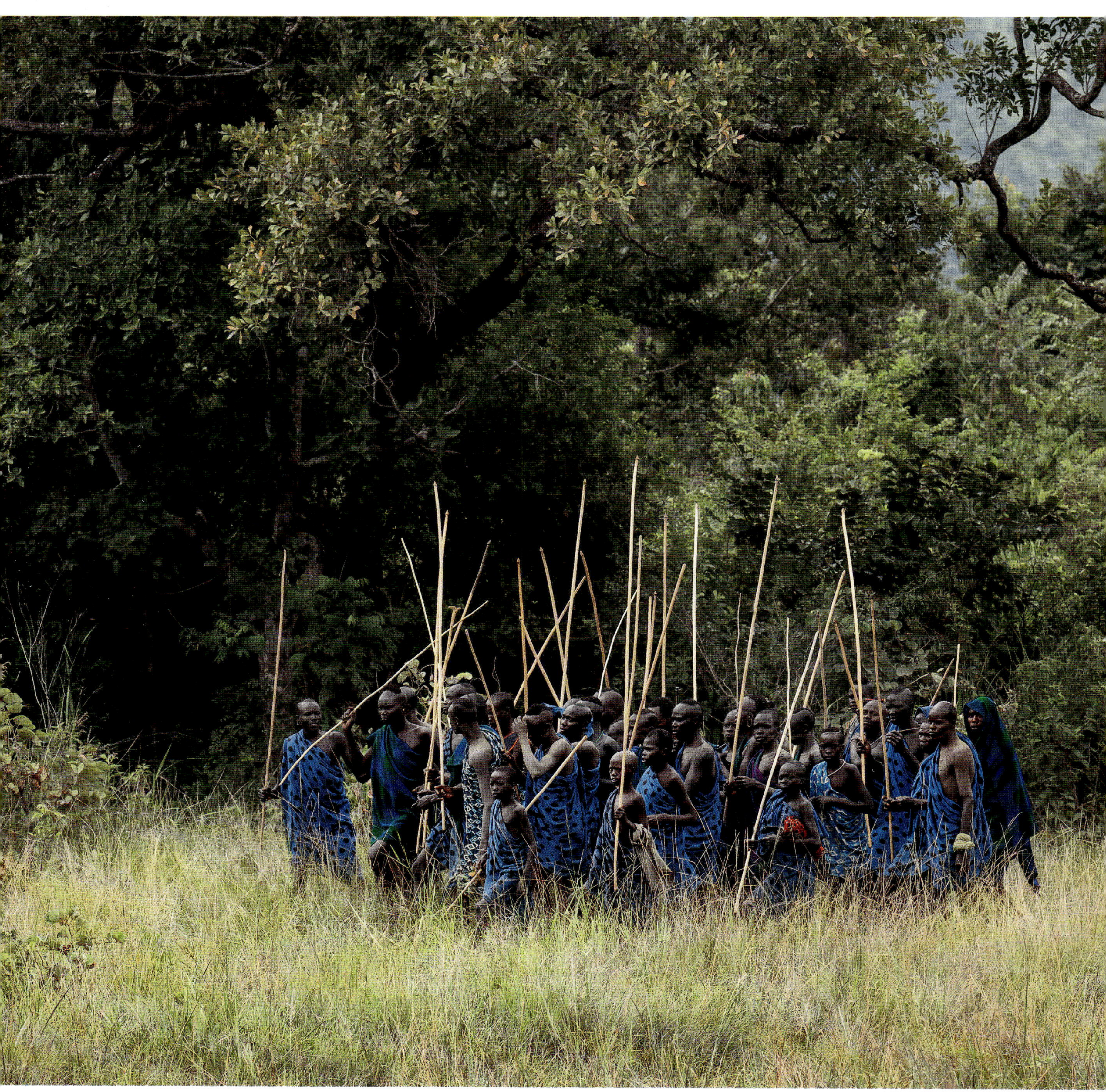

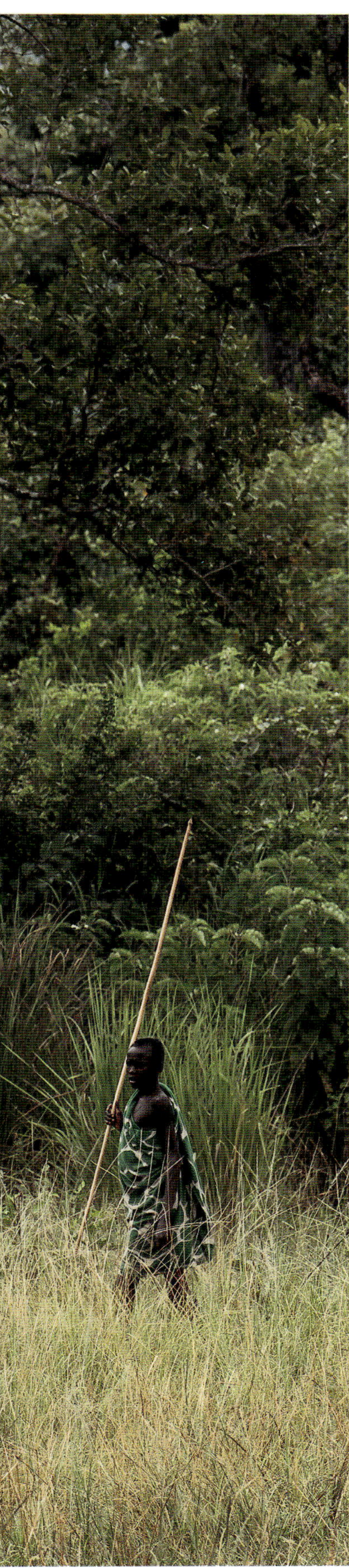

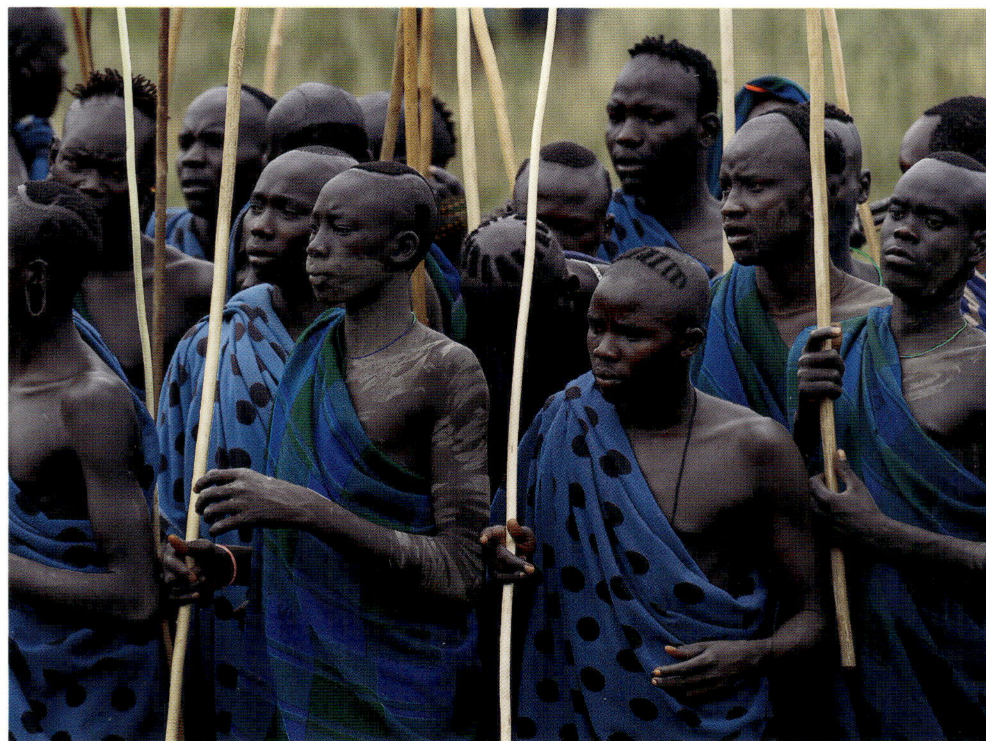

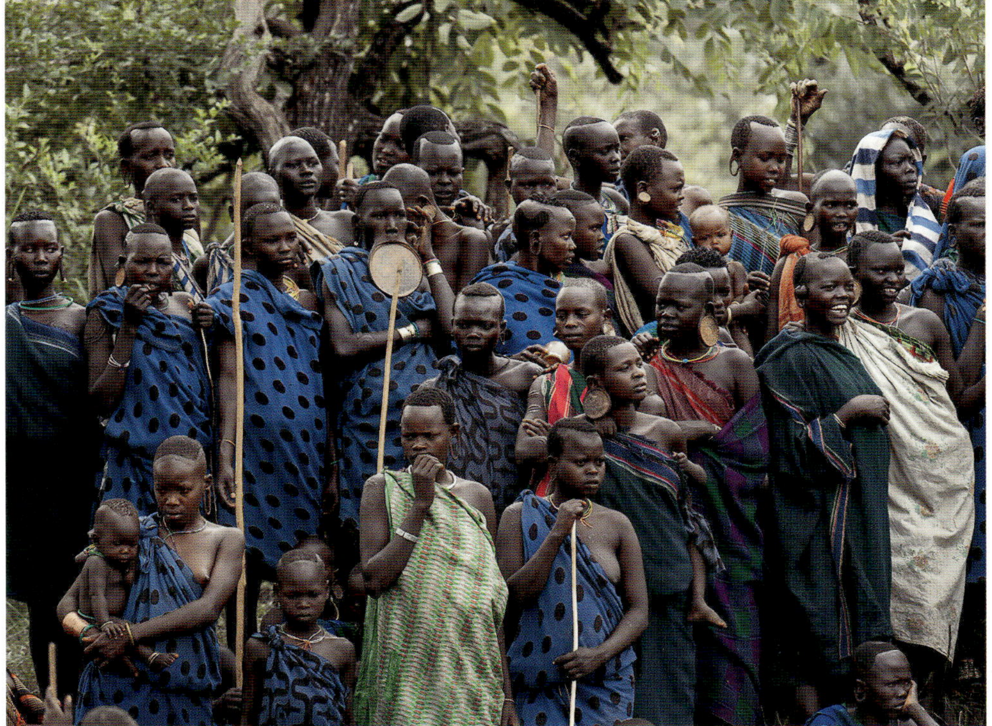

Hundreds of men from neighbouring villages approach the battlefield, singing to impress all the young women and their opponents, proving they are the best warriors.

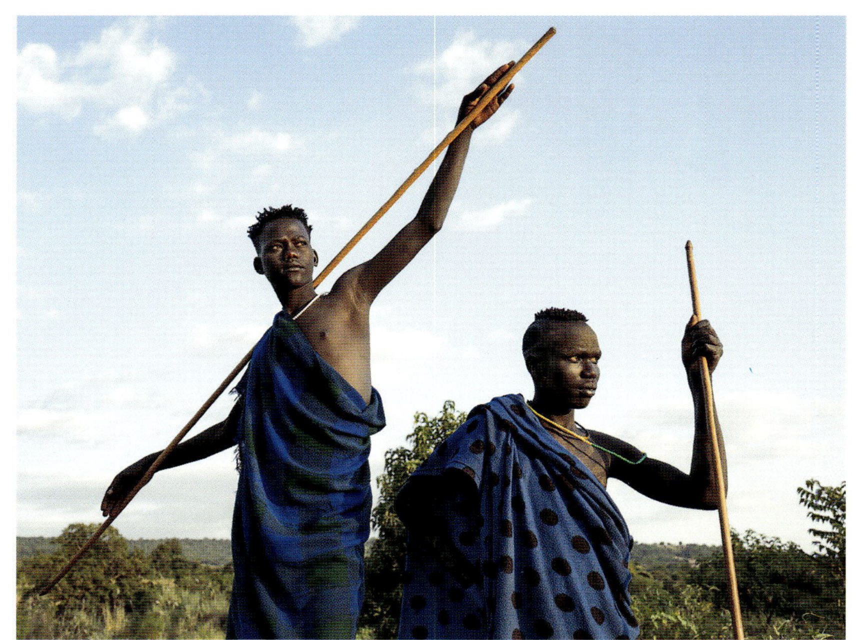

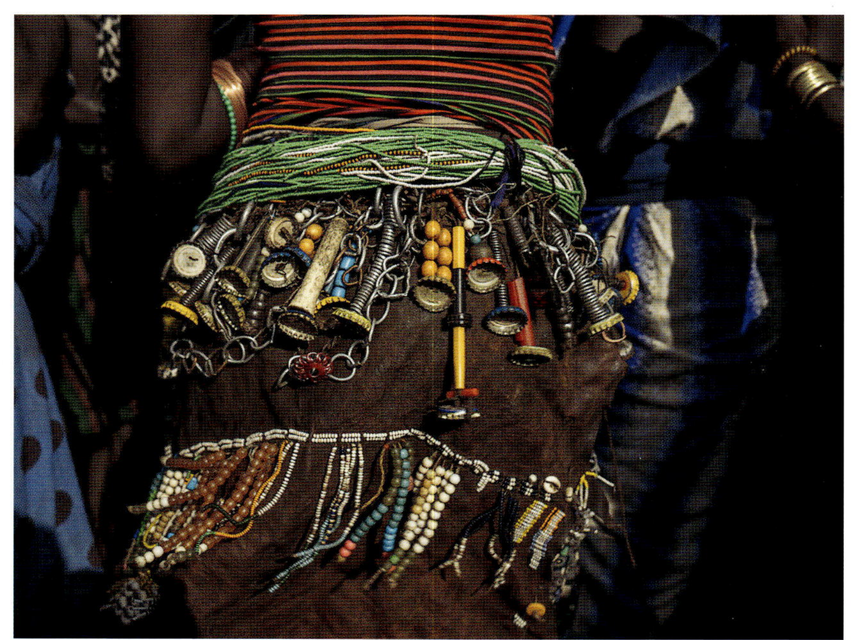

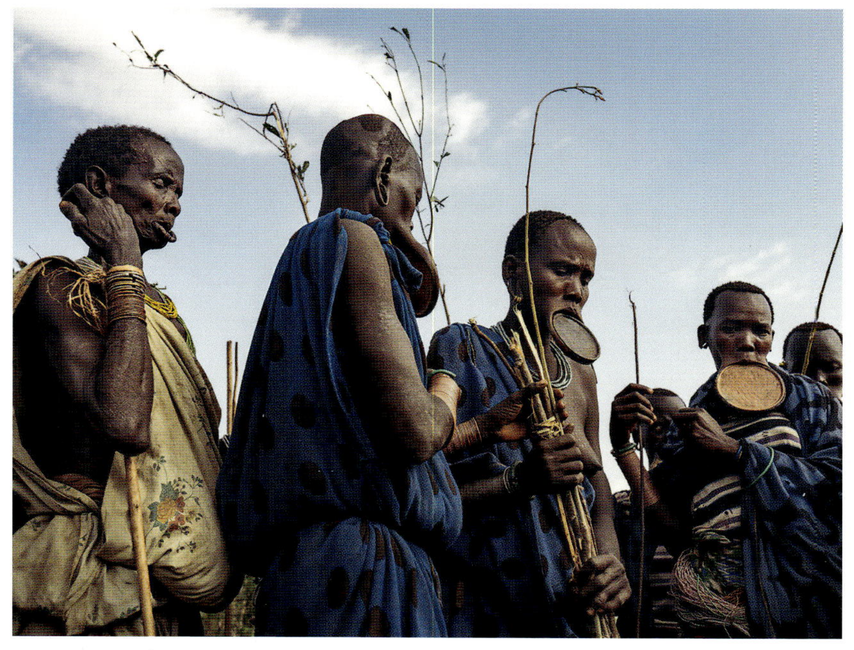

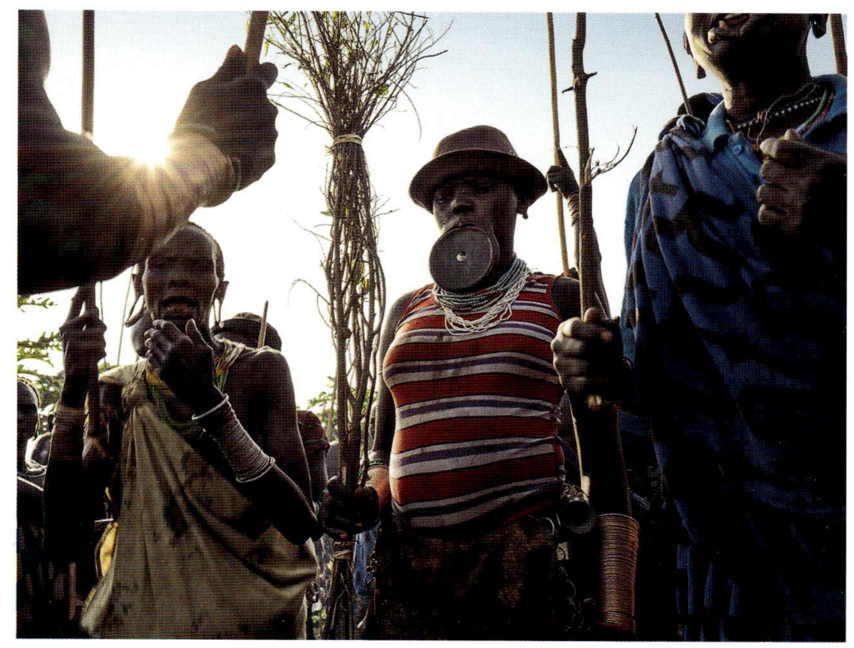

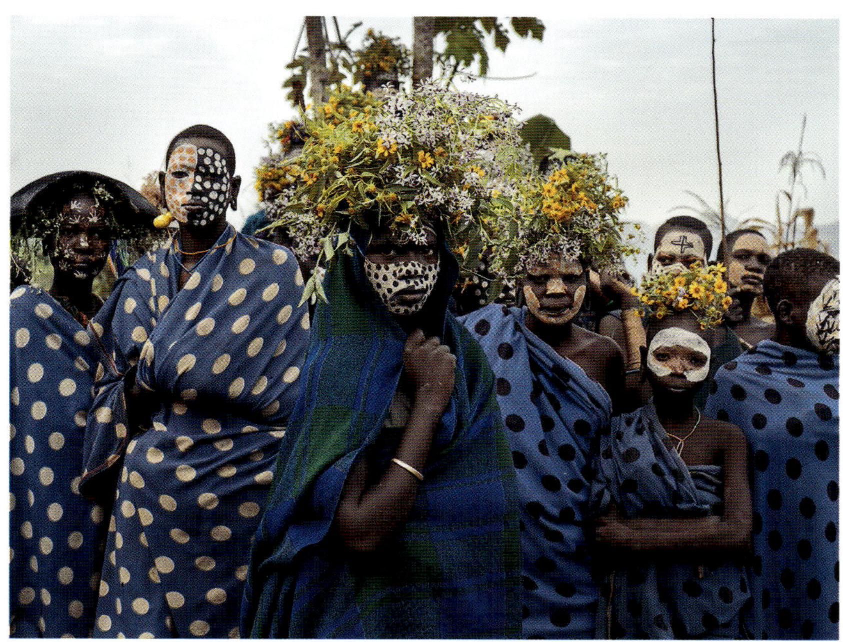

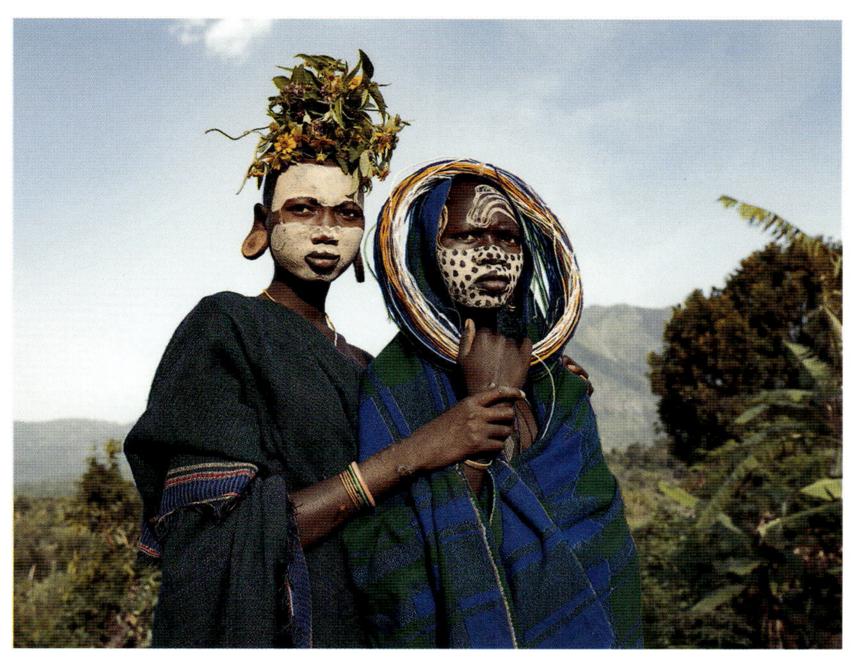

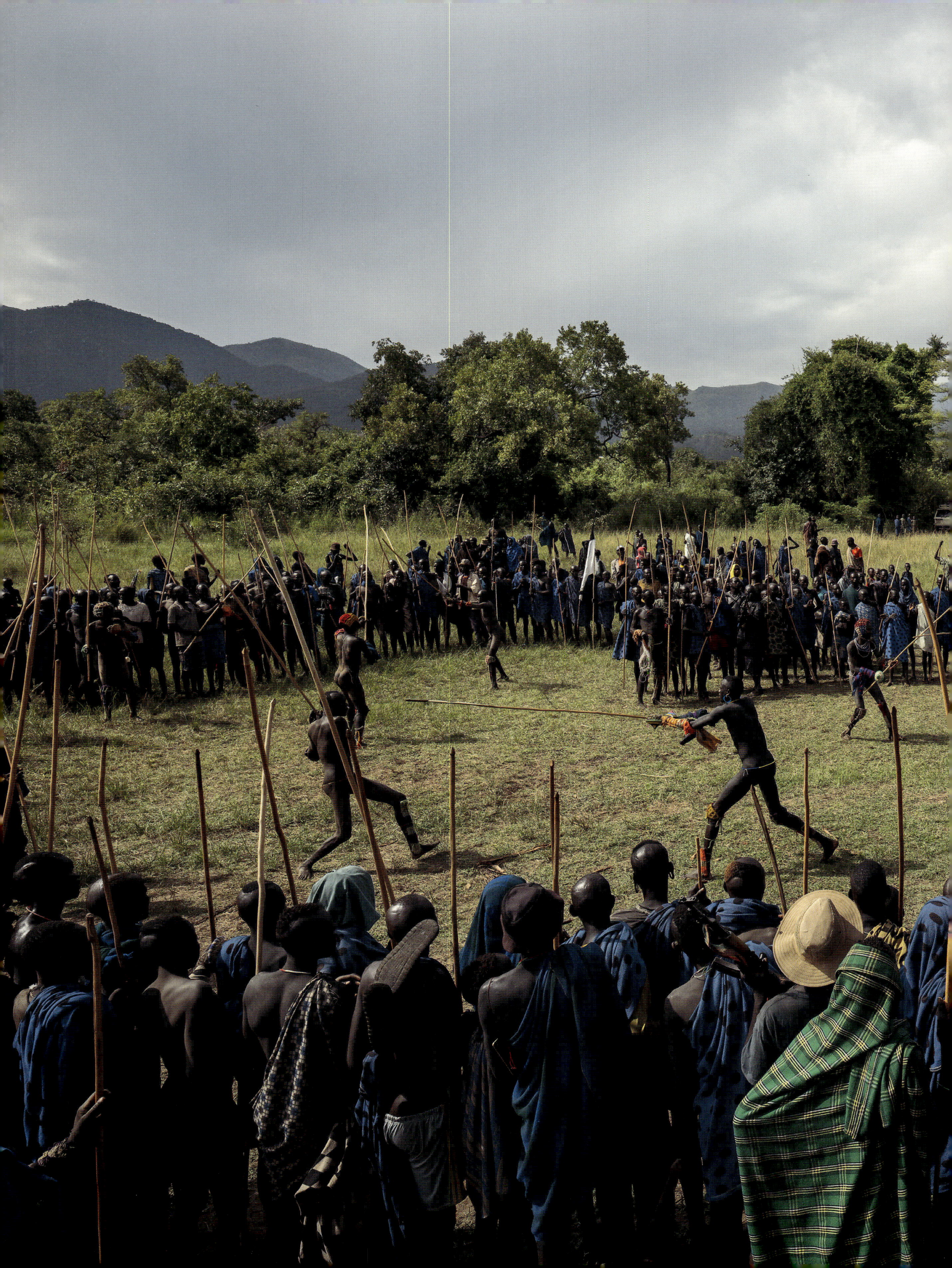

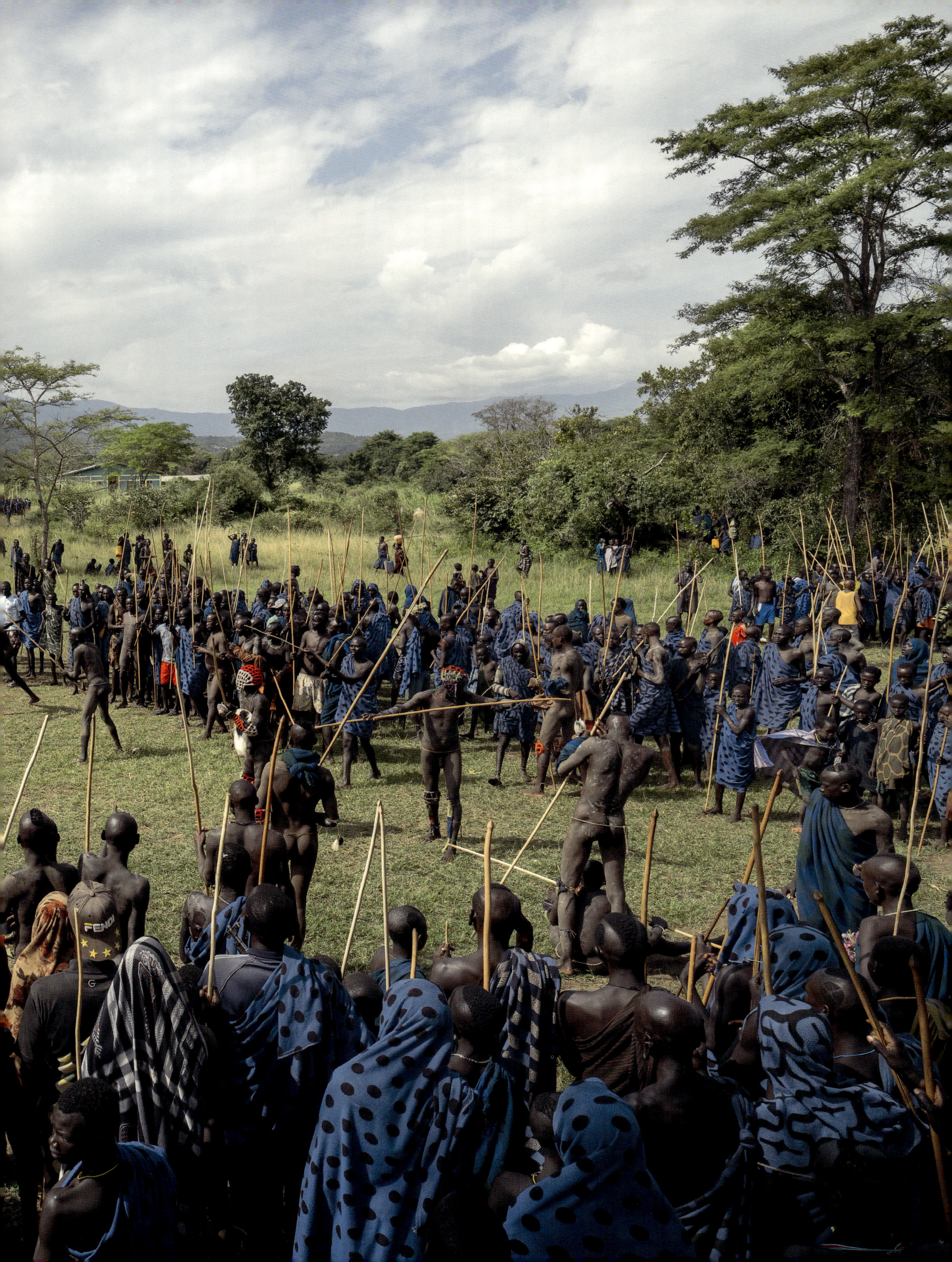

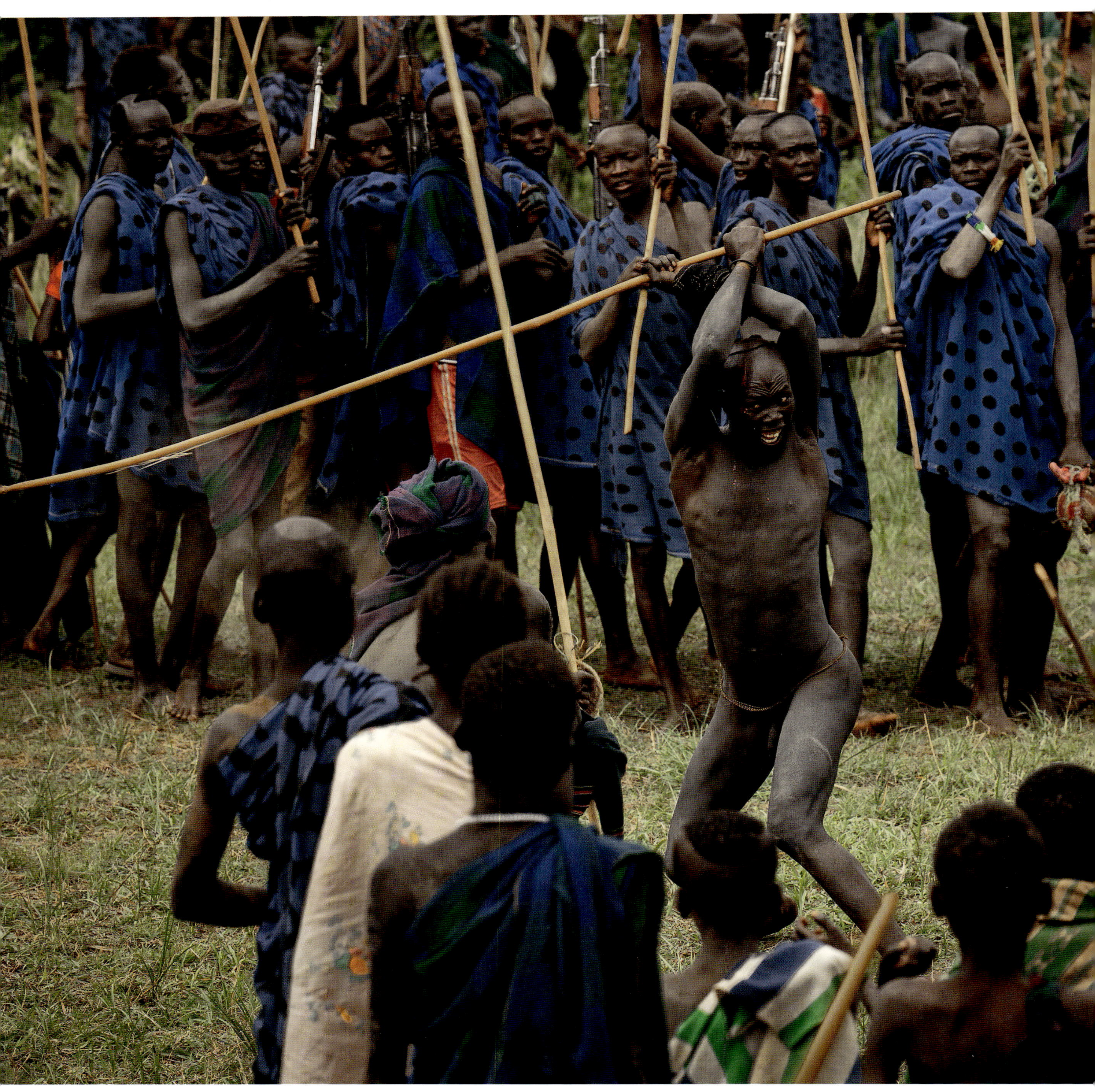

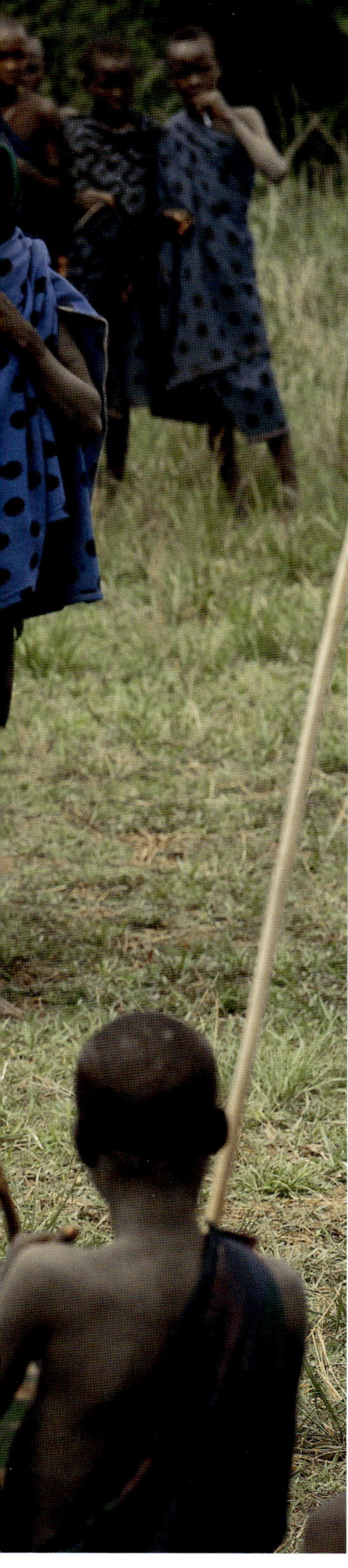

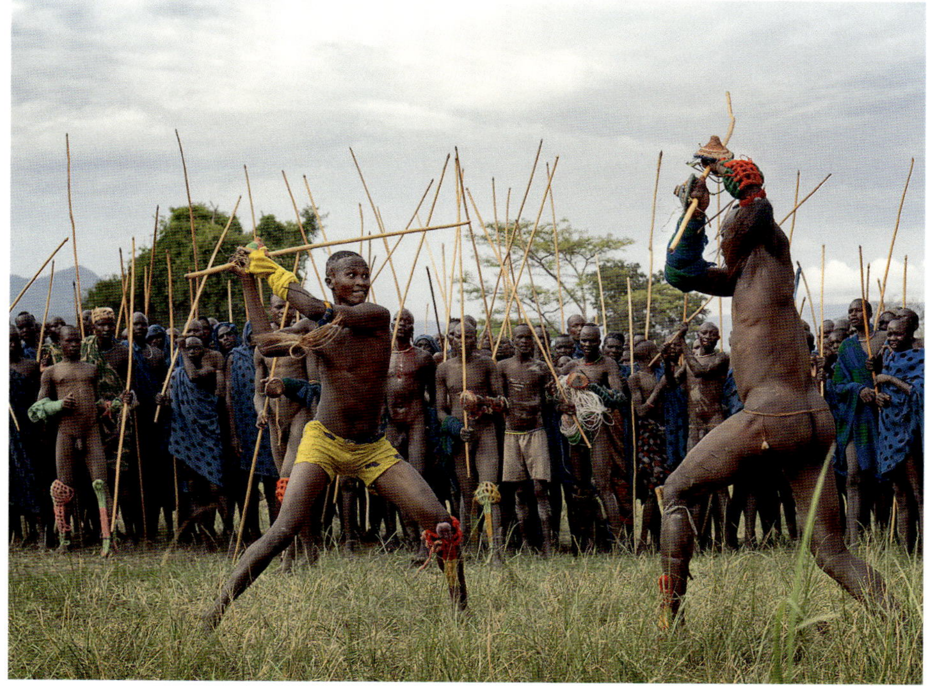

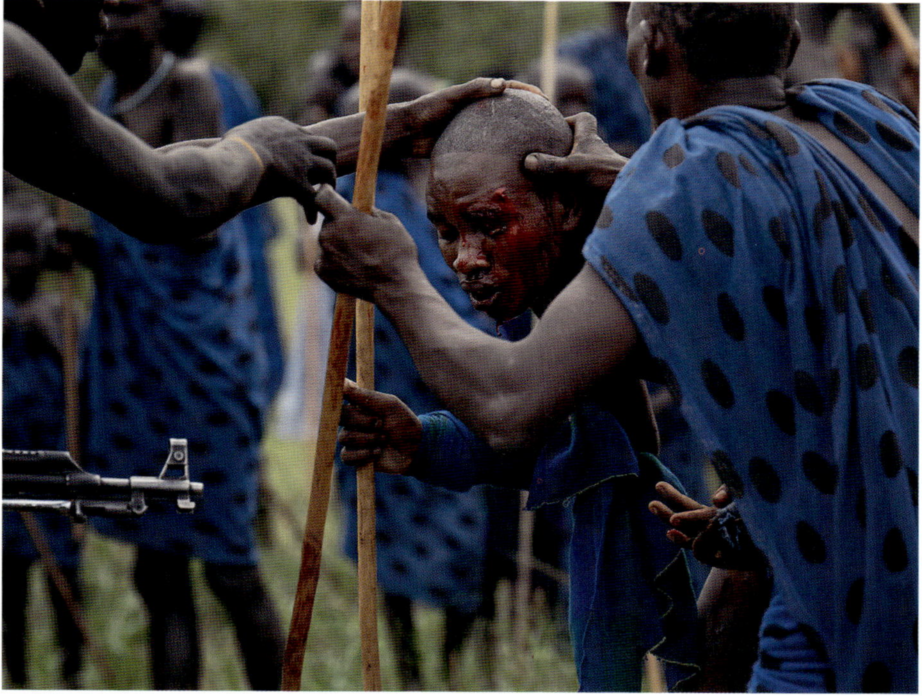

Donga stick fighting can cause severe injuries
from the painful hit of a stick or by AK47 bullets,
but beating each other to death has recently been
stopped by human rights organisations.

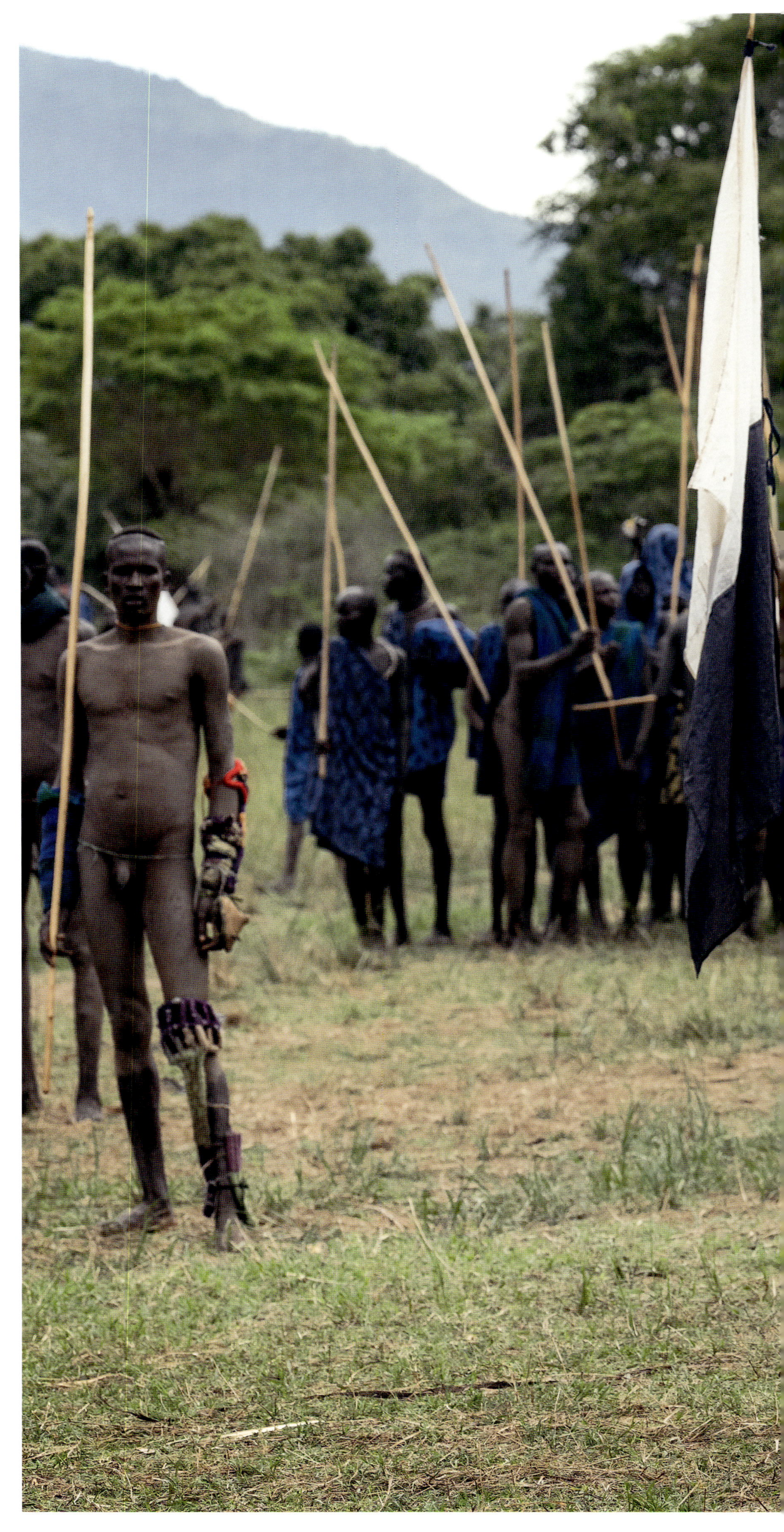

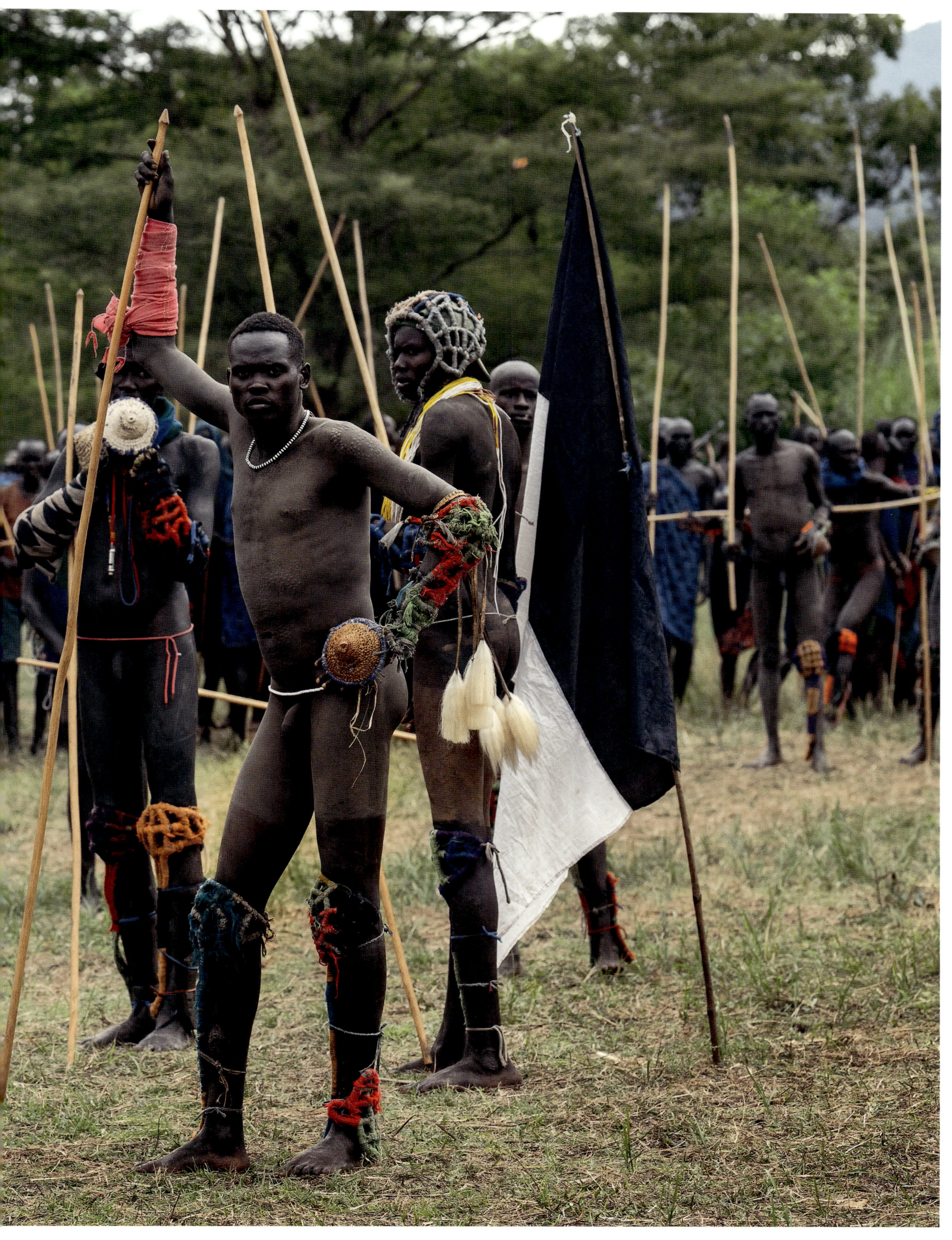

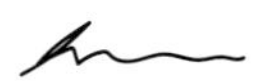

Tarahumara Runners

MEXICO

It is their way of being in harmony with nature and their landscape, a gift left to them by their ancestors.

Nestled in one of the world's most remote and extreme landscapes, hidden from sight in the sun-kissed Copper Canyon in northern Mexico, live a barely reachable people who call themselves Rarámuri, meaning 'those who run fast'. Surprisingly, these remarkable people – the Tarahumara – do not train. And yet they are legendary worldwide for long-distance endurance running.

Play is serious business for the Tarahumara people; they can spend days in celebration and later tirelessly run a marathon while continuously kicking a ball (*komakali*) around the harsh, mountainous terrain. Girls and women also compete, but instead of kicking a ball while they run, they use long sticks to toss and catch hoops. And they do all this wearing only *huaraches* (traditional leather sandals). Yet as the rapidly modernising world seeps into their playground, you see more of them running in the same plastic footwear they wear in everything else they do.

SORICHIQUE,
CHIHUAHUA

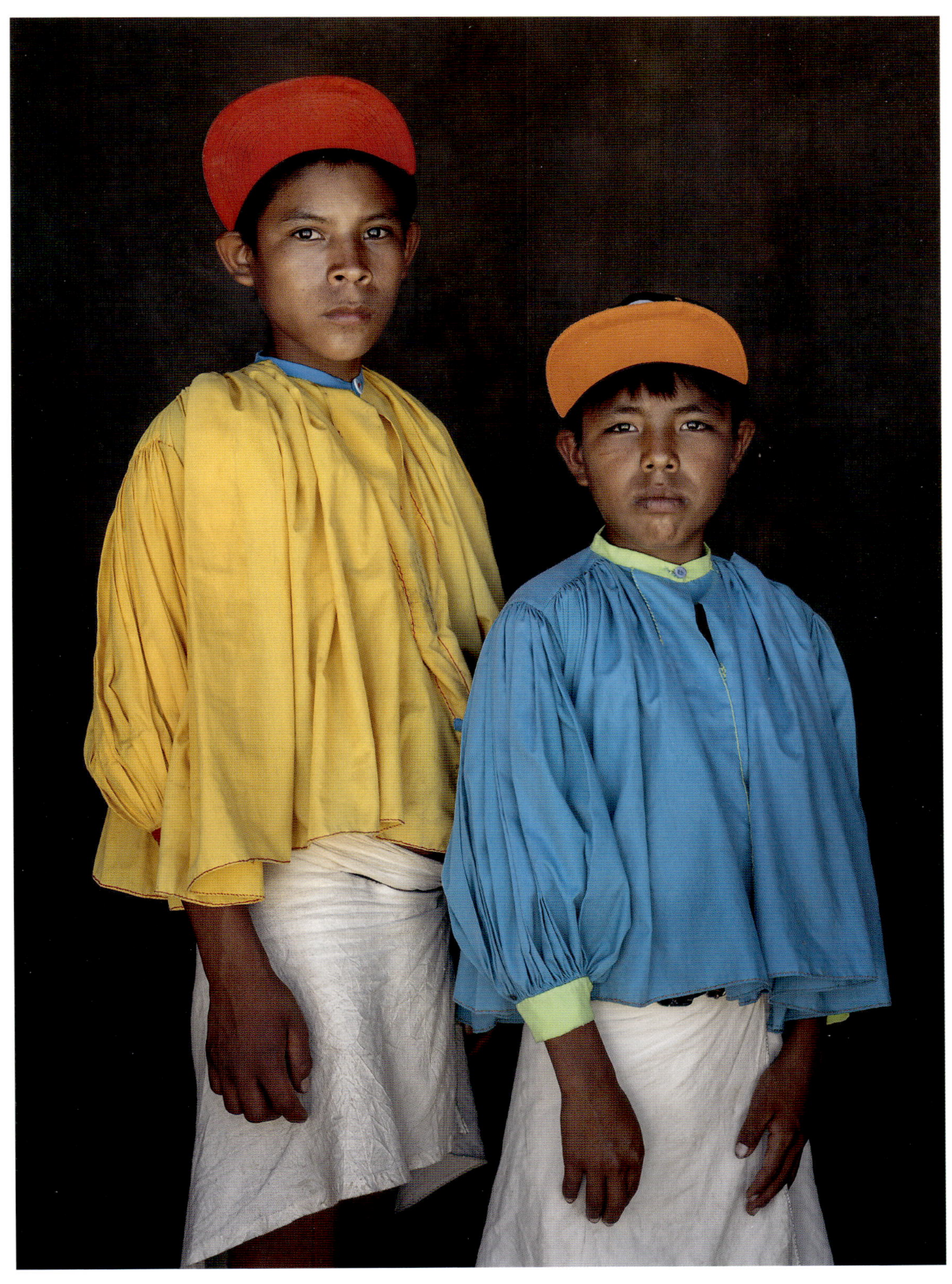

Tarahumara runners begin already running at an early age.

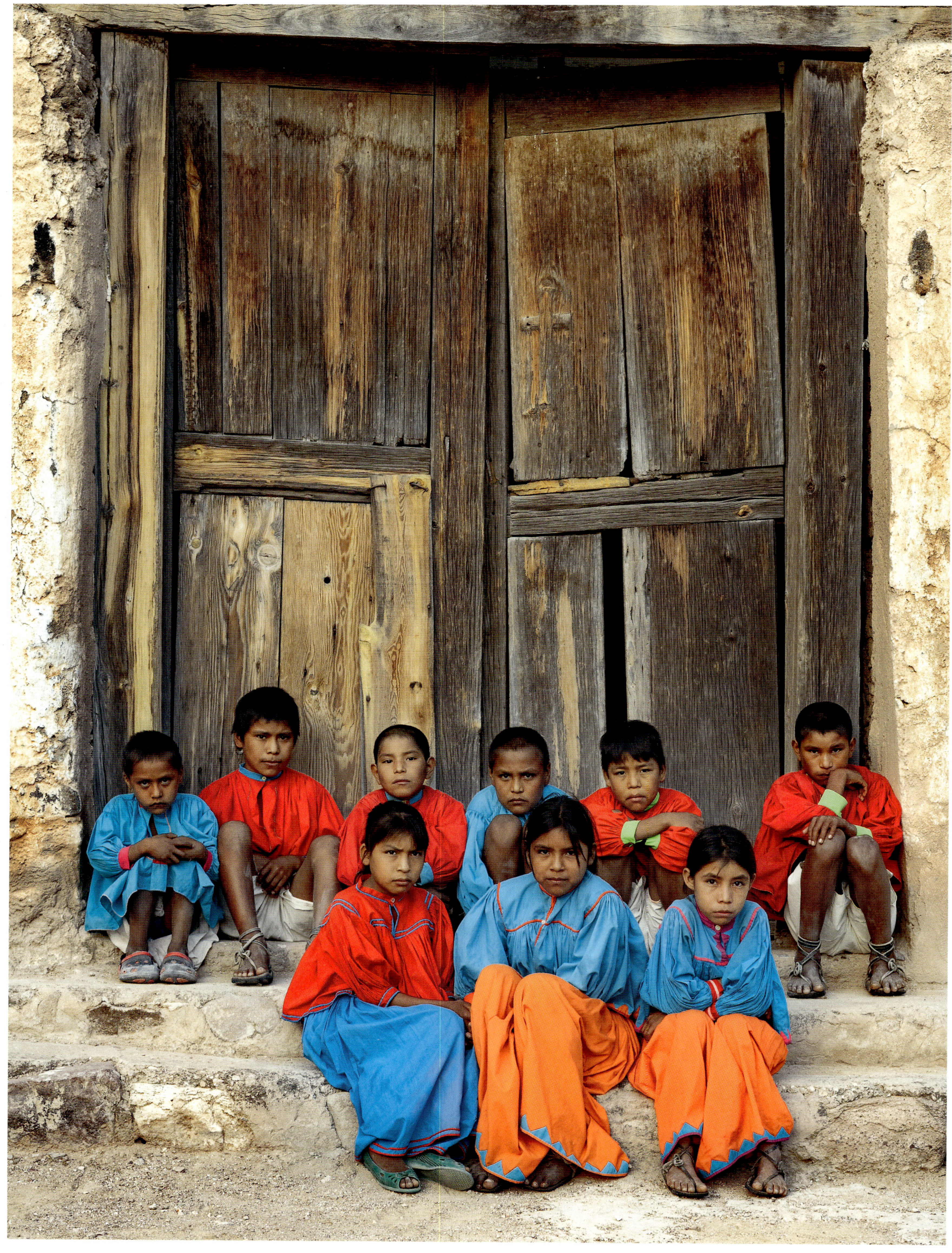

People from all over the world seek out the Tarahumara, looking for the holy grail of athletics, thirsty for answers. What secret could these indigenous people have that gives them such stamina? It is not their shoes, training or diet. Contrary to Western culture, running for the Rarámuri is not about competing to win. For them, it's a way of life; a means to get through their daily chores, spend time together, and a form of prayer blended into the spiritual tapestry of their tight-knit community. It is their way of harmonising with nature and their landscape, a gift left to them by their ancestors.

These people have been racing outside the Copper Canyon since 1927, when Austin, Texas, hosted an eighty-two-mile run featuring the Tarahumara runners. Between 1992 and 1998, around thirty-five of them entered eight ultras in America, and most of them finished in the top ten, with four wins and two record-breakers.

Arnulfo Quimare is the legendary runner who in 2006 beat Scott Jurek and has been the reigning champion of the Sierra Madre since he was eighteen. Featured in the book *Born to Run*, he's described as the 'greatest living Tarahumara runner'. Having won innumerable races and setting records in most of them, he has established himself as the number-one ultrarunner in the world. But it isn't just men who win these long-distance races.

María Lorena Ramírez brought global attention to her community when she was featured in the Netflix documentary *Lorena, Light-Footed Woman*. Although extremely shy, she is quite competitive, having won the Ultra Trail Cerro Rojo 50k in Puebla, Mexico, where she defeated five hundred athletes from twelve other countries. Shortly after, she became the first Rarámuri woman to compete in a European ultra, attempting the Bluetrail, Europe's second-highest race. The Ramírez family has a history of long-distance running. Her older brother Mario placed tenth in the 30k run in Puebla, and three of her seven siblings and her father ran with her in the Chihuahua ultramarathon.

The merging of spirituality and community is very present during a race as women surround and cheer the exhausted runners by chanting in unison *Iwériga*, meaning 'I'm sending the power of my soul to yours'. Tarahumara men proudly proclaim that *el poder de las mujeres* (the power of women) provides them with the fuel and energy to keep running by supplying *pinole* (ground corn) mixed with water throughout the race.

Strangely enough, this resilient tribe was never conquered by the ever-powerful Aztecs and, until recently, has remained relatively uninfluenced by modern Mexican culture. Despite their changing circumstances, they still consider themselves an independent nation.

Yet the future of the Tarahumara people has become shrouded in uncertainty as drug trafficking, violence, deforestation, mining and climate change threaten to destroy their way of life. One can only hope that their long, rich history and courage will allow them to keep running into tomorrow.

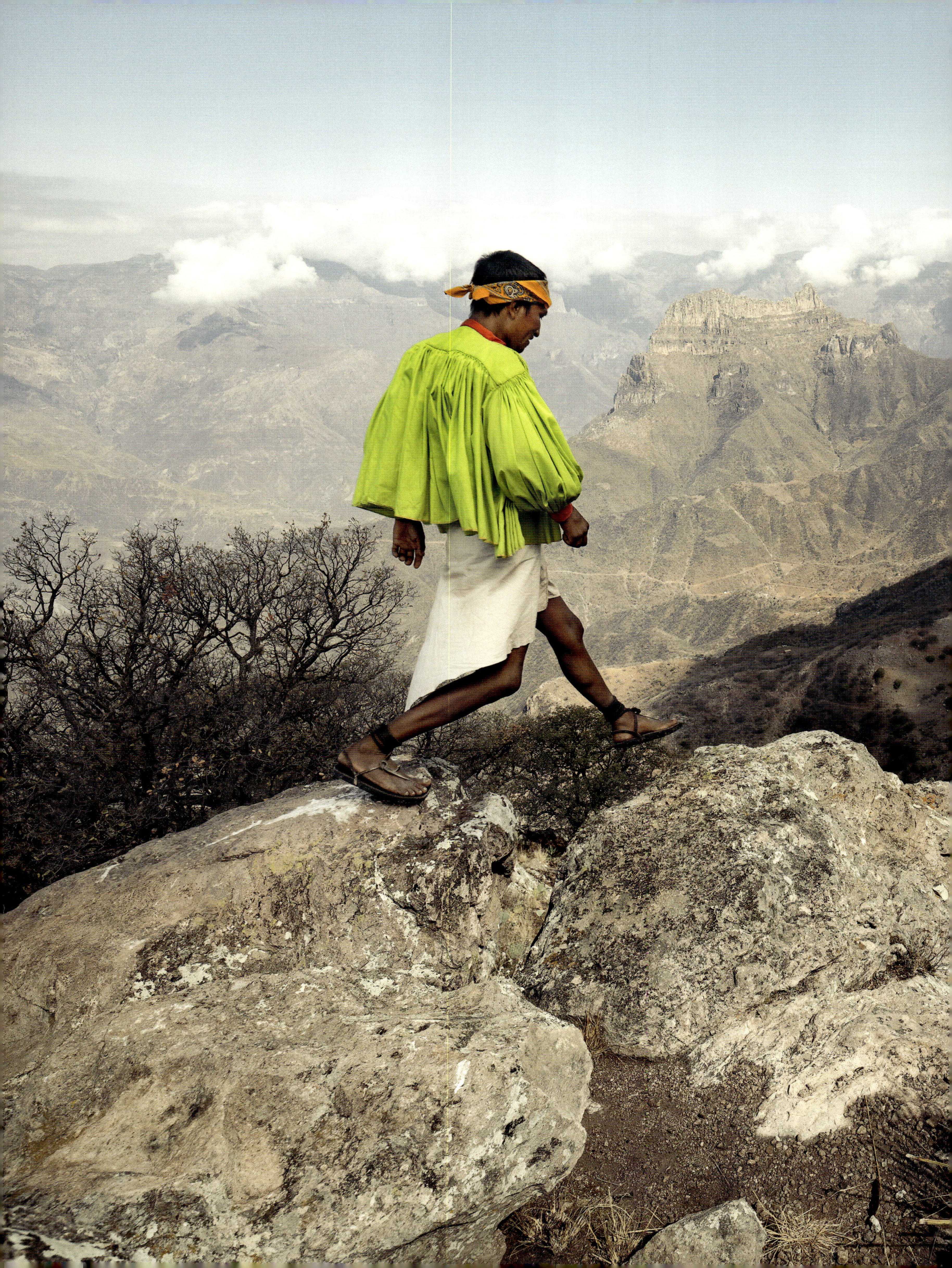

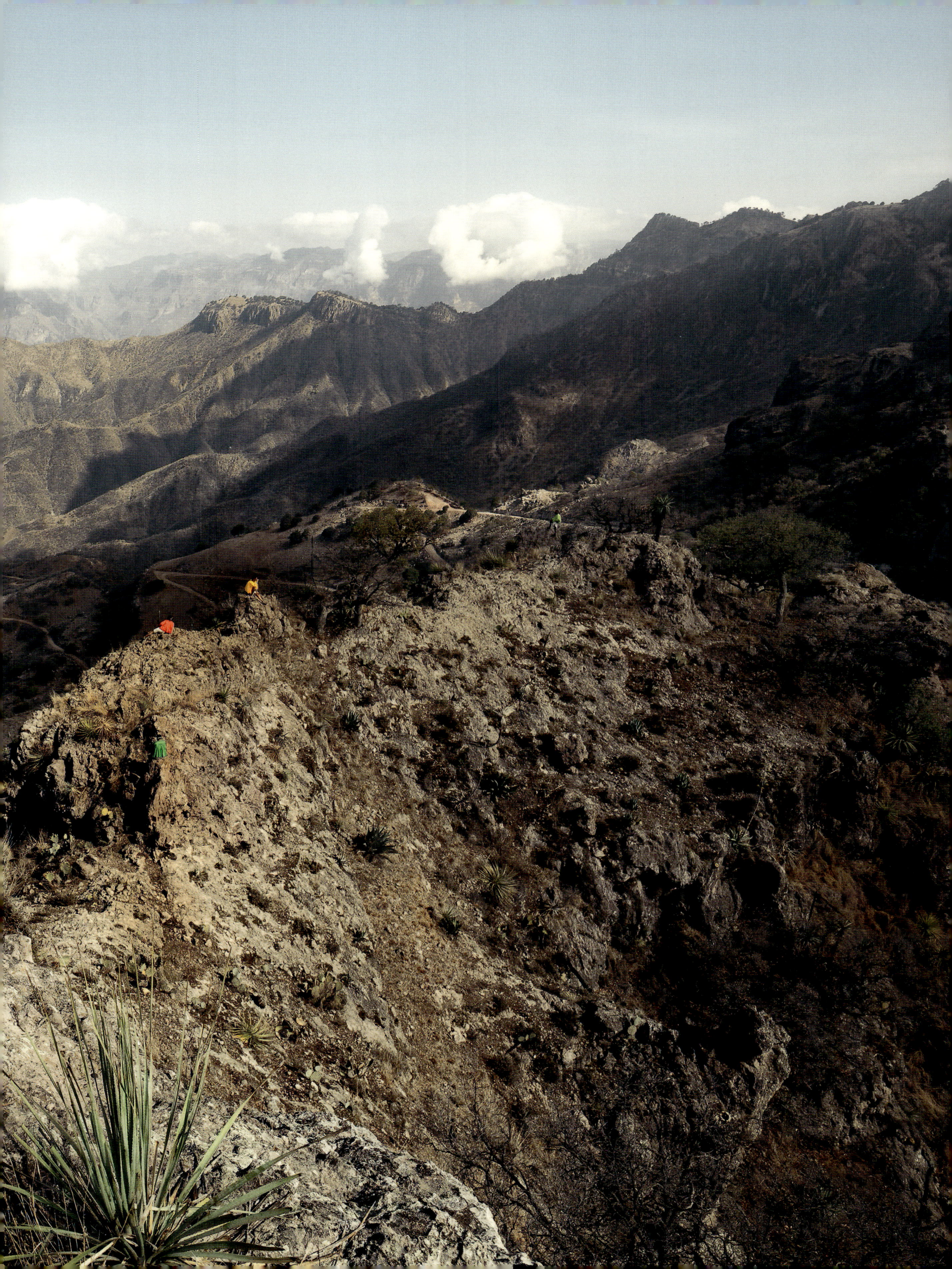

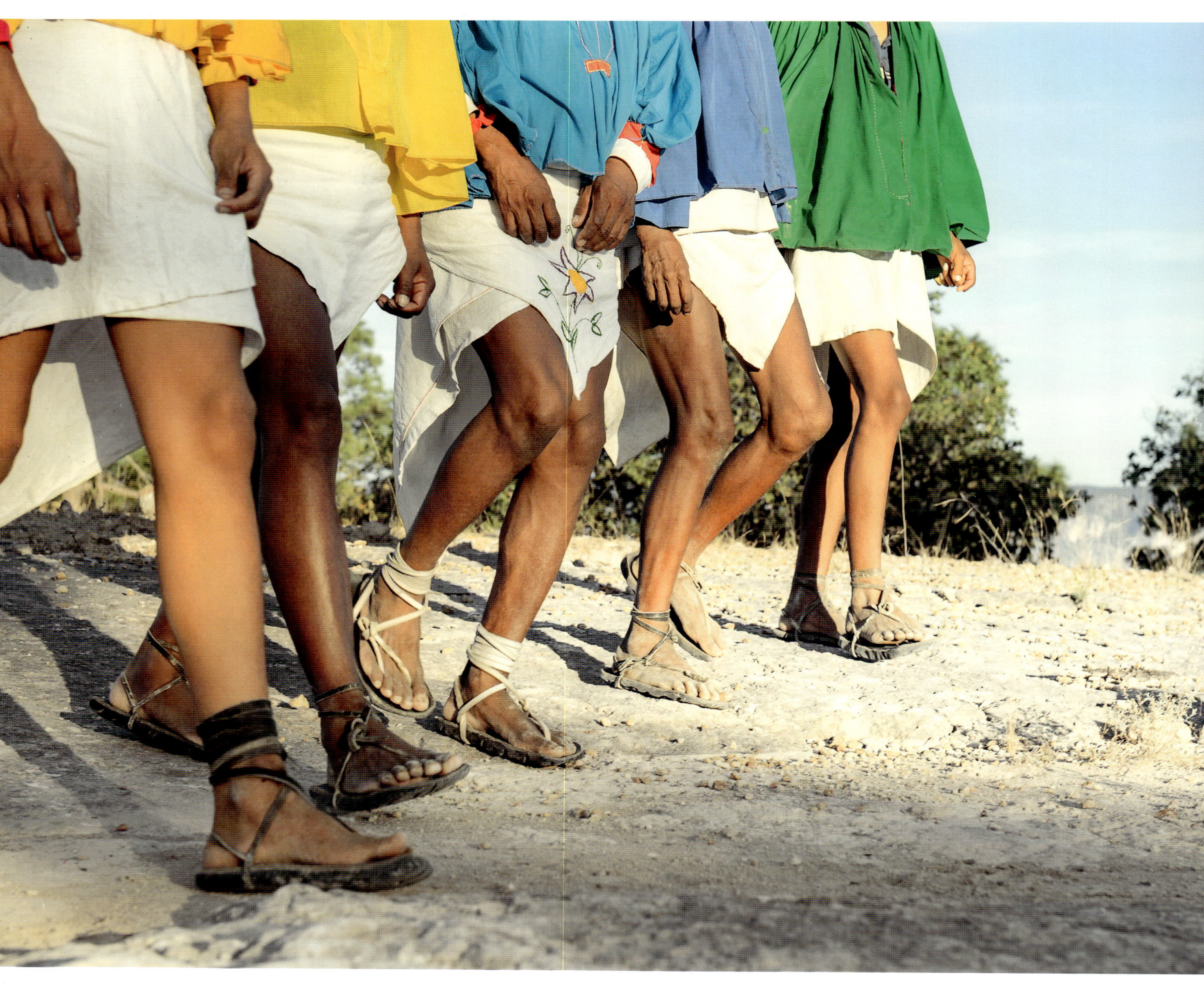

Running for the Tarahumara is an event that includes
everyone – men, women and children run together kicking
the wooden ball for hours and sometimes days.

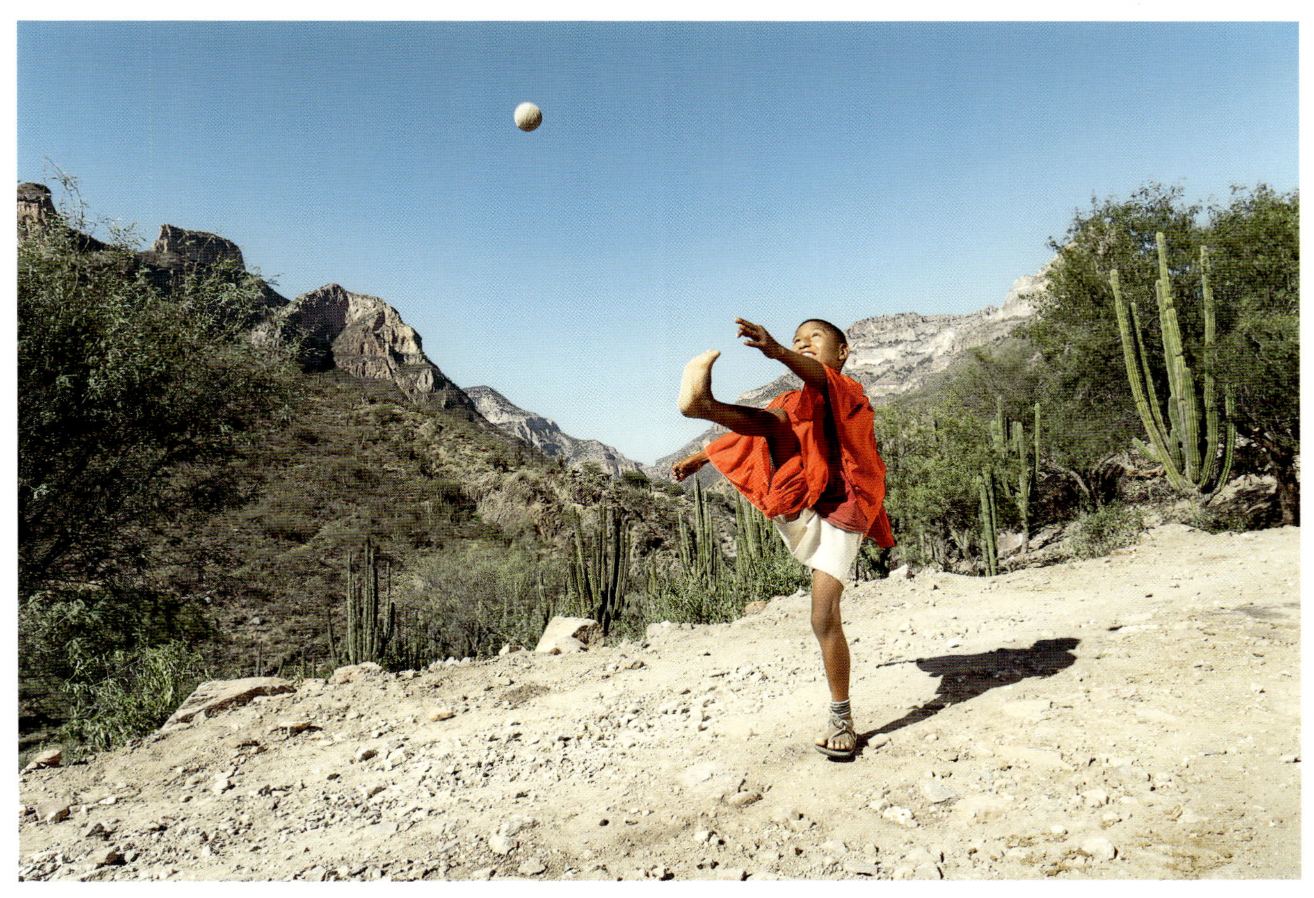

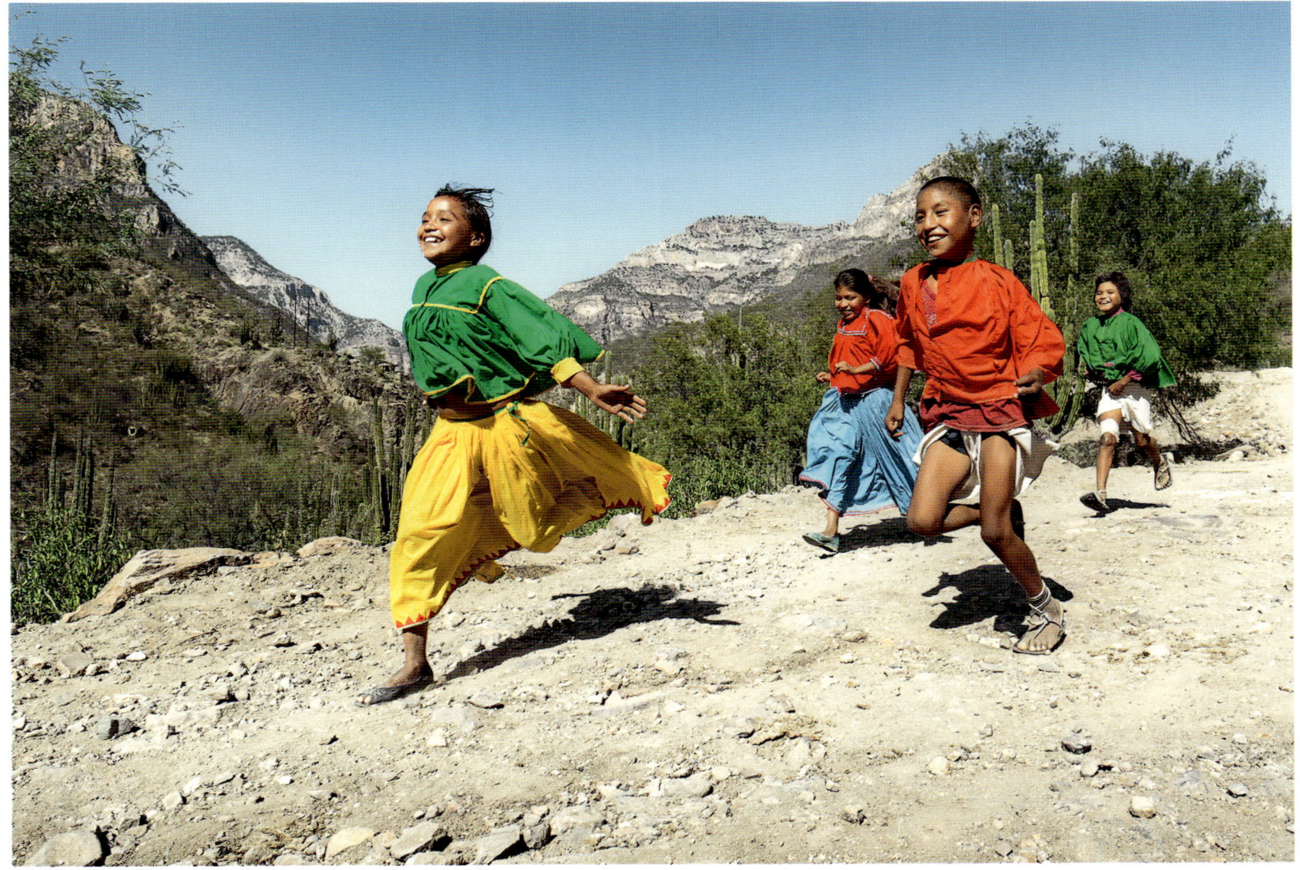

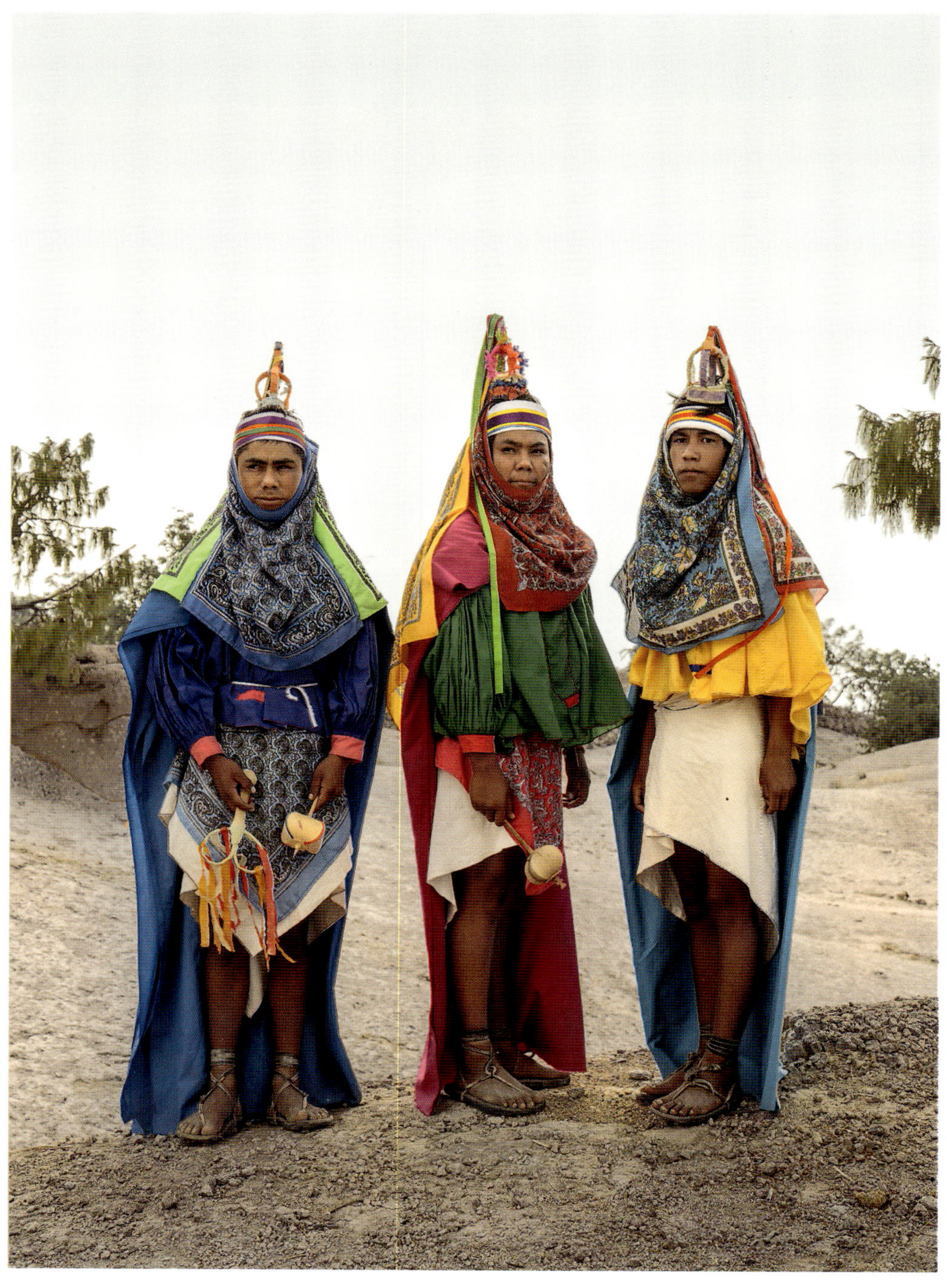

Tarahumara men are dressed in traditional, ceremonial
clothing worn for special events and dances.

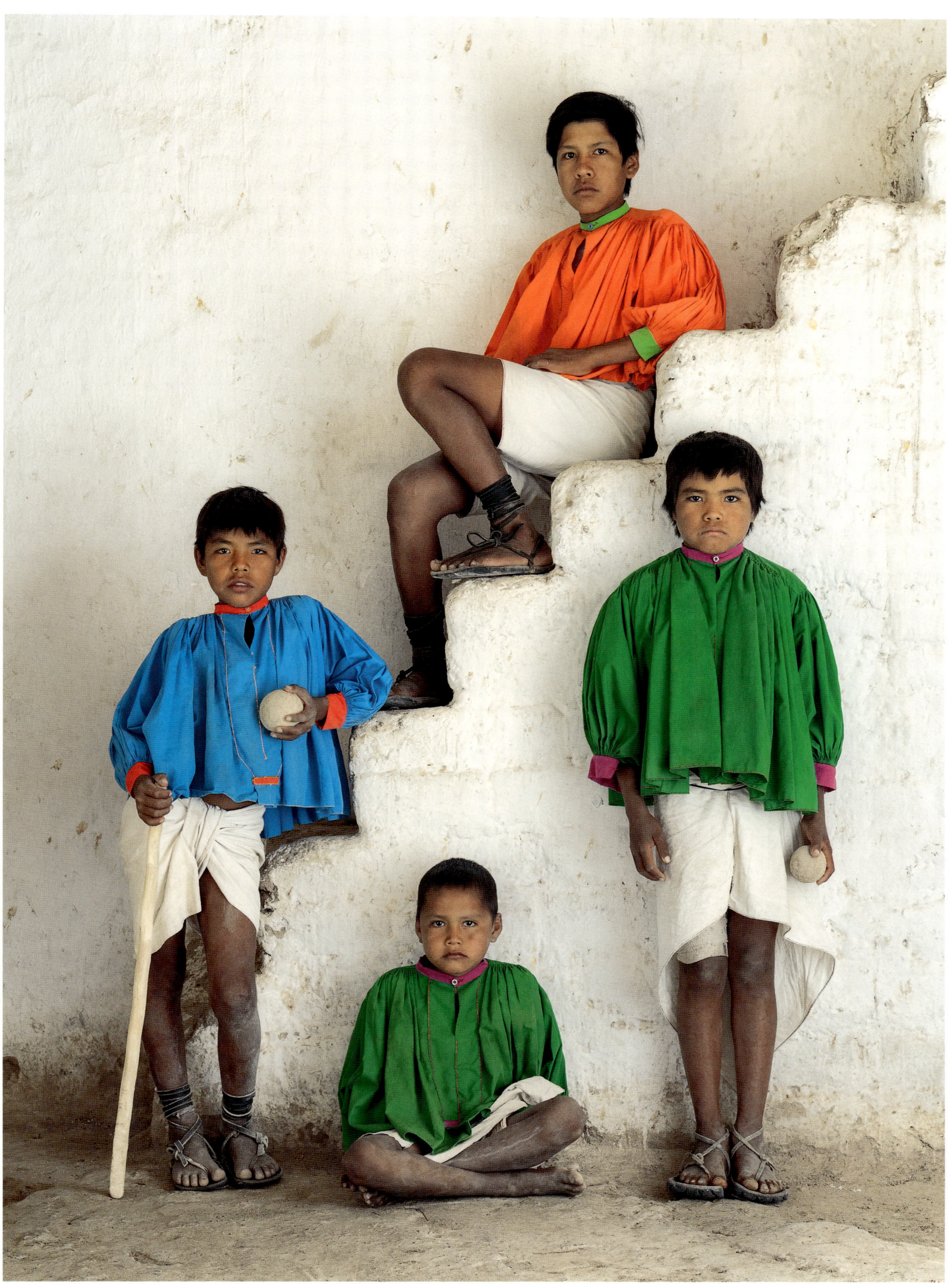

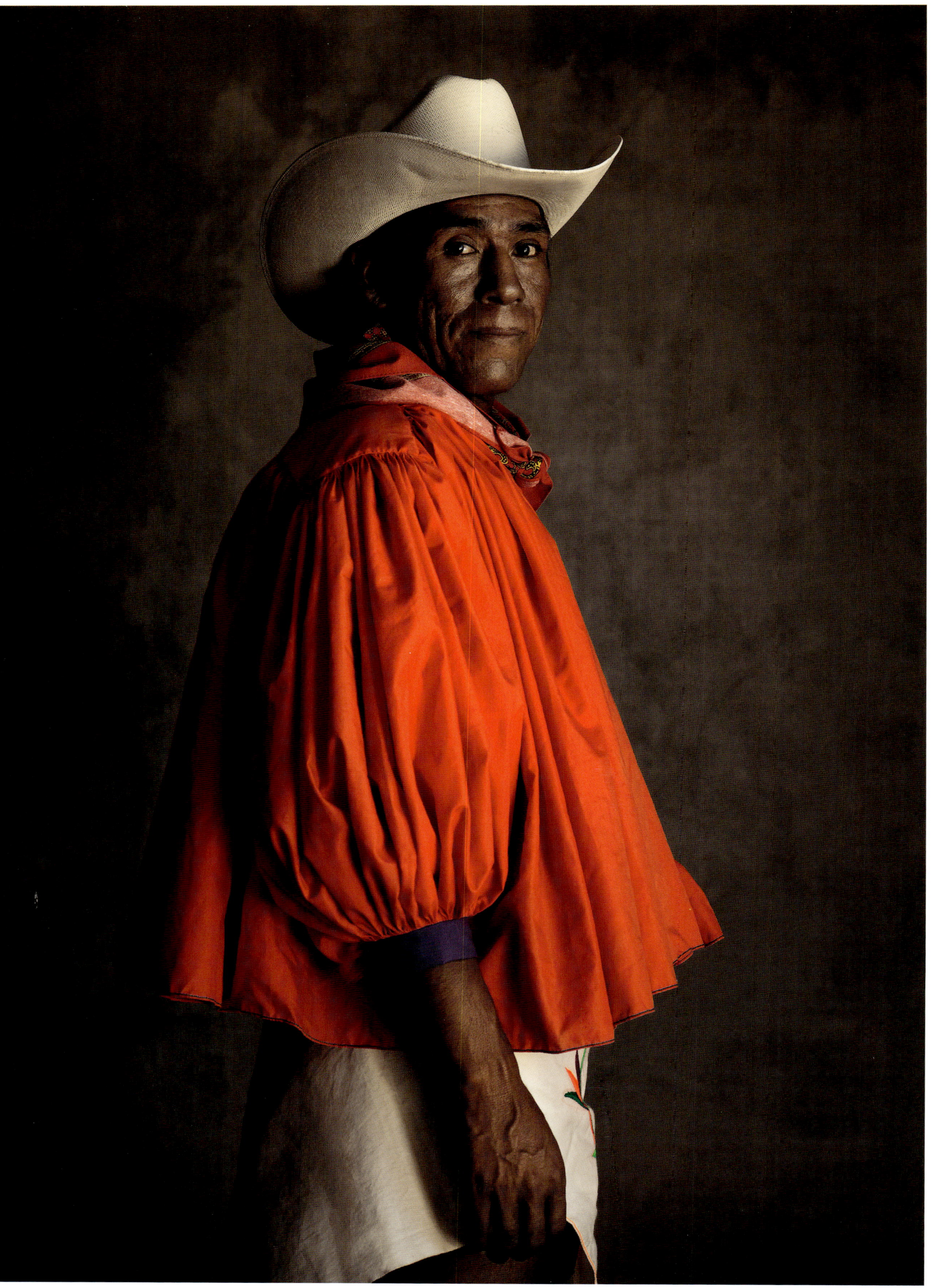

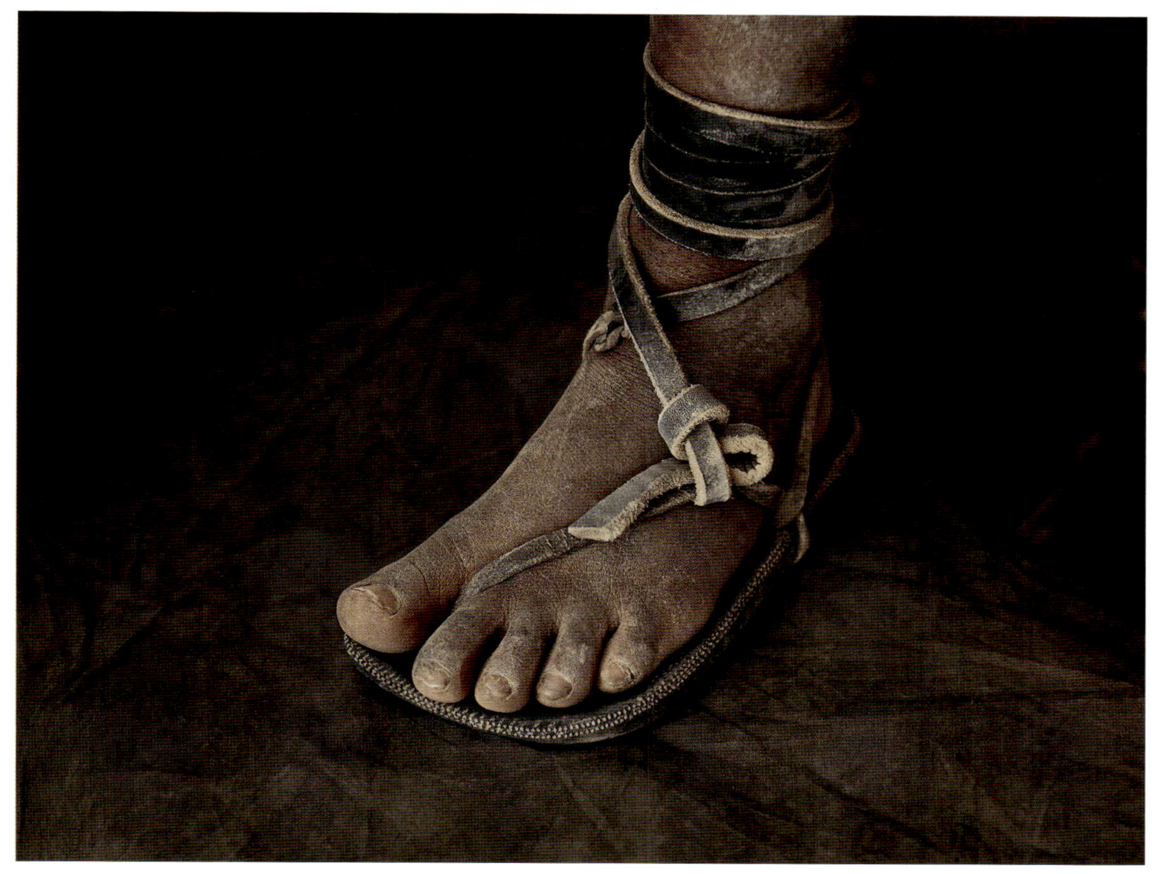

*"I love to run, and my ability to run is
God's gift, running always helps me
remember who I am as a human. When we
run and dance, we give thanks to God."*

~ Arnulfo Quimare, champion Tarahumara runner ~

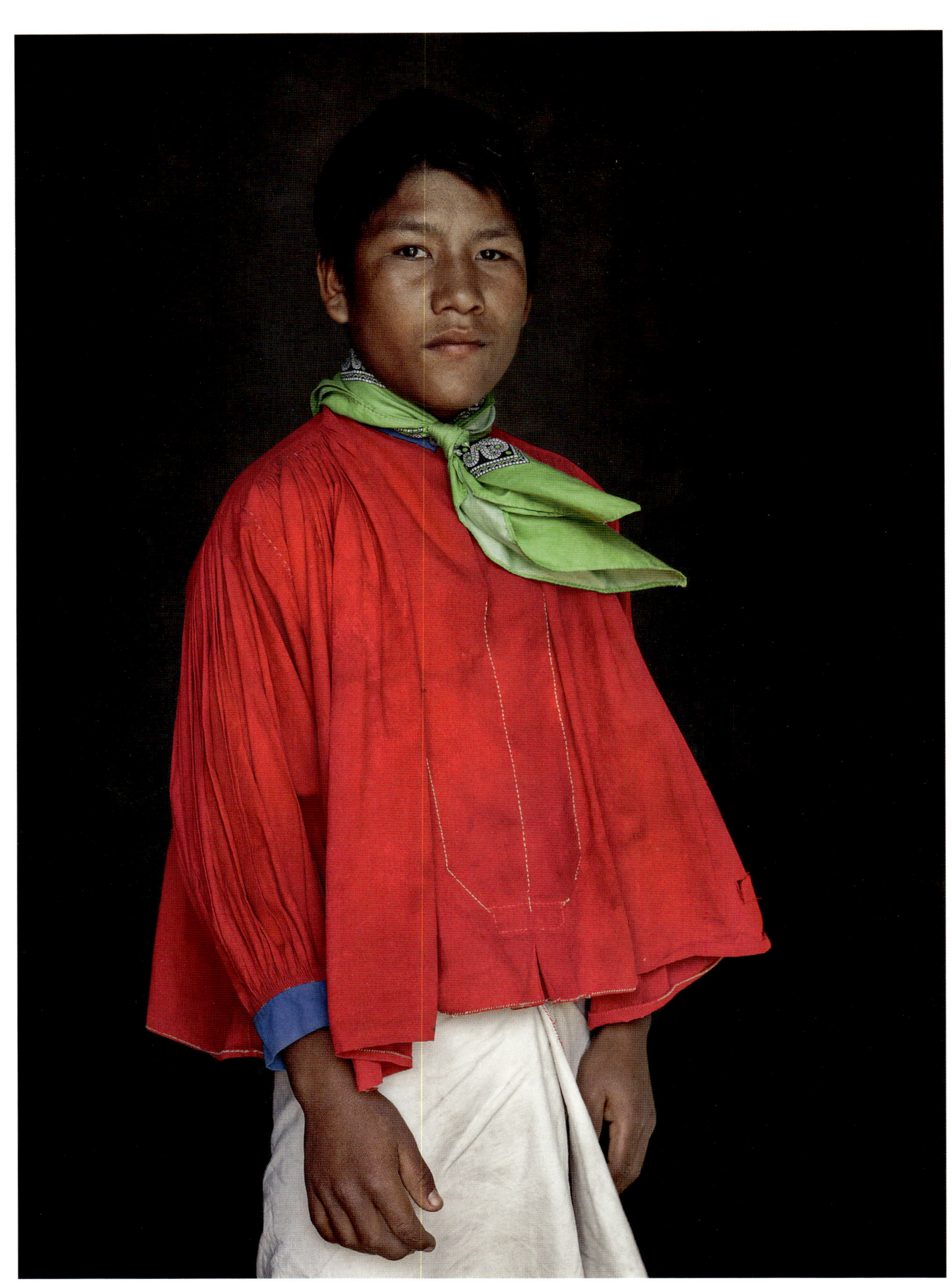

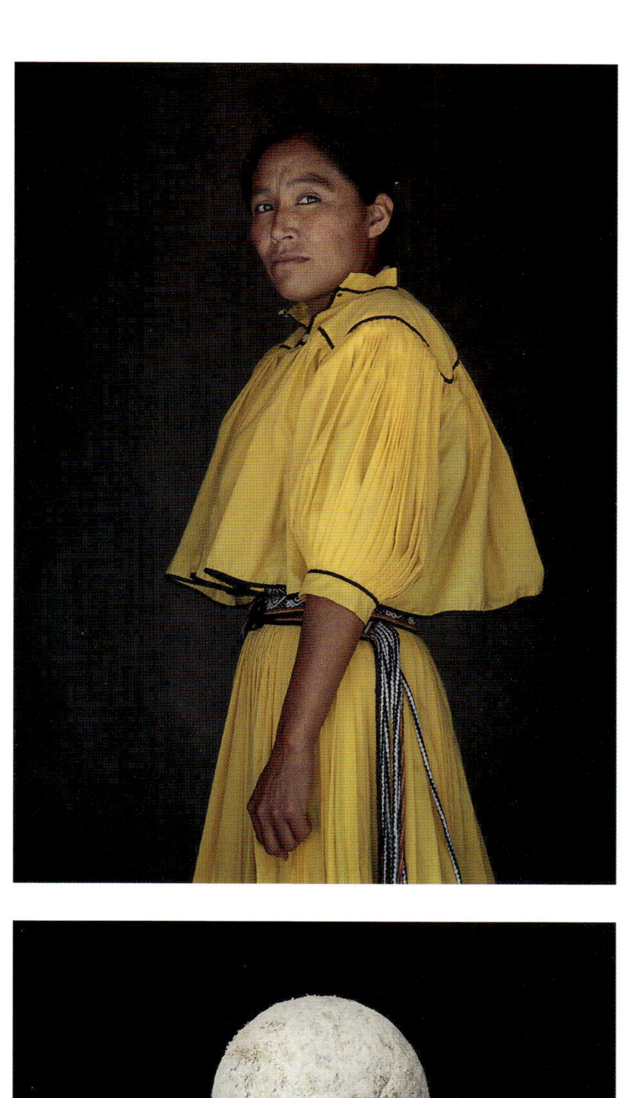
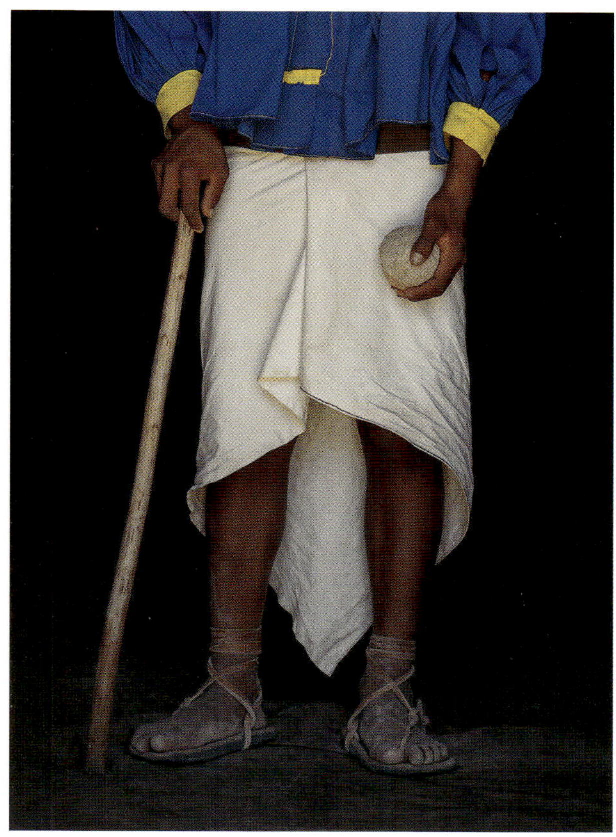
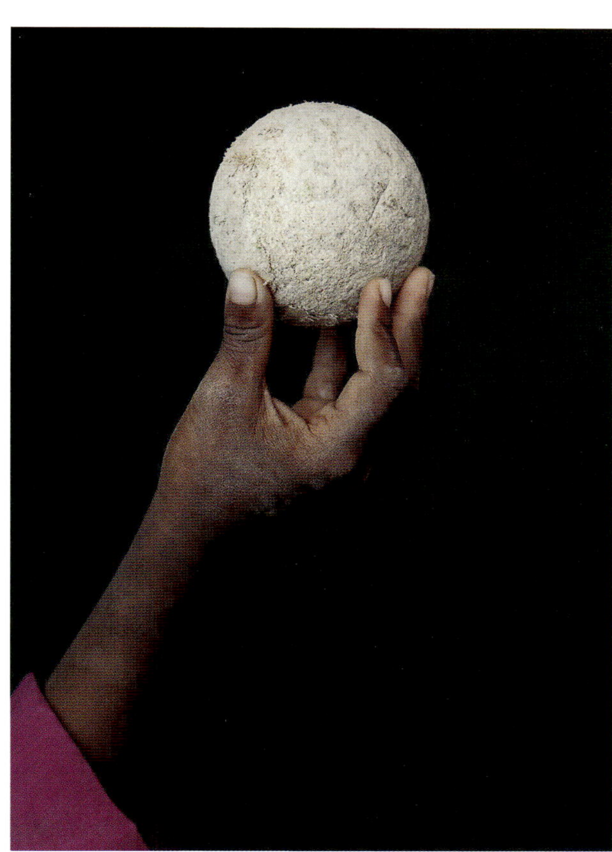
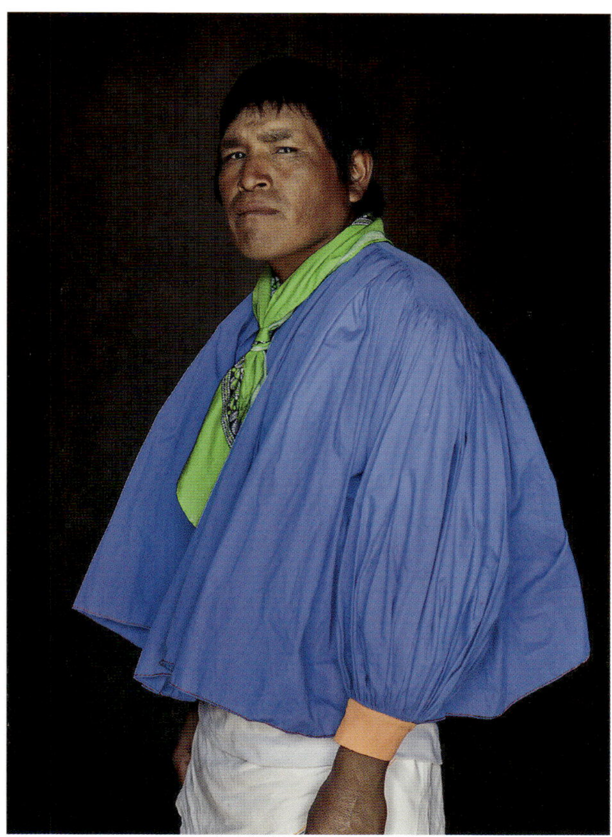

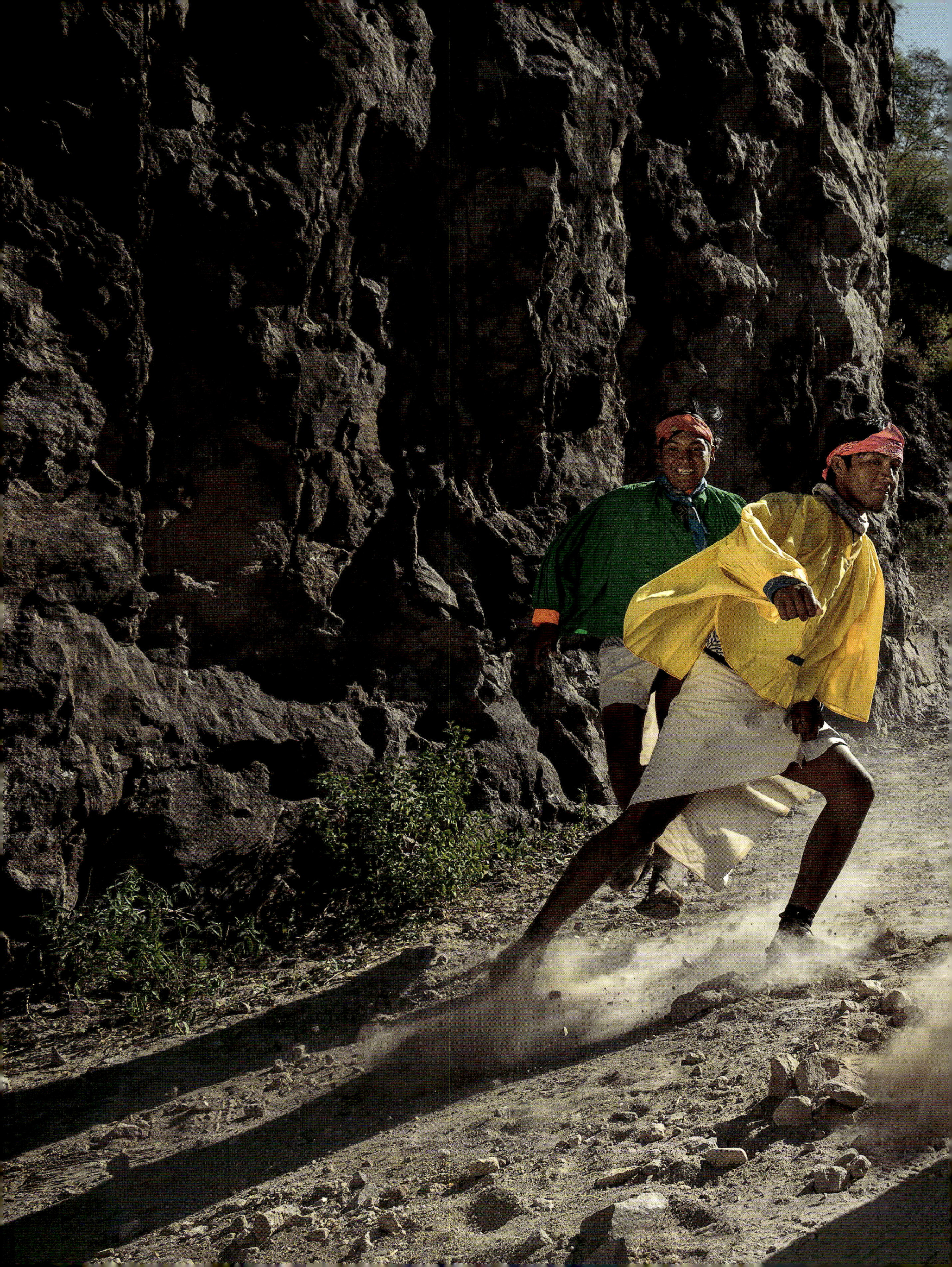

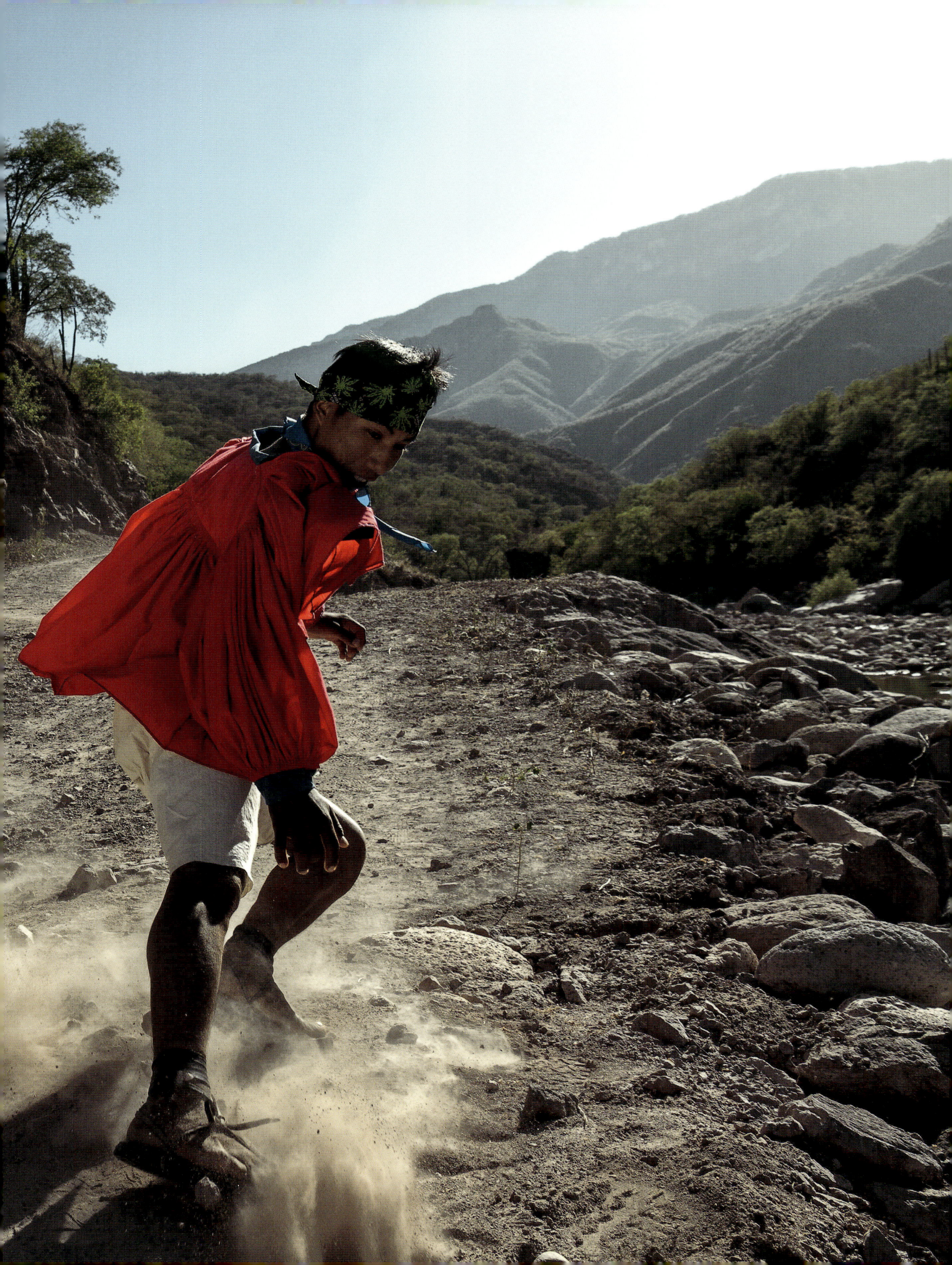

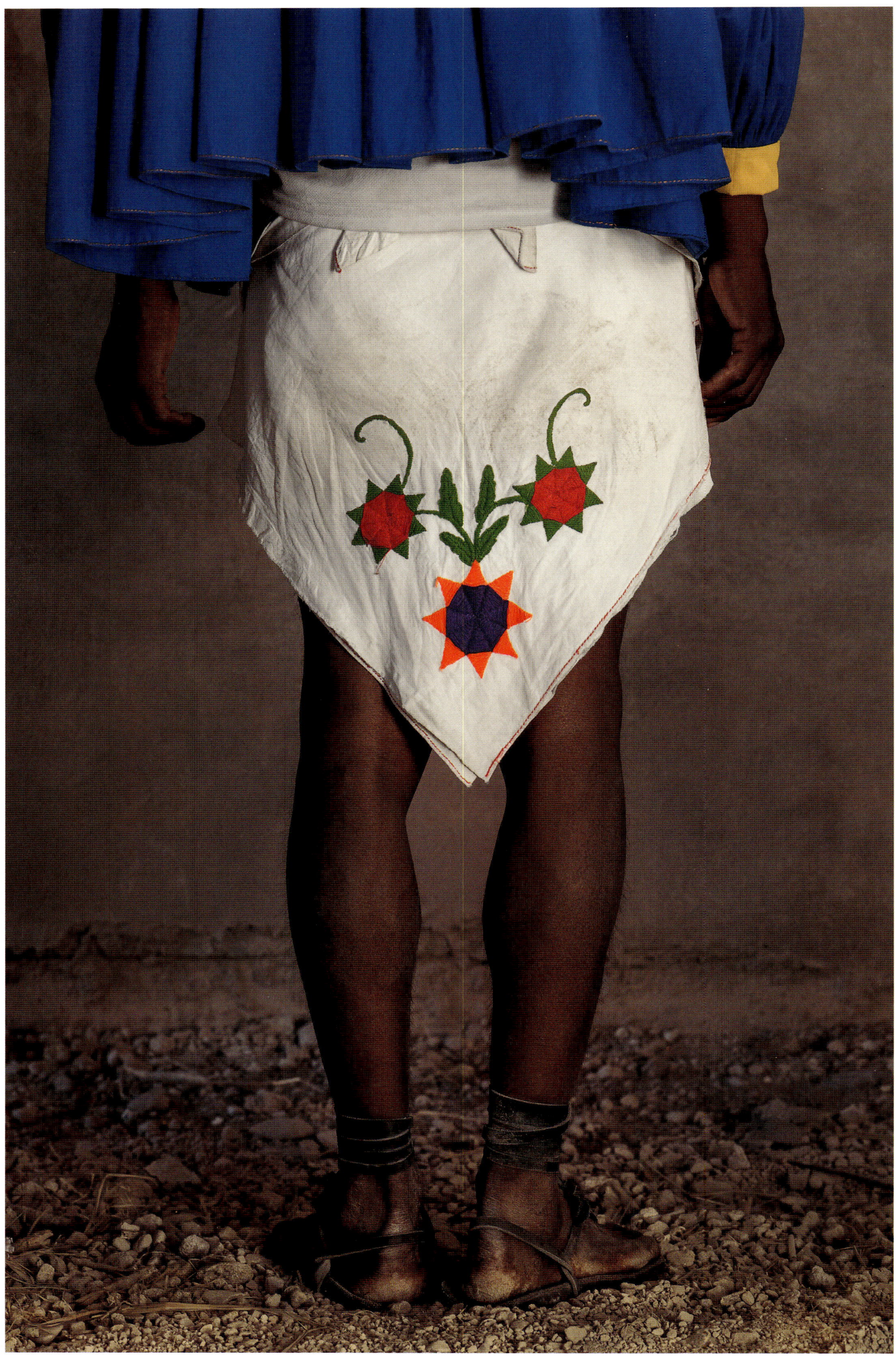

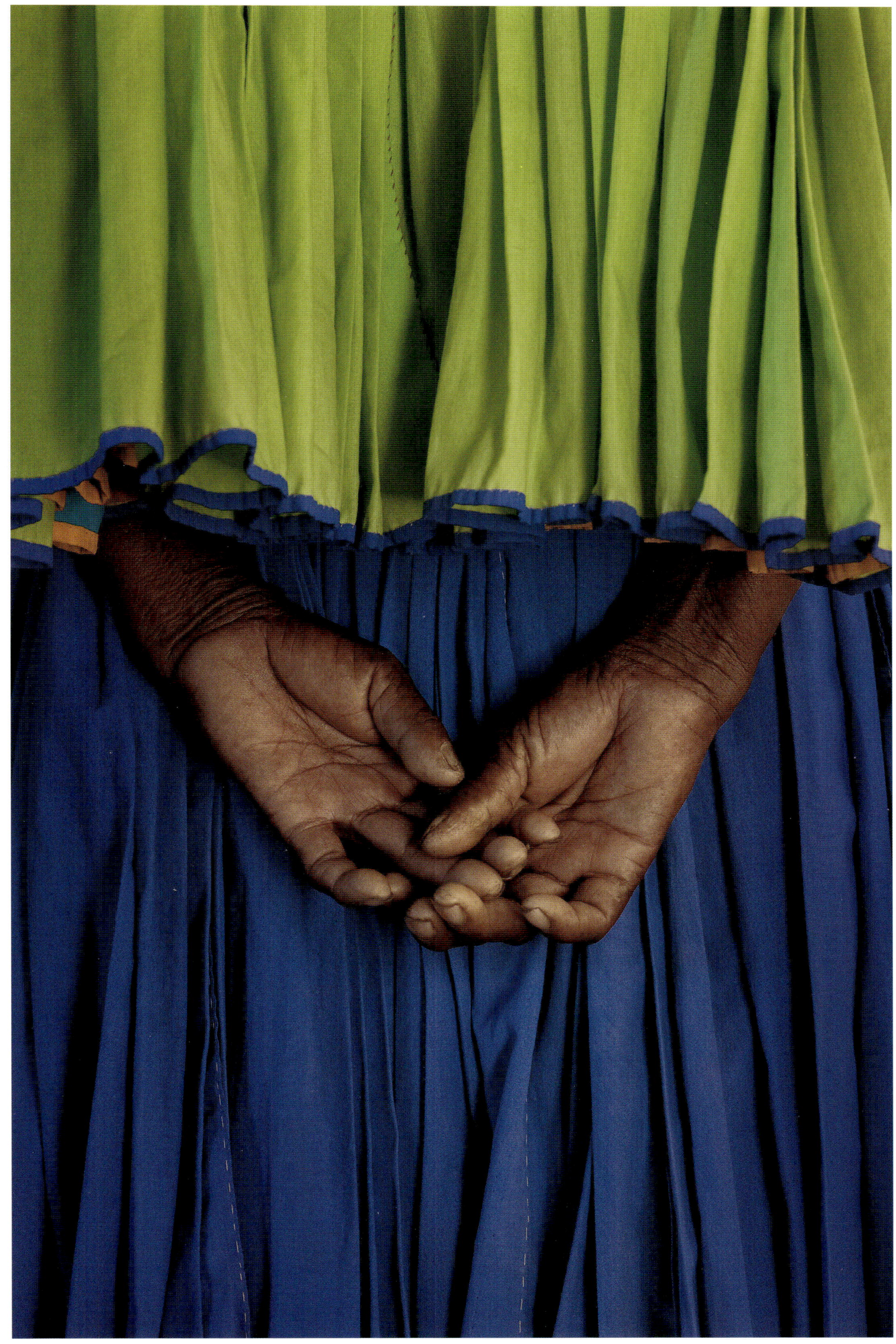

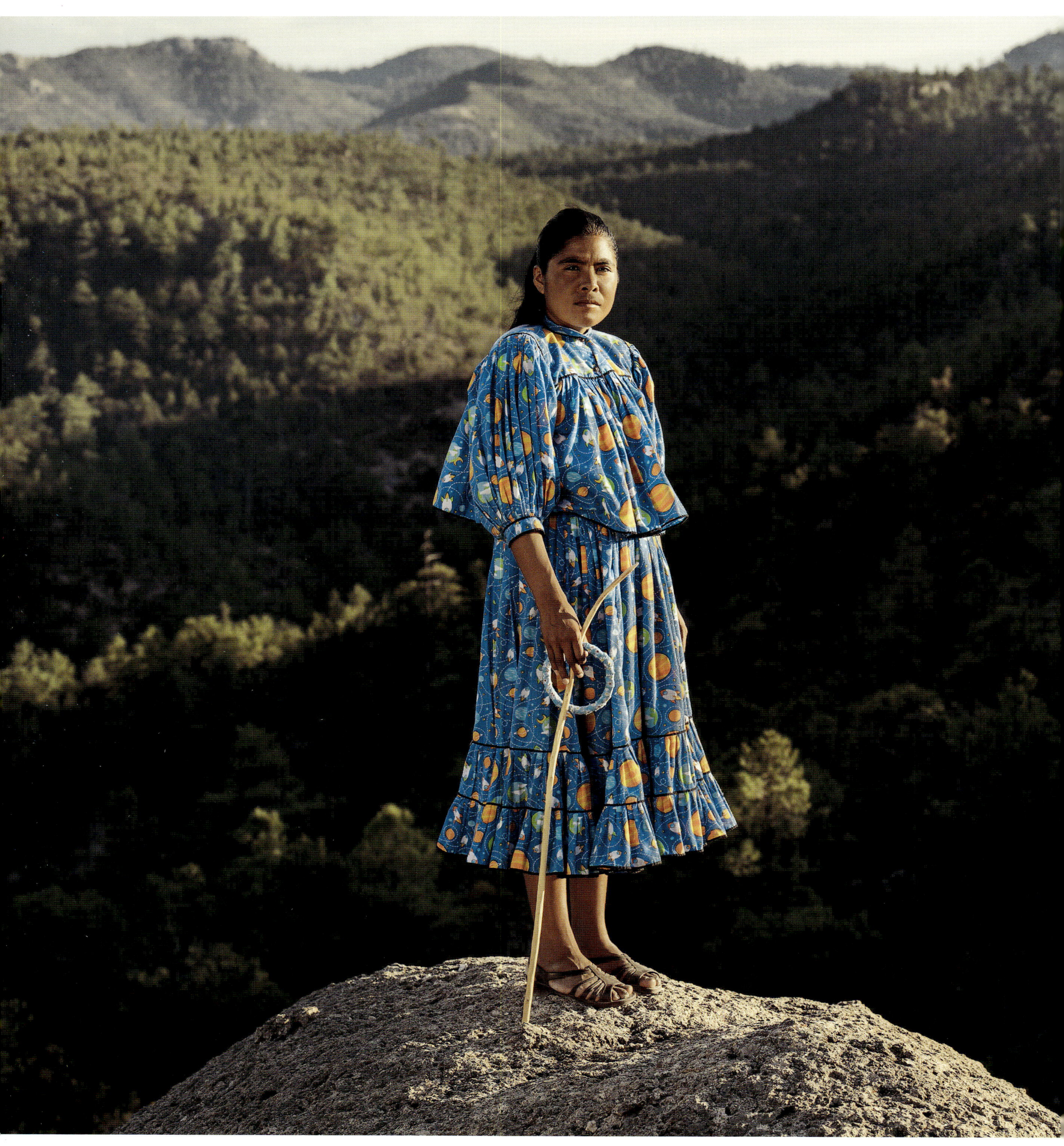

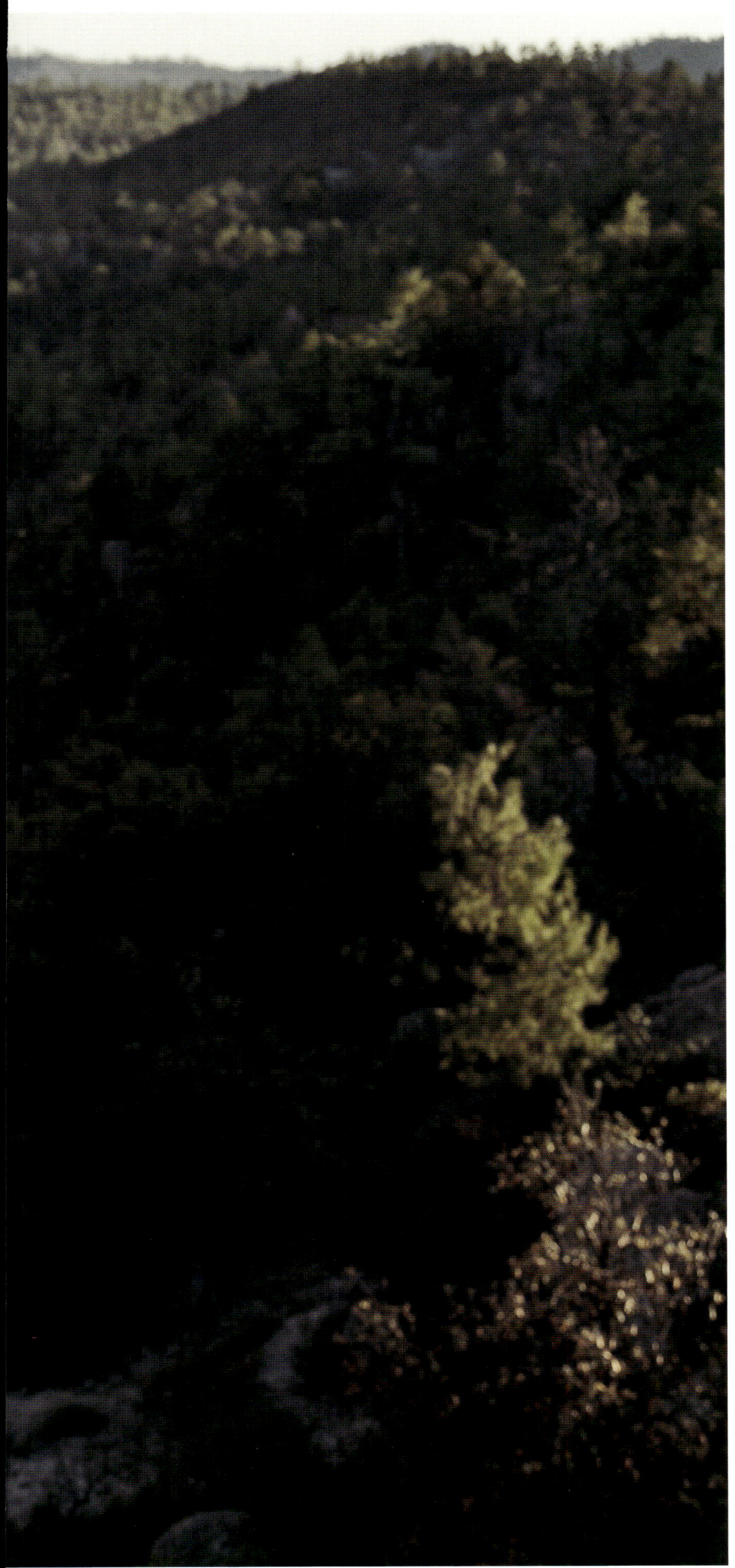

Maria Lorena Ramirez is an inspiration to her community and a prizewinnig endurance runner who beat many international opponents while running in sandals.

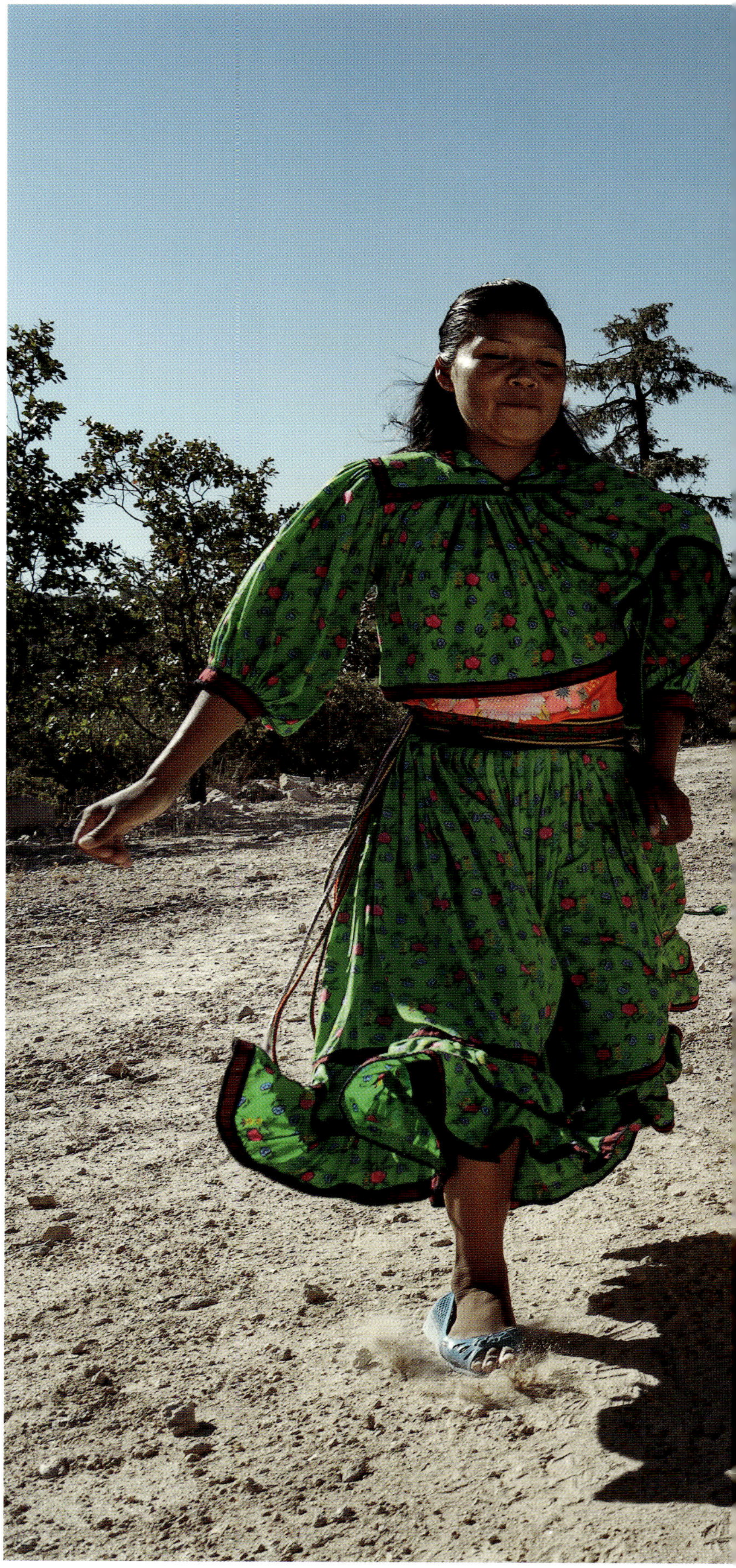

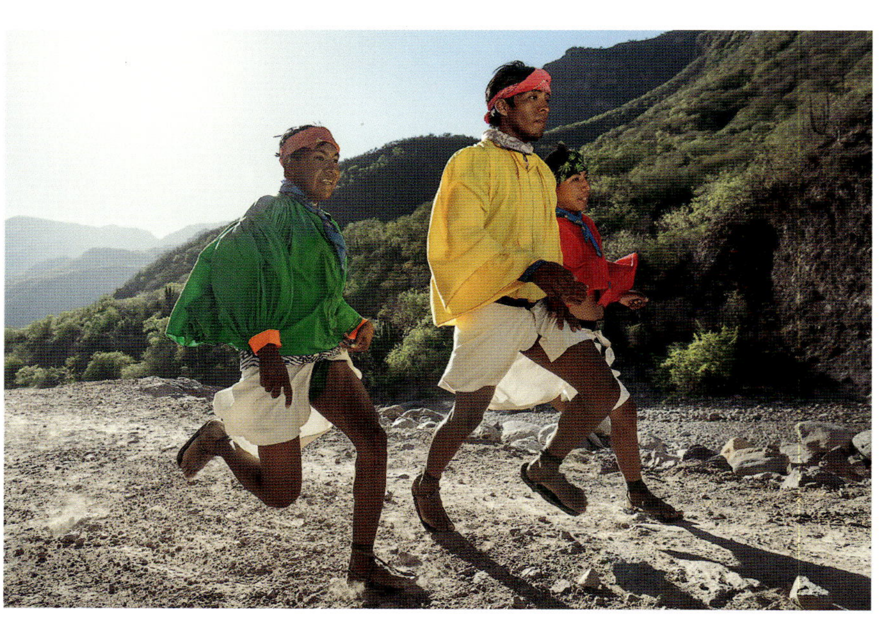
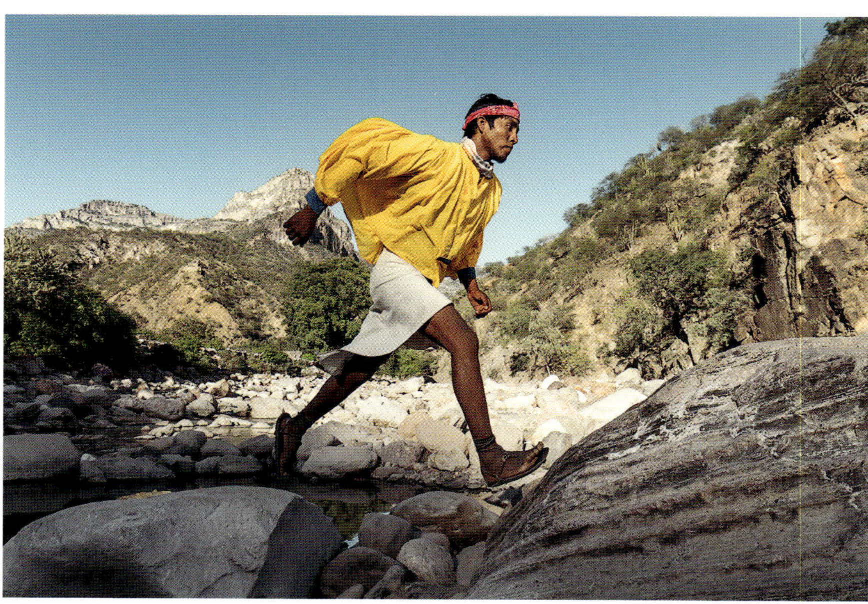

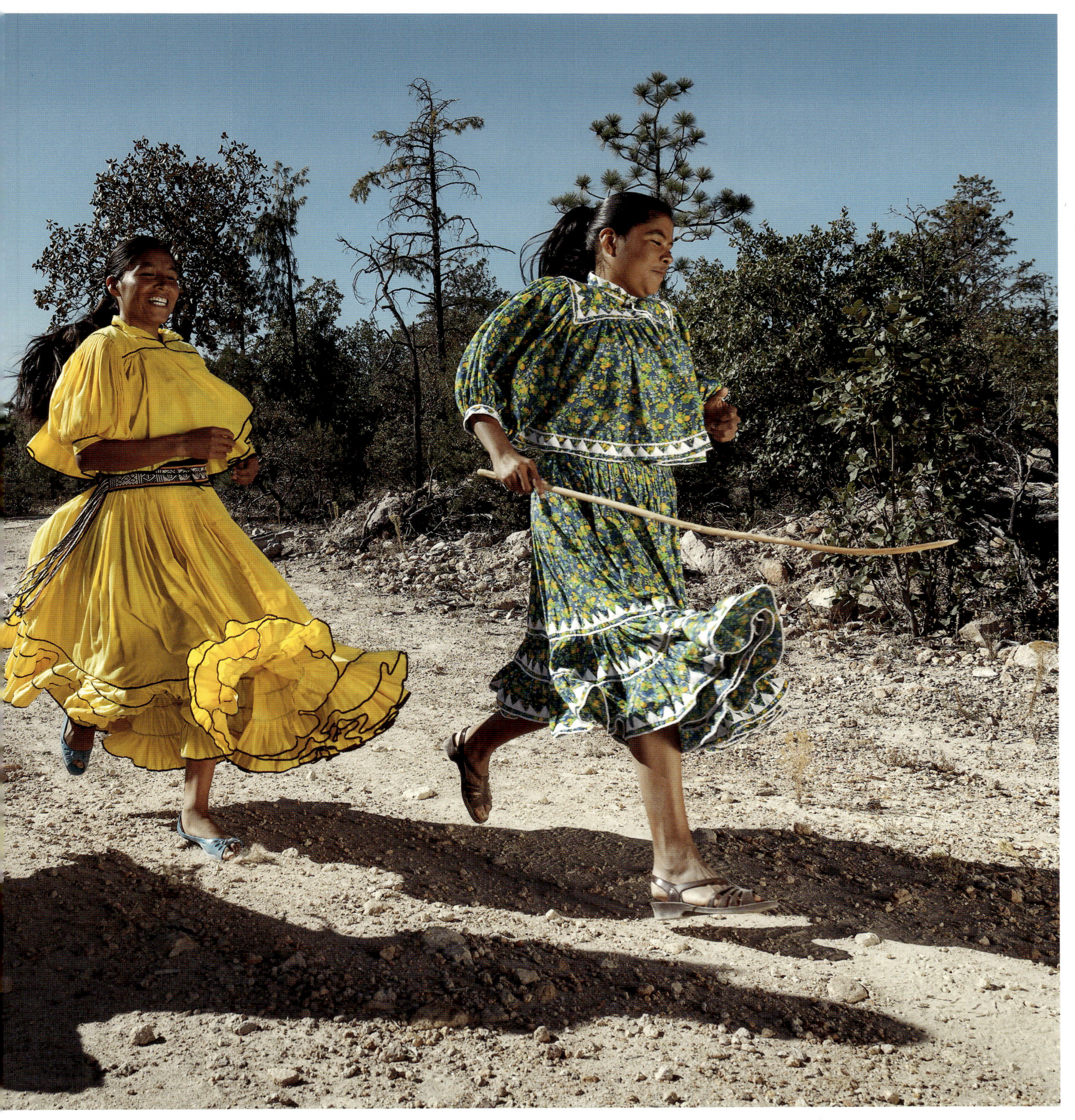

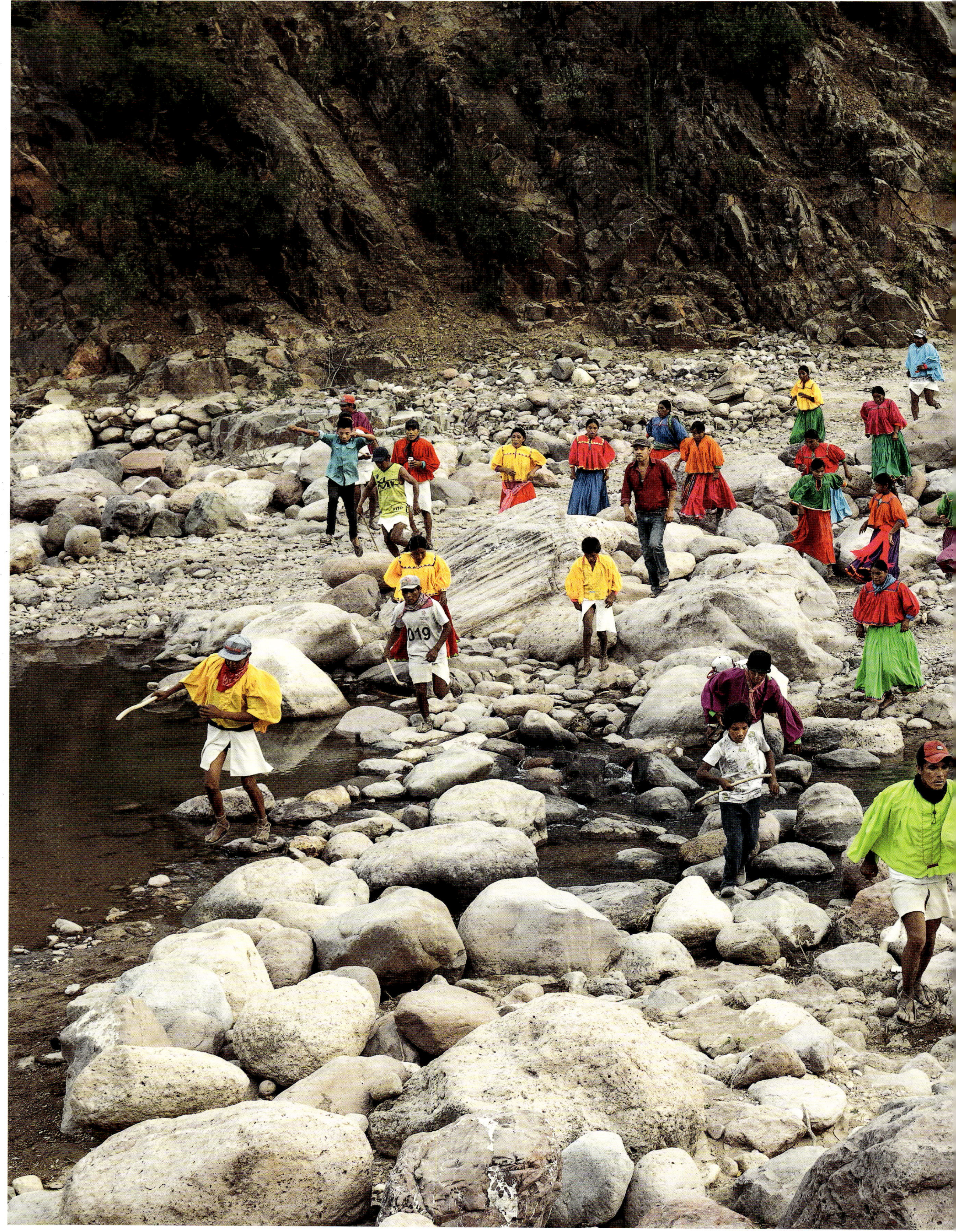

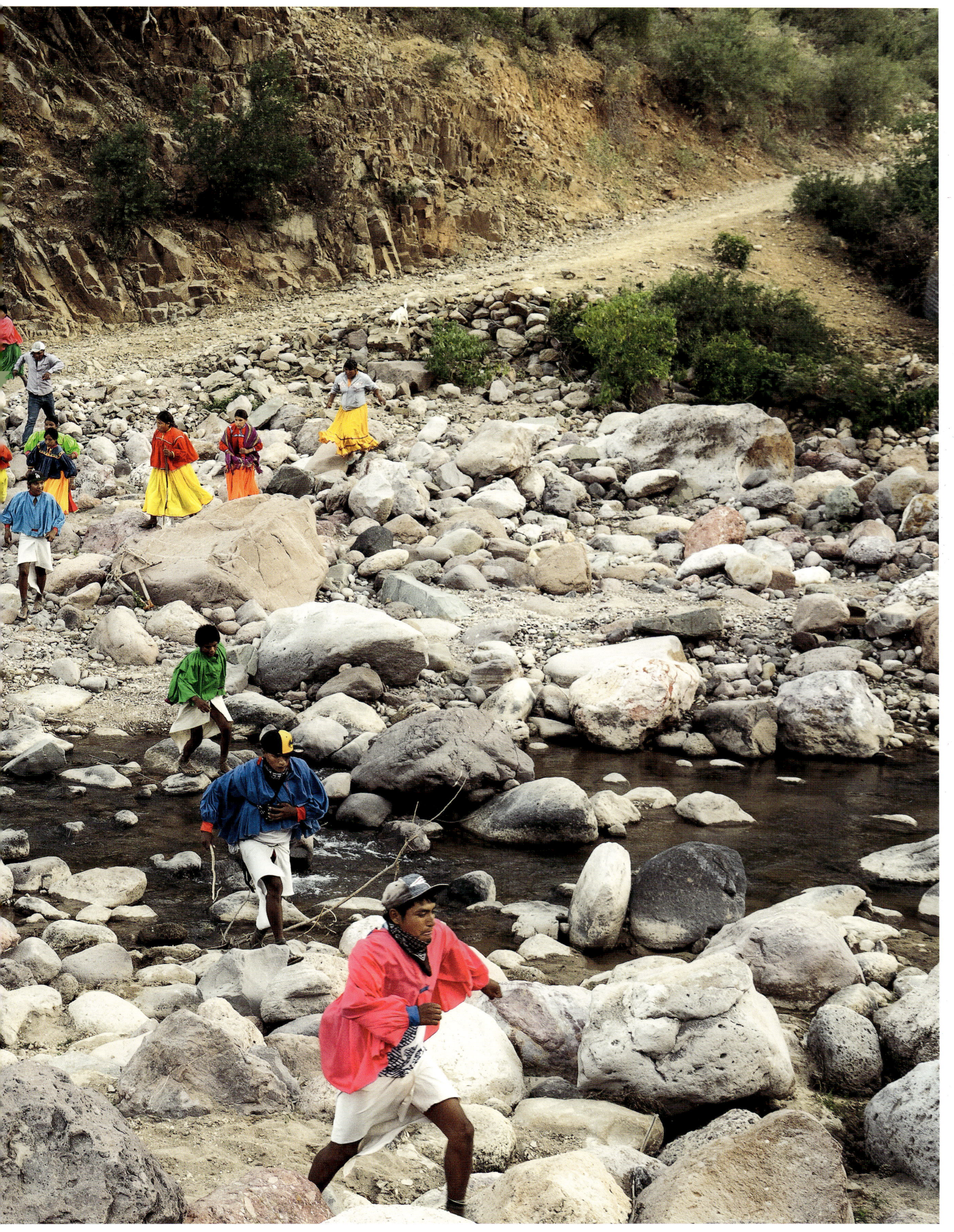

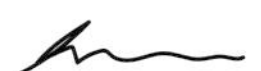

Big Wave Surfing

PORTUGAL

This playground is beyond dangerous,
it's a matter of life and death.

Tucked away in the small, unassuming Portuguese fishing village of Nazaré, the holy grail of waves lies waiting for its prey. Each year the world's most heroic big wave surfers gather in this humble town to face off against the tsunami-size monster of waves.

This playground is beyond dangerous; it's a matter of life and death. One second of panic and the sledgehammer wall of water can crush the Bravehearts of the ocean. The unpredictability of these Atlantic swells and how close they break to the shore make them the most ominous and sought-after waves on the planet.

Generations of Nazaré locals have both feared and admired this sleeping giant, witnessing their fishermen disappear into Europe's largest underwater canyon, 125 miles (201 kilometres) long and three times as deep as the Grand Canyon. Yet years ago, this picturesque fishing village, with its brightly coloured boats, traditional clothing and cobblestone streets, was virtually unknown amongst the big wave surfing community.

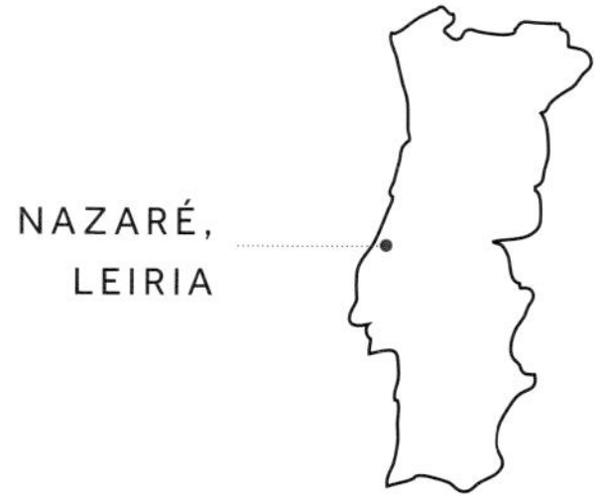
NAZARÉ,
LEIRIA

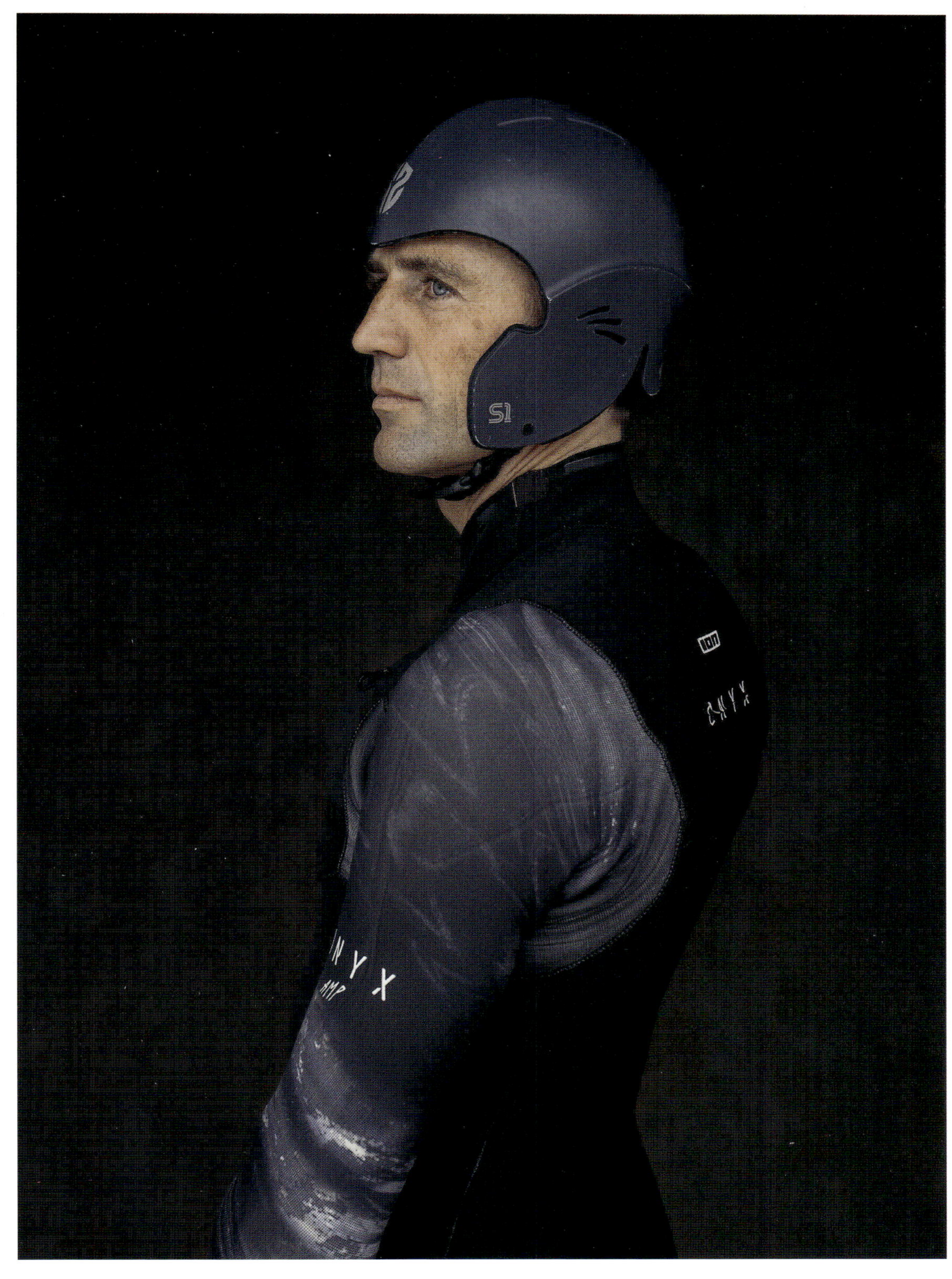

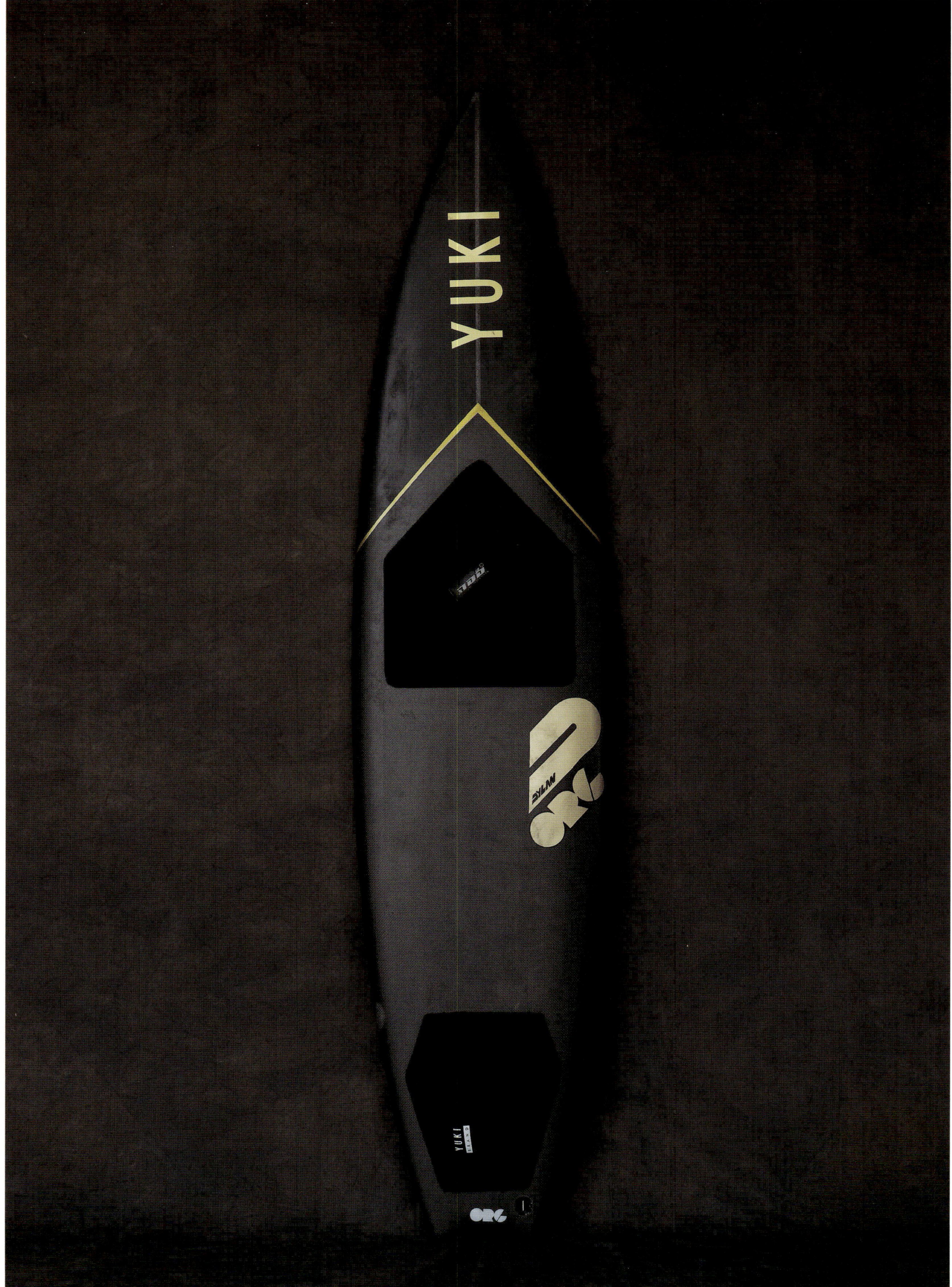

YUKI
2YLAN
ORC
YUKI
ORC

The mad-hatter attempt to surf the ocean's Everest began in 2011 with the legendary Garrett McNamara, who entered the Guinness World Records by riding a seventy-eight-foot (nearly twenty-four-metre) wave. The laid-back Portuguese village quickly became a hot spot for international surfers. In 2017, Brazilian Rodrigo Koxa raised the bar even higher when he surpassed McNamara, creating a new record for the tallest wave ever surfed at eighty feet (over twenty-four metres). Surfers are not the only wave-crazy fanatics; photographers and spectators from all over the world go to great lengths to be part of this magnificence at less than a few days' warning that the mammoth swells are on their way.

How does one prepare to go up against Mother Nature's wildest force? First of all, to survive in these unpredictable waves, surfers need to be top-notch swimmers, stay calm and sharp in critical situations, and be able to withstand massive amounts of water crashing down on them and holding them underwater for over thirty seconds at a time. Aerobic exercise, weightlifting, underwater rock running, yoga, meditation and breathwork are necessary elements of their life-and-death training. Big wave surfers are some of the best-trained athletes in the world, yet no matter how strong they are, the ocean always has the upper hand.

As with many male-dominated extreme sports, it requires a certain kind of grit, discipline, and herculean strength. So the notion of women attempting this David-and-Goliath feat wasn't readily accepted by Big Wave officials.

Brazilian born Maya Gabeira has been rocking the gender boat since her devastating near-death wipeout in 2013. She not only survived but made such a remarkable comeback that in 2017 she rode a sixty-eight-footer (20.8 metres), the most significant wave ever surfed by a woman, establishing her place amongst the giants. In 2020, she broke her own Guinness World record, in one of the closest races, by surfing a 73.5-foot (22.4-metre) wave; it was just two to three feet larger than one surfed by the French superwoman of athletes and world champion big wave surfer Justine DuPont.

Every surfer, regardless of gender, will tell you that riding the mightiest of all waves is impossible without a great team and a dedicated community. From the highly skilled jet-ski drivers to the spotters and rescue teams on the shore, this sport attracts the most selfless, friendliest, hard-working people who try to keep everyone safe while pursuing their glory.

At the end of the day, they are all just tiny specks being flung off jet-skis like rag dolls into skyscraper size waves. A big wave surfer hears the thunder of tons of water echo in their pounding heart until time stands still. In that singular moment, they are side by side with Poseidon, taming the beast, and nothing else matters.

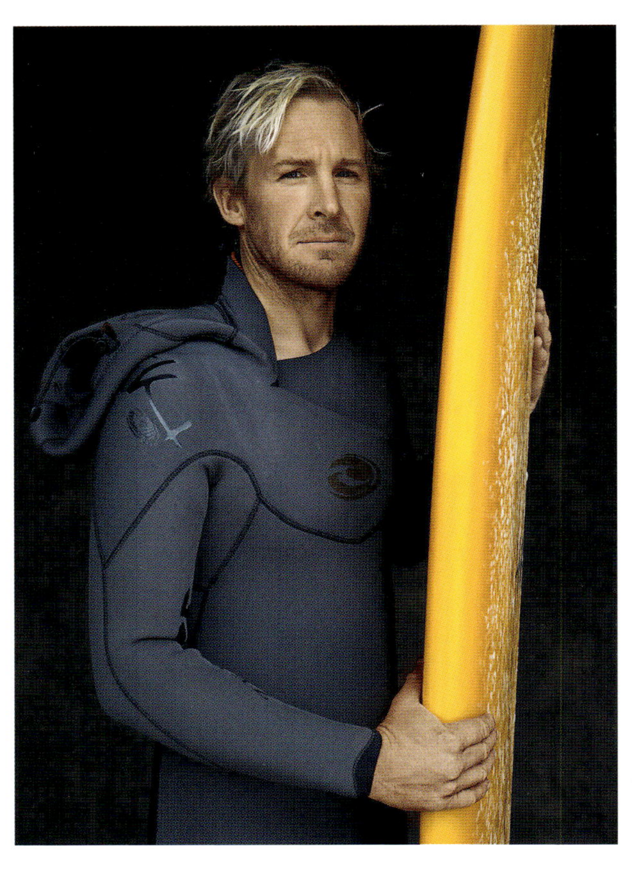
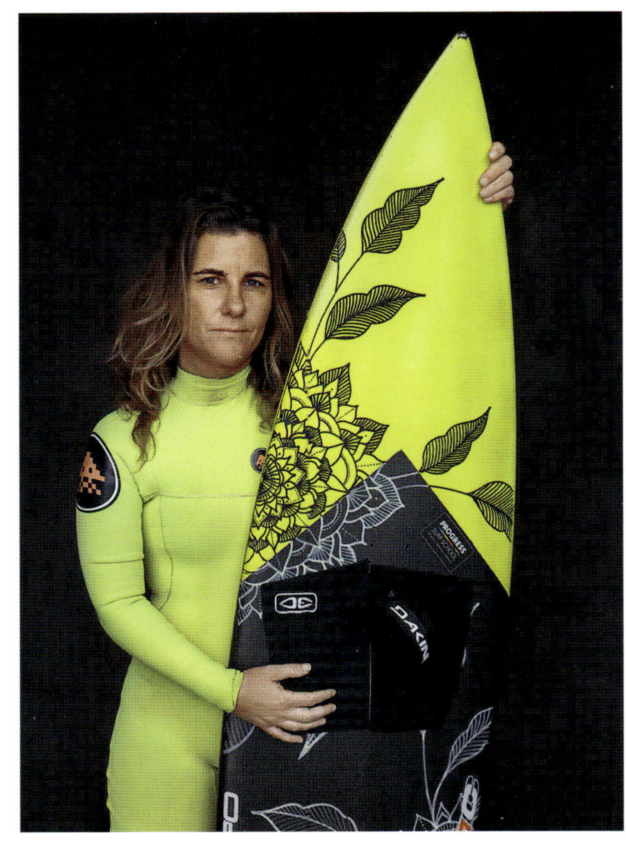
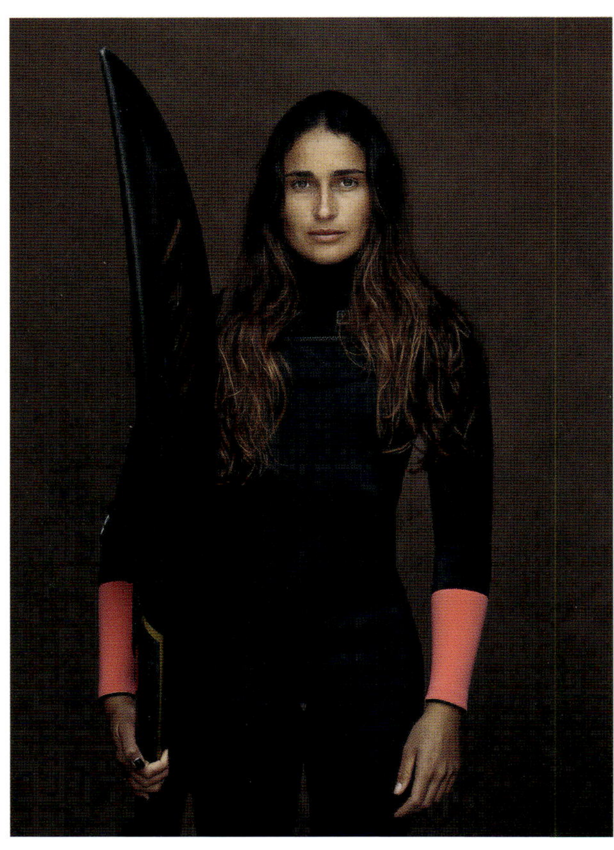
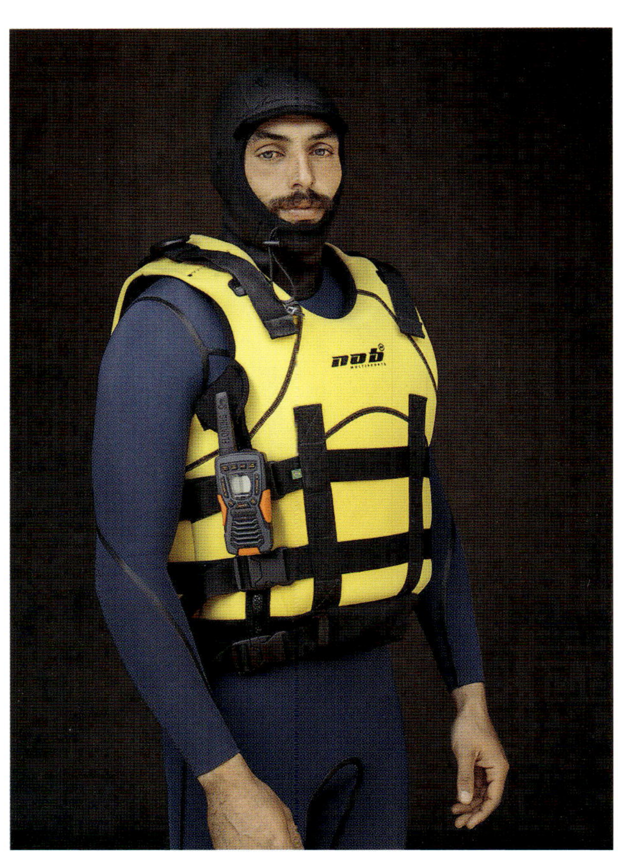

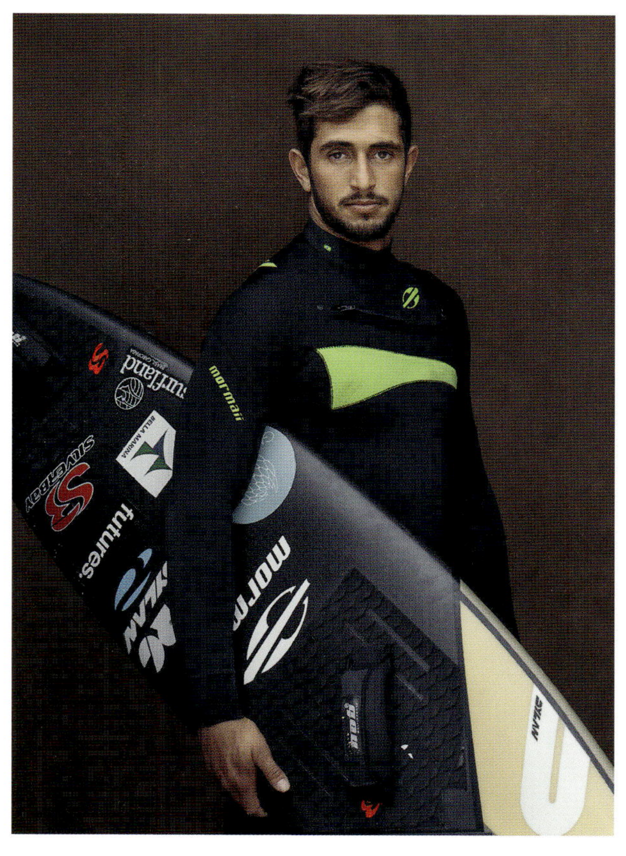
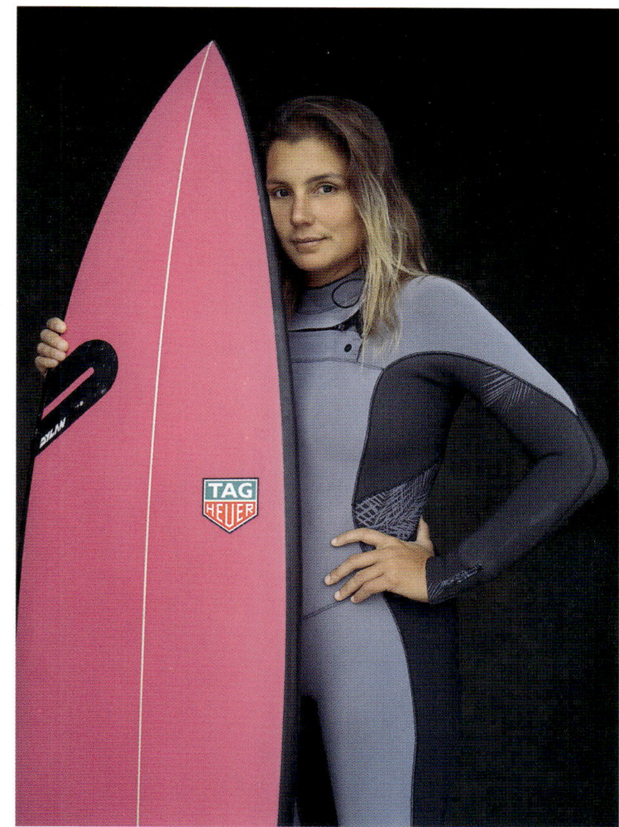
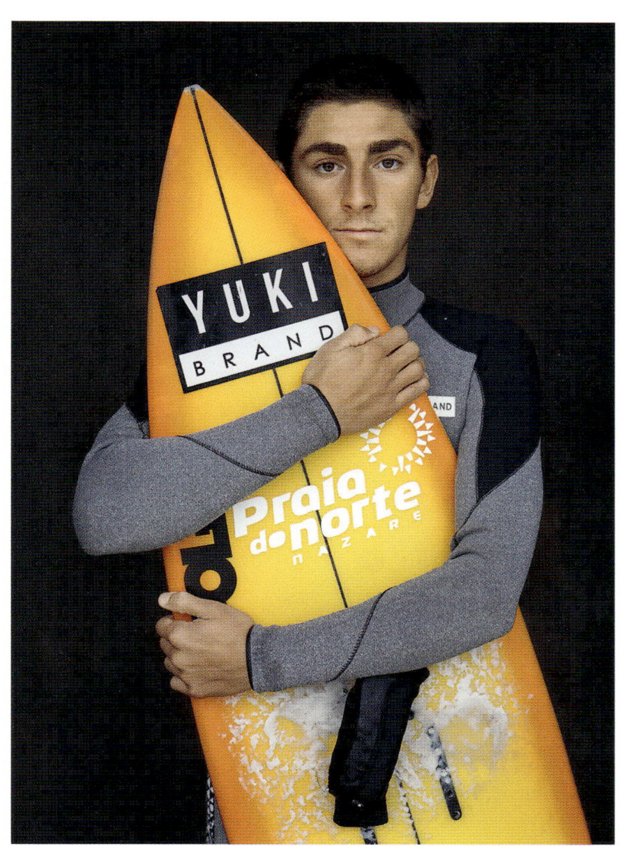
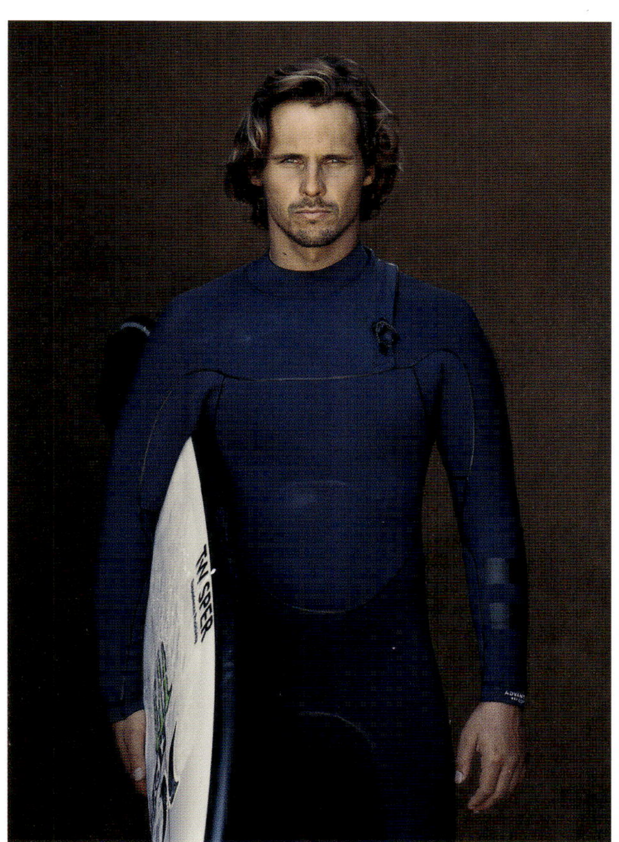

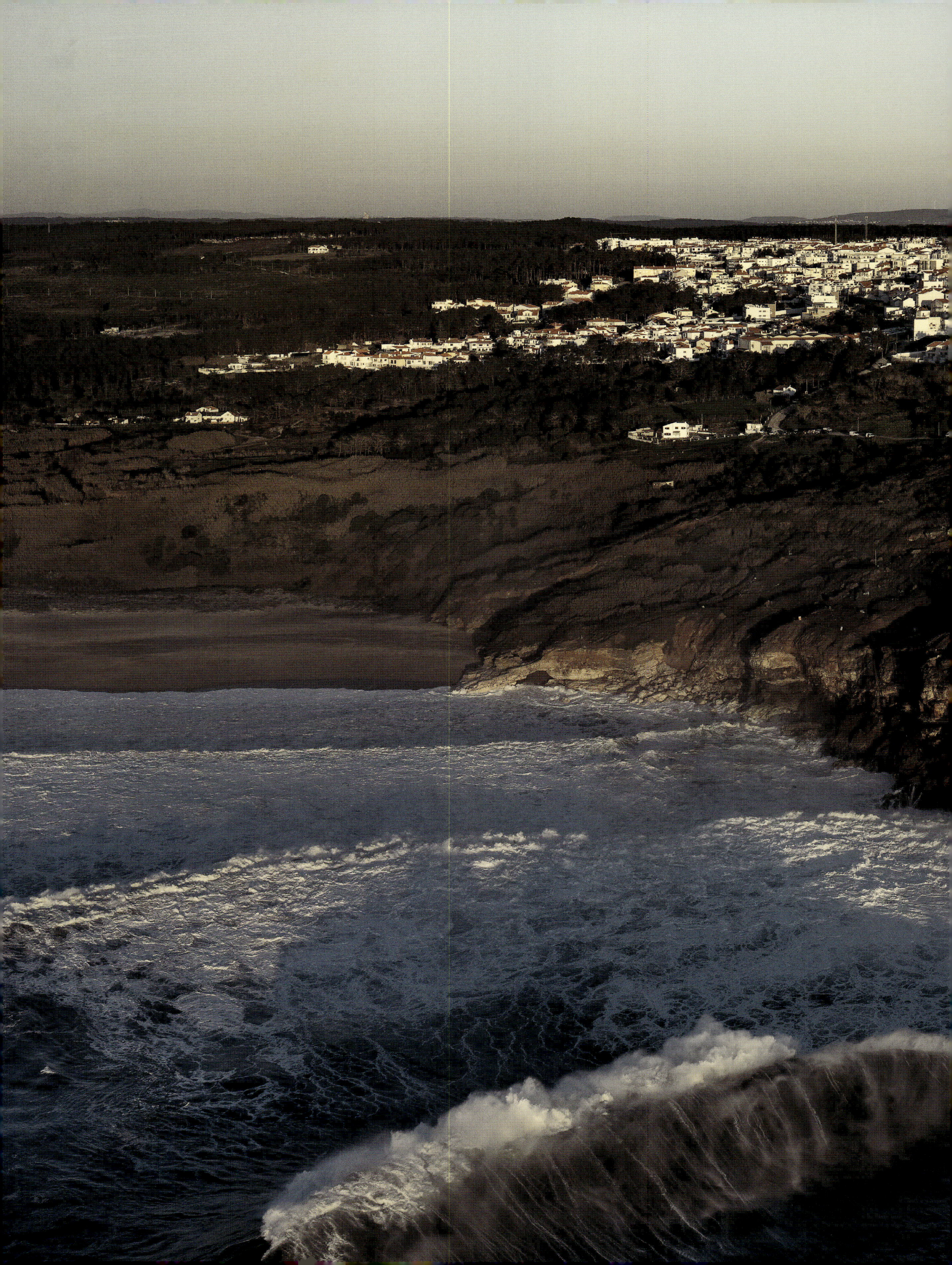

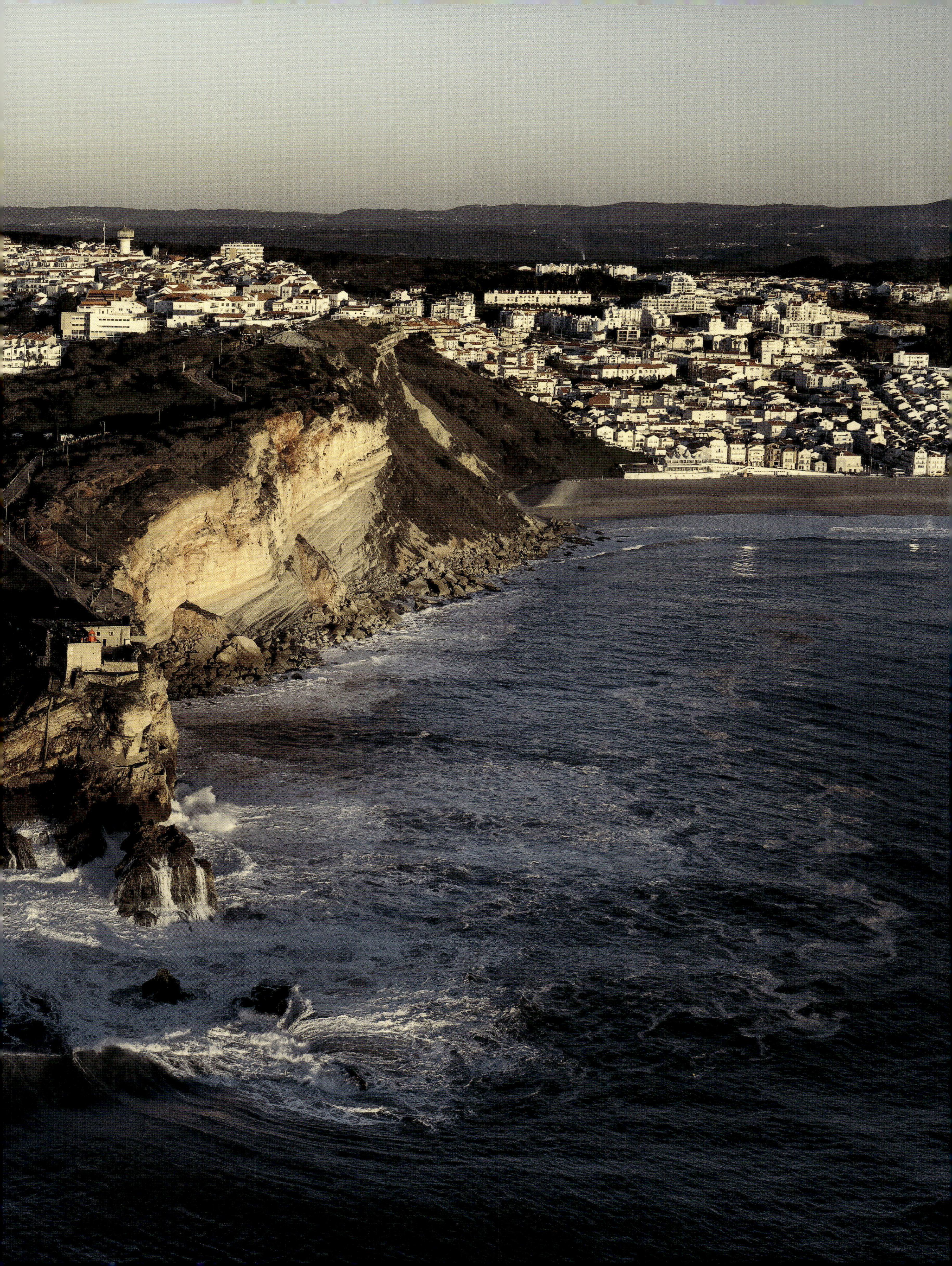

"Nazaré is the most challenging, dangerous wave I've ever surfed. It is the only place in the world where a giant canyon reaches all the way to the beach. Riding one of these waves is like being chased down by a moving avalanche."
~ Garrett McNamara ~

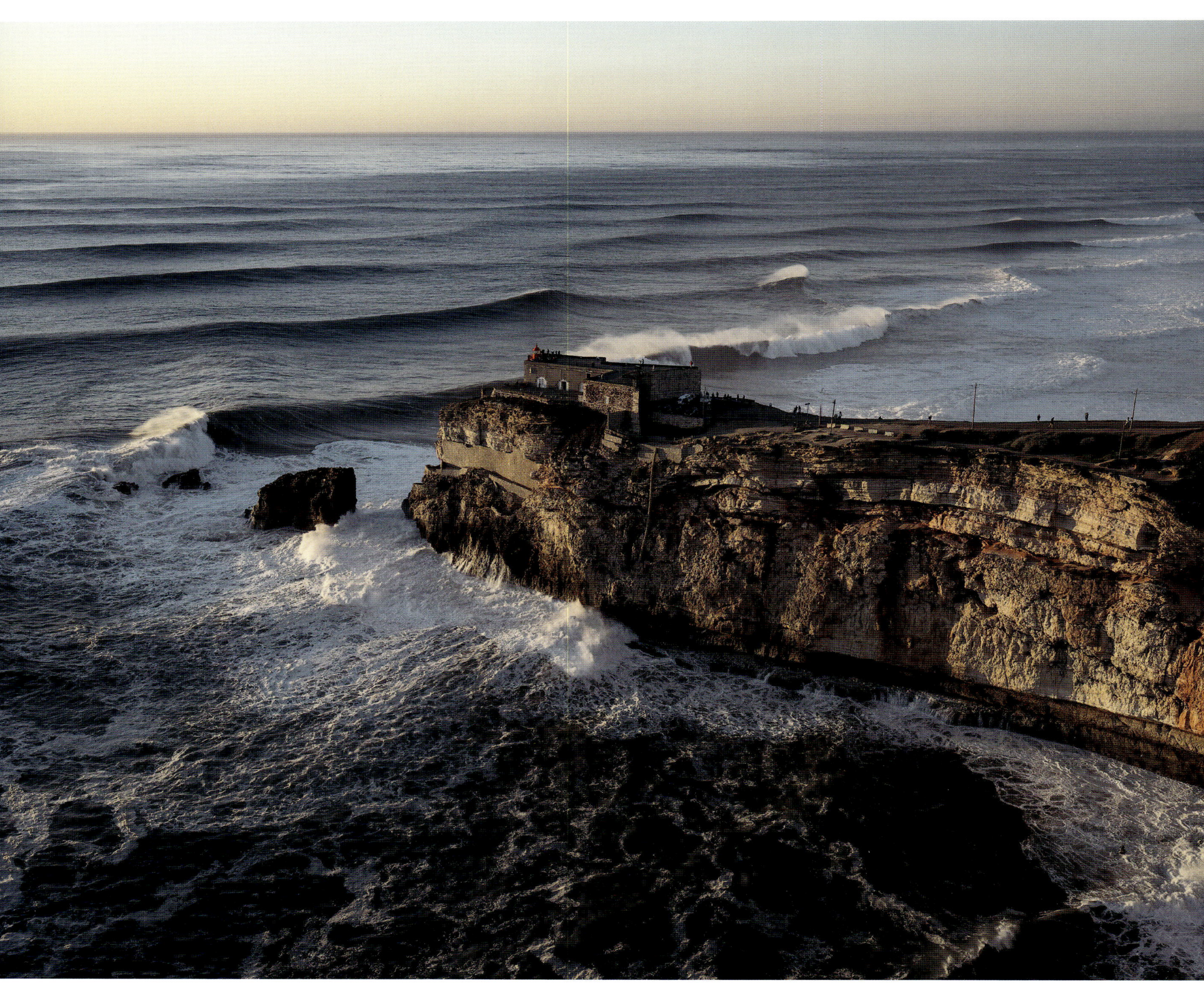

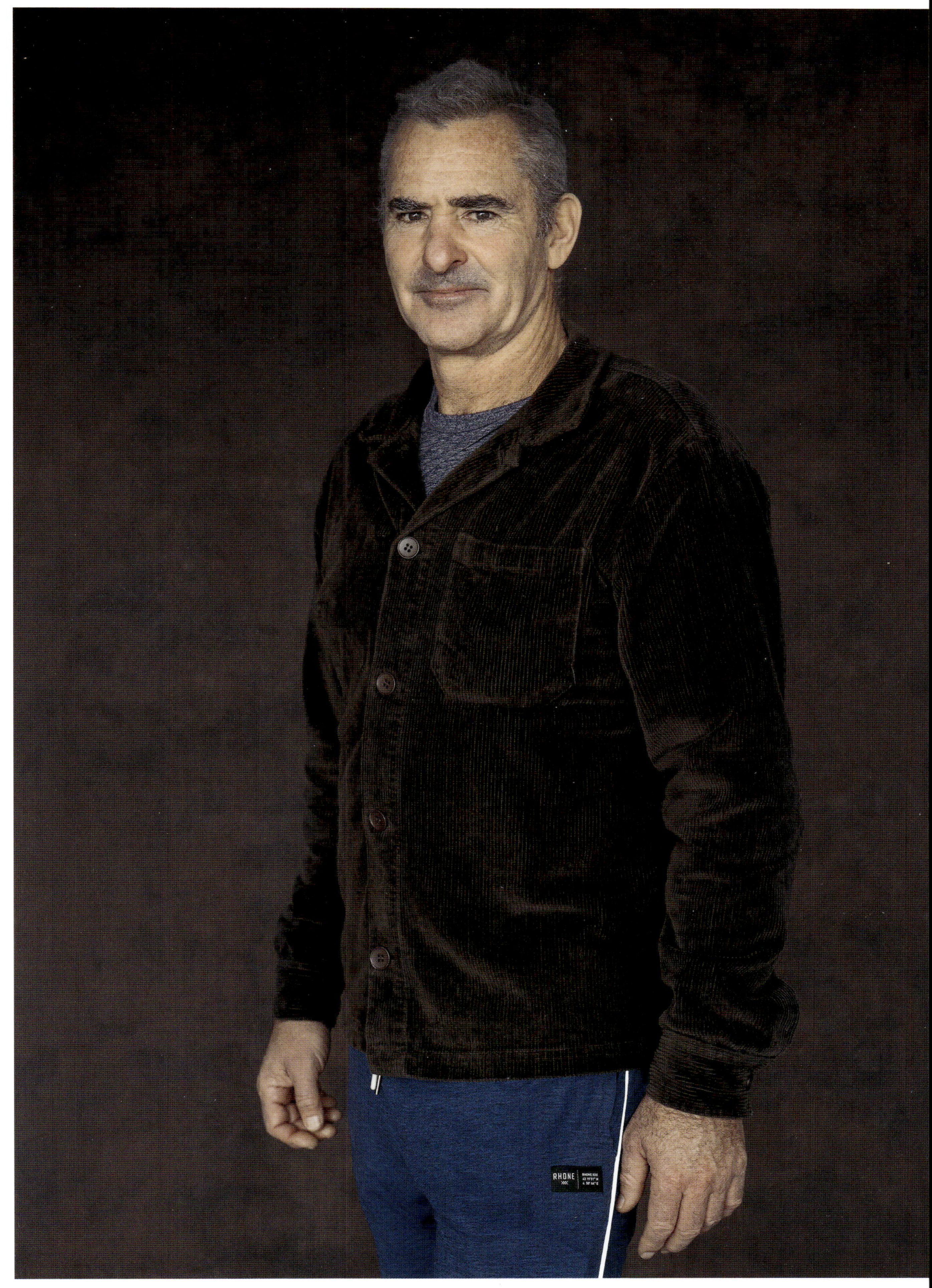

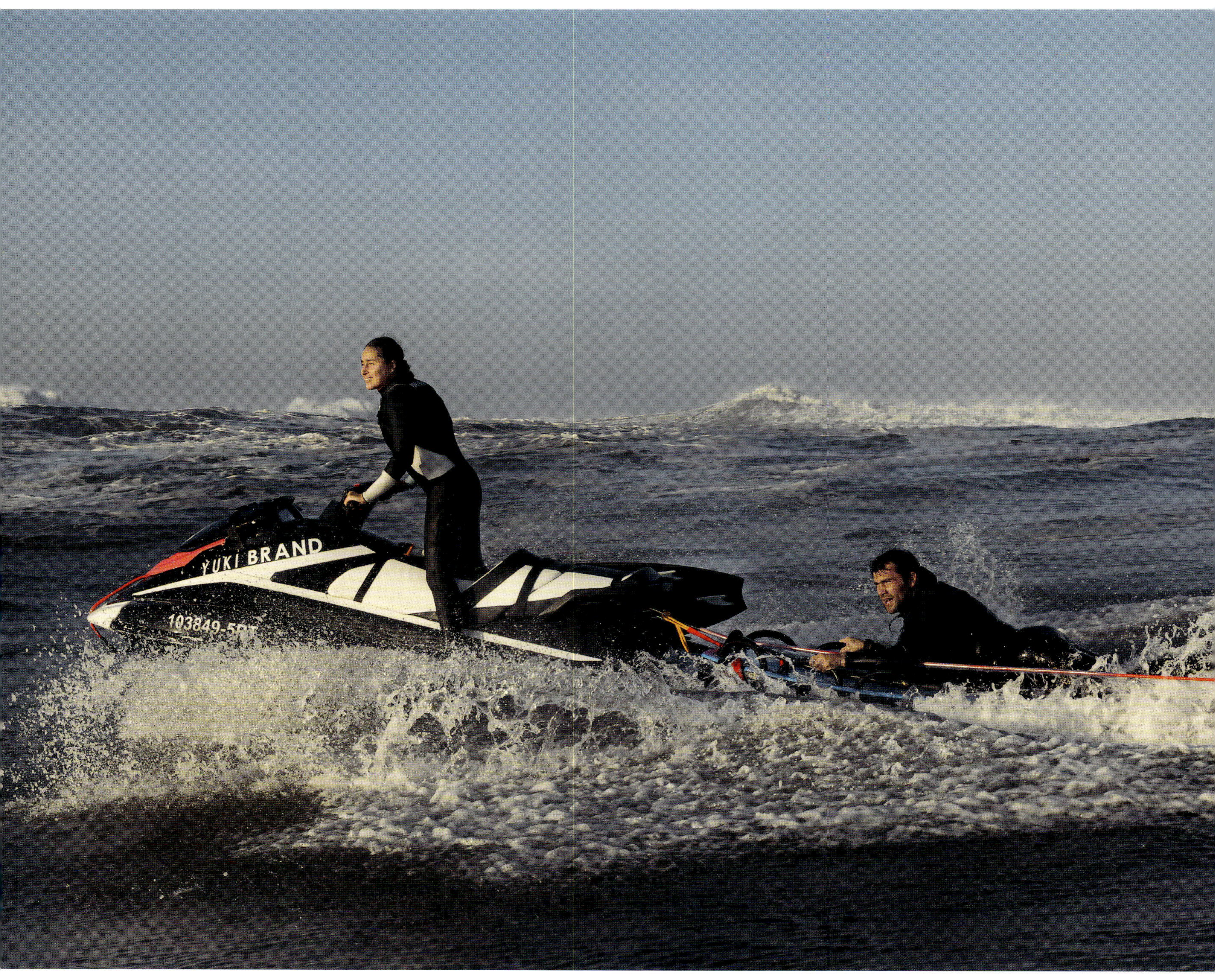

The small fishing village of Nazaré has become the hotspot for Big Wave Surfers, attracting Pro-Surfers from around the World, ready to take on the mightiest of challenges. The giant waves of Nazaré are created by an underwater canyon, with waves speeding up as they get closer to the shore, growing in power and size, making them unpredictable and dangerous.

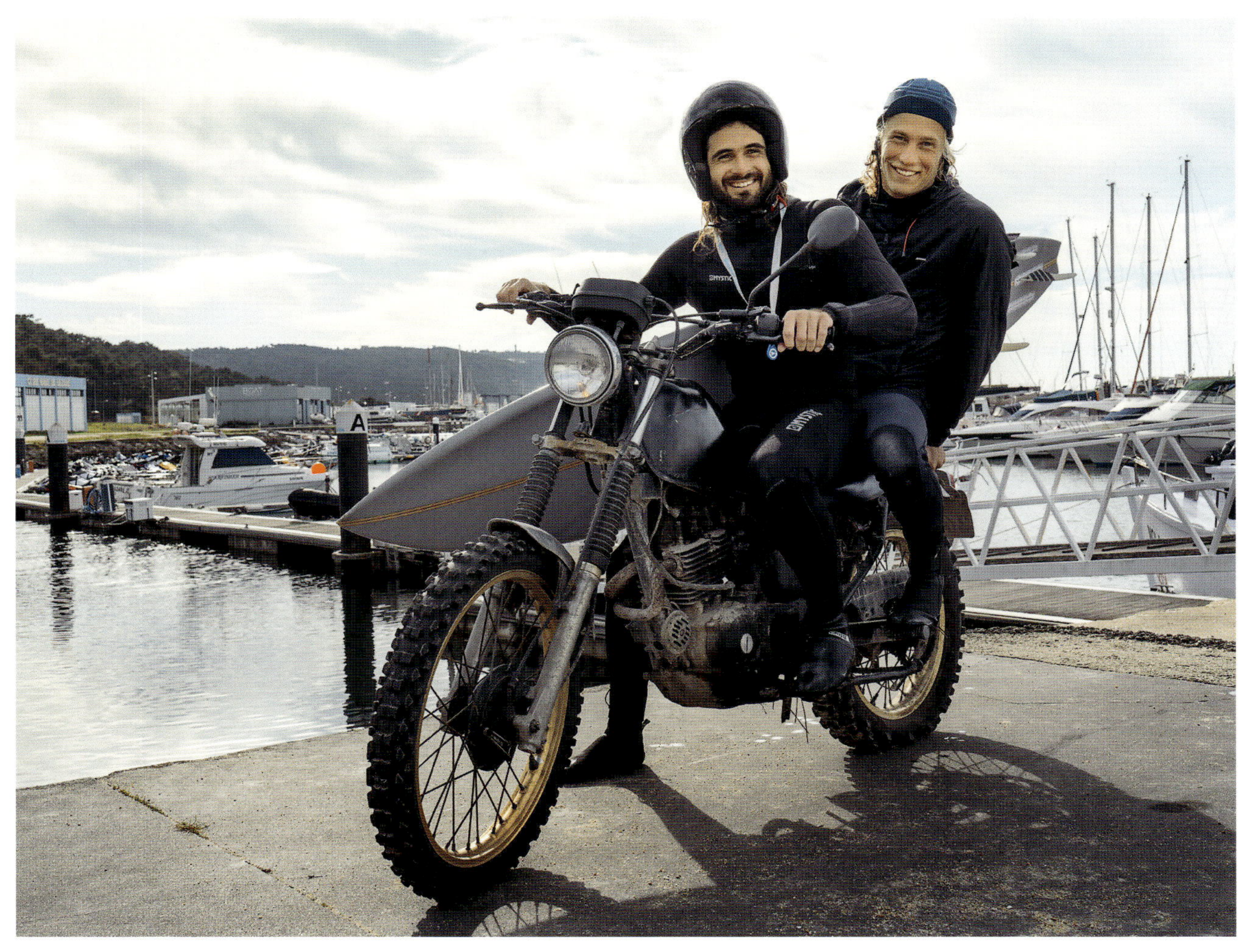

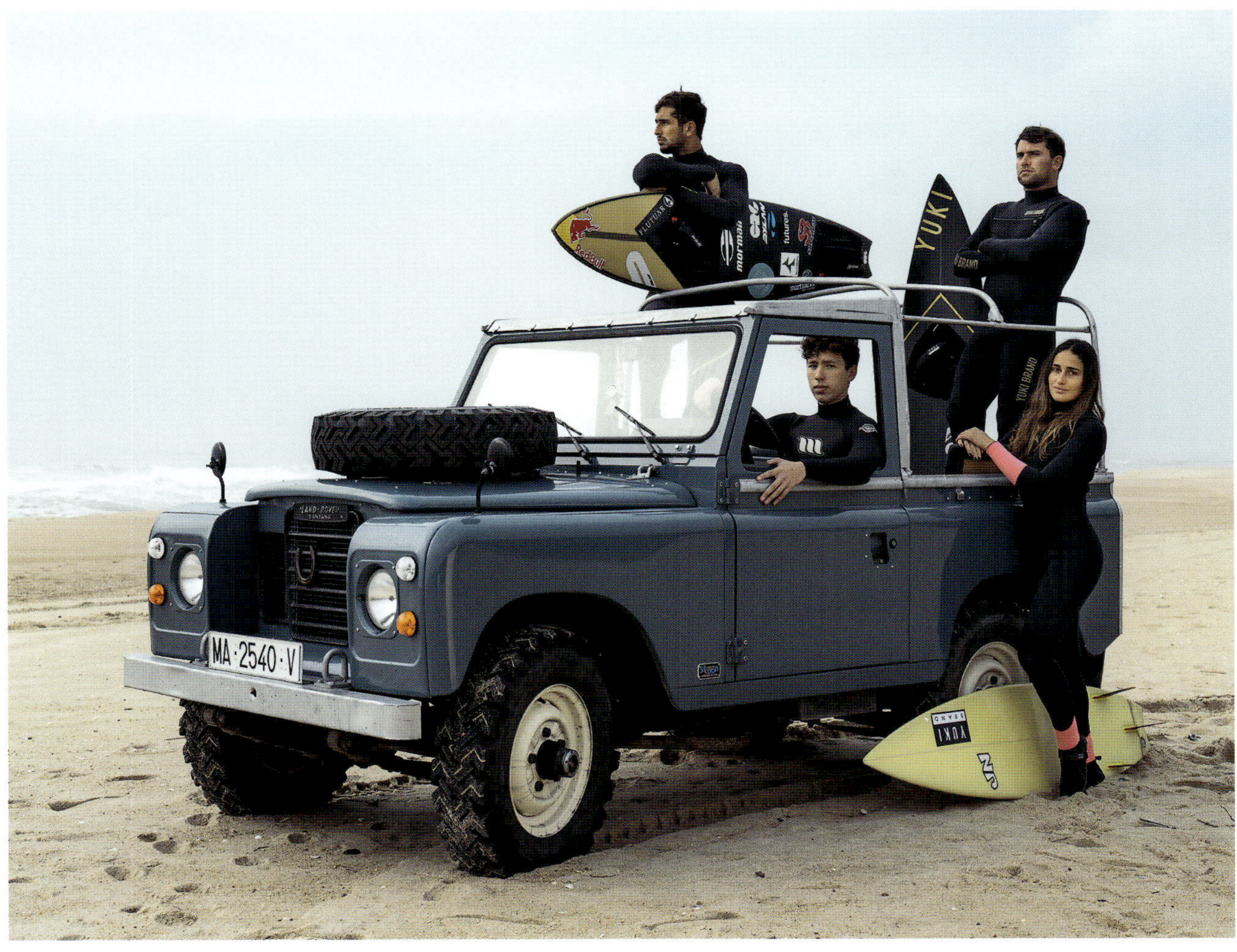

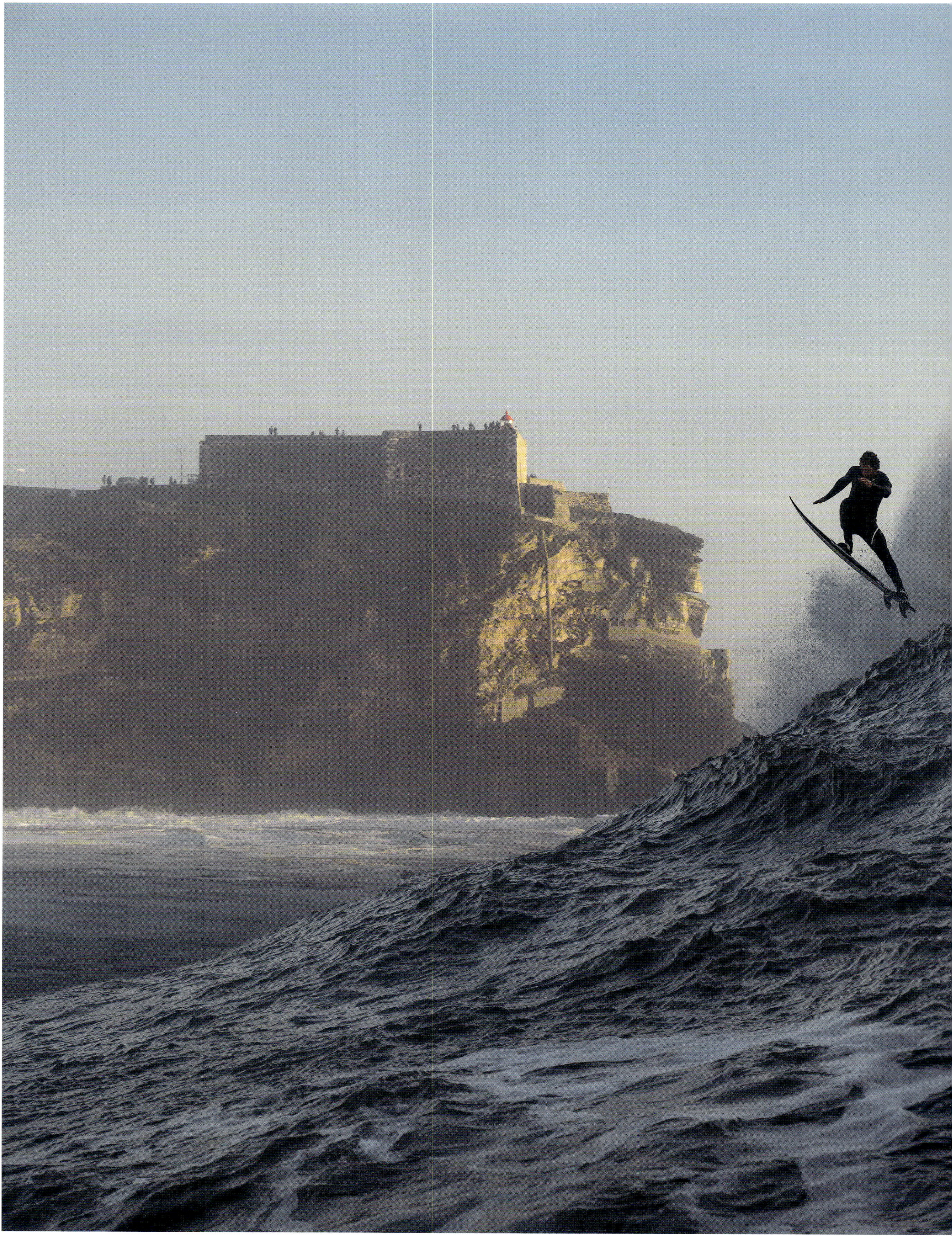

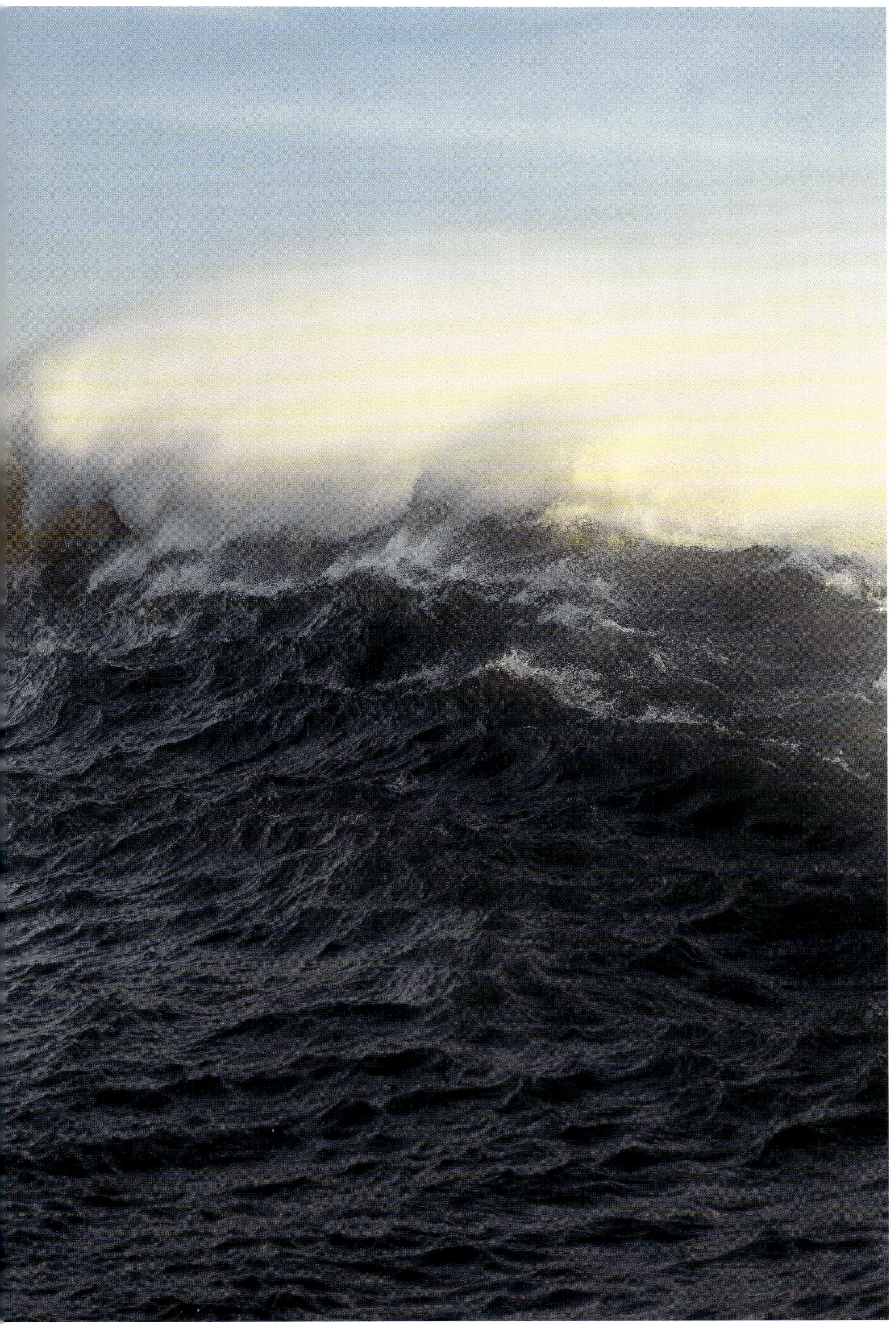

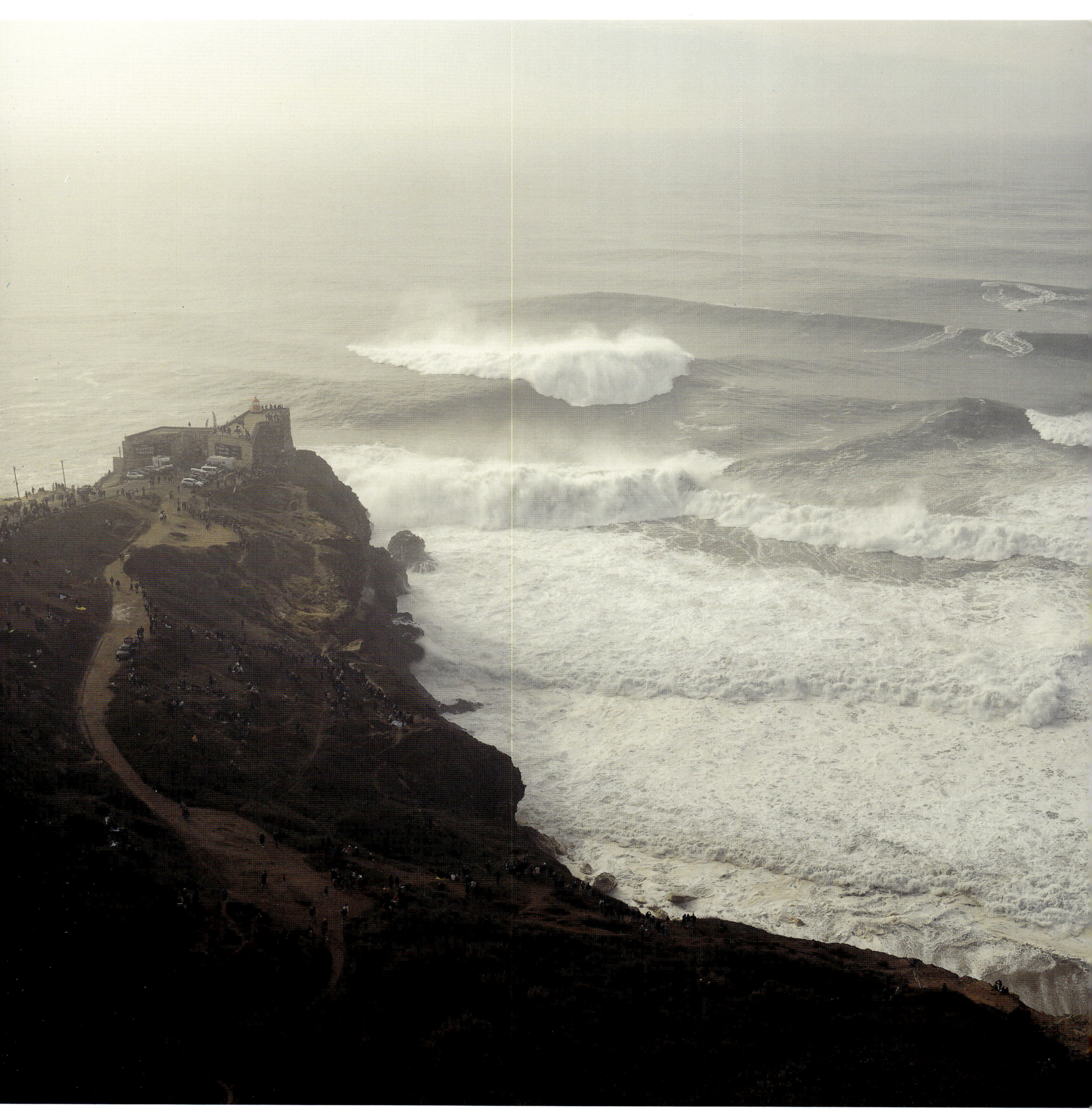

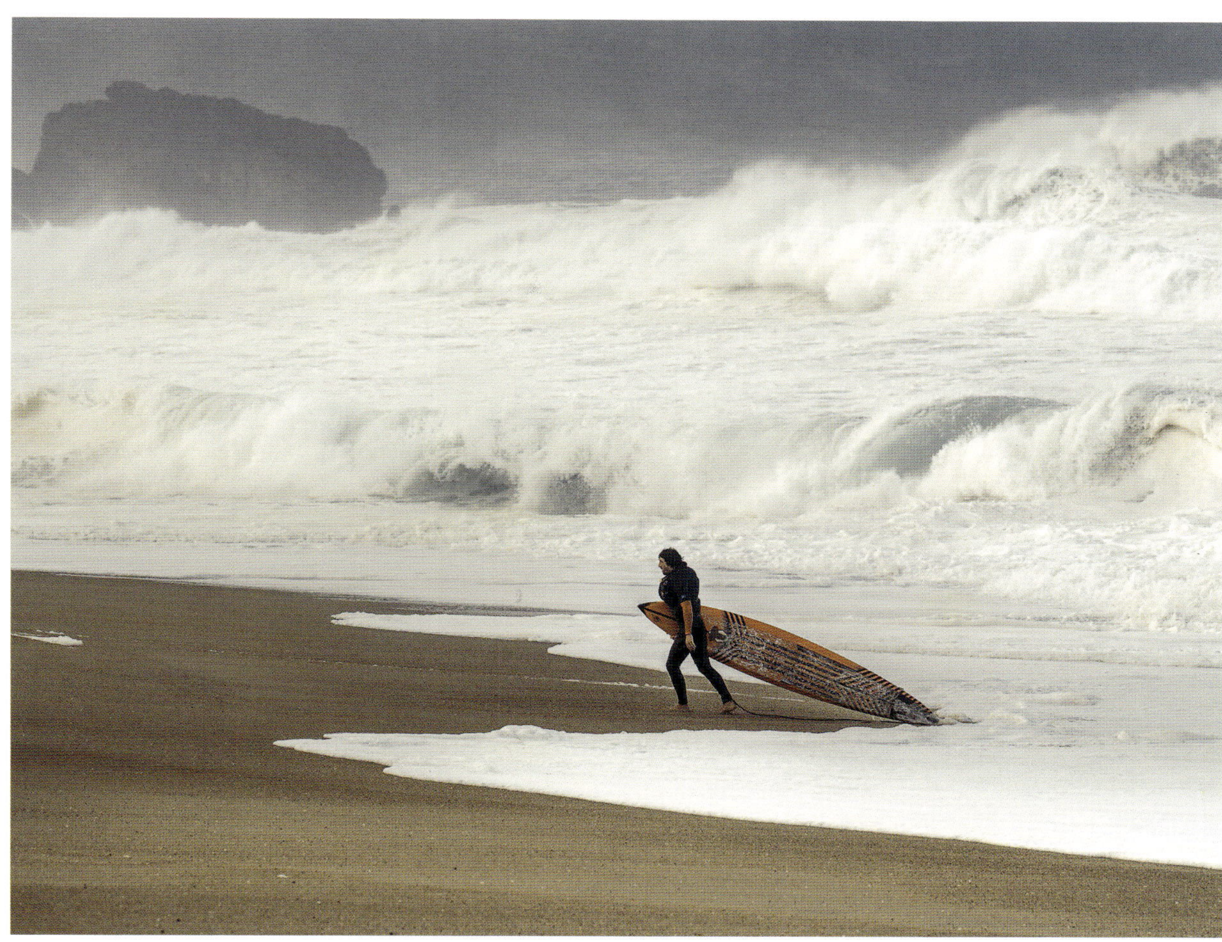

Big Wave Surfing is rarely thought of as a team sport, but the spotters, rescuers on the beach, jet-ski drivers and the local community are essential in helping surfers tackle the monster waves.

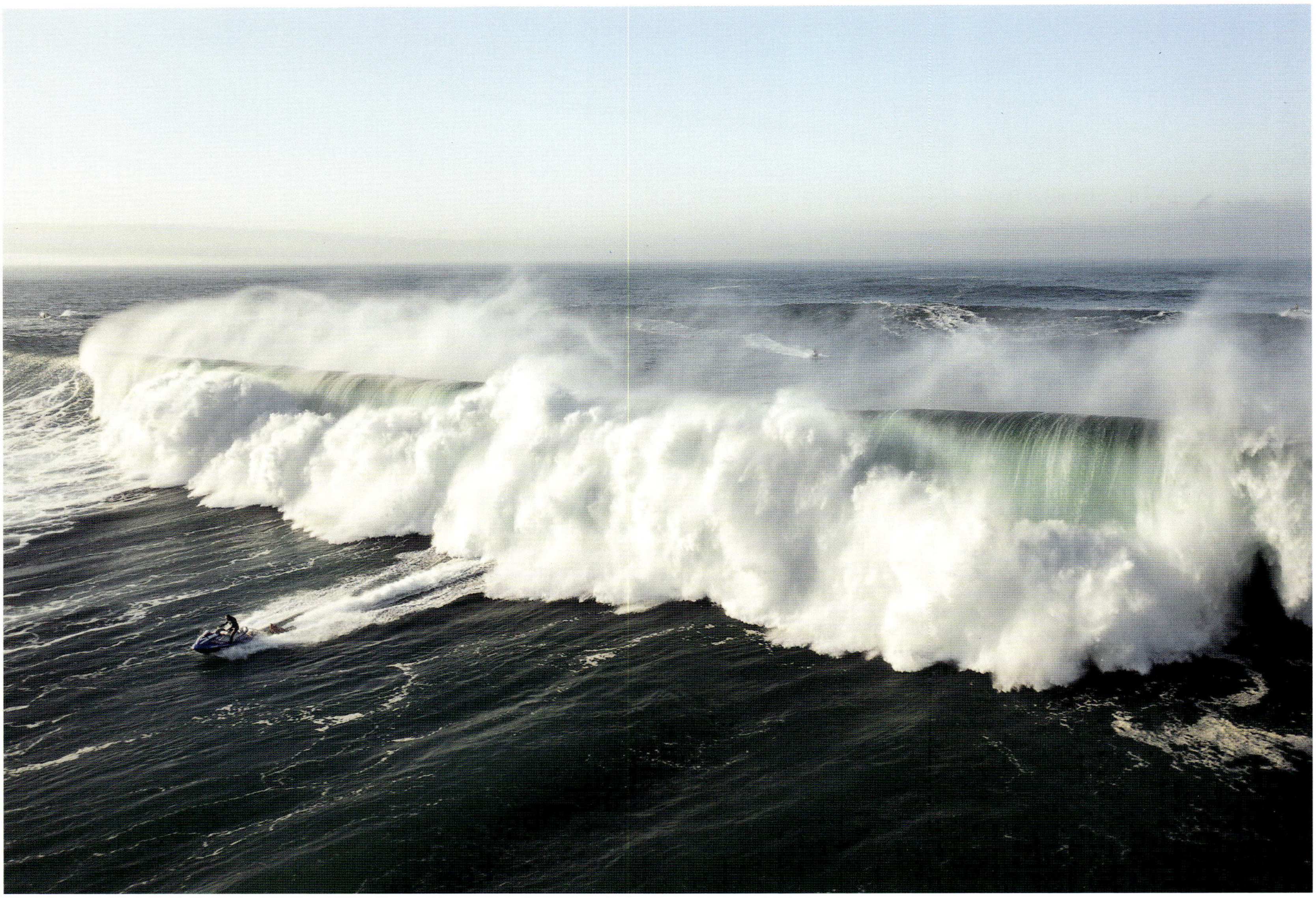

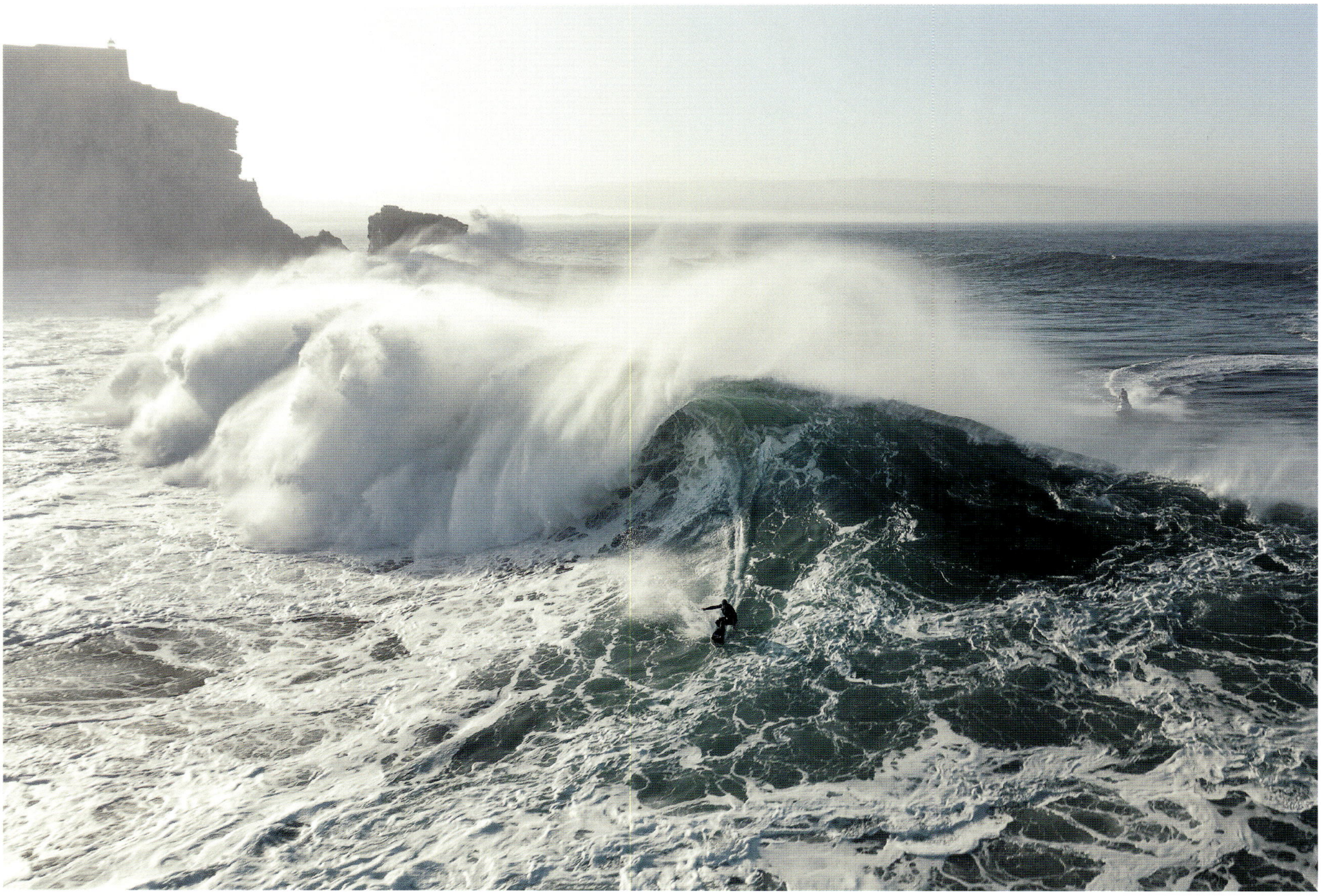

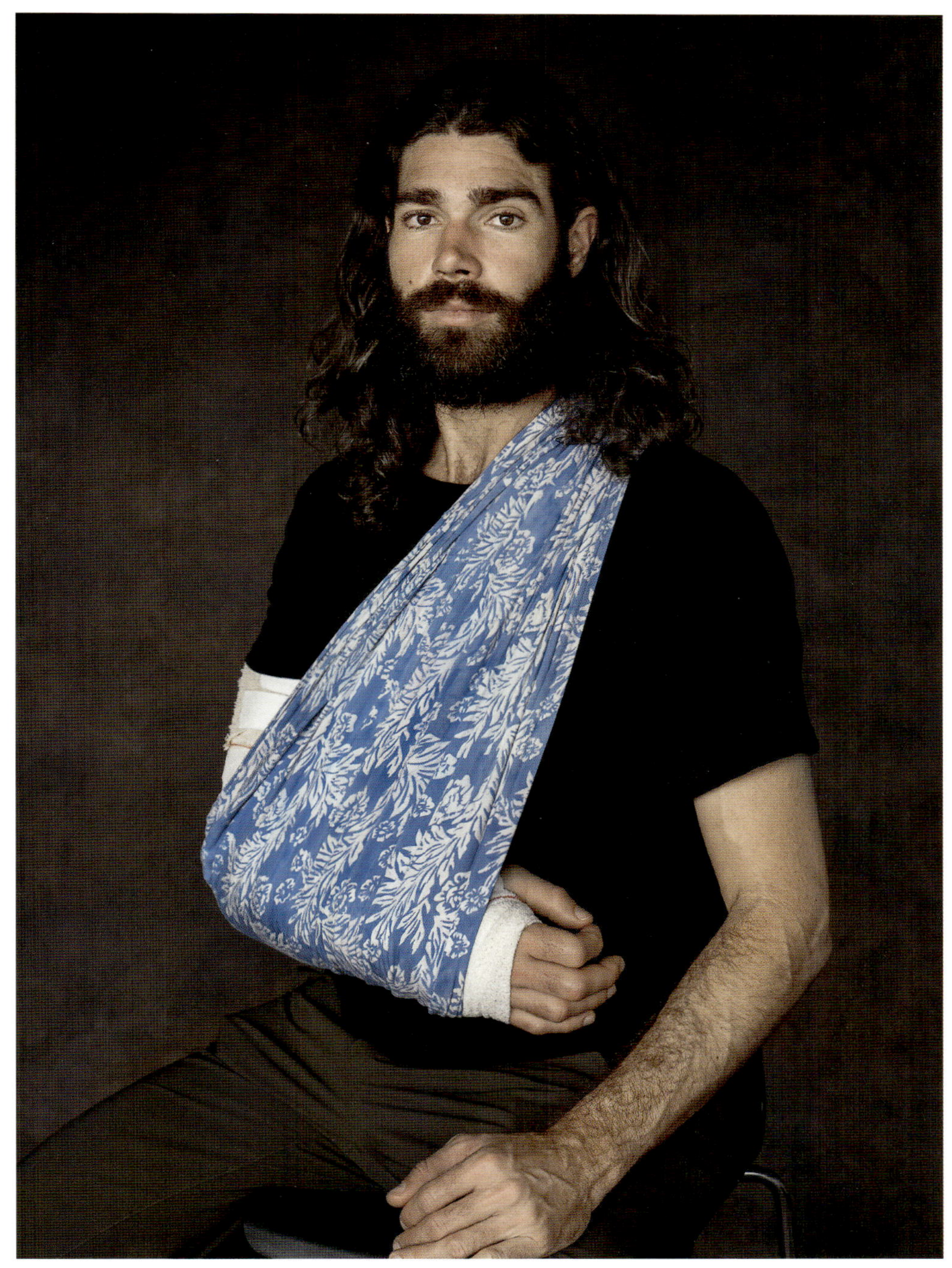

> *"The surfing accident was the most violent, traumatic, profound and humbling experience of my life."*
>
> ~ C.J. Macias, surfer, Garret McNamara's brother-in-law ~

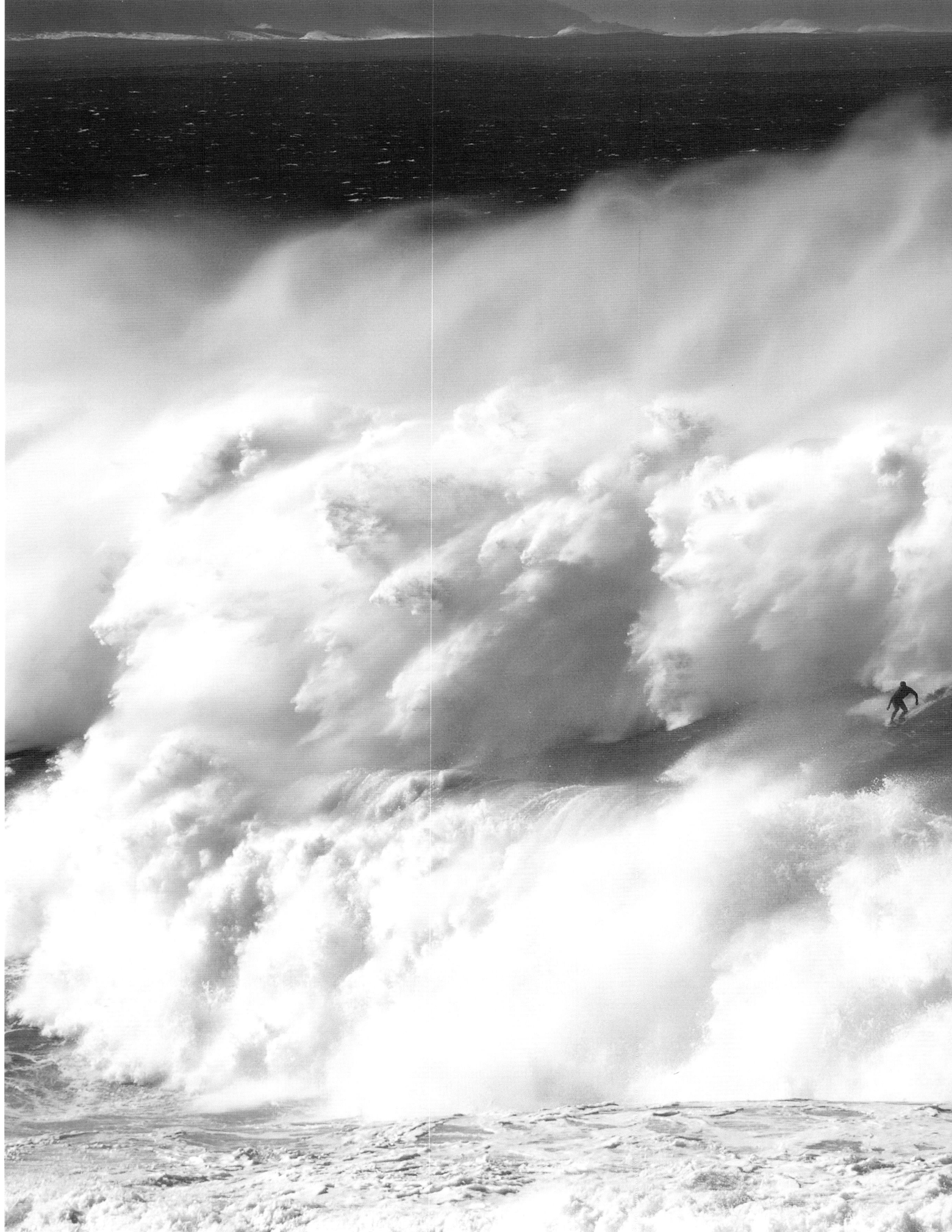

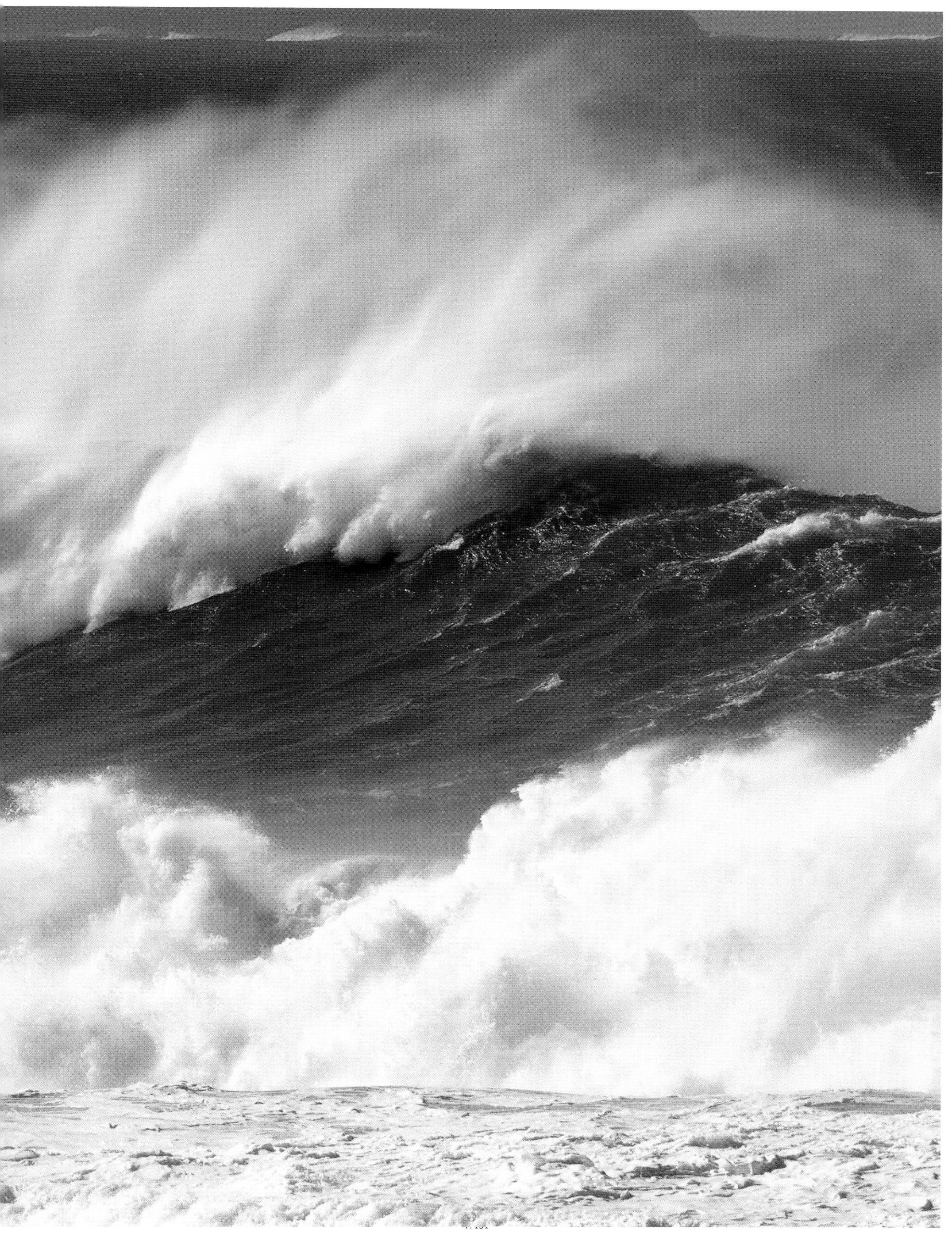

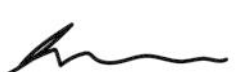

Charreada

MEXICO

It is more than a historical sport.
It is the countries pride and joy.

Bursting with vibrant hues, a rich tapestry of culture and age-old traditions, Mexico and its coat of many colours is an explosion of the senses. From its diverse landscape and ancient ruins to delicious cuisine and stunning white sandy beaches, this land of plenty is where the original rodeo and true cowboys emerged. Known as *charreada* or *charrería*, it evolved from a fusion between Spanish colonisers and the indigenous people whose land they occupied. *Charreada* is more than an age-old sport; it is Mexico's pride and joy, a national celebration dating to the sixteenth century when the Spaniards arrived with horses and cattle in tow. The Aztecs couldn't believe their eyes; to them, man and horse were one creature sent by the gods, giving the settlers the power to conquer.

GUADELAJARA,
JALISCO

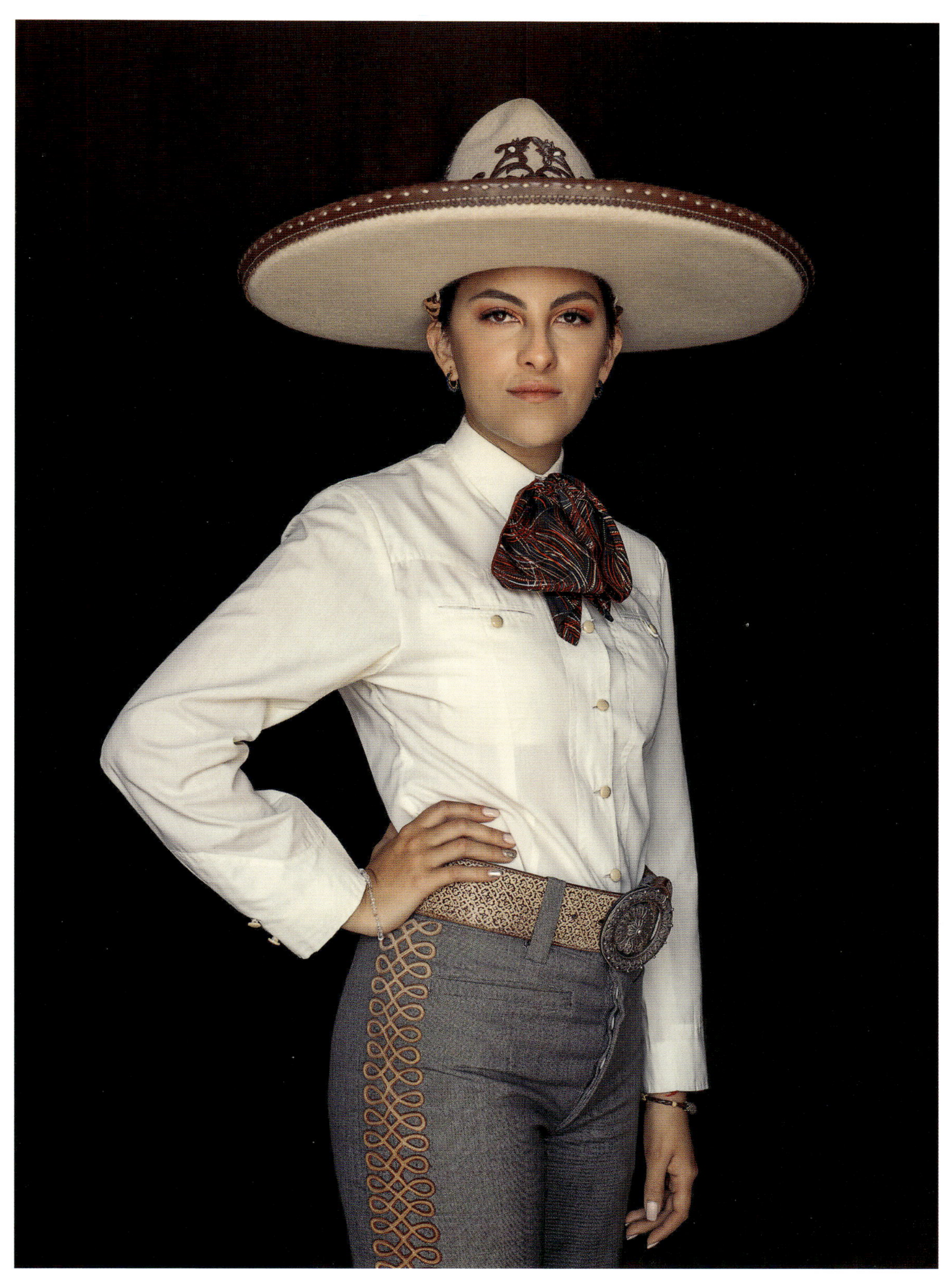

Begoña Saldaña breaks with tradition to perform male
events (suertes) such as lassoing and coleadero.

"Anyone can be a good horseman. It just takes practice, but that's not what charrería is about; it's a way of life outside the arena as well as in."

~ Raúl E. Gaona, Vice-president San Antonio Charro Association ~

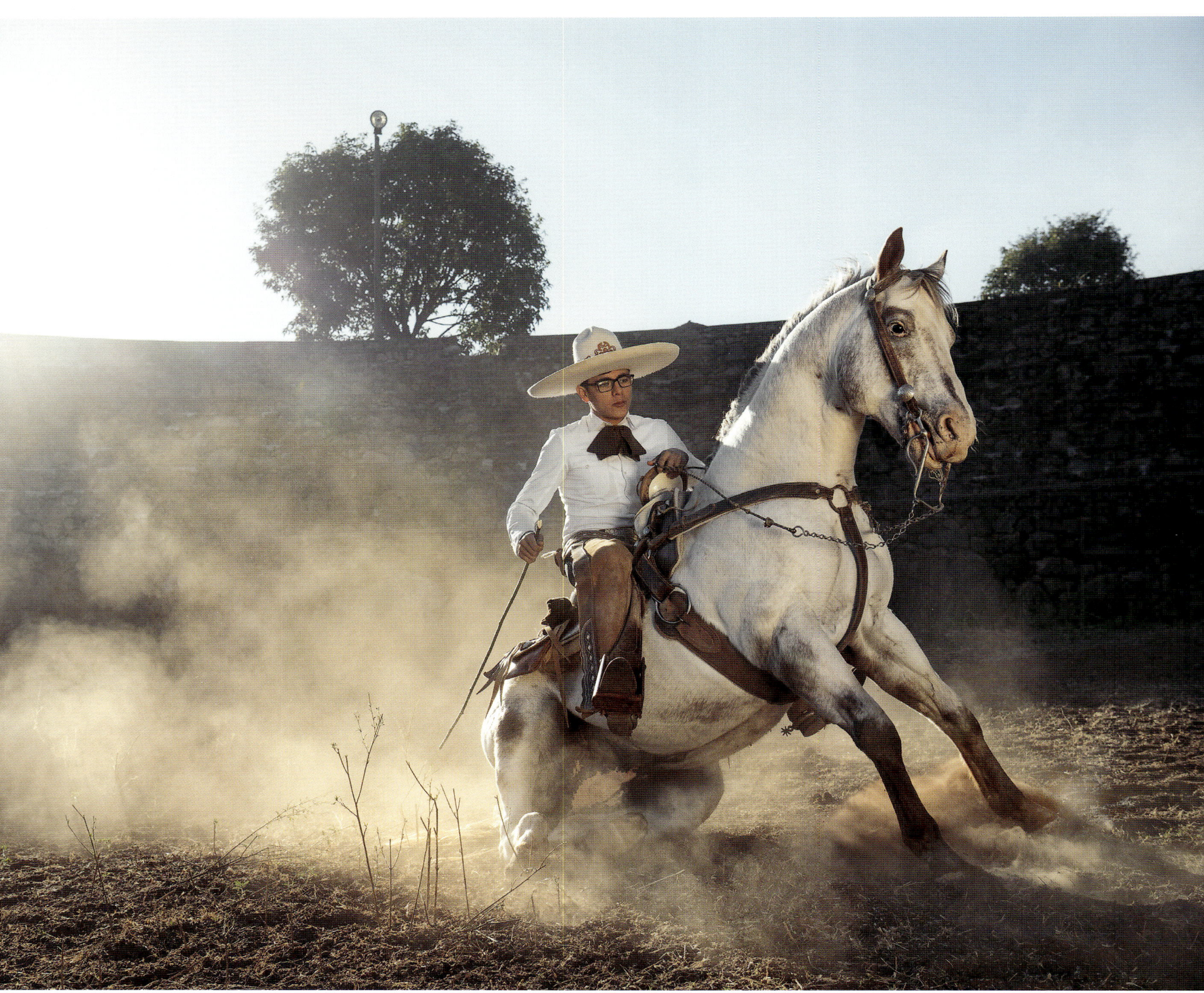

The conquistadors set up large haciendas (ranches) but soon found themselves short-handed and, despite their prejudices, were forced to hire locals. Gradually the Indigenous ranch hands proved to be expert equestrians with unique abilities and saddle styles. As their talents and popularity grew, competitions between haciendas became a source of entertainment, uniting the community while bridging the divide between landowners and their workers.

After the Mexican Revolution in the early 1900s, many estate owners reluctantly moved from the countryside into the larger cities, forced to abandon their rural customs. The fear of these practices vanishing into modernisation led to the creation of the National Charro Association, and *charrería* was then officially declared a regulated sport. It is at the heart of Mexico, deeply rooted in courage, chivalry and national identity – so much so that in 2016, UNESCO declared it part of the 'intangible cultural heritage of humanity' despite protests from animal rights organisations. But *charreada* participants will swear that they love and adore their animals, treating them like royalty and providing the best food, shelter and care.

Charreada should not be mistaken for the American rodeo found in its neighbouring country. It is not an individual sport played for money but a team competition played for dignity and honour. Another significant distinction is that *charros* (male horse-riders) don't take eight seconds to pull down a steer; they ride until the bull stops bucking. And all this is done with style, precision and the elegance of a dancer.

Charreadas are held every Sunday in Guadalajara, Jalisco – which is also home to the mariachi, and no *charreada* takes place without a mariachi band! *Charreadas* are also held in Hidalgo and Pueblo and in parts of the U.S. There are more than nine hundred associations practising the sport today. The cowboys' playground is an arena called a *lienzo*, which is similar to a bull ring, with a passageway twelve metres wide and sixty metres long leading into a ring forty metres in diameter.

Charros (male horse-riders) and *charras* (female horse-riders) begin training from the day they learn to walk. This lively familial sport has a strict 115-page rule book that both men and women must adhere to. It is a tradition that gets passed down from generation to generation.

A *charreada* begins with an opening ceremony that includes participants on horseback dressed in their finest traditional regalia, proudly parading their team banners into the arena while the mariachi band and announcer blare through the speakers. The well-groomed crowd is passionate about what they're about to see, cheering, whistling and applauding wildly while sharing food, tequila and beer with friends and family.

Once the participants have finished bowing to their adoring fans and judges, they take their places to compete in the first of ten different *suertes* (events), nine for the men and one for the women. *Asociaciones* (teams) compete for state, regional and national championships, and each contestant is evaluated on their style and technique.

Galloping at break-neck speed, the *charro* in his immaculate and intricately embellished suit and sombrero skillfully rides the horse from one end of the arena to the other. He brings the horse to a screeching halt, first demonstrating the ability to manoeuvre it to a slide stop, then to spin on its hind legs and lastly, to execute the trick of backing up. The first suerte – the *cala de caballo* – has been completed, revealing the horse and rider's expertise, strength, and agility.

The following nine *suertes* are performed in a specific order: *piles en el lienzo*, lassoing the cows' back legs to slow it down without hurting it; *colas en el lienzo*, bringing down a steer by its tail; *jineteo de toro*, riding the bull until it stops bucking; *terna en el ruedo*, three *charros* try to lasso a cow's head or horns and hind legs as it runs; *jineteo de yegua*, a *charro* must ride a bucking bronco bareback until it stops; *manganas a pie*, a dismounted *charro* attempts to lasso a horse's forelegs; *manganas a caballo*, a mounted *charro* lassos a horse's forelegs to get it to stop; *el paso de la muerte*, a bareback rider holding only the mane must chase and jump onto another horse and ride until it stops bucking. The last event and the only one women take part in is the *escaramuza* (skirmish), a show of grace and bravery in which eight women dressed in beautifully embroidered dresses and perfectly angled sombreros execute high-speed, synchronised equestrian patterns to musical accompaniment, all while riding side-saddle.

And in between all the excitement of man and beast performing high-risk feats, *'banda'* music blasts through the arena during intermission, inspiring couples to jump to their feet, displaying their salsa dancing talents in the aisles, in the true spirit of Mexico's contagious fiesta. Even after the *charreada* ends, the party goes on, with more food, music and dancing.

To witness the world of *charreada* is to experience the wild, wild west refined into an artful sport that was once rooted in colonialism. It has become the symbol of Mexican identity, a tribute to its rich cultural traditions and blended ancestry, proudly extending beyond its national playground.

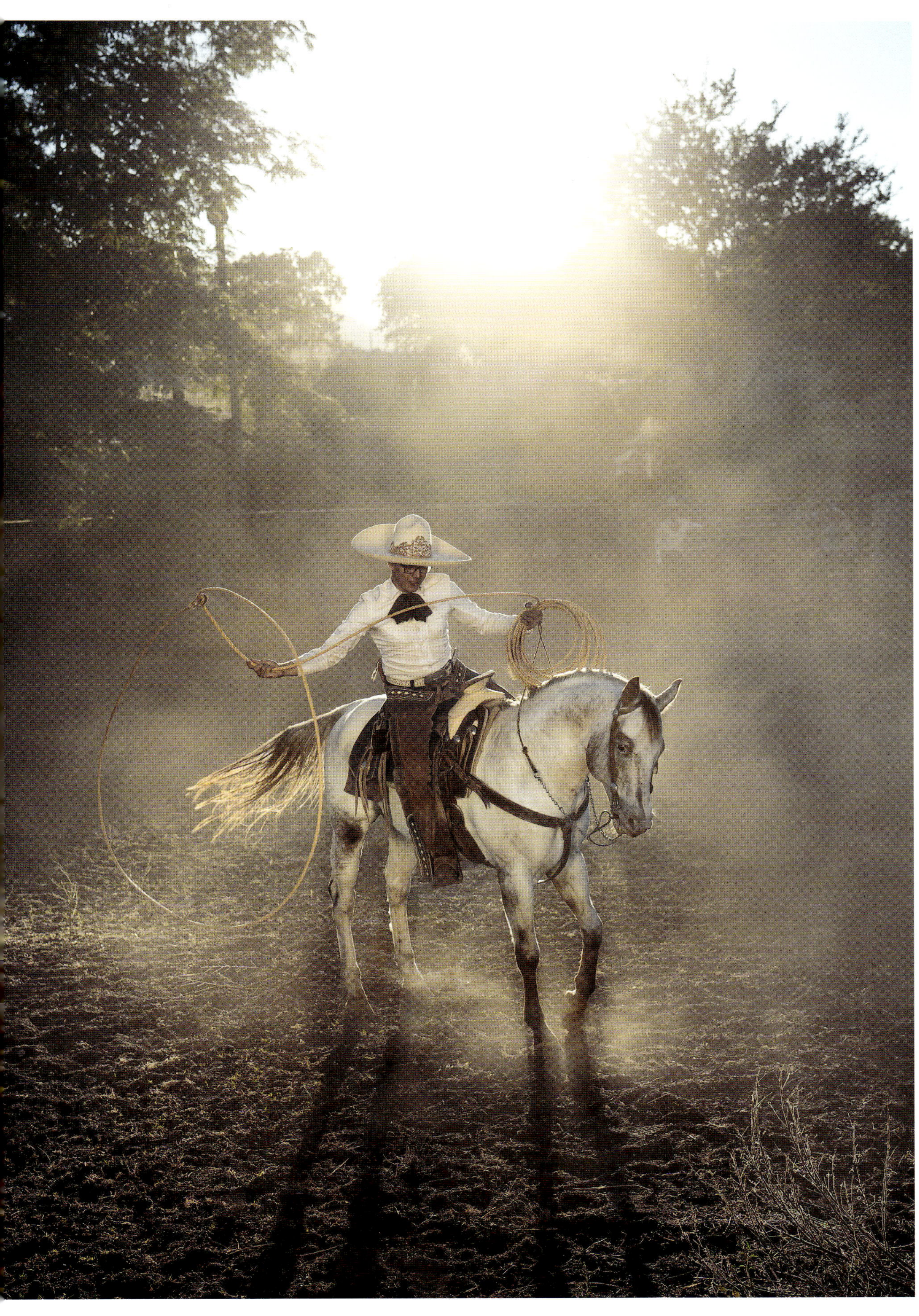

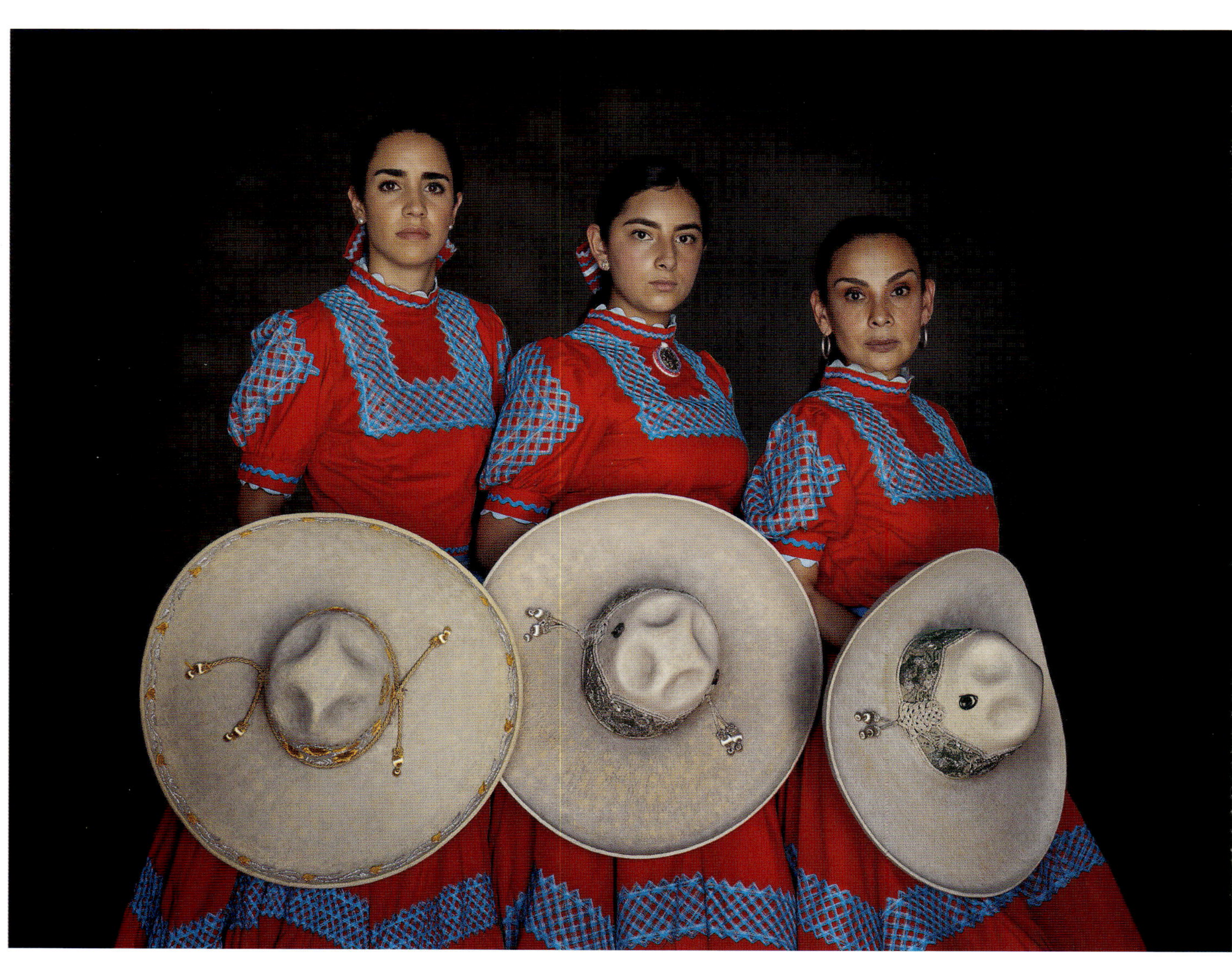

The famous sombrero's wide brim shields the face,
neck and shoulders from the sun and acts as head
protection if the charro or charra falls off their horse.

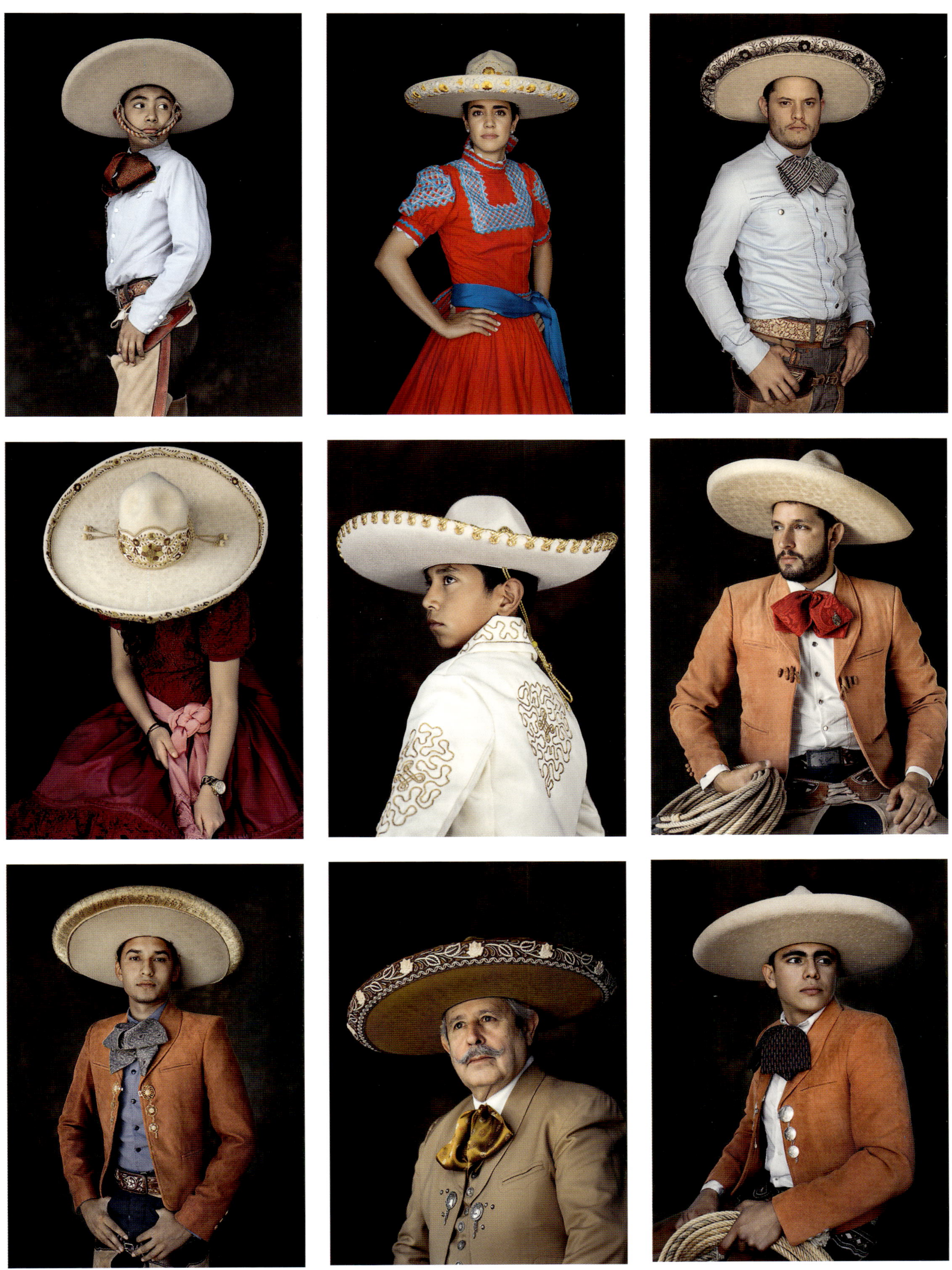

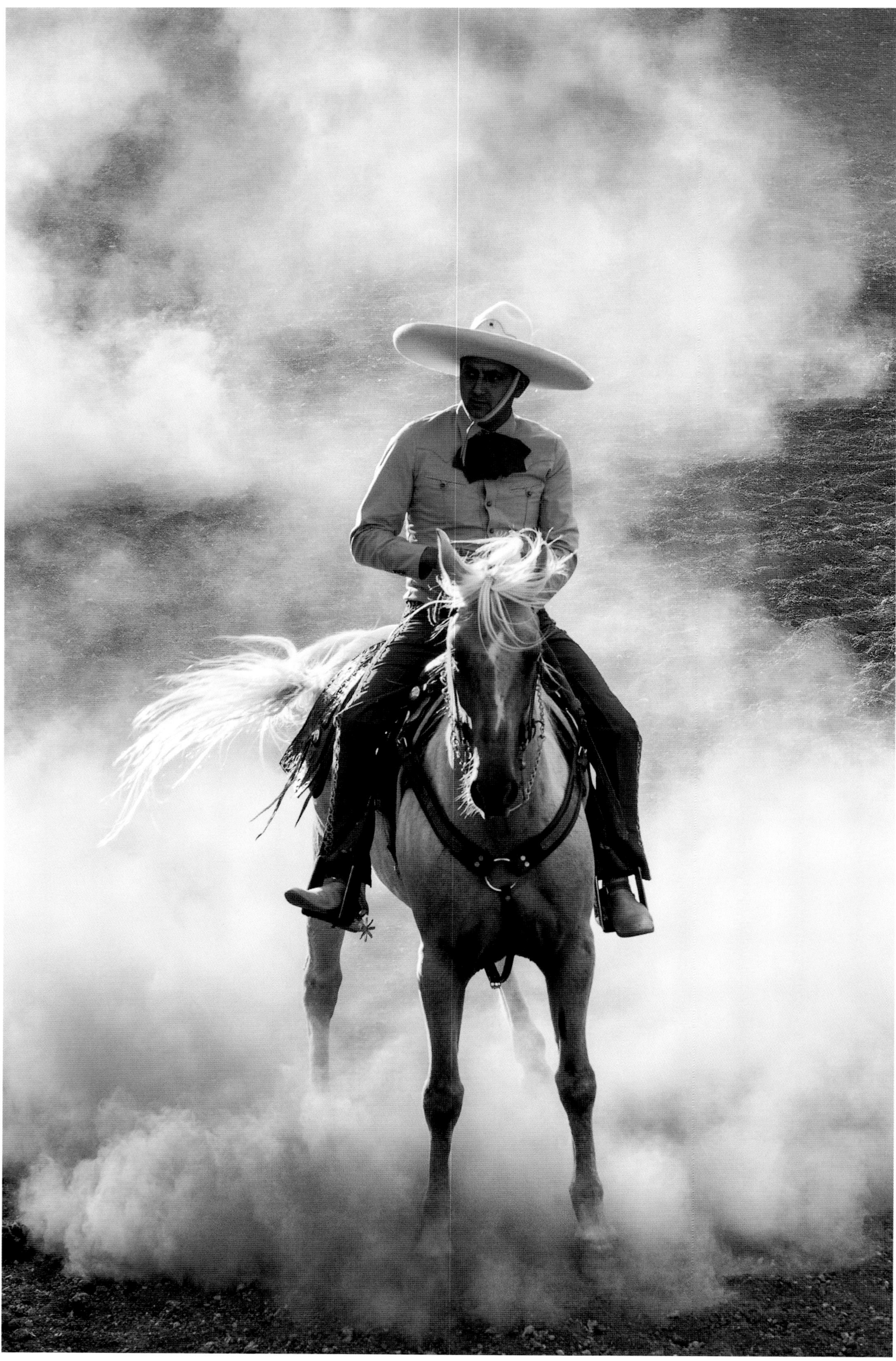

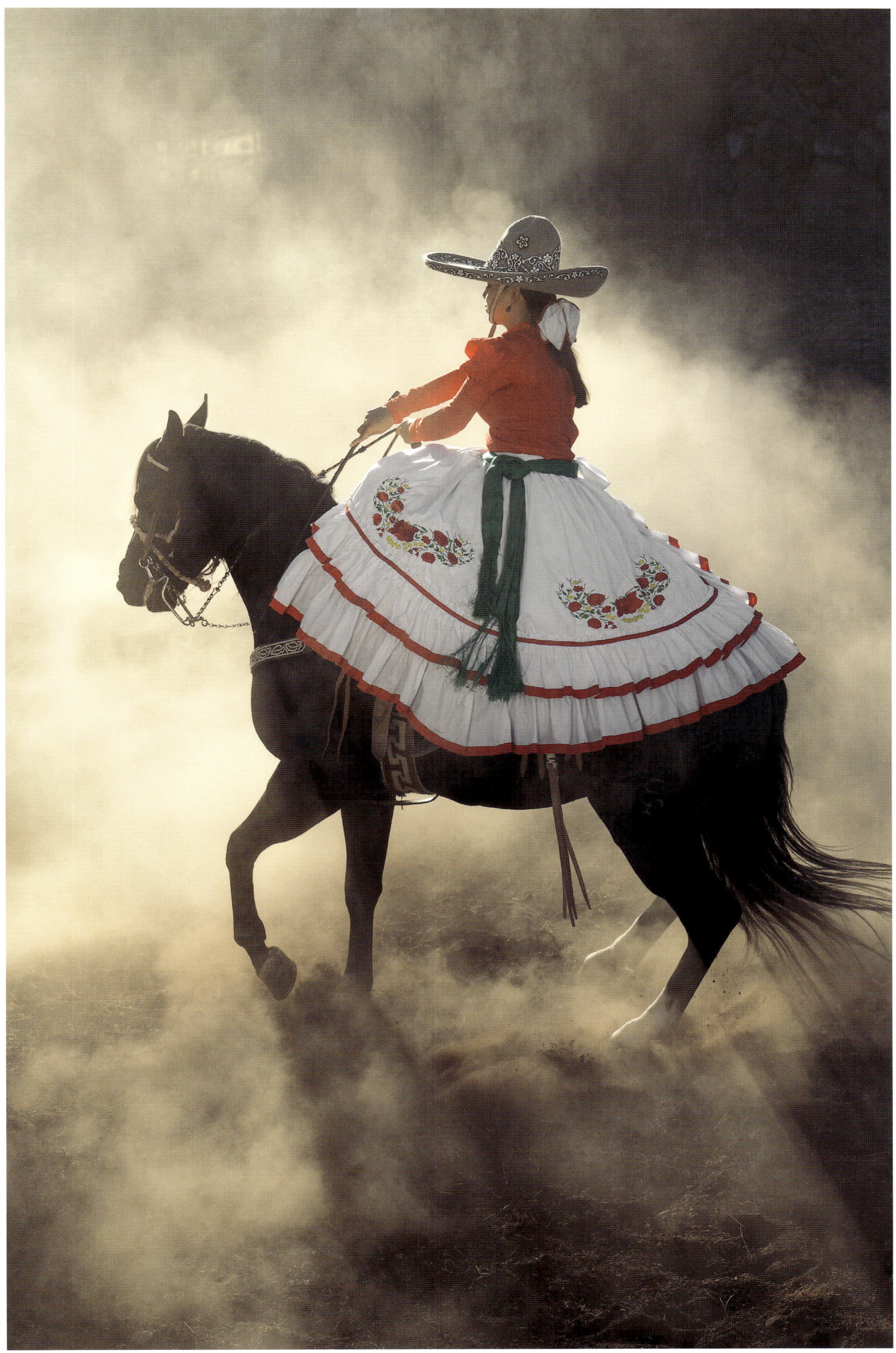

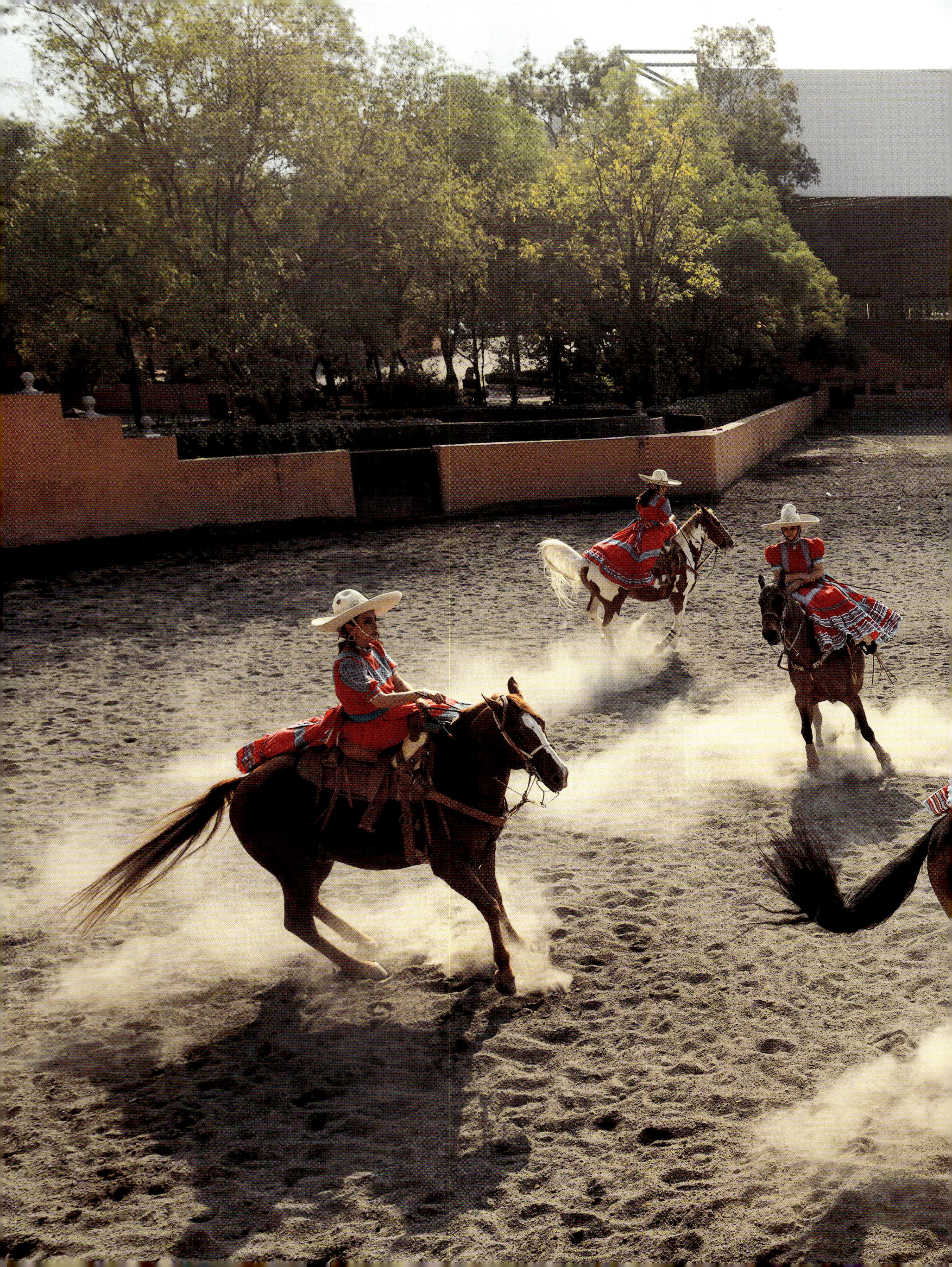

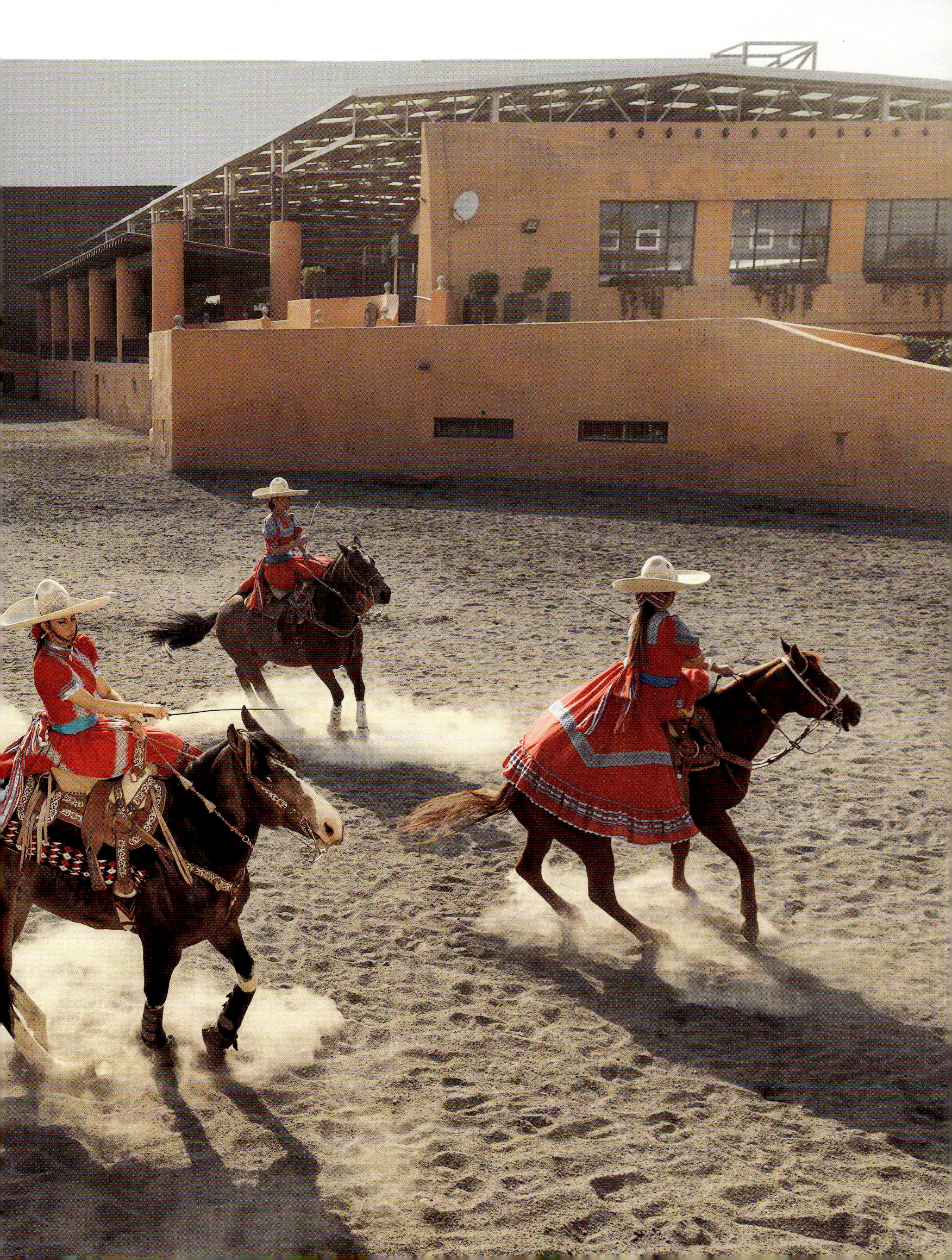

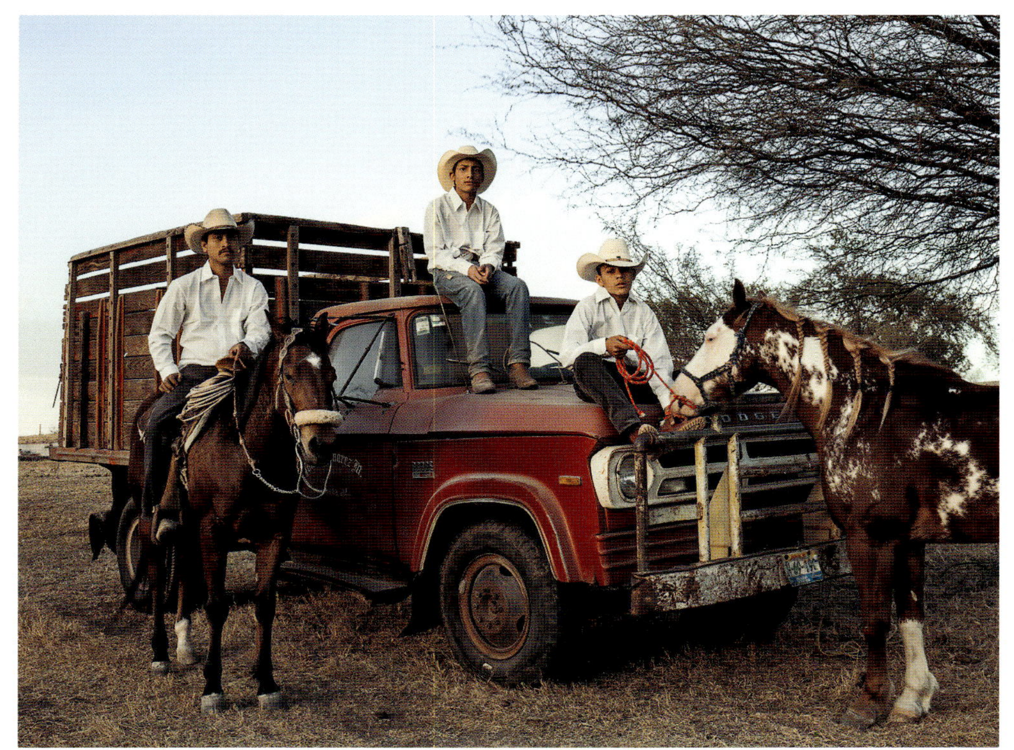

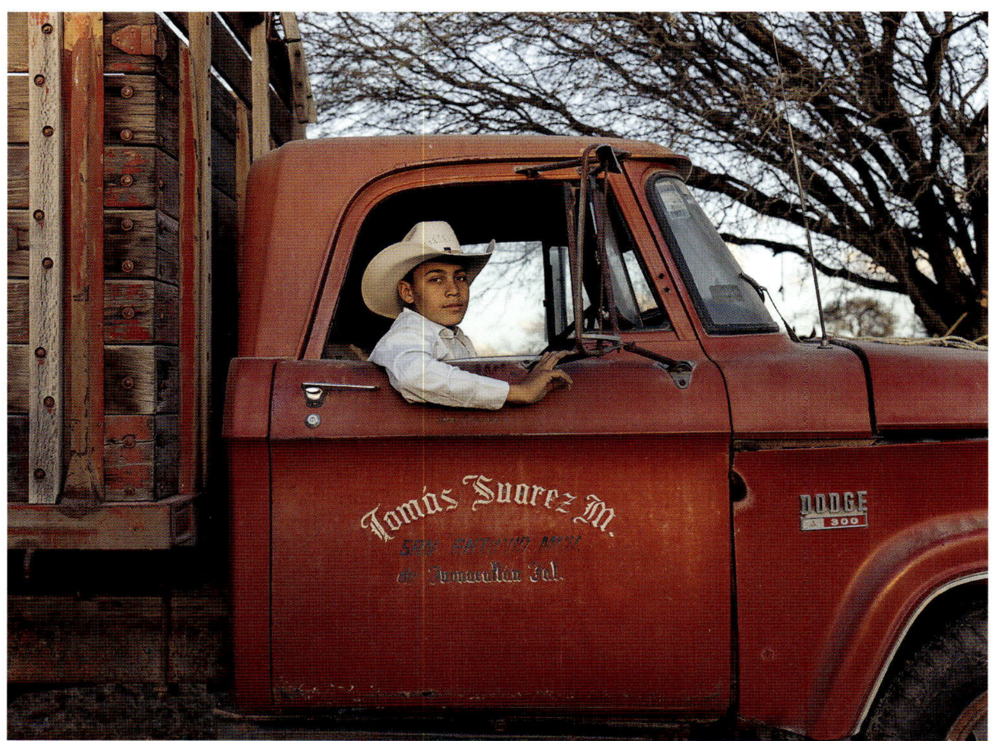

Tomás Suarez M.
DODGE 300

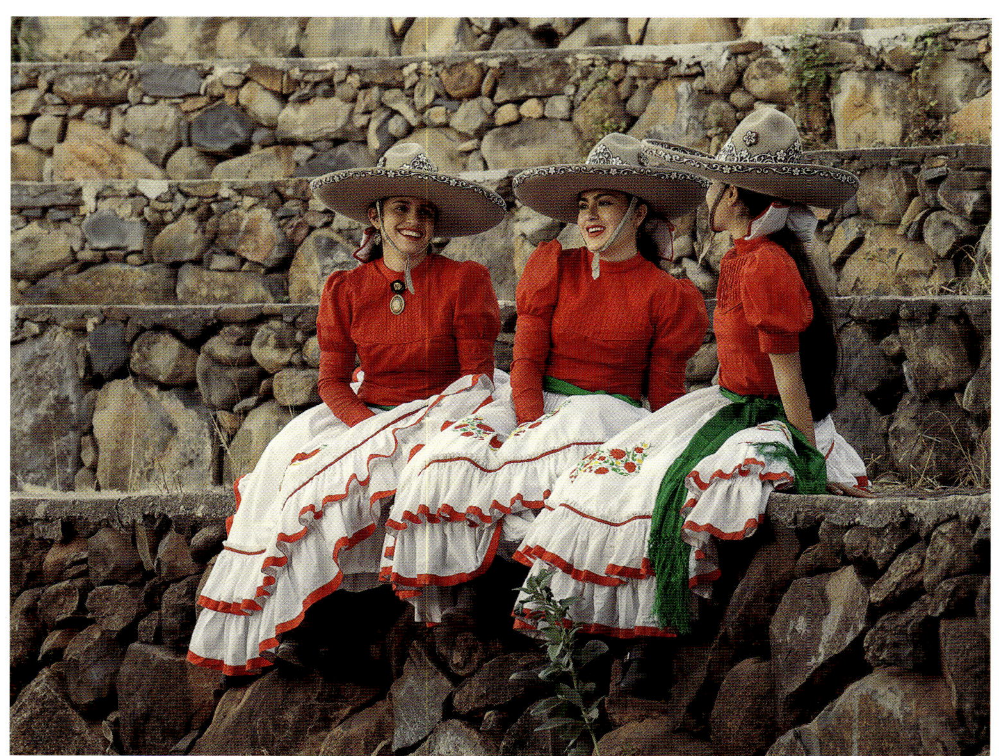

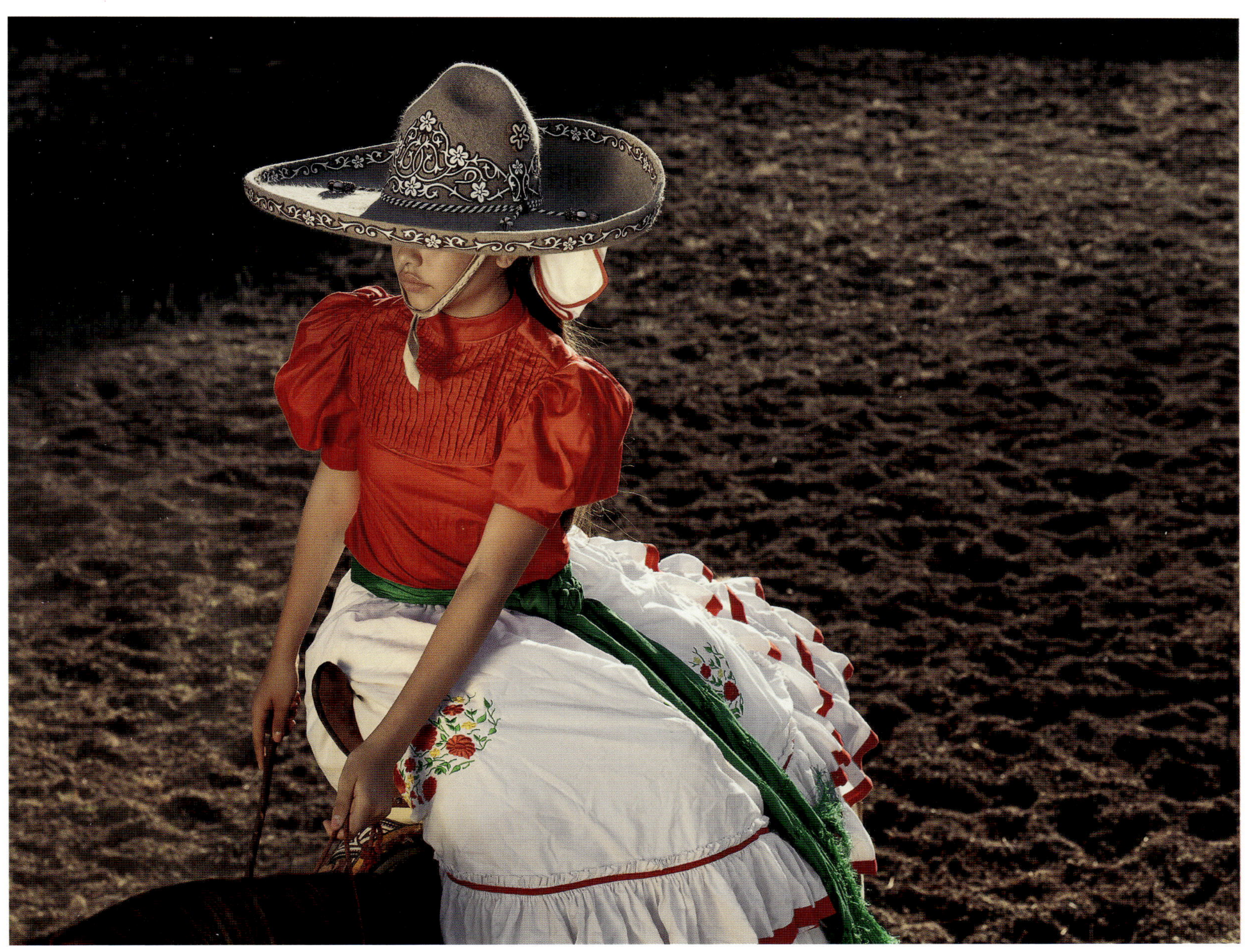

The escaramuza is the female charreria, where
women ride sidesaddle, performing carefully
choreographed tricks in their traditional dresses.

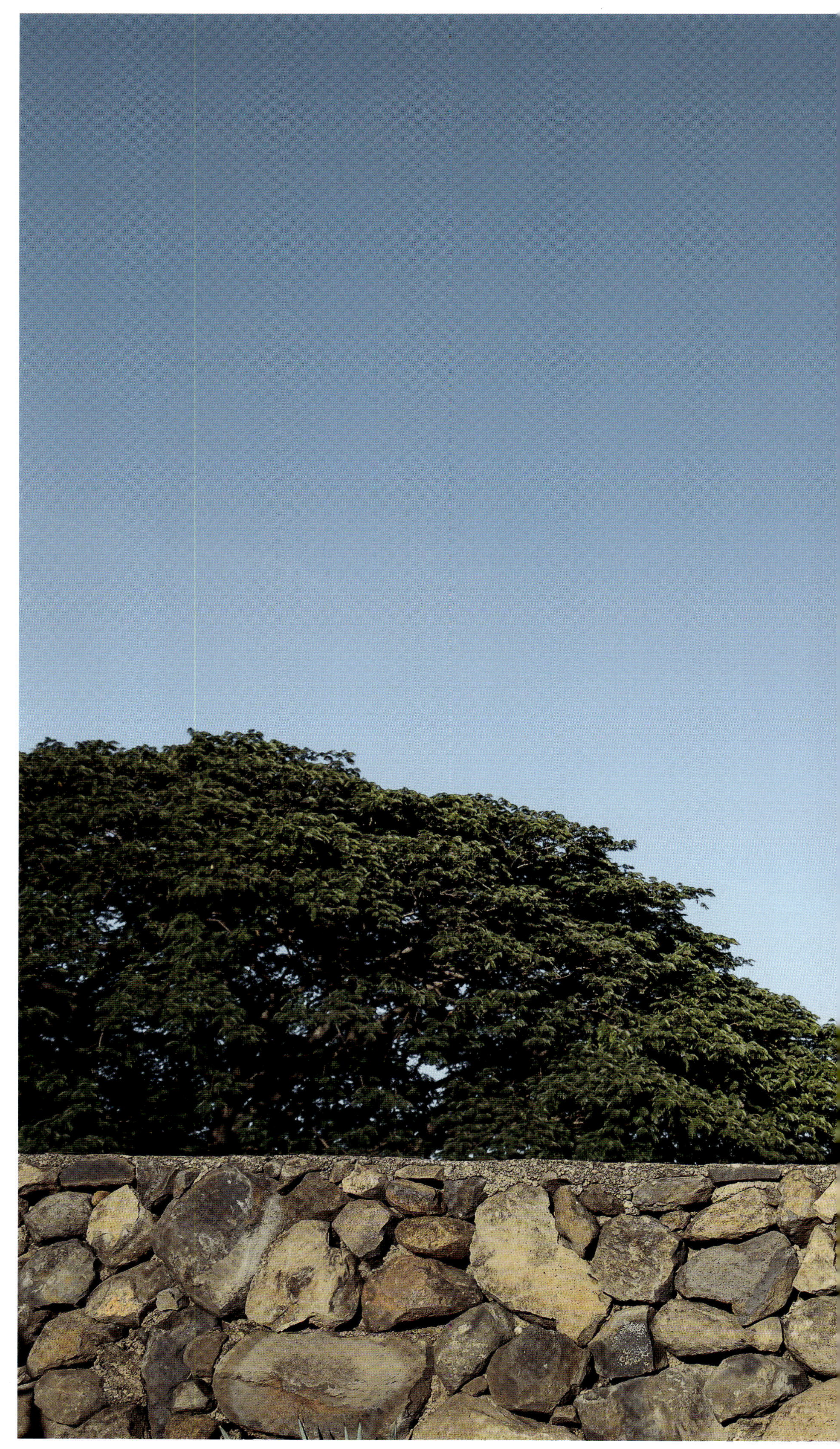

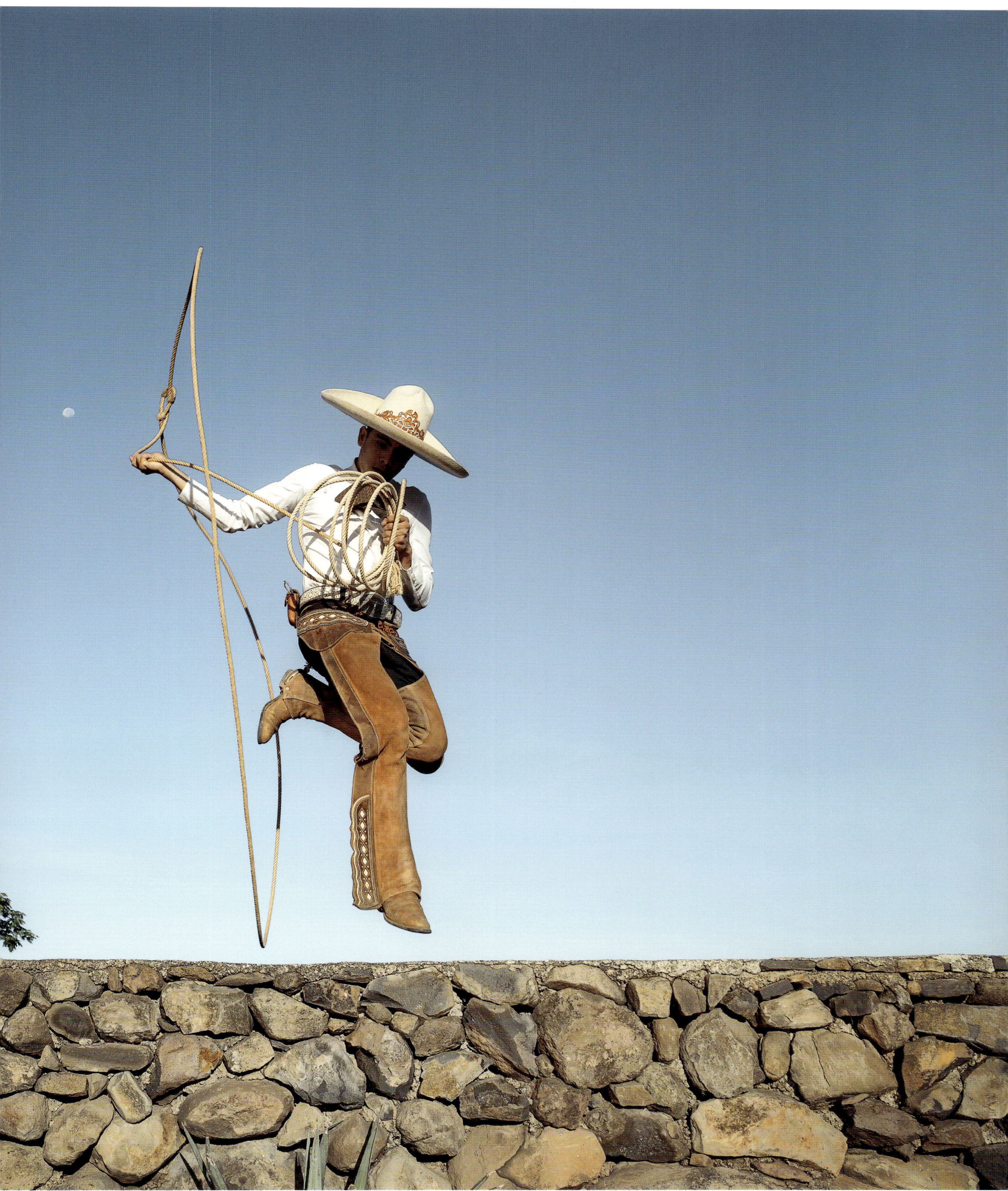

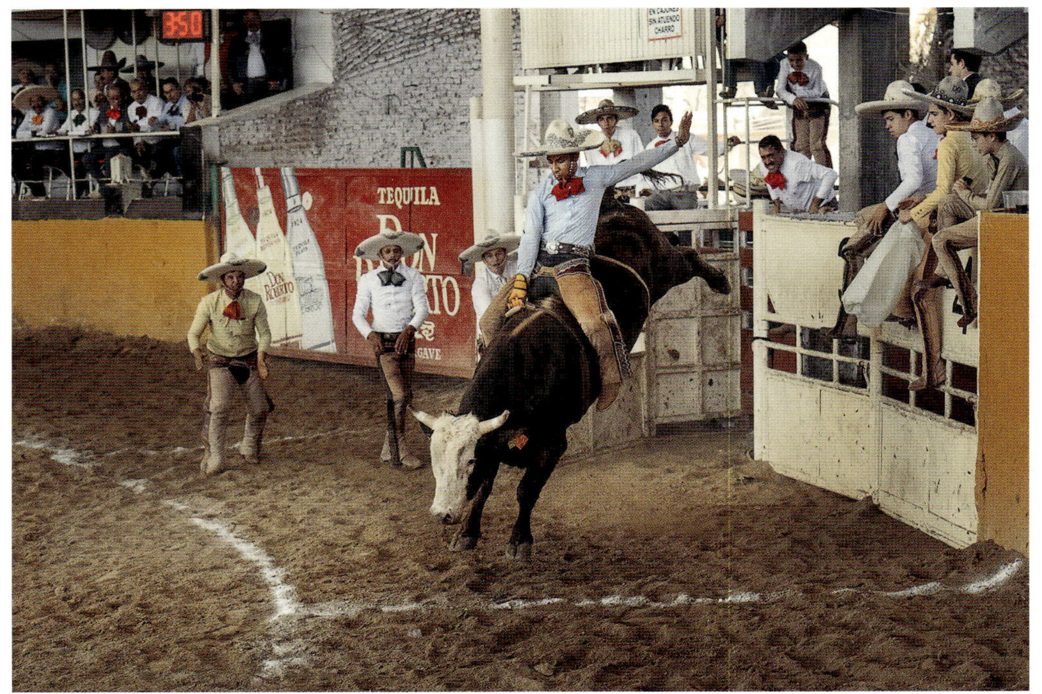

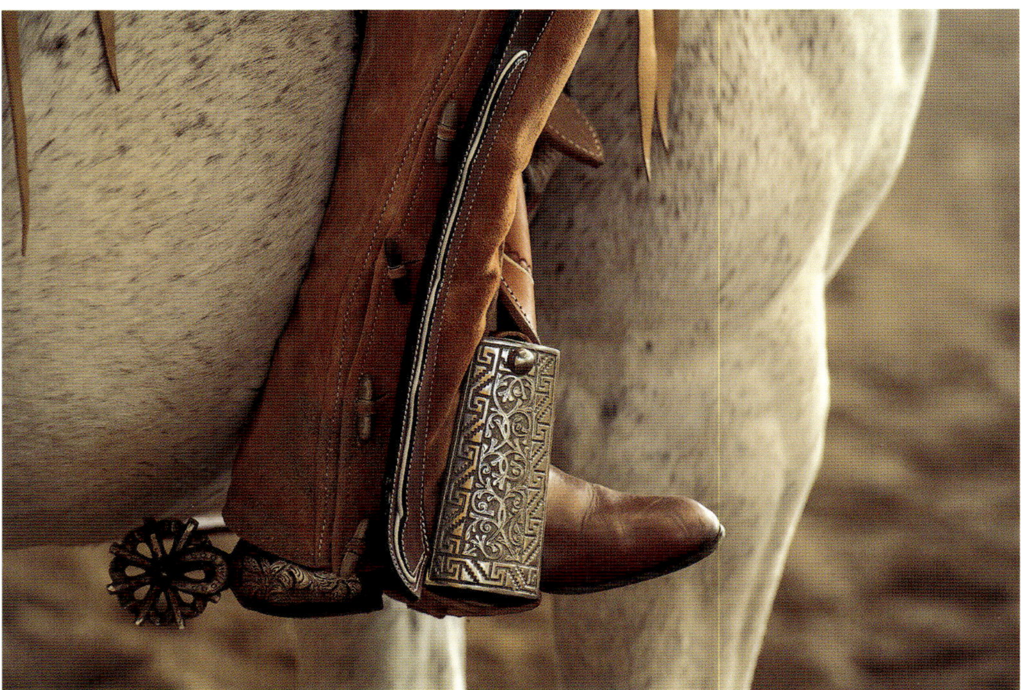

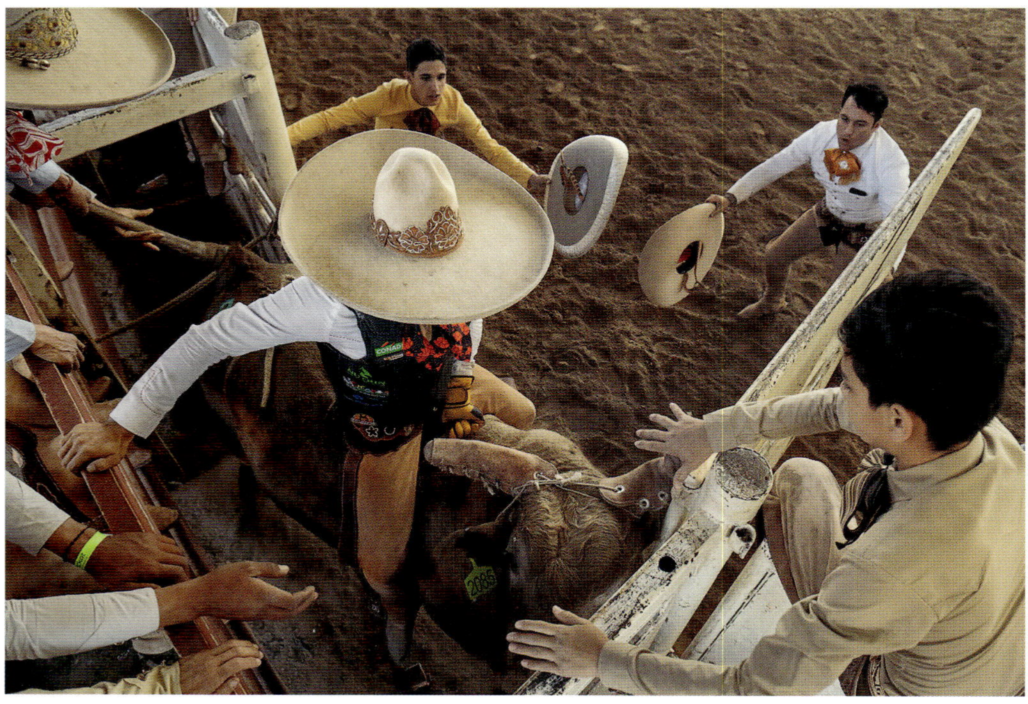

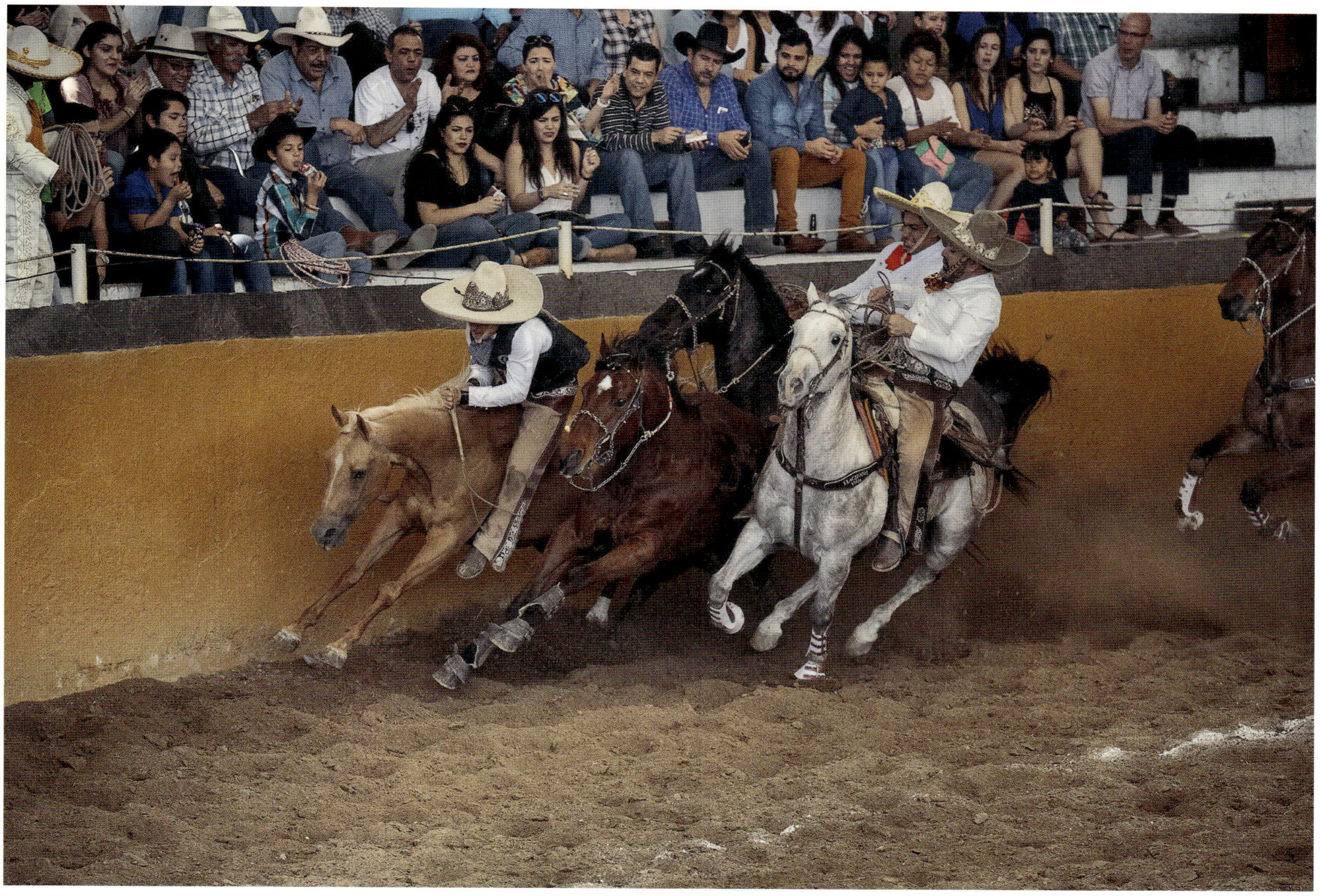

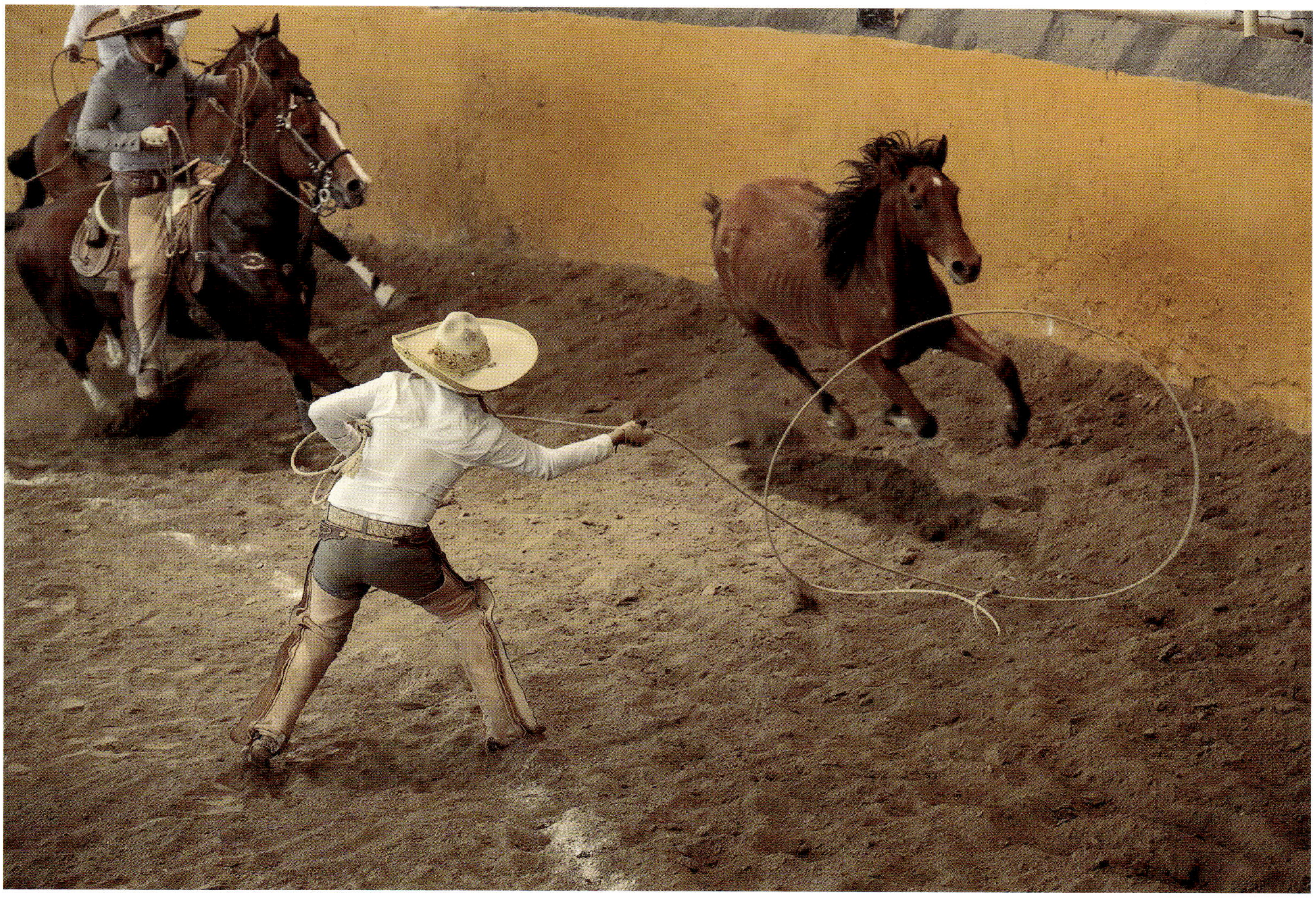

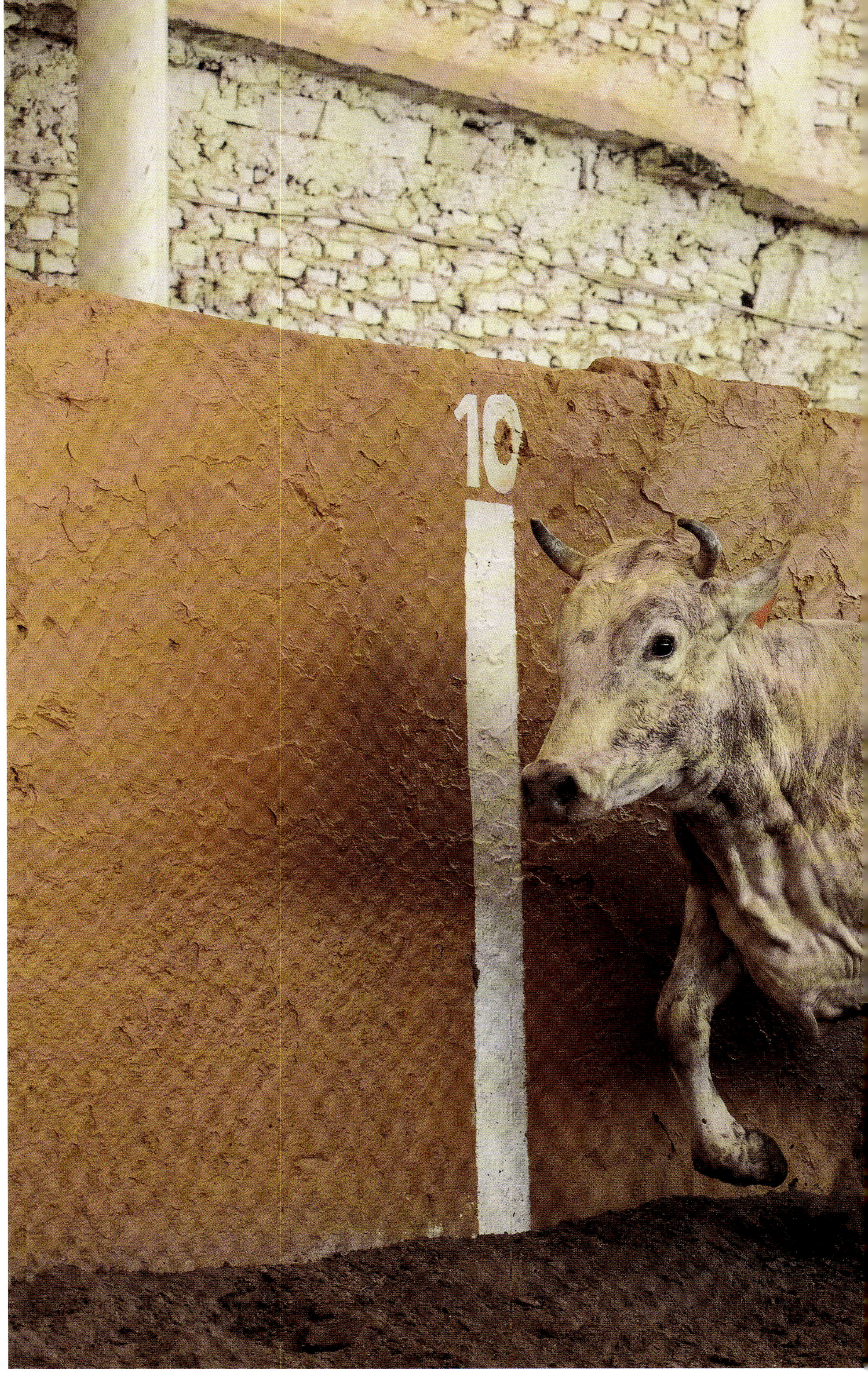
10

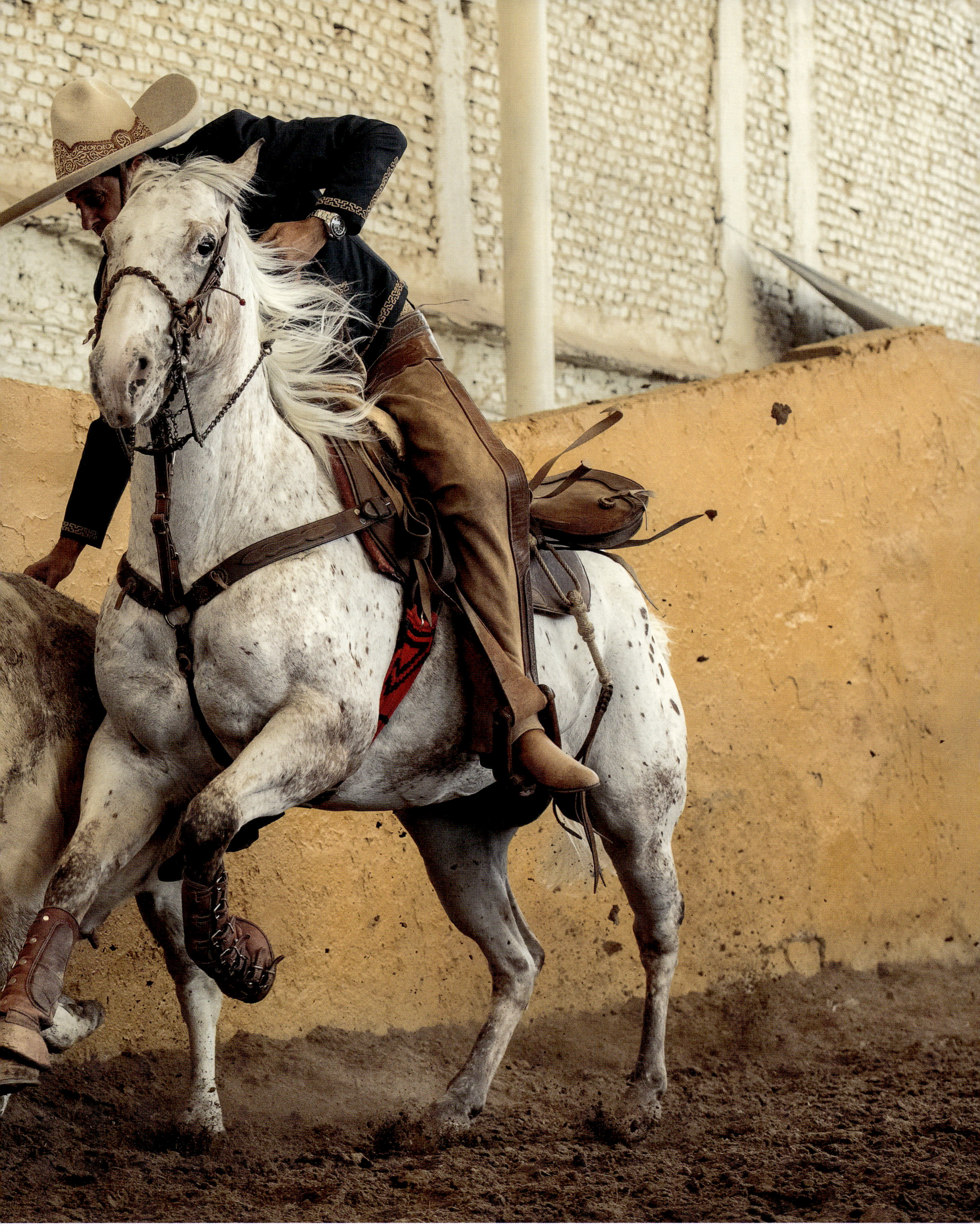

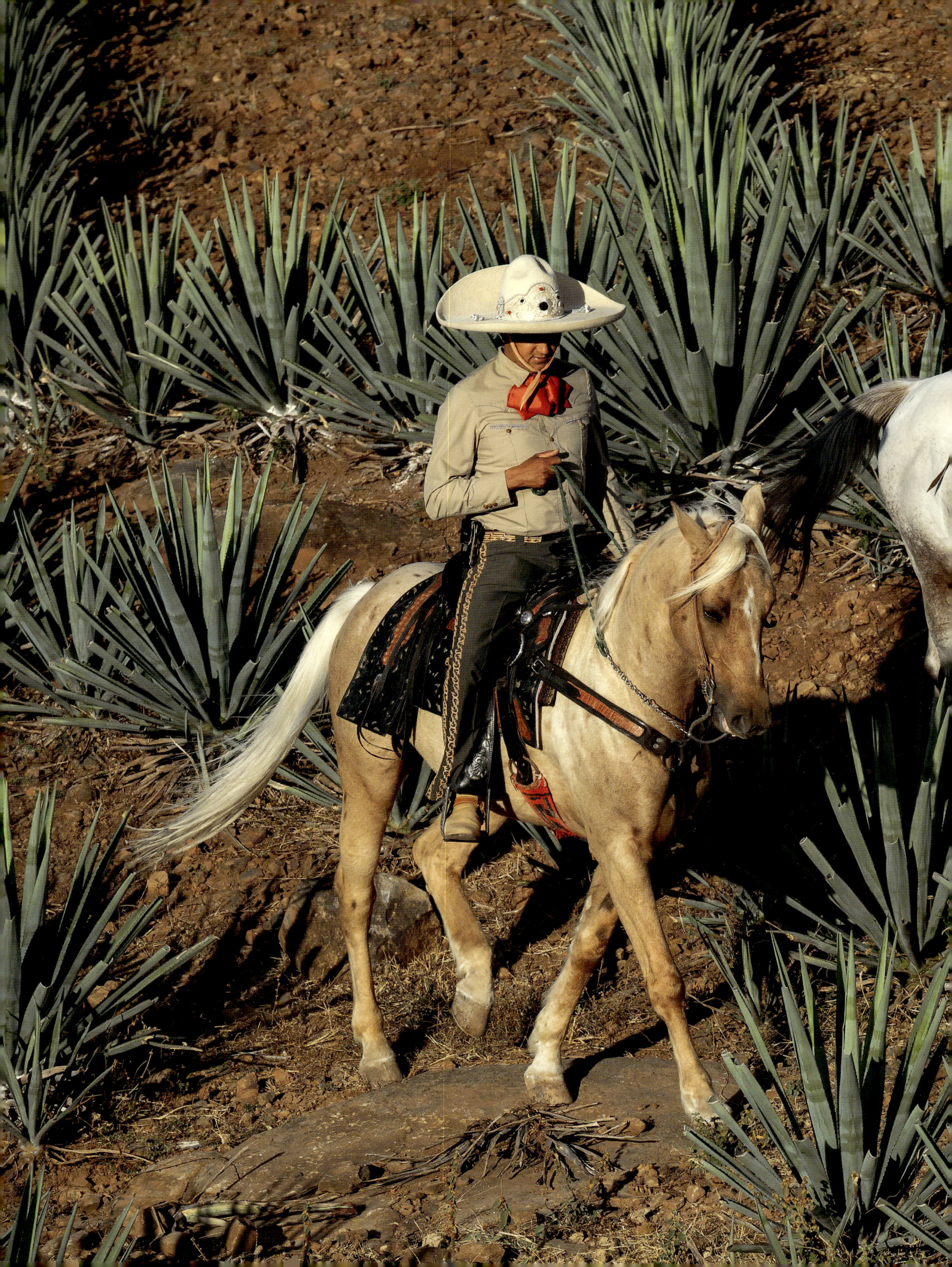

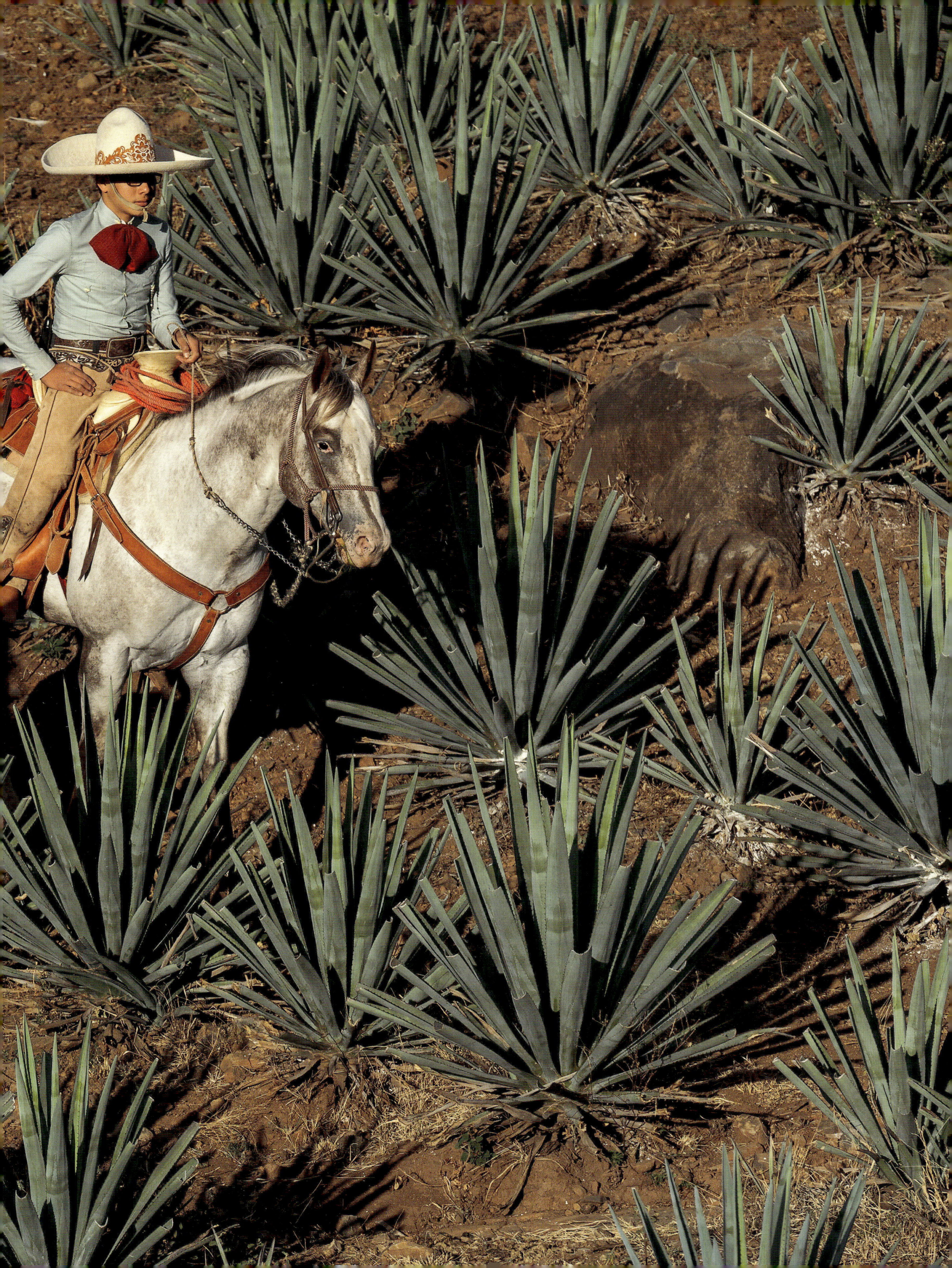

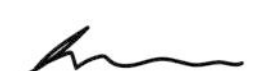

Amputee Football

NIGERIA

These exceptional athletic abilities are testaments to the
power of the human body and spirit to push beyond limitations.

Football is one of the most beloved sports in the world, attracting millions of worshipping fans. Part of its popularity is that anyone can play it; regardless of where or how one lives, whether rich or poor, all one needs is a ball. And at least one foot. In the heart of Lagos, one of Africa's most populated cities, where the rich flaunt their wealth and the poor cannot hide their lack of it, lives the remarkable Special Eagles amputee football team. This group of super-athletic, resilient men missing one or more limbs due to either childhood illness or tragic accidents have dedicated themselves to playing this globally cherished game.

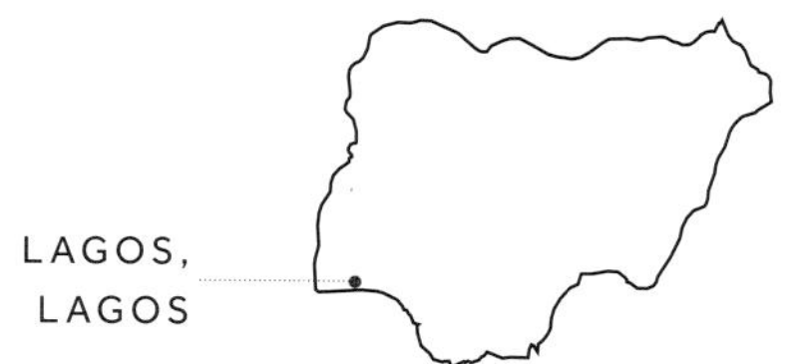

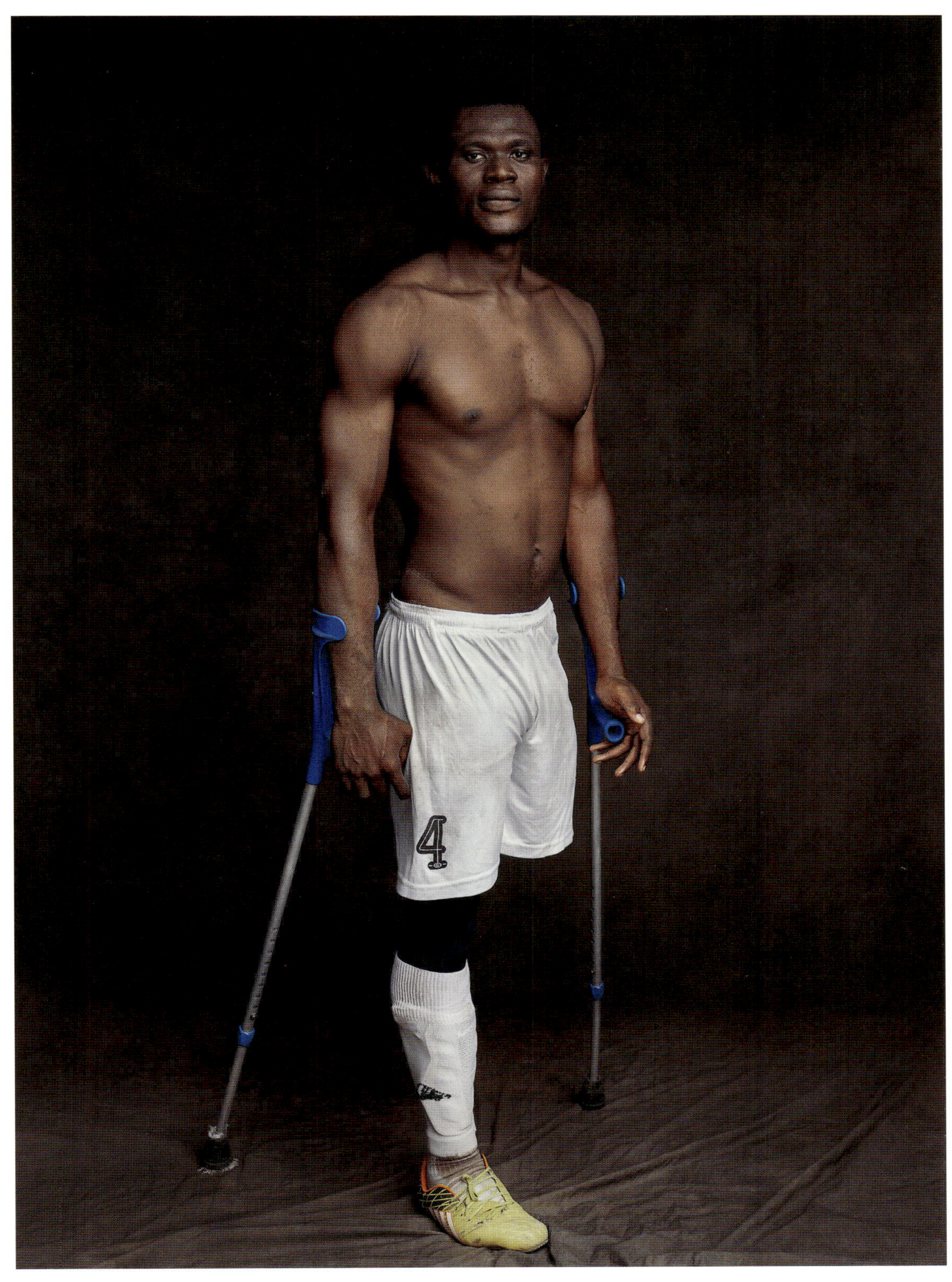

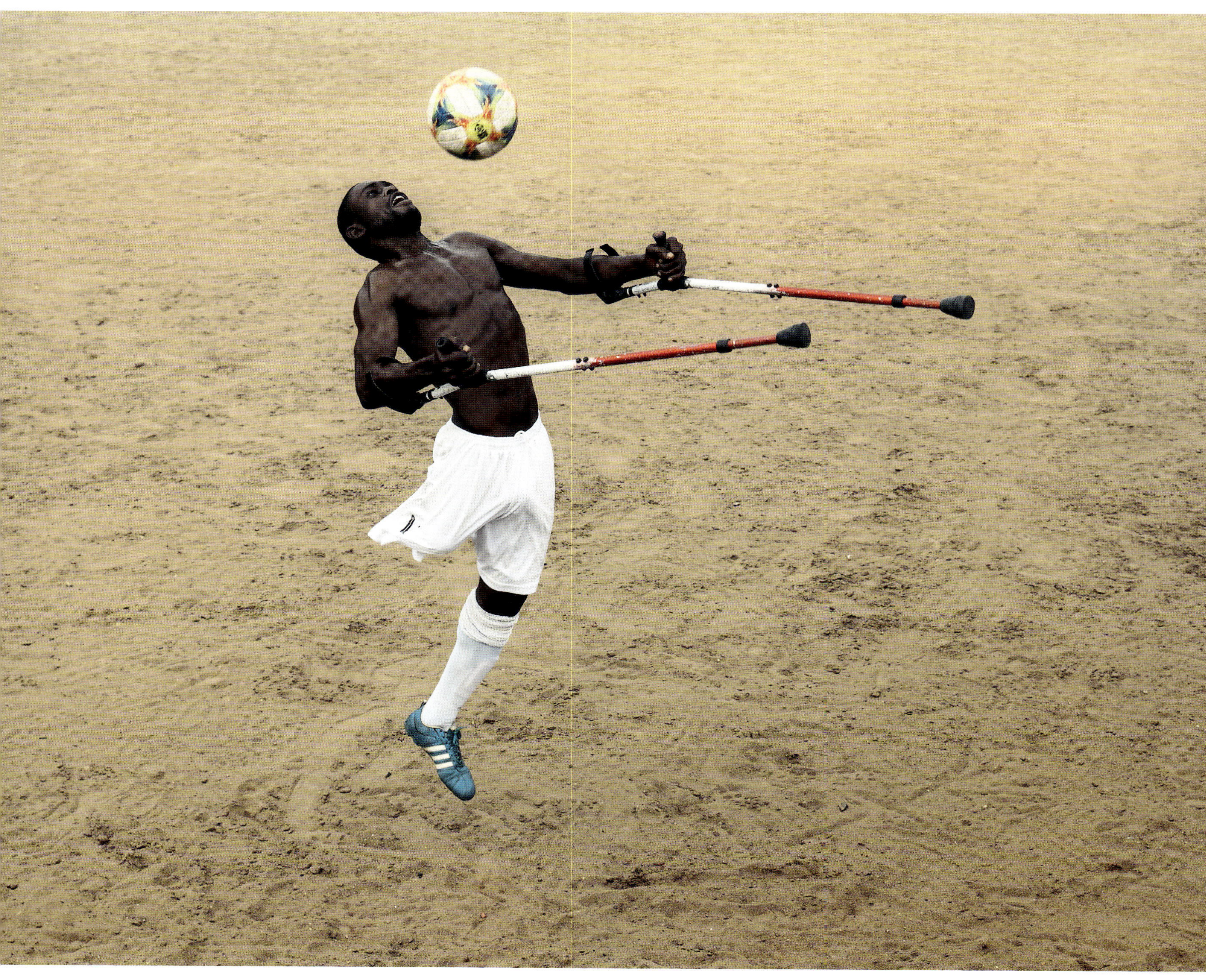

Football is one of the oldest sports, played in Britain as early as 200 b.c. Amputee football was created in 1982 by Don Bennett, a skier who lost his leg in a boating accident, and football coach Bill Barry, who helped bring international attention to the sport.

Amputee football was introduced in Africa only two decades ago. Since then, organisations have been working hard to develop this sport because so many amputees have lost arms and legs unnecessarily. Eighty per cent of amputations occurred because of accidents, infections and insufficient health care. The other twenty per cent were born with a disability due to the effects of polio. The amputee football players know that if they had been born in a different country or received proper health care, they wouldn't be in the condition they are in today. Unfortunately, the impoverished become victims of a failed medical system.

Special Eagles captain Sharafadeen Olalekan started playing football very young and dreamt of becoming a professional footballer for Nigeria. But his destiny took a turn. Injured, he was rushed to a local doctor who treated him but was unaware of a bone fracture. The fracture led to an infection, eventually ending in amputation. Olalekan's dream of being a pro player had come crashing down – until he discovered the World Amputee Football Federation. When he signed with a club in Istanbul, Turkey, Olalekan became the first Nigerian amputee player to receive a professional contract. He has dedicated himself to promoting amputee football and launched the project *Hope for the Disabled*, the first of its kind in Africa.

The Special Eagles have worked hard to make a name for themselves within Nigeria and internationally. They may be missing limbs, but it doesn't stop them from playing with incredible skill, speed and finesse. Amputee players need to sprint, swivel, dodge, kick the ball and perform expert acrobatics while balancing on crutches. These exceptional athletic abilities are testaments to the power of the human body and the spirit to defy limitations.

Amputee football is played with seven players per team (six outfield players and one goalkeeper) in two twenty-five-minute halves with a ten-minute rest. Outfield players have lower-limb amputations, and goalkeepers have upper-limb amputations. Some rules include: Outfield players cannot play with prosthetics, only forearm crutches; they cannot control, block or strike the ball or another player with their crutches; a violation results in a penalty kick and removal from the game. The playground measures seventy by sixty meters, and the goal is 2.2 metres high by five metres wide and one metre deep.

Amputee football is a tough game; it makes professional able-bodied football look like child's play. And these men play it with plenty of dignity and passion, even under the glaring sun with temperatures hovering between thirty and forty degrees Celsius.

Over the years, the team has put in hours of intense training, overcoming many obstacles with minimal financial reward. Yet somehow, they've managed to stay motivated and committed to the game. Goalkeeper Blessing Agu explains, 'We qualified for the 2007 World Cup in Turkey. We collected the visas, but we couldn't go. The second time, it was the same for the 2010 World Cup in Argentina; again, we qualified but couldn't go'.

They qualified for World Cup events three consecutive times but were unable to go due to a lack of funds. Organisers threatened to ban Nigeria from future competitions, so when they qualified for the 2018 World Cup in Mexico, they knew they had to make it there. Thankfully all the media coverage and fund-raising efforts paid off. Captain Mikel Obi from Nigeria's able-bodied national football team, the Super Eagles, generously donated tickets for the entire amputee team. The odds were stacked against them as they made their debut appearance in Mexico, and although they didn't win the cup, they managed to defeat El Salvador, a small win but a victorious one nonetheless.

That same year, the team won a silver medal at the Angola Nations Cup, and in 2019 they won yet another silver medal at the Amputee Football Nations Cup in Dar es Salaam, Tanzania. And in 2021, they once again qualified for the 2022 World Cup in Turkey.

The players dream of leaving Nigeria, hoping they'll be recruited to international teams so they can improve their lives and those of their families. An amputee's life isn't easy, but it's a monumental challenge in a city as busy and chaotic as Lagos, with few facilities and little to no financial aid for the disabled.

Disadvantages of any kind, let alone physical ones, are enough reason to fall into self-pity and despair. Yet these astounding men have found that football has given them purpose, self-worth and a reason to persevere. Together, they have created a brotherhood, embodying football's joy and spirit, where the impossible becomes possible.

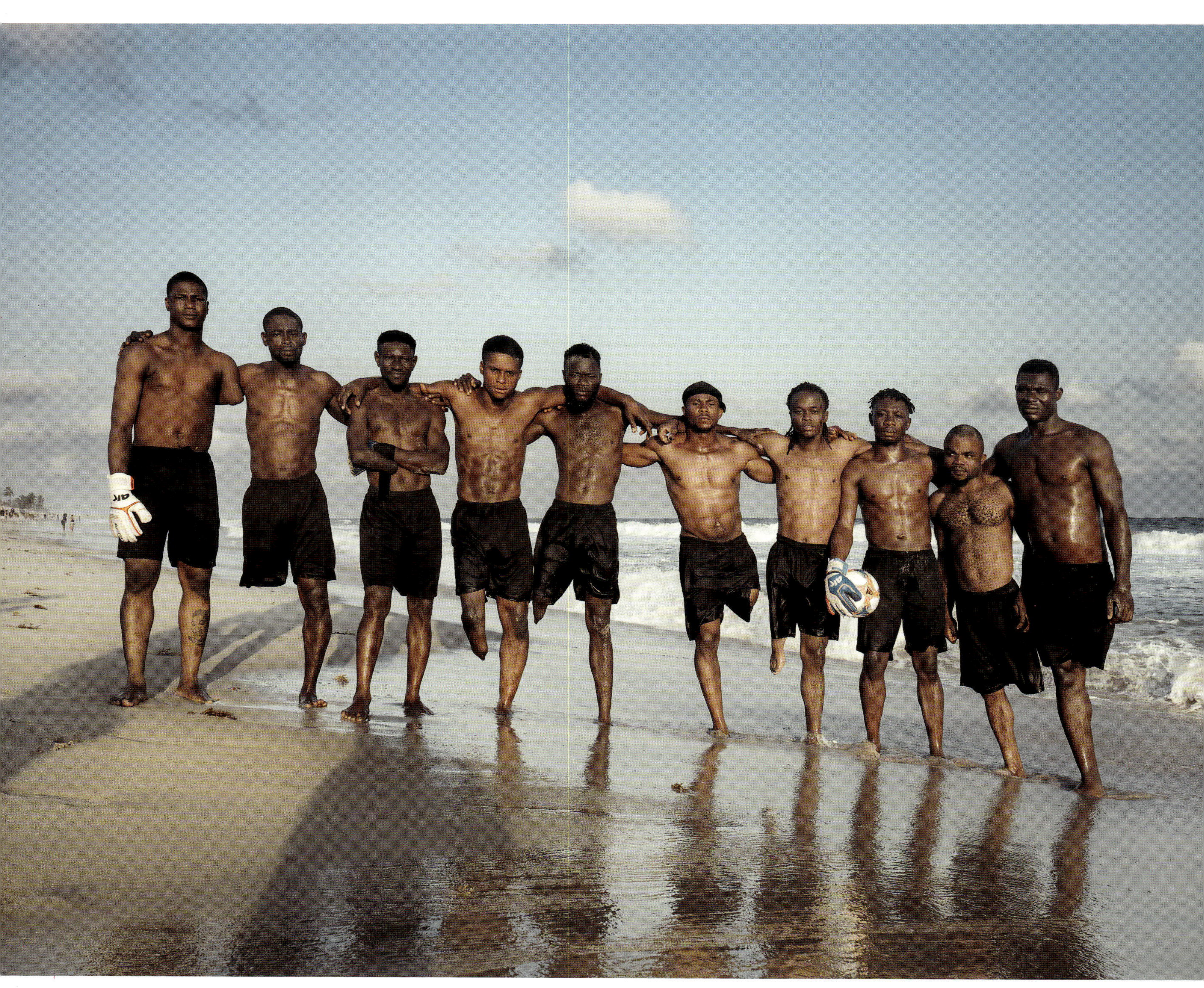

In 2018 at the World Cup in Mexico, the Special Eagles made their debut appearance, managing to defeat El Salvador, a small victory with a big impact.

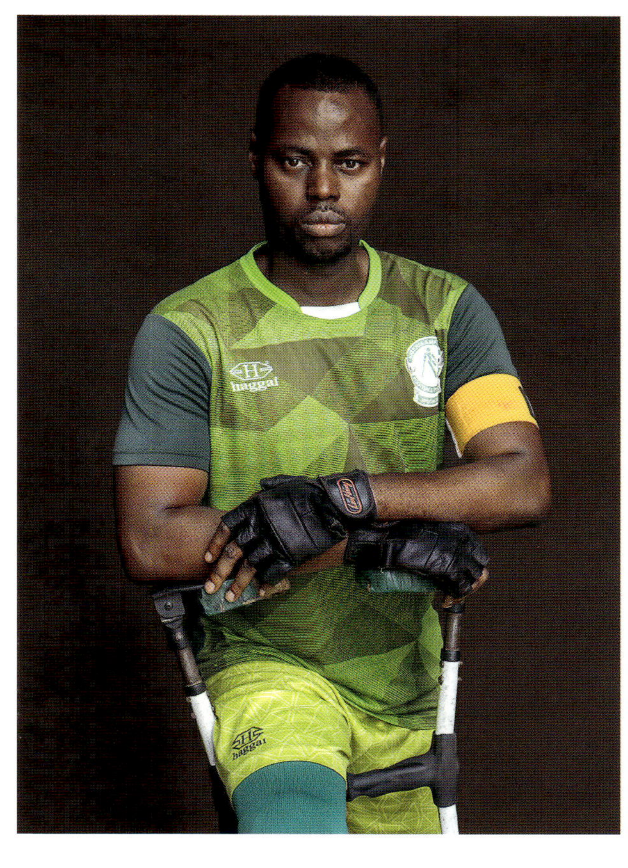
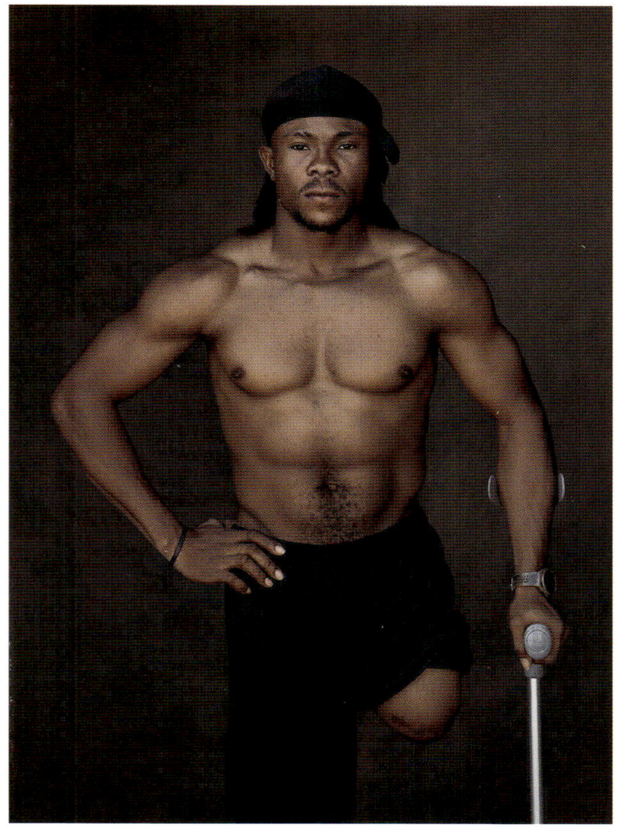
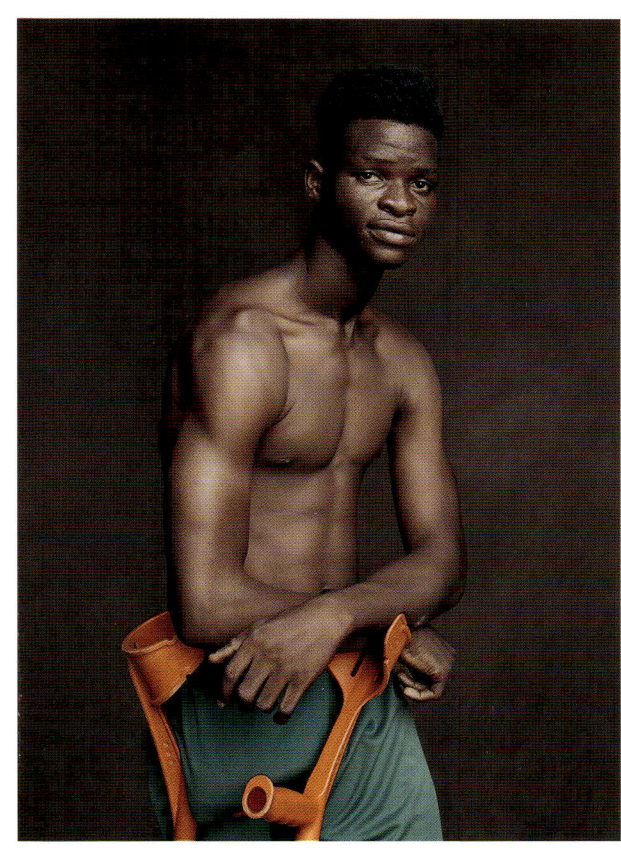
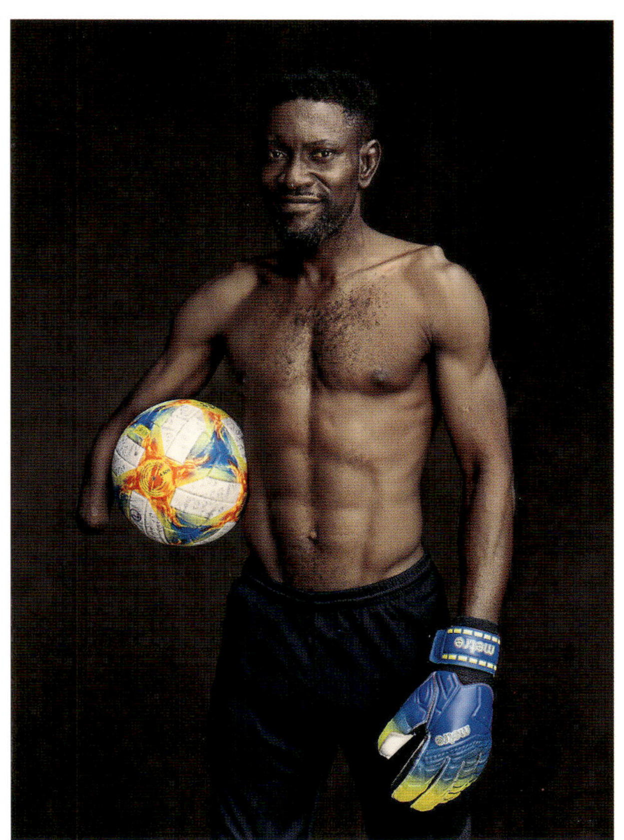

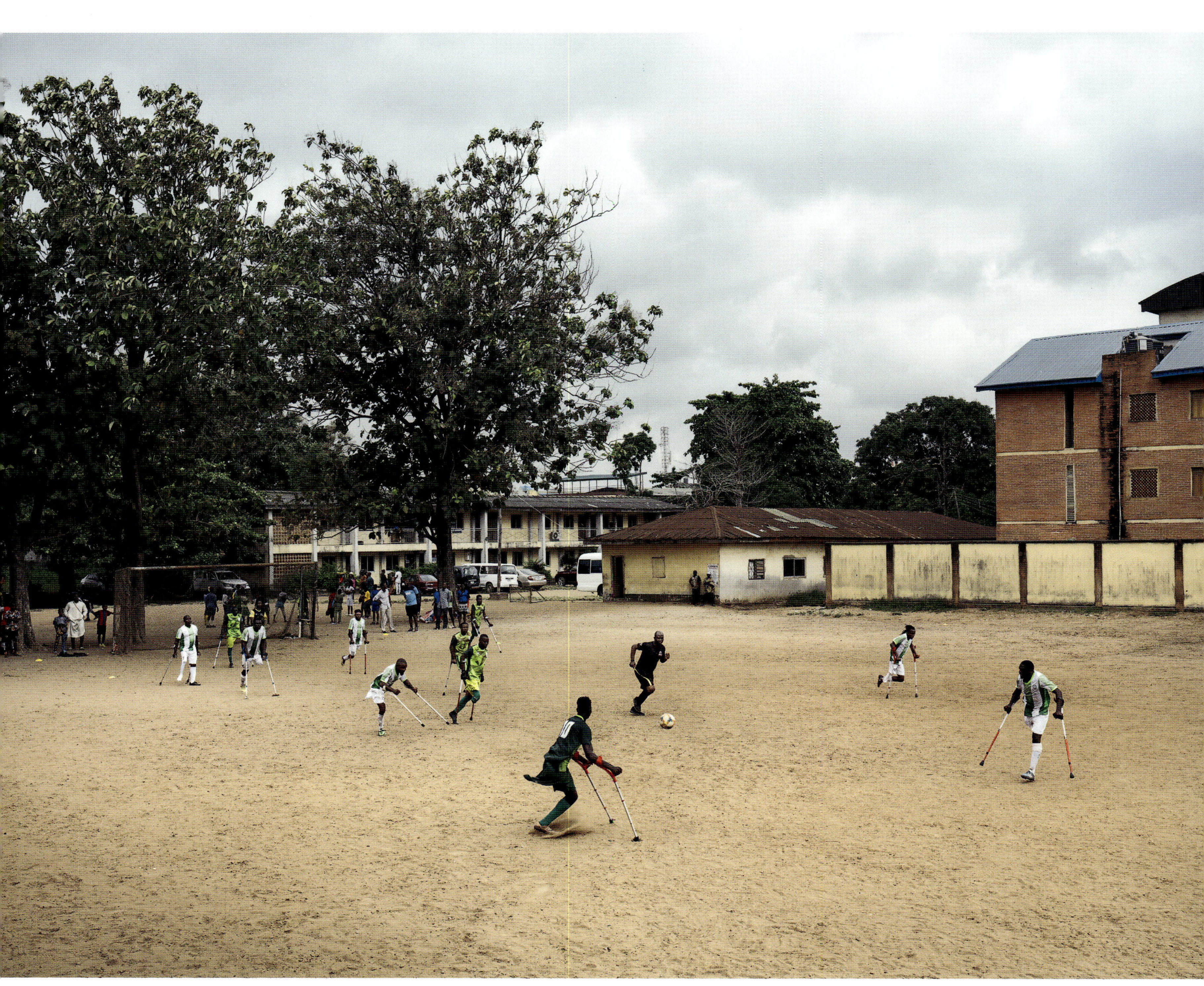

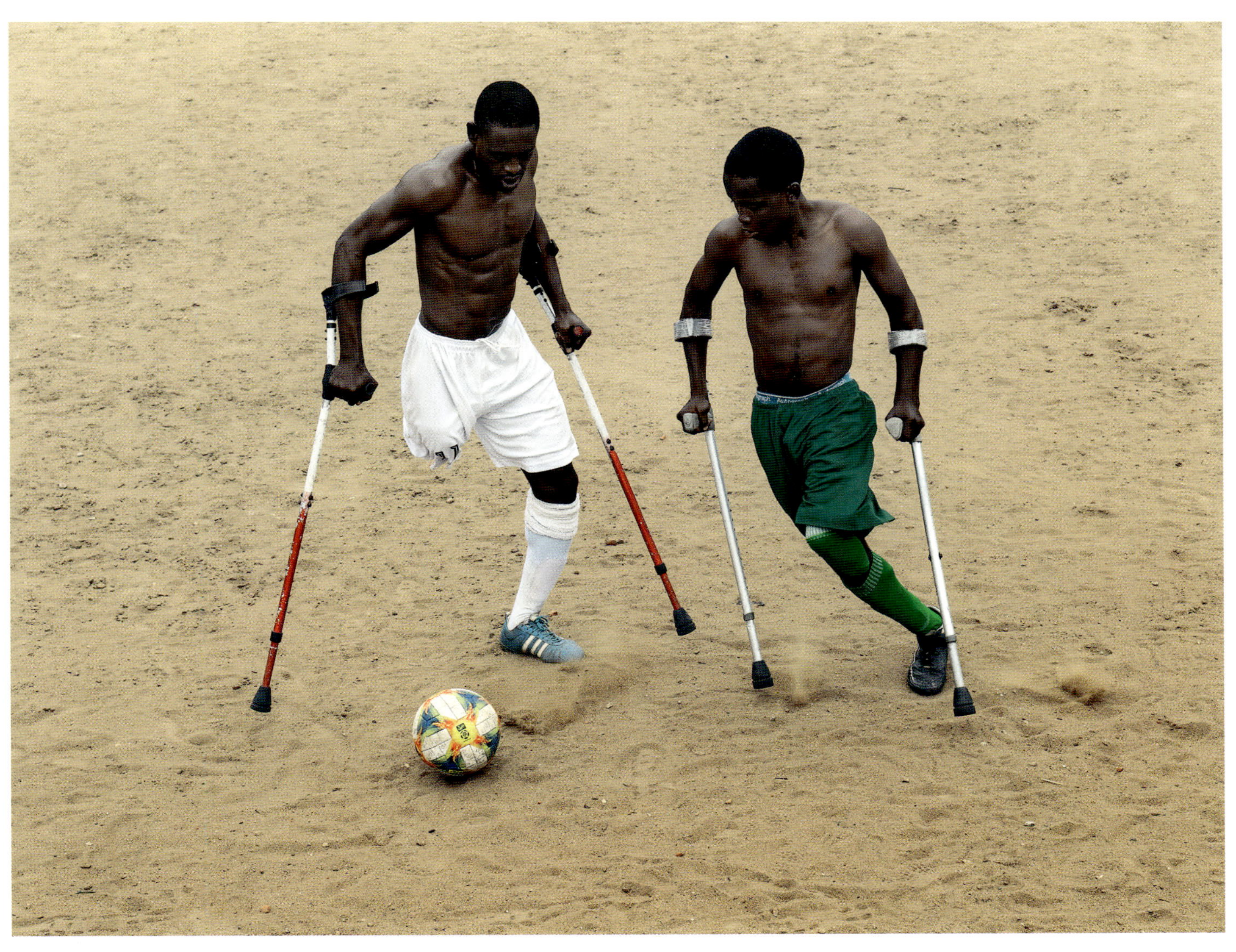

The Special Eagles team are role models for the less
fortunate, representing hope and the belief that all dreams
are achievable regardless of the obstacles one faces.

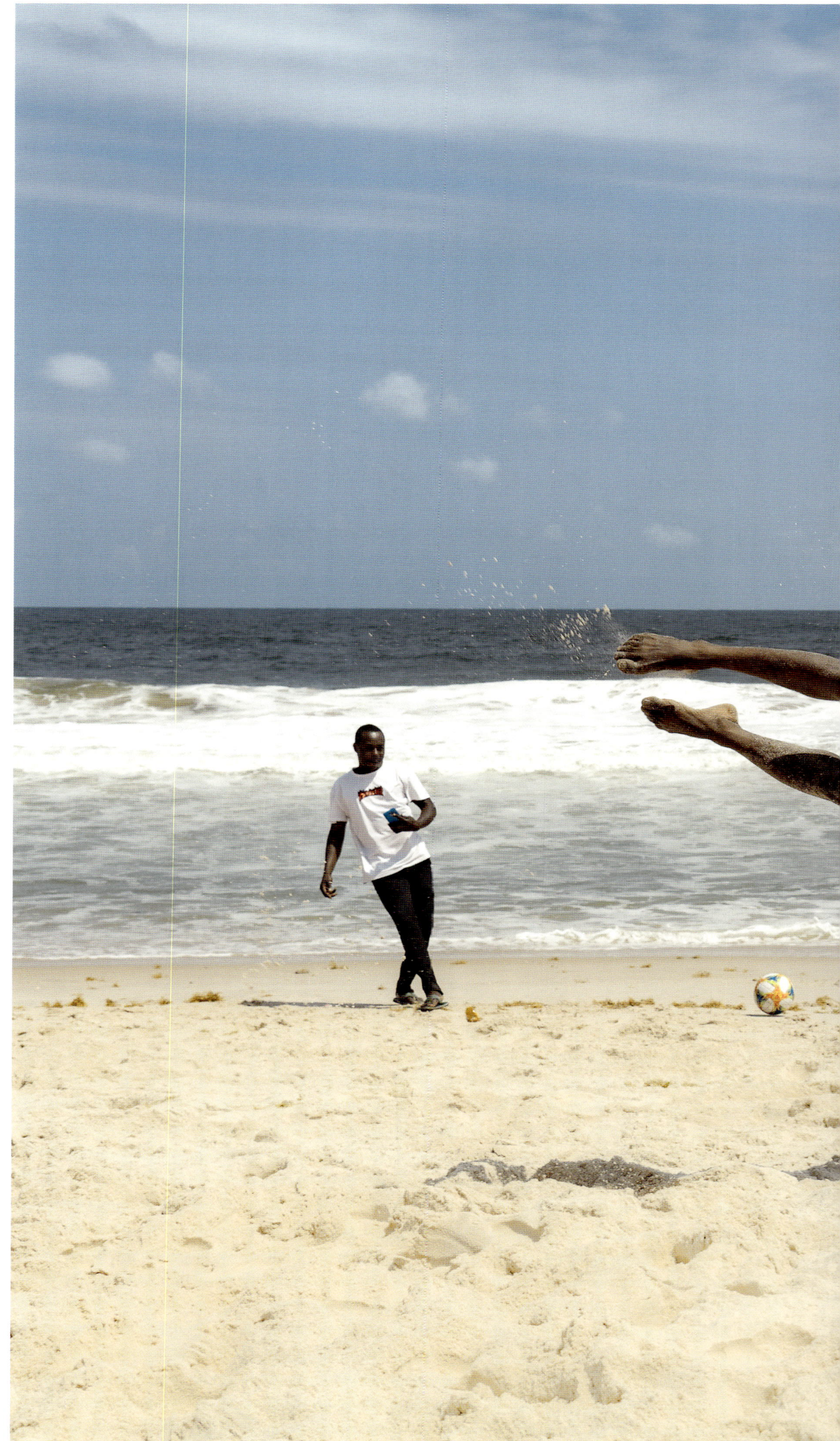

Unfortunately, most accidents
that happened on the field that
led to amputations were due to
poor medical treatment, forever
altering the course of their lives.

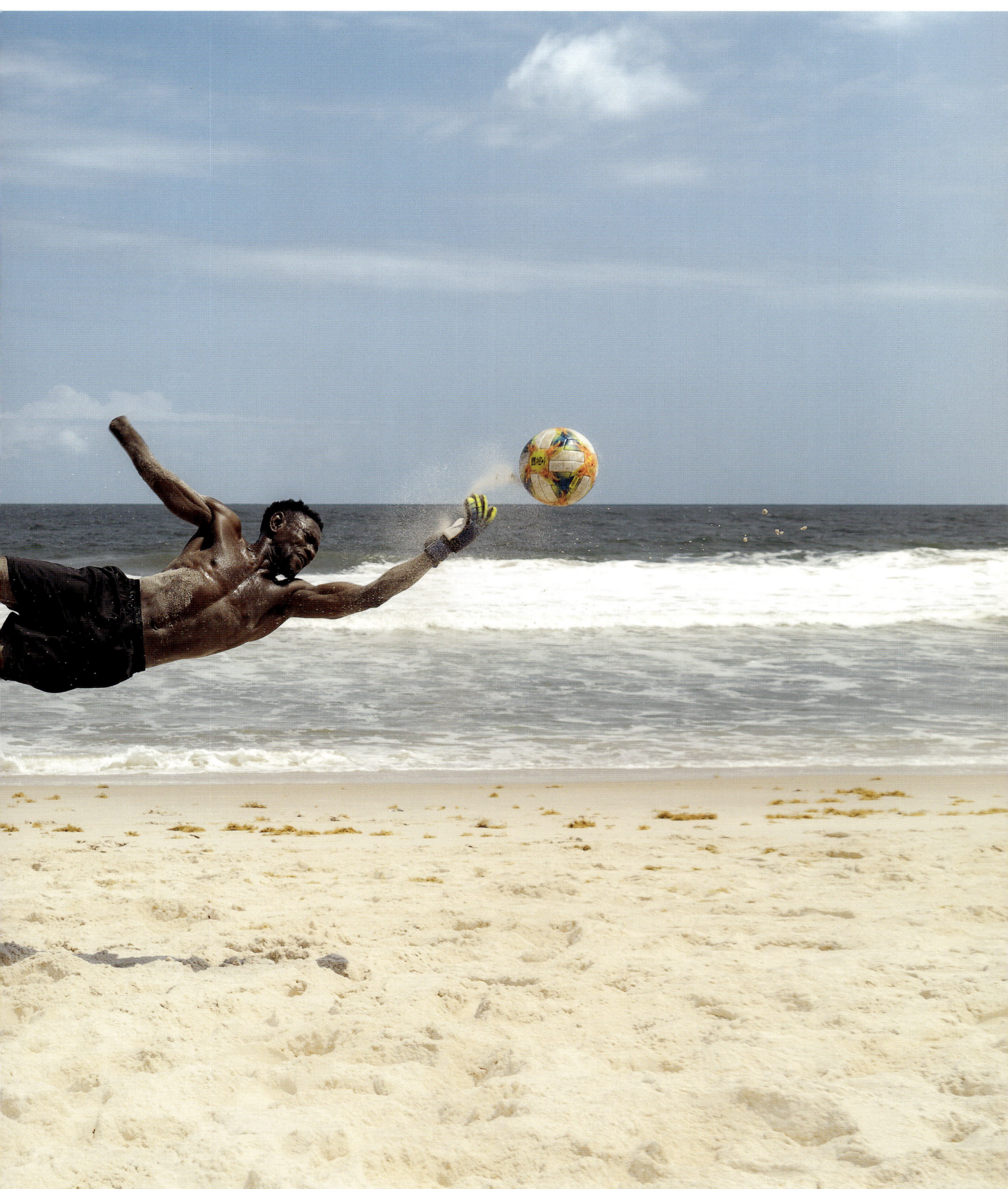

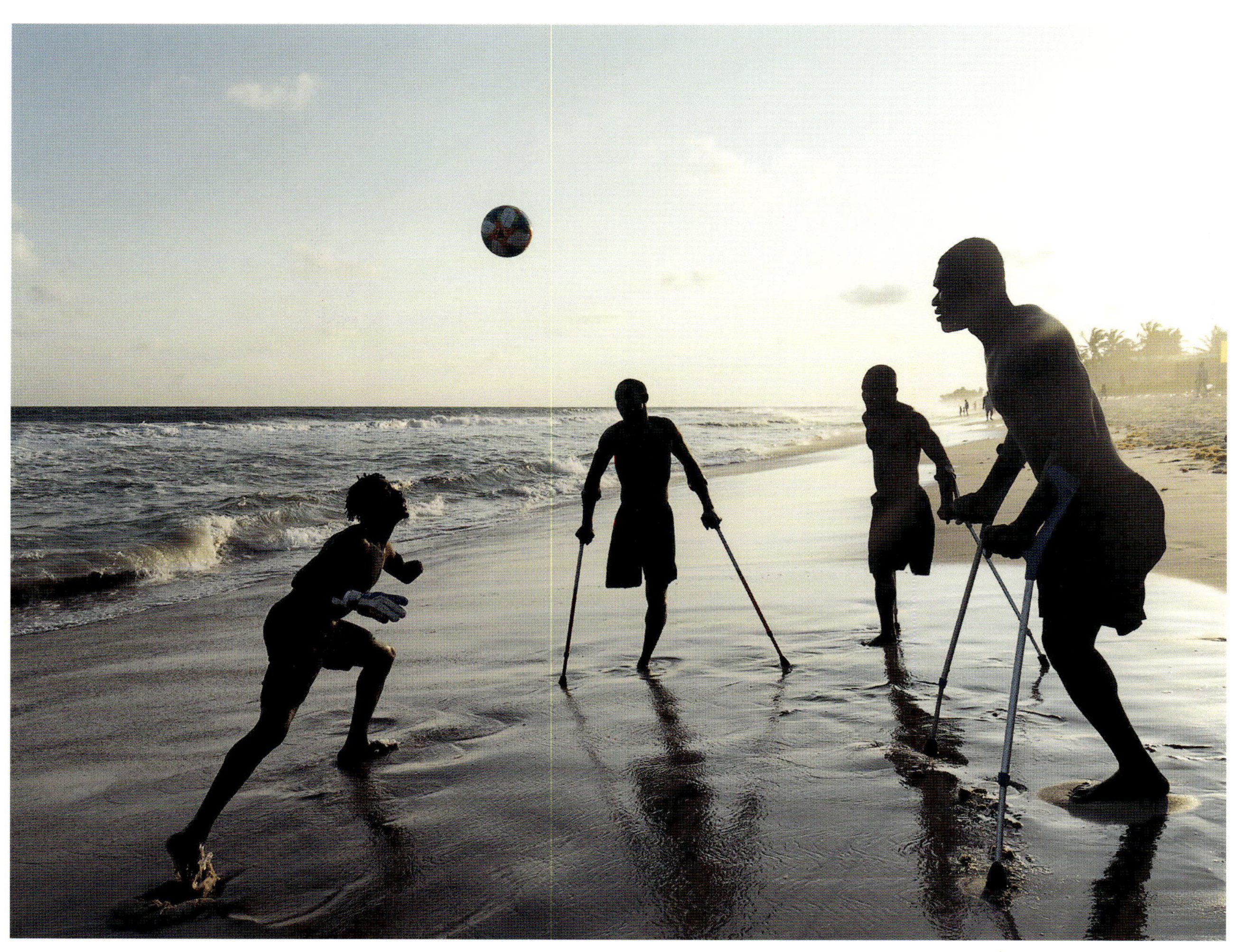

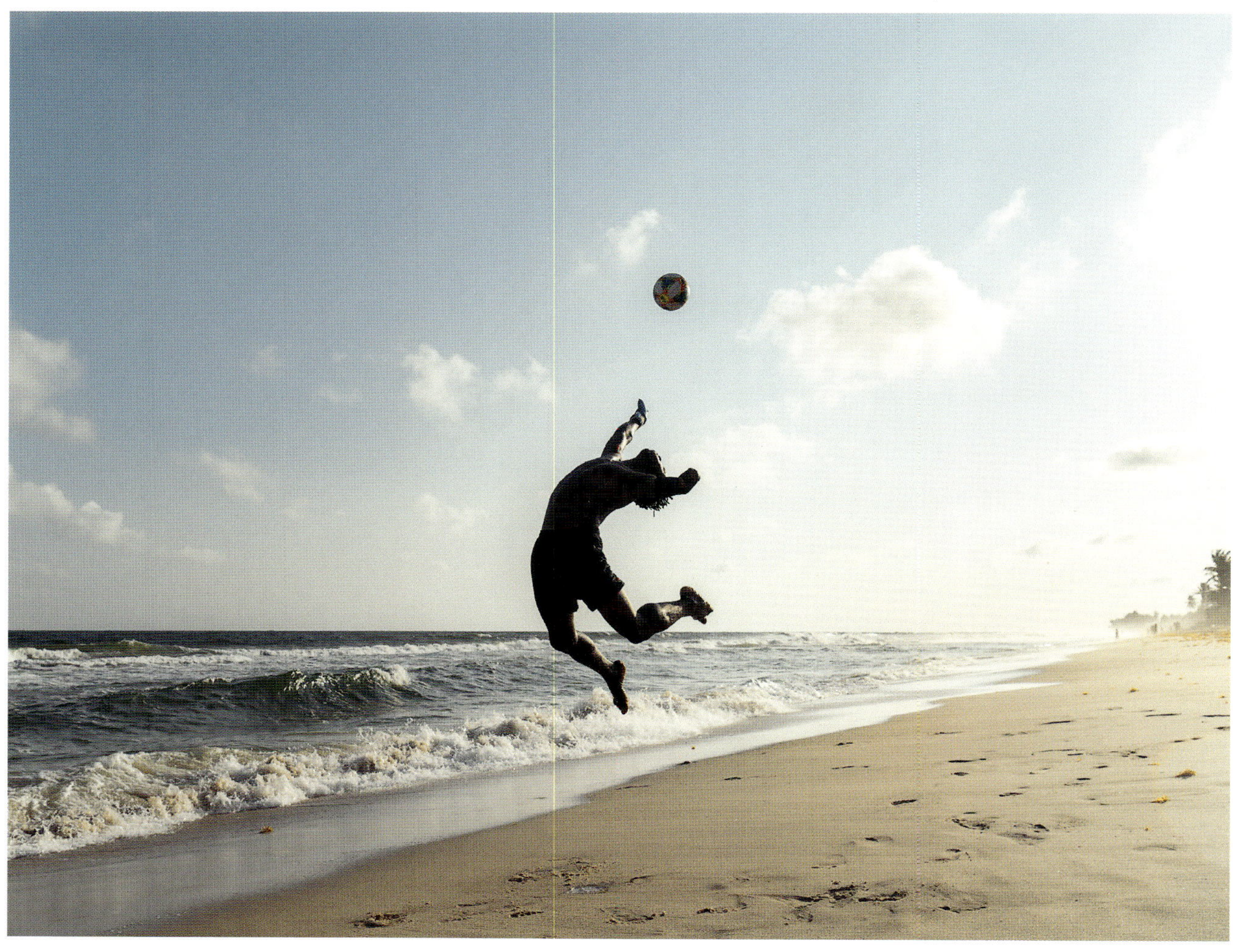

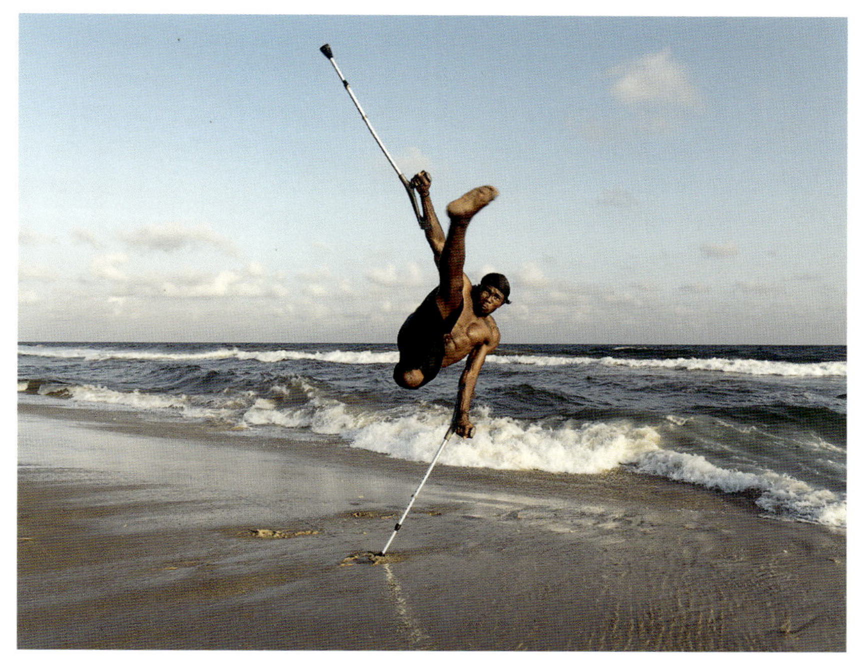

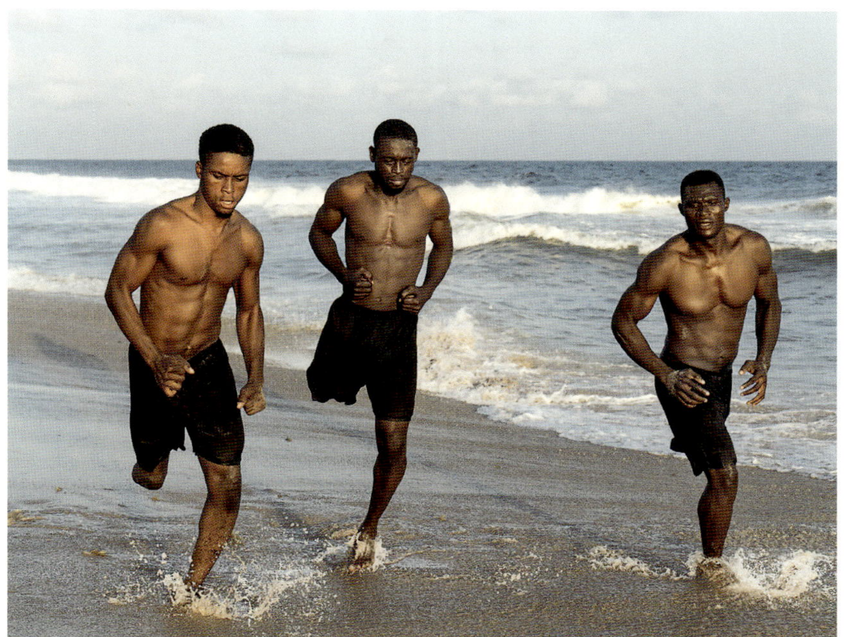

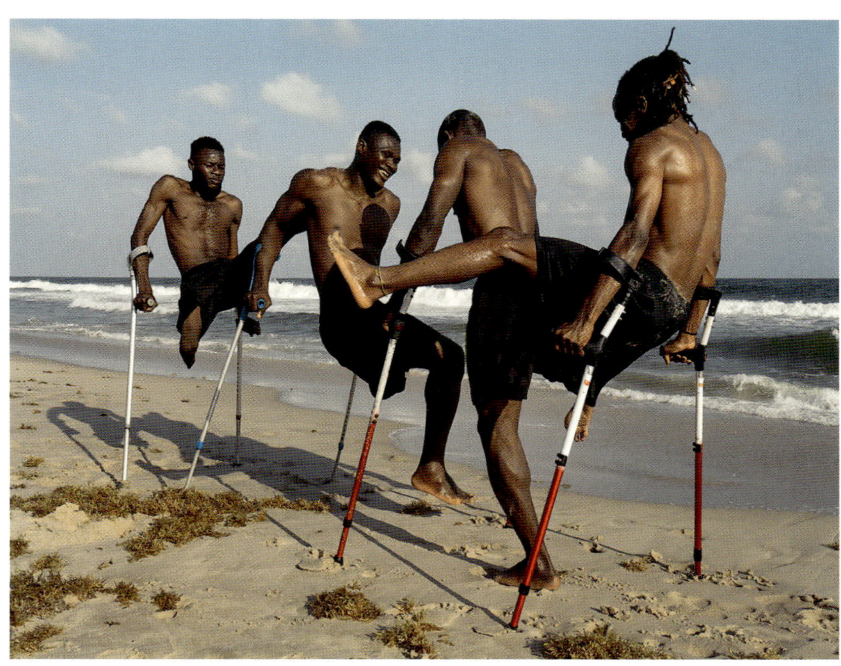

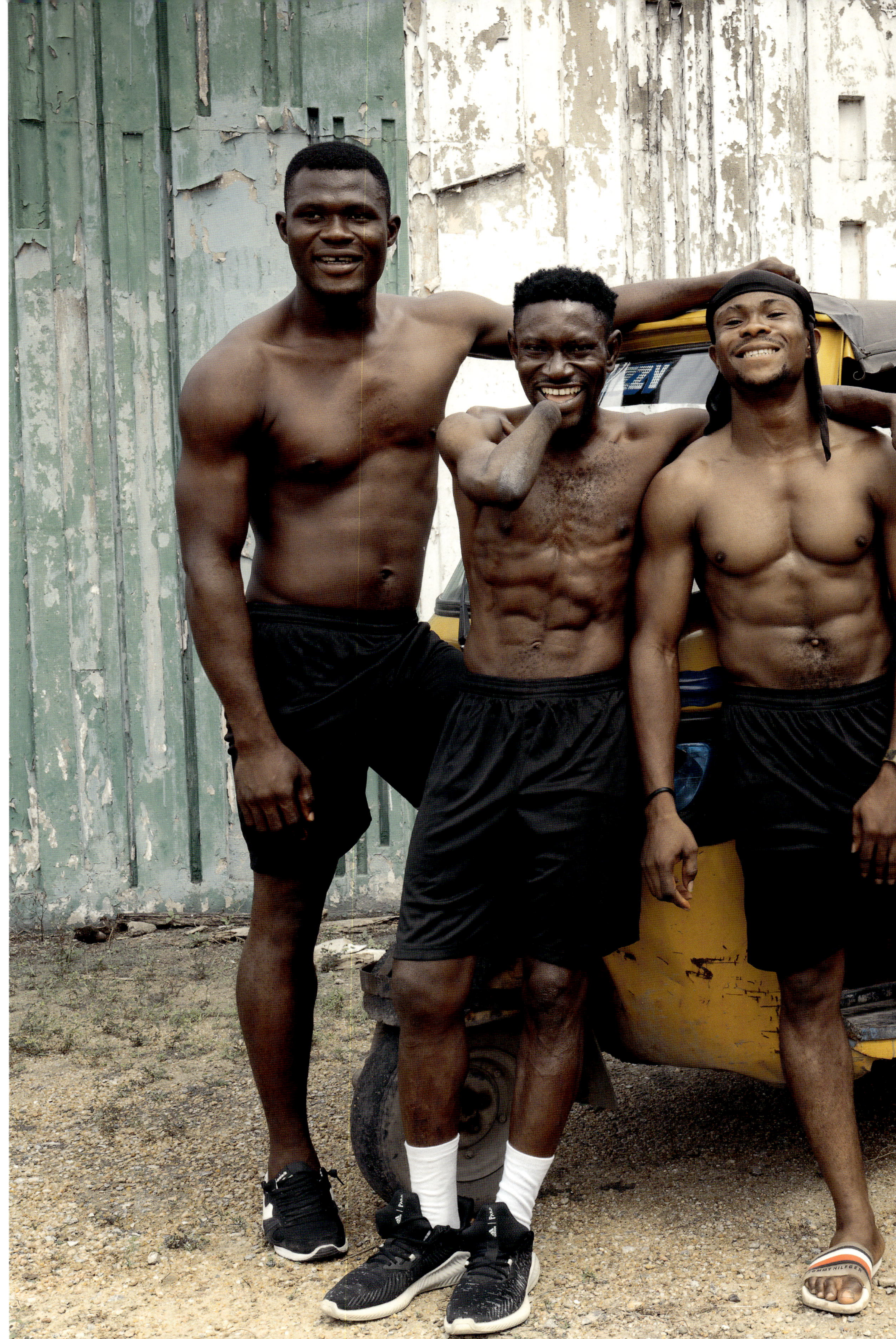

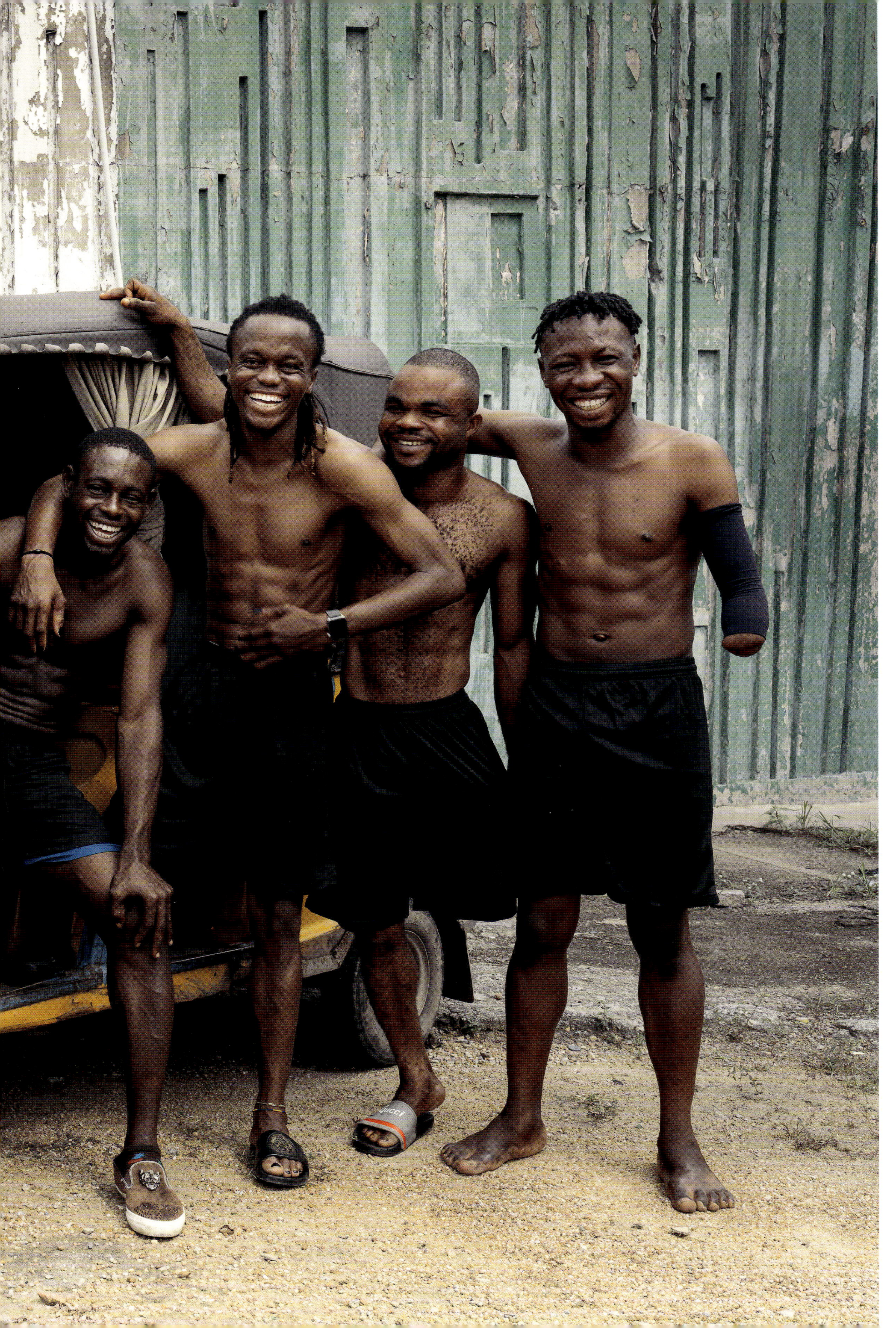

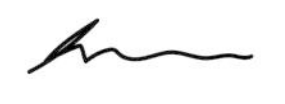

Boxing Ladies

CUBA

*An entirely new revolution is bubbling up, one of
equality and the right of women to fight.*

In the middle of the sweltering heat of the Caribbean, the battered and tattered island of
Cuba basks in its reputation for producing scores of successful boxers, winning more
Olympic medals than any other nation since Fidel Castro's revolution. But an entirely new
revolution is bubbling up, one of equality and of women's right to fight: Cuba's female boxers are trying to pound their way through the old, rigid rules that value beauty over brawn.

For over a hundred years, boxing has been a national pastime in Cuba. It grew in popularity
in the 1930s, and after the revolution in 1959, training programs were implemented
throughout the island. Between 1972 and 1980, Cuban boxers cleaned up at the Olympics
and became known for a boxing technique closely related to dance, emphasising precision and style rather than power. The father of this style is the renowned Alcides Sagarra
Carón, who played a pivotal role in developing the country's tremendous pride for its dis-
tinctive boxing tradition, which has garnered thirty-seven Olympic gold and seventy-six
World Championship medals – all won by men. With all this boxing history under the country's belt, you would think that bringing women into the ring wouldn't be such a giant leap.

HAVANA,
LA HABANA

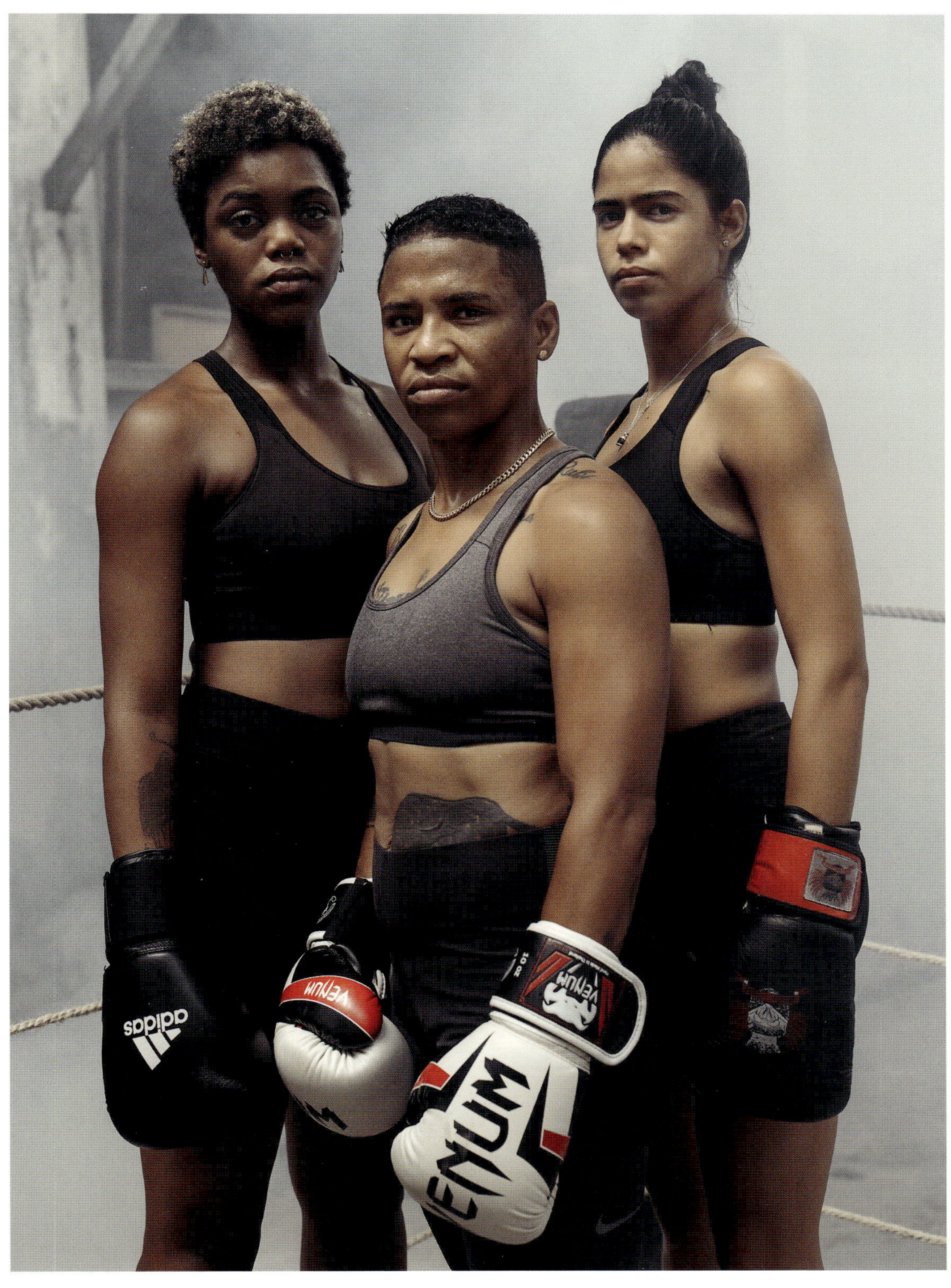

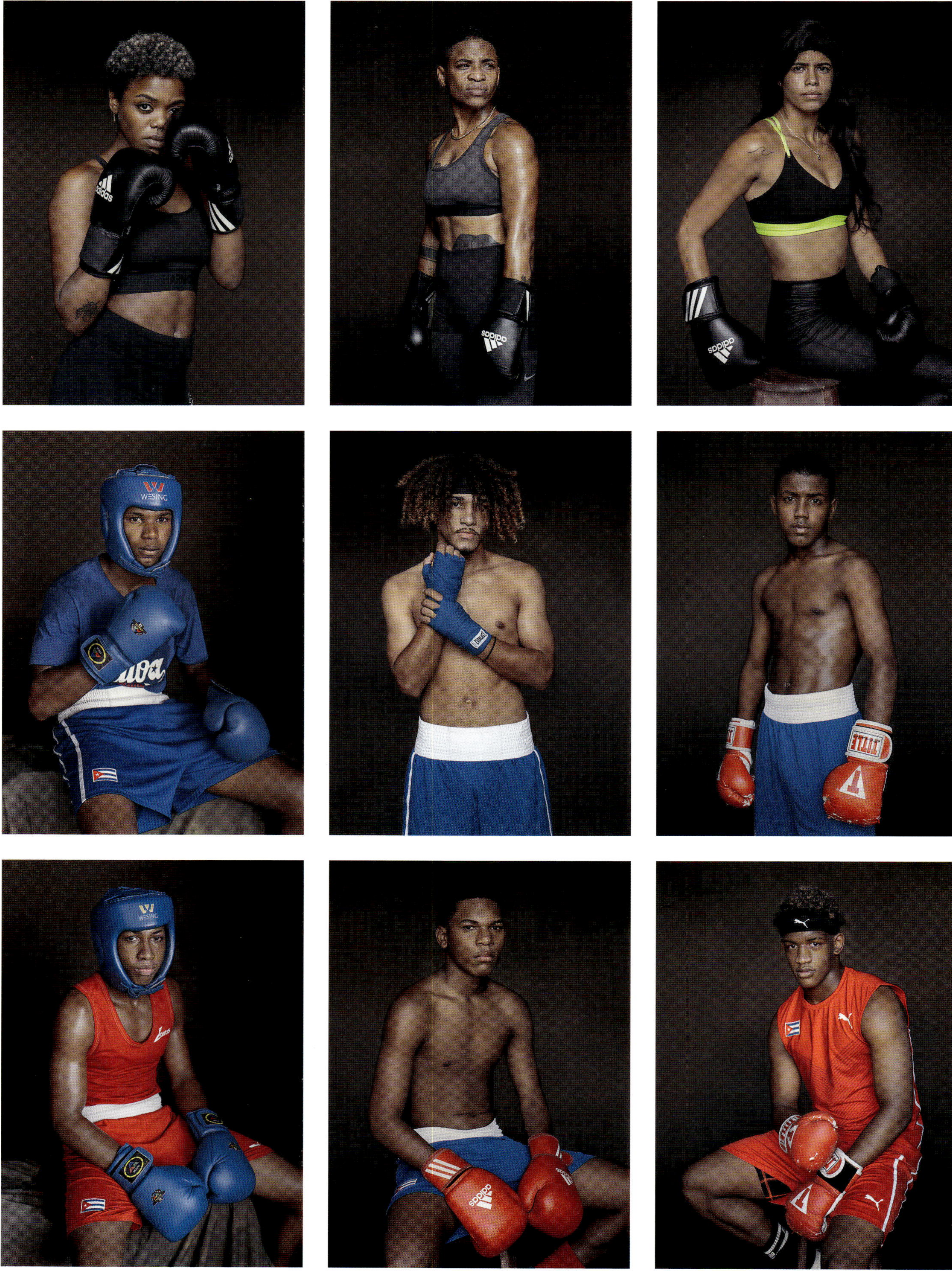

Astonishingly, Cuba is one of the few countries in the world where women's boxing remains banned despite women's participation in other Olympic sports such as wrestling, weightlifting and judo. To this day, the long-held macho belief that boxing is a man's sport and too dangerous for women persists. Raul Castro's late wife, Vilma Espin, believed that women should not engage in such activities, as they risk damaging their beauty. But these attitudes have not discouraged up-and-coming generations of female fighters; instead, such antiquated notions have awakened a rebellion.

In a world full of selfies, Botox and anti-ageing creams, it's a wonder that women still manage to rise above the sexist media and advertising; even more surprising is that this uprising is taking place in a country as isolated and downtrodden as Cuba. So what makes women want to engage in this controversial and skilful yet brutal sport that dates back more than five thousand years to ancient Sumer and ancient Greece?

With all its adrenaline, excitement, and hype, this love-it-or-hate-it sport attracts fans worldwide. For many female fighters, it's become more than just a form of self-defence – it's about athletic mastery. Young women such as Idamelys Moreno and her sparring partners Arisnelvis Capa and Arianna Arrieta have followed in the footsteps of the pioneering Namibia Flores Rodriguez, who painstakingly tried to pave their way. Unfortunately, the rusty doors of Cuban bureaucracy would not open for Rodriguez despite her years of training, skill and determination.

The birthplace of Cuban boxing sits amid colourful vintage cars, brightly painted murals, lively music and the dilapidated baroque buildings of Havana – its crumbling streets fading like an old movie star. The legendary Rafael Trejo, the city's oldest gym with its open-air arena and spartan facilities, is where male boxers now make room for their female counterparts. Olympic silver medal winner Emilio Correa Jr. is also rising to the challenge by offering them valuable tips and tricks.

'Cuban women cannot be denied their rights to participate in boxing competitions. It is only a matter of time before women take their place among the sport's icons,' says eighty-five-year-old Dr Alcides Sagarra Carón, teacher, trainer and creator of the Cuban school of boxing.

Cuba's outdated, chauvinistic playground is begging for these gutsy gals to trail-blaze their way into international rings. The last round in this fight will be to wake the country up from a century-long siesta and allow these mighty maidens a chance to bask in the sun and relish in their right to fight.

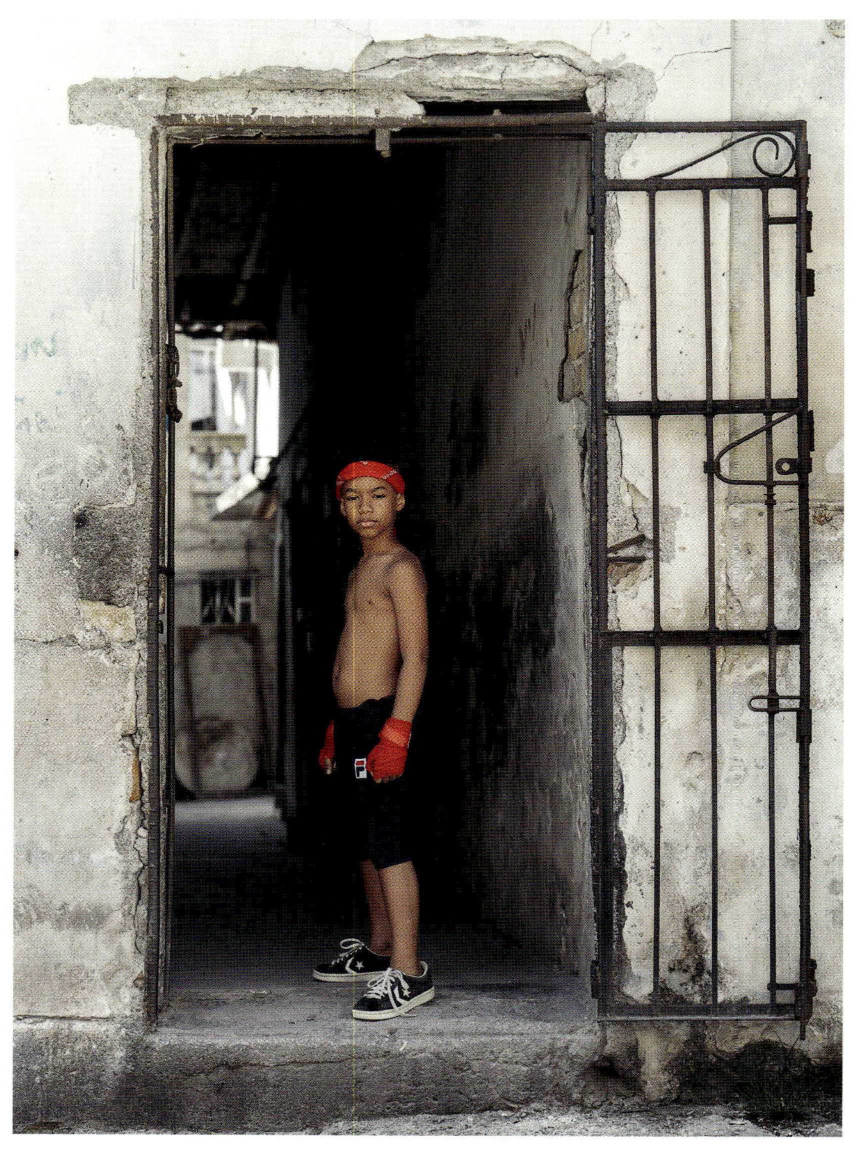

Boxing is one of the most popular sports in Cuba
after baseball, and children dream of becoming
pro-boxers, giving them a chance at a better life.

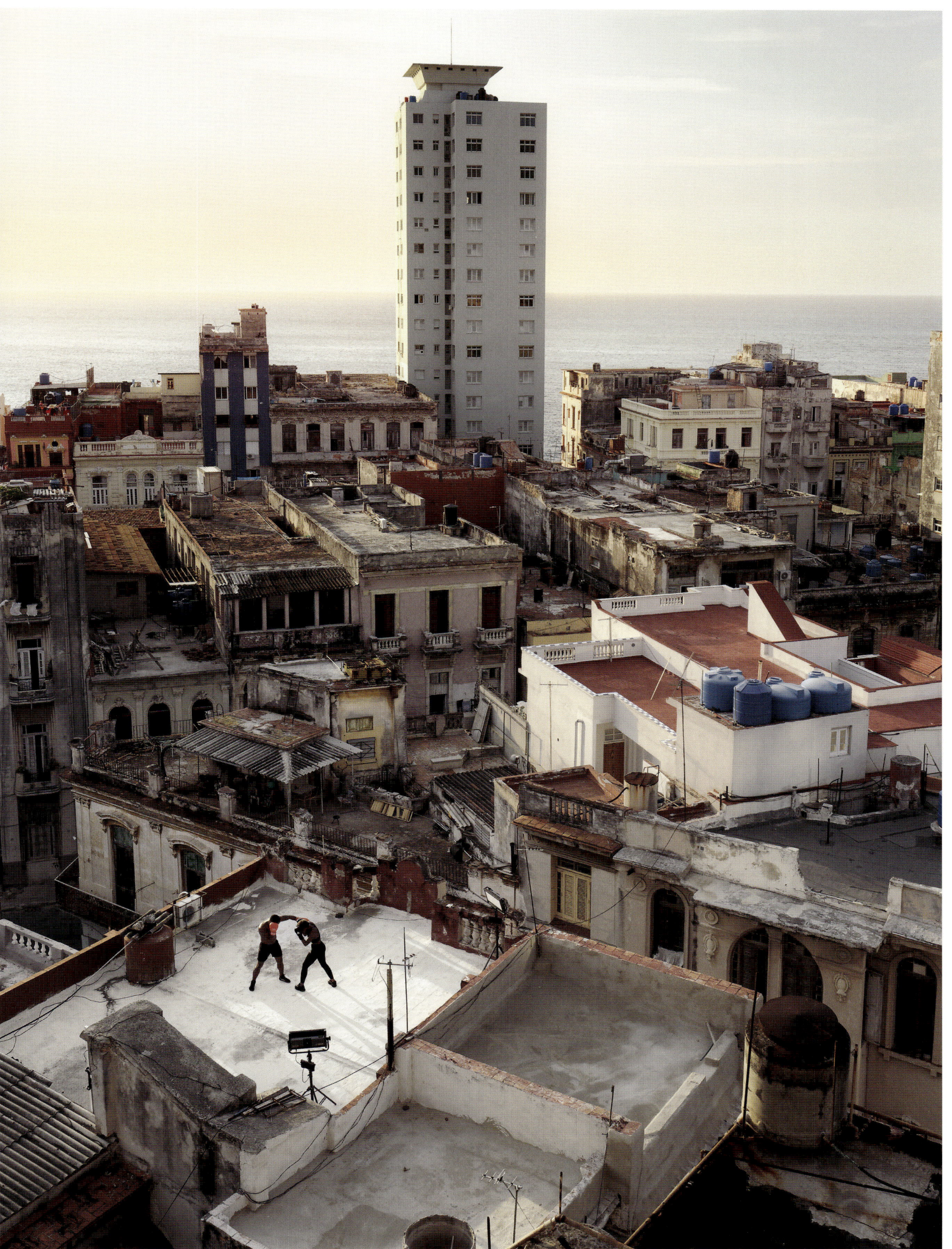

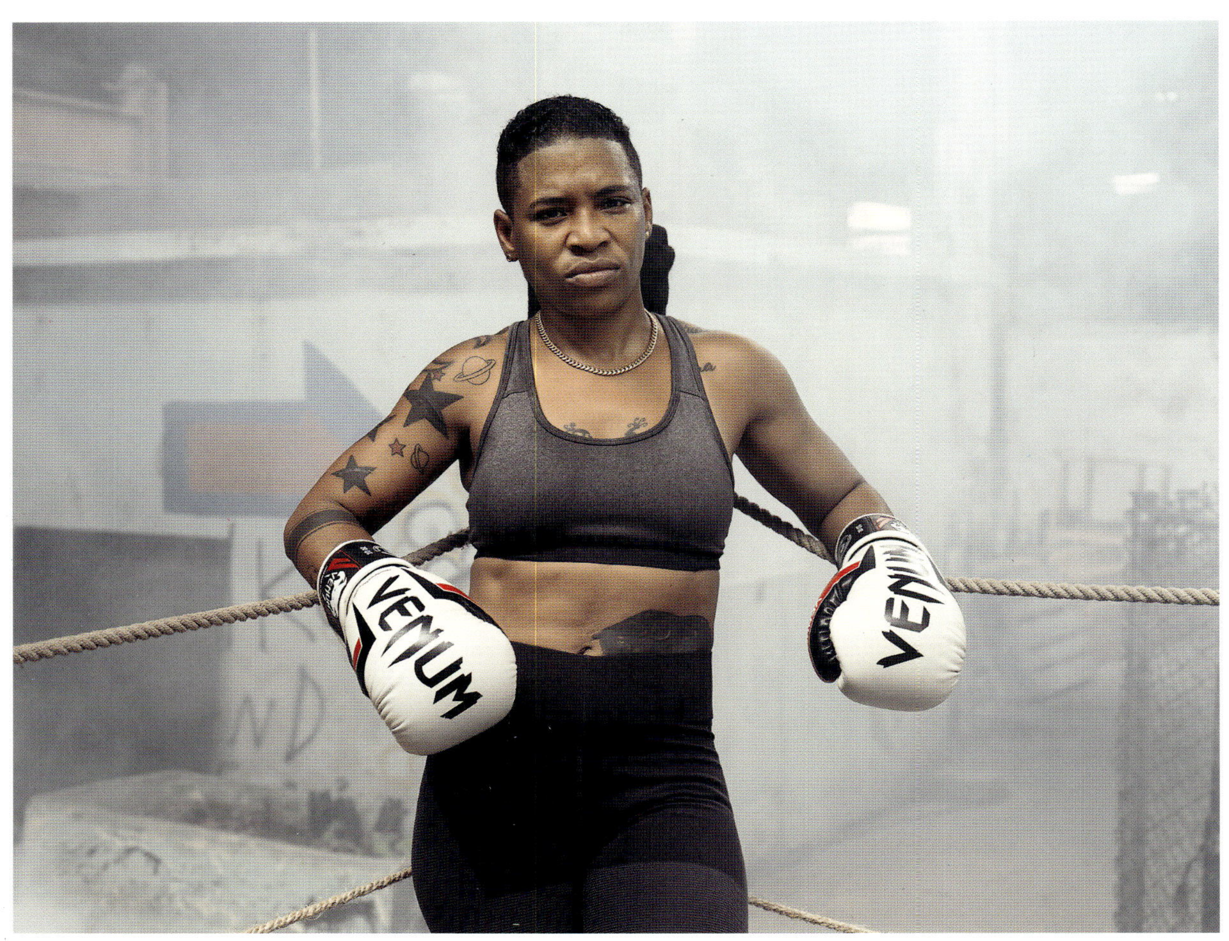

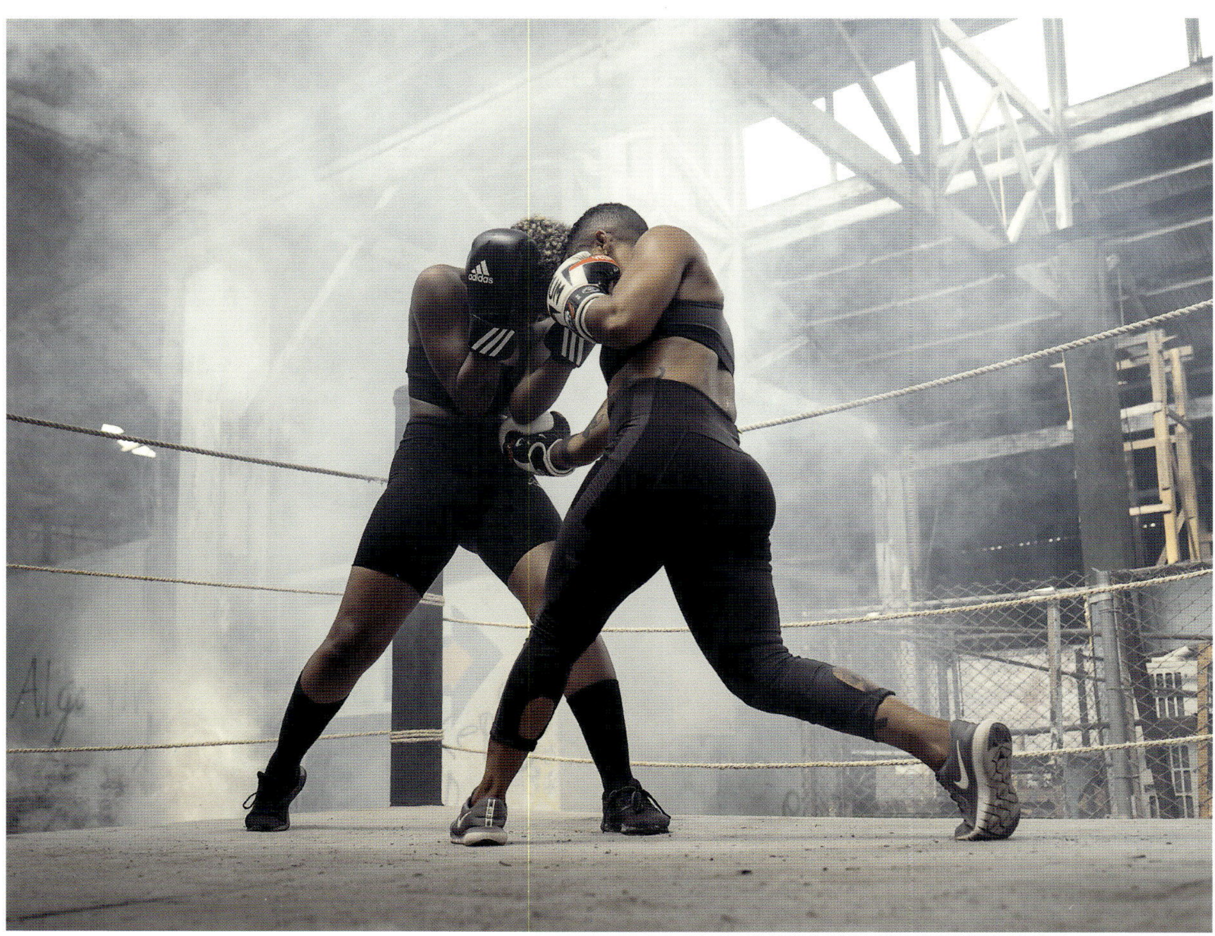

Cuba's female boxers hold onto Namibia Flore's dream
of representing their country as Olympic champions.

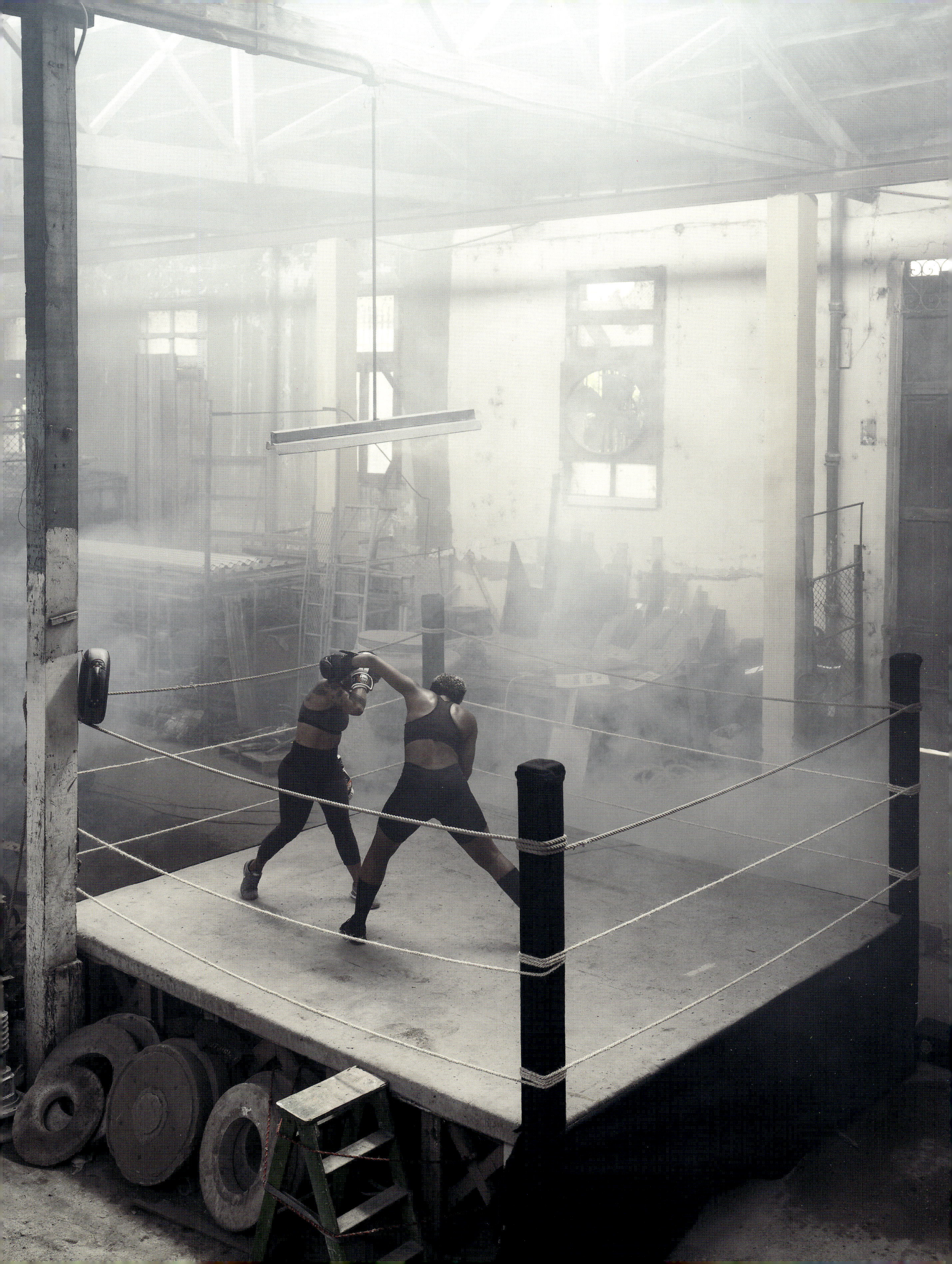

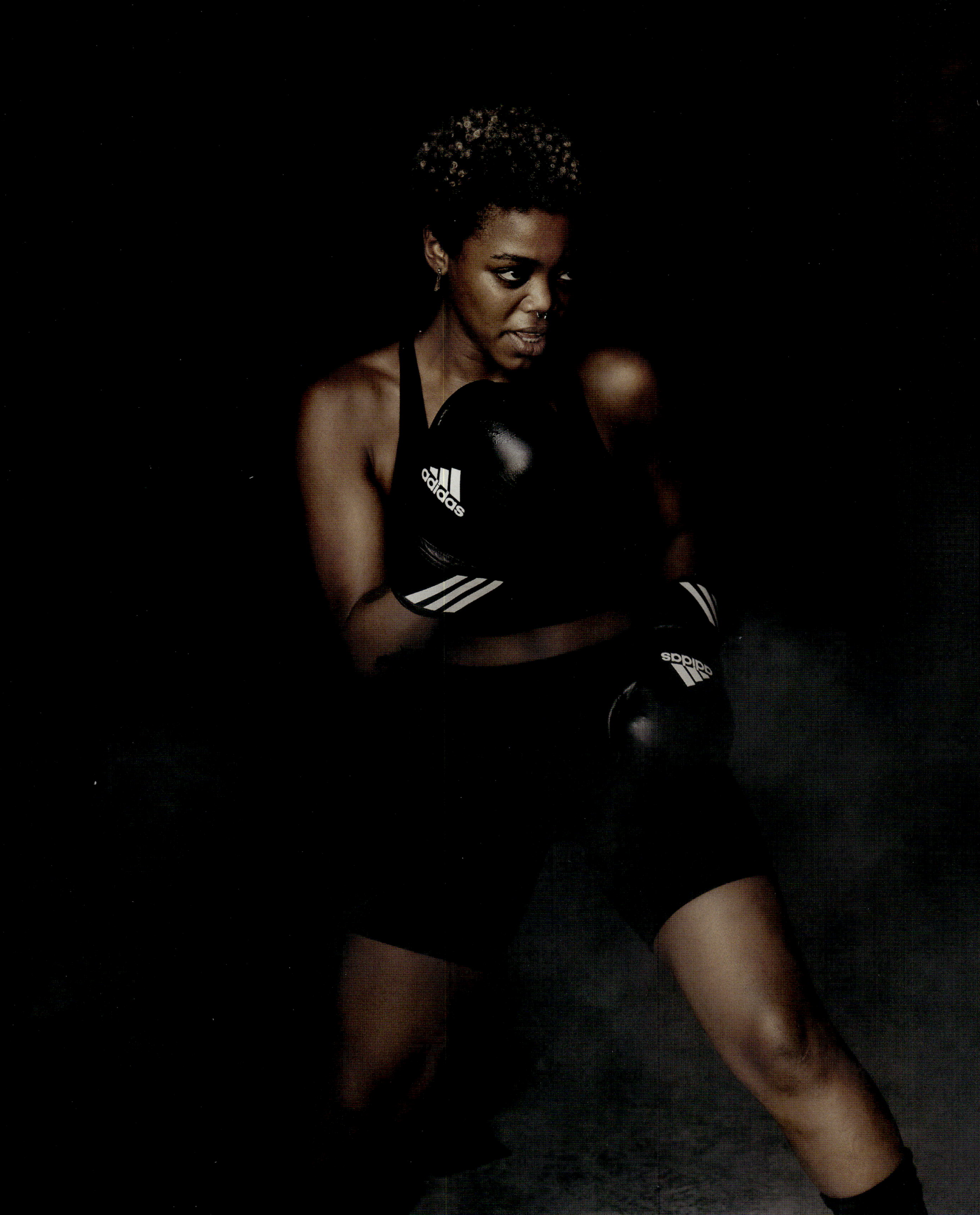

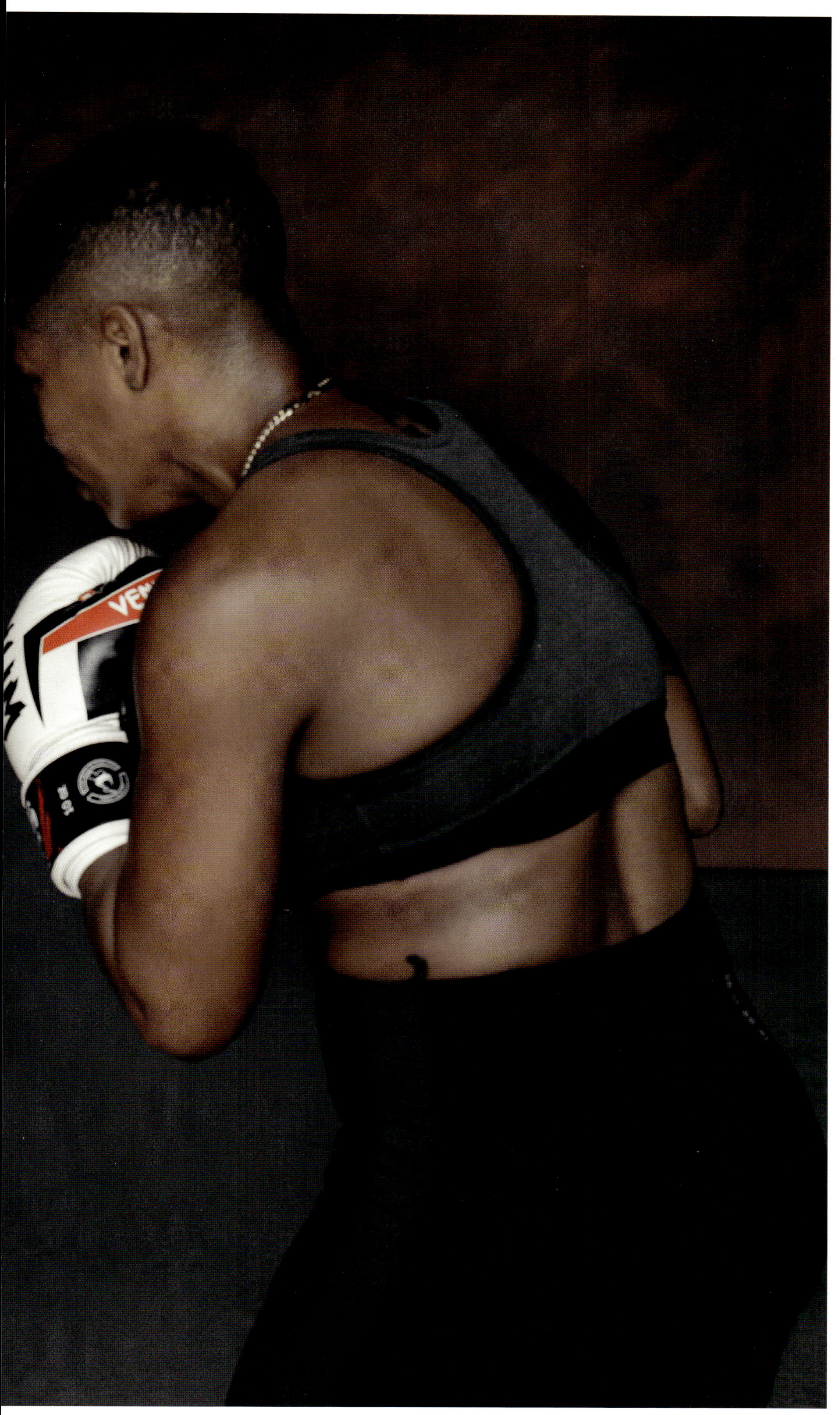

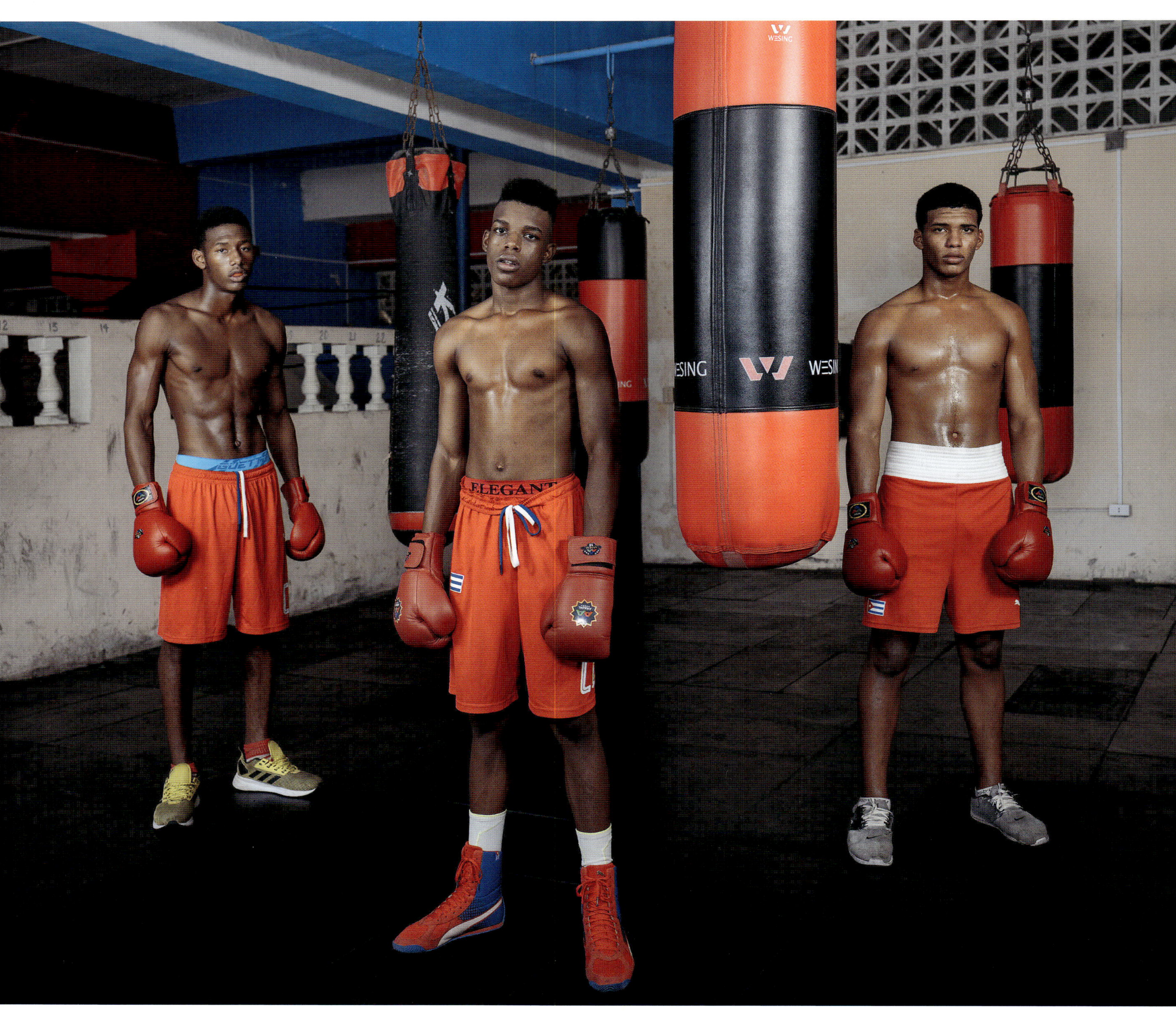

Cuba's national boxing team is one of the most successful in the world, and their secret is to start training youngsters from a very young age.

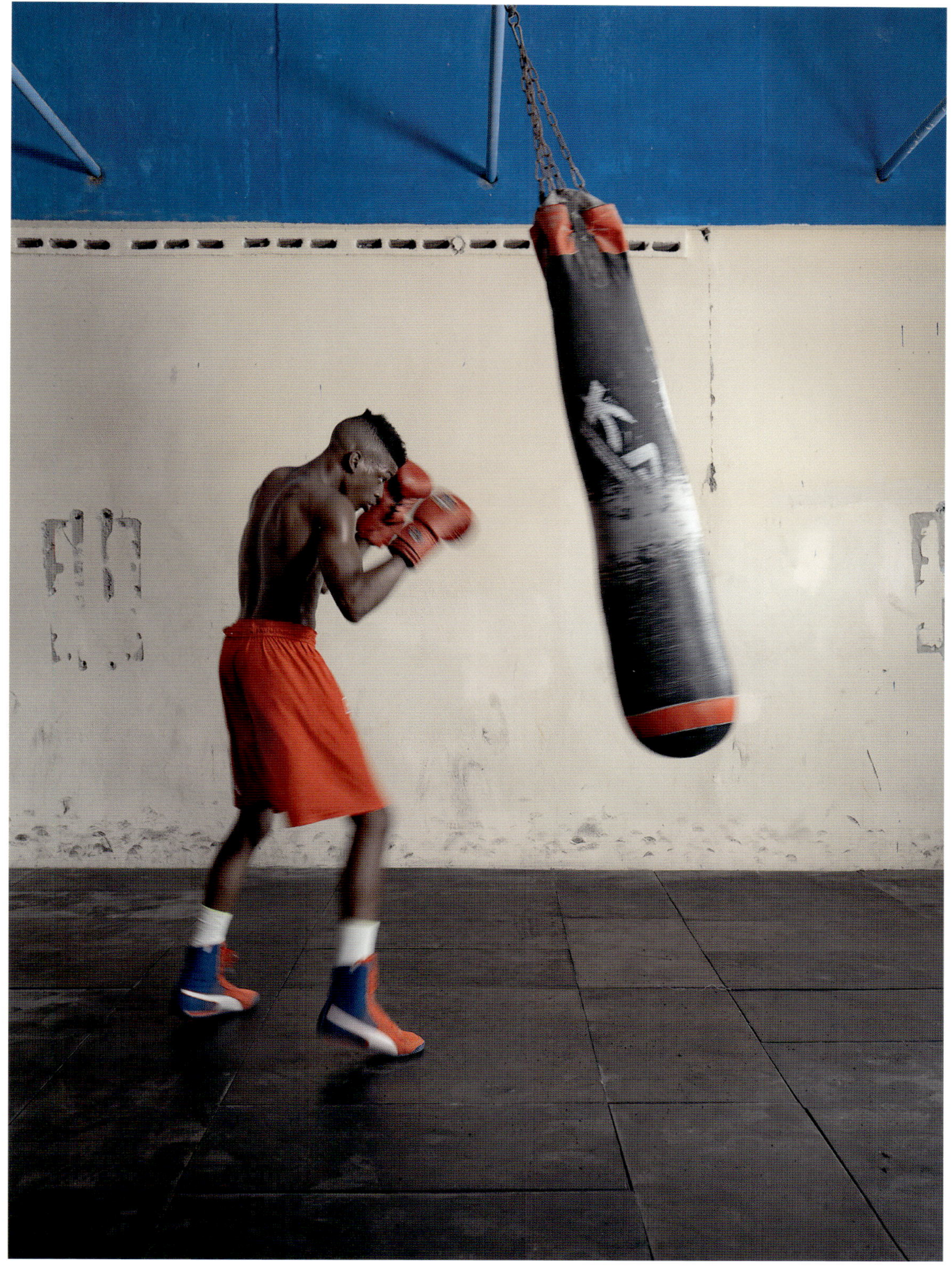

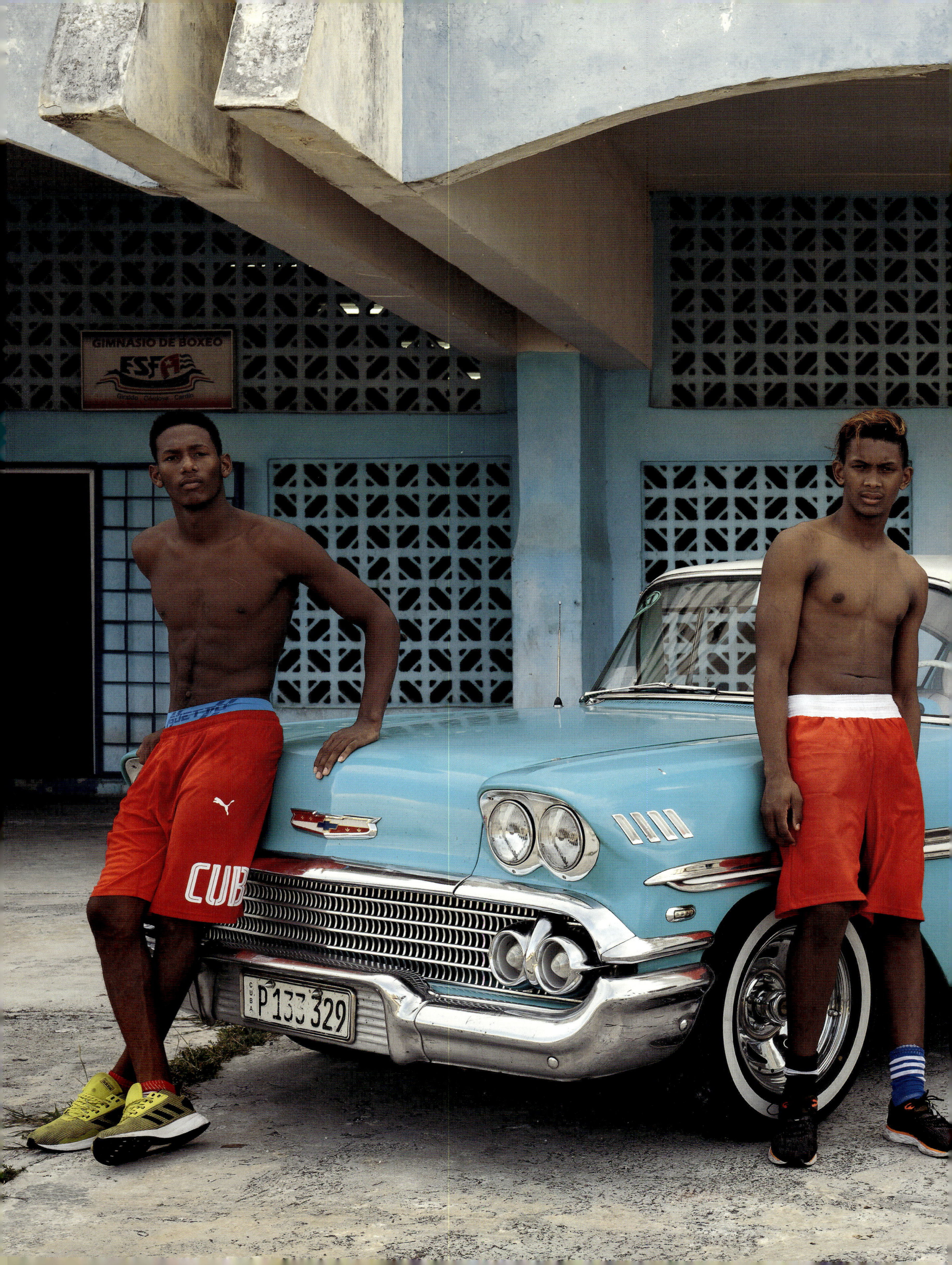

GIMNASIO DE BOXEO
FSFA
CUBA
CUBA   P 133 329

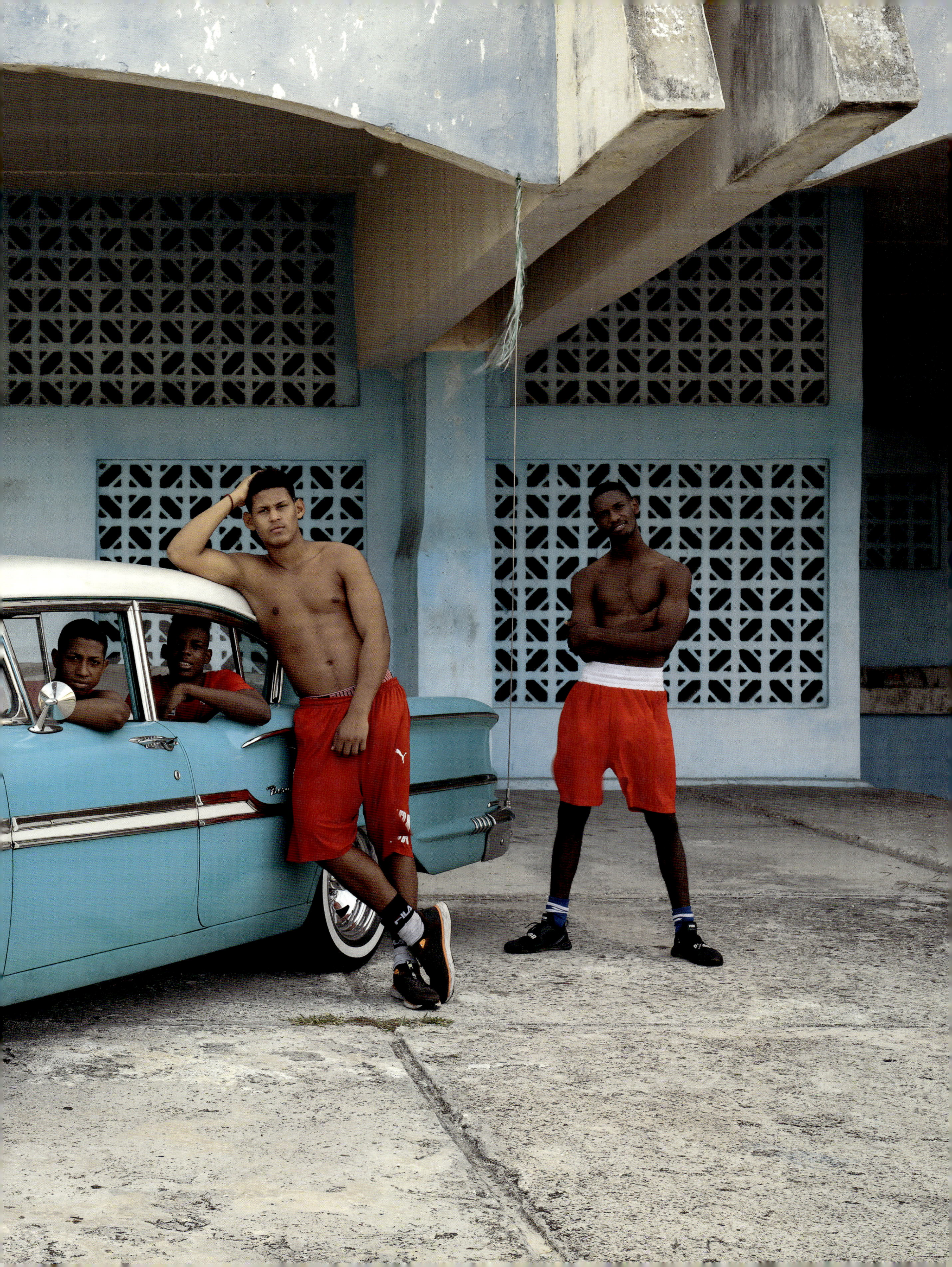

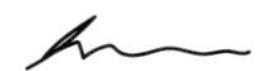

Course Landaise

FRANCE

*Both man and animal are judged on
their artistic and athletic merit.*

The eternal clash between man and beast dramatically plays out in southwestern Les Landes, France, a richly forested coastal area where the art of ducking, diving and dodging a charging cow has become more of an acrobatic feat than a blood sport. *Course landaise* is an ancient style of bullfighting that may date as far back as the Minoan civilization. Archaeologists have found ancient Greek paintings and artefacts depicting both men and women springing through the air over a charging bull – a surprising portrayal of gender inclusivity.

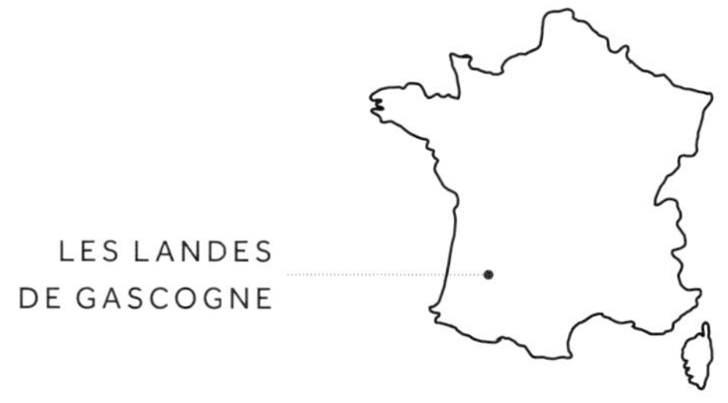

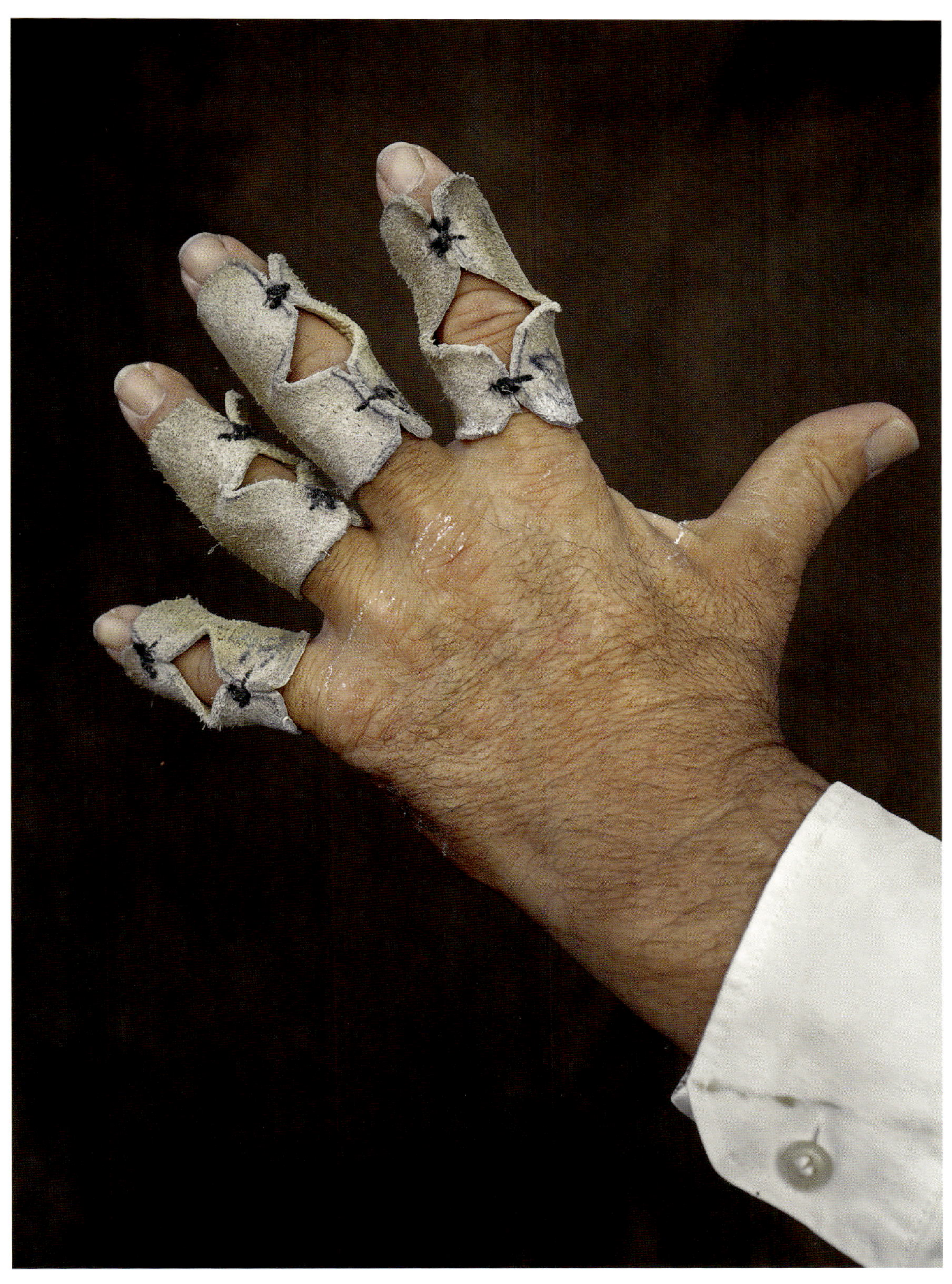

The cordier (rope operator) protects his hands and fingers
while holding onto a cow weighing over 300 kilos.

This particular incarnation of the acrobatic sport was developed in the 1400s when cows were released and ran through the streets during the celebration of Saint-Jean. It also goes back to the tradition of branding cows in the dunes, considered a less dangerous place to do so; jumping over cows in the sand then developed into a game of courage and bravery. Today, *course landaise* is an established sport with its own schools and is part of the National Federation holding regular championships. The season begins in March and ends in October, with as many as six hundred events held per year.

Unlike bullfighting, this unique sport does not involve harming or killing animals and uses cows rather than bulls. It is also so specific to the region that many French people have never heard of it. On this perilous playground, men face a stampeding cow equipped with nothing more than bravery and skill, gracefully leaping into a somersault and twisting out of harm's way within millimetres of the animal's deadly horns.

These are not ordinary cows; other breeds have been used in the game, but the *landaise* cow has endured the test of time, which is why it is the sport's namesake: *courses de vaches landaises* (landaise cow races). These specially bred cows are not reared for the dairy or meat industries; they are bred to be faster, smarter and lighter on their feet, effortlessly jumping over a two-meter (six-foot) fence. Individuals are named to gain notoriety and curry the audience's favour. The young cows enter a bullring for the first time at three or four years old and may go on competing for another ten years until they're retired to greener pastures. Some cows rise to stardom and may enjoy the spoils of an illustrious career, winning the highest honour – the Golden Horn award.

Both man and animal are judged on their artistic and athletic merit. *Course landaise* is more of a theatrical art form than a fighting sport, where courage, agility, style and speed are highly valued. The torero and the animal are not in a competition but a dance, as both perfect their moves, boldly gliding around one another in the sandy, open-air arena.

Course landaise is a community event, with big noisy groups enjoying a traditional feast at long tables, uniting family, friends and locals before the thrills of the competition. The air tingles with *joie de vivre* as everyone waits for their favourite toreros and prize-winning cows. Kicking it all off are big brass bands, playing loudly, proudly representing their locality.

As the cow stirs in the loge, its horns securely tied, *cordiers* (rope operators) and *entraîneurs* (wranglers) carefully set the stage by loosening the ropes enough for the cow to enter the arena. The *éscarteur* (dodger) taunts the cow to run towards him as he deftly changes direction in the nick of time. The cow lowers its head, readying itself to rush forward. The *sauteur* (leaper) runs directly at it, jumps straight up and corkscrews over its back, landing on his feet in enough time to swerve before the cow charges again and narrowly misses his arched back. The crowd gasps, jumps to its feet and cheers loudly as these daredevils perform unimaginable acts of bravery.

The primal desire to triumph over animals is not the only motivating factor behind this lively sport. These highly skilled athletes dedicate years of their lives to training, risking injury and possibly death to push themselves beyond their limits in search of perfection and, above all, self-mastery.

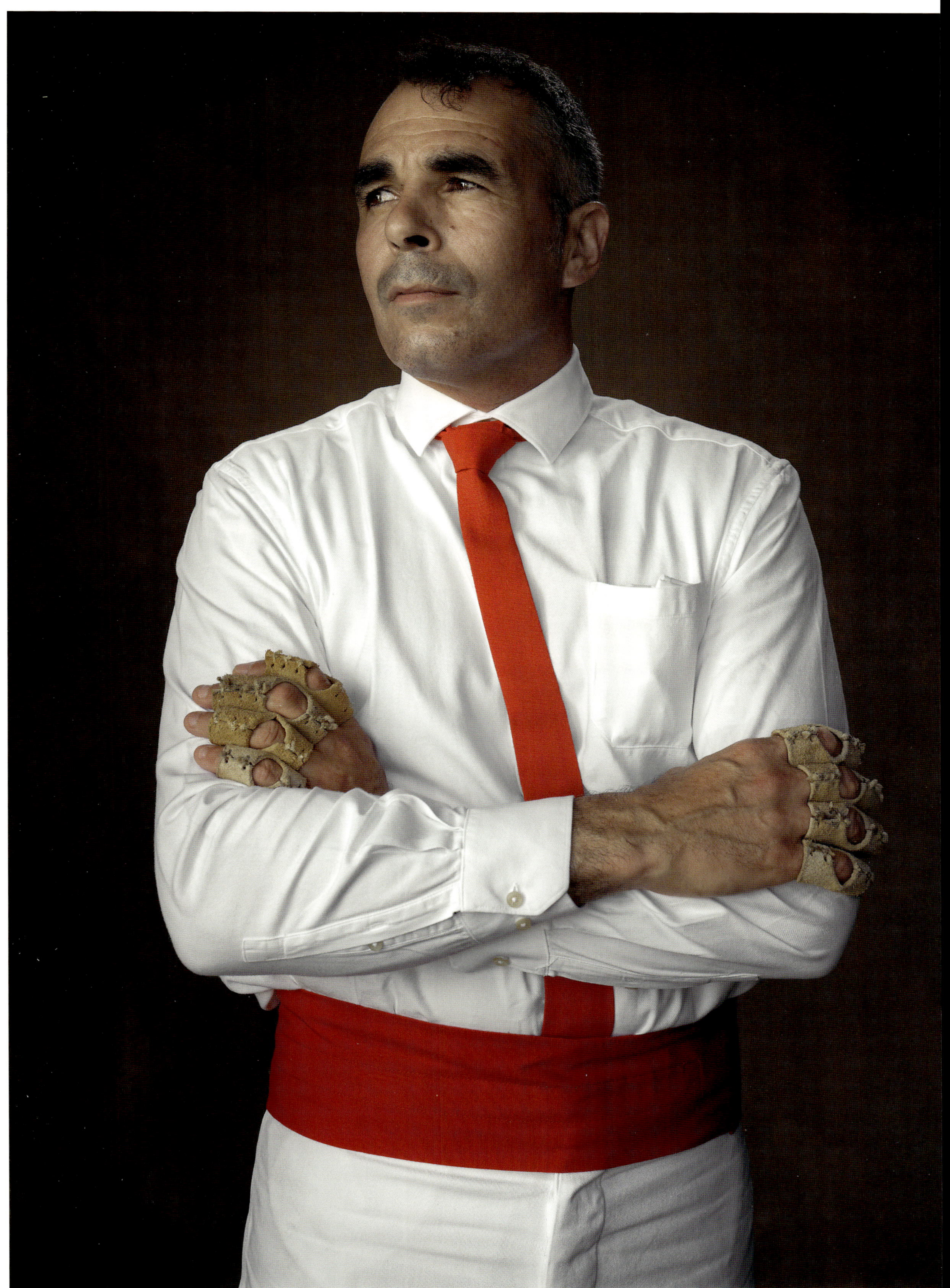

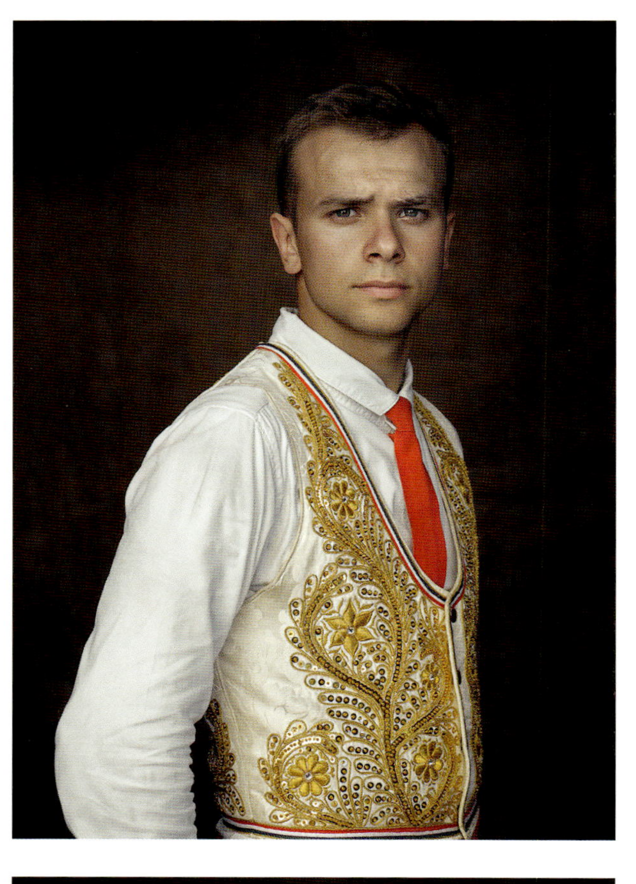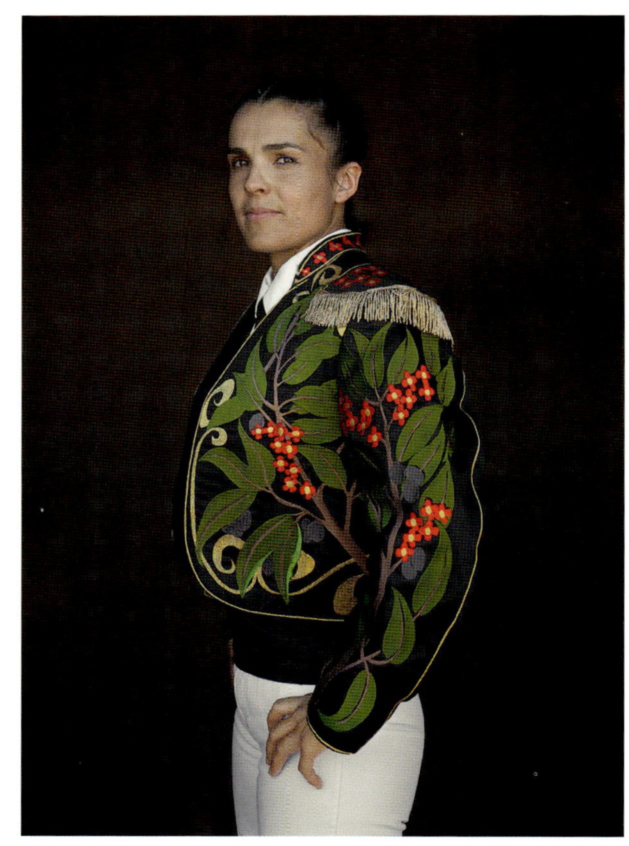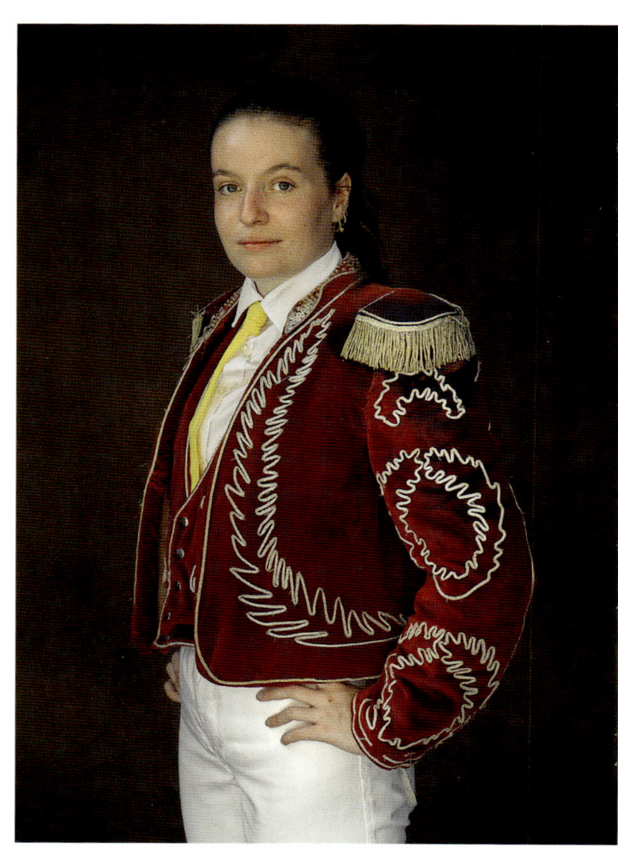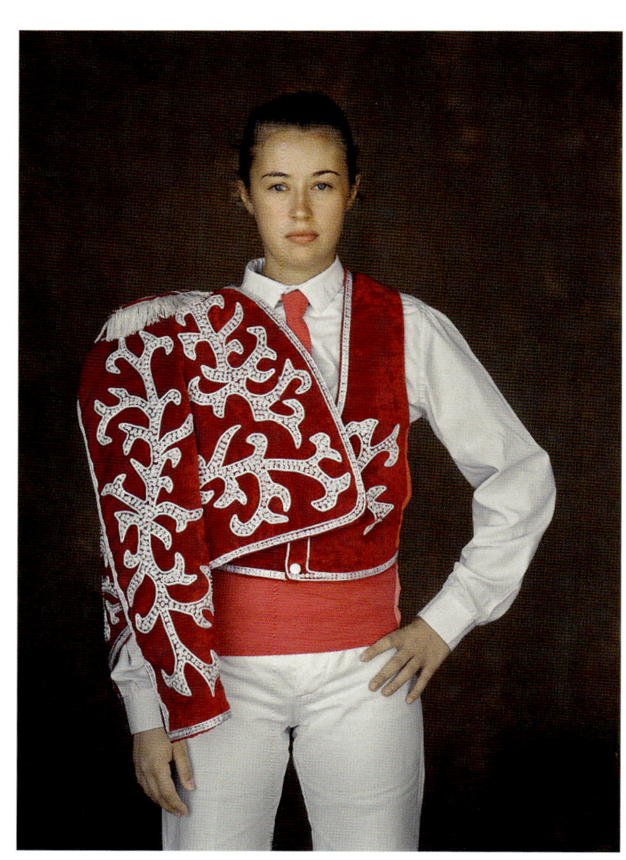

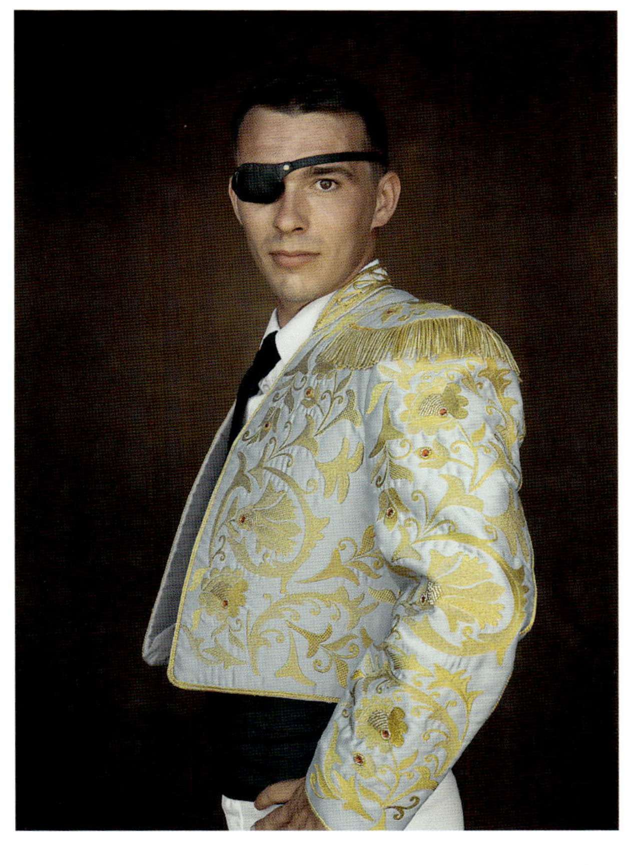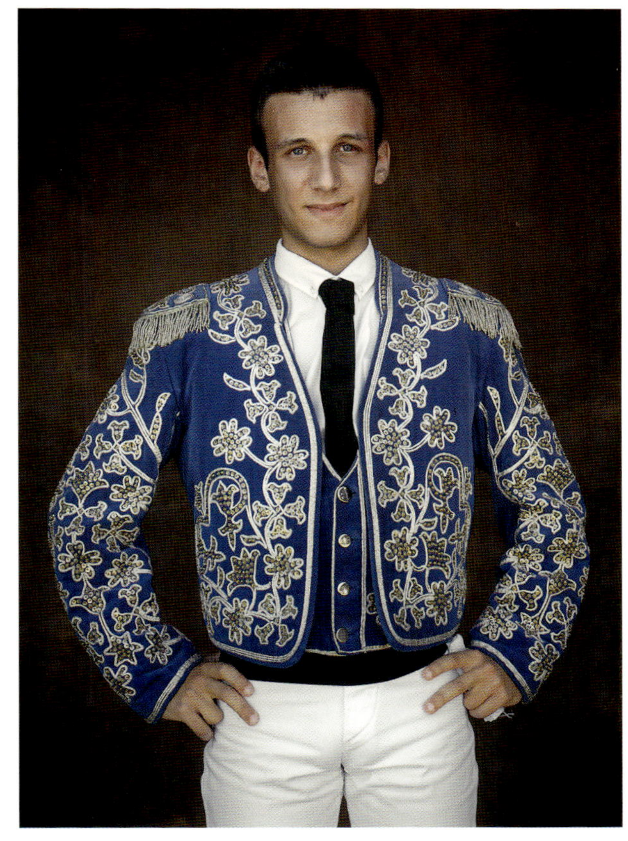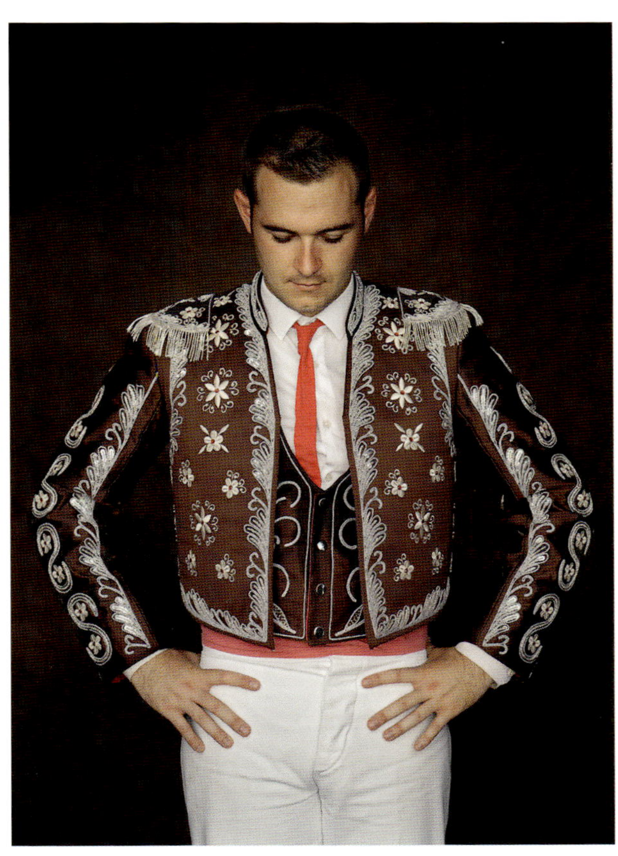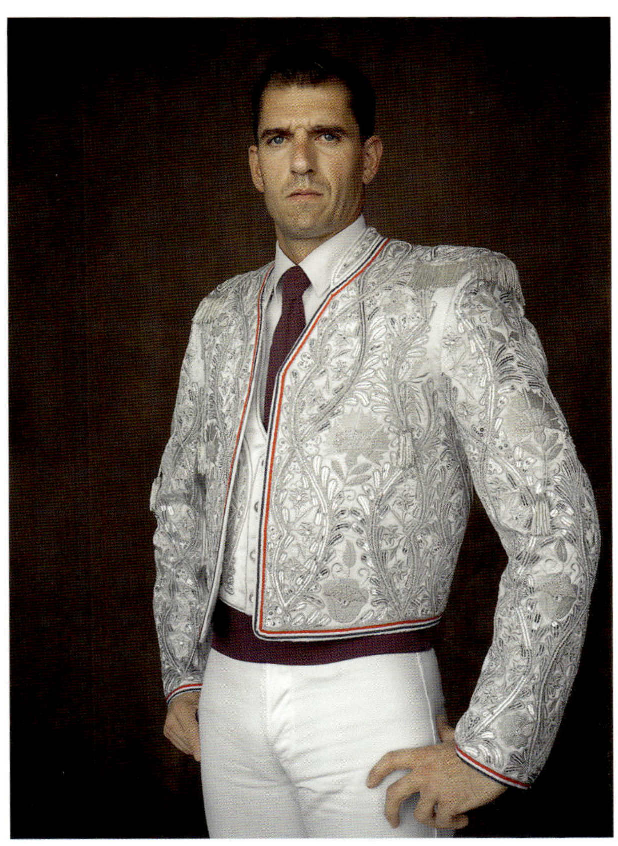

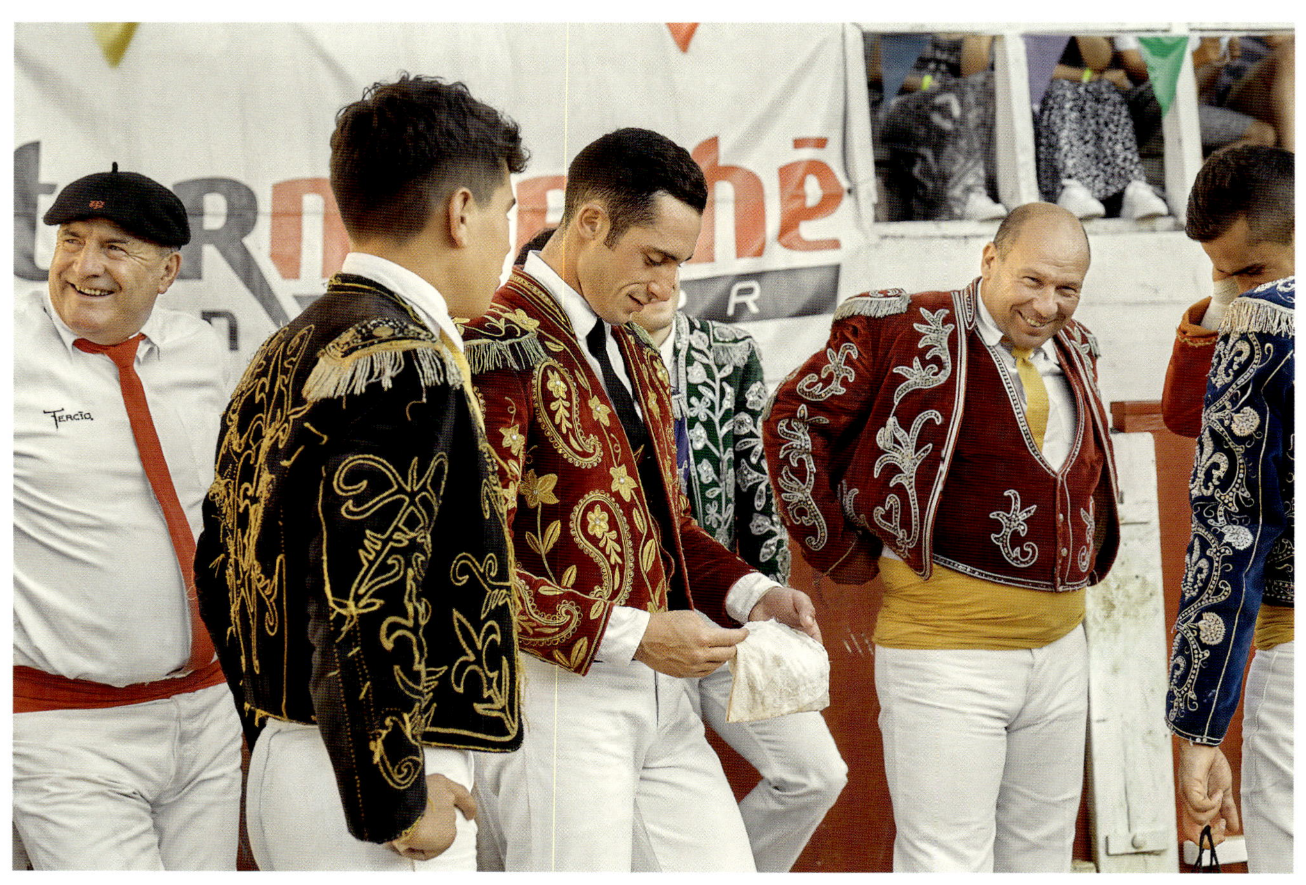

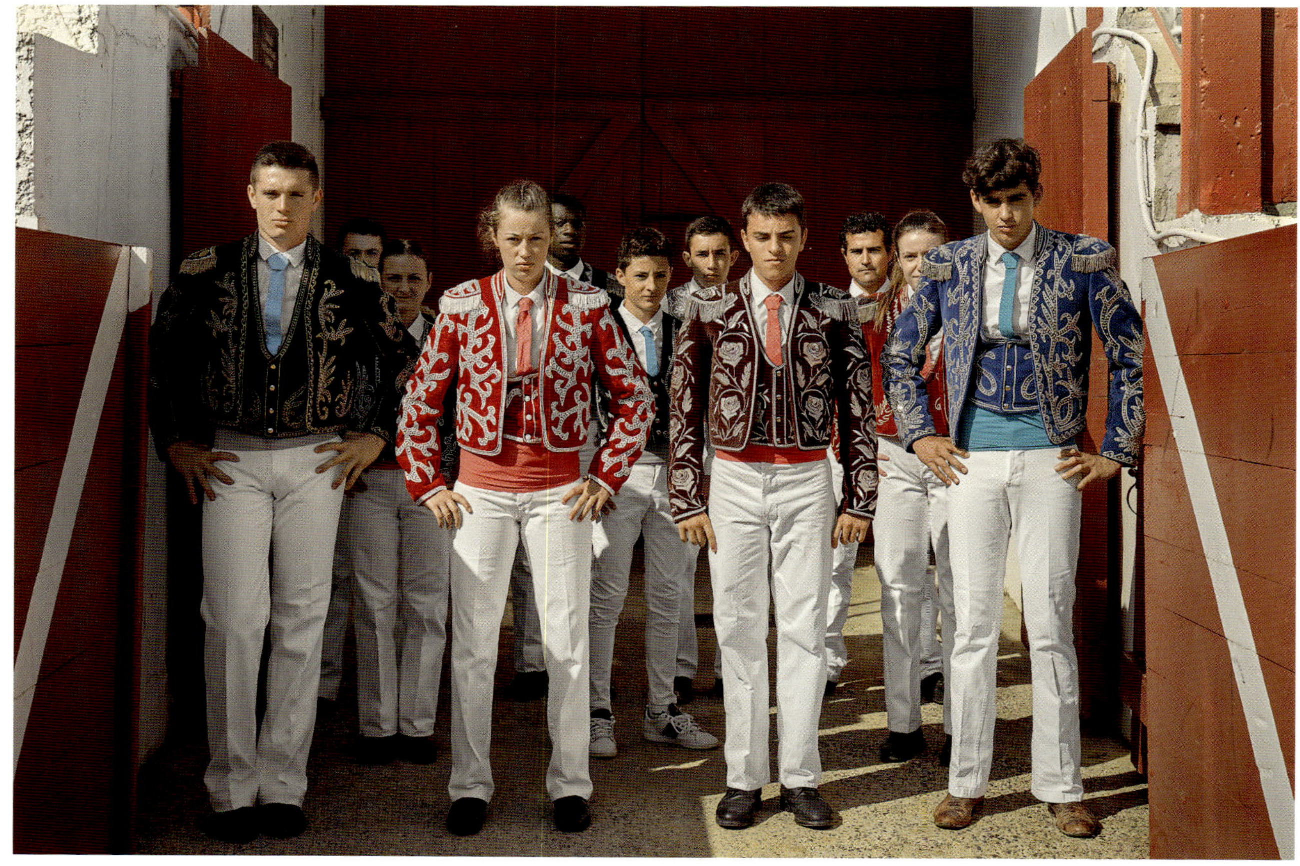

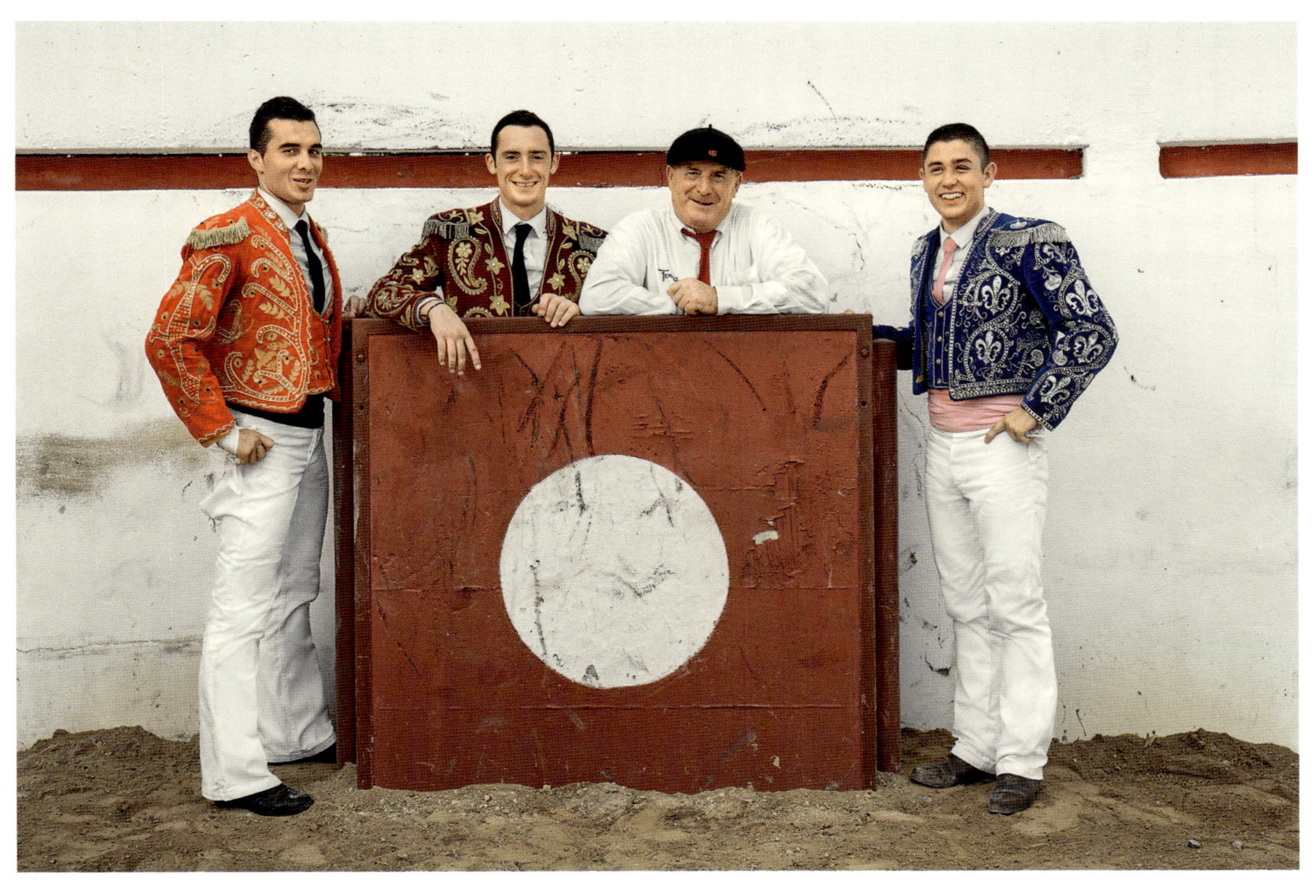

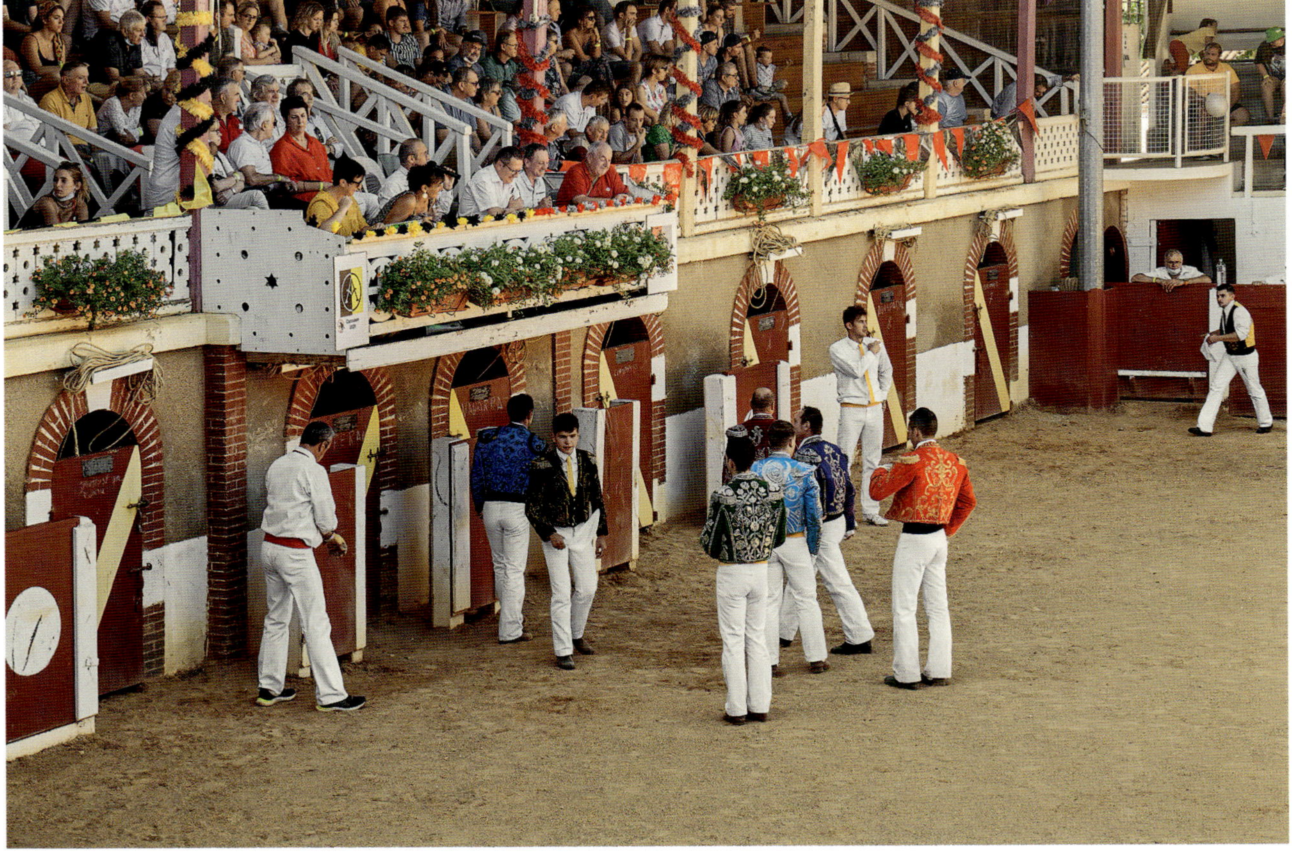

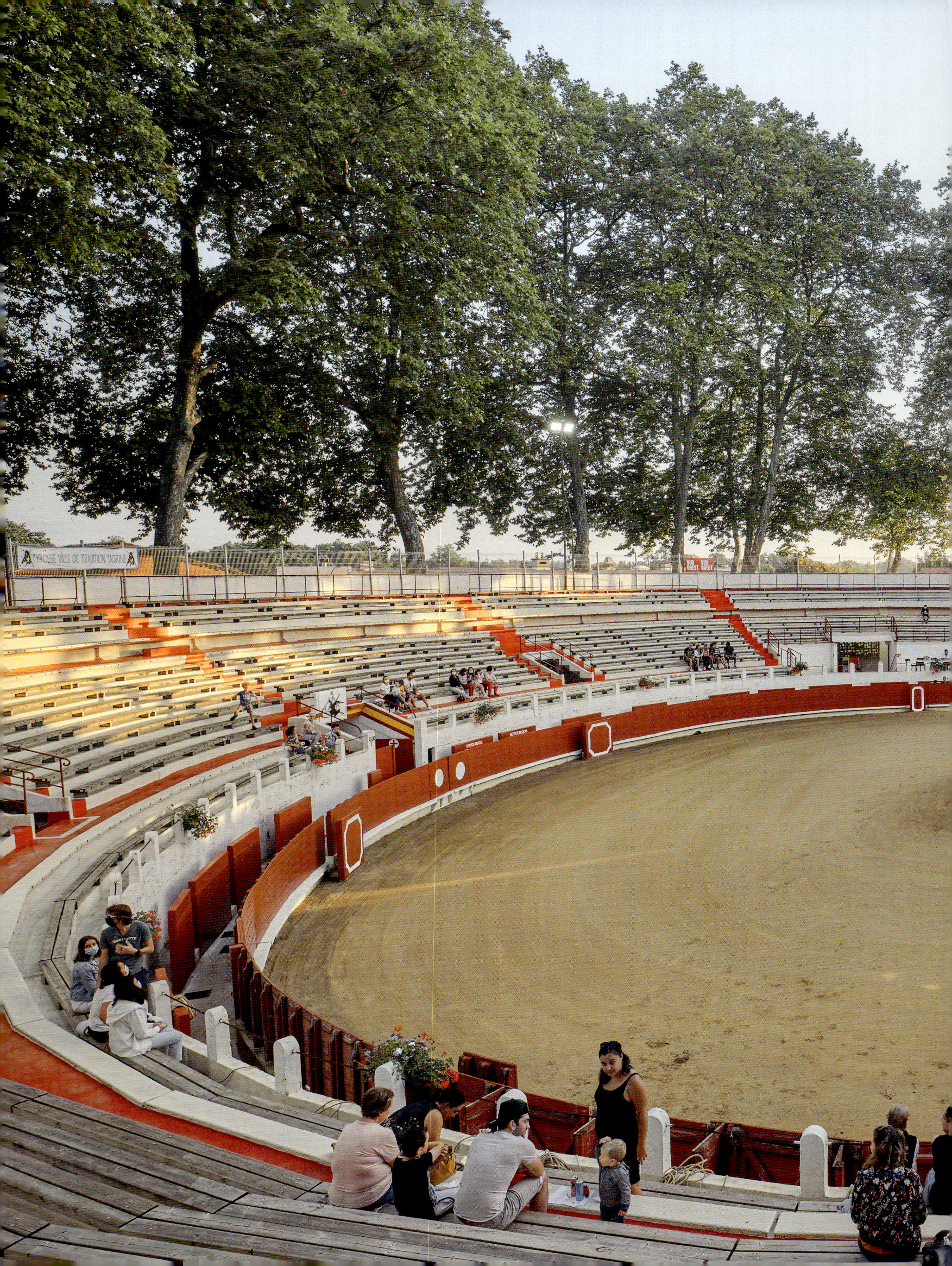

TYROSSE VILLE DE TRADITION TAURINE

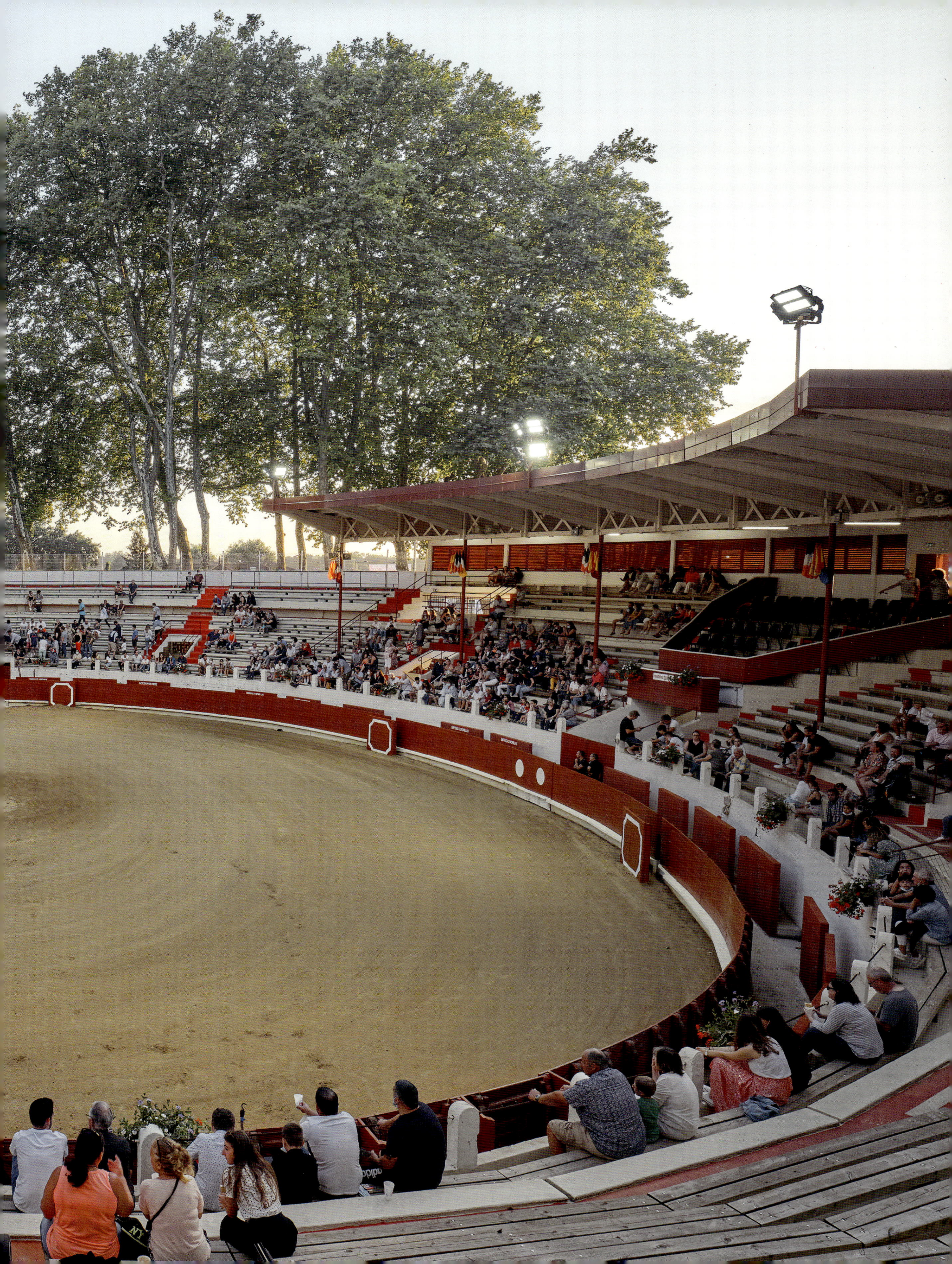

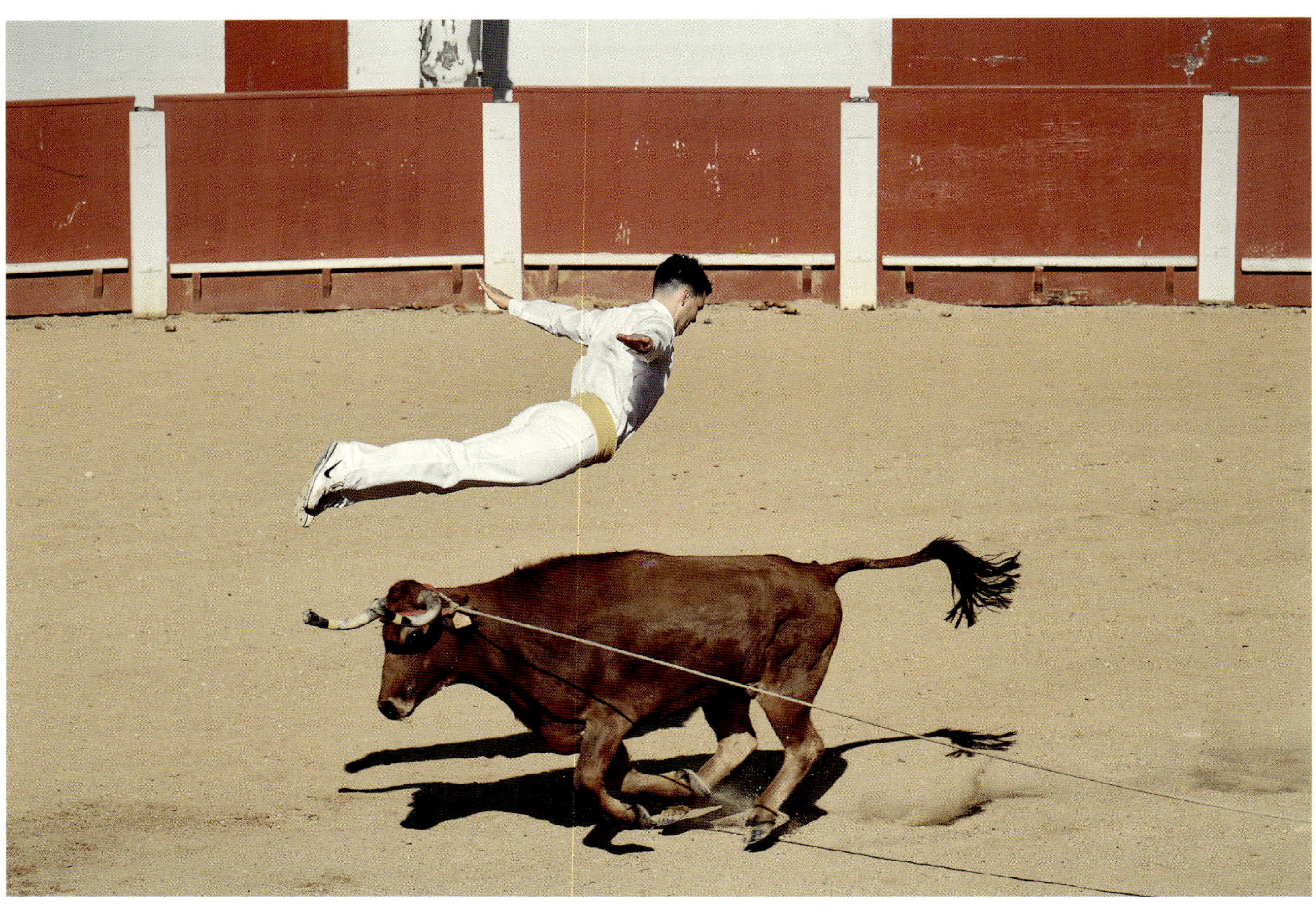

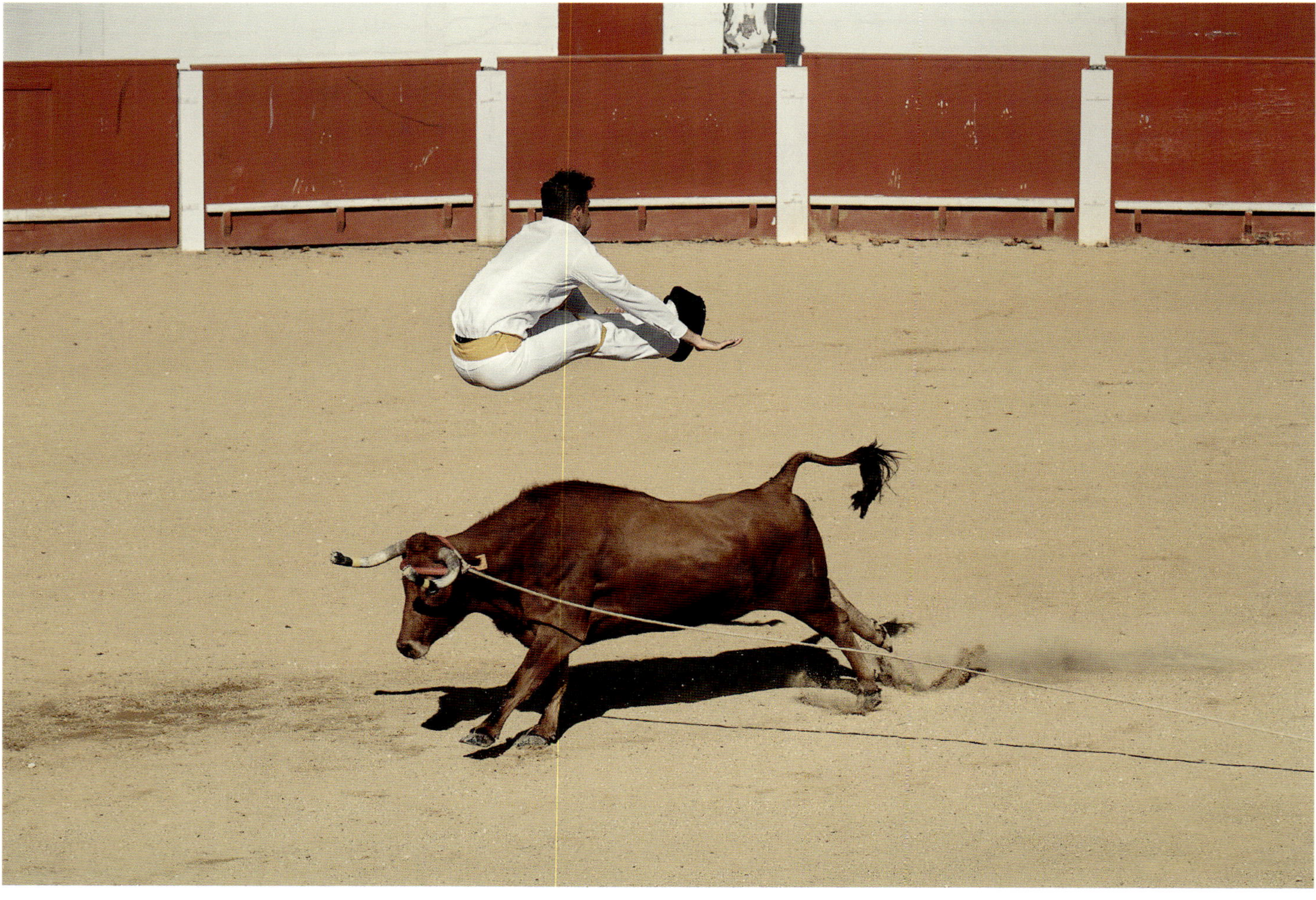

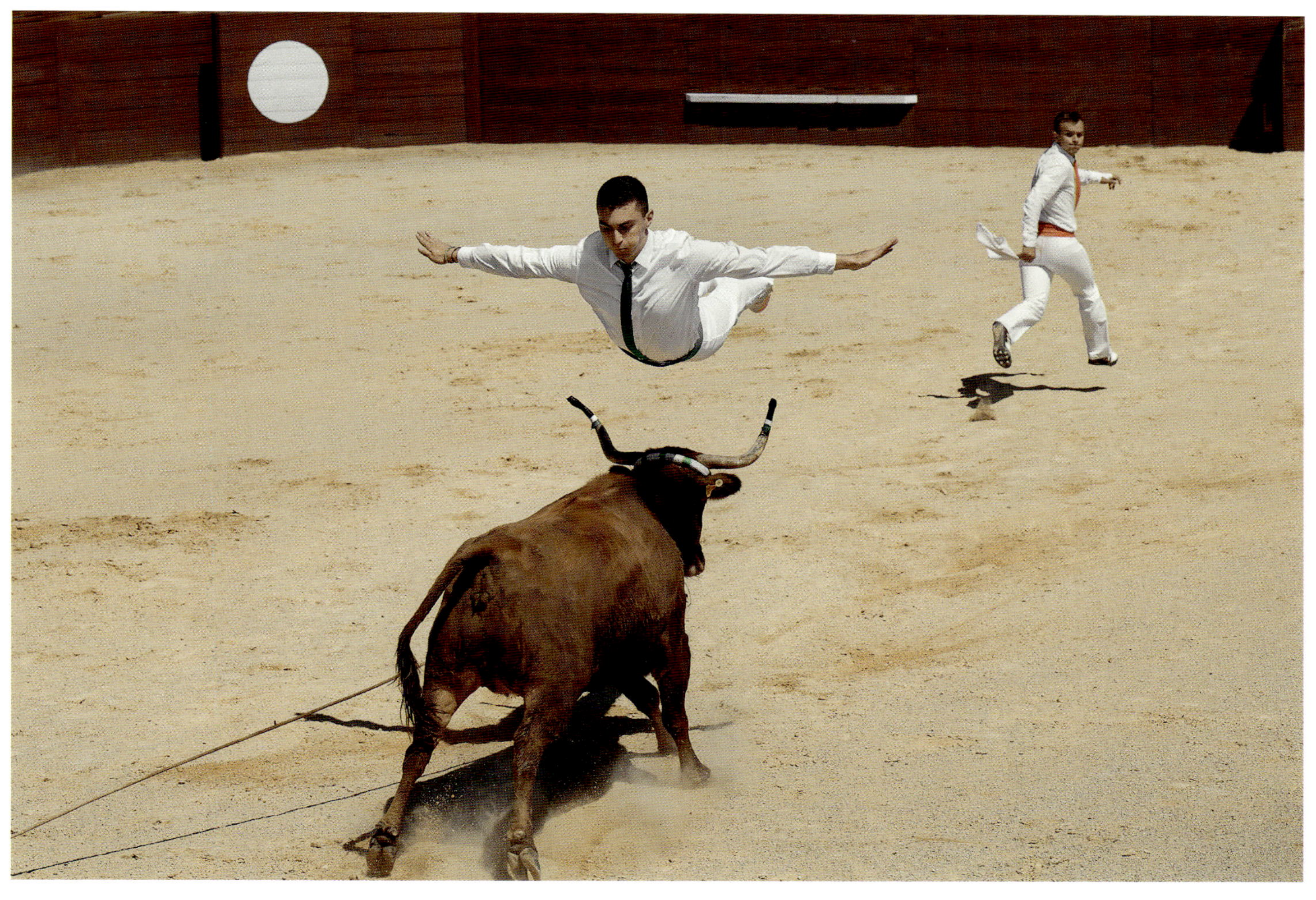

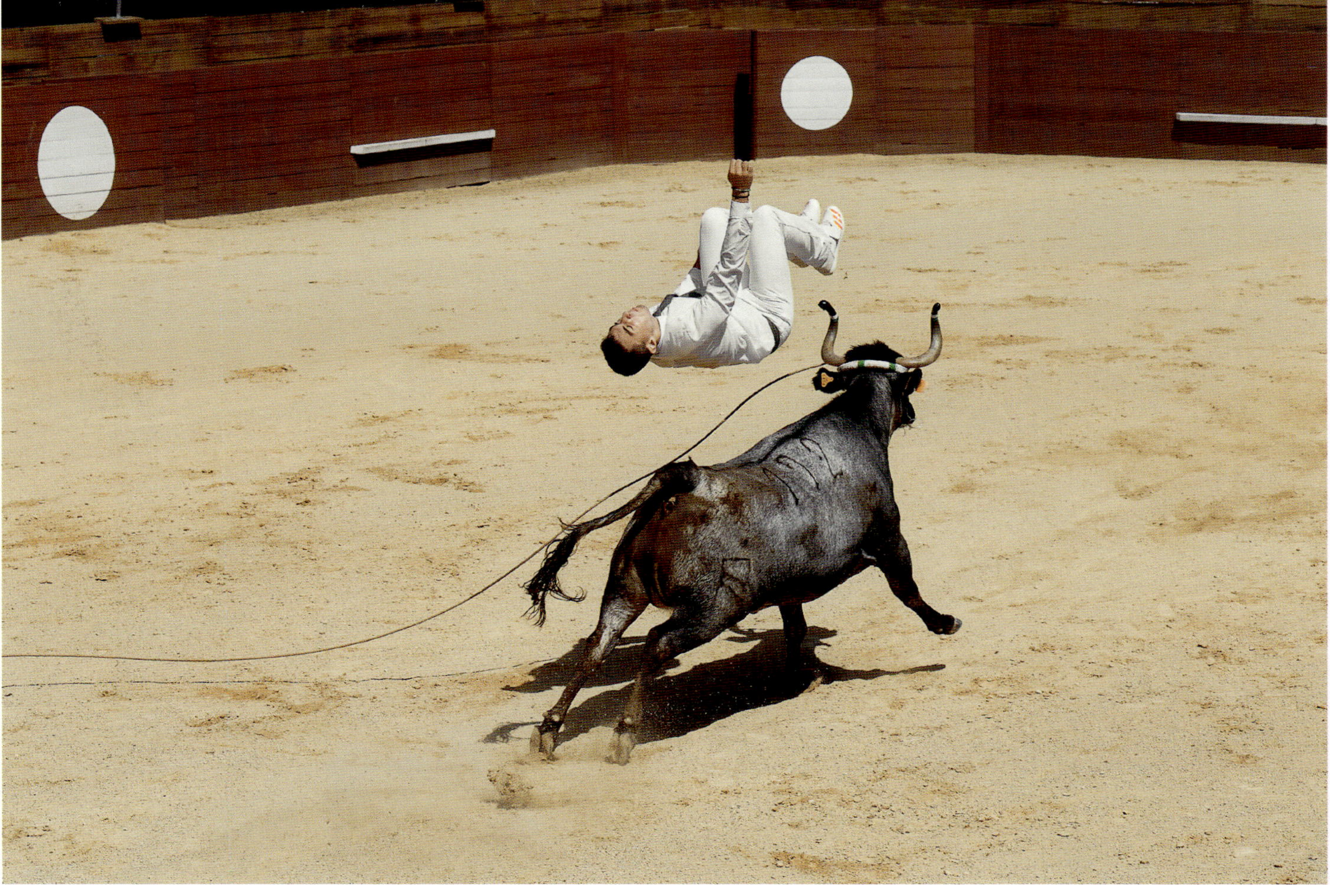

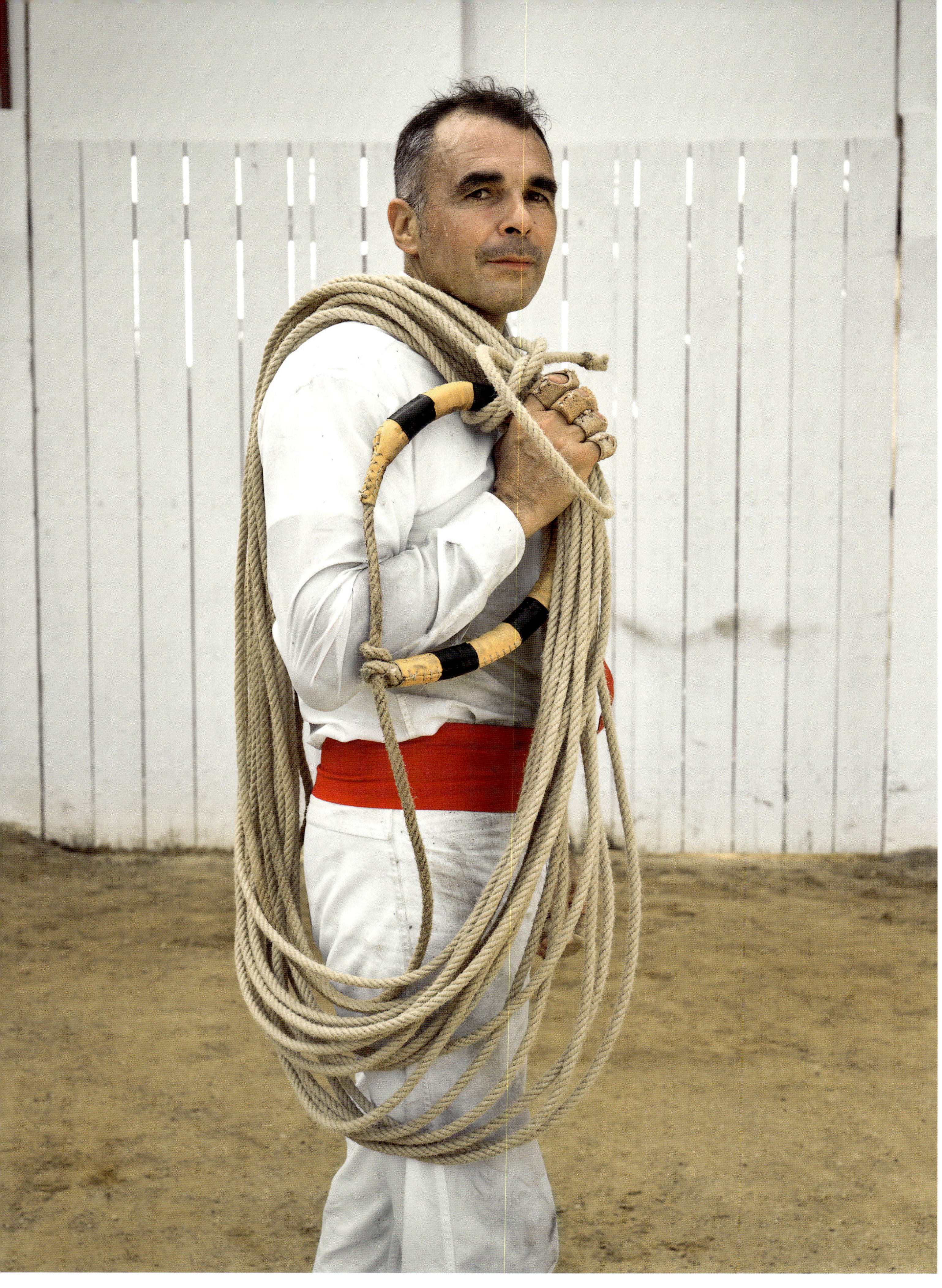

Jean Francois Deyris is a first-rate cordier (rope operator)
playing for the prominent Ganaderia D.A.L.

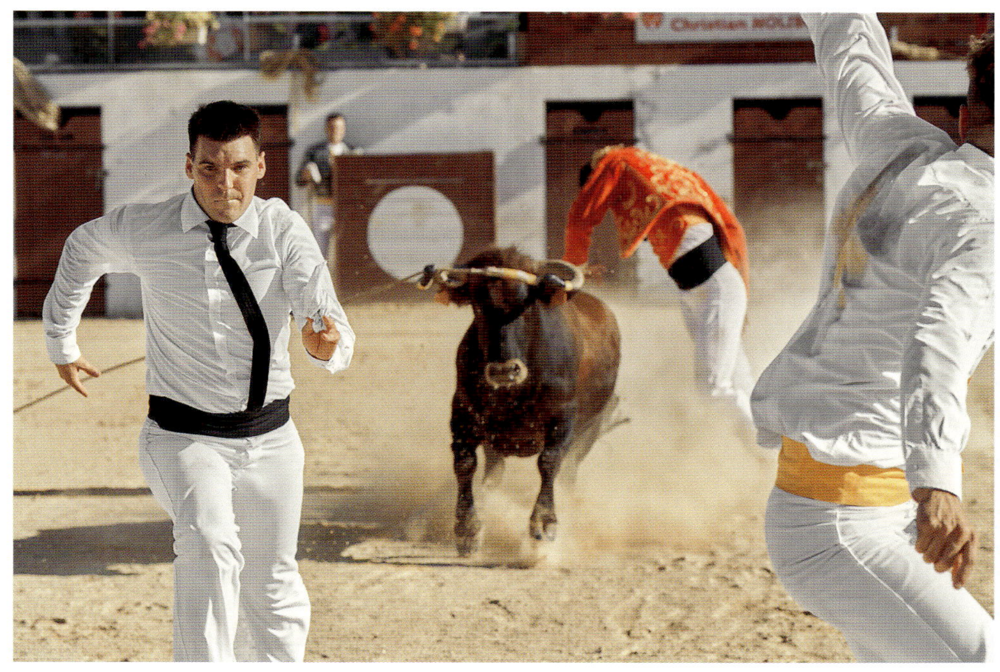

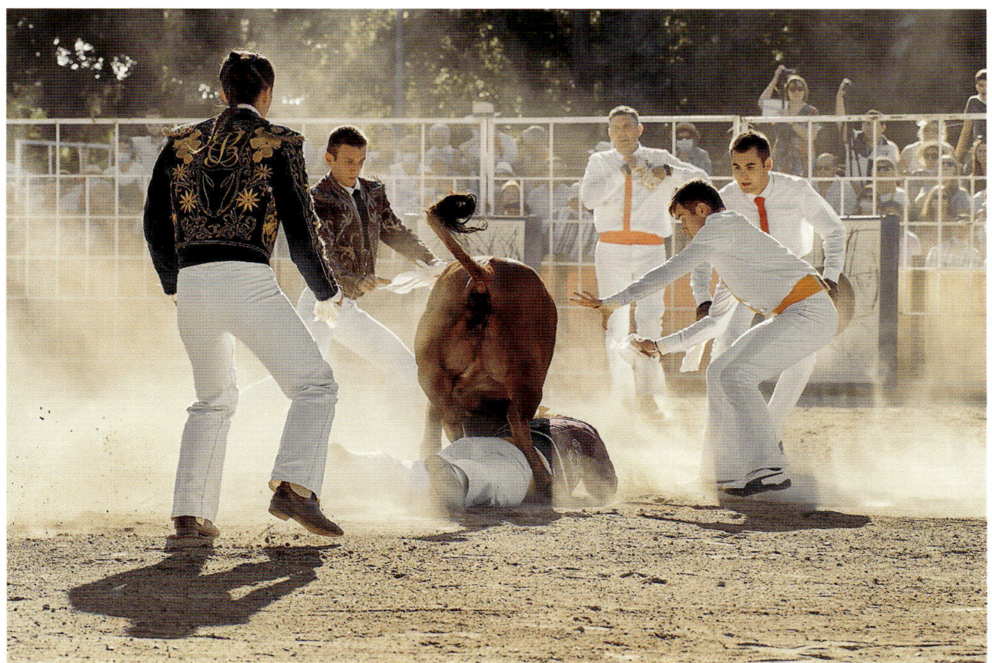

Injuries are common in this dangerous and graceful sport,
where both the performer and cow are at risk.

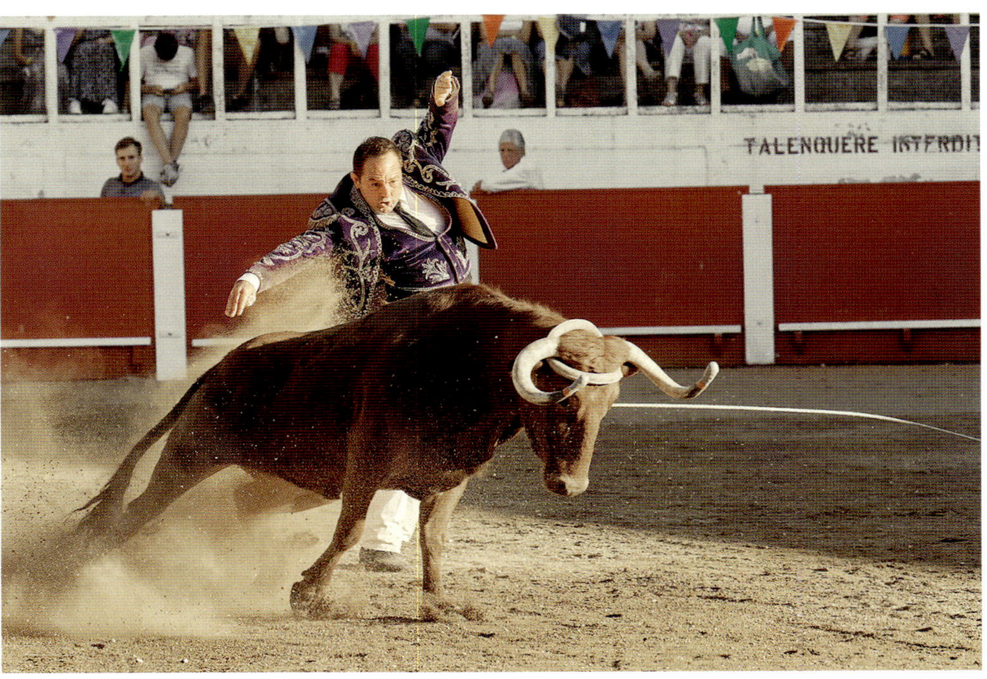

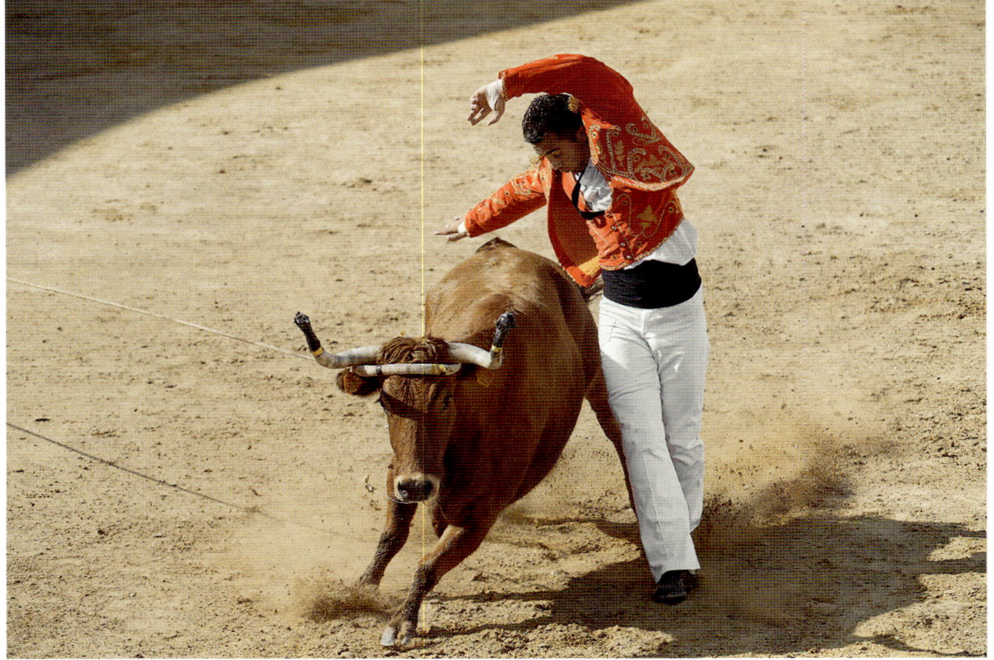

The jury gives a higher score to the écarteur
(dodger) that can perform the steadiest technique
as the animals' horns barely miss his kidneys.

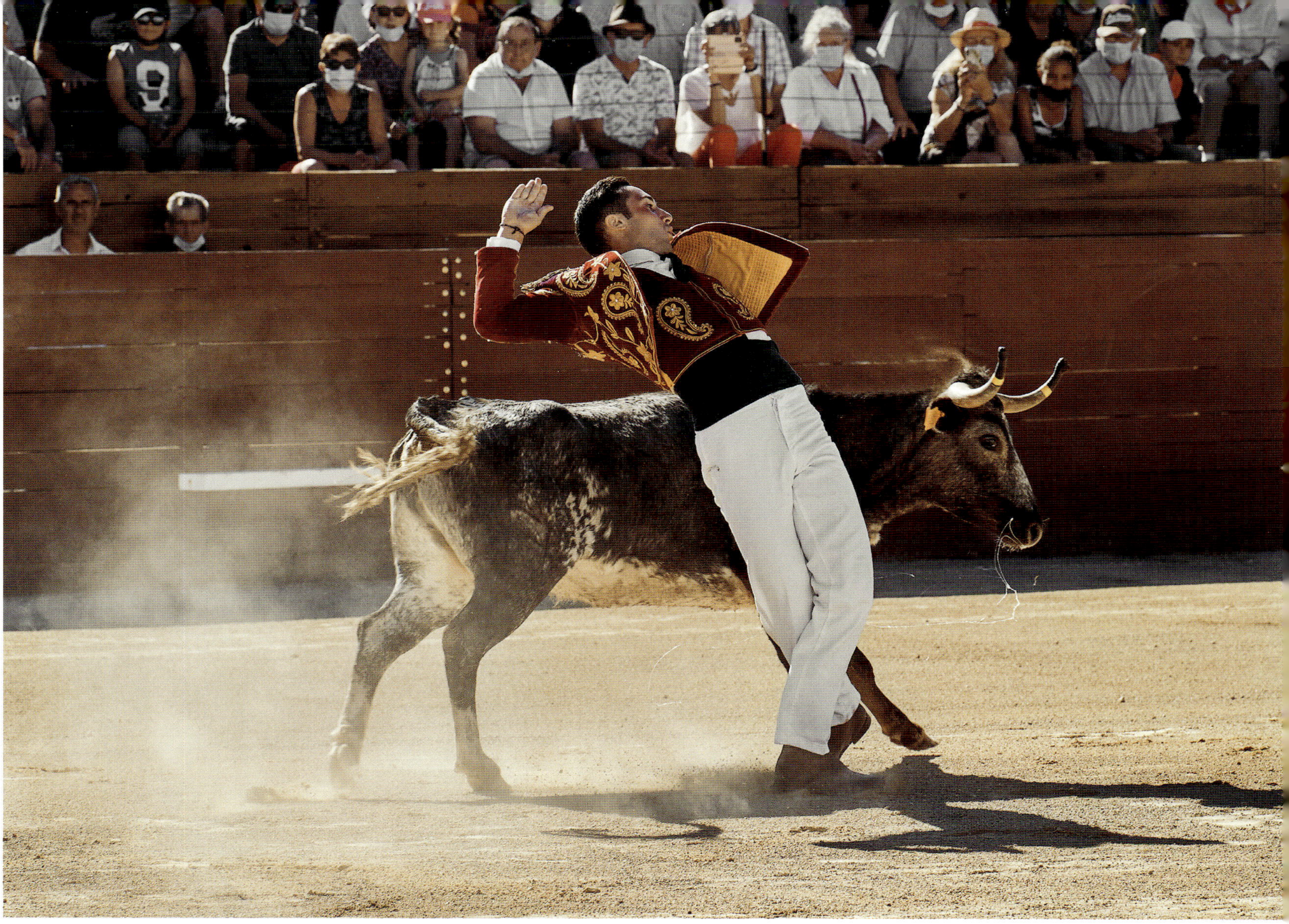

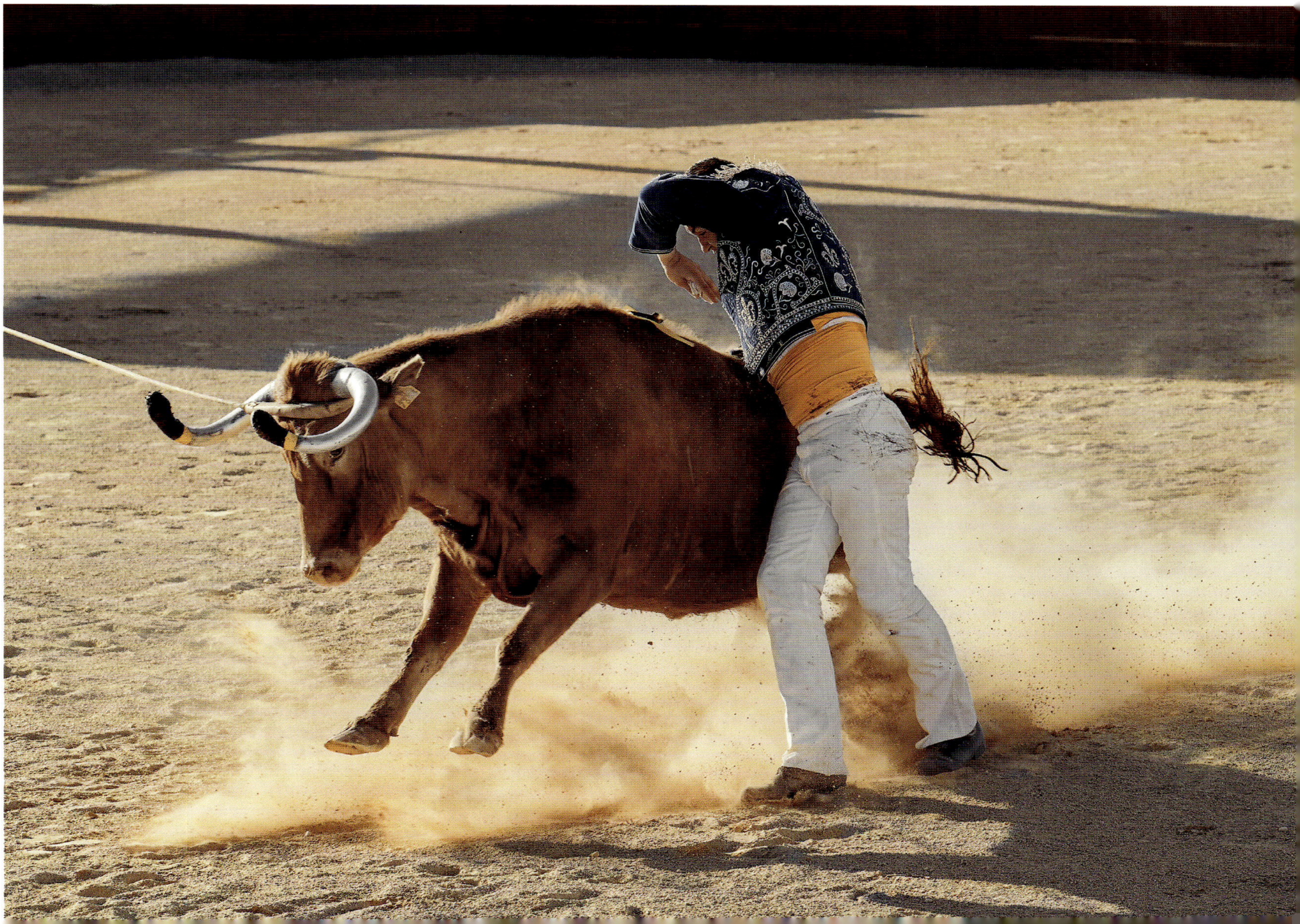

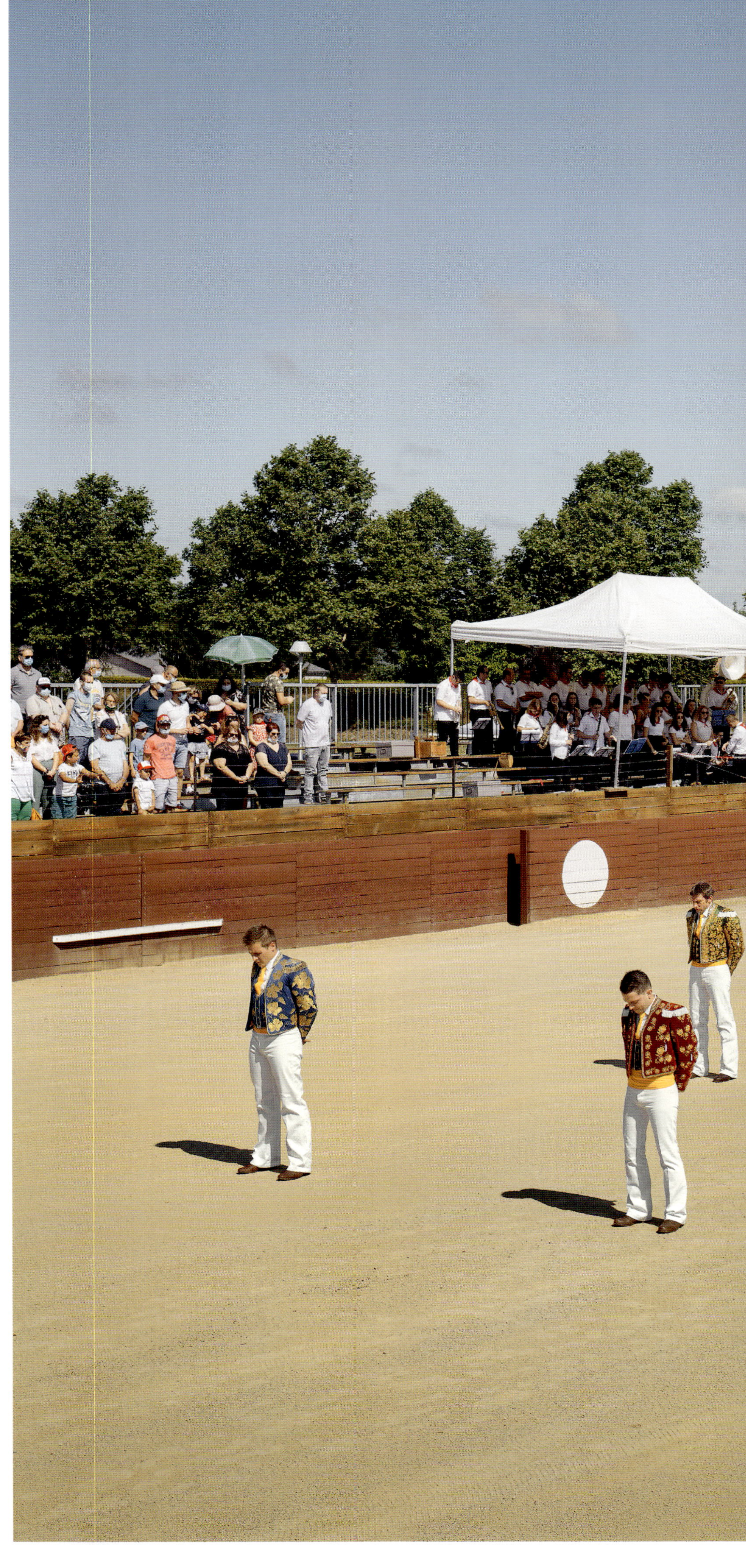

Both teams (locally known as 'coursayres')
and the audience stop to honour the game
and the nation with a moment of silence.

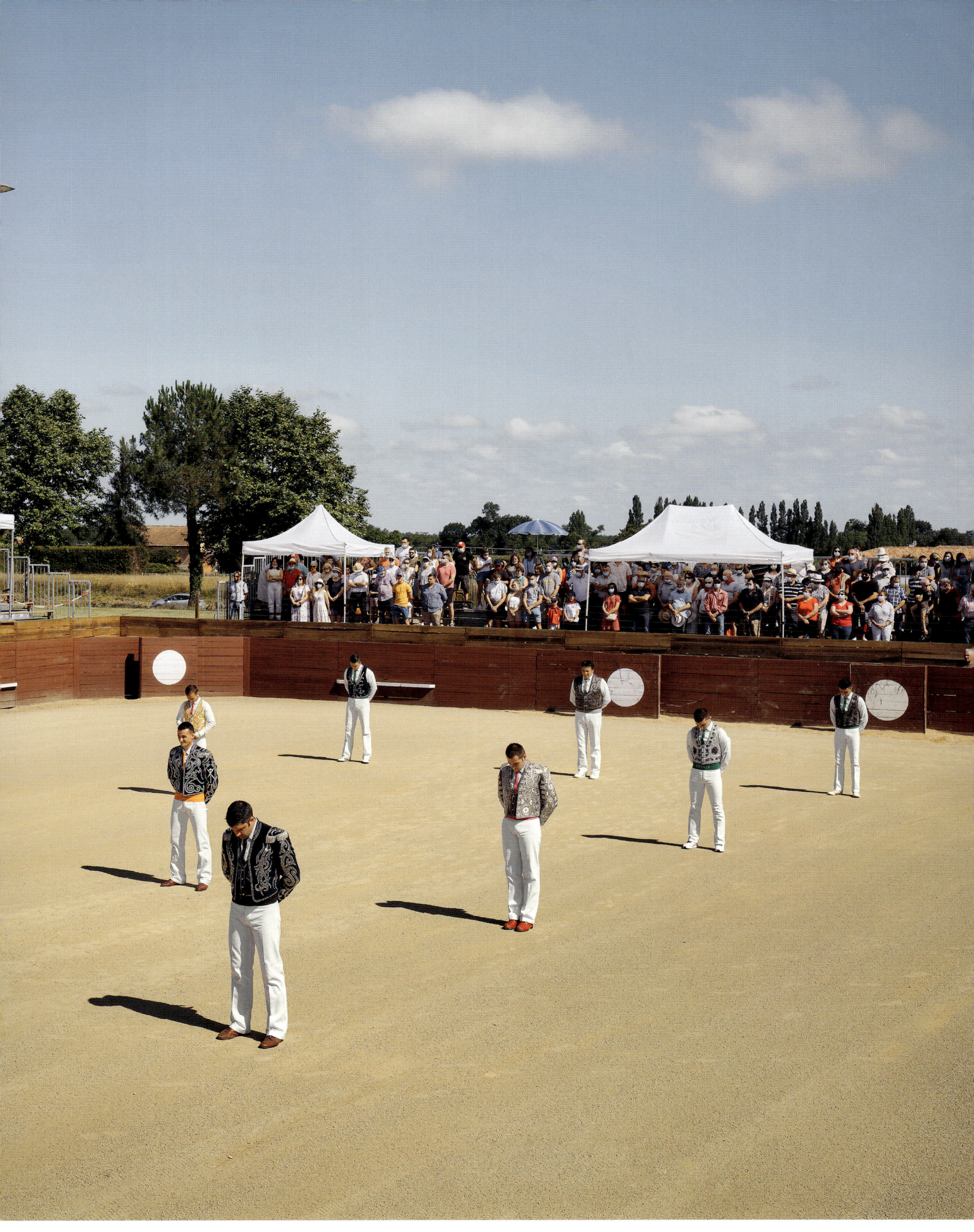

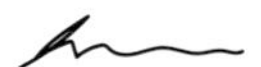

Fierljeppen

THE NETHERLANDS

It is not a sport for cowards, nor is it played for money,
instead, it is the pride and honour of the game that matters most.

They say necessity is the mother of invention, and nowhere is this more true than in the Netherlands, the most densely populated country in the world, known for its charming canals, classic windmills and tolerance for the taboo. With one-third of the land below sea level, the Dutch's sheer engineering mastery has kept it from disappearing into the North Sea. The Dutch's relationship with water has been one of ingenuity and cooperation and from this creativity sprung the country's oldest and most traditional sport – *fierljeppen* – a Friesian word meaning 'far-leaping' or 'far-jumping', giving an entirely new meaning to 'Flying Dutchman'.

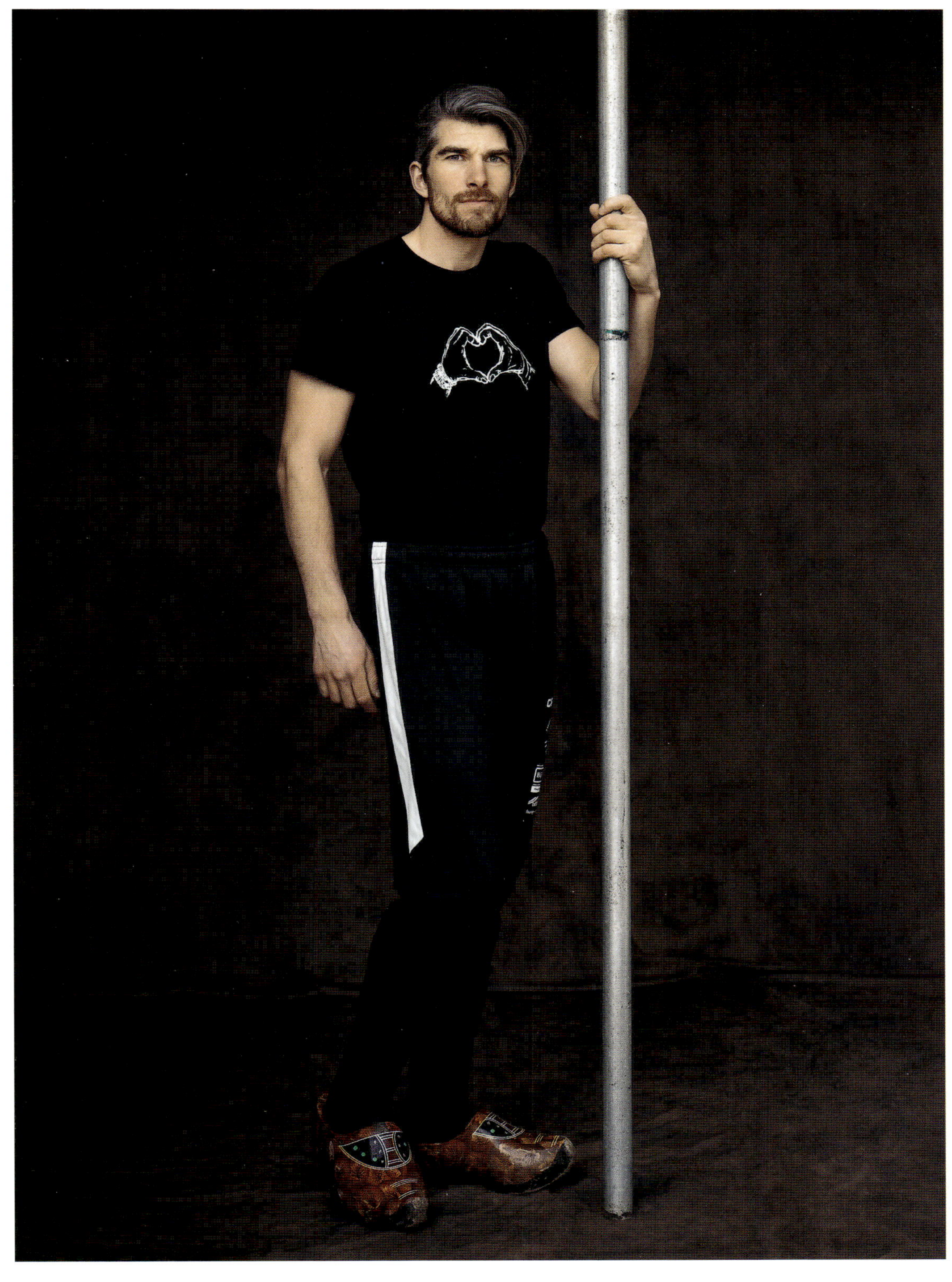

*"Fierleppen is flying for
those who can't fly."*

~ Ysbrand Galama, National Champion ~

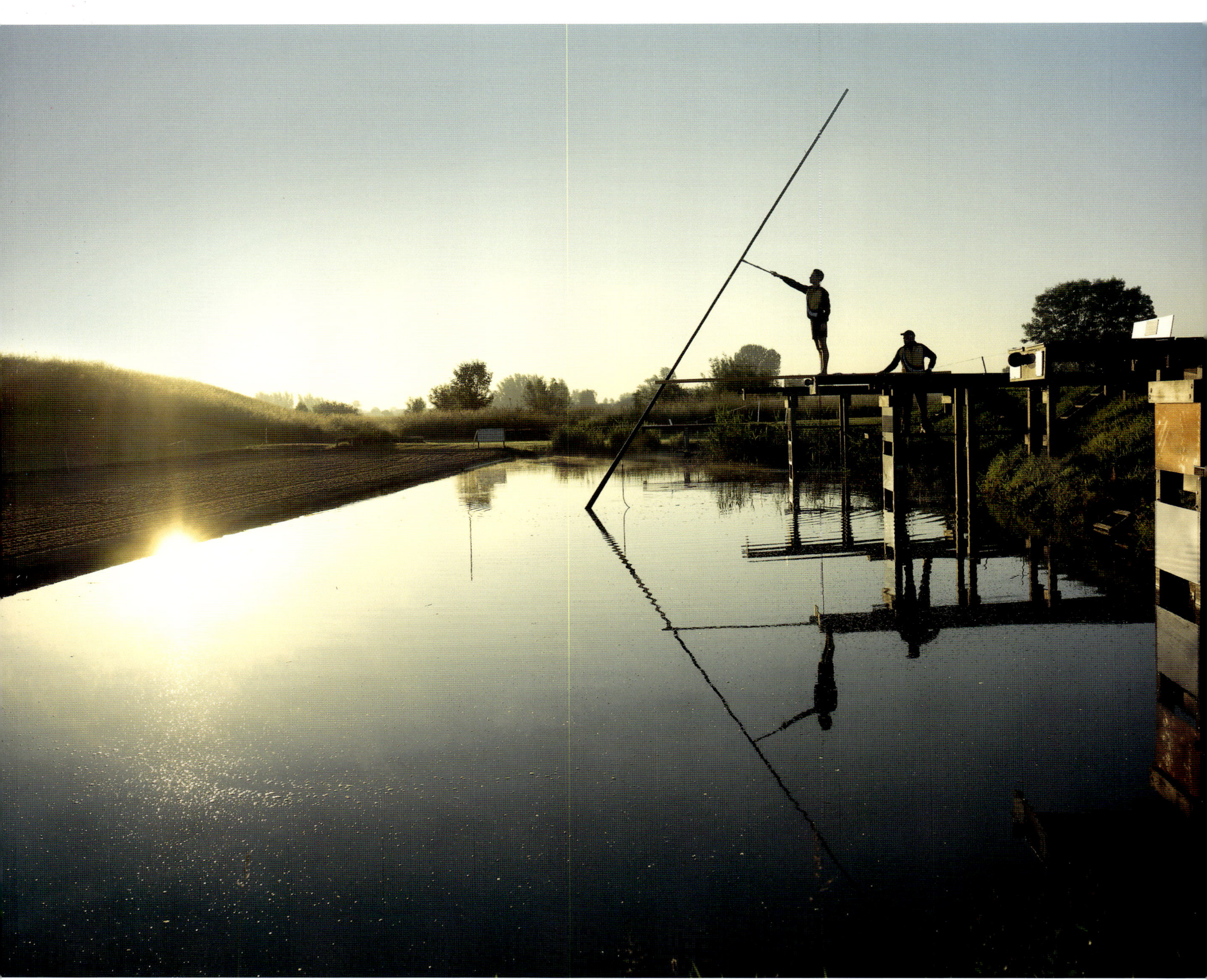

This peculiar sport traces back to the sixteenth century when Frisian farmers faced the challenge of crossing countless waterways and canals to get to their fields. They discovered that jumping over the water with the help of a wooden pole was much less time-consuming than walking around – and a lot more fun. Another motive for leaping over canals was egg thievery, part of Friesland's traditional lapwing egg hunt in which people jump from one plot of land to another, looking for eggs before getting caught by the farmer. A further testament to Dutch resourcefulness comes from a local legend. In 1575, during the rebellion against Spanish rule, a man was said to have crossed enemy lines concealing a secret message in his canal-jumping pole, proving its multi-functionality.

Eventually, as roads and bridges were built and the poles got longer and longer, hurling oneself over the water became less about transportation and more about an entertaining game requiring strength, skill and agility. The first competition took place in the village of Baard in 1767, where *fierljeppen* was formally recognized as a game. But it wasn't until 1975 that it became an established sport with documented rules, structure and regulations.

In 2006, the classic wooden or aluminium pole was replaced by lightweight carbon fibre. Switching to this modern rod meant competitors could fling themselves over greater distances. Today, the pole comes with a flat plate at the bottom to prevent it from sinking into the muddy floor of the waterway. But the world was unaware of this fascinatingly quirky tradition until 2007 when the U.S. reality show *The Amazing Race* had contestants leap across a canal during the Dutch leg of the competition. In 2018, UNESCO declared it an official part of the culture, and its popularity extended beyond the borders of Friesland to other Dutch provinces.

Fierljeppen is an odd combination of pole vaulting and long jump practised from May until September. It is not for the faint of heart, nor is it played for money; instead, it is the pride and honour of the game that matters most. The objective is to take a flying leap over the water and land as far away on the other side as possible. The athletes must run at lightning speed and have laser focus, perfect balance and the strength and coordination of a gymnast. They must not be afraid of heights either as they shinny up a thirteen-meter pole and teeter atop it until it tips in one direction or another. With beers in one hand and French fries with mayo in the other, the crowd breaks out into boisterous laughter as a jumper misses, and his flailing body tumbles through the air, splashing into the cold canal.

Set in the picturesque playground of this low-lying country, this gravity-defying sport grounded in tradition and necessity has given a whole new meaning to 'look before you leap'. The desire to catapult oneself into the air is no longer confined to Dutch tradition but has expanded into international waters, captivating the hearts of the boundless.

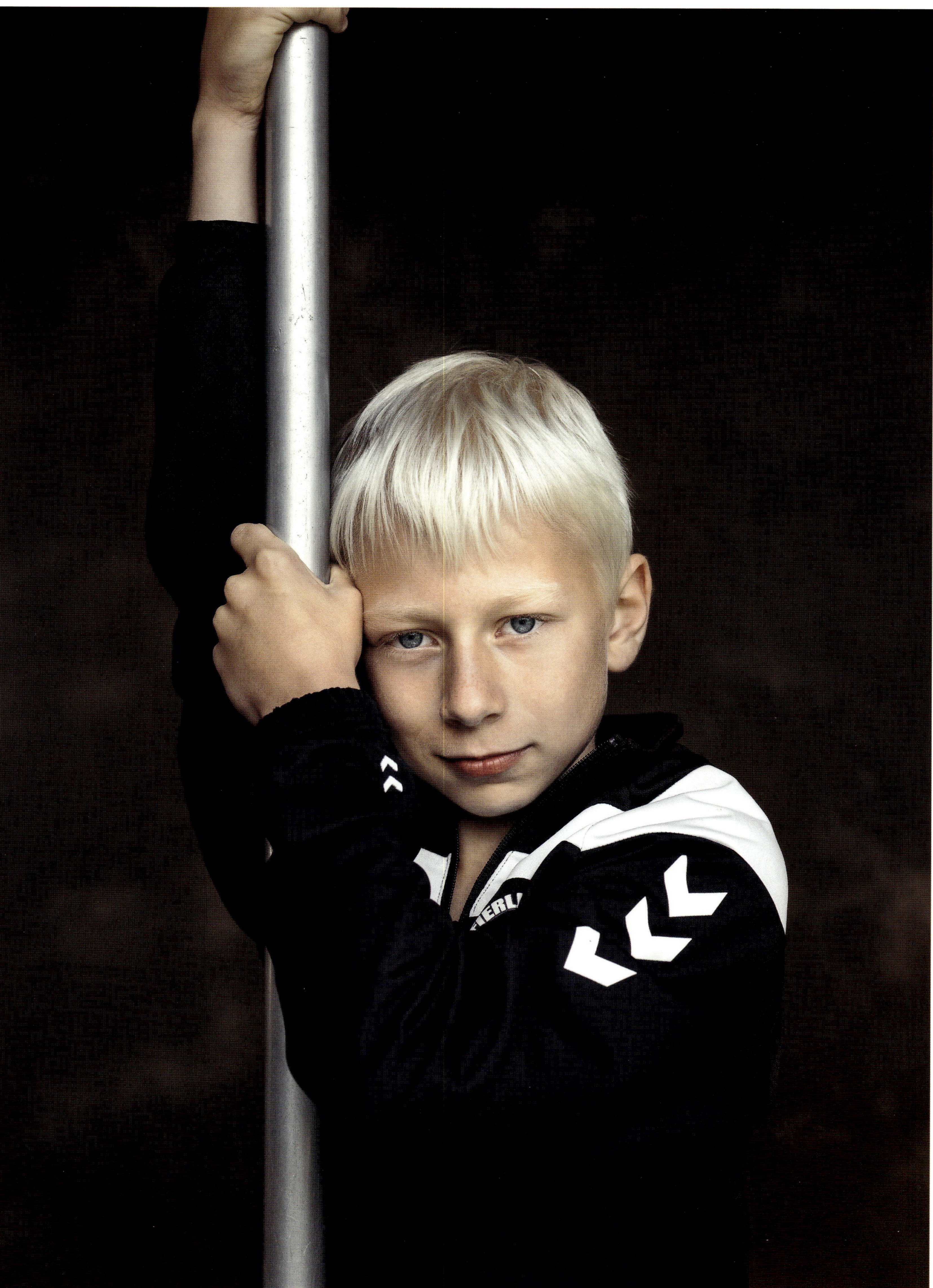

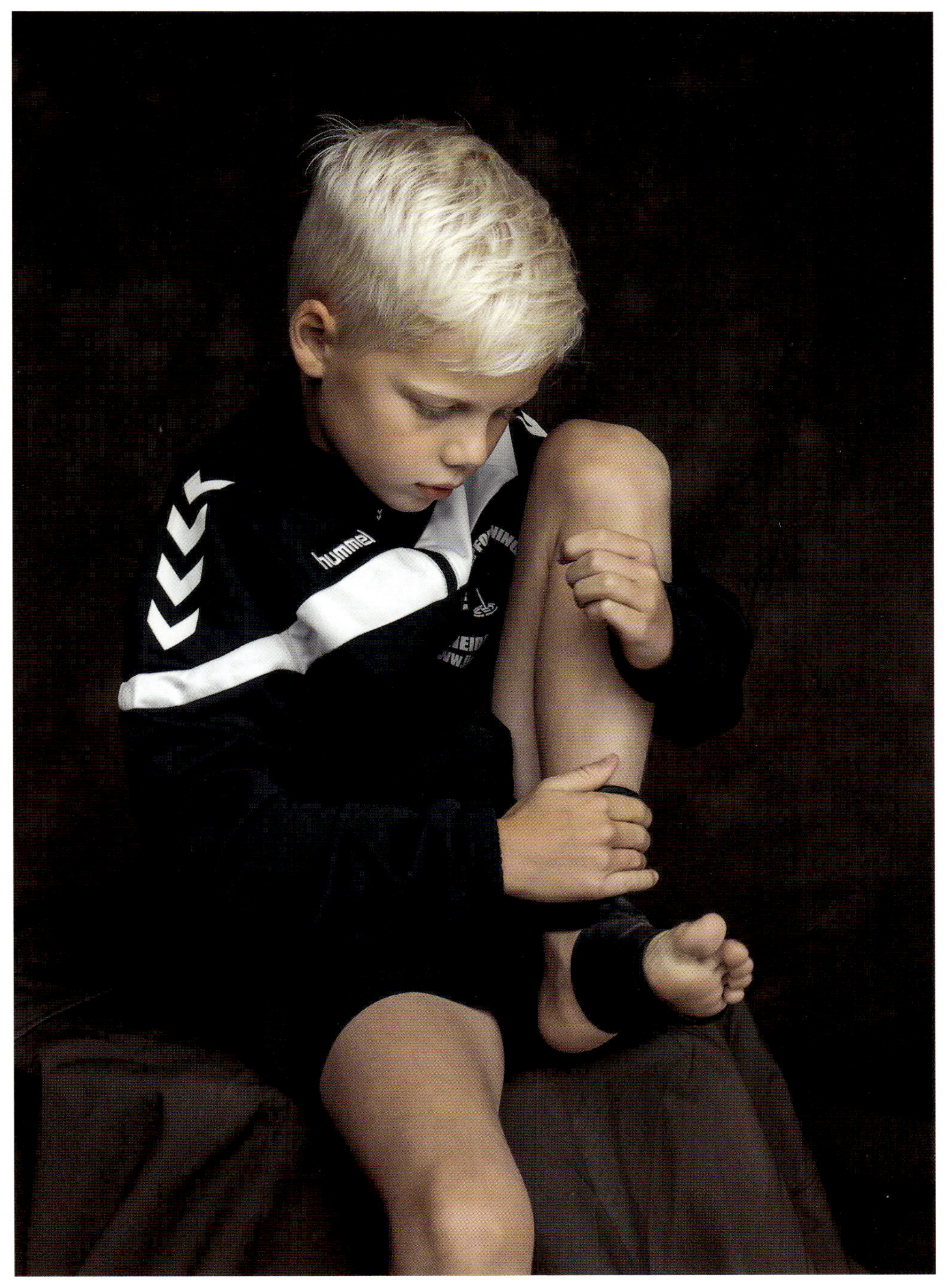

Fierljeppen players use a bicycle inner
tube to protect their ankles while jumping.

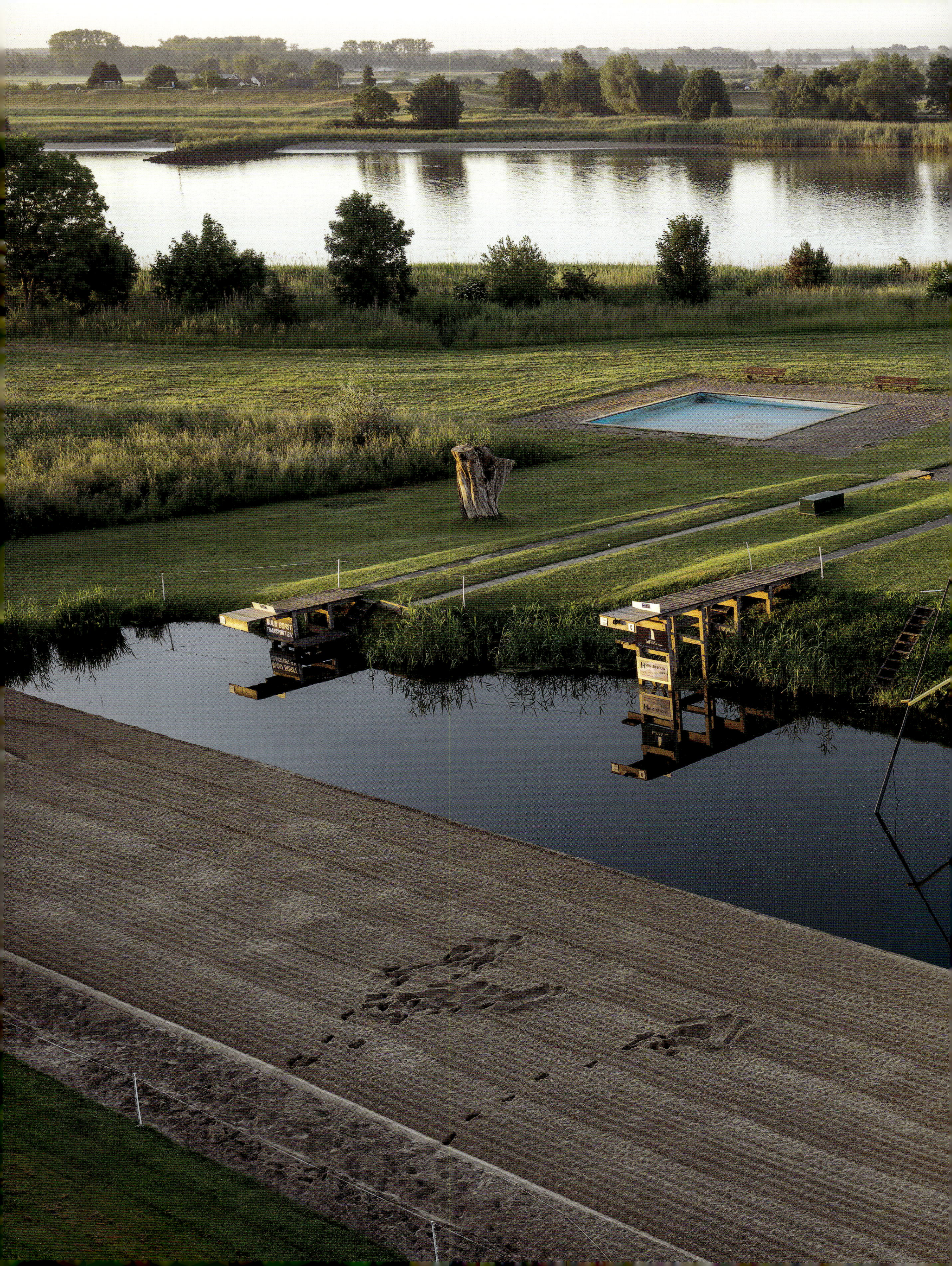

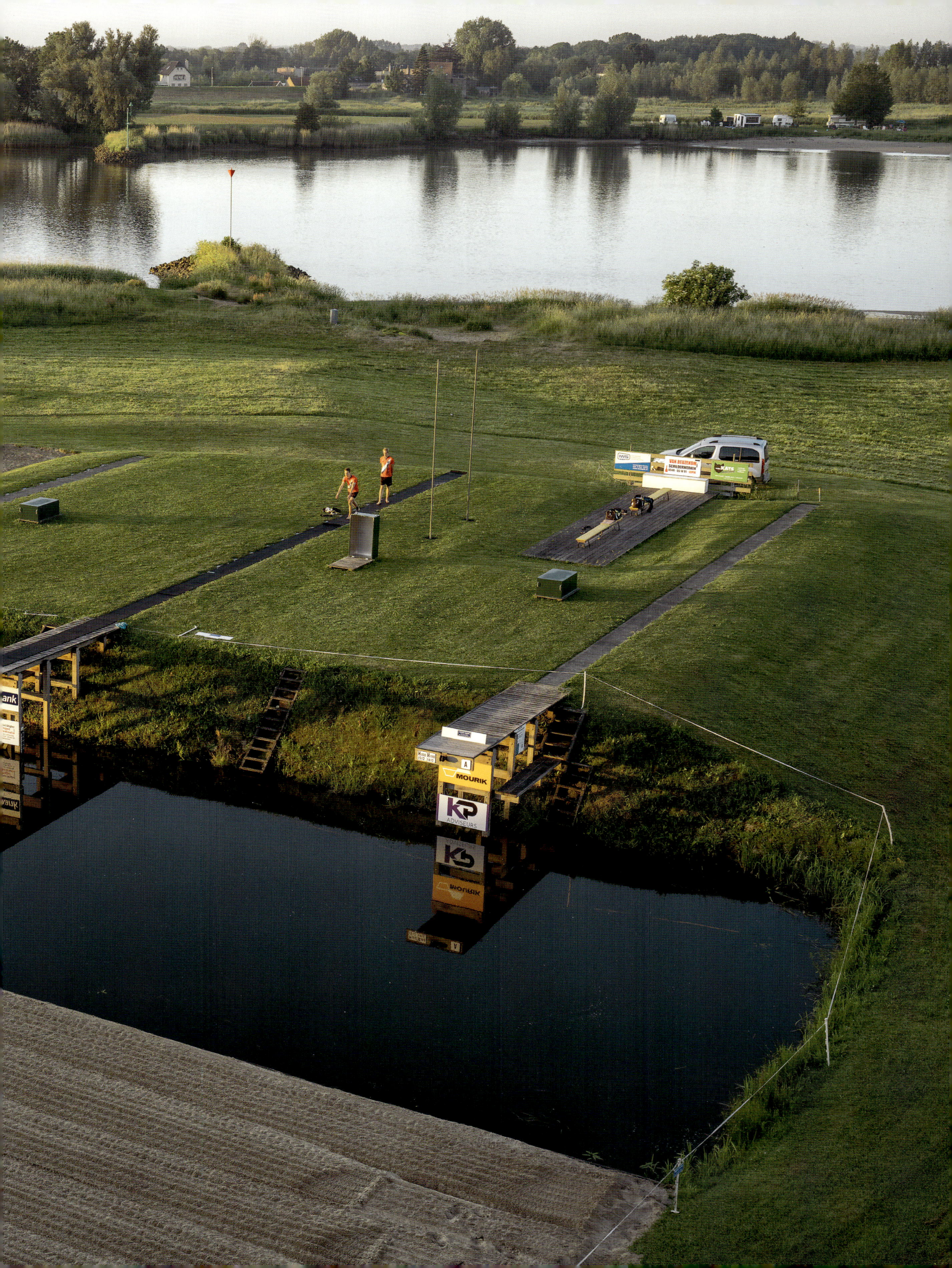

MOURIK
KP ADVISEURS
IWS
VAN BEUZEKOM
SCHILDERWERKEN
0348 · 35 14 91 · LOPIK
KATS

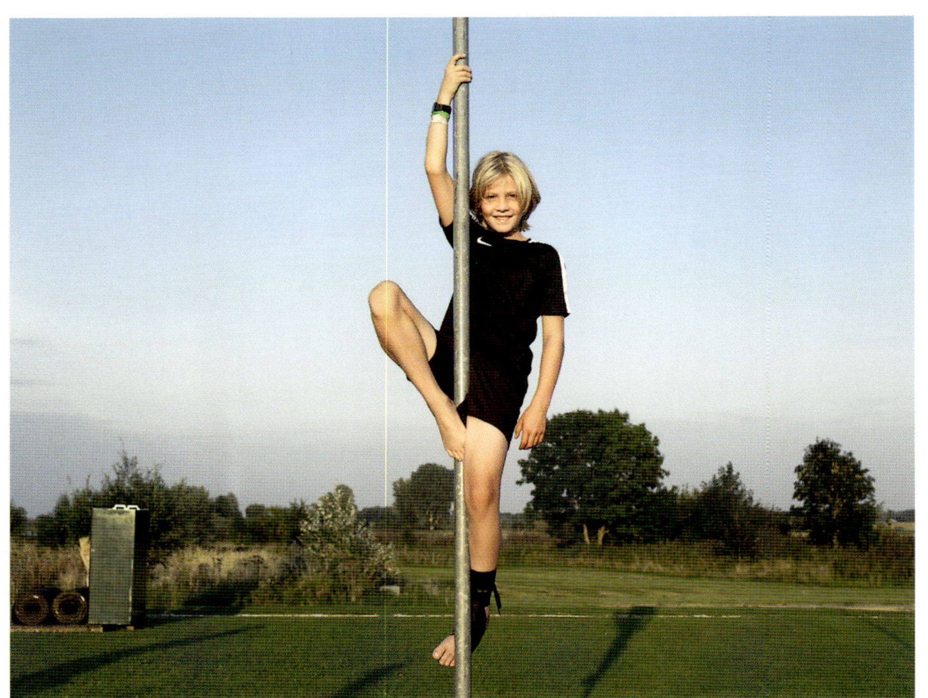

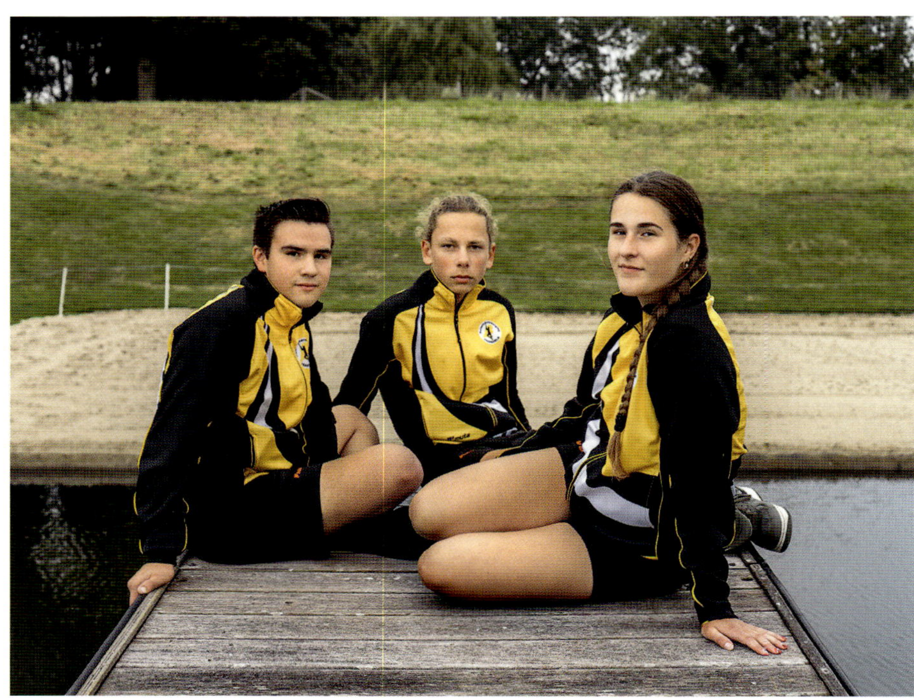

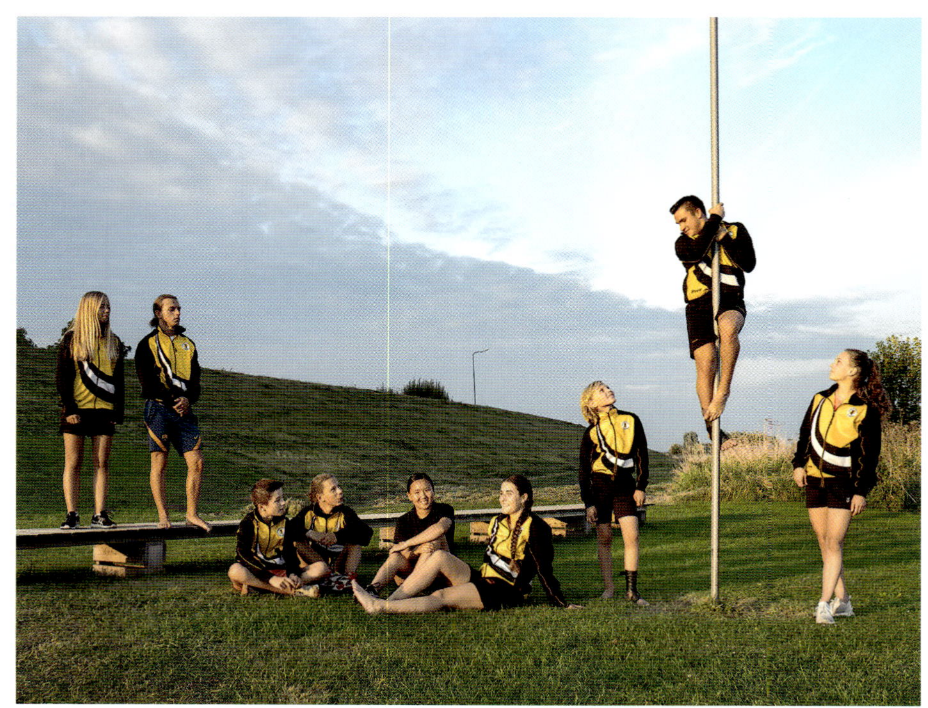

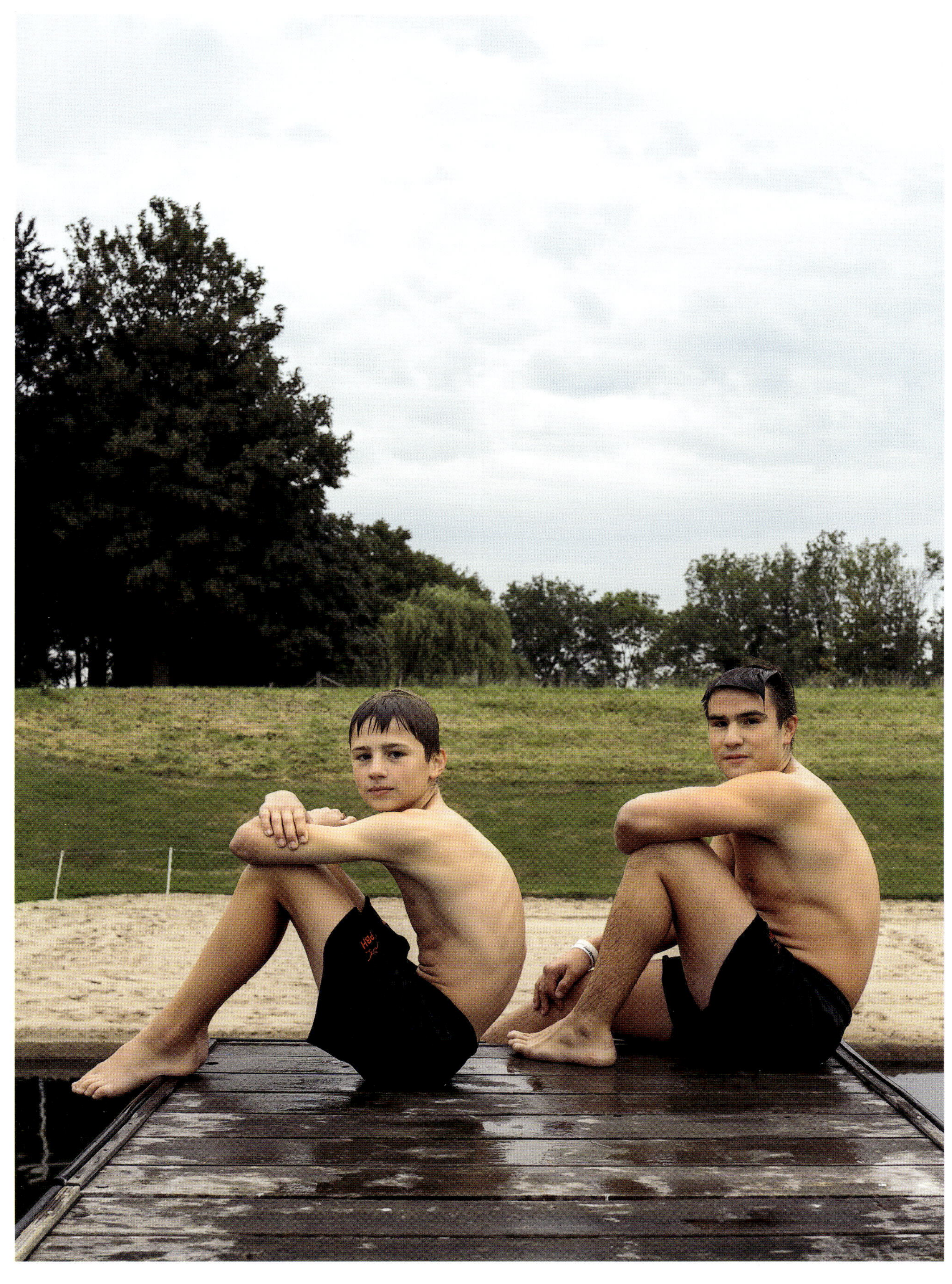

Child members of the Jaarsveld Club train
regularly and intensely, perfecting their
running, climbing and jumping skills to become
the best Fierljeppen athletes they can be.

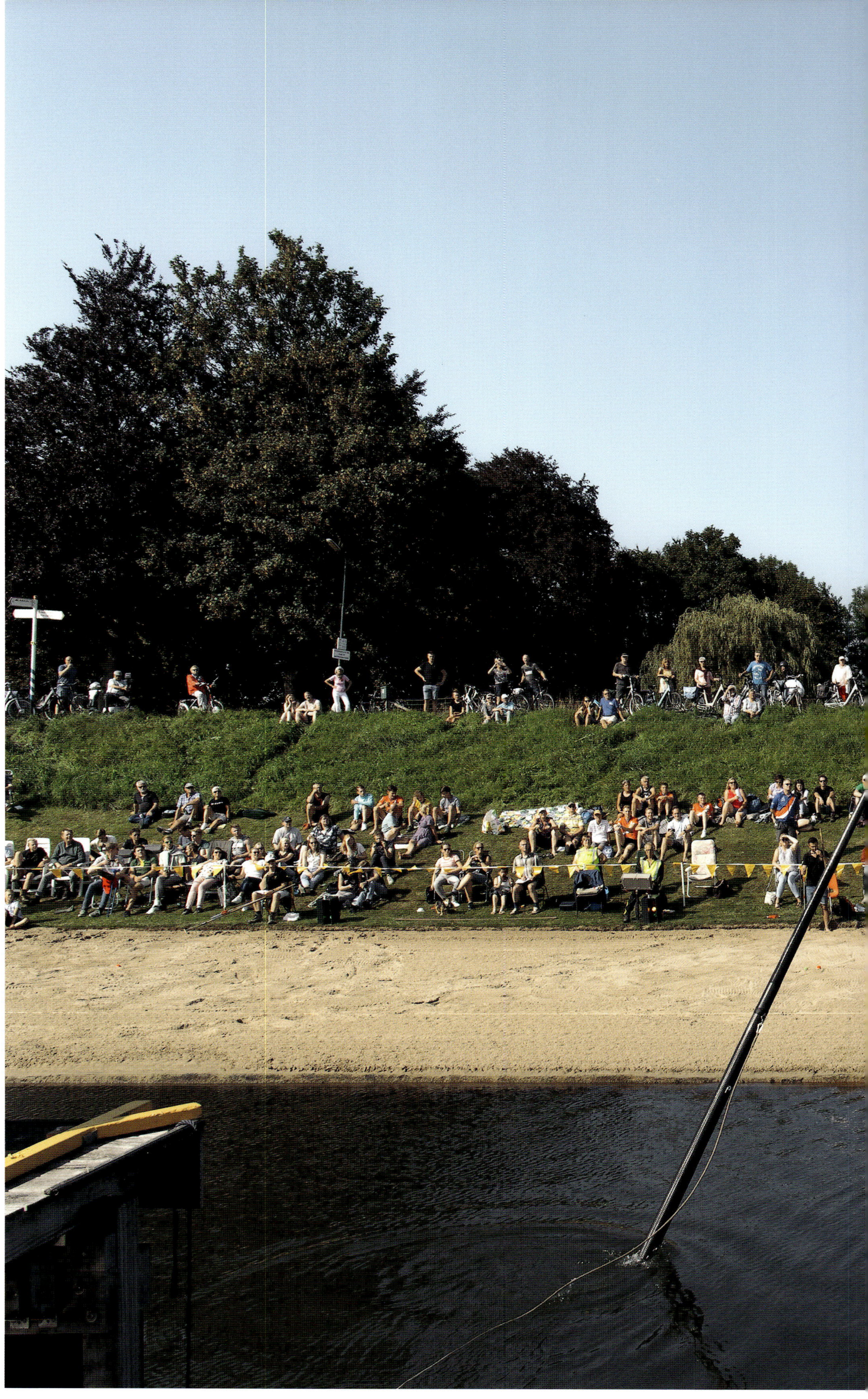

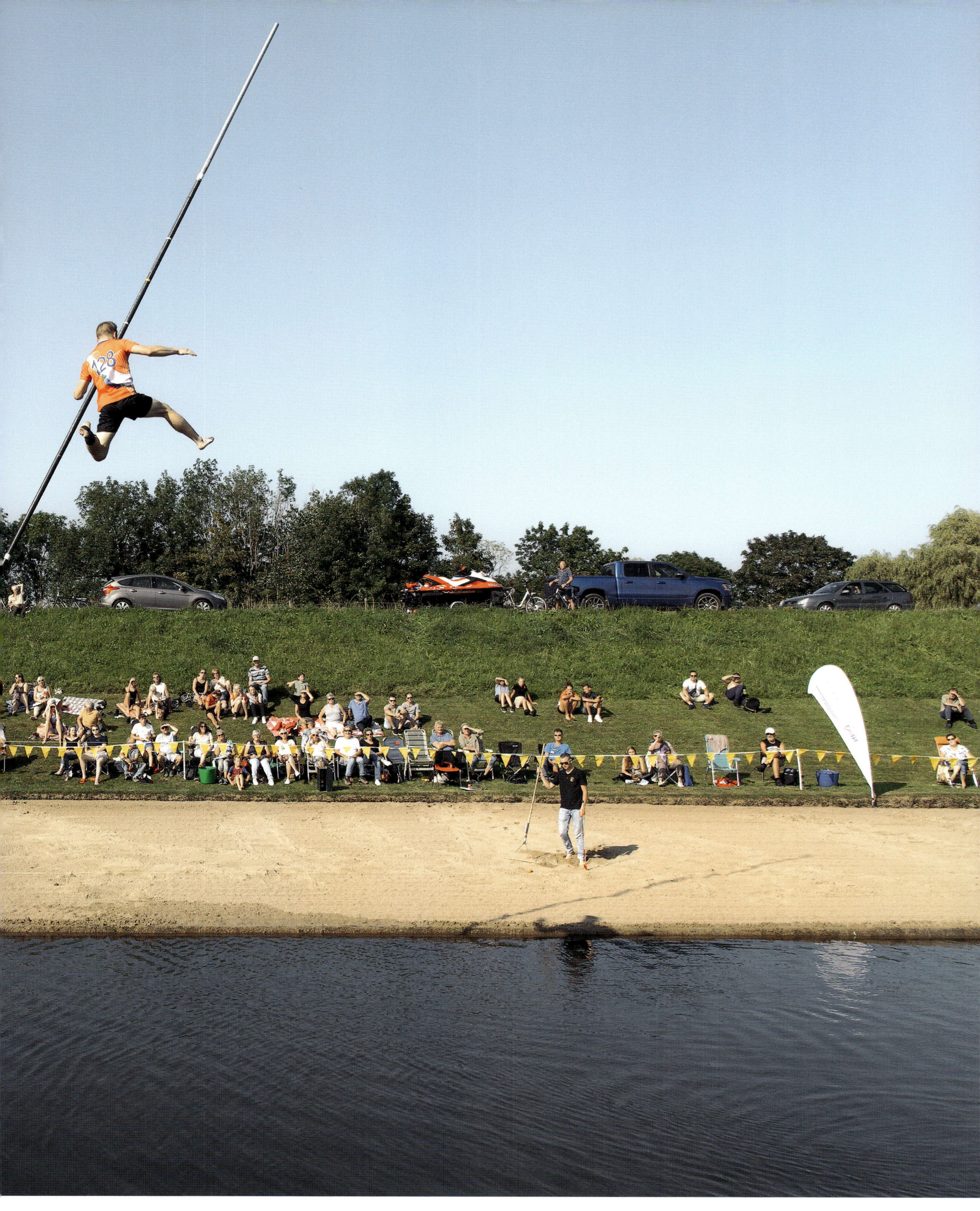

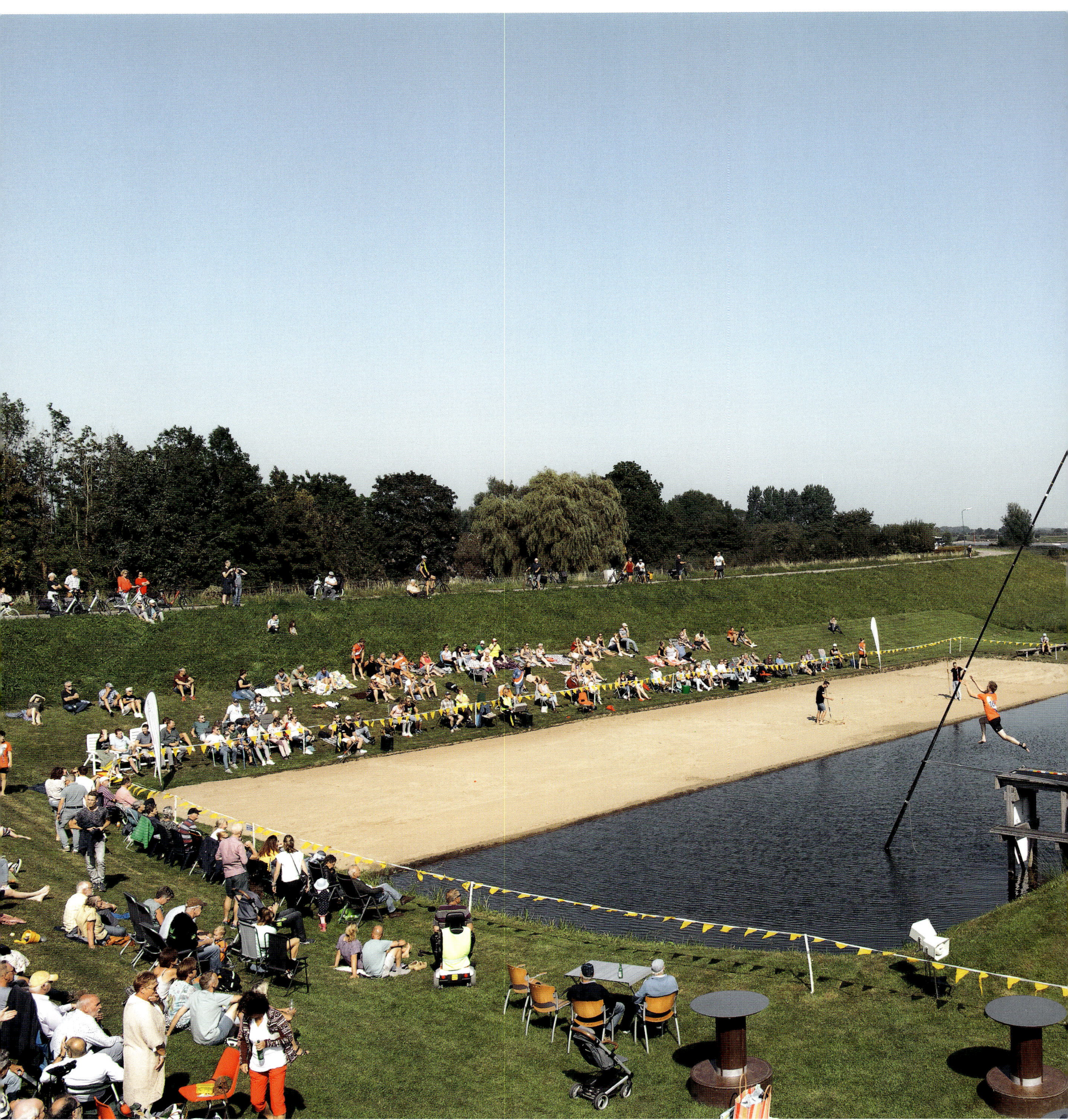

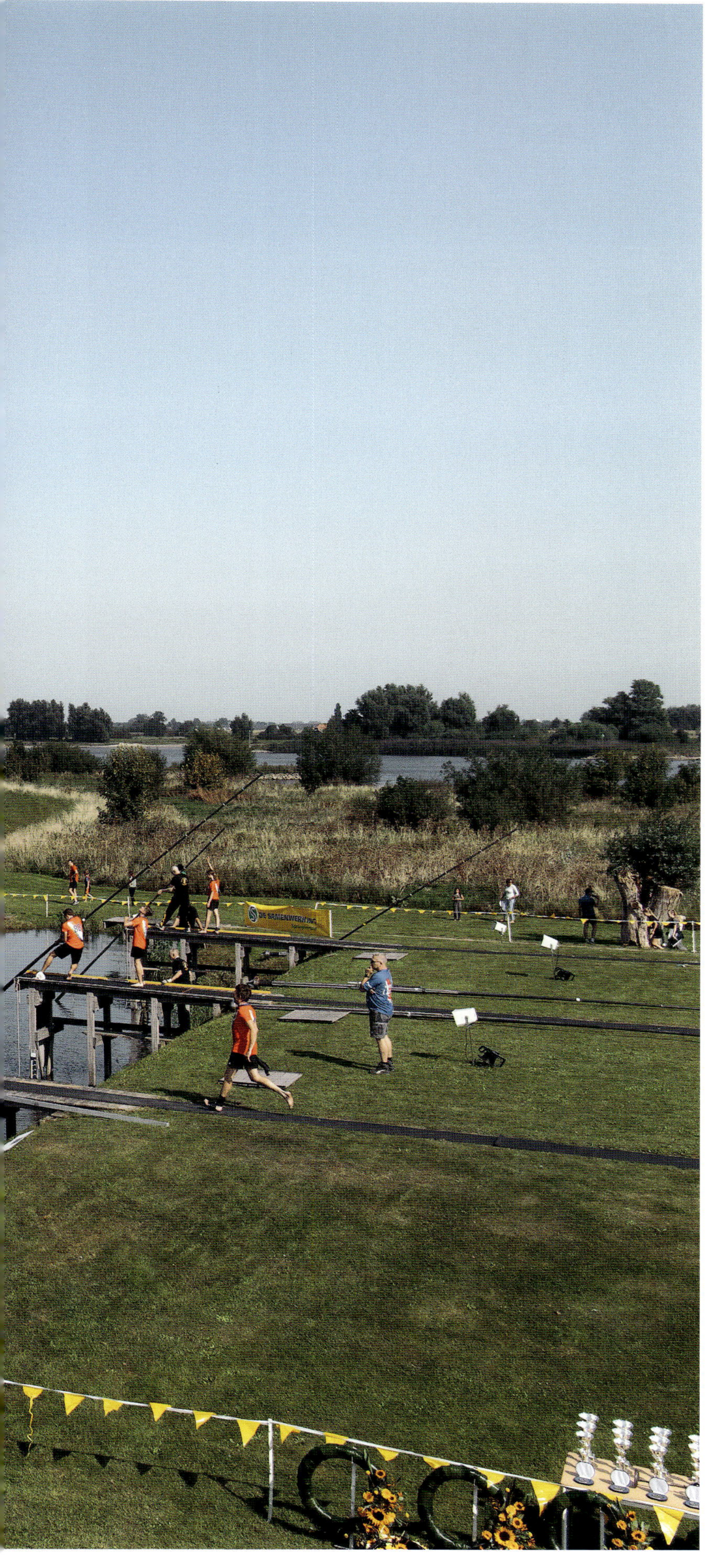

The friendly rivalry between the provinces of
Friesland and Utrecht takes on a serious tone as the
winners of the Friese and Holland Championships
try to prove who the master leapers are.

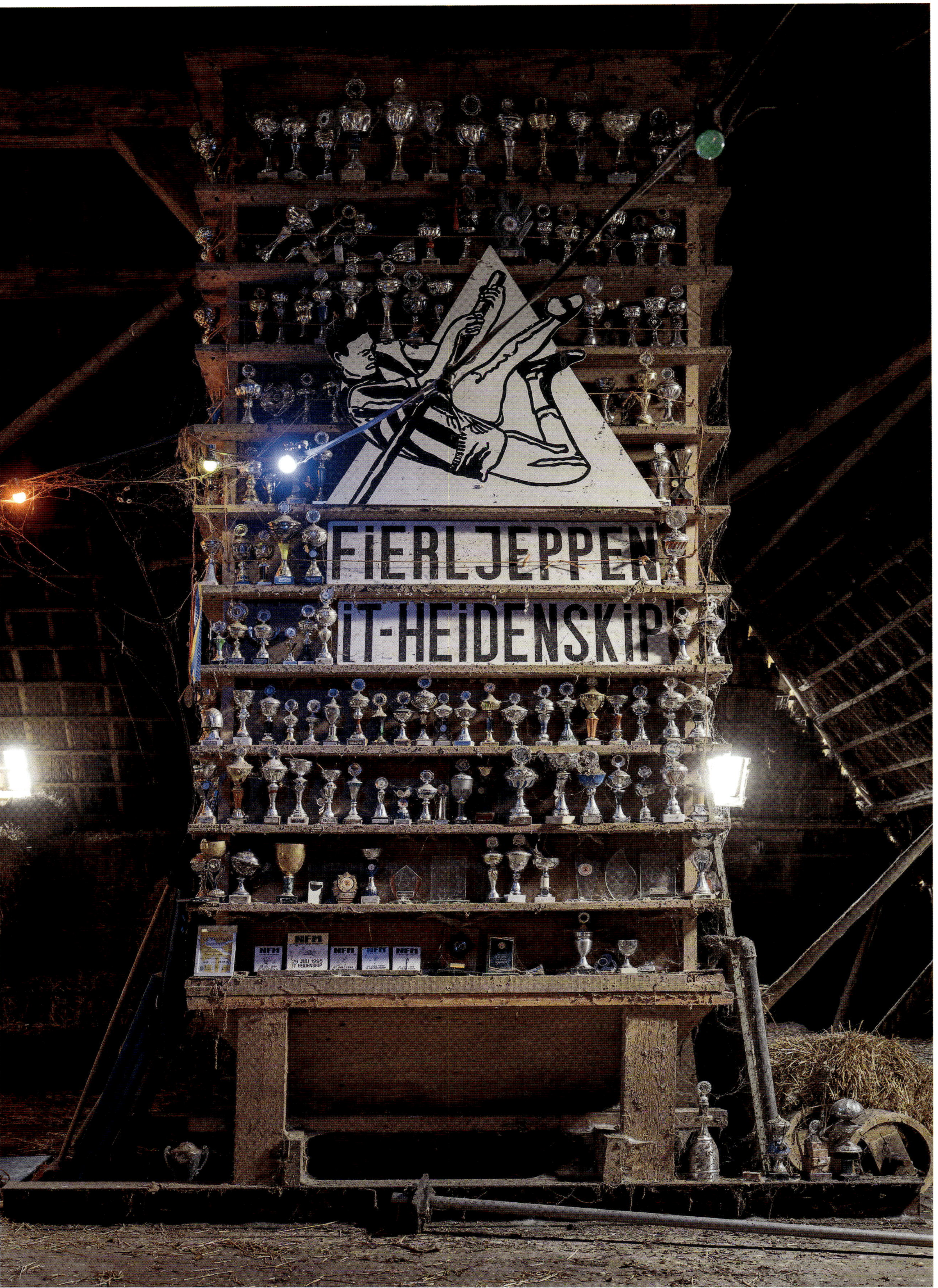

FIERLJEPPEN
IT-HEIDENSKIP

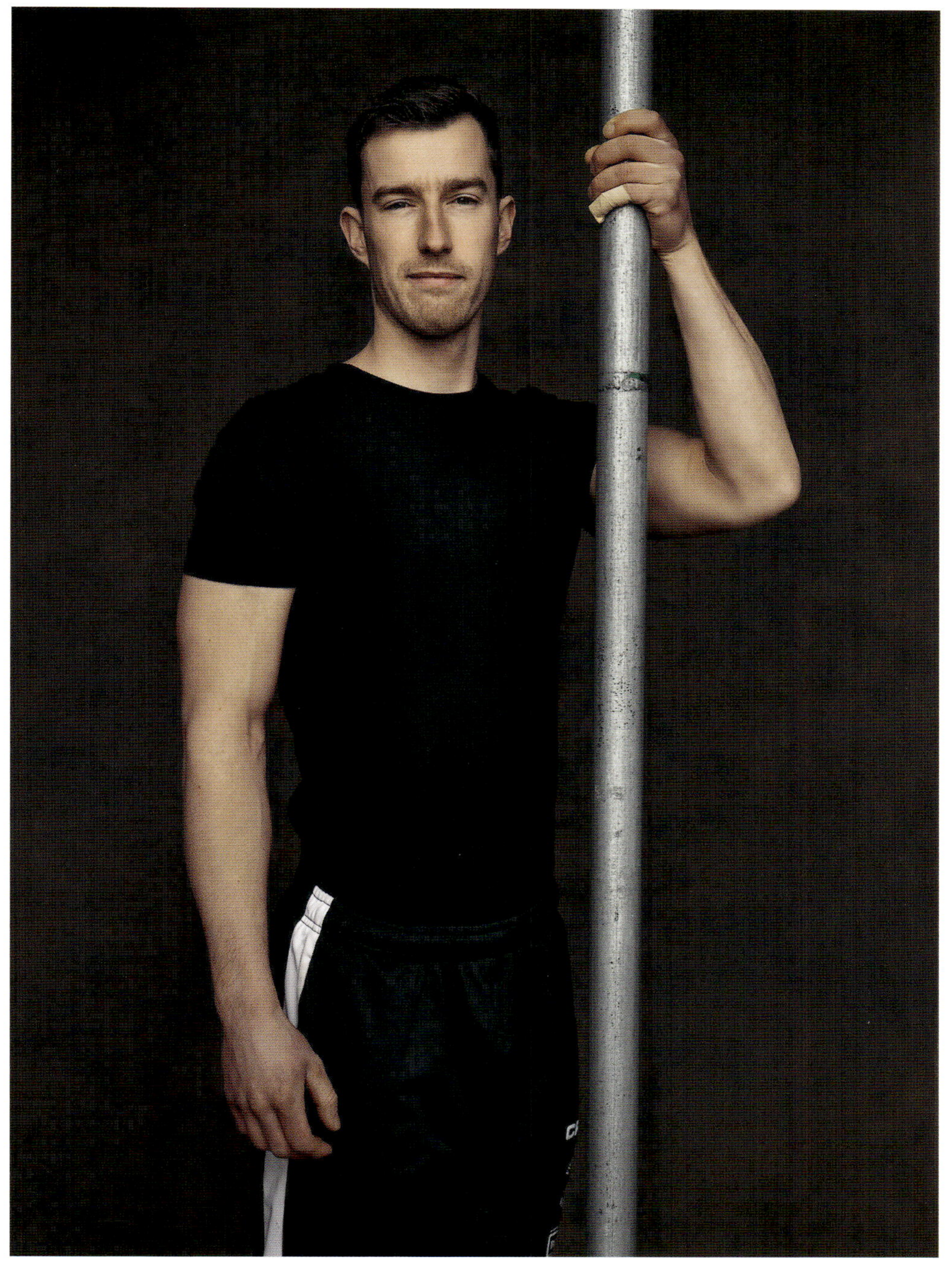

Bauke de Jong,
National Fierljeppen Champion

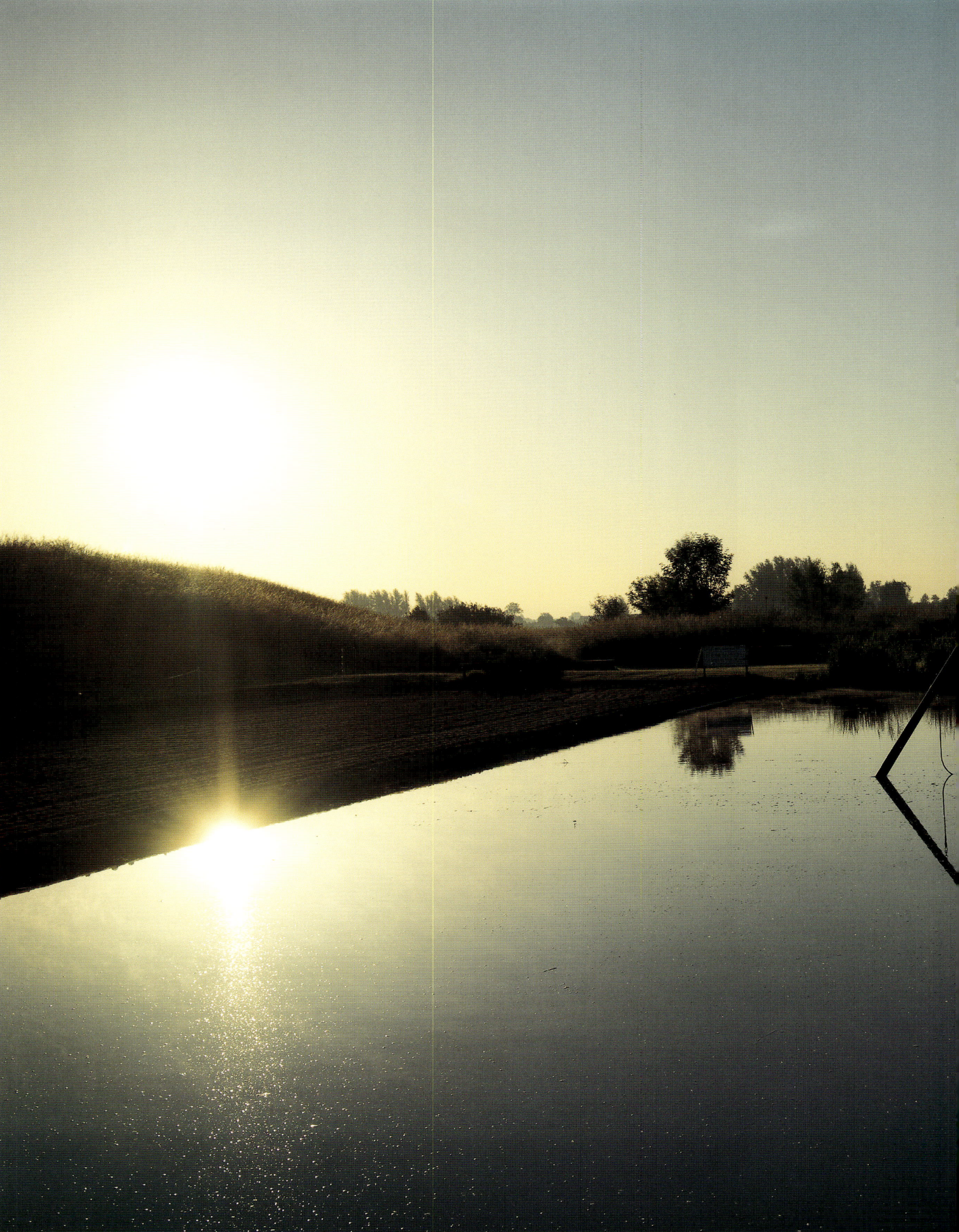

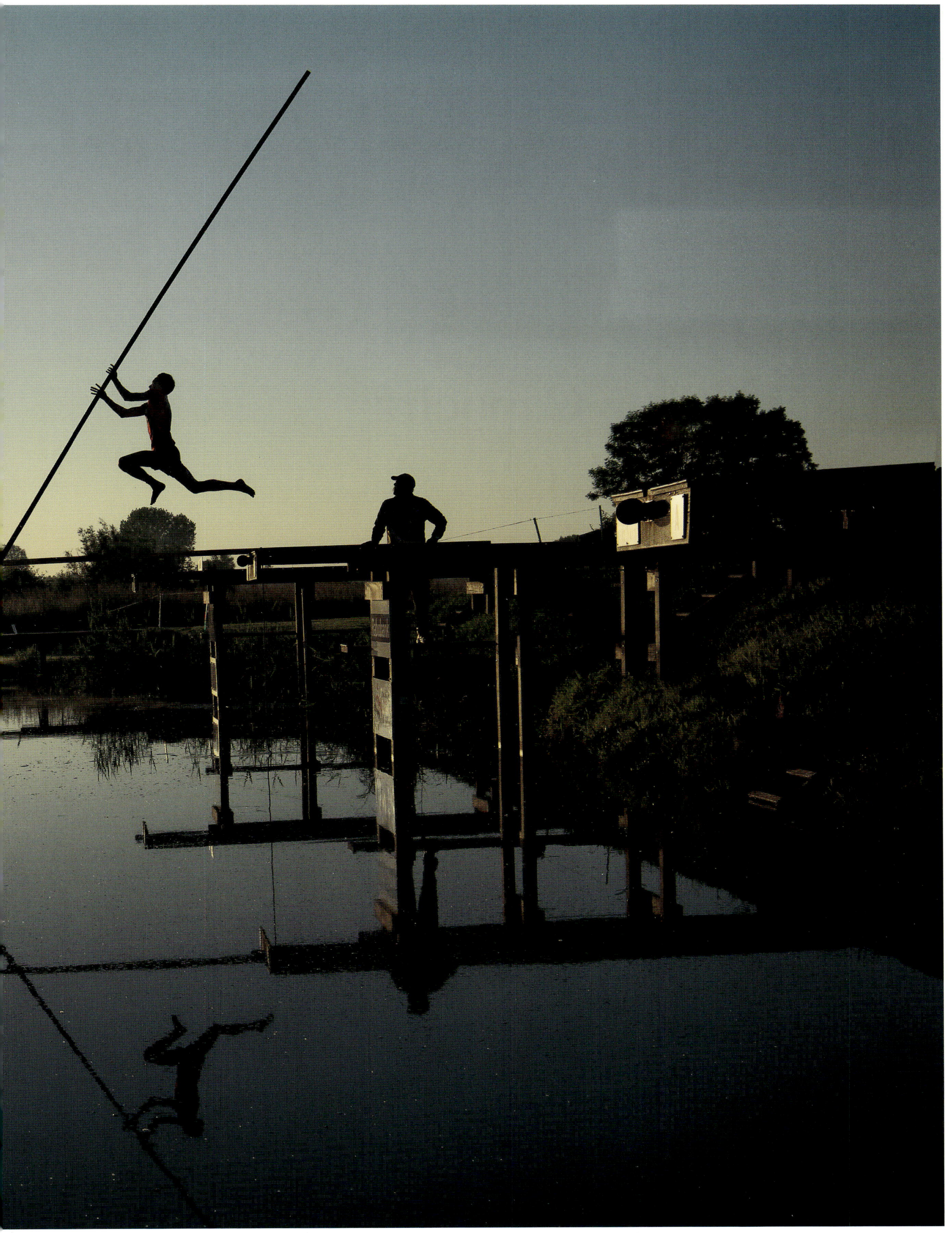

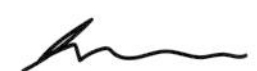

Capoeira

BRAZIL

*The pulsating rhythms of this mesmerising game sway in
unison with acrobatic kicks of precision and agility.*

Rising from the ashes of oppression like a phoenix taking flight, the pulsating rhythms of this mesmerising game sway in unison with acrobatic kicks of precision and agility. Capoeira, Brazil's most beloved, spirited martial art, camouflaged as a graceful dance, has extended its popularity far beyond Brazil's borders, bringing joy to all who play or witness it. Here, in one of the most exuberant and passionate playgrounds in the world, a place synonymous with colour, carnival and long expanses of sandy beaches, the horror of slavery has etched itself into Brazil's history. Capoeira's roots stretch back to enslaved Africans whose only means of freedom was to secretly train their minds and bodies in an act of resistance.

ARPOADOR,
RIO DE JANEIRO

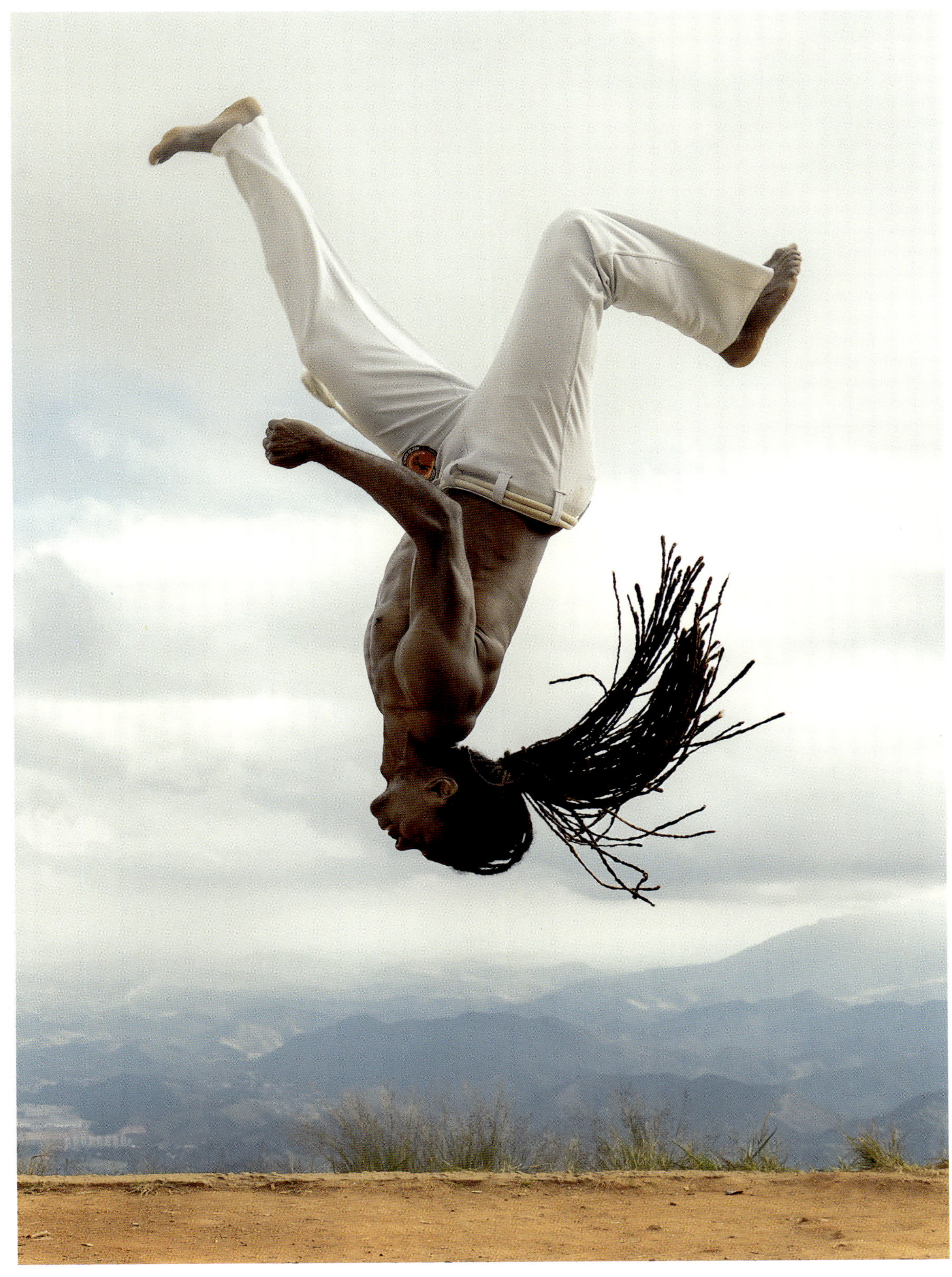

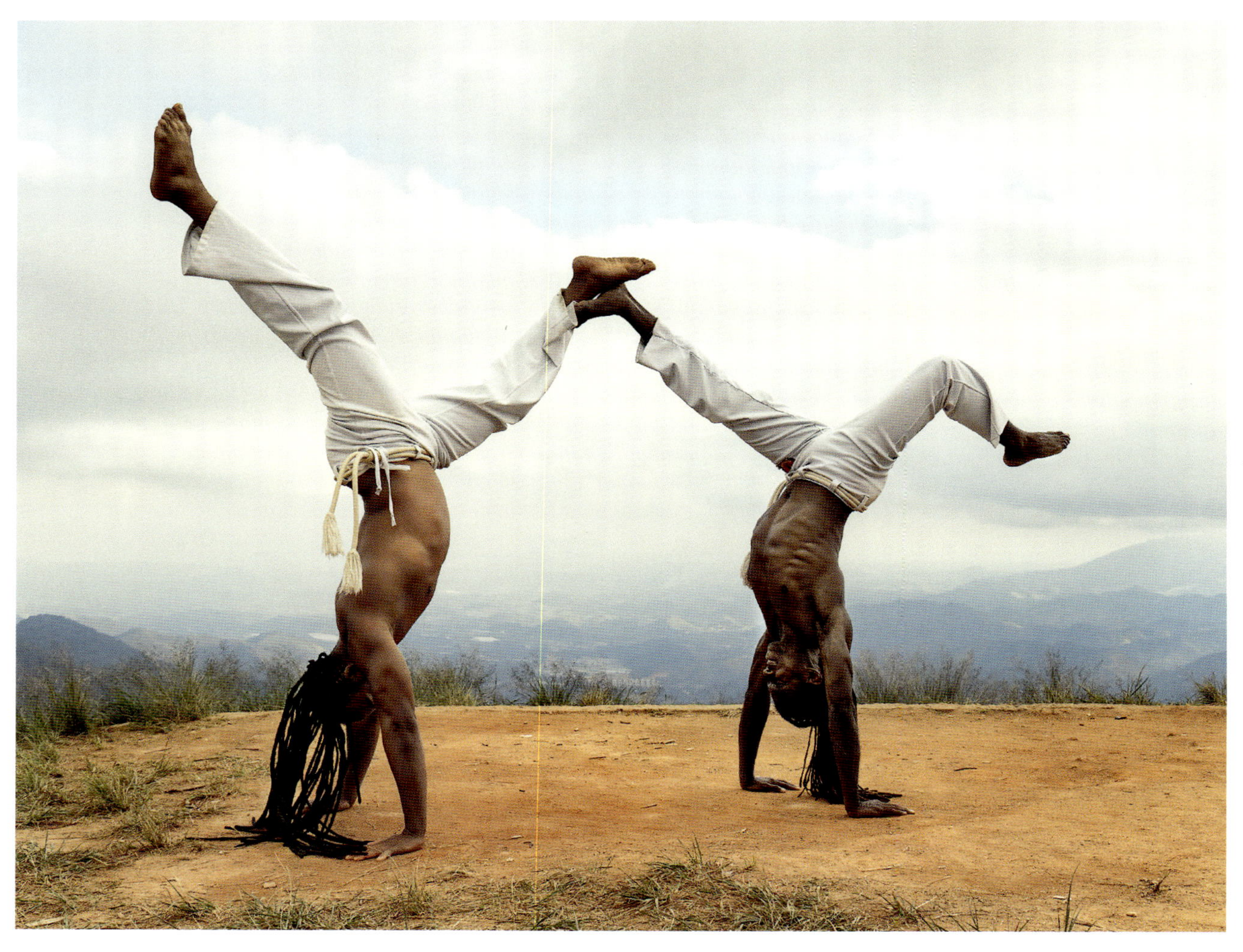

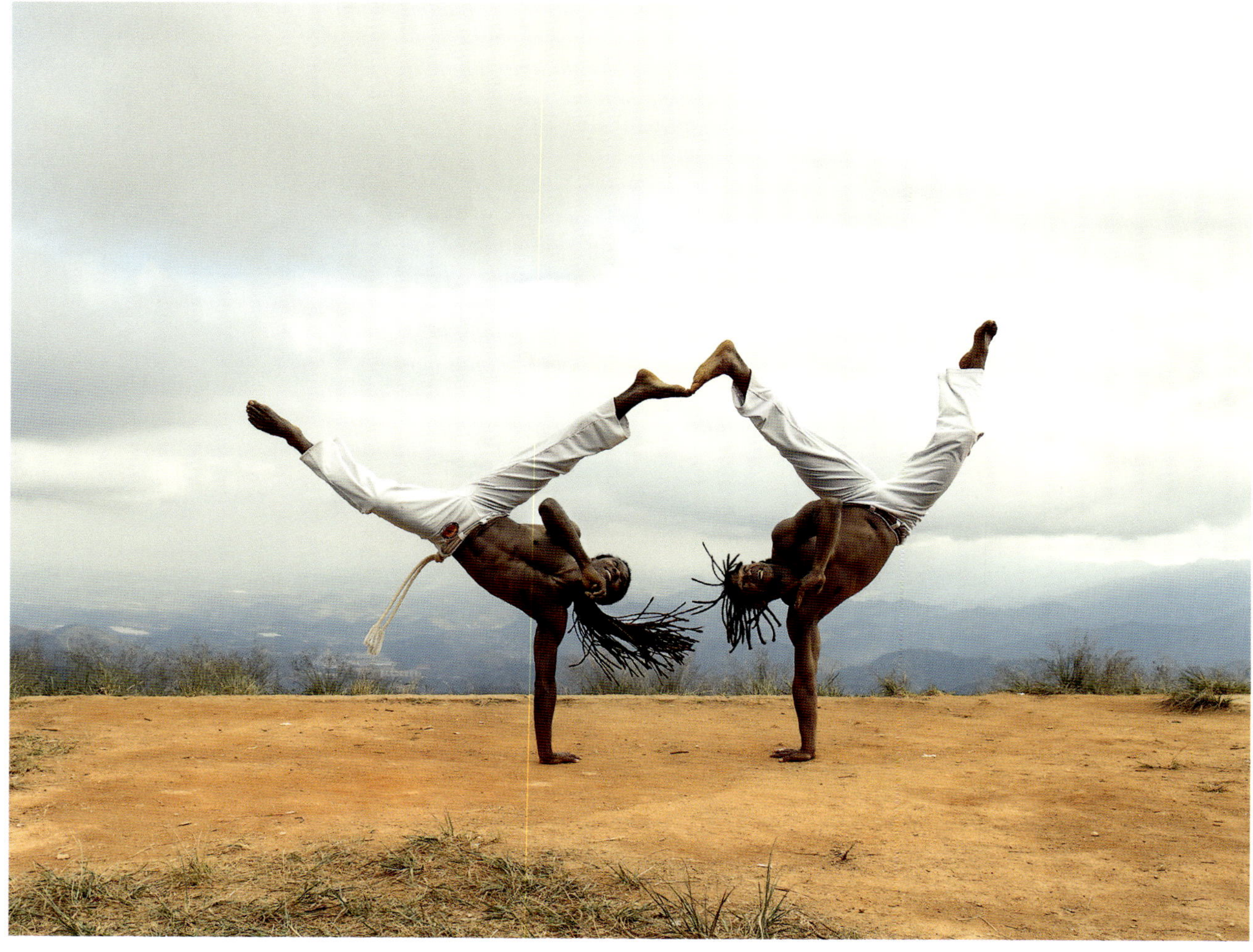

*"Capoeira is a game, it is dance, it is fight,
it is of war and it is of peace, it is of culture,
of music, it is a portion of things."*

~ Reinaldo Ramos Suassuna ~

During pseudo-celebrations, people would sing and dance in tight circles to guard and conceal the acrobatic warriors in the centre, who were fighting for the survival of their community. The *berimbau*, a single-stringed percussive instrument, was used to warn the warriors of the arrival of enslavers, giving them time to switch to a seemingly harmless dance. Despite the abolition of slavery in 1888, the Brazilian government still considered capoeira a crime; those caught practising it were severely punished, even killed. It wasn't until the 1930s that capoeira was decriminalised, and in 2014 UNESCO declared it part of humanity's 'intangible cultural heritage', securing its place in Afro-Brazilian culture.

The rules of the game are straightforward: two participants, entering a circle formed by both musicians and fighters, synchronise their movements in a simulated fight, never touching the opponent, while rhythmic music sets the tempo for the game. The surrounding players clap their hands to the beat of the drum and sing songs that reflect their historical struggle. The end of the game is marked by a fighter leaving the circle or another capoeirista jumping in to fight.

Witnessing capoeira is like being part of an ecstatic theatre performance. Everything revolves around creating *axé*, the sacred energy that makes it all happen. The stage is set as heartbeats harmonise with the sounds of the *berimbaus*, *pandeiros* (tambourines), an *atabaque* (drum) and an *agogô* (bell) echoing into the hot, thick air in a call-and-response conversation amid a *roda* (circle of capoeiristas). As a display of respect, opponents squat in front of the band leader before the improvisational game of defence and attack begins.

Outfitted in pristine white clothing and a *cordão* (a belt in the colour of the players' acquired skill), they alternate from slow rhythmic movements called *ginga* (rocking back and forth) to fast-paced action. The main objectives are to be in constant motion, avoid being a target and distract the opponent through dodges and bluffs, luring them into the open for a counter-attack. From ground rolls and leg sweeps to high-flying kicks and dizzying cartwheels, it all takes place at lightning speed, leaving spectators happily bewildered.

Mainly men play capoeira, but as its popularity spreads – it is now practised in over 160 countries worldwide – more women and children participate. Capoeira gives children a unique opportunity to creatively move their bodies while developing coordination, flexibility, confidence and a strong sense of community. The children of the favelas stand to benefit the most from this sport, giving them an escape from the drugs, violence and poverty surrounding them.

The rise in the popularity of capoeira has created new interpretations. However, the most authentic, true-to-its-roots form is still found on the streets of Brazil, thanks to its strong spiritual connection to *candomblé* ('dance in honour of the gods') – a mixture of traditional African beliefs with traces of Catholicism.

Although the iconic capoeira was born of the gravest of crimes against humanity, it has alchemically transformed hate into a captivating art form and a positive force for change that will undoubtedly continue as a cultural legacy.

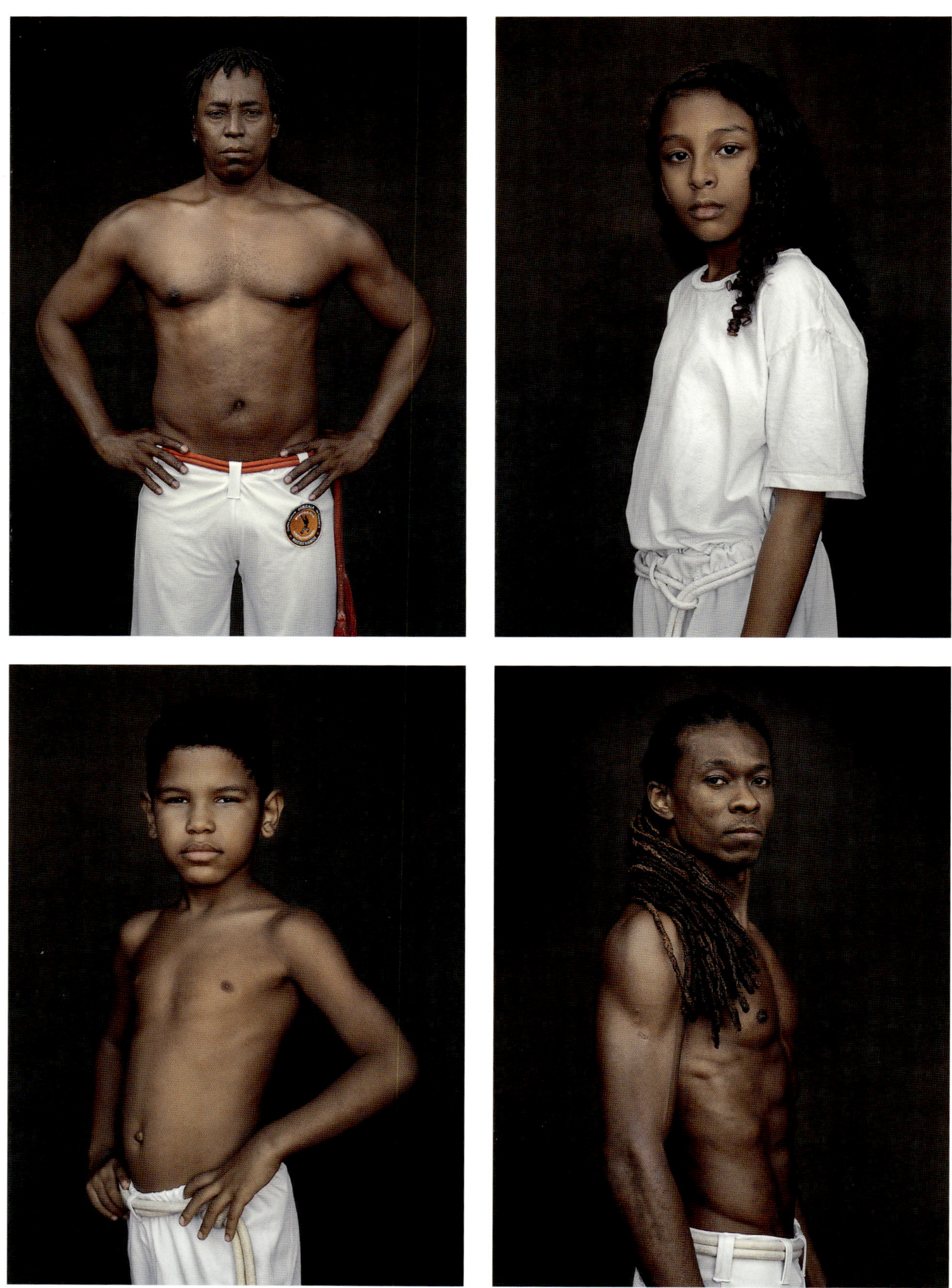

Capoeiristas must wear white pants
(abada), a white t-shirt and a belt (cordão),
specific to their experience level.

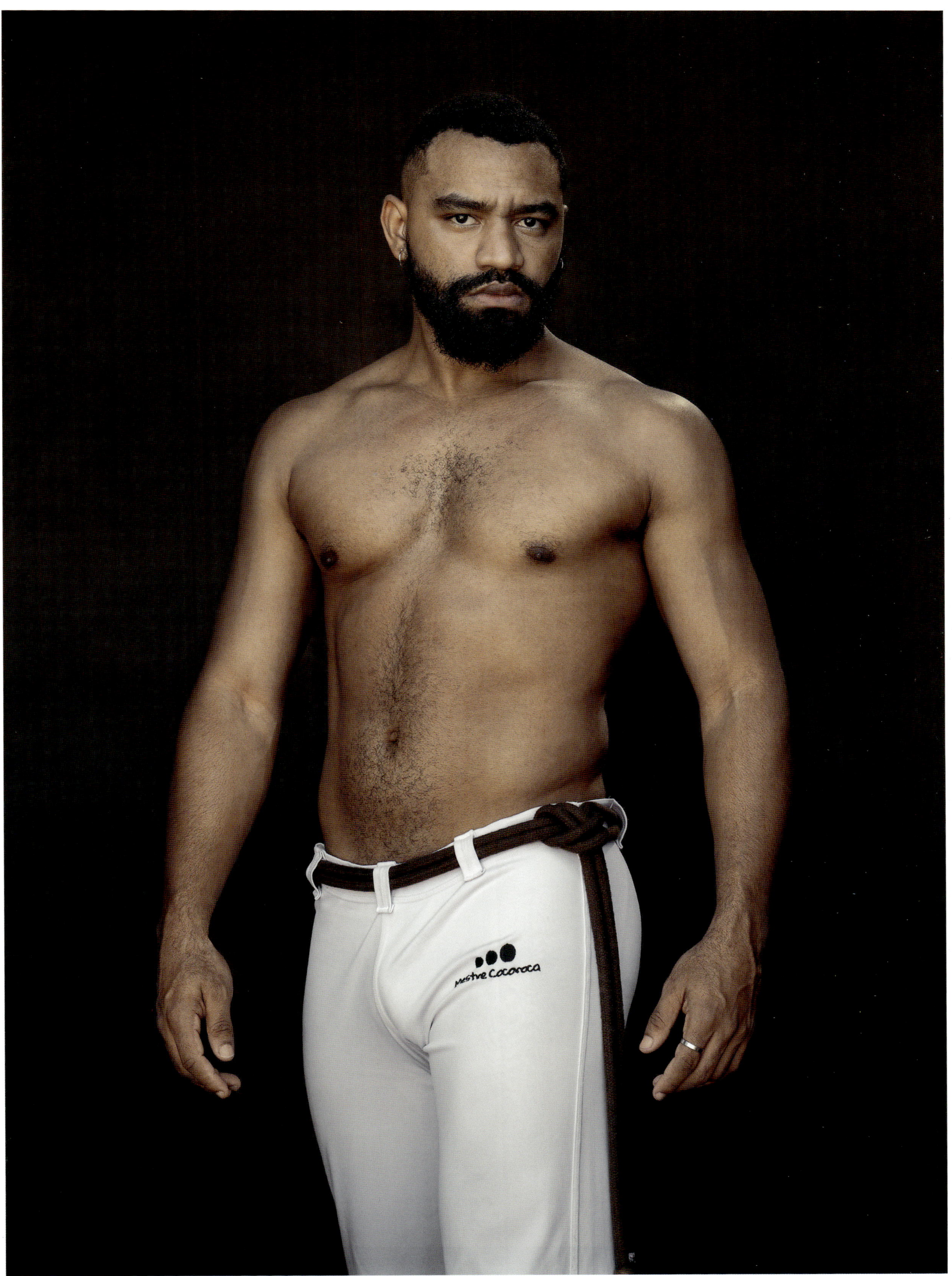

Mestre Cacaroca

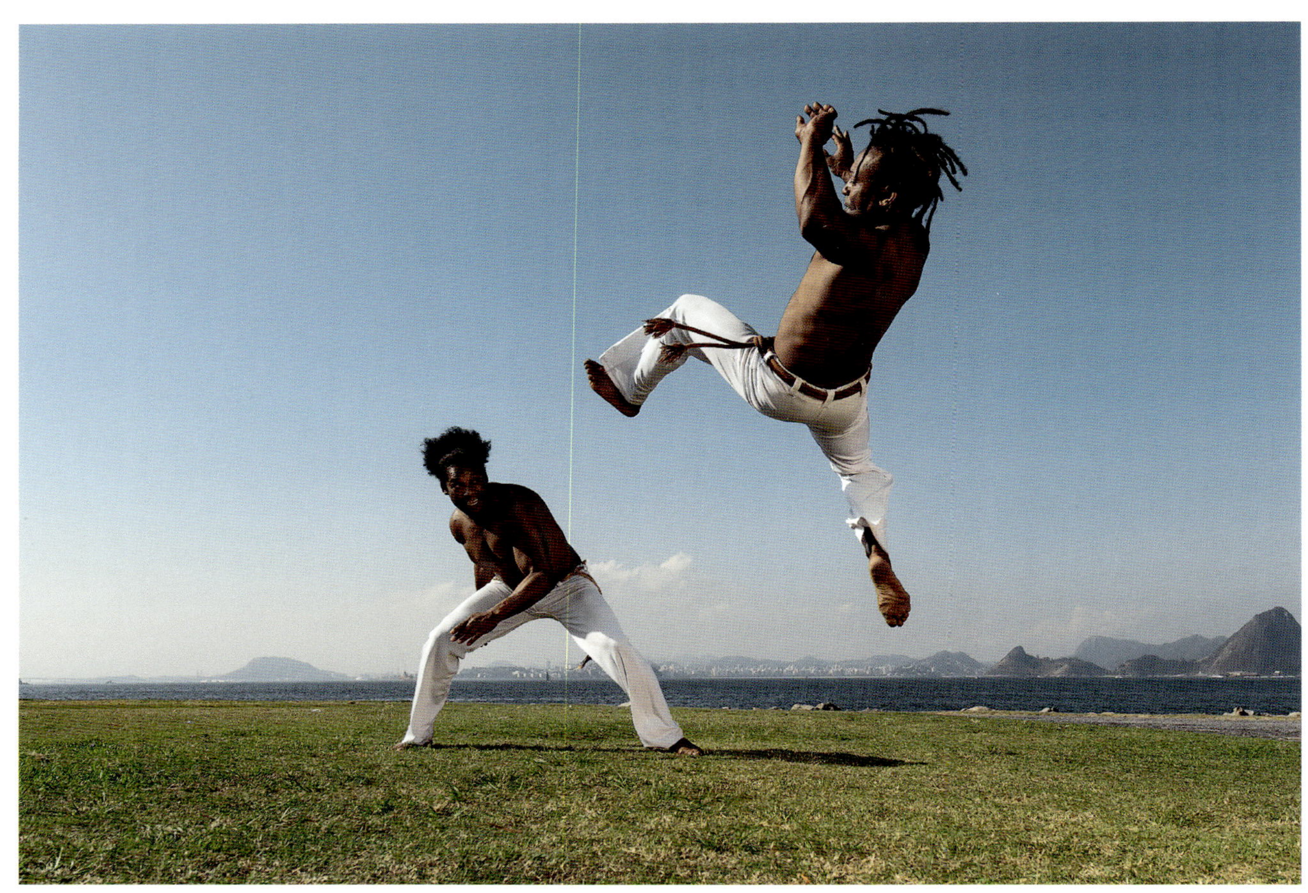

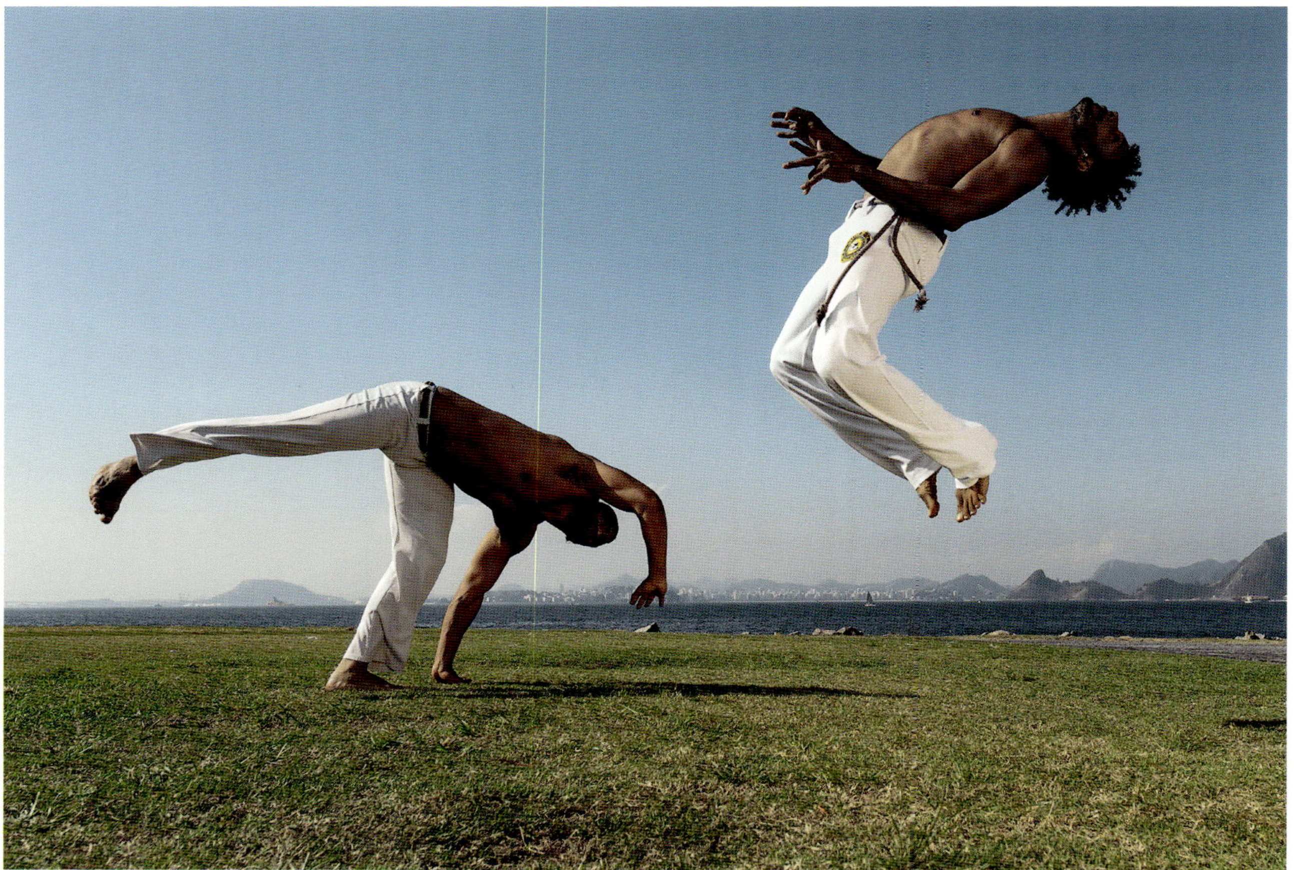

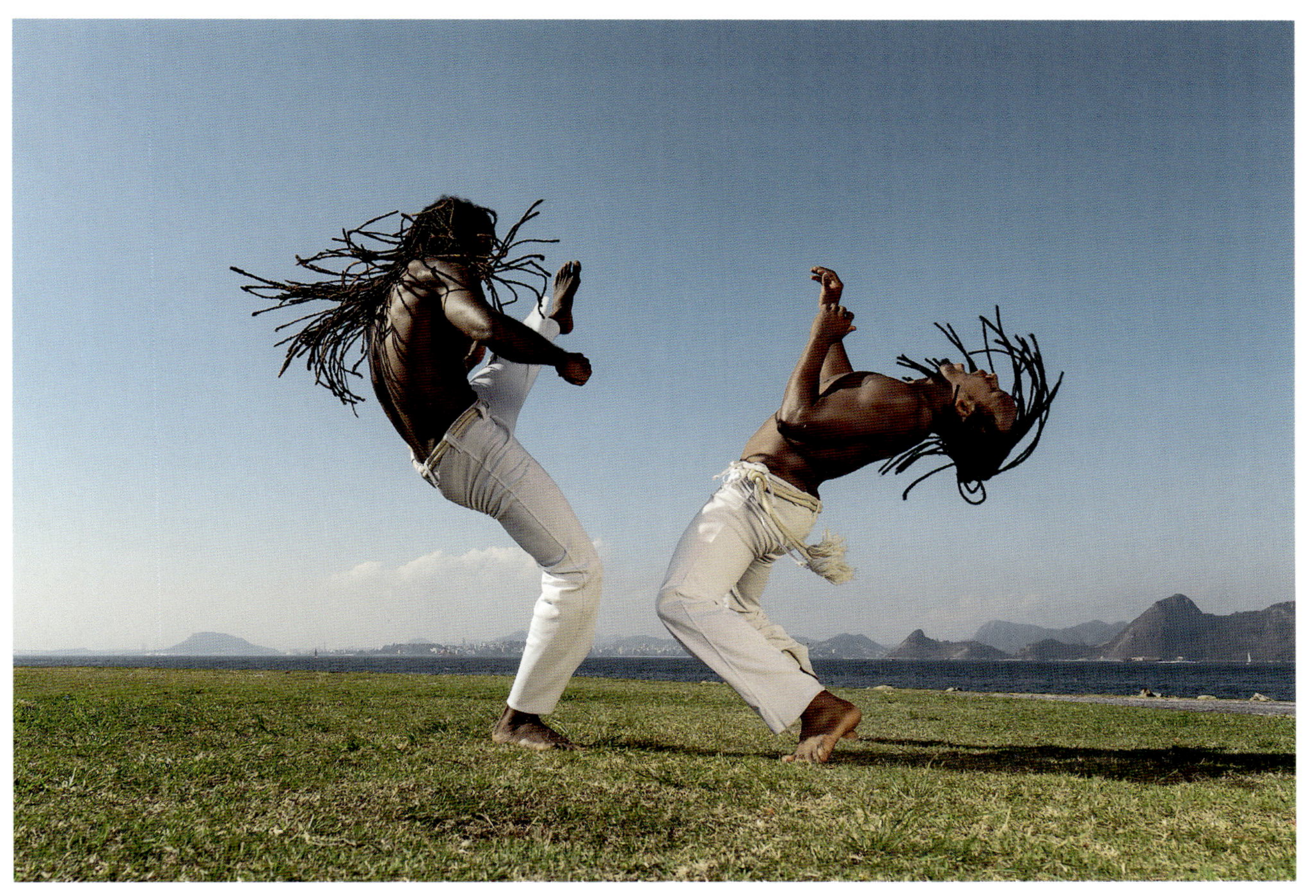

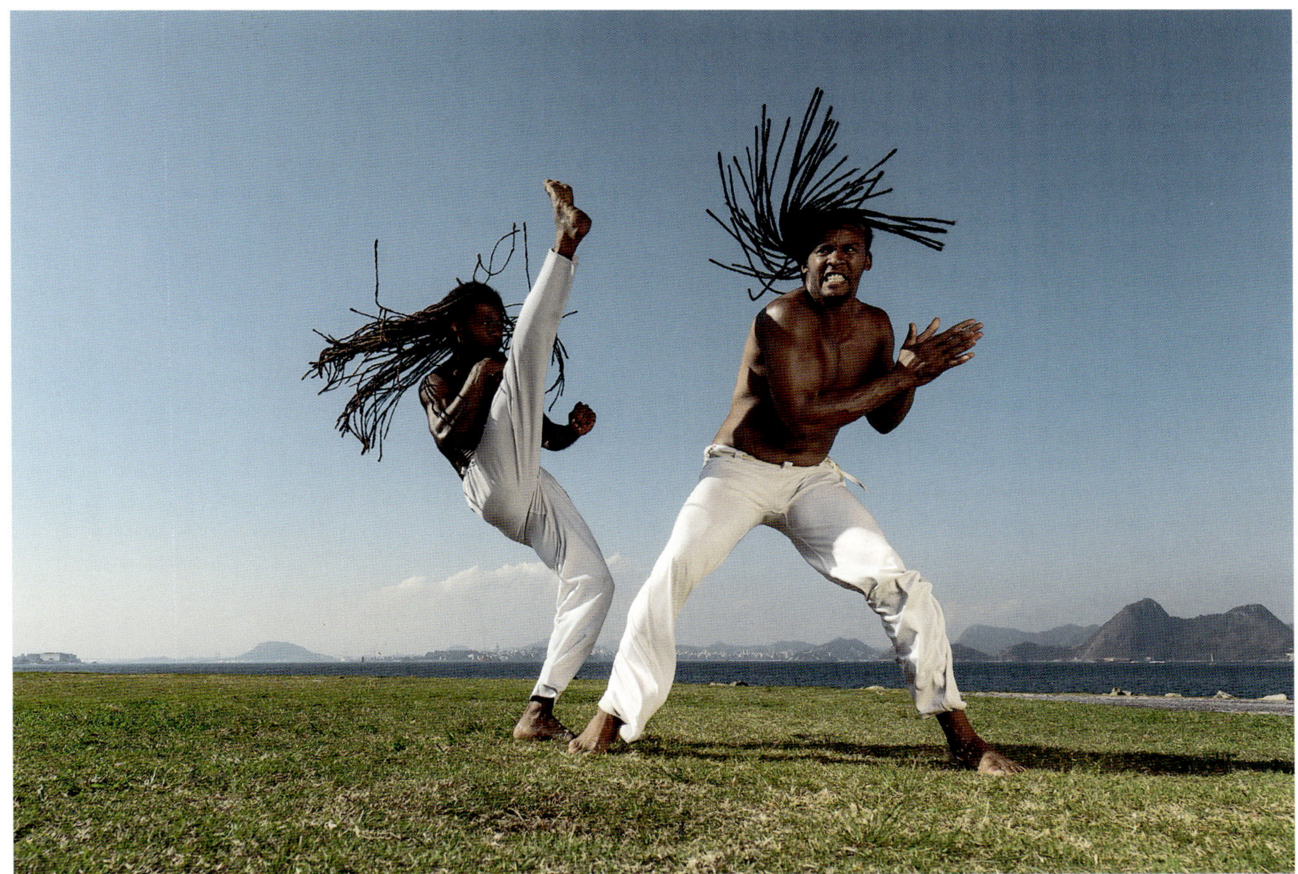

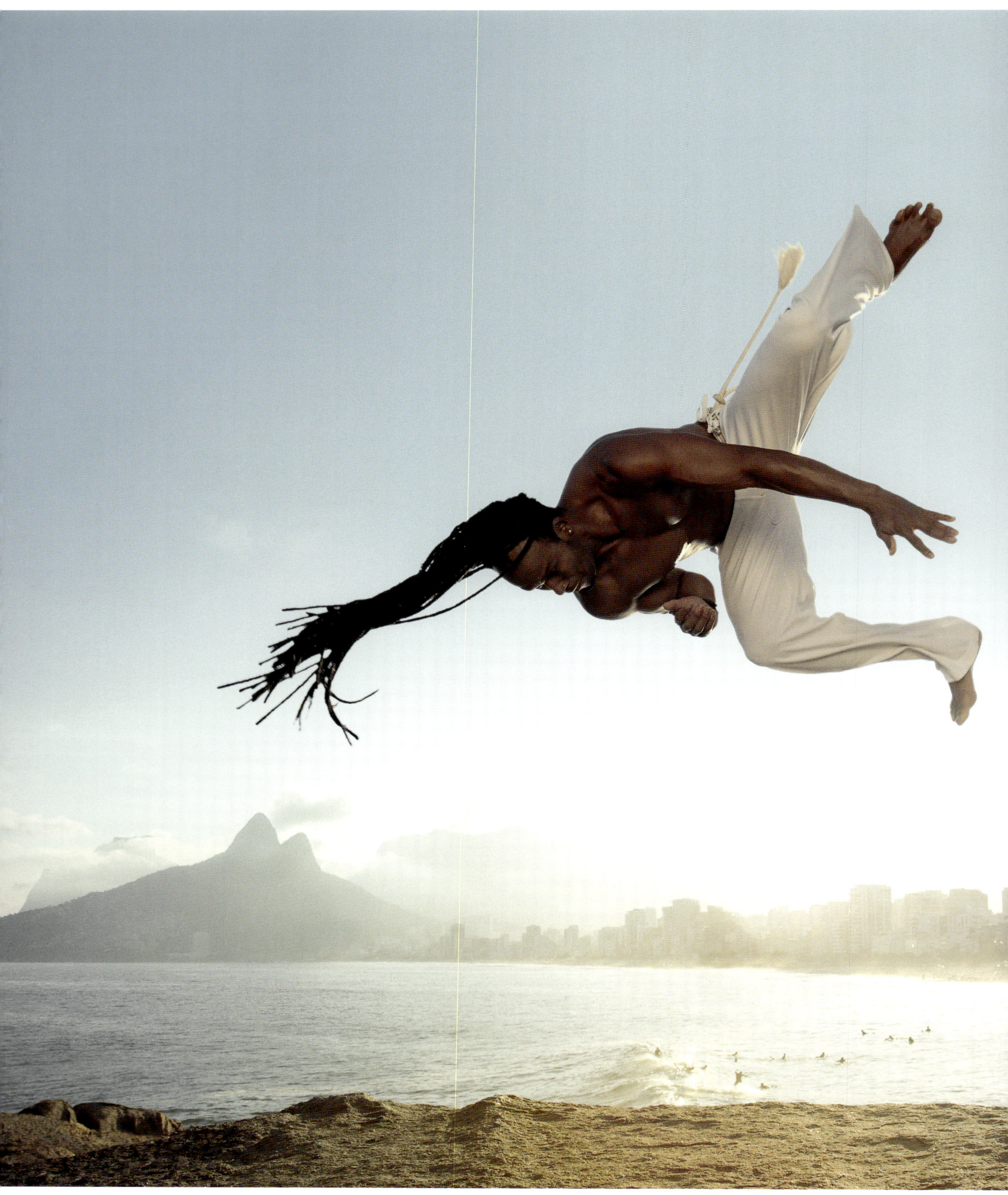

"A true capoeirista is not the
one who simply knows how to
move the body but the one
who is moved by the soul."

~ Mestre Pastinha ~

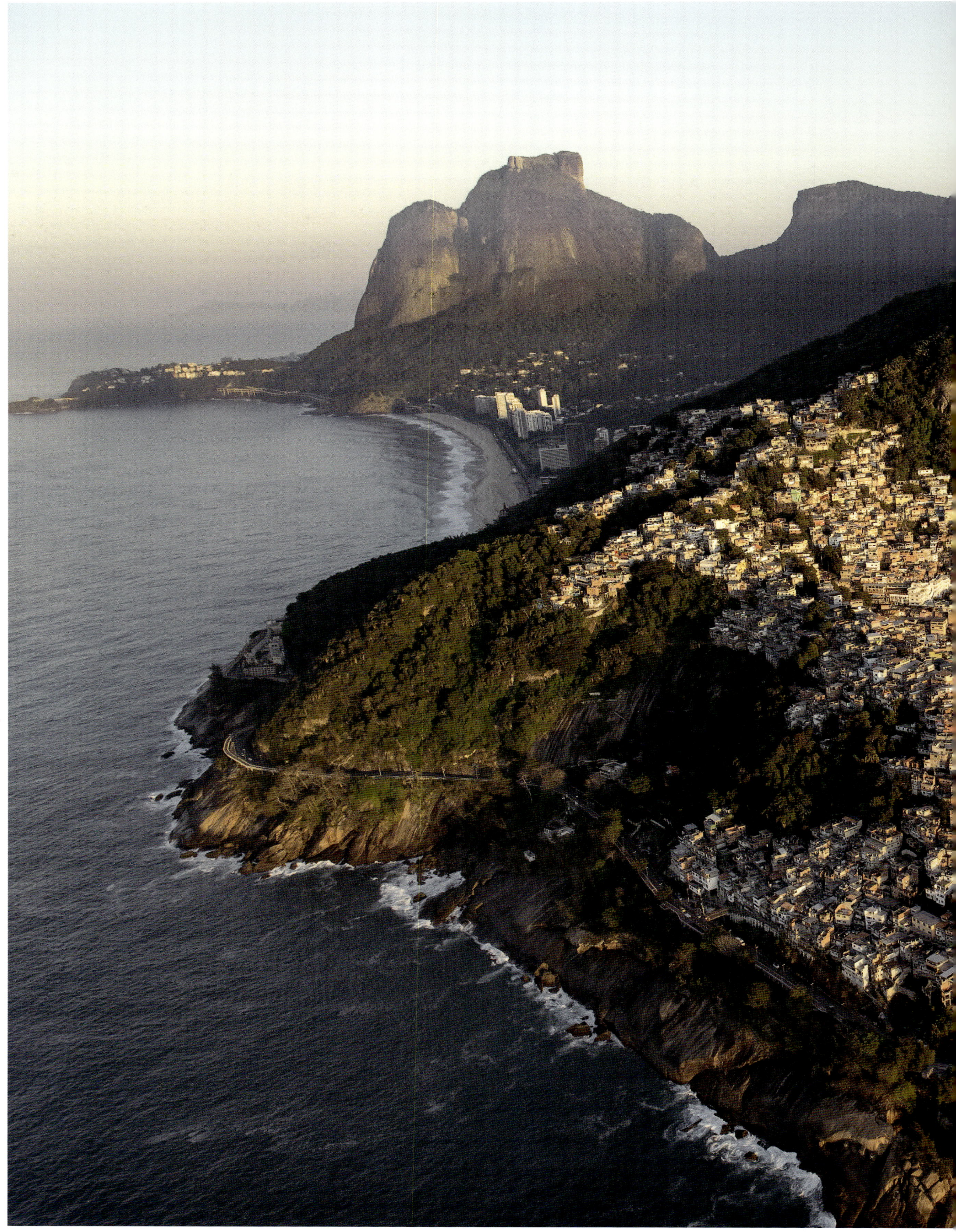

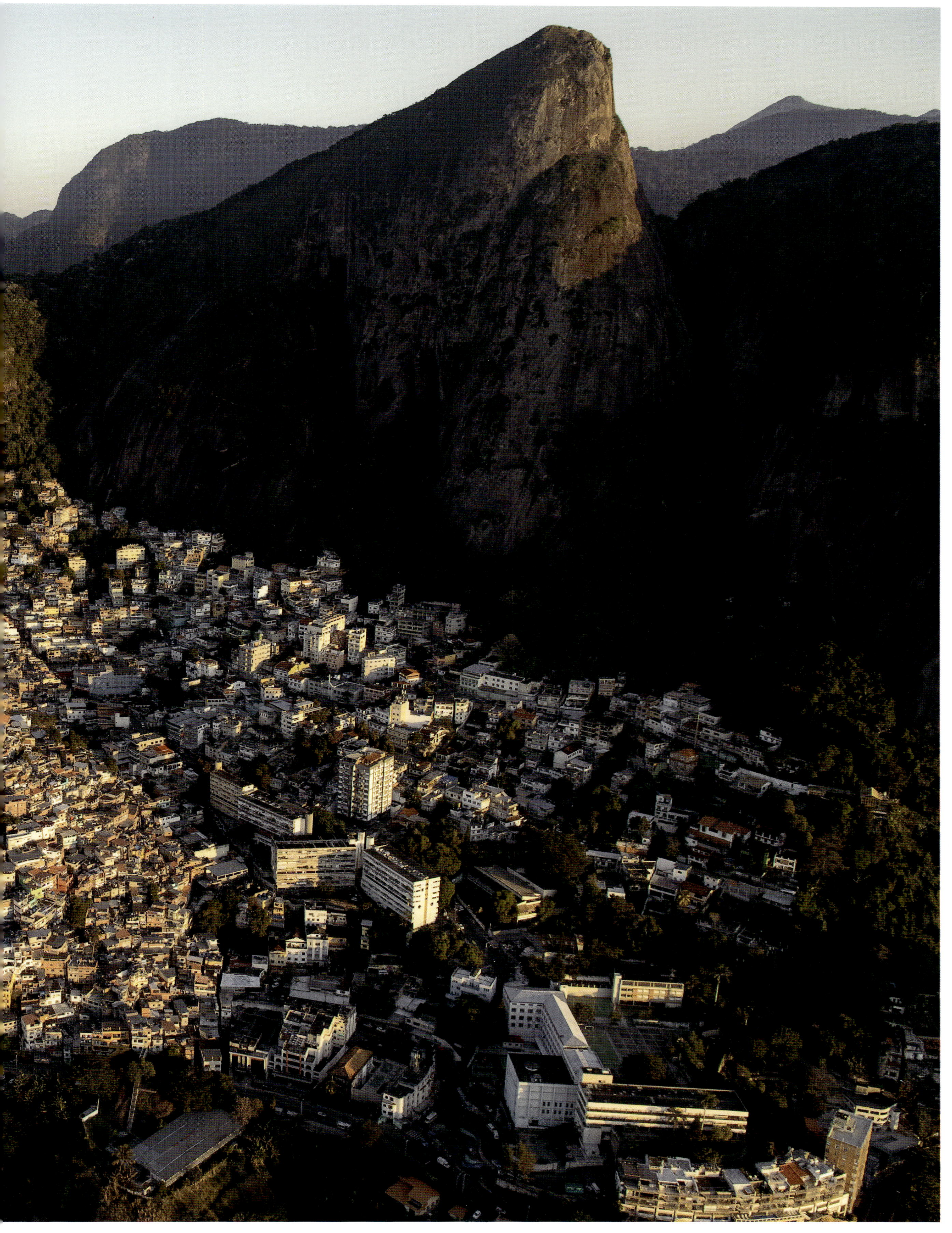

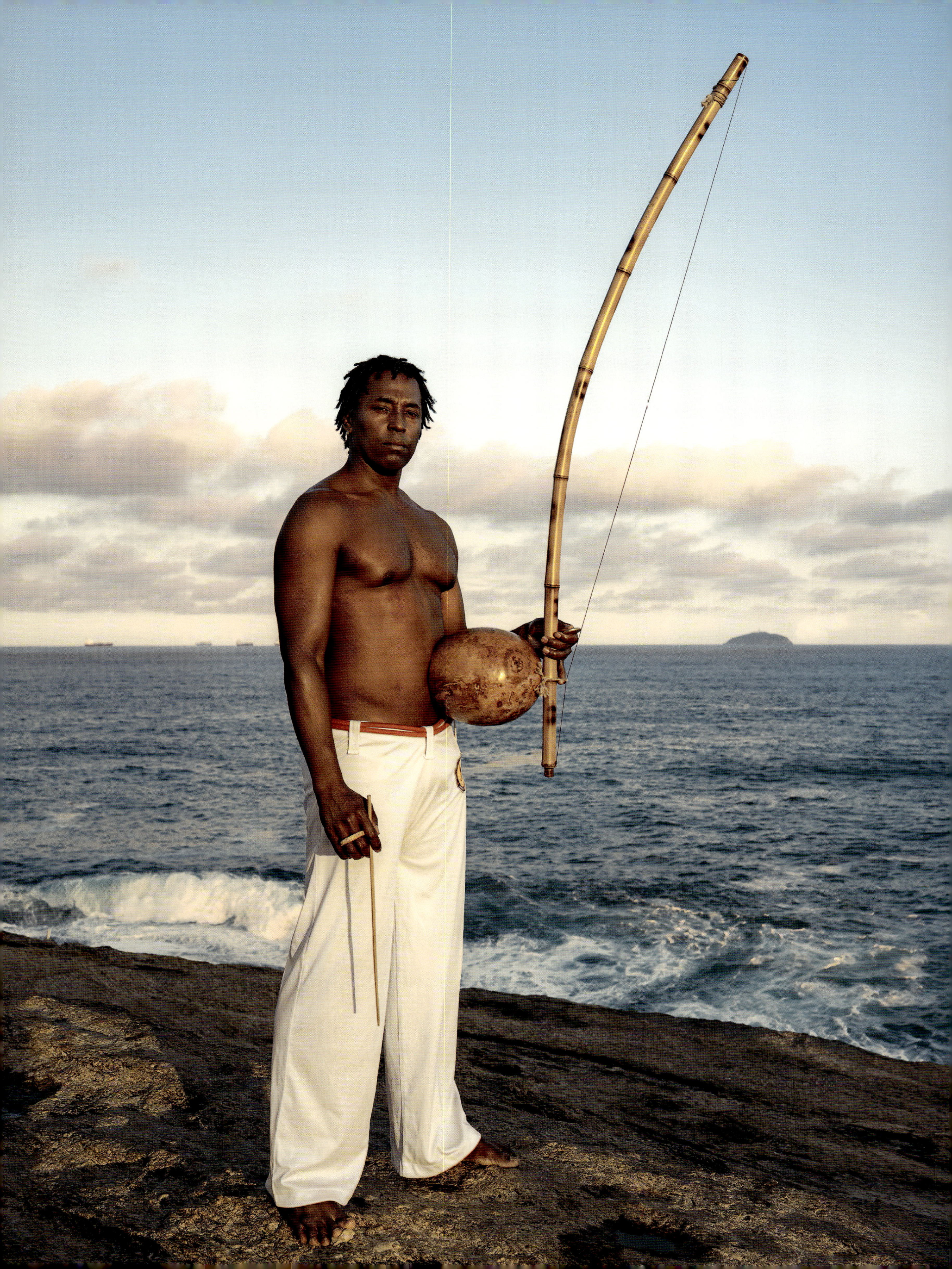

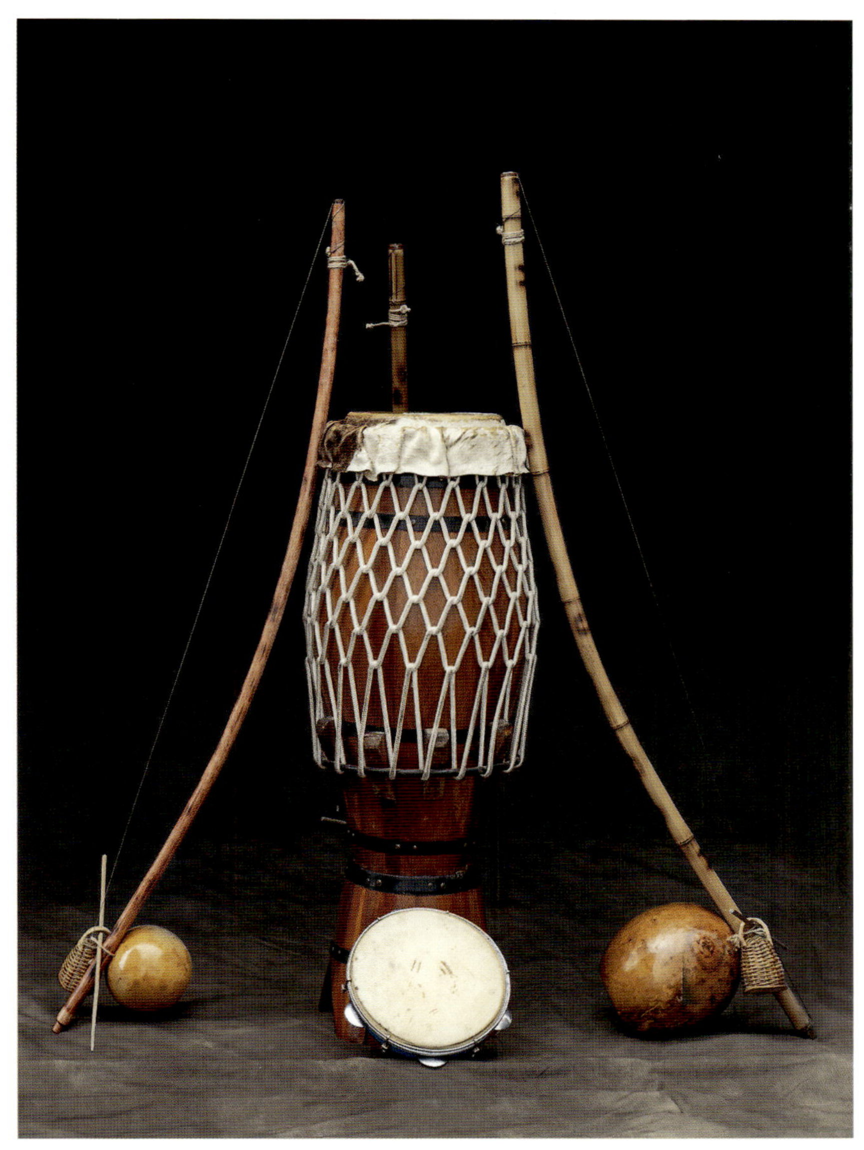

Music is essential to capoeira, expressed through
playing ancient rhythms with traditional instruments
like the berimbau, singing ancestral songs and creating
axé, the sacred energy that the sport revolves around.

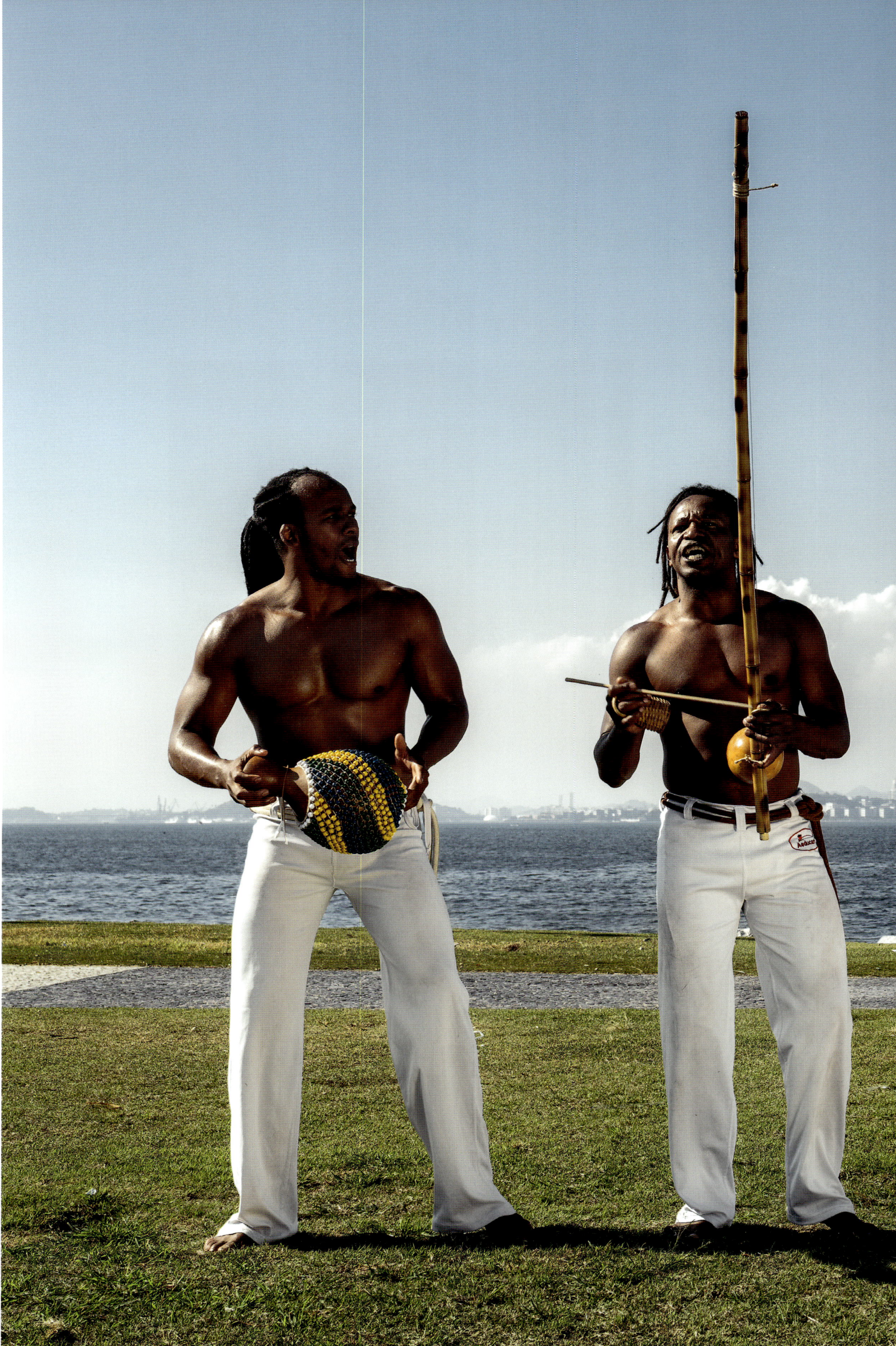

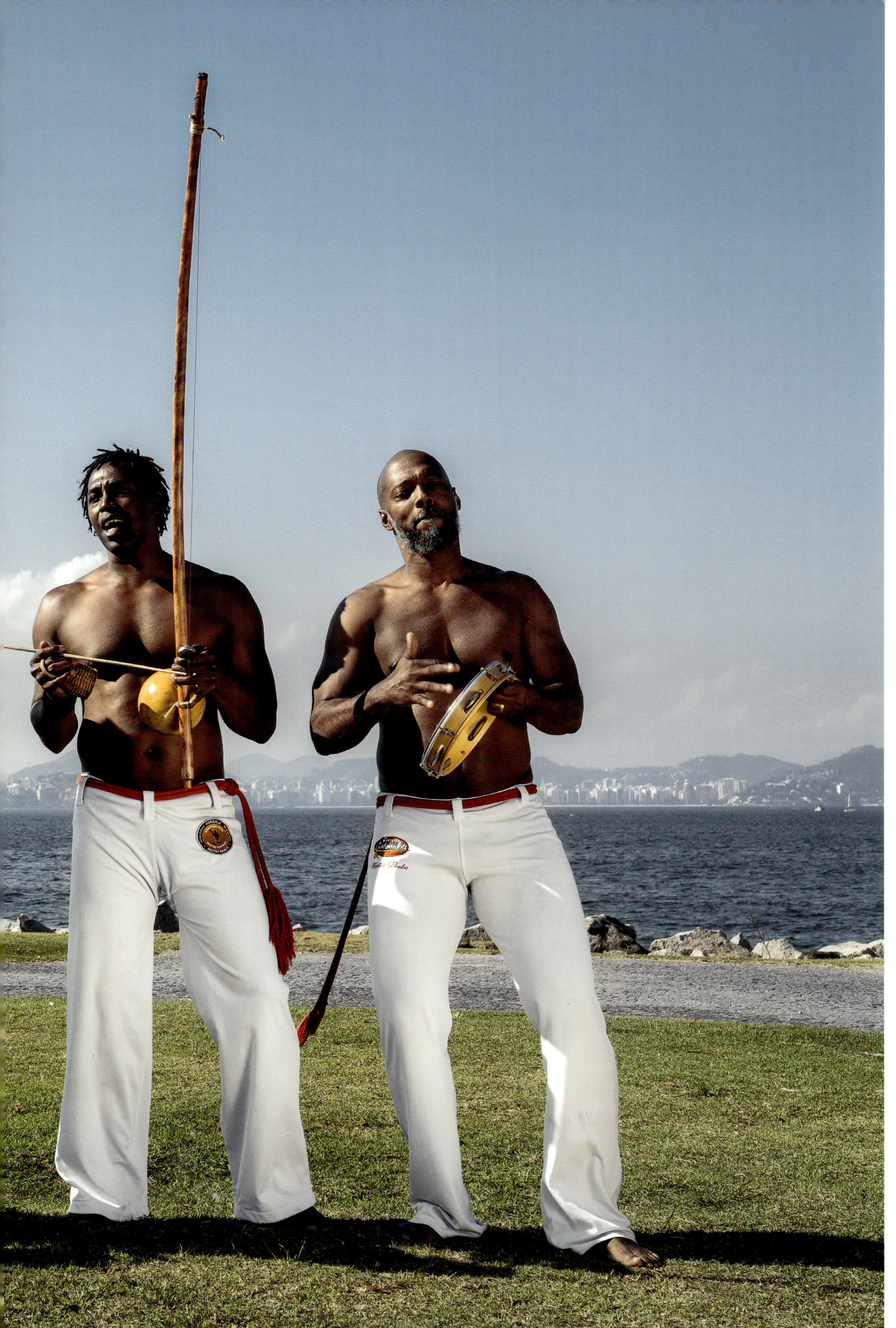

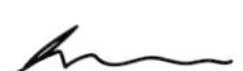

Eagle Hunting

KYRGYZSTAN & MONGOLIA

Only a person with the purest heart and sincerest
intentions can carry on this age-old practice.

In the untamed landscape of Central Asia's wild, wild east lies Kyrgyzstan. This remote, landlocked area of felt yurts, shimmering lakes and the legendary Silk Road crossings is wedged between Kazakhstan, Tajikistan, Uzbekistan and China. It is enveloped by some of the highest mountain peaks in the world. In this majestic playground where snow leopards still roam, there is a unique relationship between man and bird: golden eagle hunting. This time-honoured practice goes beyond man's domination over the birc; it is a nomadic tradition rooted in Tengrism (an ancient religion) and steeped in respect, honour and love.

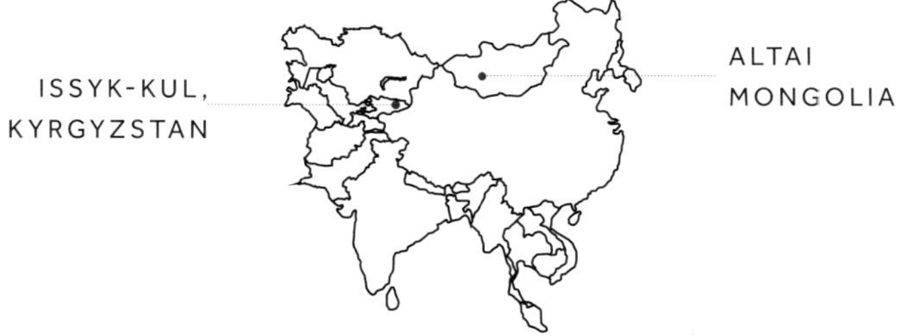

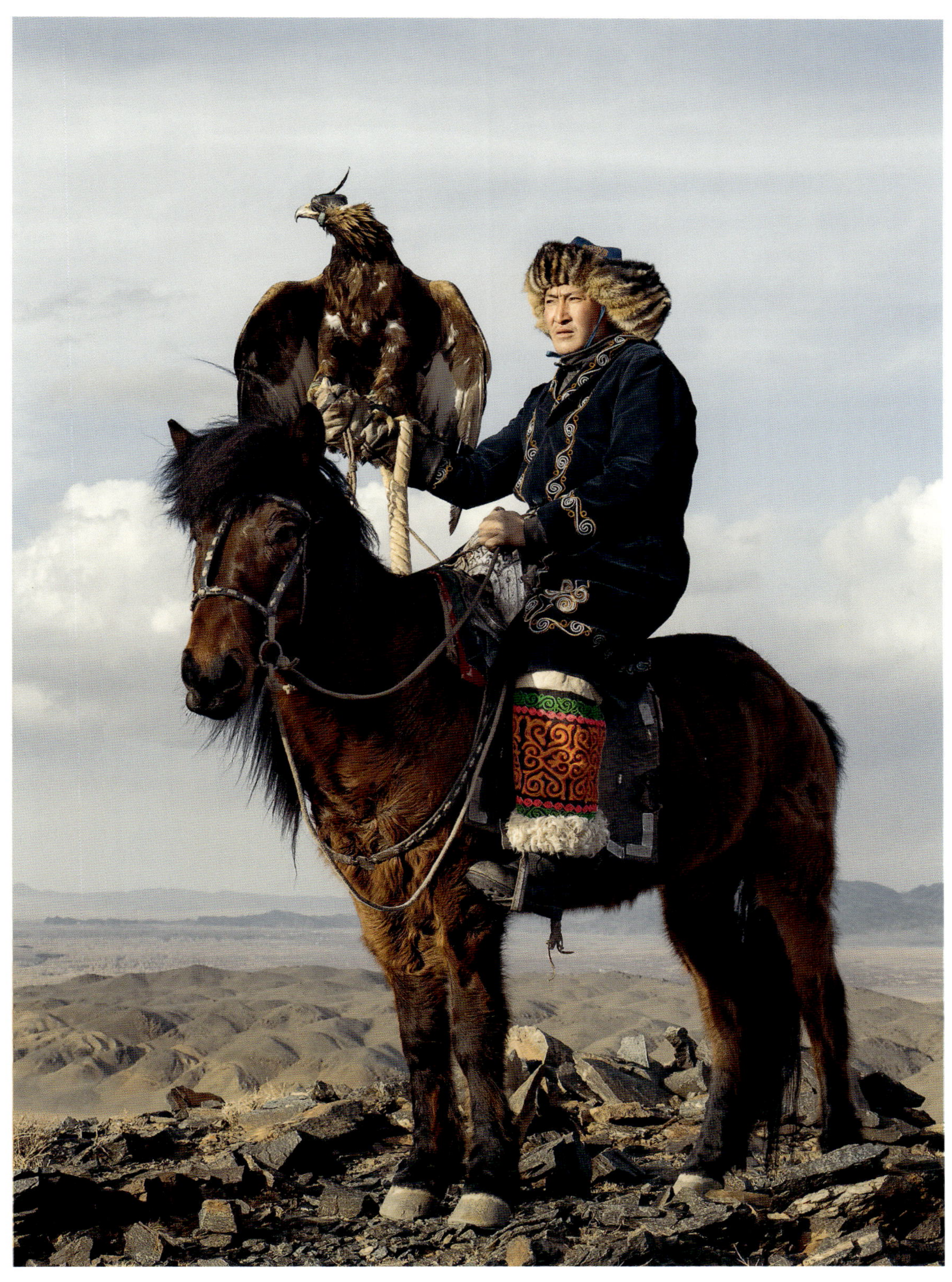

Nomads in Mongolia (the birthplace of eagle hunting) and the Central Asian steppes have been taming these giant birds of prey for thousands of years. Eagle hunting and falconry feature in cave paintings dating as far back as the Bronze Age; even the famed Genghis Khan favoured the practice.

Not just anyone can become an eagle hunter, according to master and teacher Talgar Shaibyrov, champion of the World Nomad Games of 2014 and winner of numerous awards. Only a person with the purest heart and sincerest intentions can carry on this age-old practice. Mainly boys become eagle hunters, but Aisholpan Nurgaiv of Mongolia broke with tradition to become the first female eagle hunter to participate in a competition. Other female eagle hunters came before her; evidence of this dates to tenth-century Persia. But she was the first to compete. Hopefully, other young girls will carry on the legacy that has defined this nomadic region for centuries.

The golden eagle, much more aggressive than the bald eagle, is known as the *berkut* in Kyrgyz, after the golden feathers on the back of the head. It is the most adored and preferred bird of prey for the *berkutchi* (eagle hunters). With its sharp and powerful talons, this magnificent bird has the strength, intelligence and fierceness to hunt and kill hares, foxes and even wolves. The Kyrgyz reverently refer to it as 'the bird of god'. The wingspan can reach 2.5 metres. It can fly at extreme speeds of over three hundred kilometres per hour, and its keen vision allows it to

see over distances of eight kilometres. Similar to an owl, the golden eagle can rotate its head 270 degrees and has transparent eyelids to keep dust and dirt out of its remarkable eyes.

Becoming an eagle hunter is not for the faint-hearted; it requires capturing a female eaglet from its nest and dedicating years of preparation before moving on to hunt real animals. Training begins with a stuffed fox fur fastened to a rope, so the eagle learns to fly back to the trainer's hand. The *berkutchi* must spend all their time with the bird, feeding it, singing and talking to it, so their voice is the only one the eagle obeys. Eagles will not forgive any cruelty or abuse, so they must never be punished or spoken to harshly.

The backdrop for the awe-inspiring eagle hunt is what legends are made of: the sun rising above distant, snow-capped mountains; a valley lit in stunning shades of ochre, burnt sienna and red. A soft rumble of hooves is heard as a team of men on horseback, in traditional dress, wearing *ak alpak* (tall white wool hats), emerge from the dust with their glorious golden eagles regally perched on their arms. They move as one. It is chilling to see the size of the bird up close. Although the bird sits peacefully on its owner's arm, make no mistake, this top-of-the-food-chain raptor could cause serious injury if it wanted to, making the relationship between man and bird even more impressive.

A slight movement in the distance kicks off the hunt; the Taigan dogs charge ahead to

scout the area. The hunter lets out a call. In a split second, the bird takes off, soaring high, wings fully spread, revealing its magnificence, moving at full speed with laser eyesight, ready to take down the unsuspecting fox, working in tandem with the dogs. The eagle swoops down at lightning speed with precision and skill, crushing its prey's skull with its immensely strong talons, waiting until its hunting partner arrives before feasting on its favourite bits.

Eagle hunting occurs between September and March, and it is prohibited in the spring when most animals mate and moult. Beyond hunting in the wild, official eagle hunting competitions are held in Kyrgyzstan, Kazakhstan and Mongolia. It is also part of the World Nomad Games; eagle hunters from all over the world come to compete and demonstrate the speed, dexterity and accuracy of their birds. These nomadic people believe it is more humane to use a bird of prey to hunt than to use a knife or a gun – a fair fight of animal versus animal.

After putting so much time and energy into this mighty bird, most would have difficulty letting go. But the beauty of these unwritten tribal customs, followed for centuries, is that ownership is set aside, and after a time, the bird is released into the wild. A golden eagle lives for about thirty years, so it is free for the other half of its life. With tears in his eyes, Talgar explains that when he released his most treasured feathered friend after fifteen years of collaboration, it was like saying goodbye to a family member. He often looks up to the sky, secretly hoping to meet it again.

"The lion is the king of the jungle,
but the eagle is the queen of the sky."

~ Talgar Shaibyrov ~

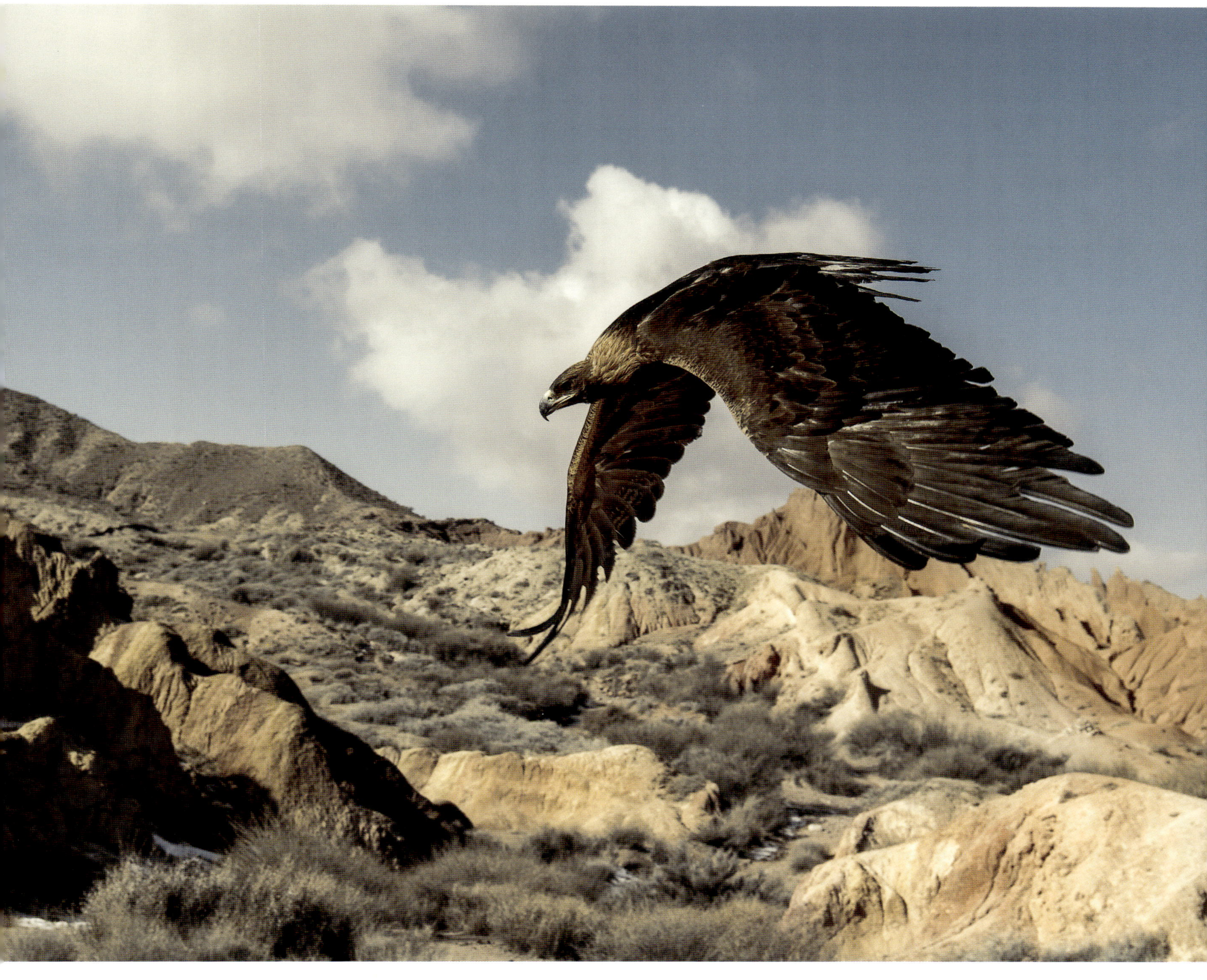

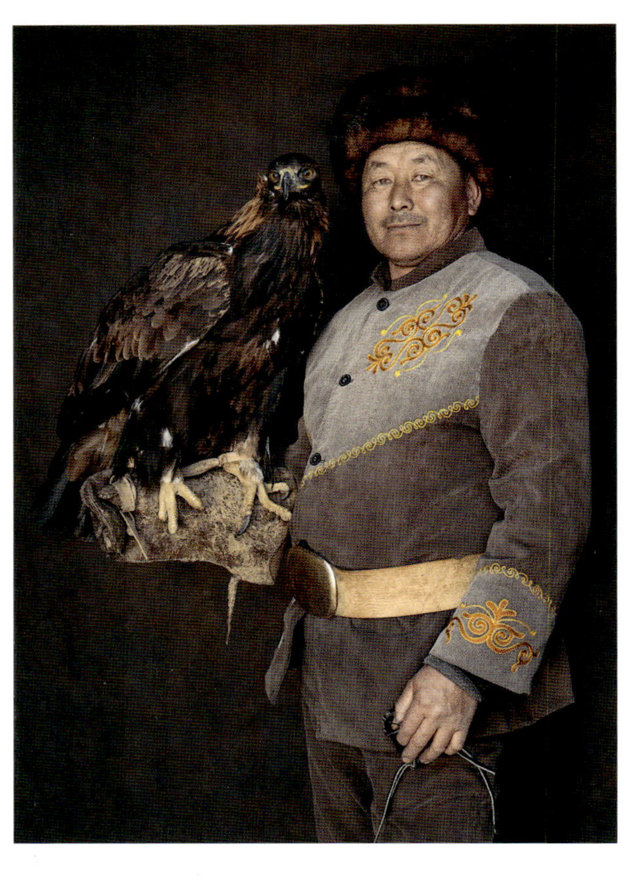
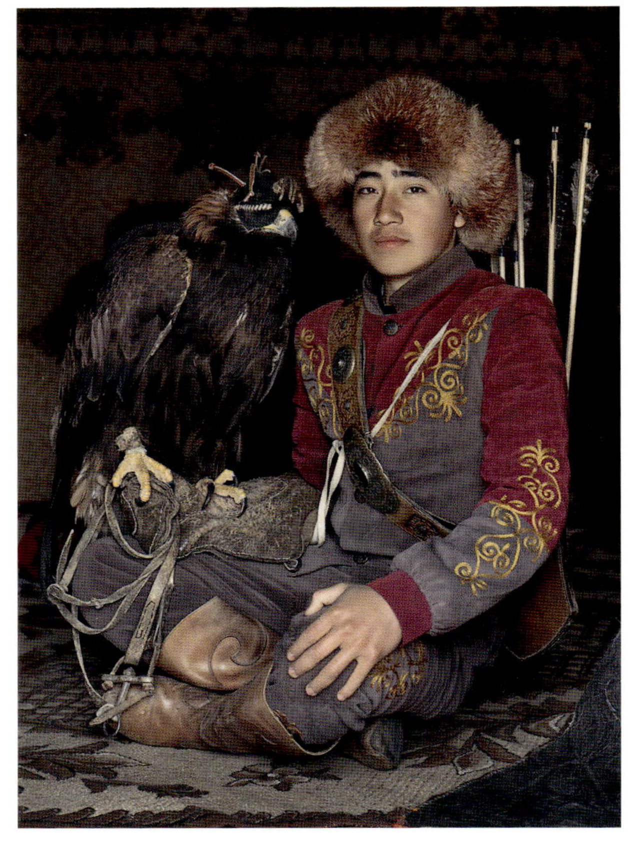
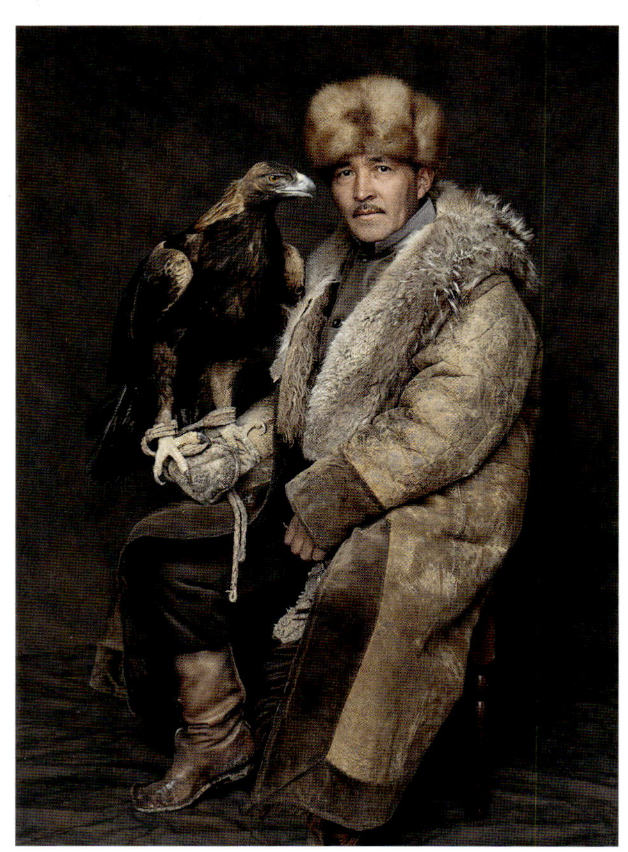
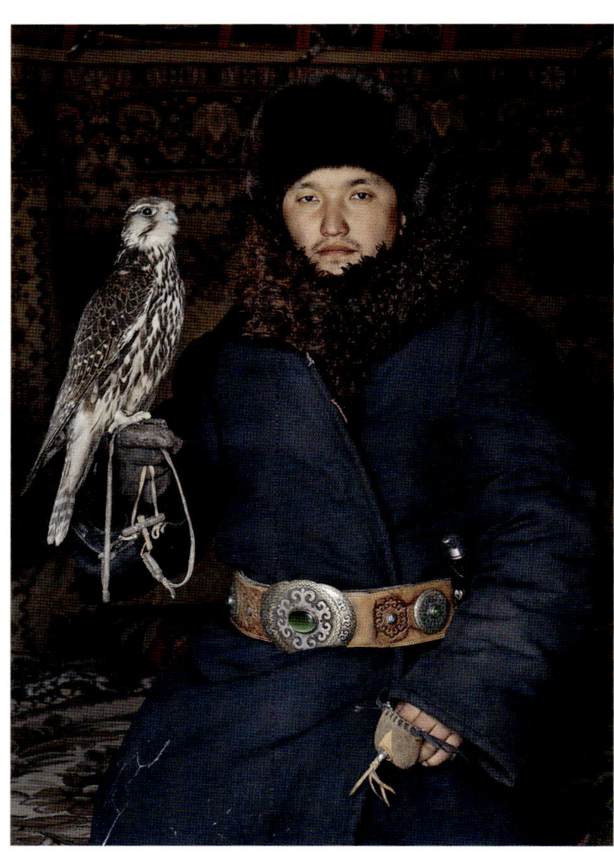

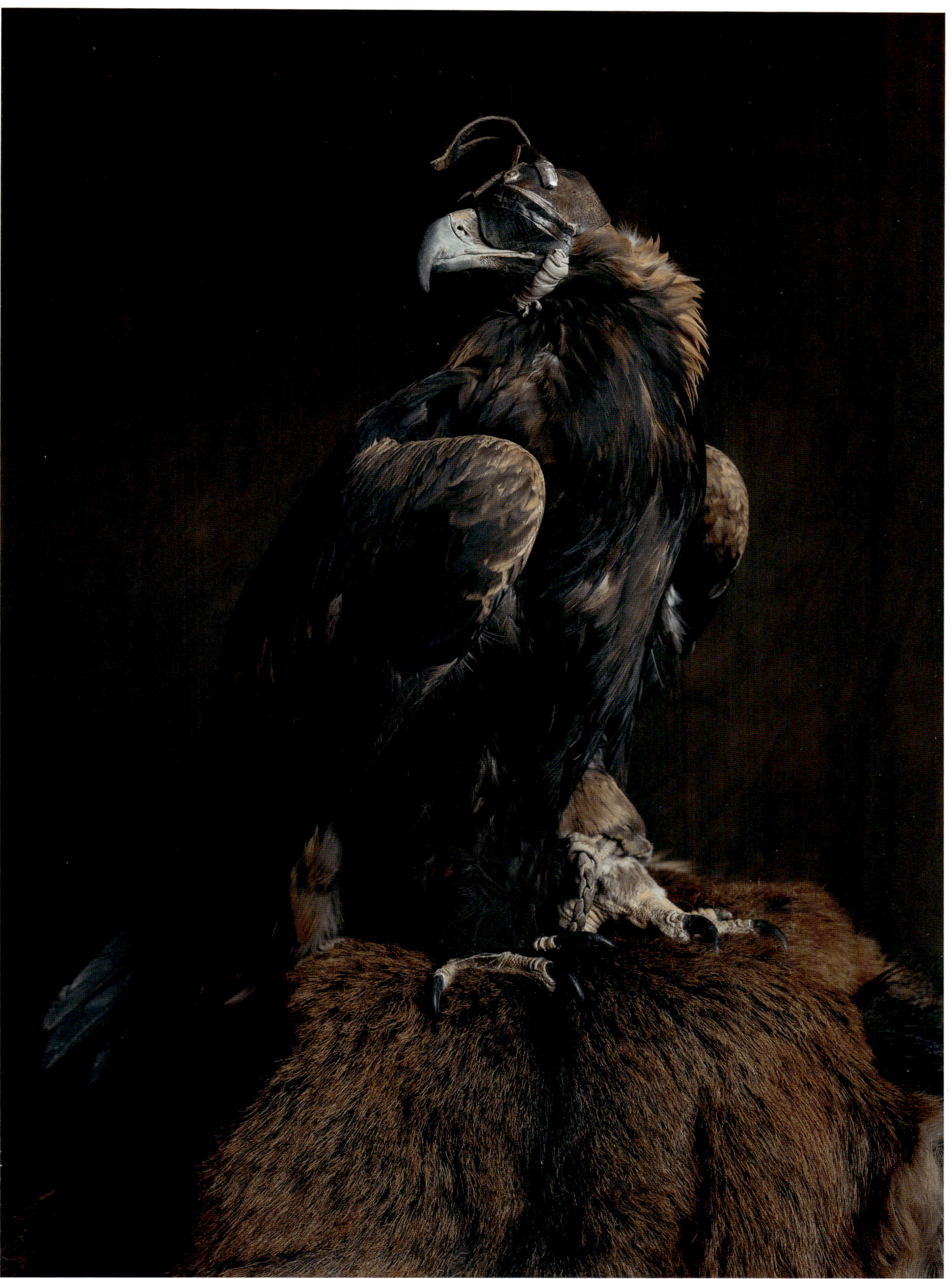

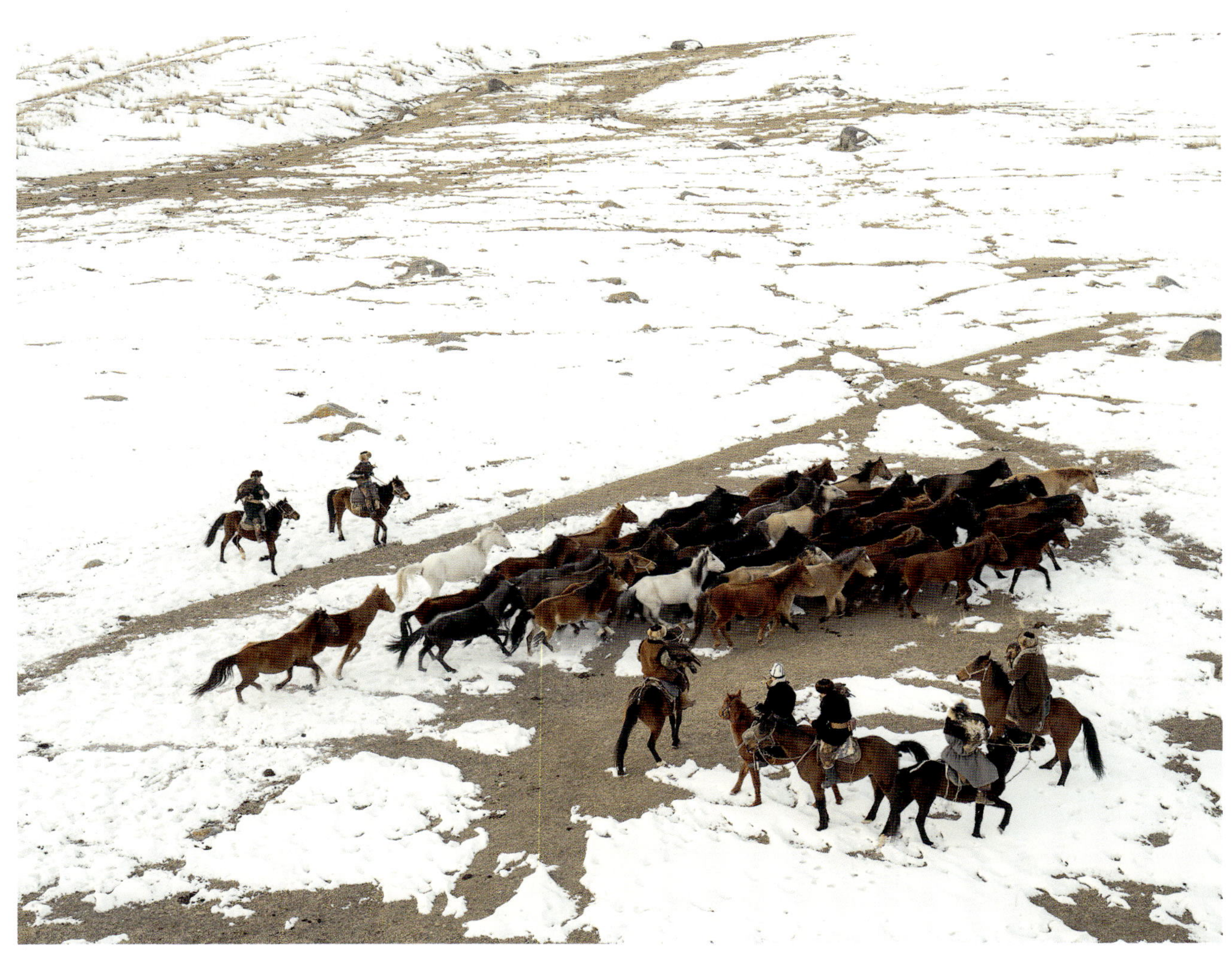

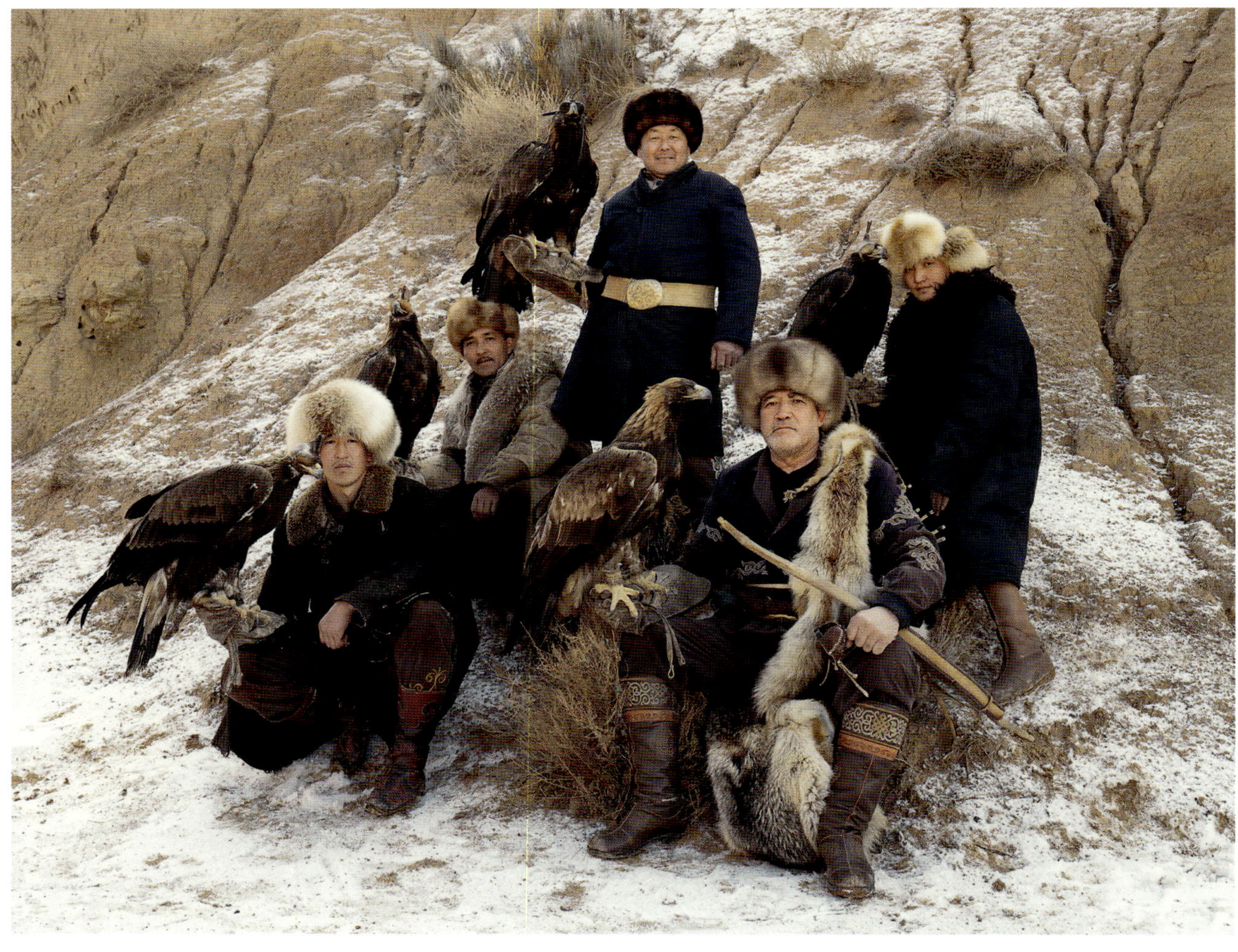

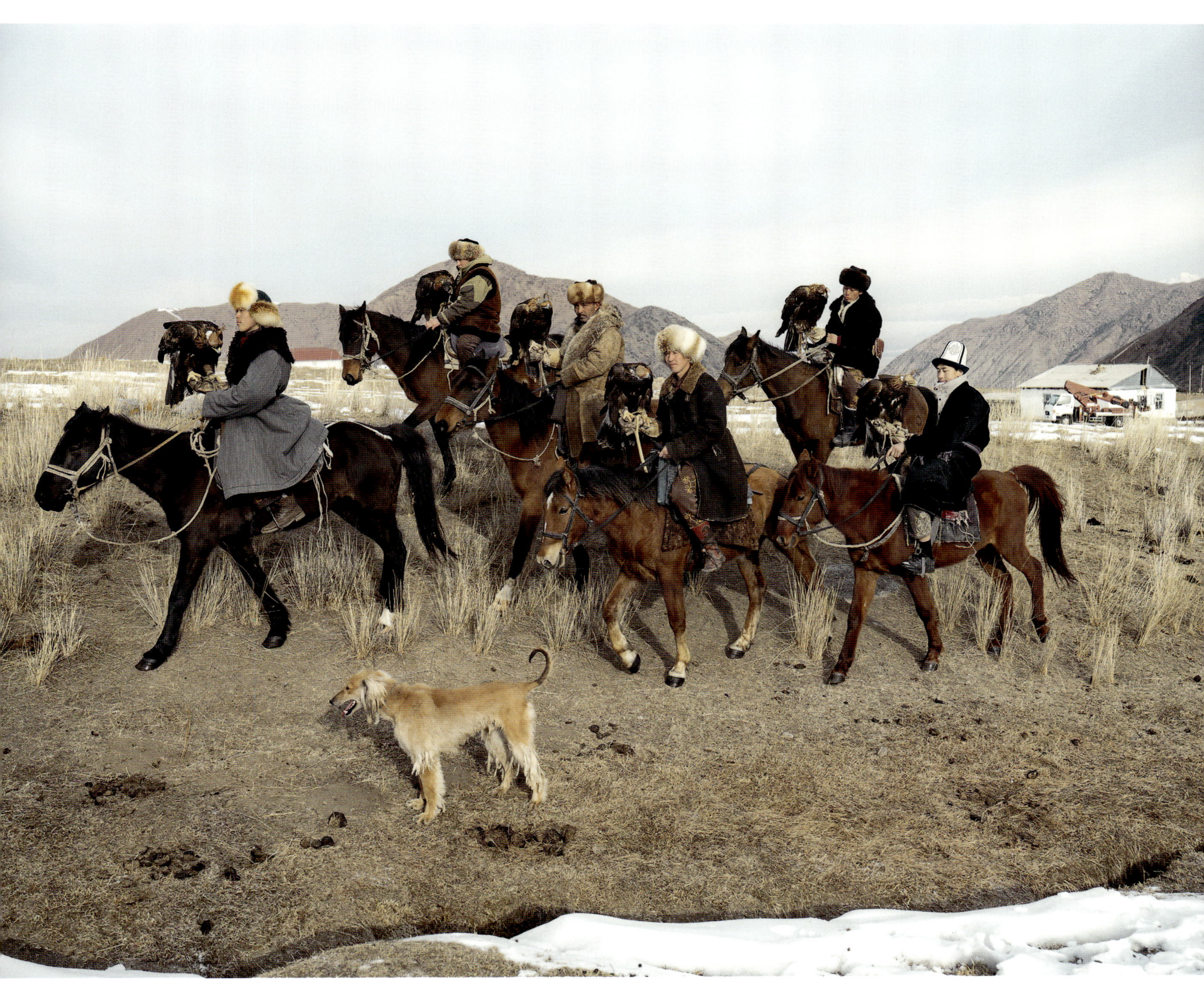

Eagles must be treated with extreme love
and care as they are very sensitive and will not
tolerate abuse of any kind or mistreatment

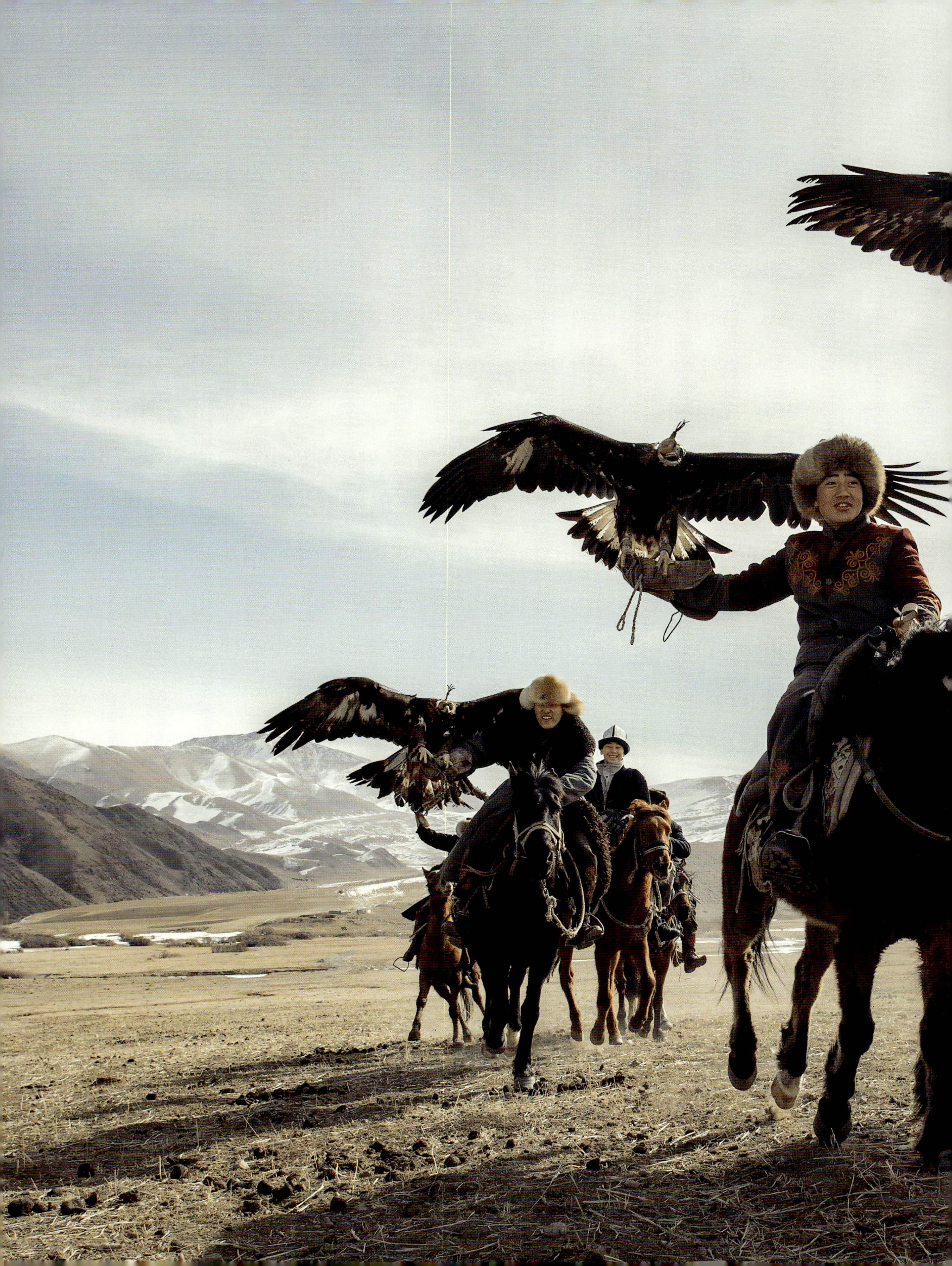

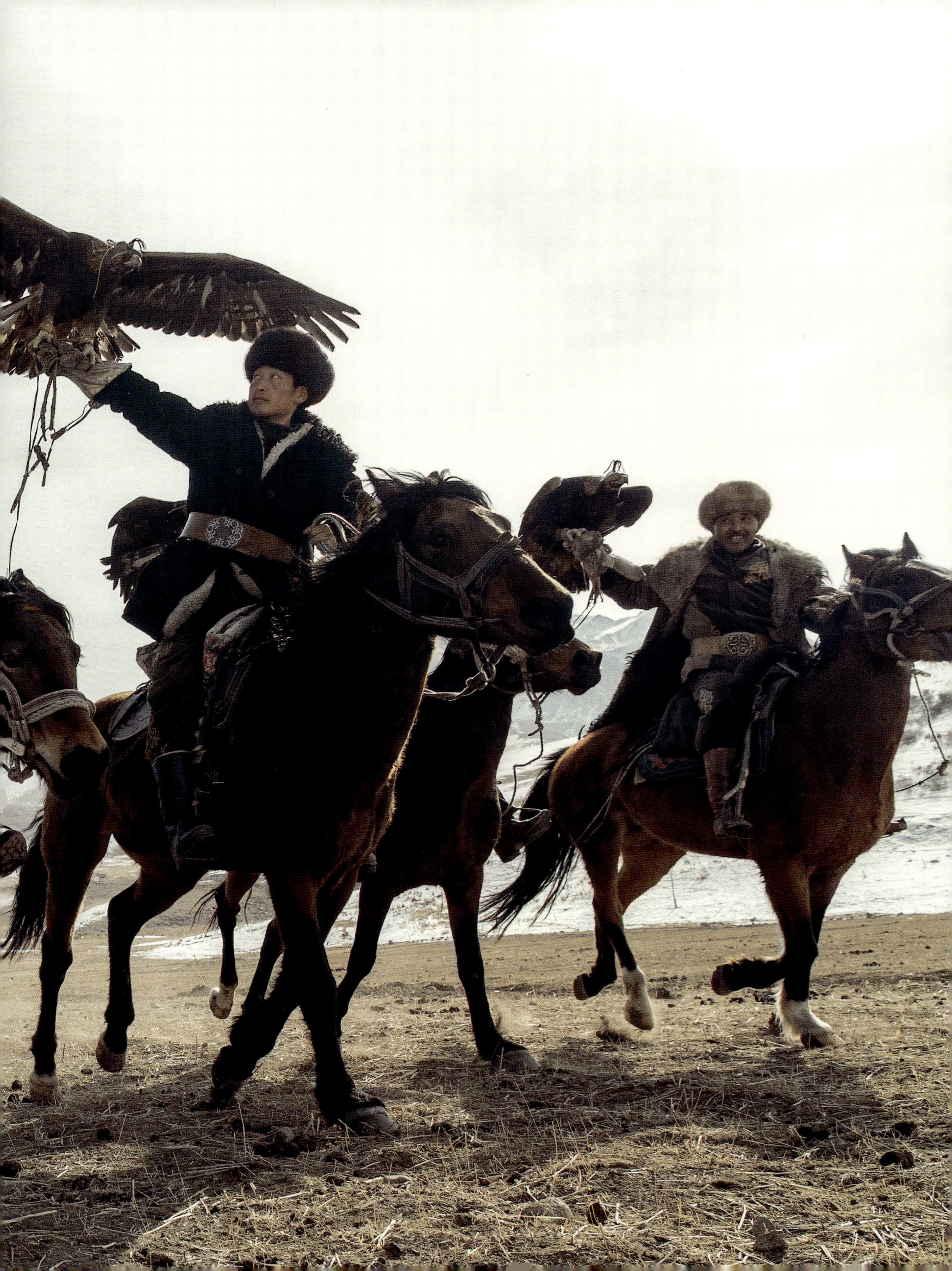

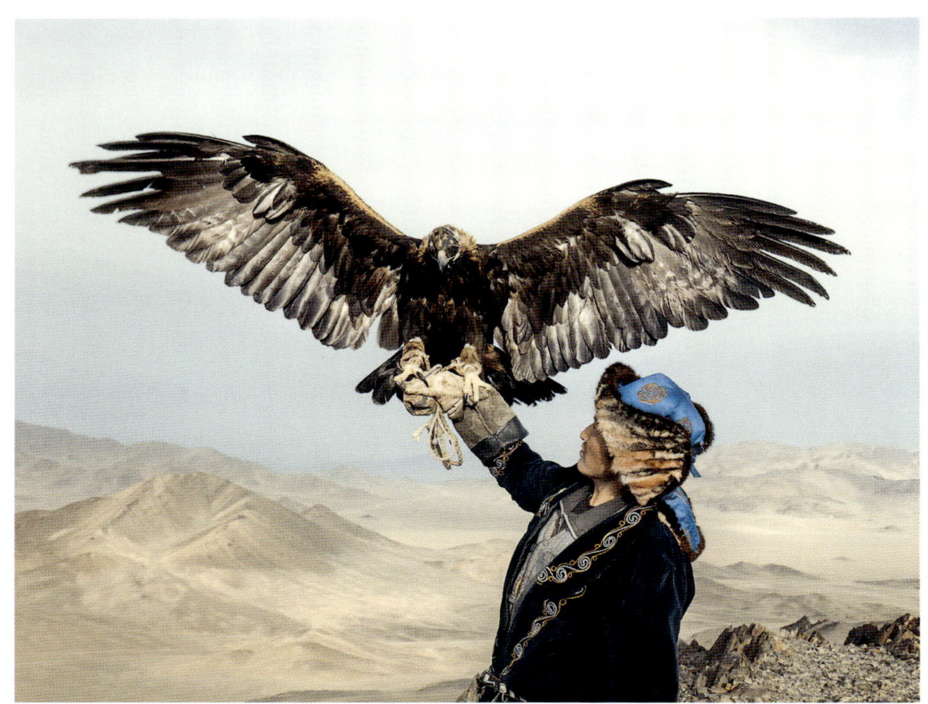

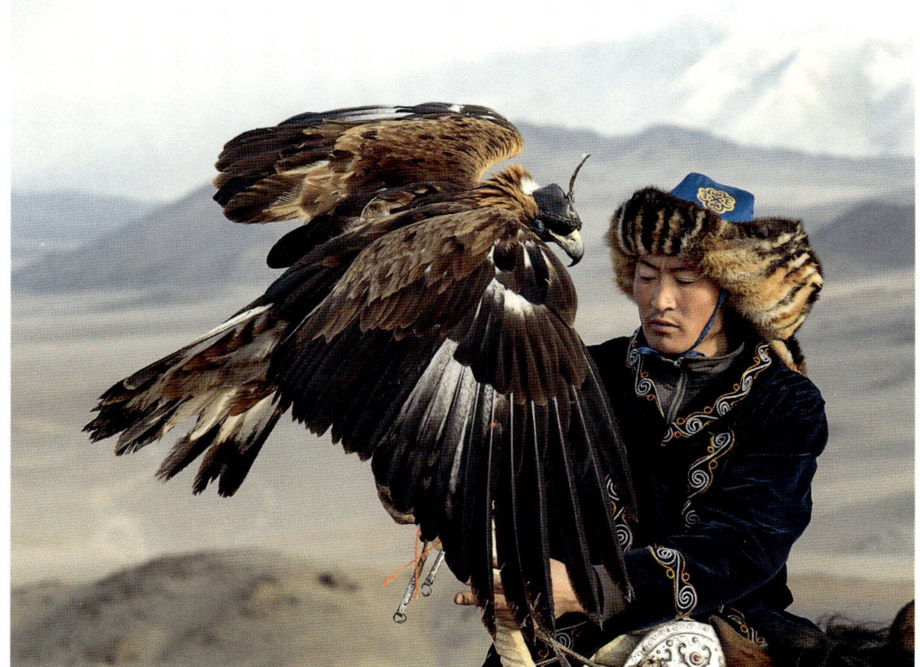

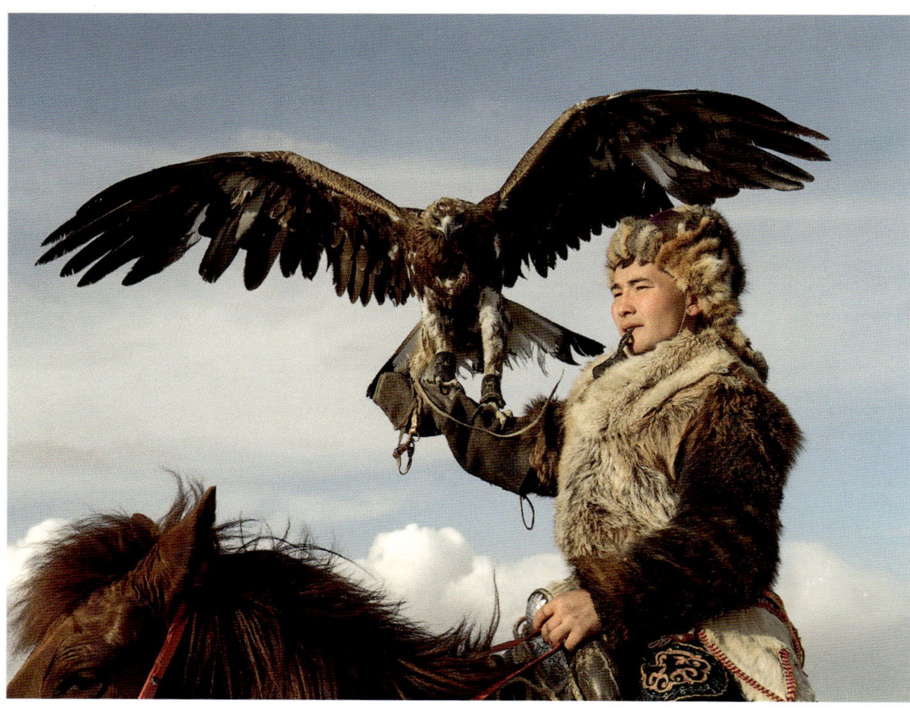

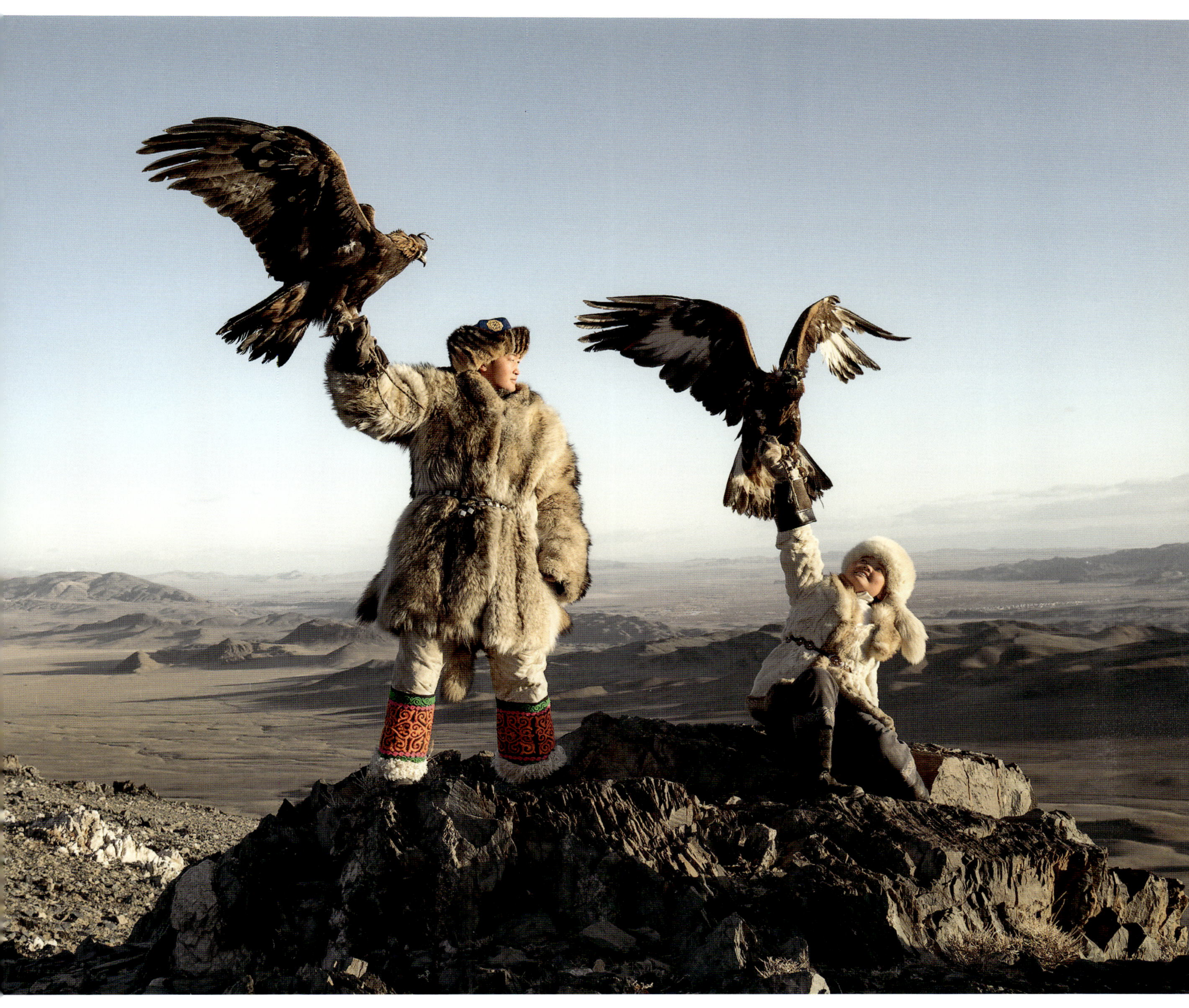

Mongolian Aisholpan Nurgaiv broke with tradition by becoming the
first female eagle hunter to participate in a competition.

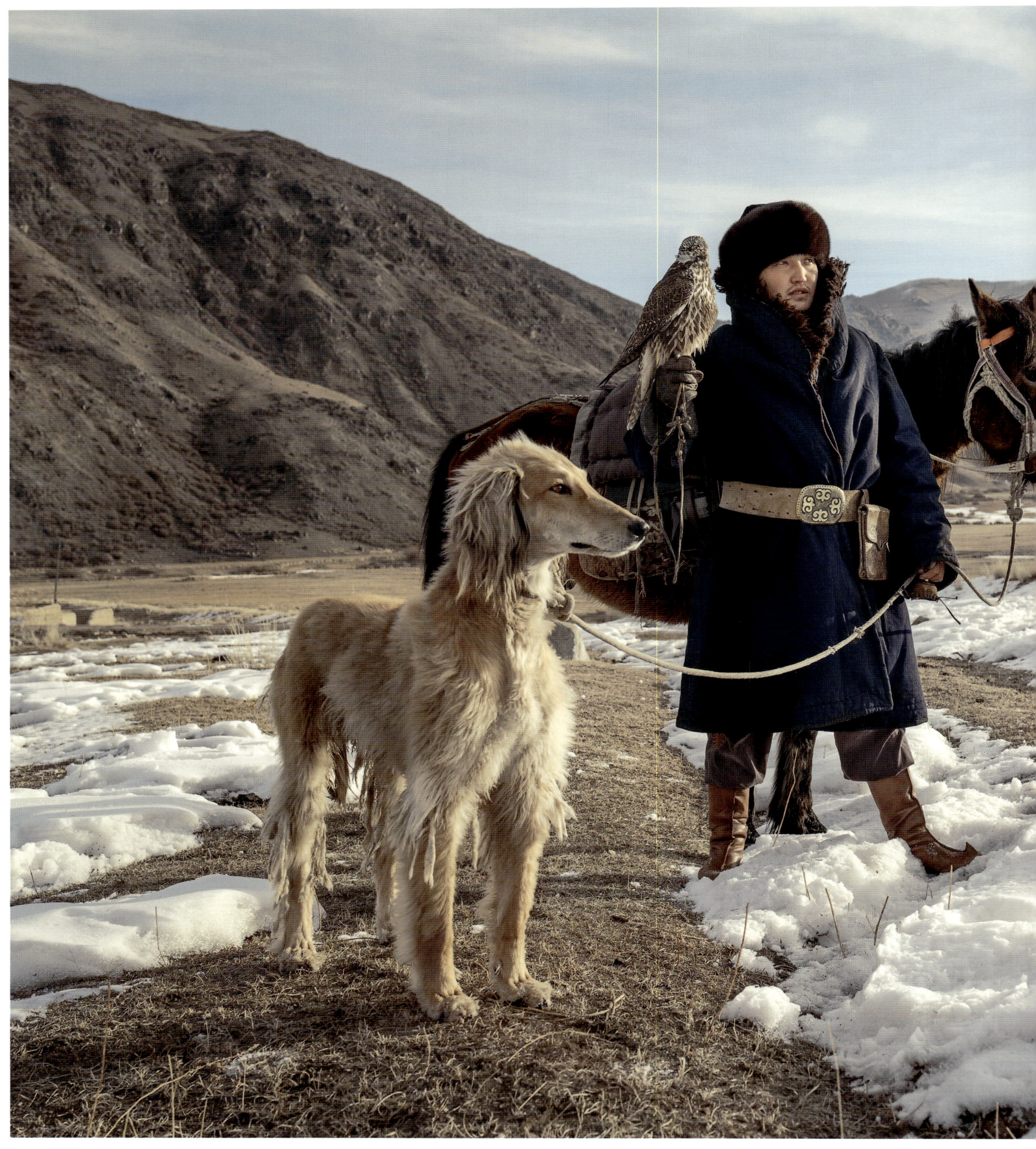

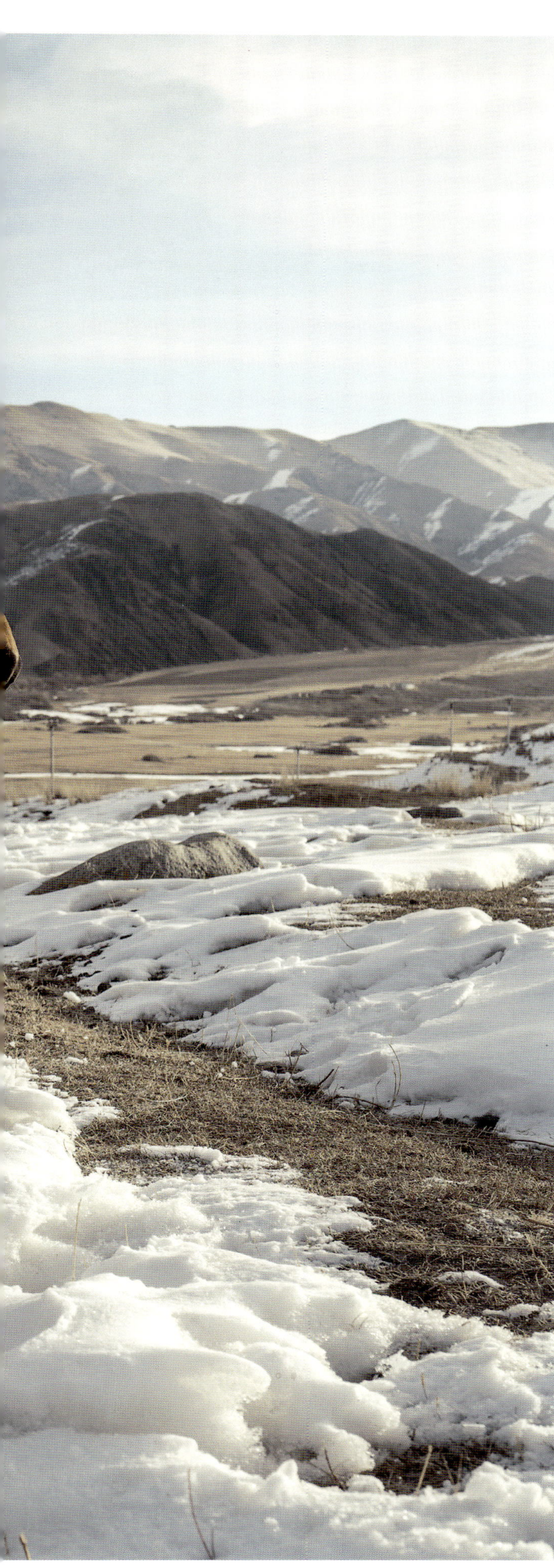

The training of a golden eagle to hunt
alongside a Taigan hunting dog and
a horse is ancient knowledge passed
from one generation to the next.

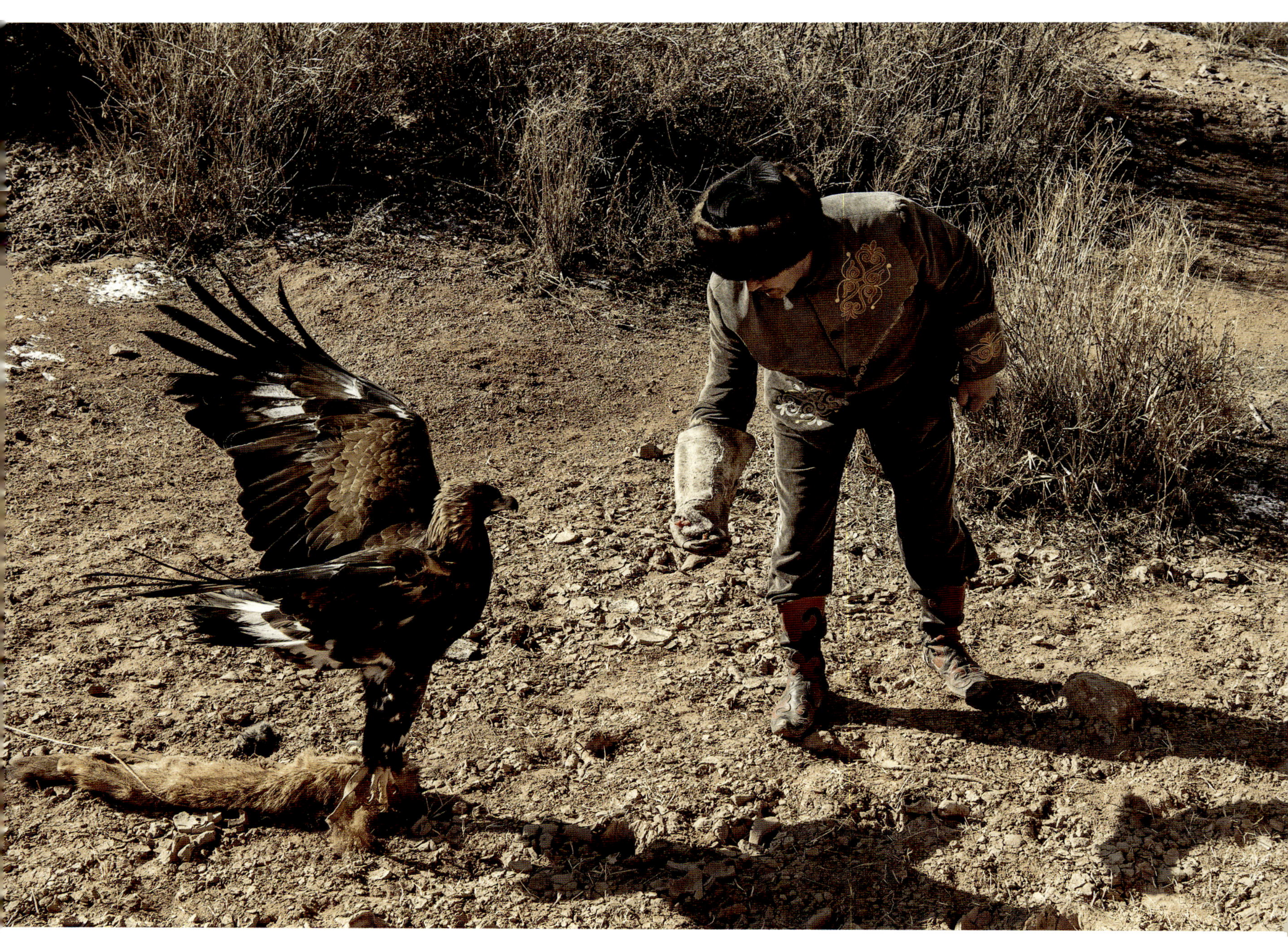

The golden eagle (bird of god) has a wingspan
of up to 2.5 meters, flies at over 300 kilometres
per hour and has extraordinary eyesight, able
to see eight kilometres in the distance.

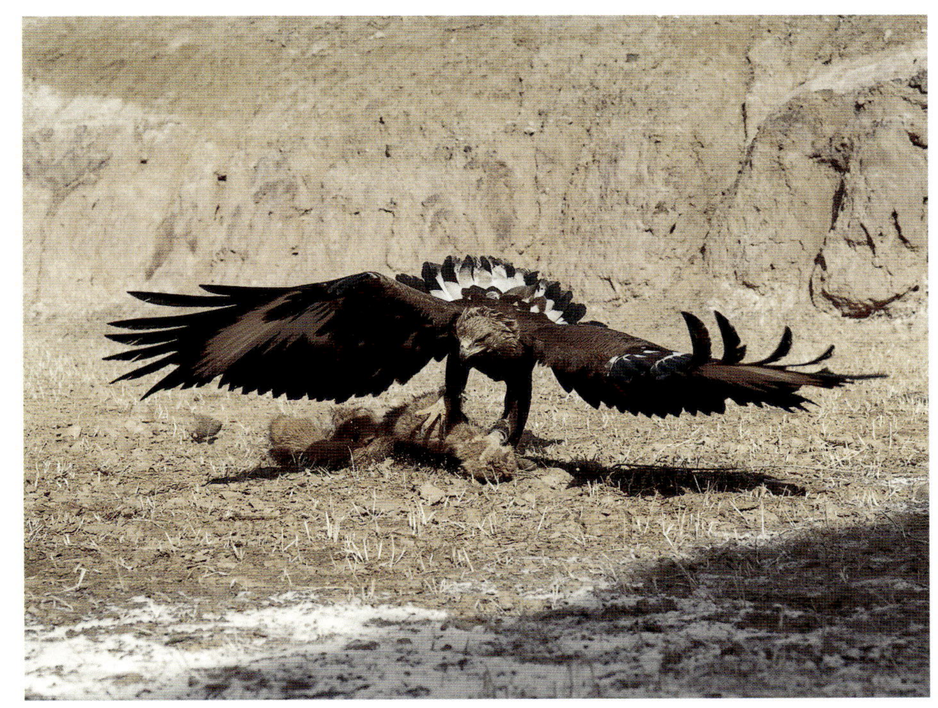

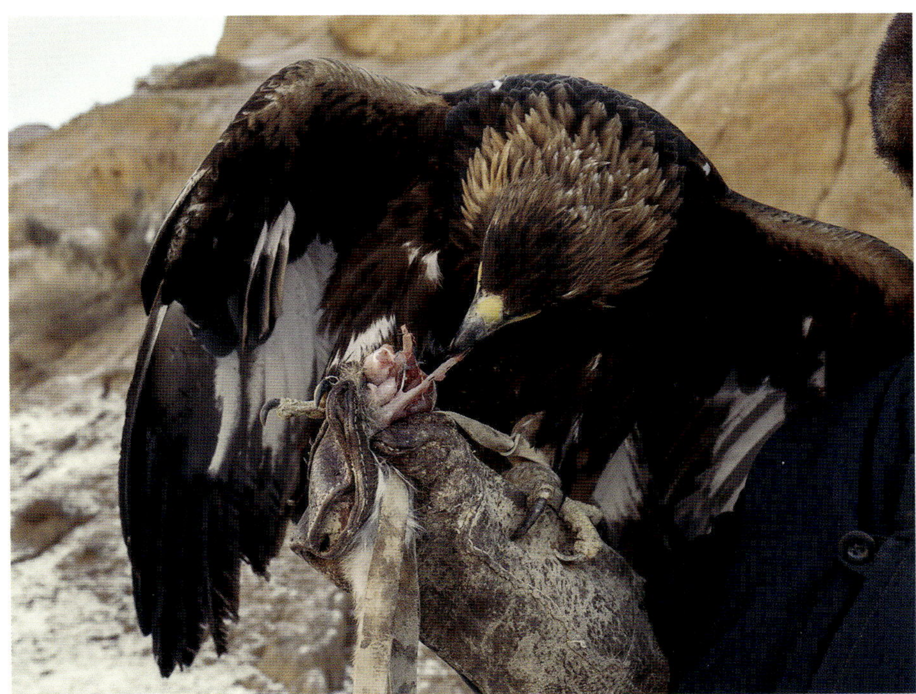

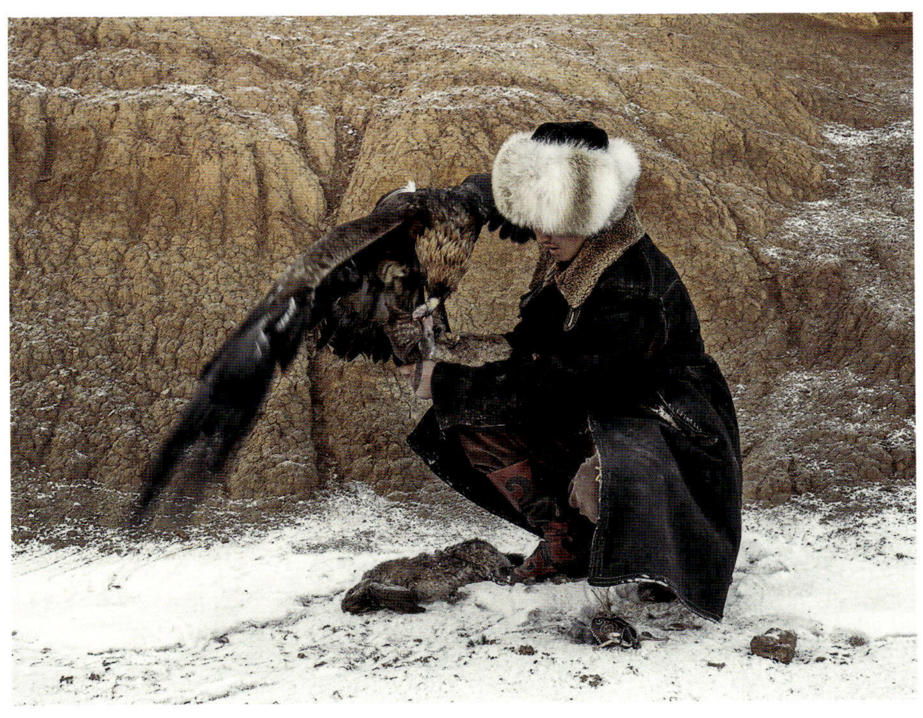

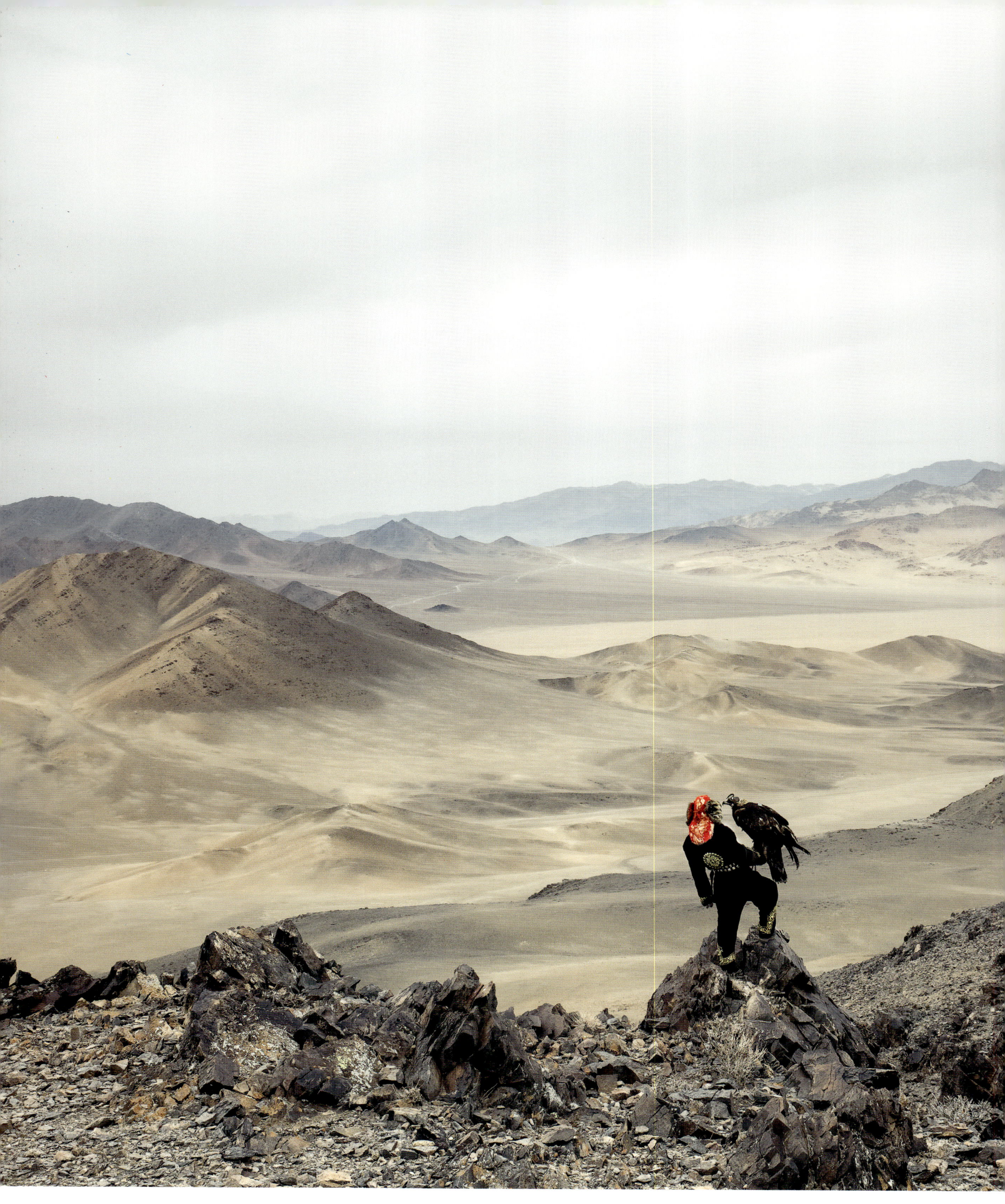

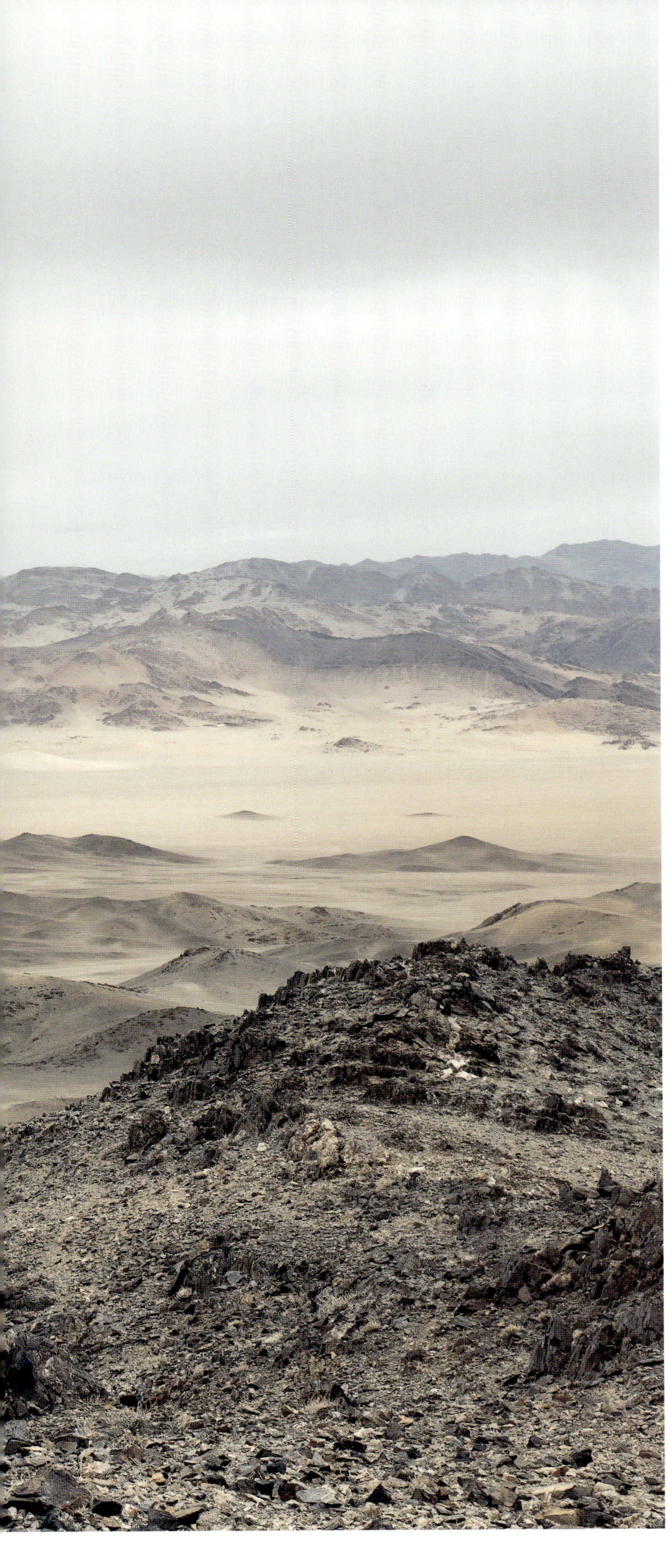

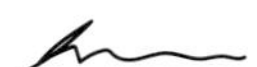

Dambe

NIGERIA

*Dambe athletes train as if their lives depend on it,
moving with focus, fury and surprising speed.*

In a land often referred to as the 'giant of Africa', highly populated with vast landscapes, live Nigeria's Hausa people forming the largest ethnic group in West Africa, a region which is home to hundreds of different ethnicities and languages. From the Hausa emerged the gritty, bare-knuckle combat sport of dambe, which has produced some of the continent's toughest fighters and is played in one of the world's most dangerous playgrounds.

Dambe, also known as *kokawa*, is a traditional martial art whose origins date back to the tenth and eleventh centuries. It stems from the Hausa butchers' caste, a group who travelled among villages to slaughter animals for festivals, weddings and funerals. They would organise fights to demonstrate their power and masculinity to potential wives.

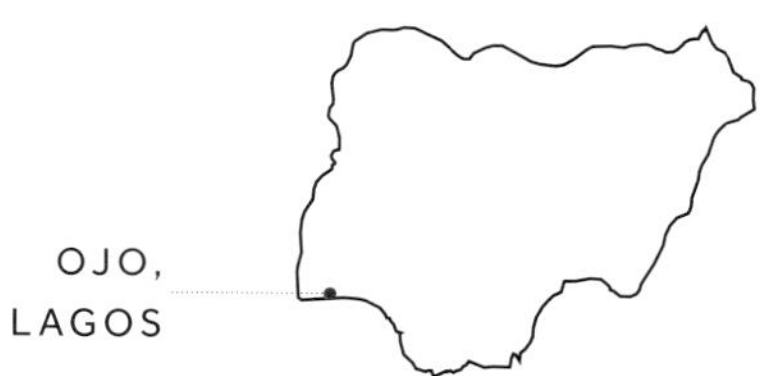

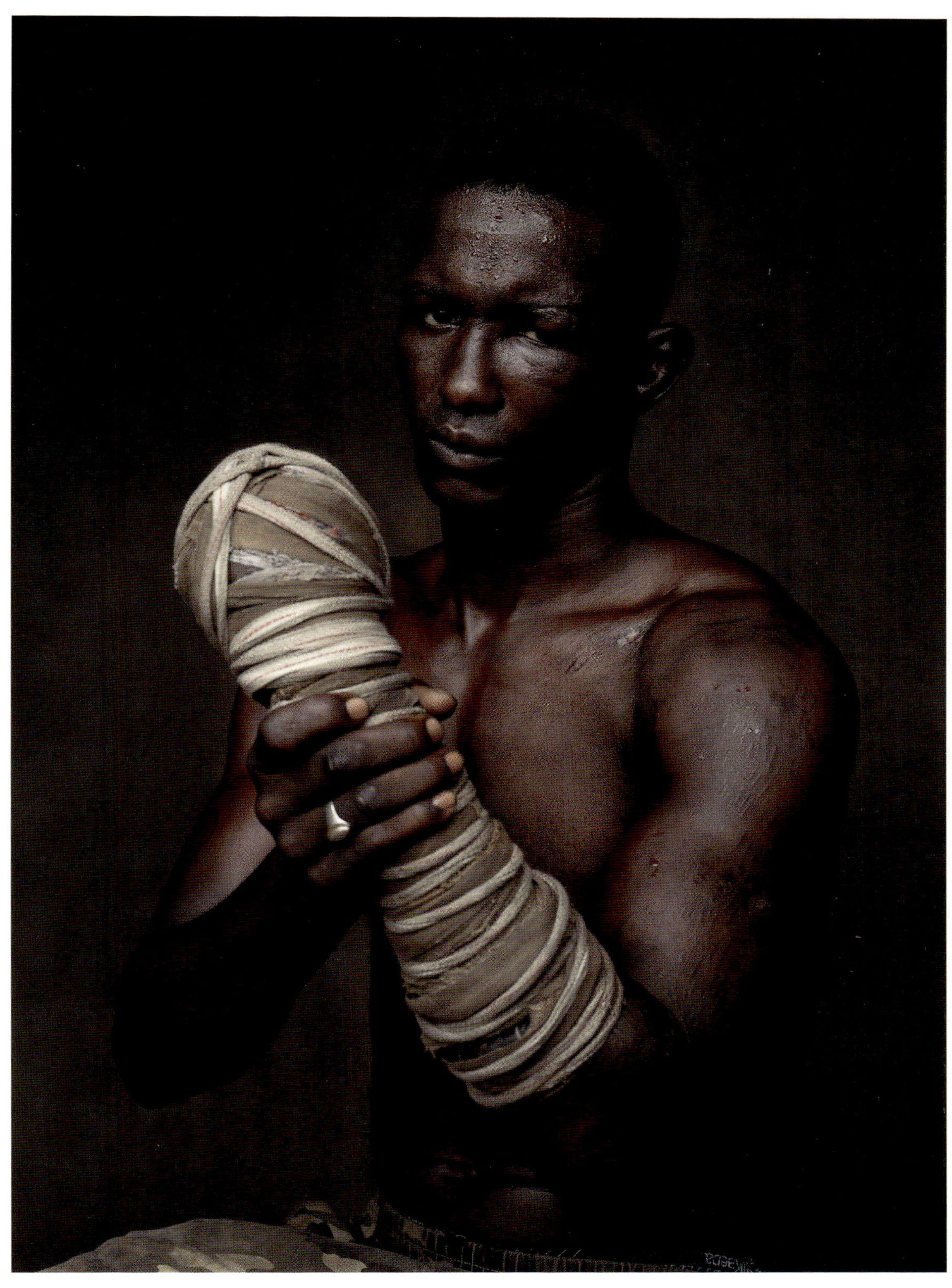

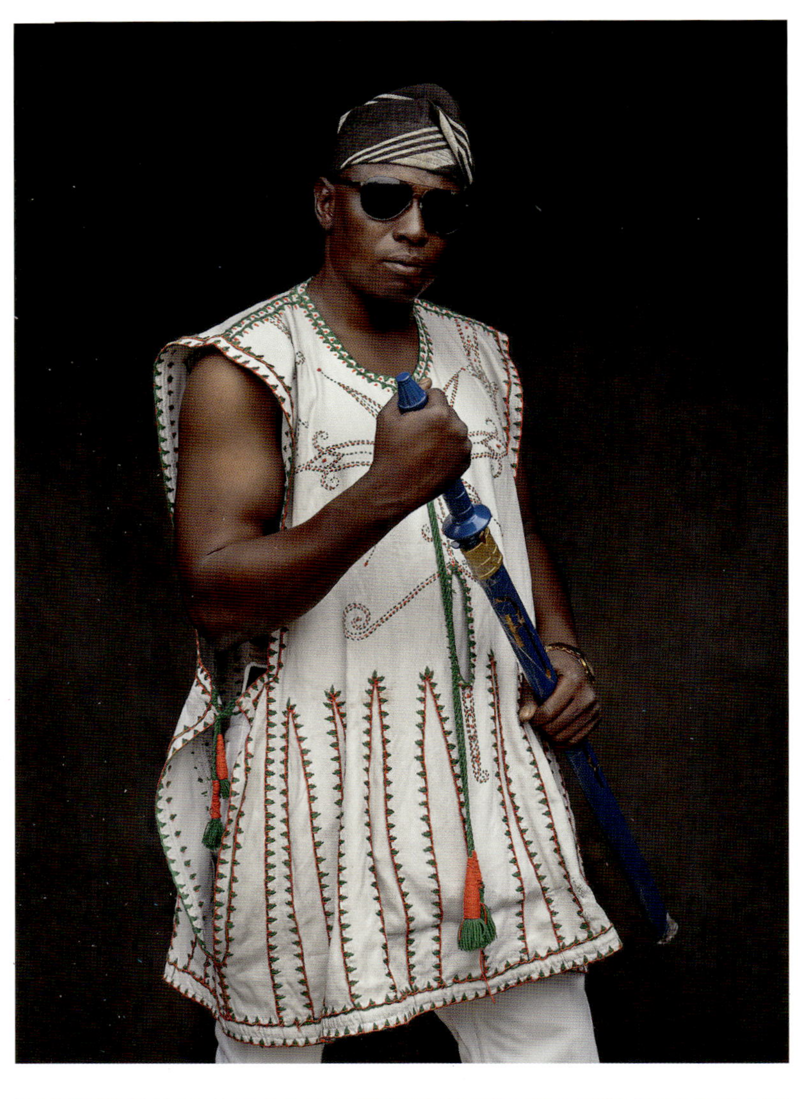
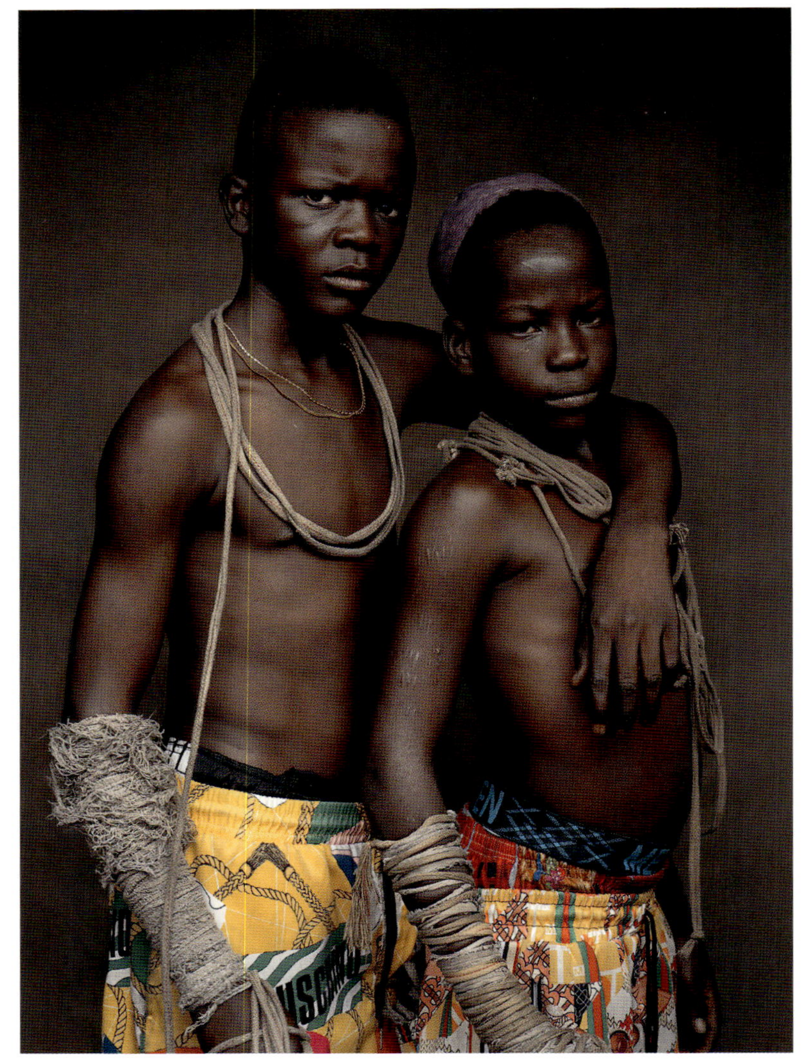
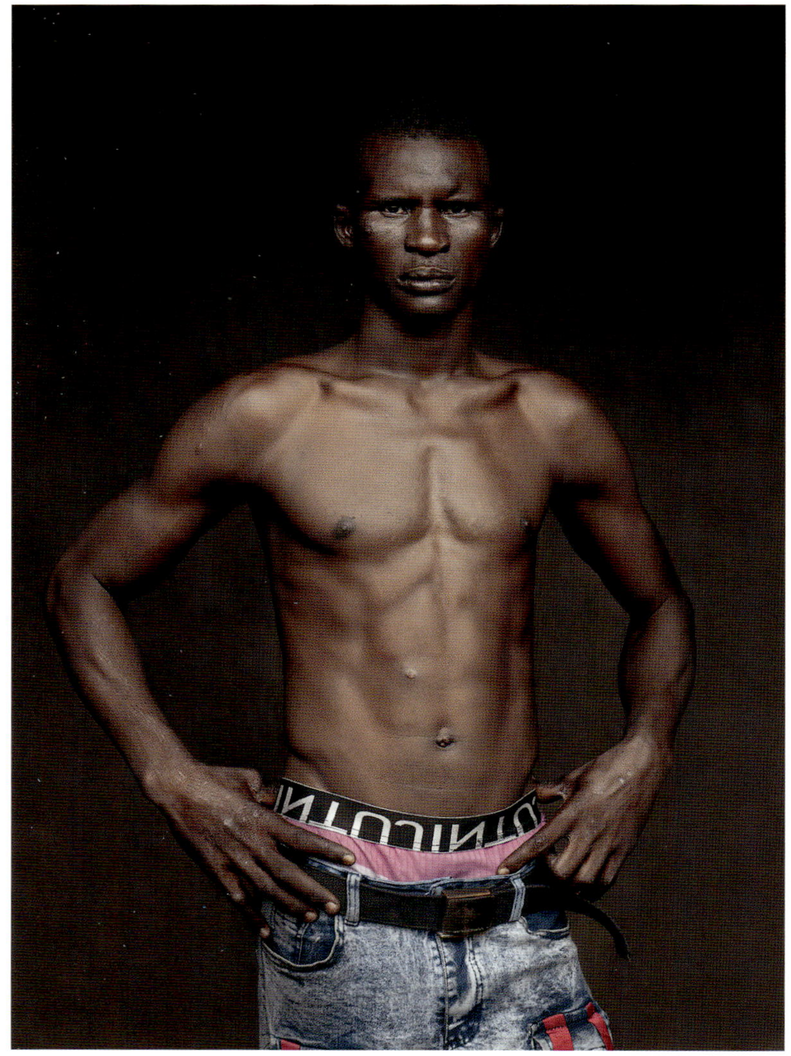
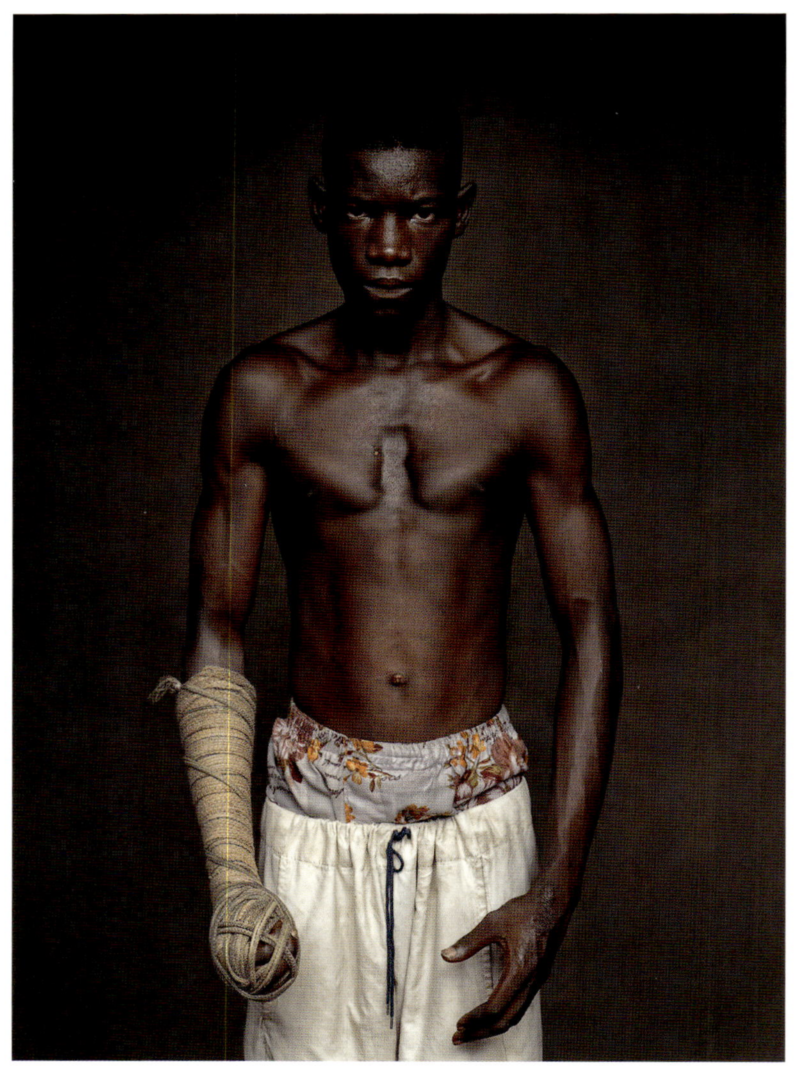

Dambe is a fierce boxing sport mostly practiced in northern Nigeria by the Hausa, but it can also be seen in the megacity of Lagos. The main objective is to knock out the opponent in what is commonly known as a 'kill' or 'death'. The fighters' only weapon is their dominant punching hand, called the 'spear' and wrapped in rope (kara); the other hand, the 'shield', is used for defence. Each match consists of three rounds wherein the boxers are allowed to fight with their head, feet and hands. There isn't a weight classification, but similar-sized men are paired up. The game ends when the boxer's hand or knee touches the ground, or the judge decides it's over. These fights are often characterised by intense brutality. But it is nothing compared to the past, when shards of glass would be wrapped up in the rope that winds around the spear hand, causing severe harm and even death. That practice is illegal today, and yet boxers still suffer extreme injuries.

On fight days, in big dusty fields with makeshift seating, large crowds gather in anticipation under the scorching sun while the modern-day warriors bind their fists in preparation for battle. The tournaments are an opportunity for commerce; people sell cigarettes, alcohol and other mood-enhancing substances. All the while, musicians play mesmerising, drum-driven music and sing songs of courage to energise the fighters. Music is an essential element the fighters can't do without; it is the musicians' job to keep them in the right frame of mind as they sing about warriors' wins, both past and present.

The fighters step into the sandy ring, their bandaged fists looking more like clubs than boxing gloves. Two men face one another, perfectly poised; the whistle goes off. A few jabs and ducks, and then one man suddenly launches a blow to his opponent's head, knocking him to the ground, and the crowd goes wild, cheering the champion.

Boys learn to fight at a very young age, observing the more mature and experienced fighters. They grow up idolising these athletes, but it's not the easiest path to adulthood. These men come from some of the country's roughest communities, and dambe gives them a chance to earn money and prestige. But the career span is short for these boxers, and most retire in their late twenties, either because of permanent injuries or, as with many combat sports, due to the long-term threat of brain damage.

Dambe athletes train as if their lives depended on it, moving with focus, fury and surprising speed. They work out intensely twice a day, five days a week, doing full-body strengthening exercises, head push-ups and one finger push-ups supporting the body's weight, all to build power in the punching arm and hand.

Besides physical training, pre-fight rituals are common. Some fighters wear charms or drink herbal tonics. Others wrap strands of animal hair around gemstones or make small incisions in their striking (spear) arm, rubbing special herbs into the cut, all for spiritual protection and a dose of supernatural power. This spiritual element makes dambe more than a sport; it's part of the Hausa culture.

Dambe fighters can win up to 200,000 nairas ($500) plus the money the audience showers on both winner and loser. Most of these men will say dambe is more than just a game; it's a lifestyle and a passion, and many rely on the money for survival. It is a poor man's sport. Despite Nigeria's oil-booming economy, forty per cent of the population live in poverty. Many of the fighters come from communities without water, electricity and healthcare. Winning a fight keeps poverty at bay temporarily, but a loss could mean doing without for weeks, so each punch determines whether they can afford food and rent.

This game is rooted in tradition but has quickly become a modern sport, attracting millions of online followers. In the dusty ring or via an internet connection, the audience watches these gladiators gamble with their lives, trying to punch their way out of the oppression of poverty and into the limelight of fame.

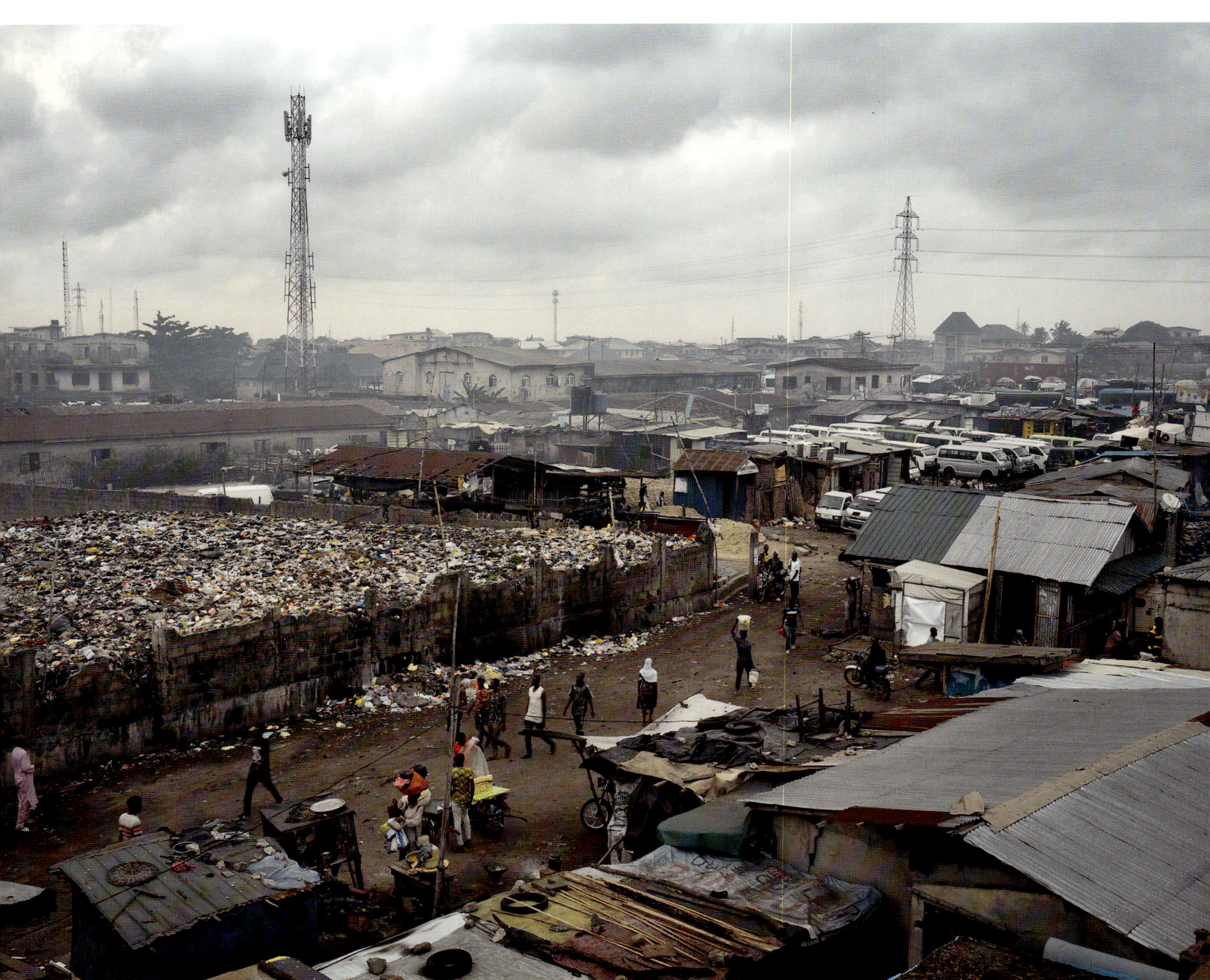

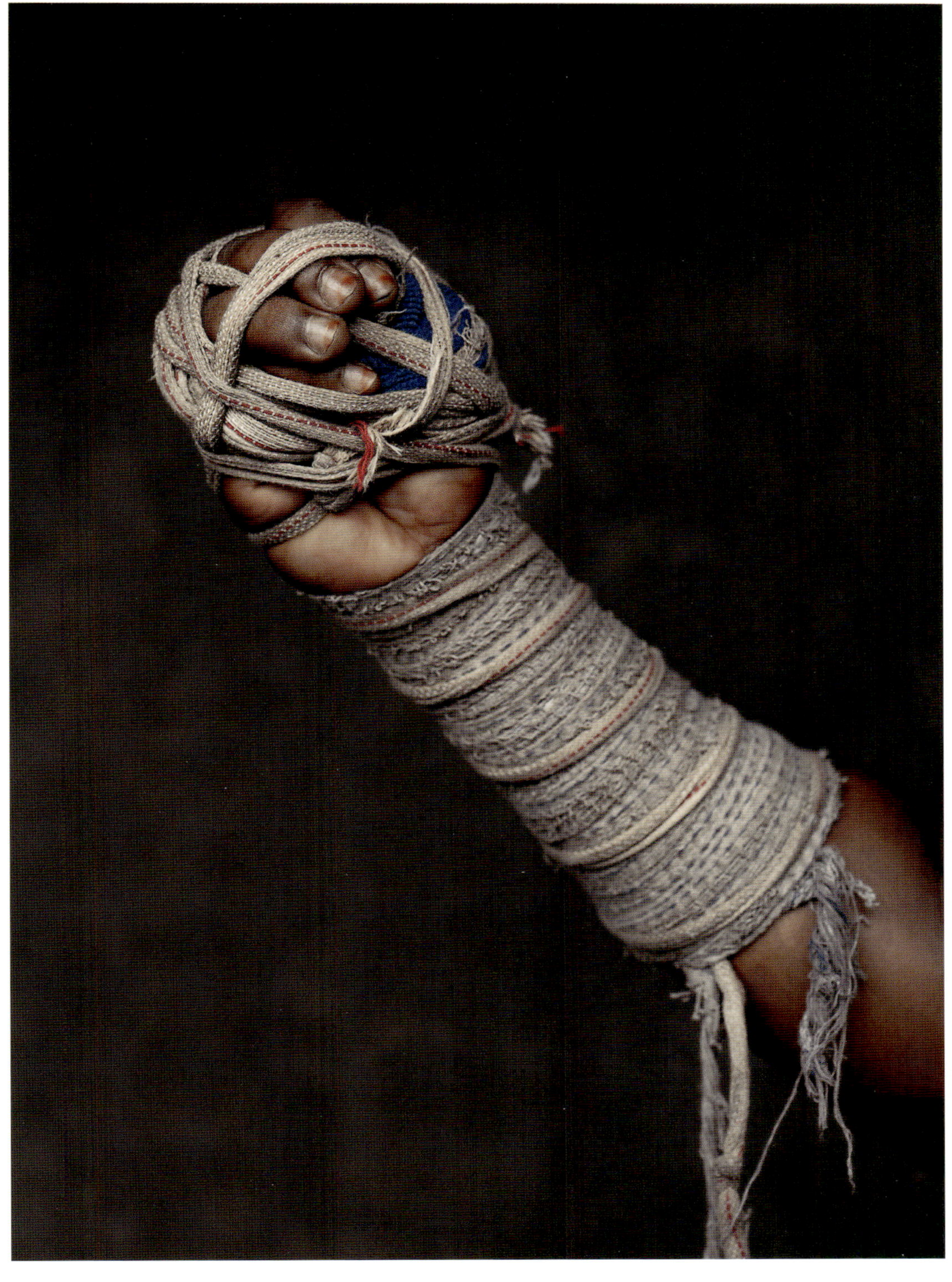

Fighters wrap one of their fists and wrists with
rope so it is as hard as a club, enough to knock out
their opponents with one punch.

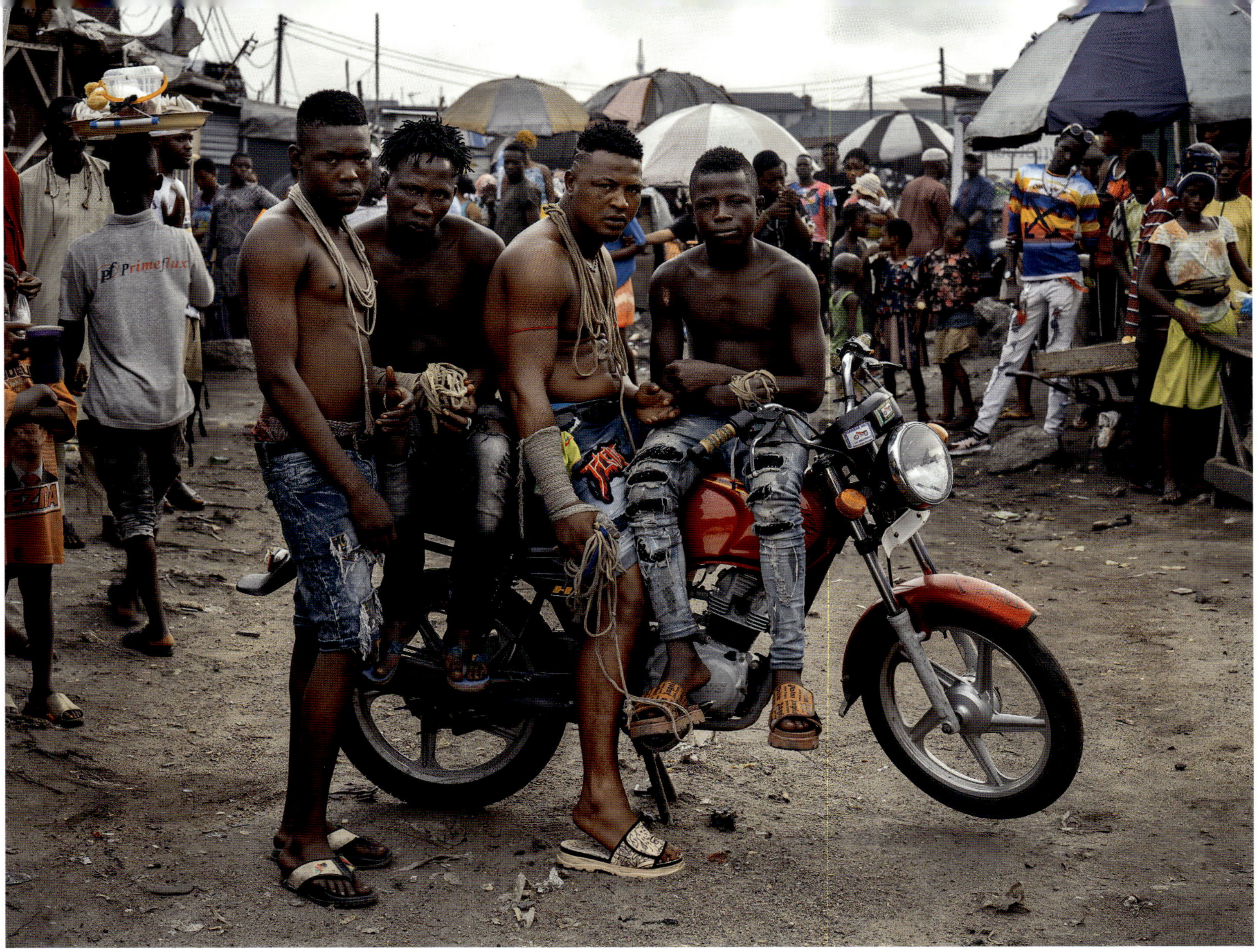

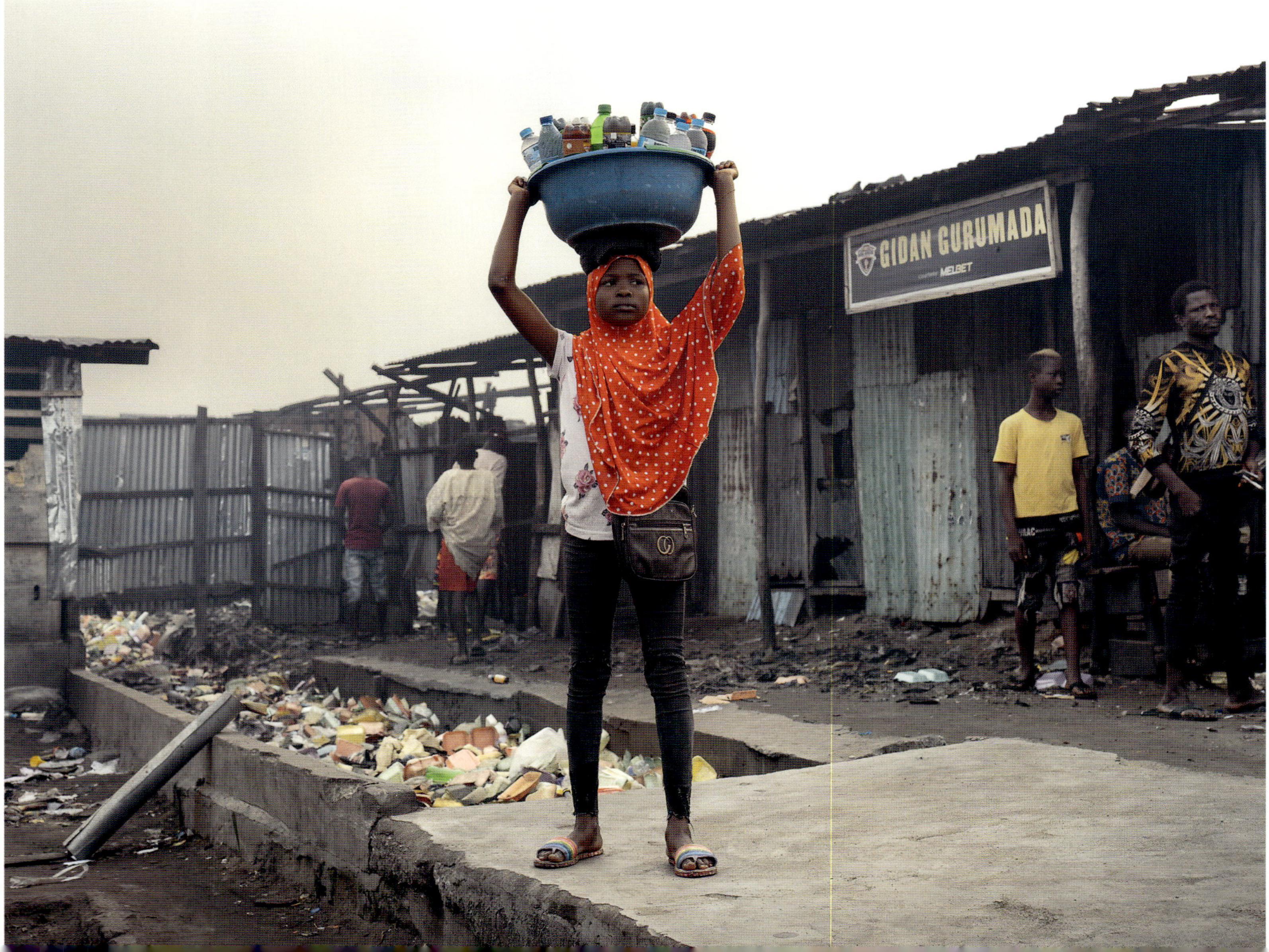

GIDAN GURUMADA
MELBET

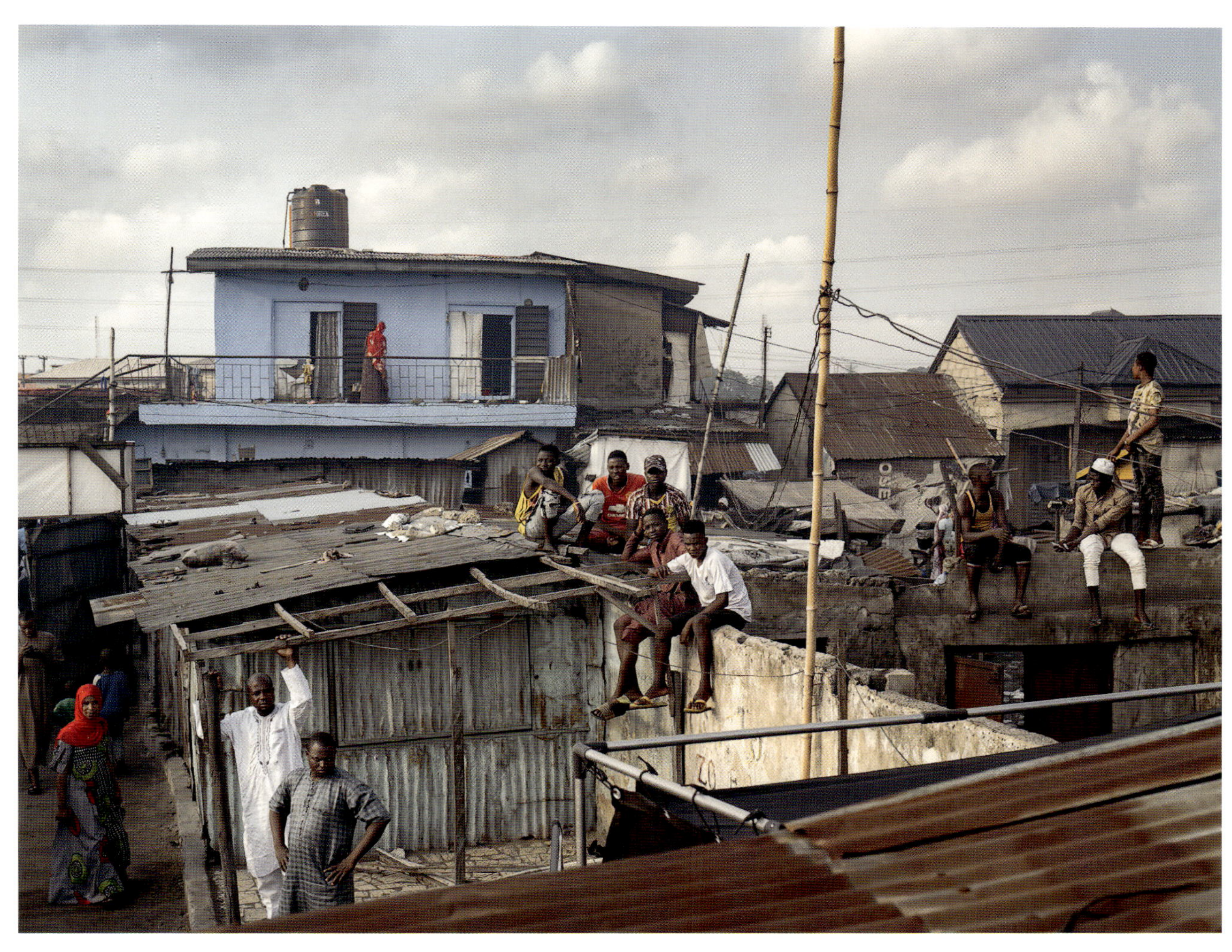

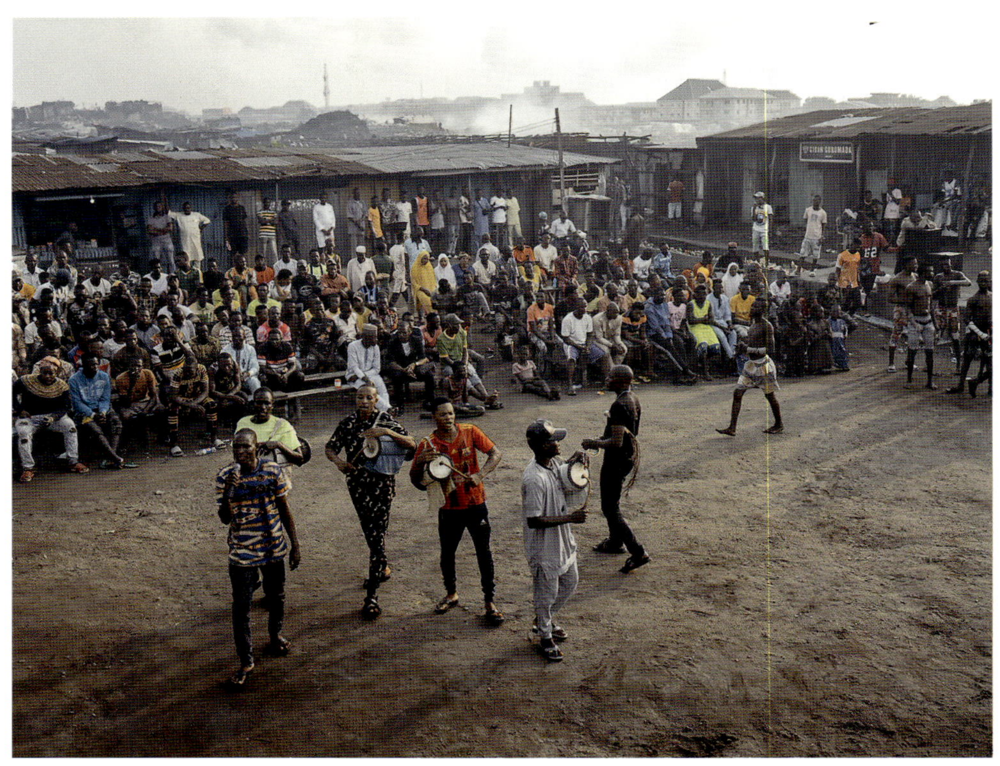

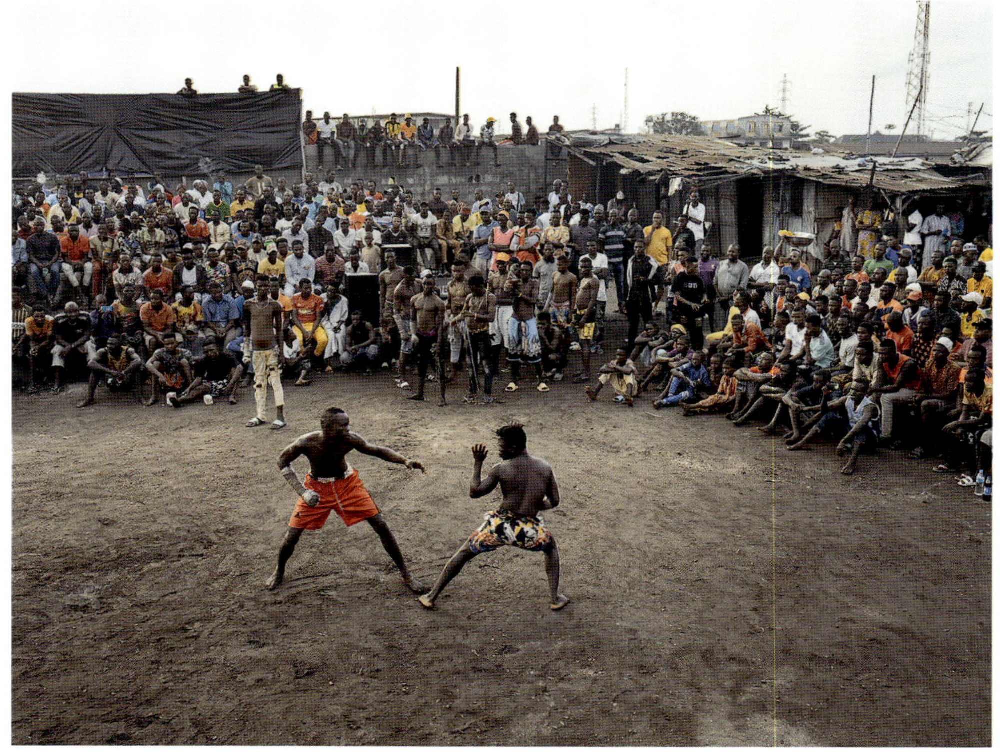

In the country's roughest communities, boys learn to fight at a young age, observing and admiring the older, experienced fighters.

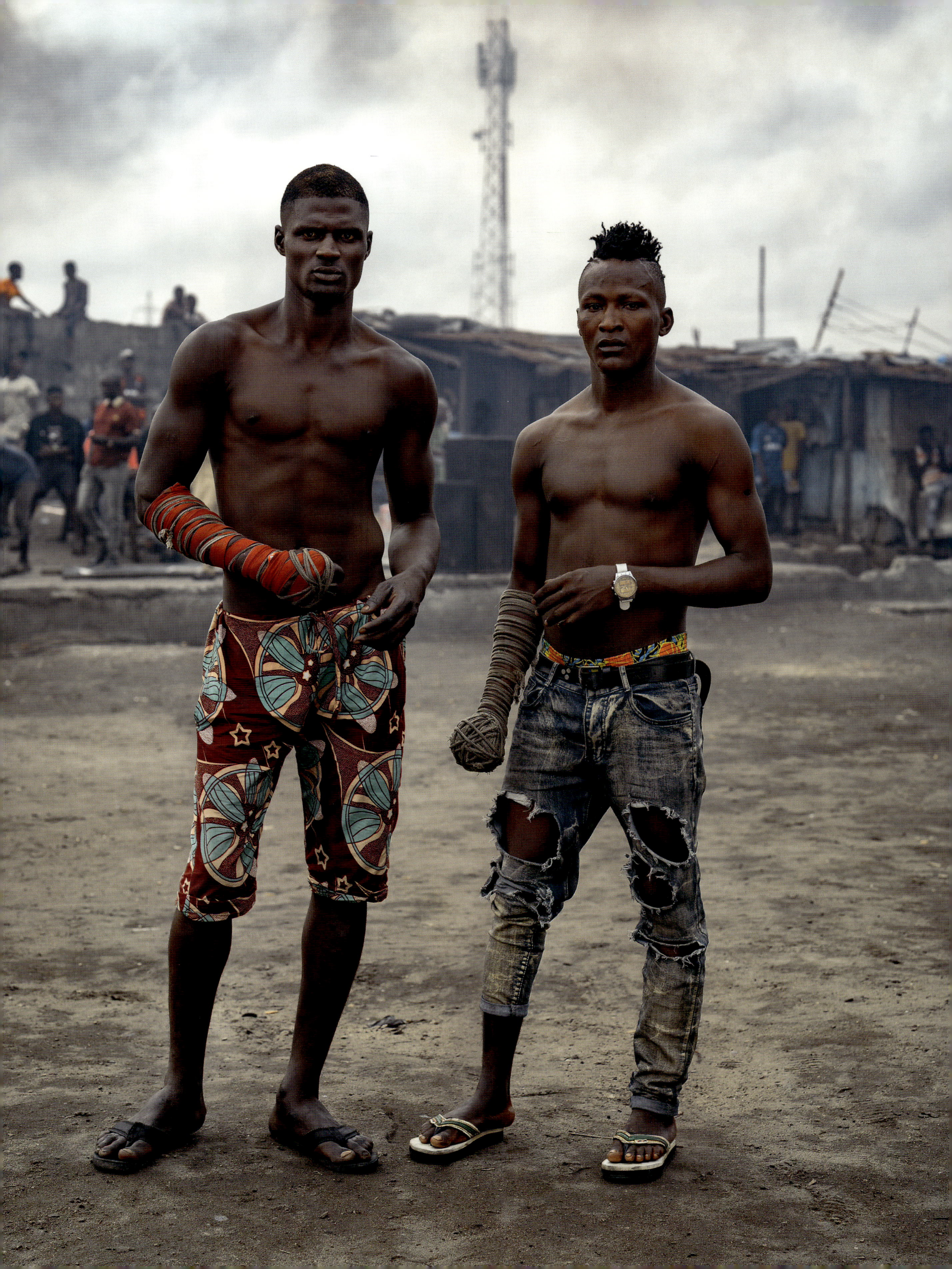

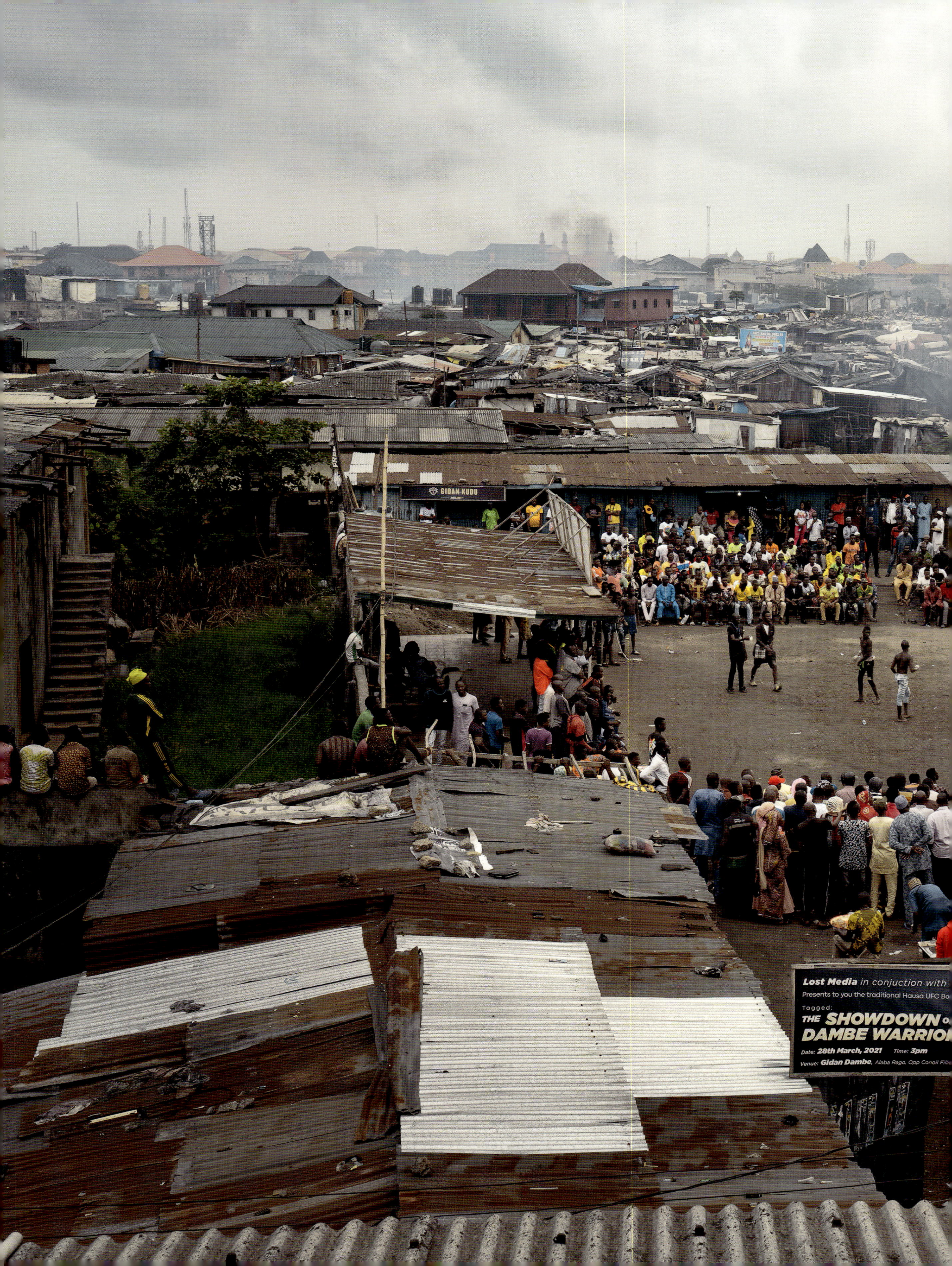
Lost Media in conjuction with
Presents to you the traditional Hausa UFC Bo
Tagged:
THE SHOWDOWN o
DAMBE WARRIOR
Date: 28th March, 2021   Time: 3pm
Venue: Gidan Dambe, Alaba Rago, Opp Conoil Fi
GIDAN KUDU

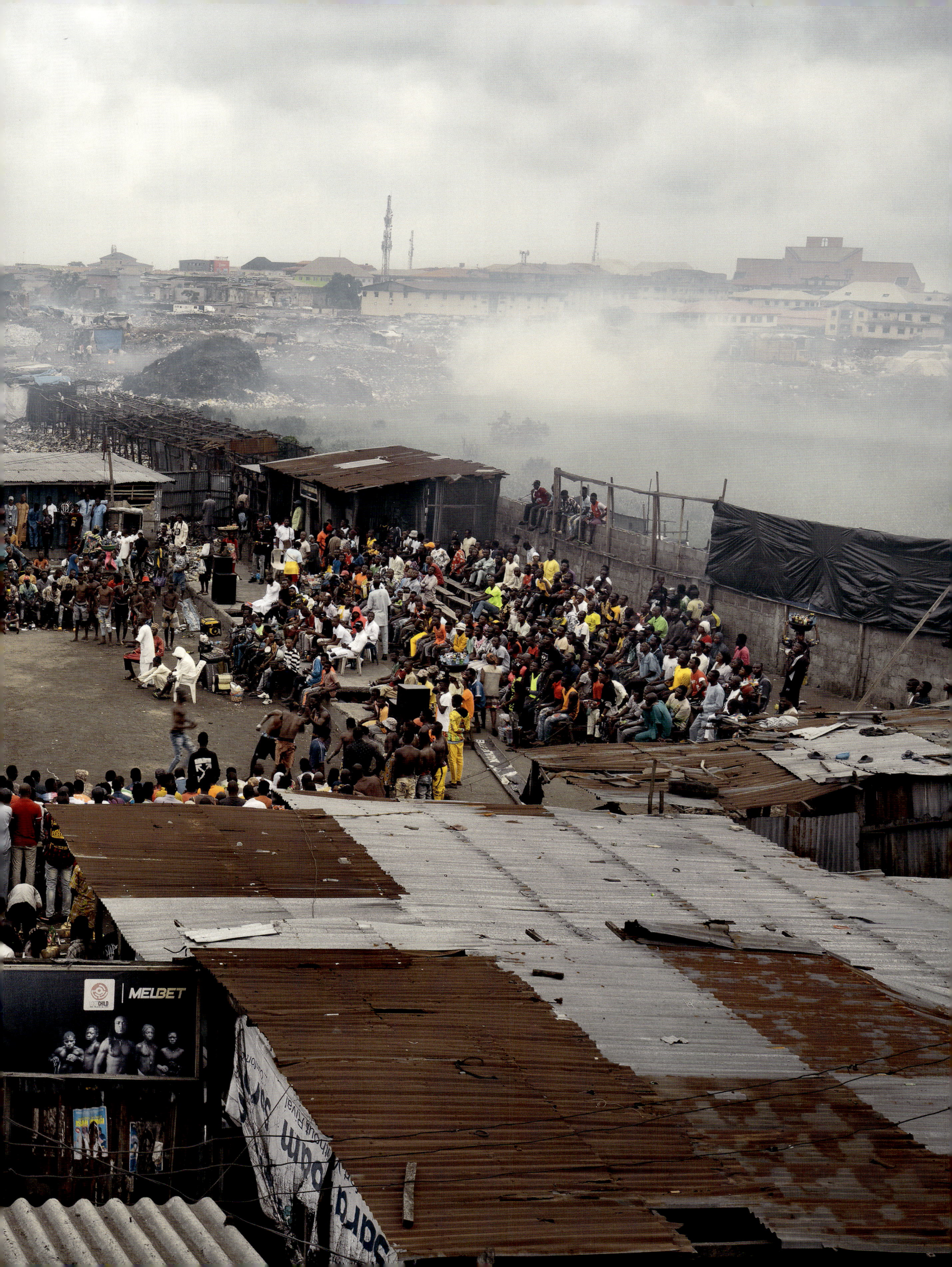

LOST CHILD MEDIA
MELBET

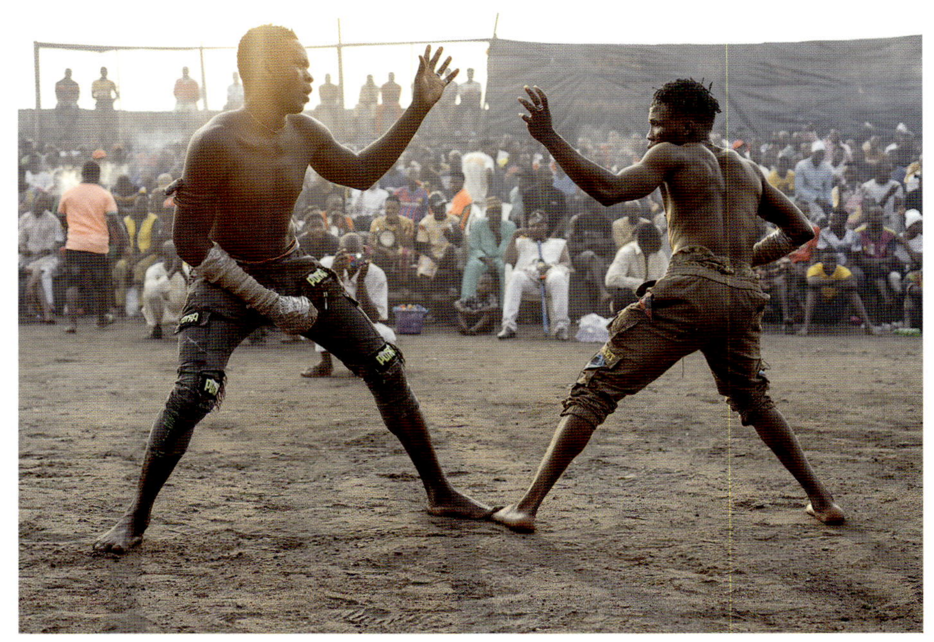

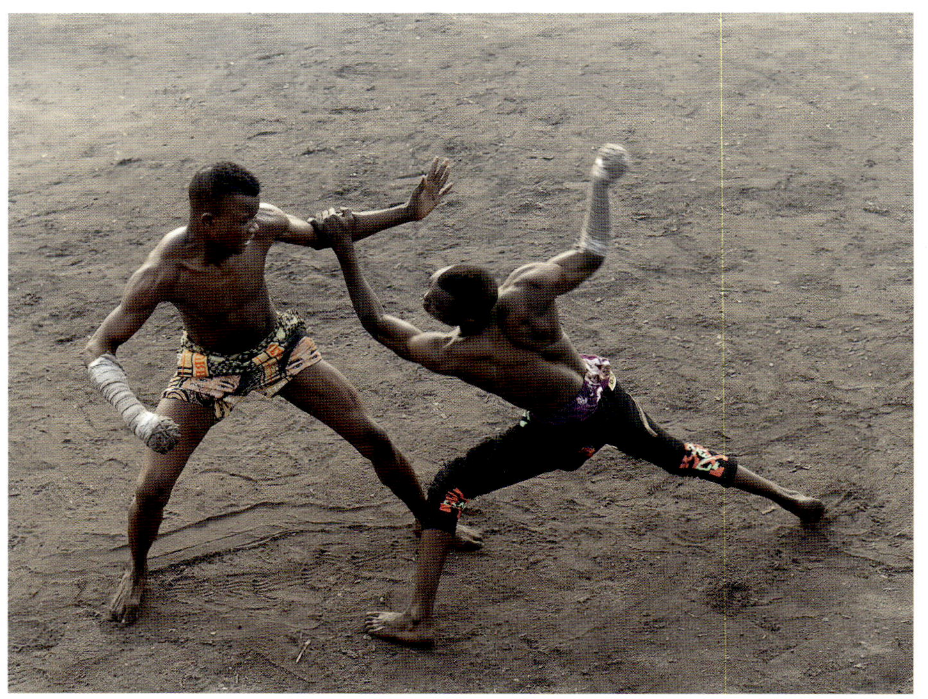

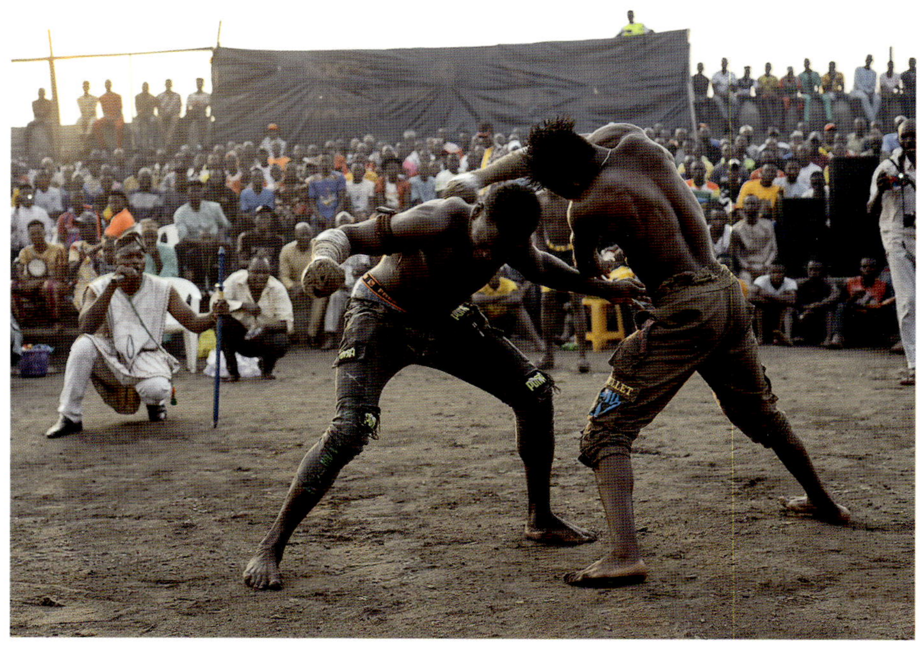

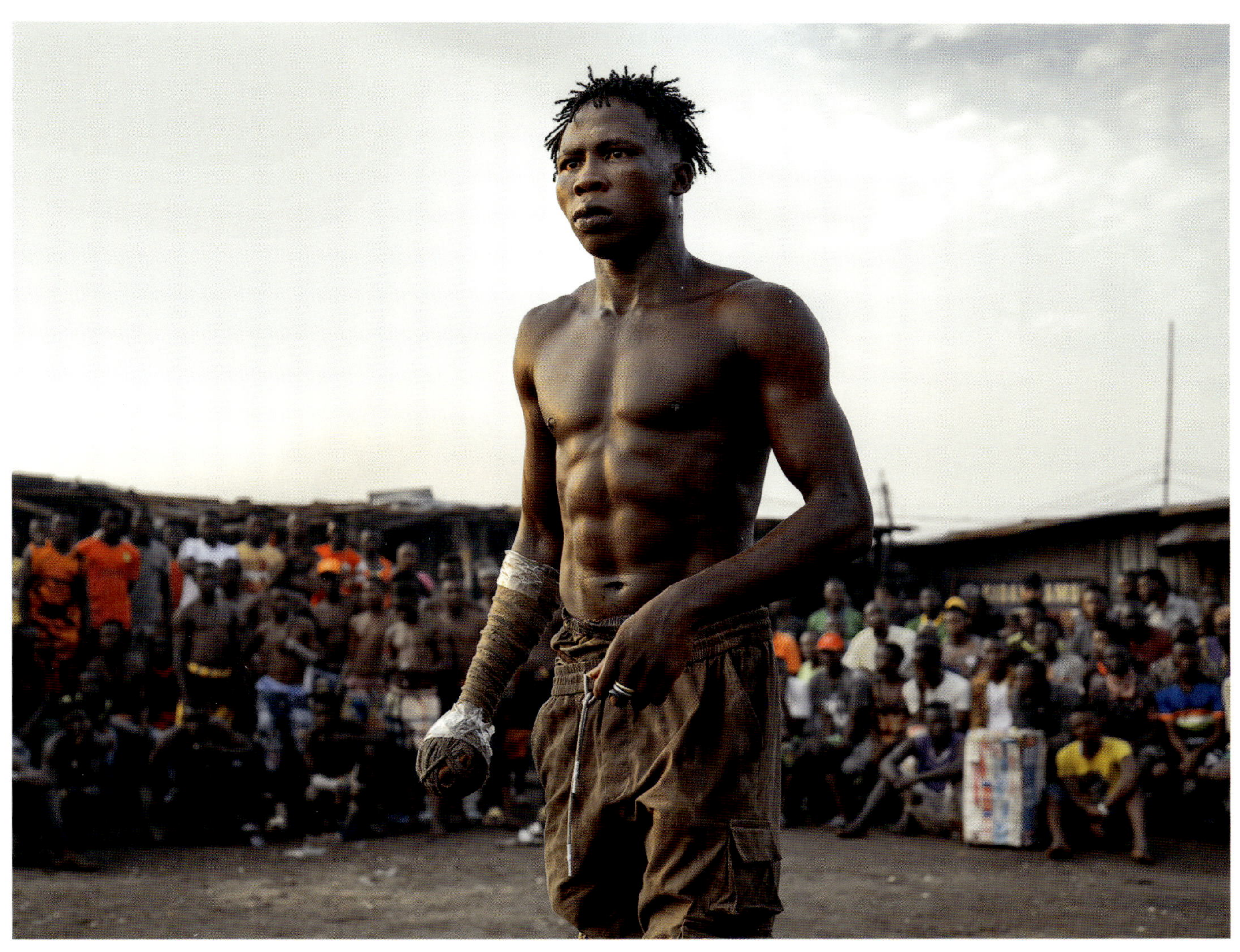

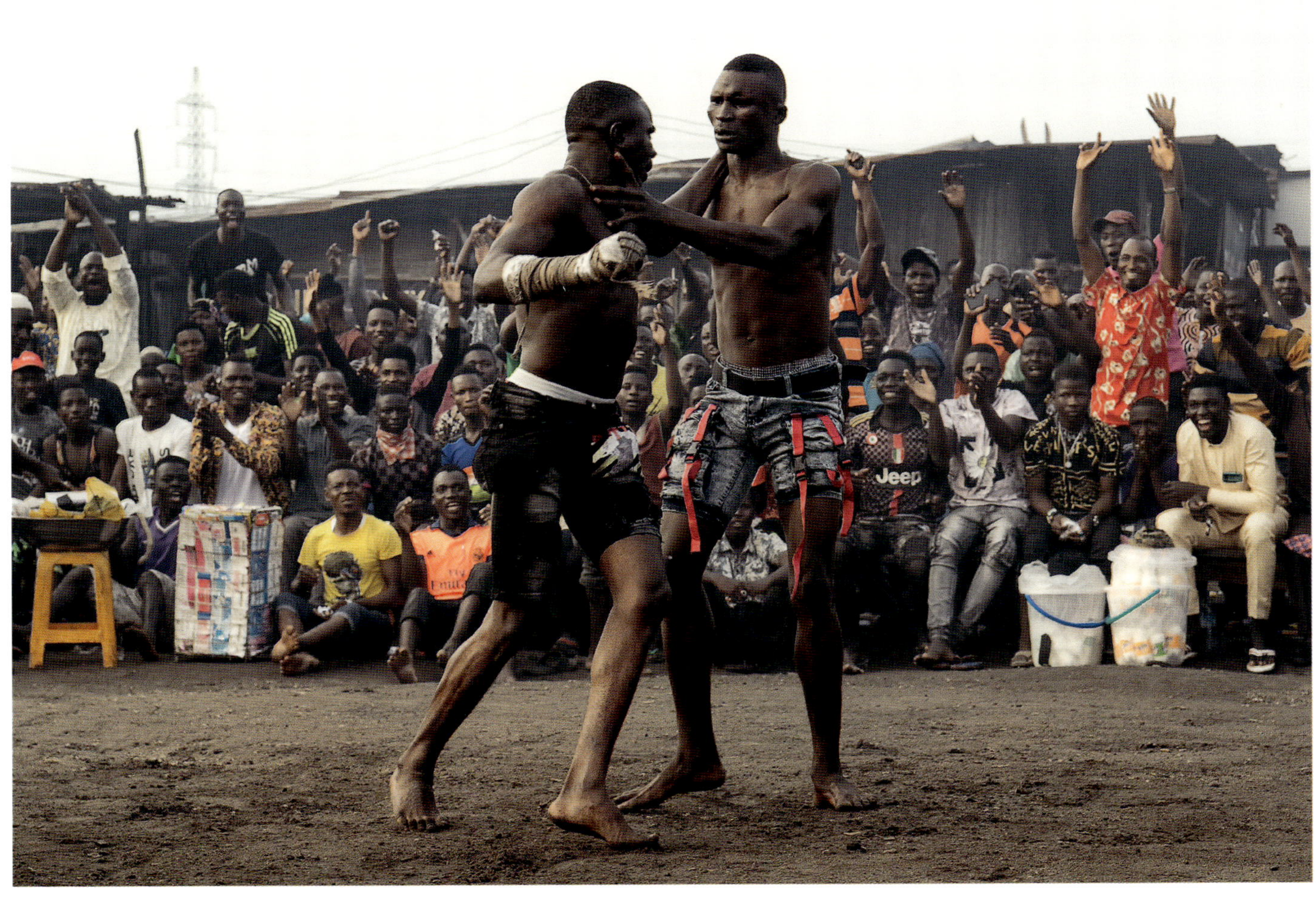

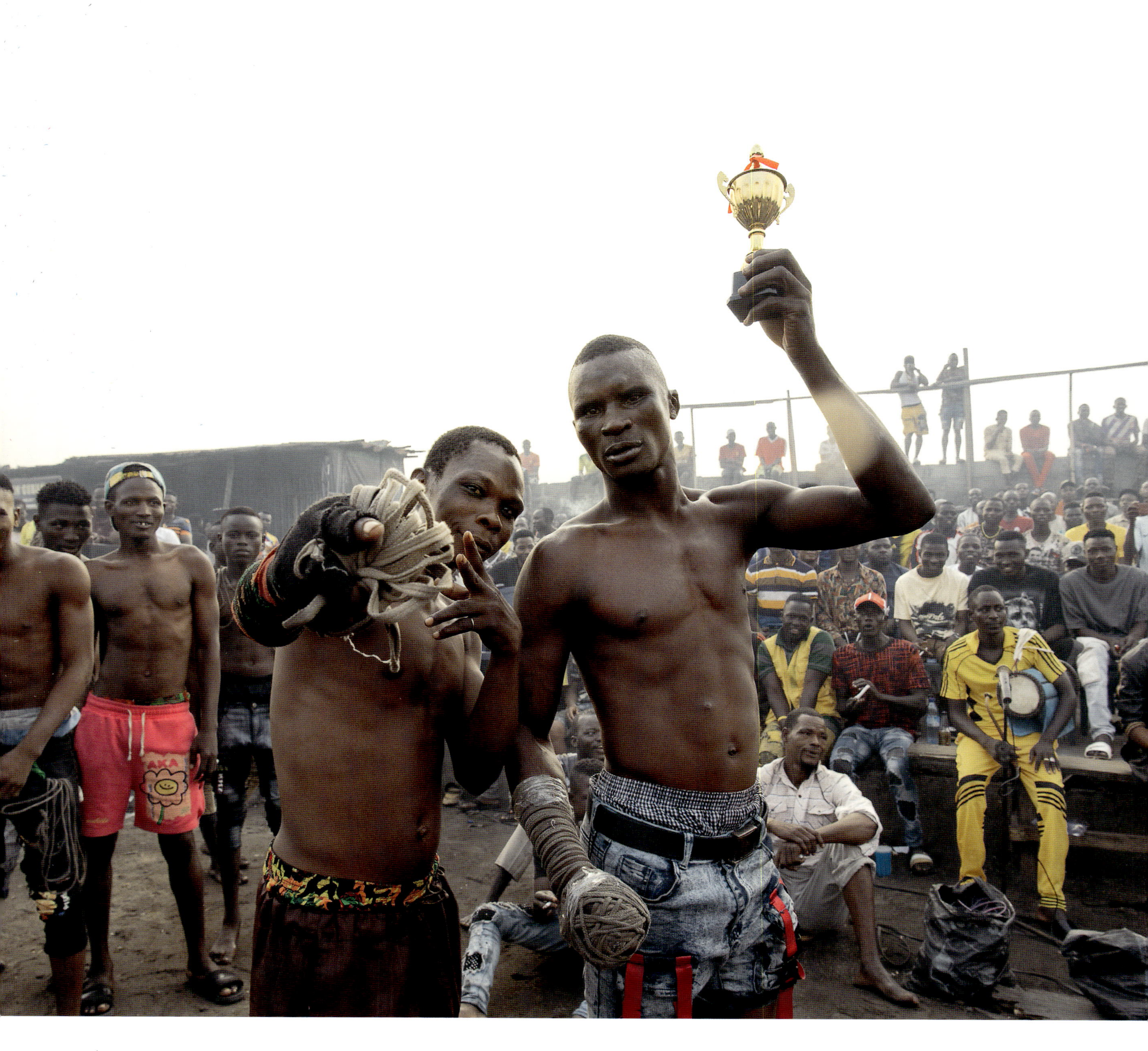

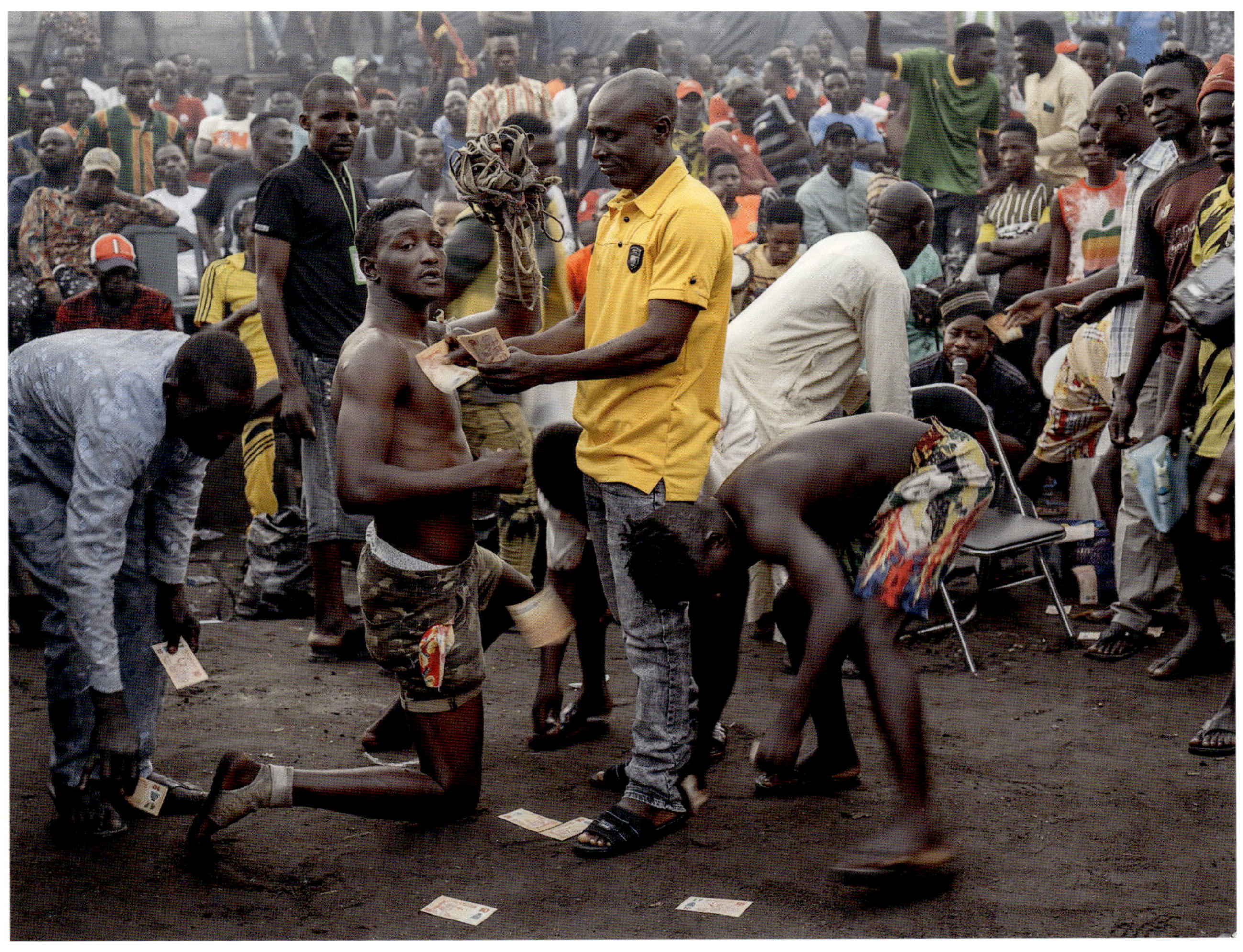

Both winners and losers of matches are
showered with money in appreciation for
their strength and courage.

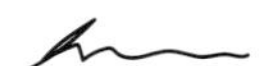

Camel Racing

UNITED ARAB EMIRATES

The unique relationship between man and animal transcends all others, rooted in the survival of the scorching sun and has evolved into an interdependent love praised by the most esteemed poets.

The myth and magic of the Arabian desert have always evoked a sense of romance and mystery, maintaining a fascination beyond the legendary tales of Ali Baba, Aladdin and Sinbad. Home to nomads and adventurers for thousands of years, this stark, alluring, ochre-filled landscape is the backdrop for the time-honoured sport of camel racing. This centuries-old tradition dates back to when Bedouin tribes would gather to celebrate weddings and other festivities. Today, the custom has become a sporting event that binds locals from across the United Arab Emirates and attracts visitors from around the world.

AL DHAID,
SHARJAH

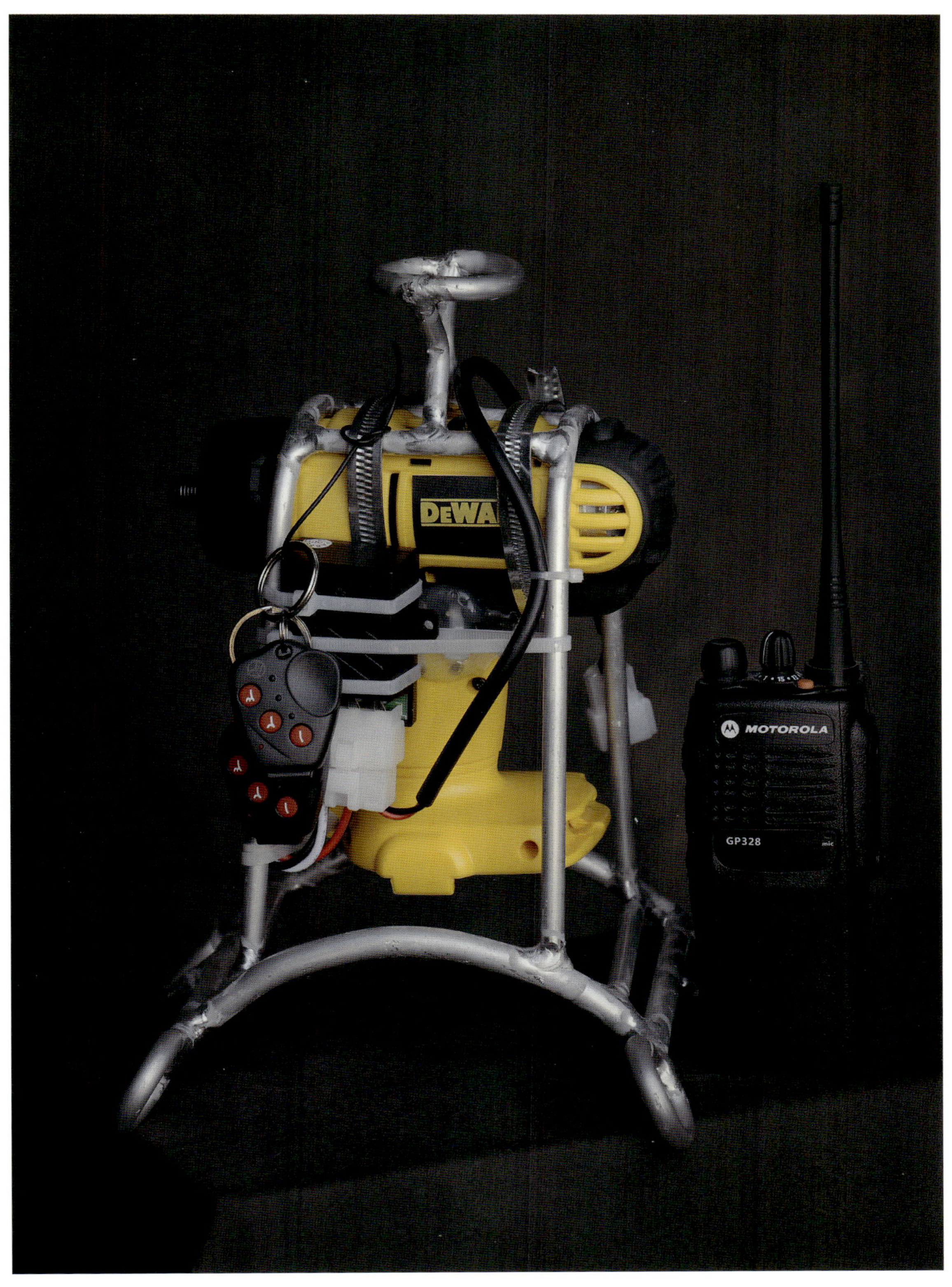

Robot jockeys, the alternative to child jockeys, are made from aluminium with built-in walkie-talkies, GPS, and a small automated whip operated via remote control.

"As a camel beareth labour, and heat, and hunger, and thirst, through deserts of sand, and fainteth not; so the fortitude of a man shall sustain him through all perils."

~ Akhenaton (King of Egypt, fourteenth-century b.c.) ~

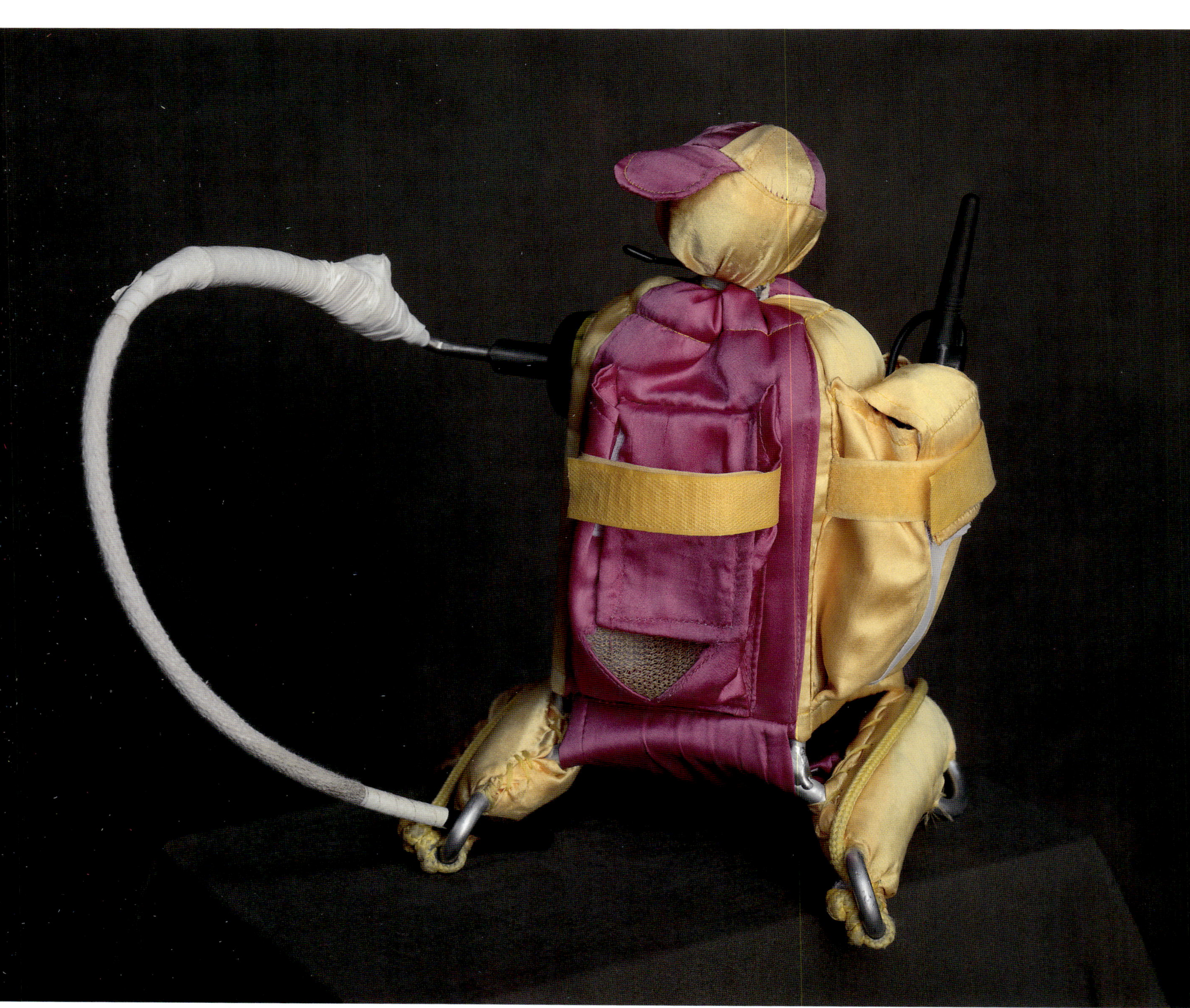

For the Arabs, camels have been a prized possession since time immemorial and were said to be God's gift to the Bedouin. Even today, as technology dominates these ancient sands, the love of camel racing continues. The unique relationship between man and animal transcends all others; rooted in surviving the scorching sun; it has evolved into an interdependent love praised by the most esteemed poets.

Only the single-humped female dromedary is used for racing, whose capacity to survive excessive heat is unsurpassable. In the UAE, there are four camel breeds specific to racing: the native *mahaliyat*; the Sudanese breed called *sudaniyat*; *omaniyat* from Oman; and the interbred *muhajanat*. Training their most prized possession begins as early as two years old. Younger camels are prohibited as their bodies are not fully developed.

In the never-ending quest for faster times and lighter jockeys, children had been groomed to ride camels since the 1970s. As the sport transformed from a Bedouin cultural event into a professional money-making industry, the demand for new jockeys attracted society's underbelly of human traffickers. By 2005 the UAE, pressured by human rights organizations,

stopped the unhealthy practice of using child jockeys. And thus, robot jockeys were born.

These toy-sized, camel-riding aluminium robots, lavishly decorated in the finest team-coloured silks, weigh around twenty-seven kilograms and are equipped with GPS and a cordless powered whip. They even have a heart rate sensor to monitor the camel's health – anything to ensure victory.

There are two major annual championships – Sheikh Hamdan bin Mohammed bin Rashid Al Maktoum Camel Race Festival and Al Marmoum Heritage Festival. Races occur in the winter, between October and April, from 6 a.m. until 9 a.m. On the day of the race, people gather before sunrise to avoid the unbearable desert heat; once the sun is up, temperatures can reach a fiery forty to forty-five degrees Celsius. Even in the early morning hours, the excitement is palpable as the crowd cheers and men in pristine white flowing robes prepare to open the gates to as many as sixty camels that are ready to run the racetrack of Al Dhaid, Sharjah, one of the most challenging in the UAE. With their long gangly legs and the teeny automated jockeys perched on their hump, the camels awkwardly bolt out of the gate. Their trainers speed alongside in shiny SUVs, operating the

jockeys via remote control and shouting at the camels through built-in walkie talkies, racing at speeds of around sixty-five kilometres an hour to be the first to get across the finish line. This male-dominated sport is part of a long tradition passed on from father to son.

In the past, winners would take home essentials such as food and livestock. Today, it's the richest purse in the world: besides trophies, winners receive cars and substantial sums of money. Owning a camel is costly; prices start at about €50,000, but thoroughbreds are worth much more, and prize-winning camels are worth millions.

Amongst the desert's beauty of dust and dunes, the landscape's harshness contrasts with the Emiratis' warmth and genuine hospitality – a nomadic people, known as some of the most resilient on earth, who have survived in this desolate environment. Consequently, family is of the highest importance to them and essential to their existence.

Despite the influx of technology and over-the-top riches, the sands of time stand still here. Camel racing reflects values and cultural practices that will keep these nomadic customs alive for generations to come.

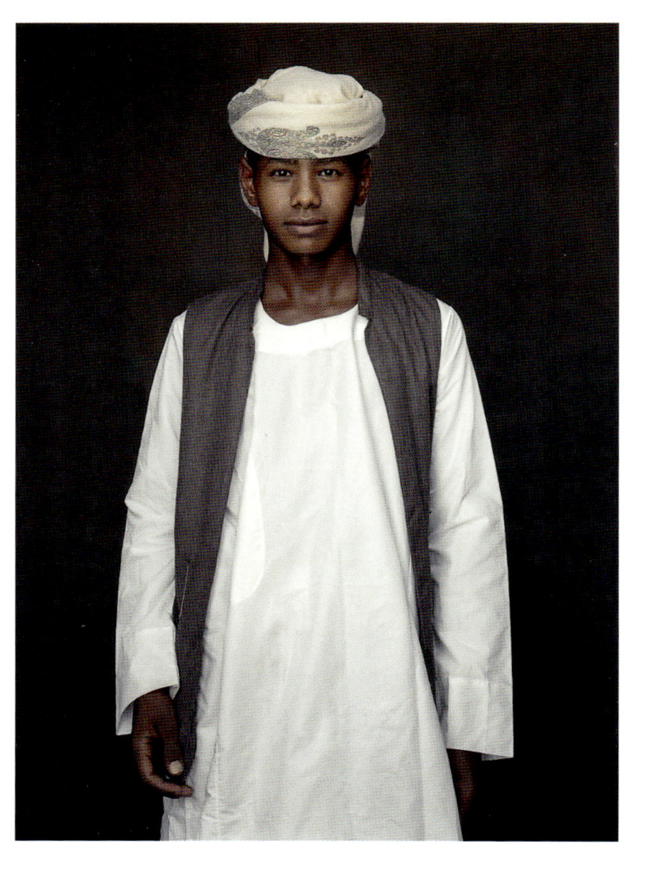
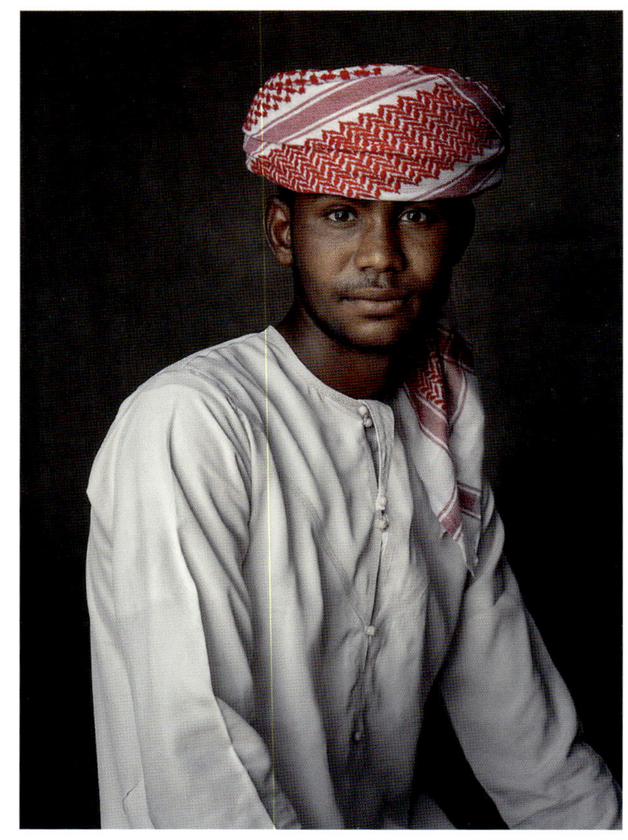
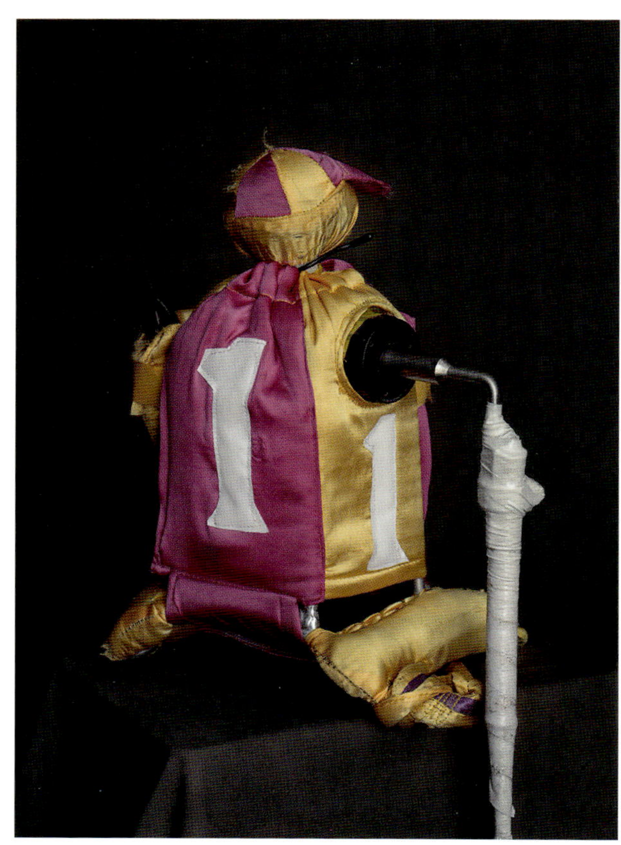
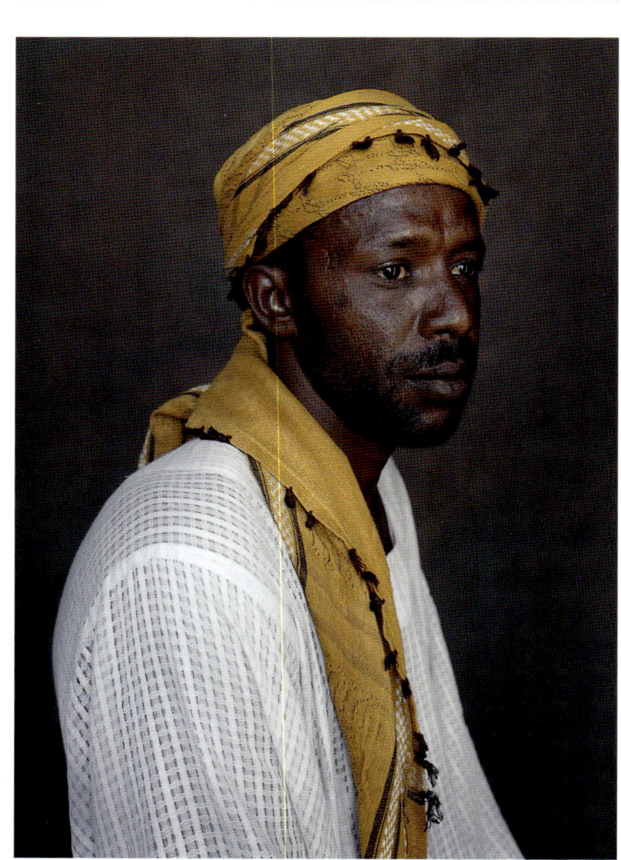

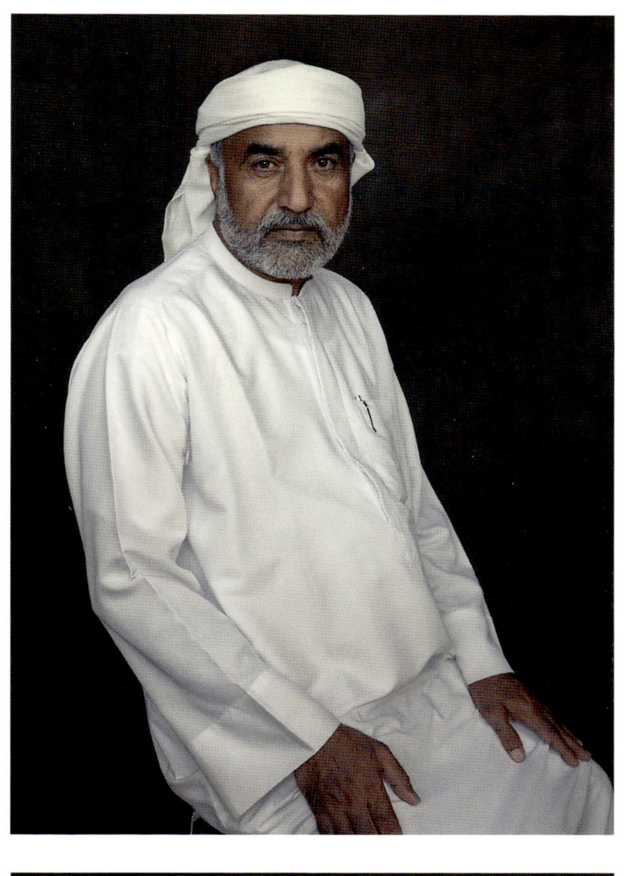
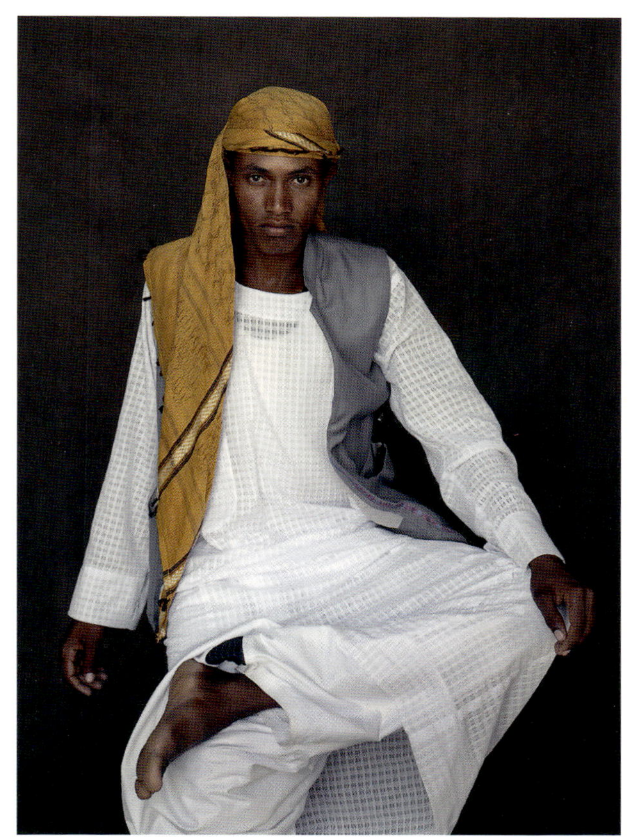
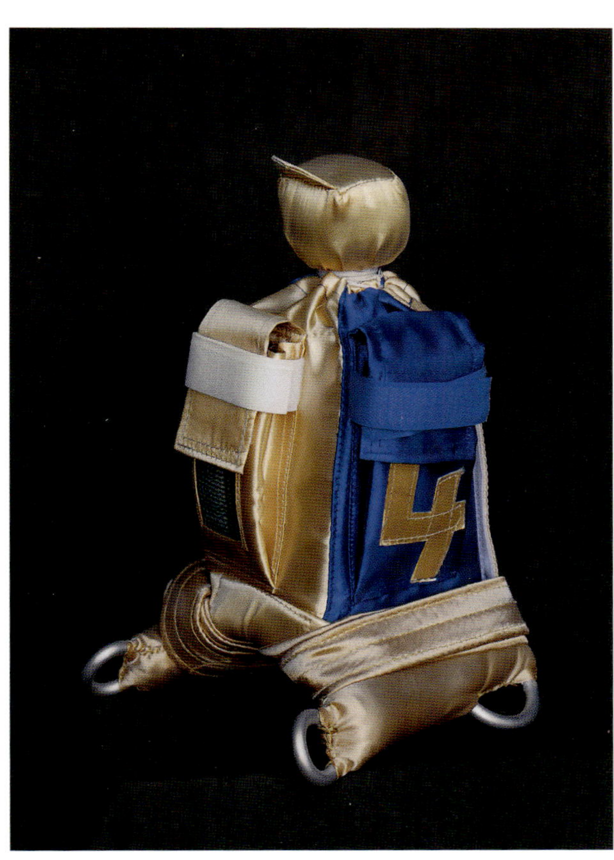
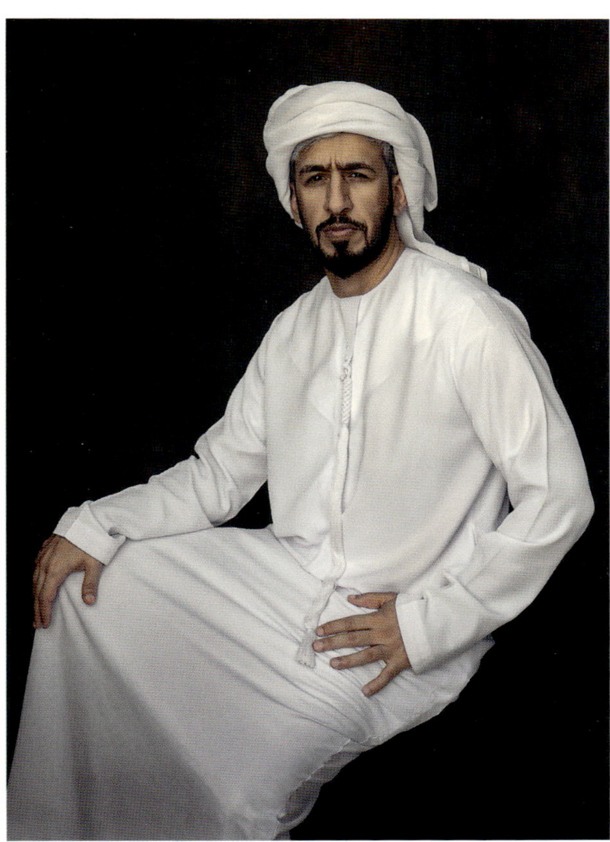

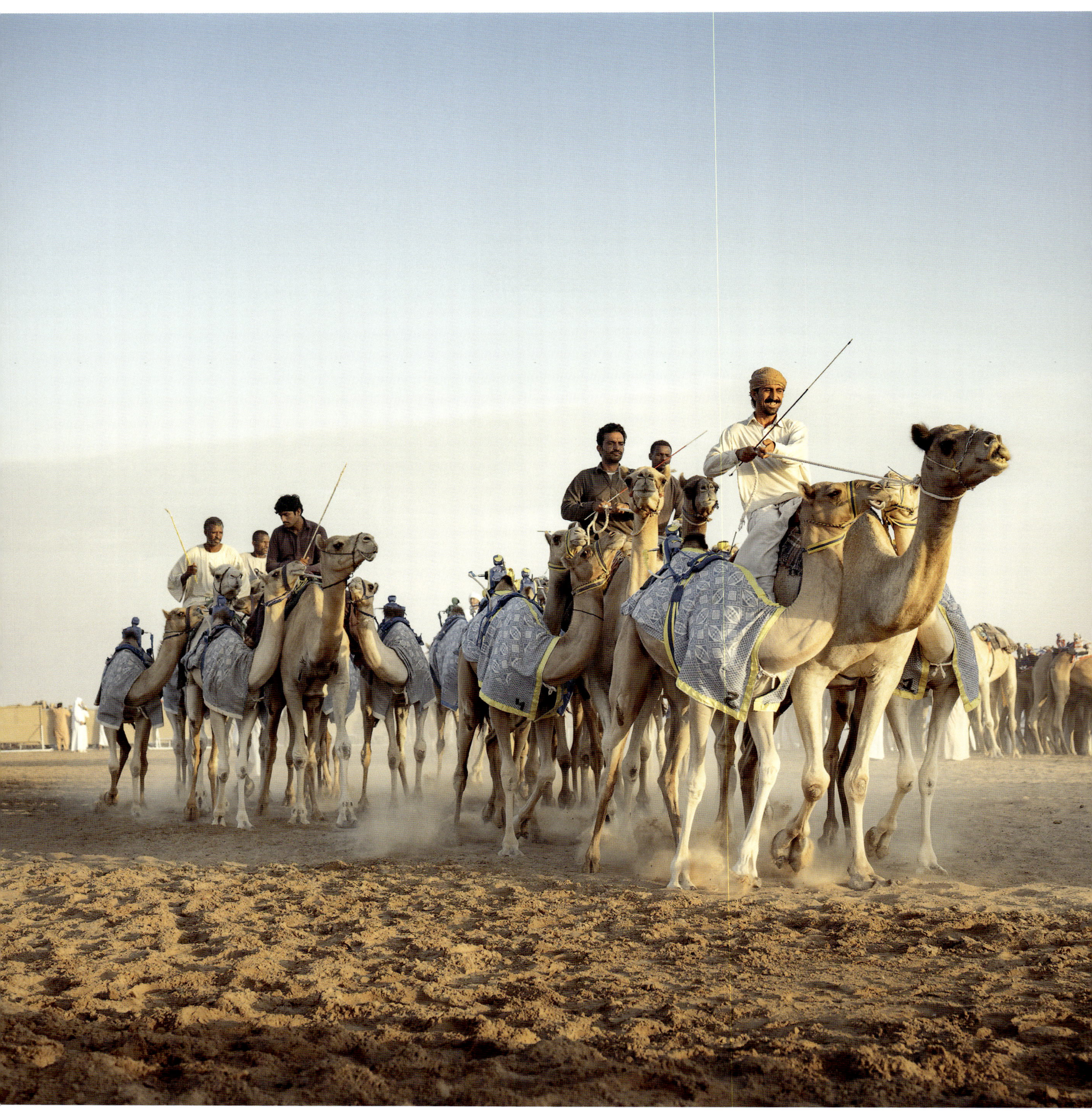

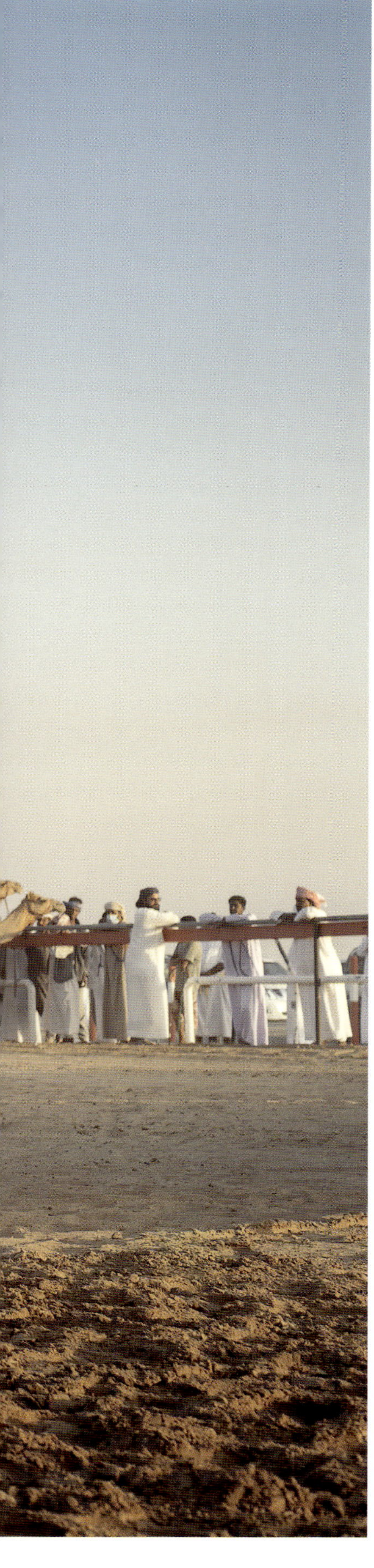

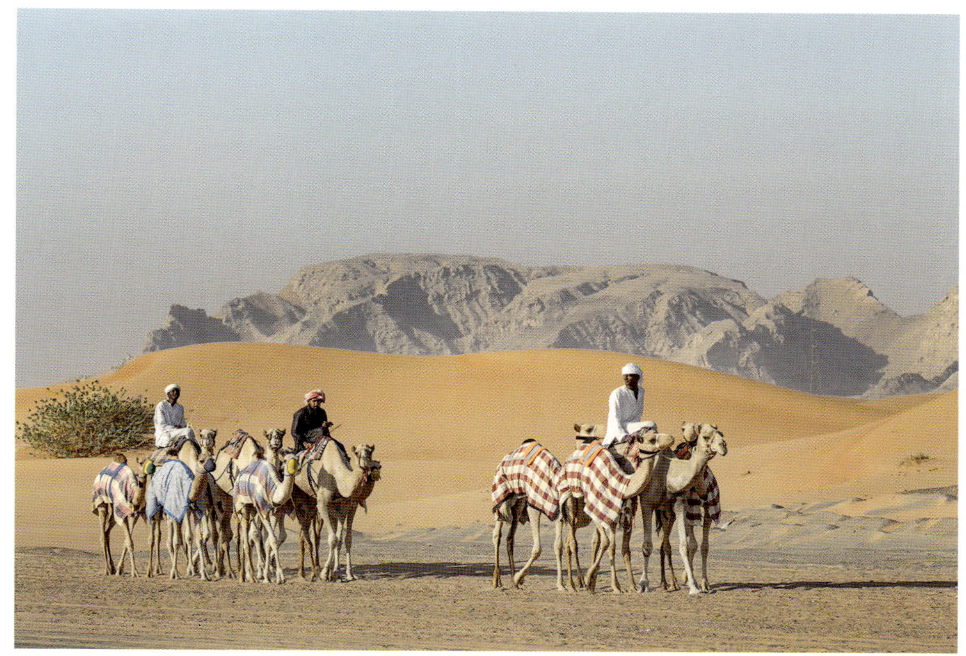

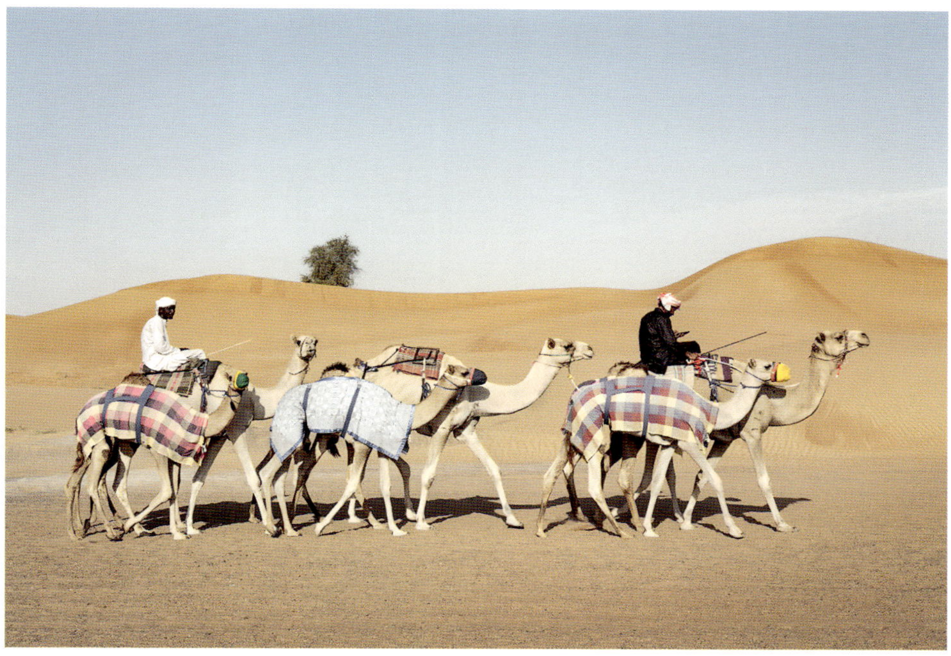

While training, camels are covered with blankets,
raising their body temperatures and causing them to sweat,
making them lighter in preparation for the race.

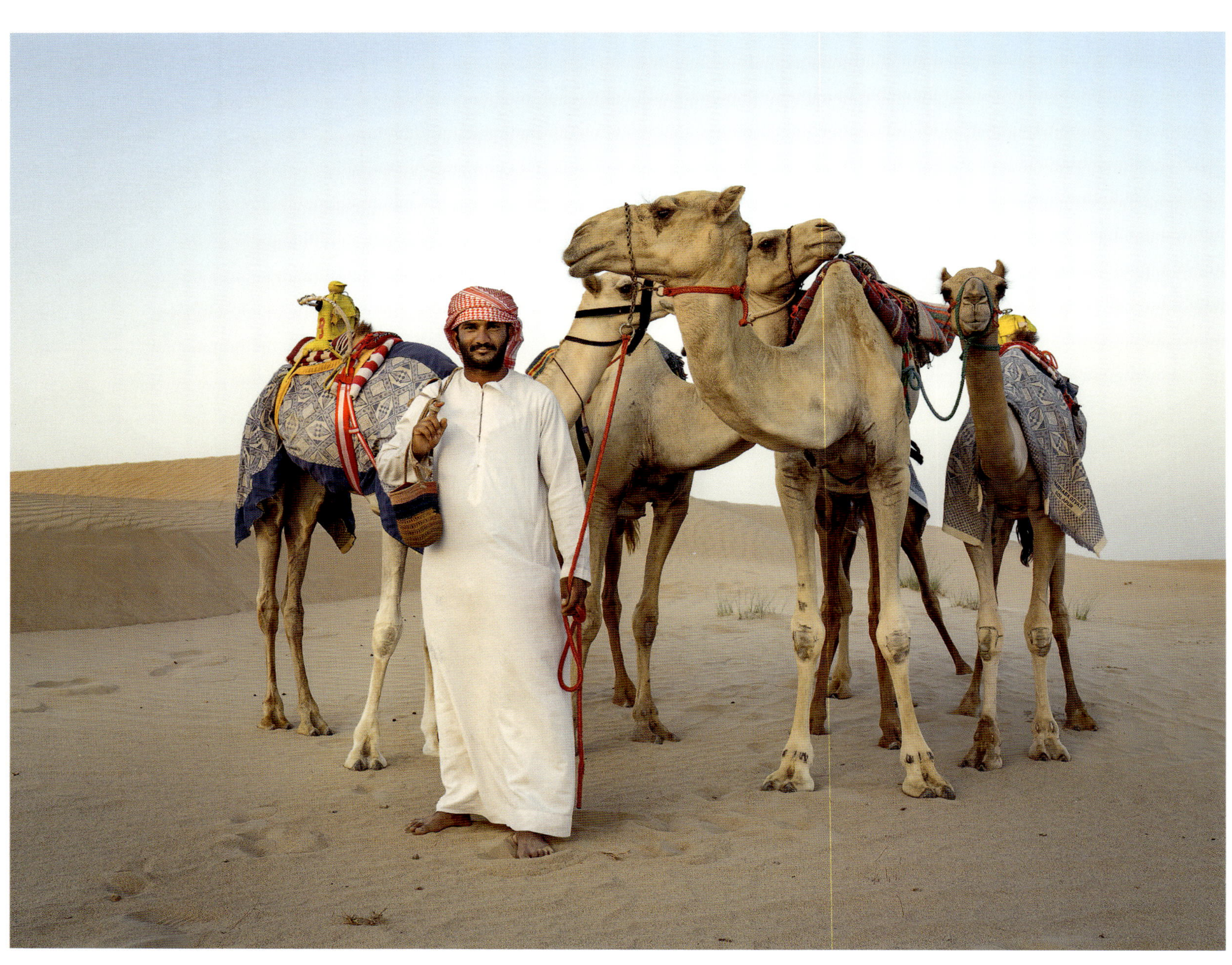

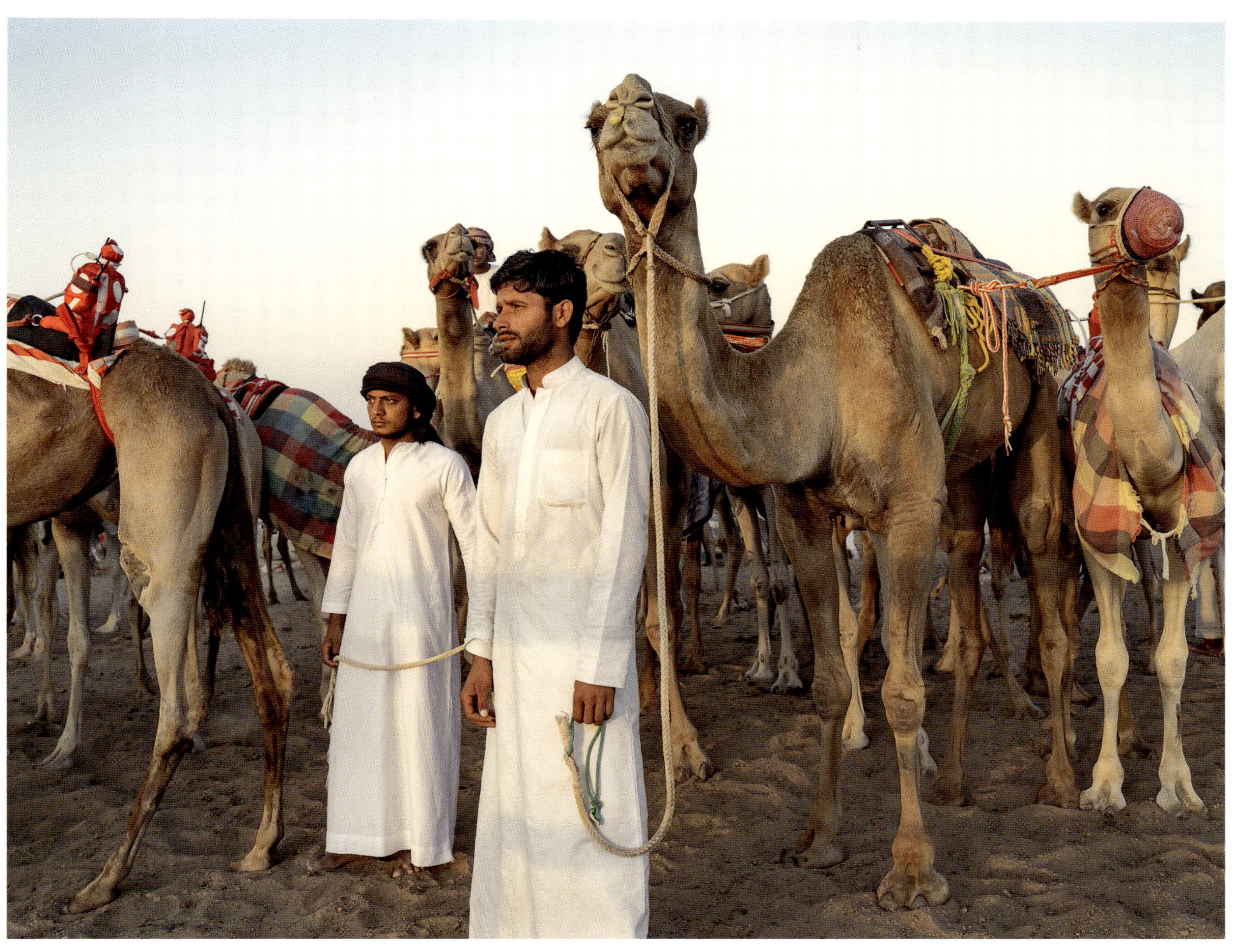

The Emiratis hire Pakistani and Sudanese men to
train the camels, arrive at the track before sunrise
and install the robot jockeys before the race begins.

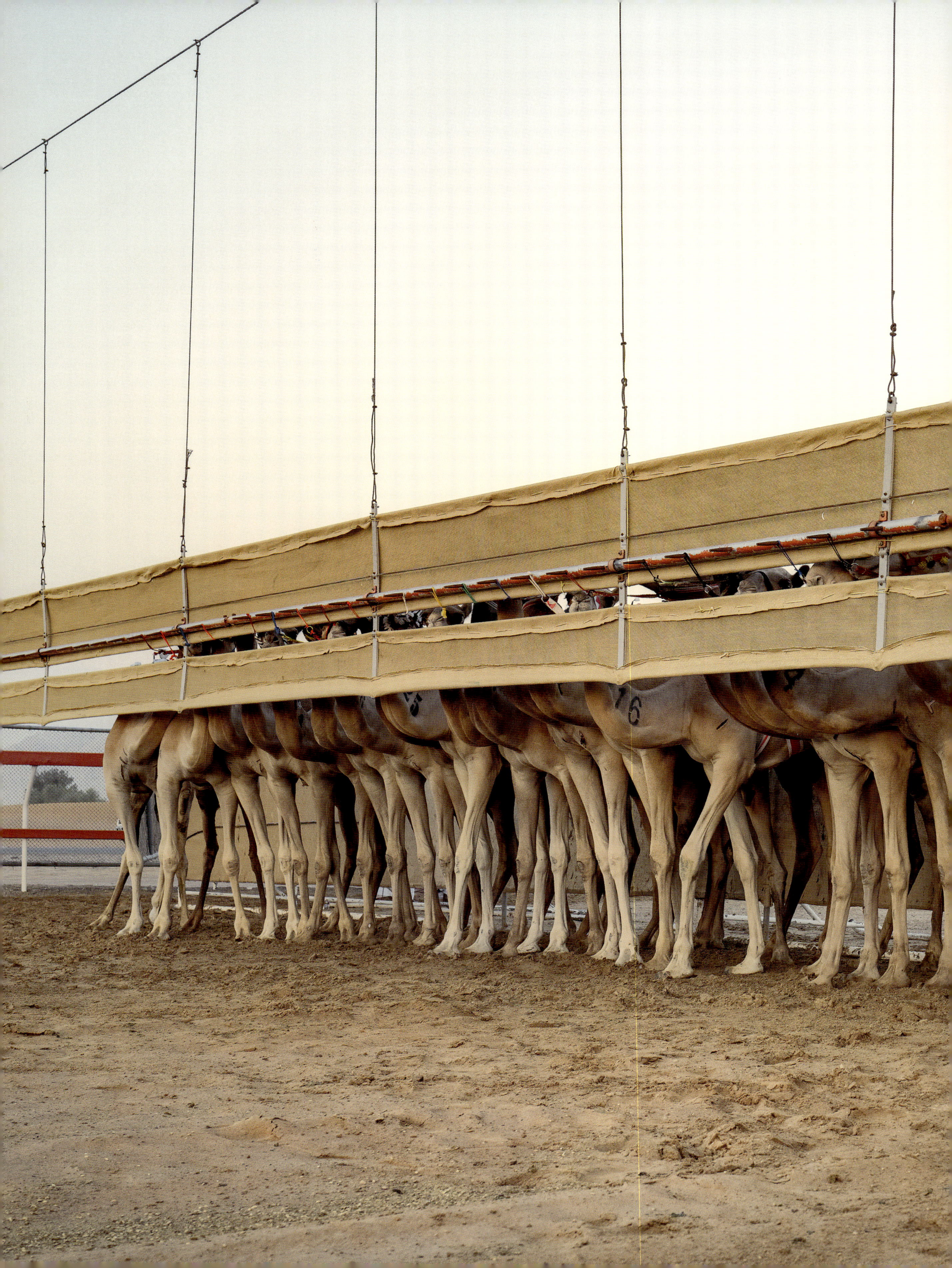

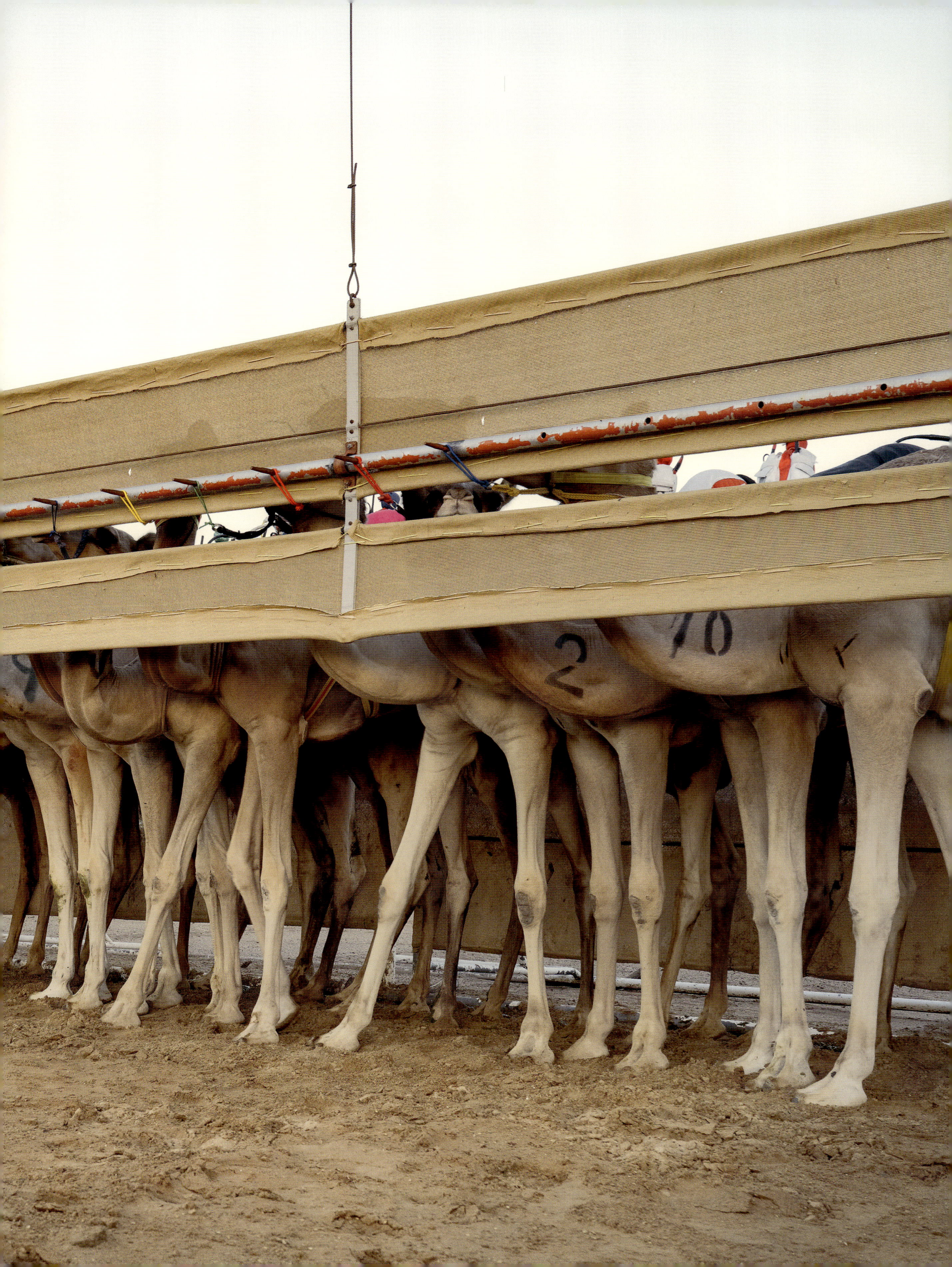

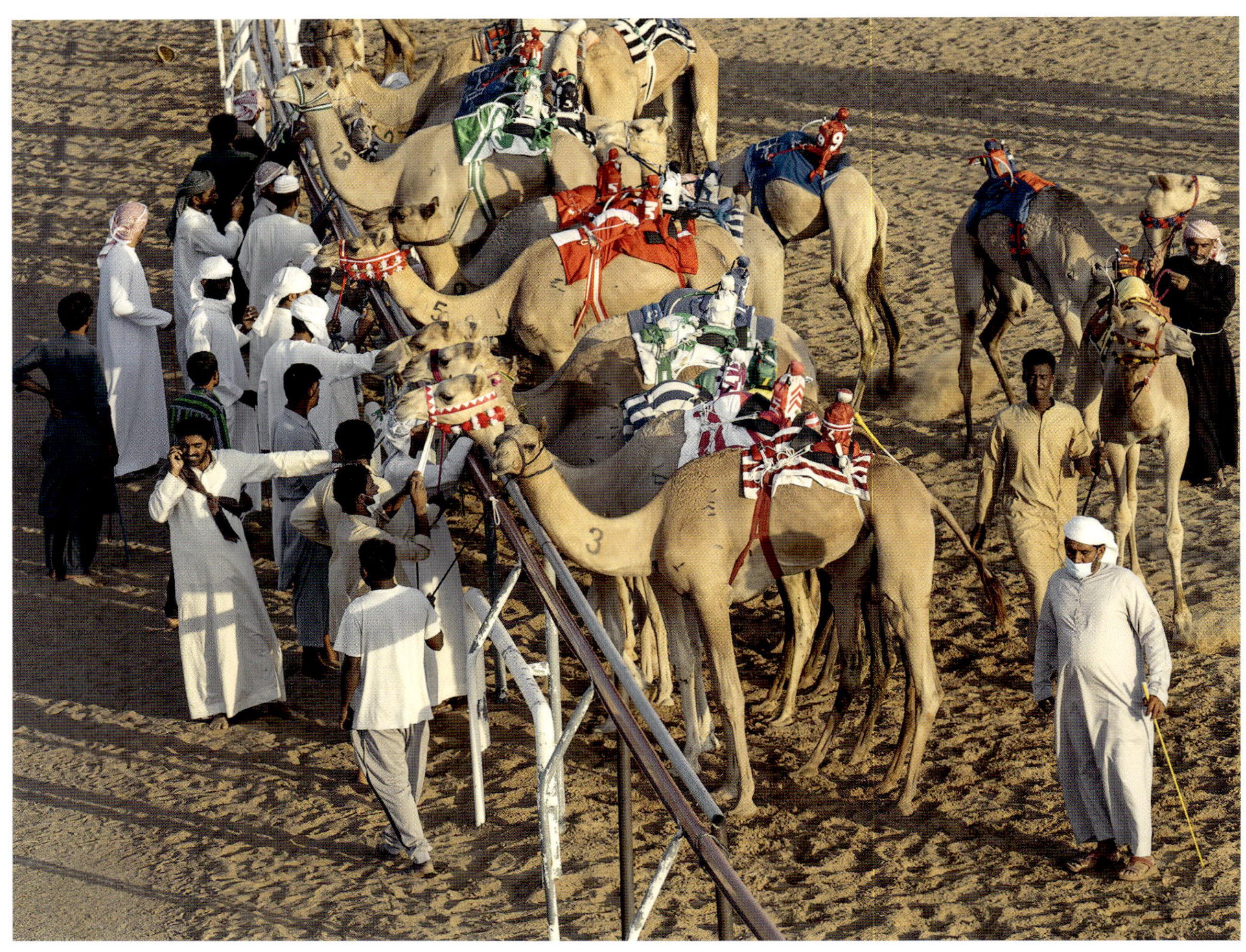

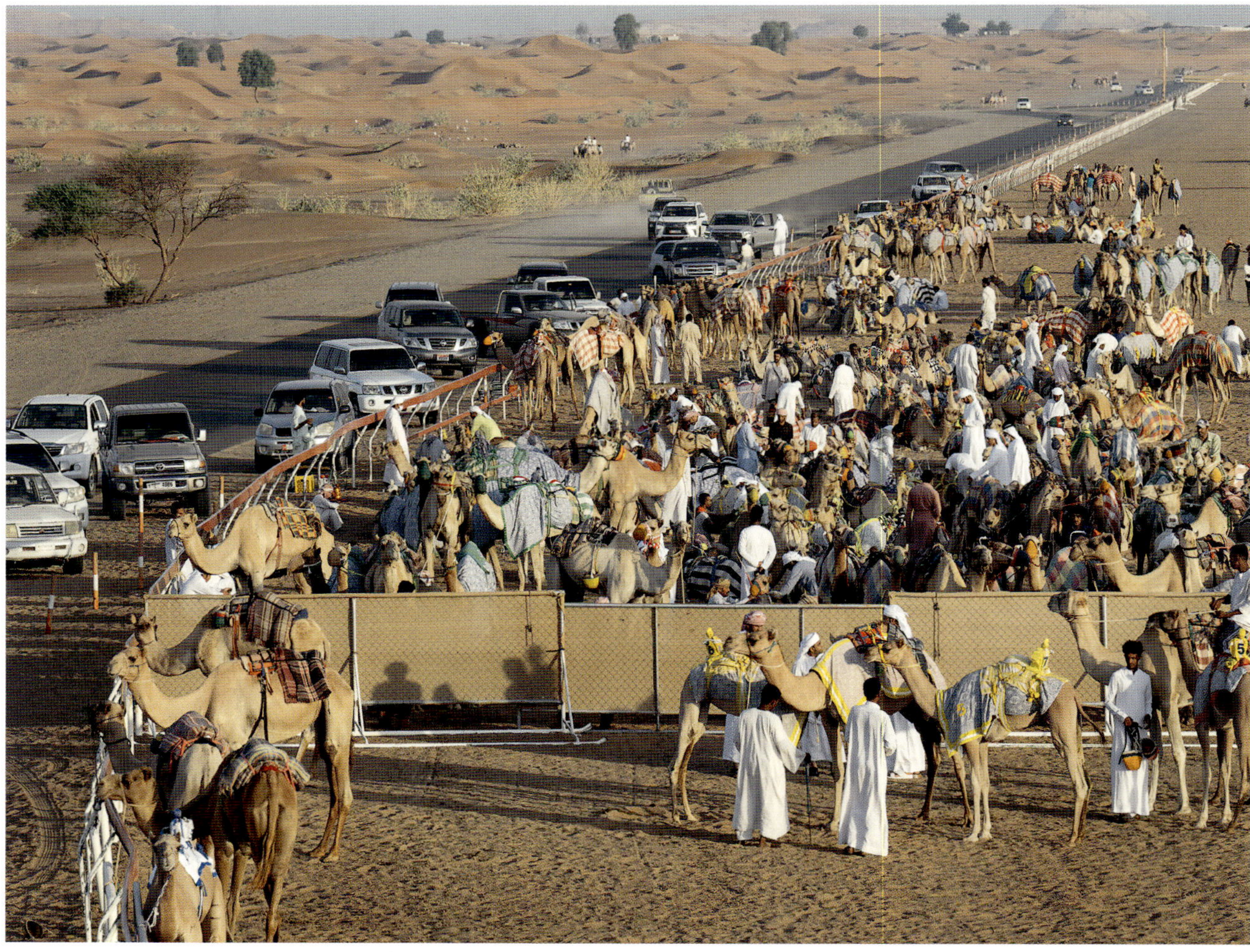

The United Arab Emirates has many camel racing tracks, but Sharjah's Al Dhaid track is considered one of the most challenging because it is heavily laden with sand.

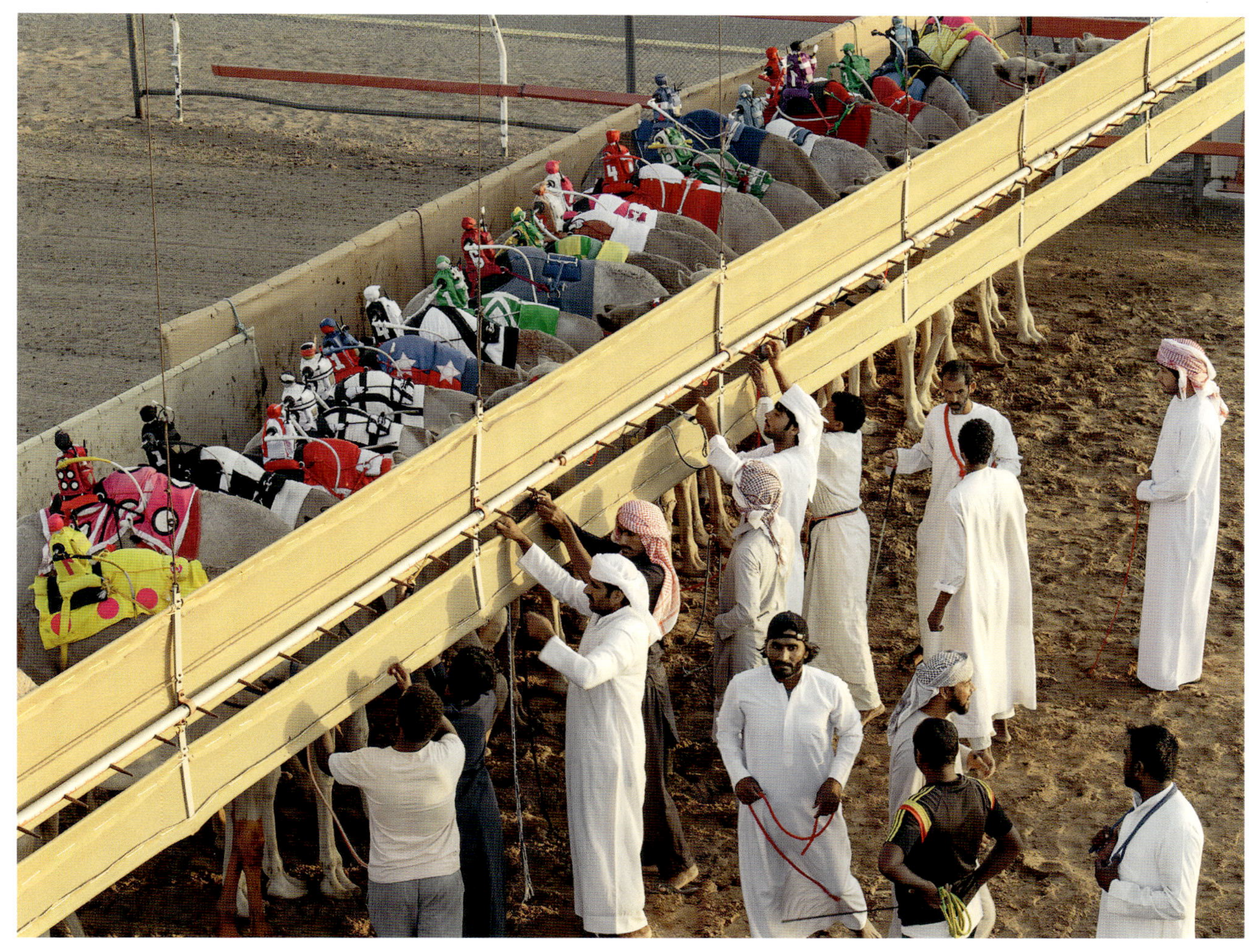

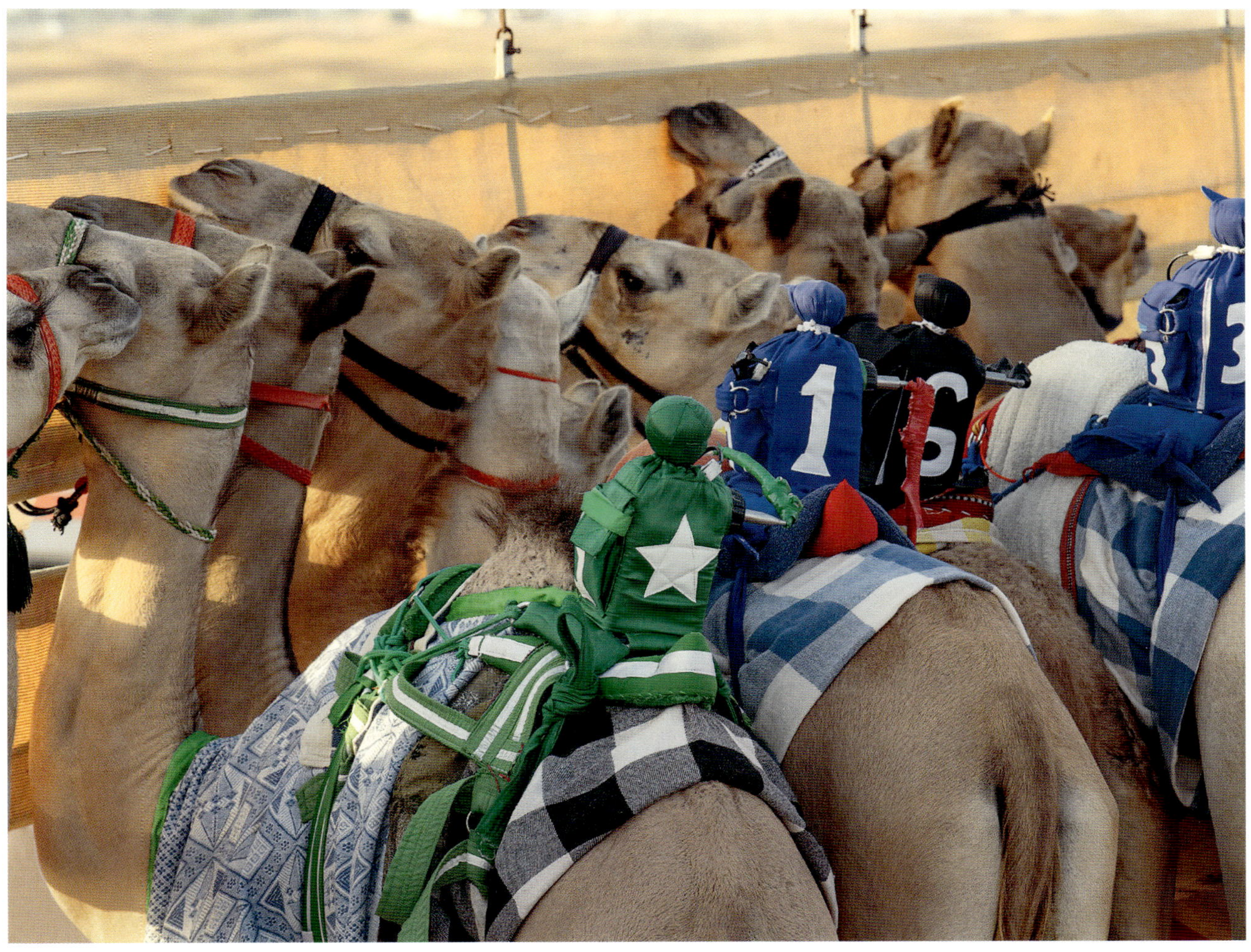

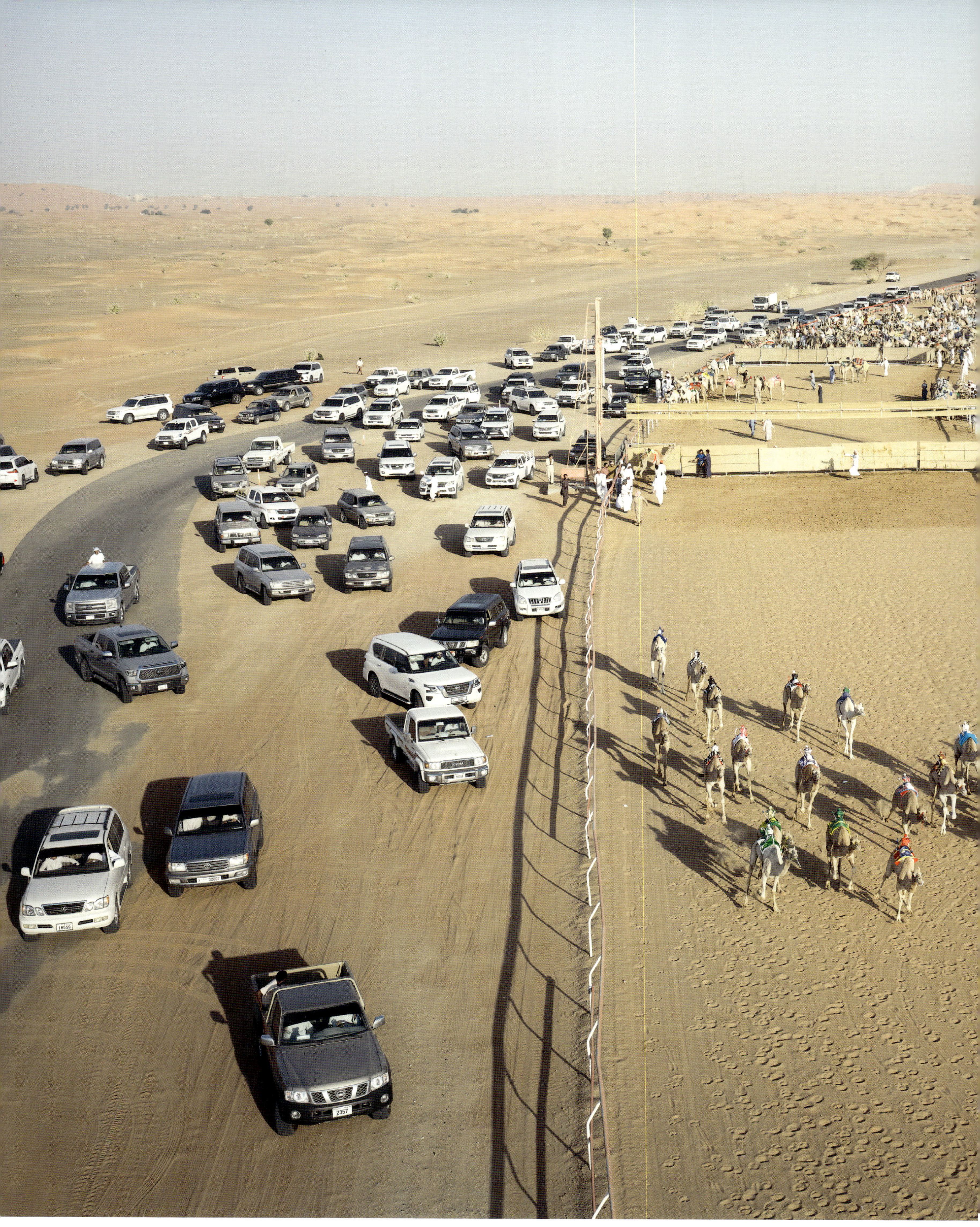

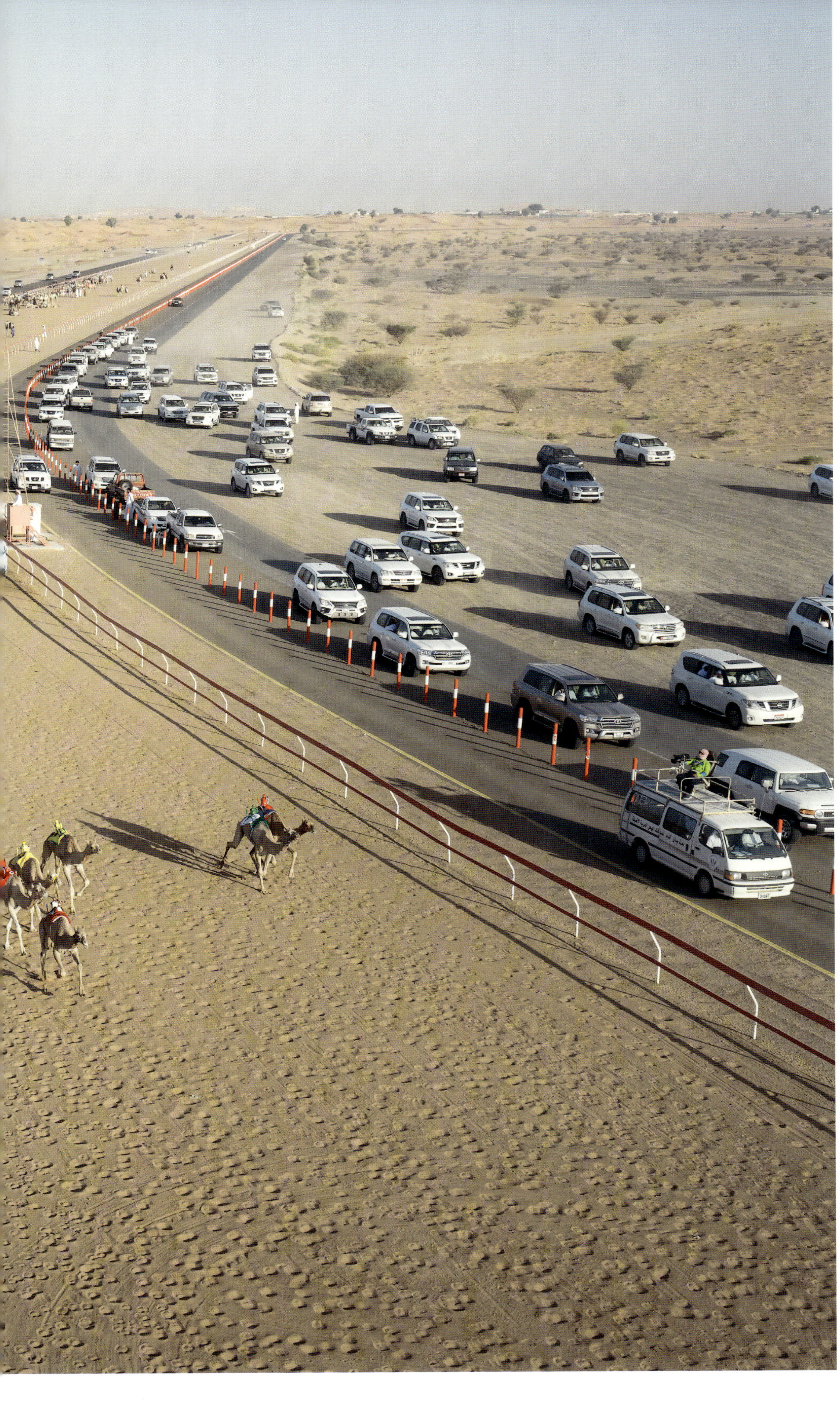

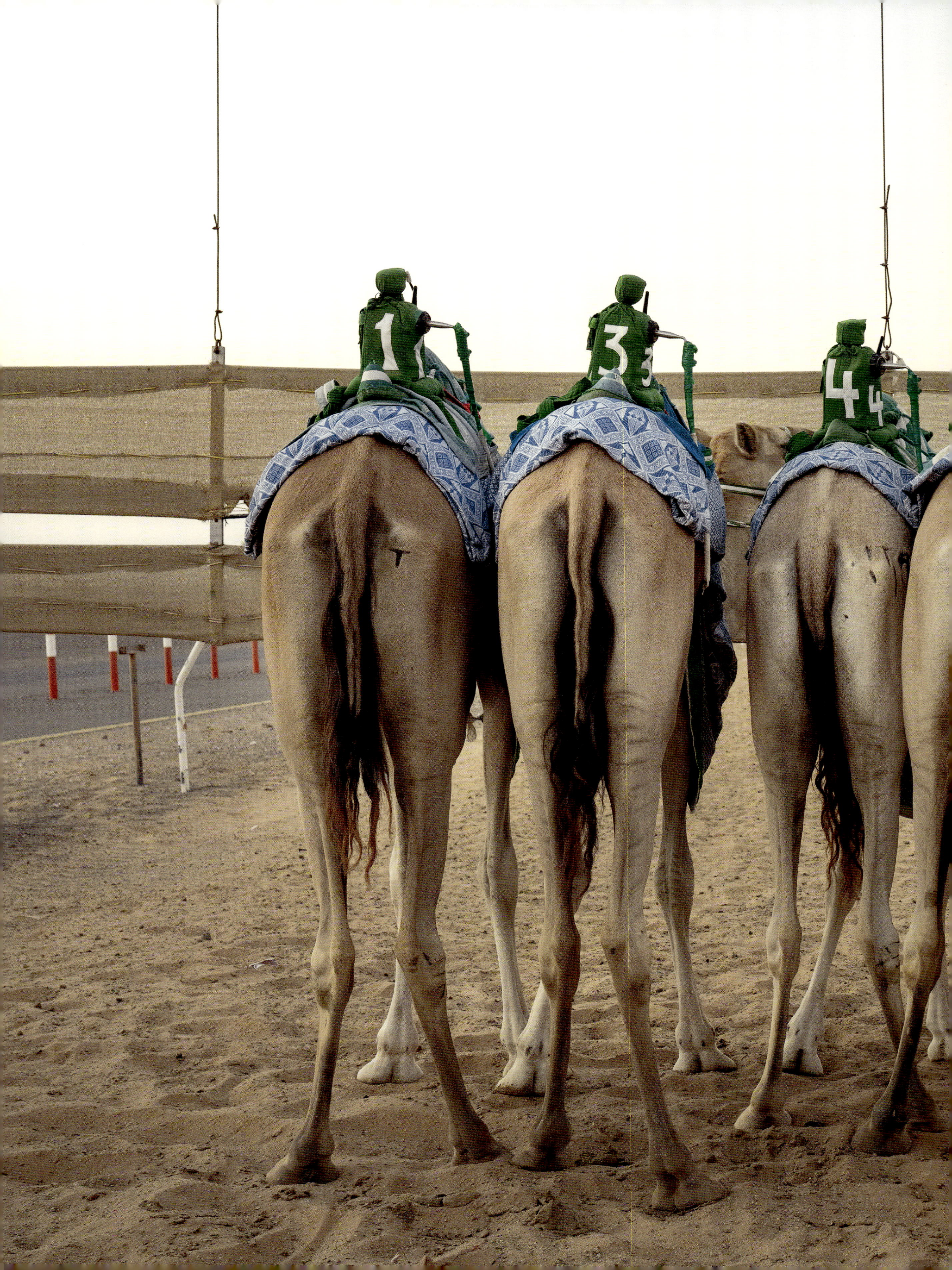

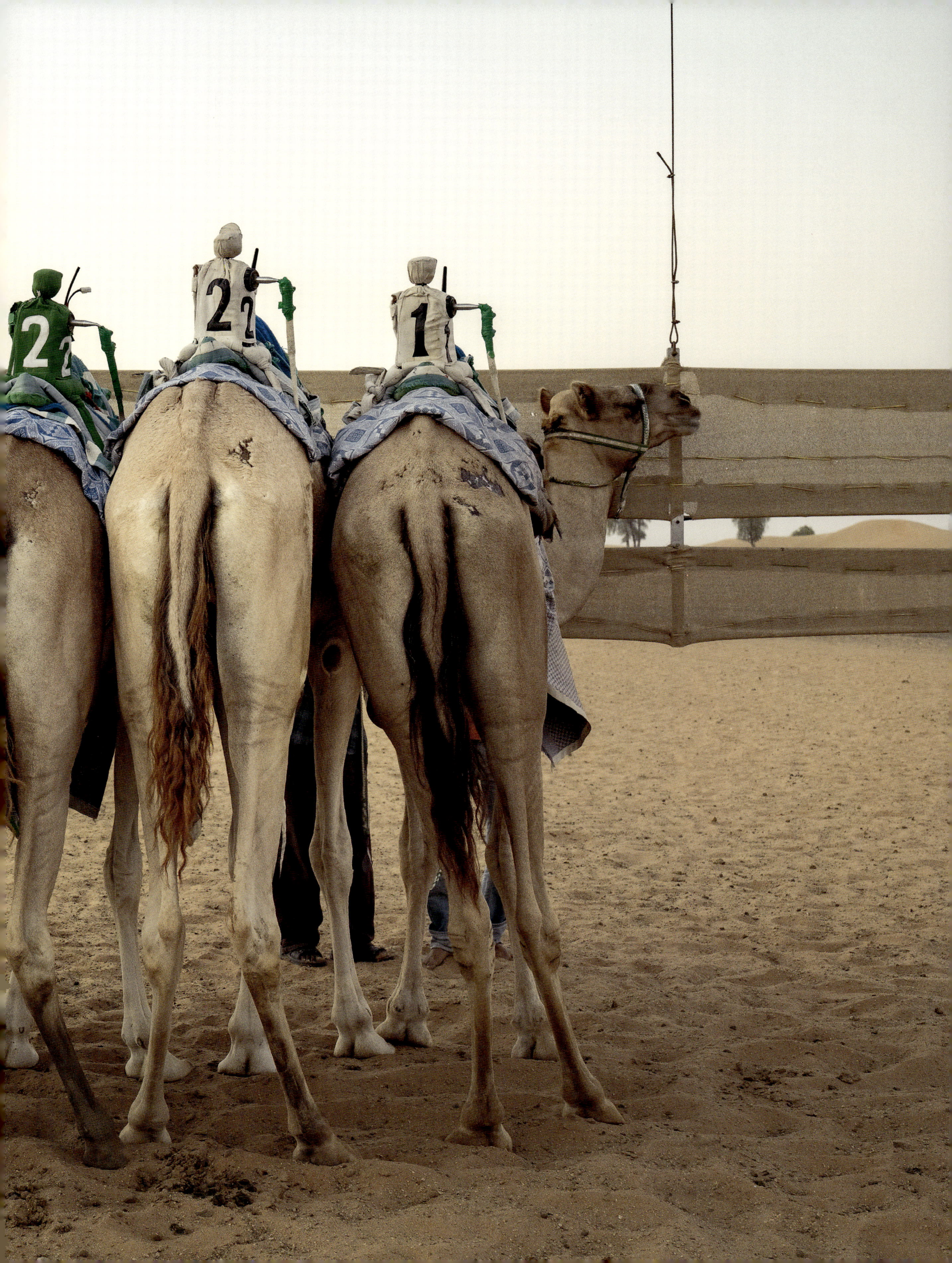
2
2
1

Acknowledgements

This book and project began as a seed of an idea, and without the support of countless individuals, it would not have grown and blossomed into what it has become today. I am profoundly grateful to everyone who contributed to the realization of this project, and I hope we will continue to grow and work together in the future.

First of all, I could not have made this book without all the incredible people I've had the honour of photographing and getting to know, who have generously shared their lives, homes and hearts with me and allowed me to tell their stories - thank you for this privilege.

Many thanks to my principal collaborator and publisher, teNeues, whose exacting and extensive skills helped make my dream a reality.

Without the Nationale Postcode Loterij there wouldn't be a book. Thank you to the team for your boundless enthusiasm and kindness, especially Imme Rog, for believing in me and my concept right from the start.

I want to extend my sincere thanks to the talented and charismatic Idris Elba, who is not only the voice of the Netflix series but also an integral part of the project. It is an honour to work with you.

I am indebted to Narda van 't Veer, my mentor, advisor, teacher – my everything. Your guidance and expertise were essential in helping to make selections from thousands of photos, bringing it all together in a cohesive form that became this book.

I am extremely grateful to my second family, the Boekhoorns, for their generosity and unwavering support throughout this entire journey. Thank you, Marcel Boekhoorn, for your financial support and for inspiring me to pursue my dreams – you've been a role model for me. A special thanks to Nicole Boekhoorn, my soul sister, for believing, investing and trusting in me and my ideas, and most of all, thank you for your friendship. I look forward to working on many more projects together.

I was blessed to have Isidoor Roebers (founder & producer of Scenery), the business brain behind the project, be there for me on every level. Thank you for always respecting and honouring my vision and helping me find the right people who helped shape this project. Without your skill, commitment, loyalty and integrity, none of this would have been possible. I hope to continue to work with you for many years to come.

Special thanks to the entire Scenery team, Lea Fels, Felix van Es, Amber Smeele, Sander Roks, Denise van den Hoek, and all the behind-the-scenes people, too many to mention.

Tomas Kaan, thank you for your cinematic vision and creative ability to translate my ideas into a Netflix series.

Thank you to Martijn van Scherpenzeel, my business mentor, who advised me throughout all of the negotiations and taught me how to navigate the business world.

Berber Bijlsma, my right-hand woman who travelled the world with me, thank you for your flexibility, patience, loyalty, competence and emotional support. Initially, you applied to be my photo assistant but turned out to be a very talented producer, for which I'm grateful. I hope we have many more adventures together.

Rose Casella, the writer of this book, thank you for bringing the photos and stories to life with your insightful, expressive and impactful writing. Your skilful mastery of words perfectly reflected what I wanted to communicate through my images. I hope we will continue to work on many more books and projects together.

Jakub Fulin, thank you for your professional photographic assistance, kindness and enthusiasm. You are always a pleasure to be around.

Annabel Verbeke, film director, thank you for your support and the fun we had on some of the first Human Playground adventures.

Much gratitude to my photo editors for everything they added to this book: thank you, Paul Roberts, for all your valuable input, Jan Stel for your superb, skilful attention to detail, which has been essential in elevating my work and Jim van Motman for your hard work, patience, continual optimism, friendship and above all, loyalty.

Rene Bierman, my photo printing consultant, thank you for improving the quality of all the prints. Your exceptionally sharp eye caught the tiniest detail, refining every image.

I want to thank the talented team at Maister for their indispensable design expertise, endless patience, creativity, and commitment to making the book as beautiful as possible.

Thank you, Annekee Gribnau and Lot Knoppers, my guides who supported and inspired my personal growth, helping me believe in myself and my work.

My heartfelt thanks to my parents, Paul and Andrea Vandenbussche, whose unconditional love and support have helped me more than I can say. Thank you for giving me my first camera. You were the ones that taught me how to work hard and still celebrate and enjoy life.

Many thanks to my mother and father in law Hilde Moreel and Wim Delporte for your loving care and support.

And to my sweet and lovely Manon Delporte, thank you for your incredible patience, understanding, love and support throughout this entire time. I love you; you're my rock.

Imprint

© 2022 teNeues Verlag GmbH

Second printing

Photographs © Hannelore Vandenbussche
All rights reserved.
Texts © Rose Casella

Coordination by Berber Bijlsma
Editorial Coordination by Berrit Barlet, teNeues Verlag
Production by Alwine Krebber, teNeues Verlag
Design © Maister
Photo Editing by Jim van Motman, Paul Roberts and Jan Stel
Color Separation by Robert Kuhlendahl, teNeues Verlag
Copyediting by John A. Foulks and Robin Pascoe

ISBN: 978-3-96171-377-6
Library of Congress Number: 2022934294
Printed in Italy by Lito Terrazzi S.r.l.

Picture and text rights reserved for all countries.
No part of this publication may be reproduced in
any manner whatsoever.

While we strive for utmost precision in every detail,
we cannot be held responsible for any inaccuracies,
neither for any subsequent loss or damage arising.

Bibliographic information published by the Deutsche
Nationalbibliothek: The Deutsche Nationalbibliothek
lists this publication in the Deutsche Nationalbibliografie;
detailed bibliographic data are available on the Internet
at dnb.dnb.de.

Published by teNeues Publishing Group

teNeues Verlag GmbH
Ohmstraße 8a
86199 Augsburg, Germany

Düsseldorf Office
Waldenburger Straße 13
41564 Kaarst, Germany
e-mail: books@teneues.com

Augsburg/München Office
Ohmstraße 8a
86199 Augsburg, Germany
e-mail: books@teneues.com

Berlin Office
Lietzenburger Straße 53
10719 Berlin, Germany
e-mail: books@teneues.com

Press Department
e-mail: presse@teneues.com

teNeues Publishing Company
350 Seventh Avenue, Suite 301
New York, NY 10001, USA
Phone: +1-212-627-9090
Fax: +1-212-627-9511

www.teneues.com

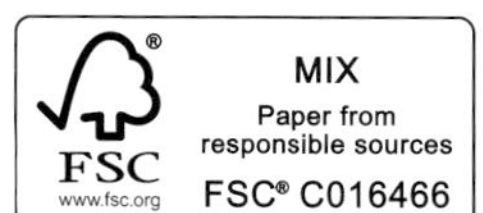

teNeues Publishing Group
Augsburg / München
Berlin
Düsseldorf
London
New York

teNeues

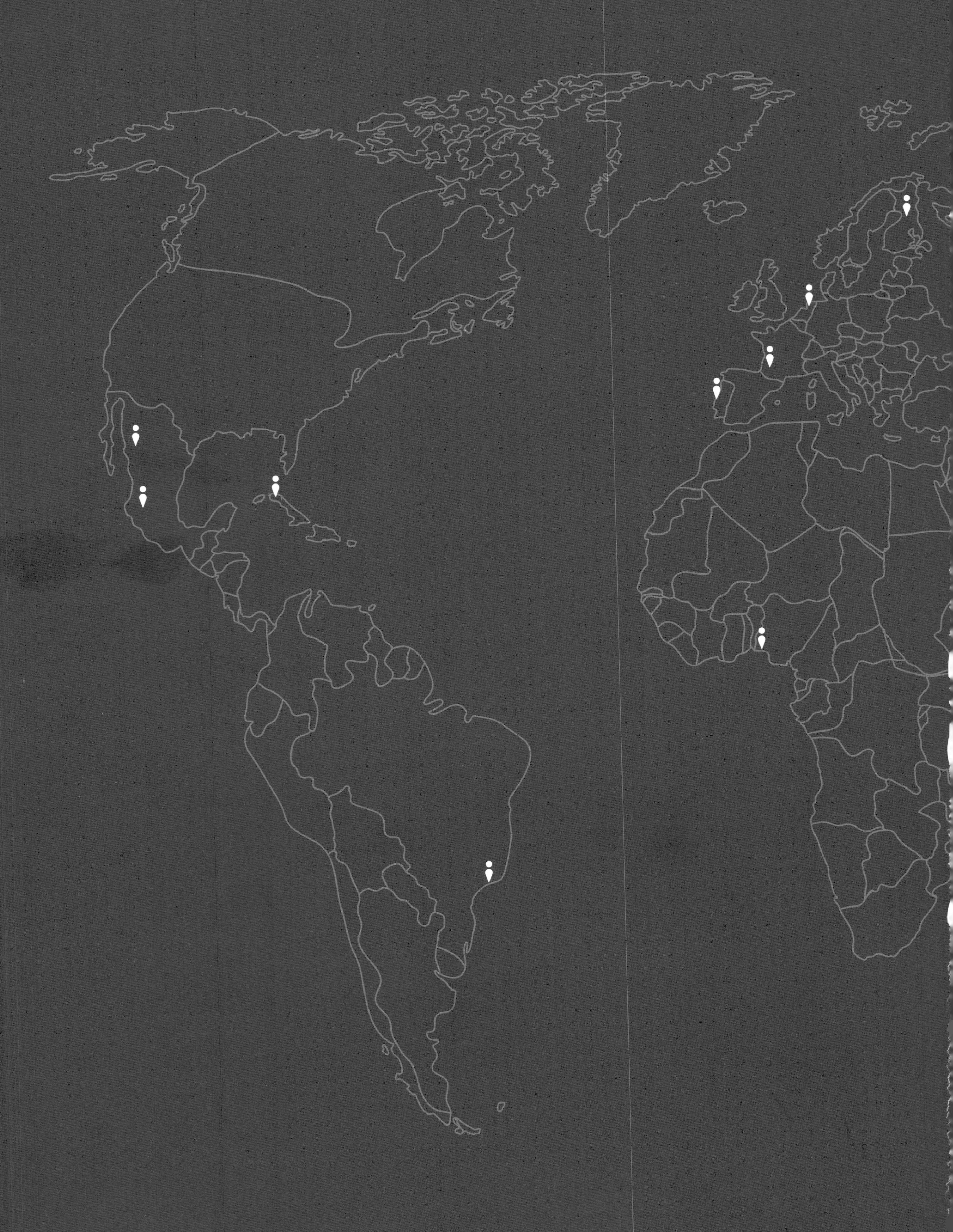